# LIGHTS AND SHADOWS

OF

# SAILOR LIFE

Clark and his friends attacked by the Natives—p 155.

# LIGHTS AND SHADOWS

OF

# SAILOR LIFE,

AS EXEMPLIFIED IN FIFTEEN YEARS' EXPERIENCE, INCLUDING THE

## MORE THRILLING EVENTS

OF THE

## U. S. EXPLORING EXPEDITION,

AND

## REMINISCENCES

OF AN

EVENTFUL LIFE ON THE "MOUNTAIN WAVE."

BY JOSEPH G. CLARK.

———

 BOOKS FOR LIBRARIES PRESS
FREEPORT, NEW YORK

First Published 1847
Reprinted 1971

INTERNATIONAL STANDARD BOOK NUMBER:
0-8369-5974-4


LIBRARY OF CONGRESS CATALOG CARD NUMBER:
70-169754


PRINTED IN THE UNITED STATES OF AMERICA
BY
NEW WORLD BOOK MANUFACTURING CO., INC.
HALLANDALE, FLORIDA 33009

# PREFACE.

In presenting this work to the public, I deem it unnecessary to enter into any elaborate explanation of its design, or offer an apology for its appearance. I have been pursuing an object which I conceive to be of the highest importance, which is the awakening of the public sympathy to the *nature and importance of the claims of seamen ;* this, in my estimation, may be best accomplished by a truthful and lucid exhibition of the "lights and shadows of sailor life." To accomplish the object thus truthfully, a thorough education in the school of experience will be the qualification which the public generally, both learned and unlearned, will regard as most adapted to such a work. At the present day, much interest is already felt in behalf of the sailor, and that interest is still increasing. It is a matter of the first importance that suitable information should be furnished, in order to give a right direction to the efforts that may be employed to elevate the character of seamen. One great truth has long been apparent to my mind, which is, that the *condition of the sailor must be improved* before his character can be very materially elevated. The gos-

1*

pel, indeed, can accomplish, either directly or indirectly, all that is expected in moral reform, but it enjoins,
with much clearness, the removal of physical as well
as moral obstacles.

Of what avail is it that the mariner is induced to
attend religious service on the Sabbath, if he mingles
with the corrupting society of the brothel the remaining portion of the time ? Of what avail is it that we
go to the sailor shivering on the beach, escaped from
the wreck, with religious books ? A dry jacket, or food,
would be much more acceptable, while moral efforts
might be appropriate and effectual afterward. This
great truth has been overlooked until quite recently,
when it was embraced by the Seamen's Friend Society. The officers of that benevolent institution have
learned the fact that every step in improving the physical condition of the sailor advances him *two* steps towards reformation,—first by removing him from his
vices and vile companions, and secondly, by inclining
him toward virtue by bringing him under the influence of the gospel.

Religion is a work in which the understanding is
concerned; no one comes under its influence without
a knowledge of it; no man will apply for pardon and
grace, until he understands properly that there is no
other hope for him. That part of our Lord's prayer,
"sanctify them through thy truth, thy word is truth,"
is sufficient evidence of the fact that any advancement
in the divine life after conversion, will be as much the
work of an enlightened understanding, as is the conversion.

The benevolent operations of the day being but a
part of religion, must be understandingly engaged in,

if they are to be auxiliaries to the conversion of the world.

The gospel comes to us in our darkness, a glorious light from heaven ; it reveals the great scheme of salvation, and at once discloses the promises of God to his people, and the means by which those promises are to be fulfilled. The means, then, like the end, are of divine appointment; hence, any efforts that may be made on the part of Zion to aid in the great gospel victory, will be effectual only as God's means are employed in the accomplishment of his purposes.

The question very naturally arises, what has the poor, despised, neglected, degraded sailor to do in the spread of the gospel ? I appeal to the Bible,—" Because the *abundance of the sea shall be converted unto thee*, the forces of the gentiles shall come unto thee." Again, the same view is repeated in that vision in which the prophet was shown the coming glory of Christ : " Thy sons shall come from far." "Surely the isles shall wait for me, and the ships of Tarshish first, to bring thy sons from far, their silver and their gold with them, unto the name of the Lord thy God, and to the Holy One of Israel." In these and other passages, we see that God has designed the sailor to act a very important part in the great conflict between sin and grace. In accordance with this view, Jesus, being about to choose his disciples, went to the sea of Galilee, and selected a small company of weather-beaten sailors as the means best adapted to the spread of the gospel.

While I would avoid every thing like egotism, and while I would not detract from the intrinsic value of the ordinary missionary labor, yet it is worthy of re-

mark, that it was to these sailors that Jesus gave his
great commission, " Go ye into all the world and
preach the gospel to every creature," a commission
for which the sailor is most admirably adapted. It
becomes a Christian duty, then, to inquire into the
condition of these individuals, and it is, partly, to give
such information, that these " Lights and Shadows "
have been penned.

The Journal of the Exploring Expedition, published by the government, being a very expensive work,
places its very important and interesting matter beyond the means of the working classes, and the scenes
and sketches which I have penned from my journal
of that cruise, will be read with interest and profit by
such as shall peruse these pages, as they will delineate the manners and customs of different portions of
the world, of whose inhabitants little has been written. The description of scenery and " life on the ocean
wave," has been truthfully penned, and the author
can, with all confidence, appeal to the experience of
every sailor for its confirmation. In the recital of the
events in which he was personally engaged, any thing
like exaggeration has been carefully avoided ; the
facts connected with the death of the generous Underwood and Henry, were too deeply engraven on his
body as well as his mind to be easily forgotten, and in
a way that renders exaggeration wholly unnecessary.
Any remark that he may make upon the officers of the
different vessels, he has given only his own personal
opinions, free from prejudice, or color of any kind,
save truth.

From the nature of their employment, seamen are
to some extent isolated, removed from many of the

influences which are adapted, in their tendencies, to refine the more ennobling sentiments of our nature, and to elevate human character. From these circumstances it seems inevitable that they should assume a kind of *distinctness*, should become a class, yet not a *caste*, to which the tendency of the past age has been so much inclined. There are peculiarities among all the varied classes and conditions of society, and this diversity constitutes the necessity of an adaptation of reformatory labors to these peculiarities. In this view of the subject, no one, it is presumed, will question the propriety of the issue of books which will be particularly interesting to the sailor as such, or those that will canvass such topics as are interesting and important, not only to seamen but landsmen. Every one who has been at all observant, must have been convinced that there has been, and still is, a manifest deficiency in this respect. It is true there have been many specimens of modern literature—" falsely so called "—in which the imagery of the ocean has been employed ; and others still, whose plots have been drawn from the incidents of the ocean, and others of a different character,—all of which are designed for the "sons of the mountain wave." Of *such* works there is an abundance.

It is not true,—as many have supposed,—that seamen can not appreciate laudable efforts, which are made to elevate the class. As among all classes of society, there is a variety here. There are those who are as degraded and brutalized, seemingly, as their native depravity can make them, reveling in the haunts of pollution and drunkenness. As accessary,

however, to this wreck of character, and blasting of
early-cherished hopes, the filching, soulless landlord,
and the wily dram-seller, have *much* to account for.
The poor, down-trodden sailor has received unnumbered wrongs from their hands, which are still registered against them in letters of fire.

Yet there is a far greater number who are high-
minded, generous and worthy, who have selected an
ocean-life—not from a blind fatality—but have been
drawn to it by a love of the grand and wildly sublime, which the ocean ever presents to the lover of
nature's wonders.   The scholar is often found here,
whose romantic predilections have induced him to
leave the halls of science, and study nature in her
more imposing forms.   There is a grandeur in ocean
scenery, a majesty in the strides of a stately ship, as
she moves, like "a thing of life," over the heaving
bosom of restless waters;—an awe in the tempest,
when the mighty voice of the Omnipotent is heard in
thunder-tones, pealing amid the roar of winds and
the dashings of billows, which can divert the man of
letters from his more quiet labors.

There are, indeed, many "shadows" in the sailor's
life, yet it has its "lights" also; and could the profession be elevated in the popular estimation, to the
position which its *importance* demands, and the talent which is already enlisted, be developed, its "lights"
would be far more conspicuous.   Indeed, when the
*efficiency* of this branch of industry is appreciated;
when the peculiar relations which the marine enterprise sustains to the advancement of civilization, and,
above all, to the *propagation of the everlasting gospel* among the benighted sons of heathen gloom are

felt, the apparent indifference of a portion of christen-
dom is wholly unaccountable. The sailor is a self-
constituted missionary, and *must* be regarded in pagan climes as the *representative* of a Christian community. He may bear the olive branch of peace to
such as are blindly bowing before dumb idols, or are
prostrating themselves before the ponderous car, to
avert the vengeance of imaginary gods, or he will
scatter the seeds of corruption, intemperance and
death. A neutrality in this matter is scarcely attain-
able. The records of the past, and the experience of
those on mission grounds, furnish sad proofs of this
proposition. Those labors have often proved apparently ineffectual, from the counteracting influences
of those who have visited missions, and have not been
guided by the pure principles of Christianity. The
pagan, in his simplicity, has shrunk in horror from
the licentiousness of those whom he has regarded as
Christians, simply because their residence is in a
Christian country.

These considerations will justify the remark made
at the onset, that no apology is deemed necessary for
any attempts which may be made to elevate this class
of our citizens,—the results of whose examples so in-
timately affect the great interests of humanity.

In order to render this work still more acceptable
to the reader, I have secured the services of Mr. J. H.
HANAFORD, a gentleman who was employed in interesting the readers of the "Light Ship," of which
paper he was the editor for some time; his sympathy
for, and deep interest and zeal in behalf of the sons of
"Zebulon;" his well-established character for morals

and religion, united with his scientific attainments, admirably qualify him to review this narrative, and prepare it properly for the press.

It is but justice to add, that the very short time occupied in its publication, with some unfavorable circumstances, wholly beyond my control, have rendered the work less perfect than it otherwise would have been. In consequence of this, some errors would naturally be unavoidable.

BOSTON, SEPTEMBER, 1847.

# CLARK'S NARRATIVE.

## CHAPTER I.

The Departure—Sermon—Ocean Scenery—Flying Fish and
Dolphins—Brilliant Phosphoretic Scene, and its cause—The
Madeira Islands—Rio de Janeiro—Ascent of the Sugar Loaf.

> Farewell to the land of my childhood and youth,
> The land of the bible, religion and truth;
> Thou bright land of blessings in every form,
> I leave thee, and fly to the billows and storm.
>
> Ye scenes of true happiness, friendship and home,
> Through which, when a boy, I delighted to roam,—
> Ye fields of sweet wild-flowers, the woodbine and heath,
> I leave ye to grapple with dangers and death.

1838. All things being ready for sea, on the 9th
of August dropped down to Hampton roads, preparatory to sailing for the South Pacific Ocean, where
we remained for a few days, waiting for a favorable
breeze.

The memorable day at length arrived for the long-
talked-of Expedition to sail. At half past three
o'clock P. M. a signal was made from the Commo-

2

dore's ship for the squadron to get underway. Accordingly, soon after the capstan was manned, and the anchor "catted," and every one seemed anxious to bid adieu to his home, since they had been so long kept in suspense, many in sight of their own "homes," without ever having the privilege of visiting their friends.

There have been various changes in this Expedition since its first organization under the command of THOMAS AP CATESBY JONES, ESQ., and six commanders have been appointed and discharged since Commodore Jones gave it up. And we were now about to take leave of our loved, our native country.

We had not proceeded far, when the wind died away and we were compelled to come to anchor, only a short distance from where we started.

Soon after, however, a breeze springing up, signals were again made for the squadron to get underway, which was immediately done, and all the vessels stood out in company. The breeze lasting but a short time, we made but little progress during the night. In the morning we were in sight of Cape Henry. At eight o'clock the ships were "hove to" and the pilots left, and by them we sent our final "farewells" to our friends on shore. At such a moment, when the last hold on our country is sundered from us, the kinder feelings of the soul are awakened. Our friends become more than ever endeared to us, and every thing connected with them wears an increasing interest. There was a sadness on the countenance of many, and a quivering of the lips.

Home! Native country! How dear to the heart. How each cherished remembrances of childhood's scenes, and loved associations of those sunny hours, come rushing up from the past, and steal into the throbbing bosom, as the ties of affection are riven. The intrusive tear moistens the eye, as early fancies flit before us, and wend their silent way down the cheek of youth,—the overflowing of the troubled waters of the soul. Affection gladly would throw her bands around the loved of earth, and draw them nearer and nearer, as the eye catches the last glimpse of boyhood's home in its faint, indistinct outline, but it is vain. The distant hum of business has died away, and the rippling of the waves, as they murmur across the prow, is heard instead. The towering spires, which point upward to the God of the "Sea and the dry land," have become dim in the distance, and familiar objects have blended in the fast fading view of the distant shore. But the fancies of the past, and endearments of home, must give place to the realities of a life on the "mountain wave."

The ship, from the gentleness of her motion, seemed less willing than ourselves, to exchange the smooth waters of the Bay and the beautiful landscapes along the shores of the "Old Dominion," for the troubled bosom and unbroken horizon of the ocean. In a few hours afterwards the shores of our happy country receded from our view, and seemed only as a speck upon the horizon.

At eleven o'clock all hands were called to "muster," where we had an excellent and appropiate sermon by our Chaplain, Mr. Elliott, who earnestly invoked "Him whom the winds and waves obey," to aid us in our arduous undertaking. He spoke feelingly of the dangers of our enterprize, and the inability of human exertions, without the aid of Him, who, when called upon by his affrighted companions, " Lord save us or we perish," bade the angry billows cease, and in a moment they were still.

At half past one o'clock, P. M. we were piped down, and at five o'clock again called to muster, when each mess was furnished with a Bible and every man with a Prayer Book.

The sea is a fit place for contemplating the majesty and power of the " Almighty," where the air is calm; where sleepeth the deep waters. What a contrast when comparing the smoothness of the sea yesterday, with the troubled bosom of the mighty deep to-day ! Now the sea is running "mountains high; "—yesterday it was hushed, and as smooth as a mirror. Through the night, nothing seemed to disturb its peaceful bosom; but now and then the gleaming of a shark, or some monster of the deep.

Some of our "green-horns" looked truly pitiful. This is nothing like what they fancied in their dreams of a sea-life in their juvenile days, after listening to the yarn of some "old tar." This is only a prelude to what may be expected before we accomplish the object of the Expedition. During the day we shipped some very heavy seas, which flooded our decks from stem to stern. During the next day the weather was clear and pleasant, with a strong breeze, sufficient for any ordinary vessel to sail at the rate of ten knots. This breeze we lost however, on account of having to lay to, for the Relief, which vessel is a very dull sailer, and besides, she is loaded as deep as she can swim. The Captain finding that he should be detained if he continued to wait for the Relief, sent or-

ders for her to make the best of her way to Rio de
Janeiro, where the squadron is to rendezvous, previous to doubling Cape Horn.

For some time during the latter part of August,
that " Queen of months " for an ocean life, the ocean
around us was enlivened by immense numbers of
flying fish. This is a beautiful animal about six
or eight inches in length, and of slender and delicate
form. Until now, I had an impression that it received its name from springing into the air for a moment
only, and then sinking into its native element; but for
several days, flocks of forty and fifty, and even of a
greater number, have risen about our ship, and flown
yards before descending again.

When in this situation, a person ignorant of their
nature could not distinguish them from birds of the
same size. The large transparent fins which they
use in flying, have every appearance of wings, and
when in a direction opposite to the sun, their whole
bodies are of a most dazzling silver white.

But in this case, as well as in that of the dying
dolphin, we have been led to commiserate as well as
to admire. At most times, when these little creatures
take flight, it is only to escape from some devouring
enemy in close pursuit.

We have often caught a glimpse of the dolphin
darting through the water under them, as they have
skimmed along its surface; and once, after watching
with delight the lengthened course of an uncommon-
ly beautiful fish, as time after time it dipped for a
moment but scarcely touched the waves before it rose
again, and seemed to exert every power to pursue its
rapid way, we saw it fall directly into the jaws of

2*

some ferocious monster, which, as if doubly ravenous from the chase, leaped partly out of the water to receive it. They seem peculiarly ill-fated; not unfrequently a flight from their enemies exposes them to the rapacity of others equally destructive, and they become the prey of gulls, cormorants and other sea fowl, hovering over the water for food. In their ærial course, they also often come in contact with vessels, and fall helpless captives on their decks.

It is pleasing, after a long seclusion from the society of our fellows, save the few with whom we come in daily contact, during the monotony of a routine of duties peculiar to a squadron like ours, it is pleasing under such circumstances, to greet a brother man. He may be an entire stranger, with whom we can have no cherished reviews of the past; can gather no gems from the sunny scenes of childhood, —perchance he is from a distant clime, has his local prejudices, his sectional animosities, yet he is a brother sailor, and is greeted with the tokens of friendship.

During the first of September we were favored with fine weather and fair breezes, and were making rapid progress toward the place of our destination. It is under such circumstances that the sailor feels buoyant. He sees no darkening clouds about him, no lightning's glare, no yawning abyss beneath, ready to engulf him in the depths of ocean's bed, but his bark moves onward in stately grandeur, a " thing of life." He feels a pride, known only to the sailor.

At eleven o'clock, September 9th, all hands were called, when we had a sermon from our Chaplain, from James 5 : 6, 12. His discourse was directed principally against profane swearing. Such services effectually call to remembrance scenes of the past and awaken the better feelings of our nature.

In the afternoon, we passed in sight of Pico, one of the Western Islands.

On the following day the lookout from the mast-head reported "land ho," which proved to be the Island of Saint Michaels, another of the Western Islands, and on the twelfth we were off Saint Michaels. Saint Michaels is a high and mountainous Island, and at the distance we were from it, has a dreary appearance. But I am told that it is extremely fertile, and produces excellent fruit and wine.

September 4th. This morning we had the first sight of a dolphin, one of the most beautiful of the inhabitants of the sea. The usual length of this fish appears to be about two feet. In its shape it bears but little resemblance to the representation of it seen on vases, &c., and in marine emblems, and armorial bearings, but is very similar to the white salmon trout, found in fresh water lakes. When swimming in the water, its colors appear exceedingly delicate and beautiful. The head, back, and upper part of the sides, vary from the hue of burnished steel to that of deep azure and nazarine blue, shading off toward the under part in pea green and light yellow. The dolphin is often taken with a hook and line, but this morning one was struck with a harpoon and brought upon deck. I hastened to witness its colors while dying. I found them to be as truly beautiful as they have been described, consisting of rapid transitions, from the deepest purple approaching to black, through blue, green, gold of different hues, and several shades of silver, to almost a snow white, and then to

purple again.   The sight, however, was painful from
a kind of sympathy with the beautiful sufferer.   I
could but feel that the gratification of my curiosity
was at the expense of its life.

The colors soon became less and less brilliant, and
in five minutes entirely disappeared.   A large school
of boneto was sporting about the ship in company
with the dolphin.   They are a very active fish and
frequently throw themselves several feet out of water.

In a water spout we have had one of those phenomena, characteristic of the region in which we
then were.   It was at too great a distance to be seen
very minutely; the end nearest the ocean was scarcely
perceptible, though the agitation of the water under
it was quite evident, the upper extremity terminated
by a tubular expansion, similar in form to the large
end of a trumpet, in a heavy black cloud.   The part
clearly visible was about three hundred feet in length
and the cloud not less than fifteen hundred feet in
height.

There was a shower of rain almost immediately
afterwards, of the largest drops I ever saw.   It was
perfectly calm, and the ocean glassy as a mirror,
which made the appearance of the rain, as it struck
the surface of the water, singularly beautiful, as far
as the eye could reach.   The whole sea seemed a
plain of glass studded with diamonds of the first magnitude.

At ten o'clock at night, the exhibitions of the day
were followed by a phosphoretic scene of unrivaled
beauty and sublimity.   I have often before observed
luminous points, like sparks of fire floating here and
there in the wake of our vessel; but now the whole

ocean was literally bespangled with them, notwithstanding the smoothness of the surface. There was a
considerable swell of the sea; and sparkling as it did
on every part as with fire, the mighty heavings of its
bosom were indescribably magnificent. It seemed
as if the sky had fallen to a level with the ship,
and all its stars in ten fold number and brilliancy
were rolling about with the undulation of the billows.
The horizon in every direction presented a line of uninterrupted light, while the wide space intervening
was one extent of apparent fire. The sides of our
vessel appeared kindling to a flame, and the flash of
the concussion gleamed half way up the rigging, and
illumined every object along the whole course of the
ship. By throwing any thing over board a display of
light and colors took place, surpassing in beauty and
brilliancy the finest exhibition of fireworks. The
rudder too, by its motion, created splendid corruscations at the stern, and a flood of light, by which our
track was marked far behind us. The smaller fishes
were distinctly traceable by running lines, showing
their rapid course; while now and then broad gleam-
ings, extending many yards in every direction,
made known the movement of some monster of the
deep. But minuteness will only weary, without conveying any adequate impression of the scene.

It would have been wise perhaps only to have said
that it was among the most sublime scenes which nature herself ever presents. The cause of this phenomenon was long a subject of speculation among
men of science, but is now satisfactorily ascertained
to be sea animalcules of the luminous tribe, particularly the species Medusa.

Captain A. K. Long, of the ship Relief, took great pains in examining this subject with great minuteness.

The weather is still favorable, and the breeze propitious. At daylight the island of Madeira, just appeared in sight, was looming above the watery horizon. About three o'clock, P. M. we came up with these justly celebrated islands, and I need not attempt a description of the sublime and picturesque scenery, or the rich and highly cultivated hills. At sunset we arrived off the town of Funchal, and came to anchor in Funchal Roads near the town.

Soon after coming to anchor, we received a visit from the American Consul, who frequently visited our ship during our stay.

The Madeira Islands consist of Madeira Parto Santo and the Desert Isles. Madeira, the principal island, is distinguished for its wines, whieh are exported to various parts of the world; its capital is Funchal.

These islands belong to Portugal, and have a population of ninety thousands, including blacks.

After our arrival here, the officers and scientific gentlemen were busily engaged in examining the islands, and making observations, and measuring the height of some of the loftiest mountains. The weather was fine and beautiful, and the country in every direction was clothed in green verdure. Our ship was furnished with a plenty of excellent beef and vegetables, and also fruit in abundance. I suppose there is no place in the known world which produces finer beef, vegetables and fruit, than this island.

The island is under the government of Portugal, and the natives seem to be quite loyal to the present Queen Donna Maria. Its capital, Funchal, is a handsome little town, containing some six or eight thousand inhabitants, who seem to be a gay and lively people, and remarkably hospitable. Like other Spanish and Portuguese towns, it has its number of churches and convents, which were mostly illuminated the first part of the night.

At two o'clock, P. M., on the following day, we weighed anchor, and bid adieu to this truly beautiful island—squadron in company.

After leaving Madeira, we had delightful weather with fine cool breezes. At four o'clock, P. M, we passed the Island Mayo, one of the Cape de Verd Islands, and at midnight lay to off the Island of San Jago, the principal Island of the Cape de Verds.

October 6th, we were off the island. At nine o'clock, A. M., came to anchor off the town of Porto Praya, and soon after received a visit from Mr. Gardener, American Consul.

Cape De Verd Islands, discovered in 1460 by the Portuguese and still subject to the crown of Portugal, form a group of about twenty in number, including those of a smaller size, which are unimportant. They formerly contained a population of about twenty thousands, but at present are very sparsely inhabited. They are all more or less mountainous, with scarcely enough vegetation to support themselves and cattle. The people, isolated as they were from the world, with most of the channels of communication cut off between them and the other countries, are dependent chiefly for whatever sustenance their own islands do

not afford, upon vessels casually stopping at them.
The trade is generally carried on by barter. From
the time of their first discovery they have been subject at intervals to severe drought and famine. The
rain of heaven is often withheld for several years in
succession, at which time all the sources of fertility
are dried up, and the people and their cattle perish
for the want of food and .water. It is not surprising
to learn that so many have perished from famine.
The most deadly famine took place in 1832, when one
half of the inhabitants lost their lives, and all their
cattle died. Large donations were made in New
York and other parts of the United States for their
relief, with which provisions were purchased and
sent them.

Coffee and sugar are raised in some parts of the isl-
and, but not in any abundance. We saw herds of
cattle and some thousands of goats grazing on the declivities of the mountain. The inhabitants, from in-
termixture, have become almost of the negro complexion and features.

Porto Praya is the capital of San Jago.

On the 27th of October, we got underway and
stood out to sea with a pleasant breeze. On the 29th
a sail was reported in sight, and, as we were near the
coast of Africa, we were suspicious that she was a
slaver. Spy-glasses were eagerly raised, and her
manoeuvres closely watched; however, she soon ran
away from us.

On the 12th and 13th, large schools of dolphin
played about our vessel, and a number of them were
caught, and notwithstanding our medical officers said

they were sometimes poisonous, they were eaten without feeling any inconvenience from them.

Nothing of importance occurred until near the close of November, when land was reported, which proved to be Cape Frio, a high and irregular point of land forty miles distant. On the same evening, we came to anchor in the harbor of Rio de Janeiro, after a passage of ninety-five days from Hampton Roads. Found the United States ship Independence and a number of English and French ships of war, also merchant ships of all nations.

Two days after my arrival I embraced the opportunity of visiting the shore, and commenced my observations upon the Brazilians.

On entering the capacious harbor of Rio, you pass the frowning batteries of Fort Santa Cruz at the foot of Signal Hill on the right hand, and on the left Fort Saint Lucia, built on a small island near the main land, and another small one a little to the eastward of Sugar Loaf Hill, so called from its shape, which is one immense isolated rock, and lifts its almost perpendicular sides to the clouds, a lower tier of which perpetually crowns its barren head. It is about one thousand feet high, said to have been inaccessible to all save an Englishman, who by some mysterious means ascended it, and raised thereon the flag of his country, as a proud signal of his exploit. Whether he fell from the rock into the deep beneath, or was slain by some hired assassin, is not and probably never will be known. Some of the officers of the Expedition have succeeded in reaching its highest summit, and there unfurled the "star-spangled

3

banner;" they remained upon it all night, and in the morning descended again and returned in safety to the ship.

———

# CHAPTER II.

Description of Rio de Janeiro—Emperor's Palace—Celebration of the Emperor's Birth—Imperial Church Chapel—Church, and the Vow of the Empress—Sectional differences—Funeral occasion.

> "I love the blue waters! their deep maddening roar,
> Is food for a spirit unbounded by shore;
> Thy whirlwinds may shriek—thy lightnings may flash,
> Yet safe o'er thy bosom, old ocean, I'll dash."

Rio de Janeiro is built at the entrance of a bay one hundred miles in circumference, intersected here and there with small islands covered with evergreen. The city contains about one hundred thousand inhabitants, including the suburbs Gloria Hill and Botofoga.

The buildings are of stone, three or four stories high, the streets very narrow and long, wearing an unpleasant and sombre appearance, produced by the wide-spreading and clumsy verandahs that disfigure almost every street. Like the generality of Spanish and Portuguese towns, it is extremely filthy, and for the want of the indispensable conduits in cities, to wit, *sewers*, the streets become the common receptacle of excrementitious abomination and filth. The slave population, and it is very considerable, is altogether more miserable and wretched than any thing my imagination could have previously depicted. The slaves are driven about the streets, yoked together by dozens, with a necklace of iron almost as delicate and slender as our chain cable, each carrying on his head a ten gallon bucket of water, and some with bags of coffee and other heavy loads on their heads. All slaves are in a perfect state of nudity, except the covering afforded by a small piece of dirty rag which is tied about the loins. The noise which they make when departing in droves from the public fountains, gives the most perfect idea of a pandemonium that can well be imagined.

The Emperor's Palace is in full view from our ship, and is opposite the only landing for boats on the beach. I had paid it a visit, and taken a full view, both interior and exterior. The fact that it is a palace, is the only thing that recommends it to a passing notice.

It formerly was the residence of the Vice Roy, and for such a dignitary good enough. The present Emperor does not reside here, but has his palace in the suburbs of the city. He is a young man of about nineteen years of age ; his father, Don Pedro the first, abdicated the crown, and he became the natural successor when quite an infant ;—since that time the kingdom of Brazil has been governed by a Regency.

Yesterday was his birth-day, on which occasion he paid a visit to the city in commemoration of that event. The streets, through which he passed, were handsomely decorated with flags, artificial flowers and tapestry of different hues and shades. Arches in several places were built across the streets through which he passed on his way to the old palace, and were decorated with every thing which the imagination could devise. The square in front of the palace was literally filled with spectators of all shades and colors, anxiously waiting to get a glimpse of his Royal Highness, as he entered the palace. This novel scene did not attract my attention, and I saw but little in it that was at all interesting, therefore I did not remain long to gaze on it. The ships in the harbor, as well as the city, were richly dressed in flags, and at twelve o'clock a royal salute was fired from all the batteries, and answered by the vessels of war in the harbor.

But to return to the description of Rio. The palace is a parallelogram of about two hundred feet in length and one hundred and fifty feet in front. It is enclosed, but contains a court yard in the centre, on one side of which is the Senate house,—the house of Deputies being a mile distant in the Campo de Aclangao—and on the other a splendid church belonging to the Carmonite monks, adjoining the beautiful little imperial chapel. It is said that this church was built by the late Empress Don Pedro, in consequence of a vow made to the goddess of fecundity. The story runs thus;—she had been married some time without becoming a mother, and in a fit of united piety and philoprogenitiveness, she vowed that should she be served as Sarah of old was, she would build a church on the glorious occasion. Her prayers were heard, and she became a mother, and as truly did she build this pretty little church as commemorative of this

miraculous event. This story is figuratively told by
six or seven statues of the Empress, placed in the
church in appropriate niches, on the right hand side
as you enter, beautifully modeled and richly decorated with diamonds; all are arranged in the delineating
style, singularly indicative of the event which they
are designed to describe hieroglyphically. The his-
toric delineation is ingenious and skilfully develops
the different eras; and the last one as you approach
the altar closes the representations, by presenting the
heavenly babe full of infantile beauty and plumpness,
in the joyous arms of the certainly handsome and
modest young Empress.

No person may deny but that this is a perfectly
natural scene, and also a truly modest one, to those
who are accustomed to look upon it as a miracle
rather than a mere picture of " the fancy;" but in a
country like the United States, where a rigid code of
delicacy is so strictly observed, certain things would
be viewed with horror, that in another are looked
upon coldly, as capable of exciting neither animal
passion or latent curiosity.

In fact, local custom is the only true standard of
delicacy, and as every country has its customs, so
has it also a different scale of modesty, and peculiar
motives of social intercourse. Take for example two
ladies, one a North, and the other a South American,
equal in their country's refinement and cultivation of
mind, yet I dare affirm both would be simultaneously
shocked at each other's want of delicacy upon many
occasions. This, of course, must be peculiarly observable in the inhabitants of isolated countries, where
intercourse to any considerable extent is impractica-

3*

ble.  Generosity, truth, gratitude and honesty, are
intrinsically the same in every section of the world,
but that which we understand by the name of modesty, or female purity of action, varies with latitude
and climate, and in fact is almost provincial in its definition.  The South American lady, who jumps into
her saddle, rides off on horseback like a man, with a
poncho thrown gracefully over the shoulders, may
have as lofty notions of true delicacy as she who flirts
along Broadway or Washington street, attended by
one who apparently has as good a claim to a forest
origin as the noble animal upon which he rides, and
over which he seems to wish for a superiority, from
the fact that he is the director, not the directed.

Whilst one day standing in the church and looking
with a delightful eye upon some truly splendid and
masterly pieces of scriptural paintings, a corpse was
brought into the aisle and laid near the altar.  The
friends of the deceased arranged themselves on each
side of the way from the door to the altar.  No female was present, as I have elsewhere observed on
many like occasions.  Wax candles were brought
and handed around weighing upwards of ten pounds,
which were six feet long, they having been previously lighted.  The priests made a grand entry from the
sacriste, dressed in full splendor of sacerdotal attire,
some with service books in their hands and others
bearing gold and silver censers, which sent forth in
downy clouds, the combined odors of myrrh and
frankincense.  The pall was removed, the coffin was
opened, and holy water sprinkled upon the satin
robes of the dead.  I looked around me for tombs or
for the grave, but saw nothing of either.

The priest carried the body three times round the enclosure, and at last deposited it in a niche in the wall, merely large enough for the coffin, and here with a hammer and a trowel the masons completed the interment.

It is no doubt known to some of our readers, and to some it may not be, that Bonaparte sent from the court of Portugal, King John and his wife to the court of Brazil. King John was the first European monarch who sat foot upon the American Continent. He made Rio de Janeiro the seat of government, and during his reign the court of Brazil was proverbially one of the most licentious upon earth. King John himself was one of the greatest libertines that the world ever produced, and stopped short of nothing to satisfy his sensual pleasures.

I visited the shore on the 10th and again witnessed the brutal manner in which slaves are treated. Could the abolitionists of the United States witness the evil of slavery, as it is seen in all its deformity here, they might more strongly enforce their favorite doctrine. Indeed, one who has been accustomed to slavery from his childhood, as it exists in the United States, might be shocked in walking the streets of Rio, at the abject condition of the slaves, and the brutal manner in which they are treated. When the slave becomes diseased he is cast on the world, to get his living in the best manner he can; and many would actually die from want, were it not for the charities of the monastic establishments, and the small sums occasionally contributed by strangers. I have frequently been accosted by these pitiable objects, and as I have thrown them a few vintons, a smile of joy would illumine their countenances, as if some dread apprehensions had been removed from their mind. Notwithstanding their charitable institutions, great numbers die annually from their deplorable condition. It is said that thousands of these miserable objects are transported annually into this kingdom, although it is a contraband trade.

Since our arrival, two slave vessels have been brought into port by an English man-of-war brig.

Rio de Janeiro is celebrated for its many and magnificent churches. The people generally are strict Catholics, and droves of them may be seen every morning entering the church to pay their early devotions at the holy altar. The English and American residents have a neat little church near the public gardens, enclosed by an iron railing, with a yard in front, paved with granite. It was built in 1820, and will hold about five hundred people very comfortably. The clergyman is of the Episcopal order, and is supported by the English and American residents and by the English government. The city is ornamented by several fountains made of granite, which are supplied with water from the neighboring mountains, by means of an aqueduct some miles in extent, similar to those mentioned in Roman history. It is the best specimen of architecture of which Rio can boast. Several other public buildings are to be found here, such as a Museum, a Public Library and a number of convents.

Since our arrival here, Captain Wilkes has been on shore with all of his scientific instruments, making observations.

At nine o'clock, A. M., January 7th, a light wind

springing up we weighed our anchor and proceeded to sea—squadron in company. We were now favored with fine weather and a moderate breeze. At four o'clock, P. M., we were just losing sight of the coast of Brazil. The bleak and lofty mountains were fast receding from our view, and in a short time were entirely swallowed up in the distance. The first part of this month was peculiarly pleasant ; but we were destined, however, to experience some little change. How very illustrative of human life! The morning of the 15th set in cloudy, and at eight o'clock A. M., commenced raining with considerable wind, which soon increased to a gale. At ten o'clock all hands were called to reef topsails, when we got a severe pelting of rain. This, however, from its frequent occurrence, the sailor thinks but little of. His life is emphatically one of toil and hardship. And yet amid all of his privations, he receives comparatively but little sympathy from those who are so dependent upon him for the luxuries, and to some extent, the necessaries of life. While the sensualist is feasting upon the delicacies of distant climes, as the highest gratification of which his nature is susceptible, like the swine that feeds voraciously upon the bounty shaken in plenty from above him, knows not and cares not from whence they came, or with what toil they were obtained. Appetite, beast-like, must be gratified, and thoughts of the sailor are as unusual as emotions of gratitude, in such depraved bosoms. Yet a brighter day is about to dawn upon the sailor; his cries are to be heard, and his claims acknowledged.

We had at this time nearly the same kind of weather that we generally have in the United States in the latter part of March. At ten o'clock, spoke the American whaling ship Leander of New York, six months and a half out, with three hundred and twenty barrels of sperm oil. Shortly after, spoke a Dutch brig bound to the Falkland Islands.

Just as we had finished our breakfast on the morning of the 21st, the appalling cry of "a man overboard!" resounded throughout the ship. We immediately hove to, and he being a good swimmer, reached the man-rope at the gangway in safety.

An effort to give a just description of scenes like this, although, in this instance, we were unusually fortunate, need not be attempted. It will prove a failure. The feelings of one struggling against the mighty power of overwhelming billows, with no gleam of hope from his "little world" from which he has been suddenly ejected; tossed and driven upon a wide expanse of waters—to appreciate the thick-crowding emotions of one under such circumstances, there must be something approximating nearer to the reality than the tame and unmeaning recital of the narrator. The gloom which pervades the surviving crew, when even "one of the few" is taken hurriedly from them, is not easily described. Even the loss of *one*, forms no inconsiderable fraction of such a miniature of the community. In the usual routine of duties, it is often observed that one is far from them and sleeps beneath the ever-restless bosom of their chosen element.

Our latitude was now forty-one degrees south, temperature ranging from sixty-five to seventy degrees. A seal was seen playing in the wake of our vessel; this circumstance induced us to believe that land was not far distant; whales have been seen sporting about in every direction, and also several sharks paid us a visit alongside and waited on the top of the water some moments for something to satisfy their voracious appetites.

At daylight on the 25th, land was reported from mast head, and at five o'clock we came to anchor in five fathoms water, off Rio Negro, coast of Patagonia. Immediately after dropping anchor we had a severe gale of wind and rain, which induced us to make speedy preparations to brave the dangers of an ocean life.

After our arrival here, our scientific gentlemen went ashore in quest of objects in their different departments, and the other officers were busily engaged in surveying, &c. There is a considerable Spanish settlement on this coast, about twenty miles from the mouth of the river, and also a village of from one to two thousand inhabitants, the principal part of whom are soldiers. The squadron, when it appeared off the harbor, caused considerable excitement among the inhabitants; the most of them fled into the country; mistaking us for a French squadron, with which nation they are at war. They soon found out their mistake and returned. There is a monthly intercourse from this port to Buenos Ayres, to which government this colony belongs. This region of Patagonia abounds in all kinds of game, excellent horses and horned cattle. Our men brought off several armadillos and young ostriches, and some ostrich eggs for curiosities.

January 30th. This morning a strong gale sprung up, blowing immediately on the land, which, from our exposed situation, compelled us to get underway and beat out to sea.  The Peacock in company; also the brig Porpoise—the two latter being compelled to slip their cables and leave their anchors behind.

On the following day, however, the weather so far changed, that we thought it advisable to return to Rio Negro, in order to get a boat's crew that had deserted from the boat and been left behind.

Having succeeded in regaining the men we again got underway and stood out to sea; squadron in company.

The weather now begins to grow cool, the thermometer ranging from forty-five to fifty degrees in the shade on the spar deck, and between decks at sixty degrees.

Our ship glides through the water like a thing of life.  At sunset there was a large school of porpoises alongside, and we succeeded in taking one, which made a fresh "mess" for all hands.  The flesh of the porpoise has no appearance or taste of fish, but more resembles beef;—only it is much darker.  I tasted some of it and liked it very much.  Our latitude about this time, by observation, was fifty degrees thirty minutes south, and our longitude sixty three degrees thirty minutes west.

At midnight of the following day, we had a partial view of the rugged peaks of Terra del Fuego, and at eight o'clock, A. M., entered the straits of La Maire.  The land here presents rather a dreary appearance; the high peaks on either hand are covered with perpetual snow, although it is mid-summer here.  At sunset we passed the straits, and again entered the open sea with land on the starboard bow.  We hove to off Cape Horn, the night being dark and blustering.

We made but little progress after weighing our anchor on the following morning, in consequence of the unfavorableness of the weather. The country here presents nothing but snow-clad mountains and barren rocks: no sign of vegetation, except here and there a stunted tree.

We were passing Cape Horn, within a few miles of the shore, with studding sails set on both sides. It is very seldom that such a thing happens, for Cape Horn is denominated the "stormy Cape," as vessels seldom, if ever, pass it without experiencing very boisterous weather. It was cloudy and nearly calm however, on the 17th, and we were engaged all day in beating up to our anchorage.

After a weary and sleepless night in working the ship up here, we dropped anchor about six o'clock in the morning in sixteen fathoms water. This was a most delightful day, thermometer in the shade, sixty four degrees. The bay and country around had quite a different appearance from what I expected.

At noon a native canoe came alongside, having on board two men, one woman and a child, but we were so busily engaged mooring the ship, that we could pay no attention to them.

Here also our officers and scientific gentlemen went on shore, and killed a number of geese, ducks, and shore birds, but with the exception of one variety, to which we gave the name of steam boat geese, are much smaller than ours, and of a richer plumage.

The Relief was ordered from Rio de Janeiro to run a line of soundings along the coast of Patagonia, and

4

also to examine the shoals which are said to exist on
that coast.   This work was performed much to the
satisfaction of Captain Wilkes.   She stood several
times close in to the coast of Patagonia, and twice so
near that the lamas could be seen feeding in herds on
the declivities of the hills.   She came to anchor twice
along the coast; the harbors were unprotected from
the violence of the waves, therefore she could not remain at anchor long enough to examine the shores or
any part of the interior.

She visited most of the harbors in the straits of Le
Mair, which we passed without noticing, and had intercourse with the natives.   The principal one was
Good Success Bay.   On the 2d January, she anchored
in this bay and in the evening Captain Long, accompanied by some of the officers and scientific gentlemen, visited the shore.   They landed in a cove near
the southern end of the bay, where they found a
stream of water about forty feet wide, which discharges itself in the bay :—the water was of a dark
color, but of an excellent quality.   Some of the party
attempted the ascent of the highest mountain.   They
found the ascent, in consequence of the vegetation
and looseness of the soil, extremely laborious.   But
by perseverance they succeeded in gaining the summit, when they found themselves amply repaid for
their trouble, in the romantic and picturesque scenery
which the country afforded.   They had also a commanding view of the bay, and an indistinct view of
Staten Island, besides several small islands that in-
terspersed the bay.   Some of the party took their guns,
expecting to find plenty of game, but were disappointed, for not a living animal of any kind was seen.

# CHAPTER III.

Interview with the Natives—Orange Harbor—Interview with
another party of Natives—Return of a part of the Squadron—
Valparaiso—The Cemetery.

" And over head
And all around, wind warred with wind, storm howled
To storm, and lightning, forked lightning crossed,
And thunder answered thunder, muttering sounds
Of sullen wrath."

Next morning we got underway and stood out of
the harbor with a fine breeze, but it soon died away
and the ship drifted back into the bay and we again
came to anchor. At six o'clock several natives were
seen coming near the ship, and in order to attract our
attention, commenced a piteous yell. This not a little surprised them, for no sign of a native had been
seen on the preceding day.

Captain Long, accompanied by several officers,
left the ship in three armed boats for the purpose of
having communication with them. On landing, the
natives came running towards them and showed evident signs of their being welcomed to their shores,
and commenced crying " Cuchillo! Cuchillo!" and
as cuchillo is the spanish for knives, and as Waddell
in his book says they have many Spanish words in
their language, it was thought at first that they were
asking if we have any knives to sell; but when

knives were shown them, they still continued their cries.   When a looking glass was shown them and a string of beads, they appeared pleased, but still the word was kept up during the whole intercourse, and it was impossible to learn its meaning.   Our own words they would easily repeat and even seemed to understand some of them.   They set great value on steel and iron, and would readily exchange their bows and arrows for a piece of iron hoop or a few rusty nails : some of the arrows were neatly made, with flint heads.

This party consisted of fourteen men, and with the exception of the chief, were all young, well made and good looking.   They were full six feet high, well modeled, and had very pleasing countenances.   They all had their hair cut short on the top of the head, and their faces smeared with a kind of clay, something like red ocre.   Their dress consisted of a single guaco skin, which, when put properly on, covered their bodies as far down as the knees; but they were not particular on this point, and often exposed themselves to a shameful degree.   Most of them were troubled with a disease of the eye, which may perhaps be attributed to their long winters, when the ground is covered with snow, which dazzles their eyes in the open air.   It seems quite evident that they have had intercourse with the Europeans before, for the report of guns did not frighten them in the least.   All endeavors to entice them on board proved unavailing; they shook their heads and pointed to the woods, and then ran some distance from the boat.

From here the Relief touched at New Island, and came to anchor and examined the shore, but found no natives. From the marks that were seen, it is very evident that natives had been recently there.

Her next place of anchorage was in a small bay about twenty or thirty miles from Orange Harbor, called Nassau Bay. They were there visited by natives entirely different from those seen at Good Success. She had scarcely got her anchor down when a canoe full of natives came alongside,—three men, one woman, and a child. Upon invitation, two of them came on board without hesitation or dismay, and Captain Long was not a little surprised to find them so different from those seen at Good Success. They spoke an entirely different language, were of a low stature, ill shapen and desperately dirty. So great indeed was the difference, that no room was left for doubt but that those seen at Good Success were natives of Patagonia, and had wandered there in quest of game.

Orange Harbor is a large and spacious harbor, situated at the deep and extensive bay of Nassau, and protected from the violence of the waves by a small island called Burnt Island, on which the Relief had a light house erected for the use of the squadron, should they arrive in the night time. It is intersected by many small bays or harbors, suitable for boats to enter for wood and water. The most convenient one is Dingy Cove, situated nearly at the head of the bay, in which boats may enter and fill with wood, cut from the banks. The neighborhood is plentifully supplied with wood, but this is the most convenient place to get a supply. Game is found here in great profusion, and water in abundance, of an excellent quality. This is the harbor where the celebrated cir-

4*

cumnavigator, Captain James Cook of the British
Navy, anchored and refitted ship previous to his Antarctic cruise, on his second voyage of discovery.
Subsequent explorers have anchored here and refitted.
Captain King of H. B. M. ship ———, has been on this
coast for several years surveying. He also made this
his rendezvous, and by him it was accounted the best
harbor on the coast.

Fish are found here in great abundance, and of an
excellent quality,—as good, if not better than our pan
fish at home. The first few days after our arrival
we had very boisterous weather, but it soon became
more moderate. Early in the morning a canoe came
alongside with six natives, five men and one woman,
bringing with them spears and a necklace made of
shells, which they readily exchanged for pieces of
cotton and pieces of an old iron hoop. They were
invited on board, but at first, only one would venture.
This was a young man of about nineteen years of age
and rather good looking. They were evidently of
the same race as those seen at Nassau Bay. They
spoke the same language and dressed and walked
like them. The woman was old, ugly and as muscular as any of the men, and with them partook of
an equal share of the labor of the paddle. They all
listened attentively to the flute and guitar, and even
attempted to imitate the songs accompanying the music. Every new object they saw attracted their attention. They were conducted to every part of the
ship, and shown every thing considered at all attractive. Their canoe was constructed of strips of bark
sewed together, and so frail and leaky that one had
constantly to keep bailing to keep it afloat. It was

about twenty-five feet long and three wide. The bottom was covered with a layer of clay about one foot thick, and on which a fire was kept burning and around which the indians were constantly hovering. Our friends, the natives, left us about one o'clock, P. M., and landed nearly opposite the ship, where they built a large fire.

On the 25th of February, the United States Ship Peacock, William L. Hudson, Esq. commanding, Brig Porpoise, Charles Wilkes, Esq., commander in chief; Schooner Sea Gull, Lieutenant Johnson, started on a cruise to the Polar regions. As the Porpoise passed out of the harbor, she was successively cheered by all the squadron. The Vincennes, in charge of Lieutenant Thomas T. Craven, was left in this harbor to await the return of the Squadron. All the sick and invalids from those vessels bound on a cruise, were left behind for the purpose of recruiting.

At six o'clock, A. M., January 6th, the store ship Relief got underway and stood out to sea, bound on a cruise to the straits of Magellan. She had on board a number of our scientific gentlemen, and also the fleet surgeon, Doctor Gilchrist.

Since our arrival here we have generally experienced milder weather than was expected in such a high latitude. It is such weather as we generally have in the United States in the latter part of February. We caught daily a plenty of fish and killed an abundance of game.

We were again visited by a party of natives in several bark canoes who came alongside, and upon invitation a number came on board. As soon as they came on deck their vociferation seemed to increase with their astonishment, and it may be added, their pleasure; for the reception they met seemed to create no less joy than surprise. Whenever they received a present, or were shown any thing which excited fresh admiration, they expressed their delight in loud and repeated ejaculations, which they sometimes continued till they were quite hoarse, and out of breath with the exertion. The noisy mode of expressing their satisfaction was accompanied by jumping, which continued for a minute or more, according to the degree of passion which was excited, and the bodily power of the person who exercised it. The old man was rather too infirm to express the full amount of his gratitude, but still did his utmost to go through the performance.

After some time passed upon deck, during which a few bows and arrows, and one or two skins were bought from them, they were taken down into the cabin. The younger ones received the proposal to descend rather doubtingly, till they saw that their old companions were willing to set them the example, and they then followed without fear. They were, like our former visitors, almost in a perfect state of nudity. Still the women possessed an uncommon share of modesty, and seemed perfectly conscious of their exposed situation, for not one could be induced to come on board, though presents were repeatedly offered them as an inducement. There were one or two children in the number, whom they seemed to treat with great tenderness. A blanket was given to one of the women, and she had no sooner received it, than she wrapped it around her child. I was much astonished to witness the modest behavior of these poor savages, as quite the reverse might be expected from beings so literally in a state of nature, and ignorant of social intercourse.

We had much amusement with the men who came on board. We dressed them up in sailors' and marines' clothing, and then took them before a looking glass, that they might view their altered appearance.

The only word of their language that I could distinguish was " *Yam Mah Scooud,*" which words they repeat when asking for any thing. They are a set of poor, miserable beings, but very innocent; they did not touch an article that was not given them. About four o'clock they left the ship and encamped on shore opposite to us. The only dwelling which we could discover that they inhabited, was made of the branches of trees.

March 13th. The natives paid us another visit this morning, expecting to get another load of presents, but were disappointed. They had pulled off the clothes that had been given them the day previous, and came as naked as when on their first visit. This was done no doubt to excite our sympathy and solicit charity. It is very surprising how these poor, miserable beings can subsist, with but little covering to protect them against the inclement weather which prevails here during the entire year. Their principal food is shell fish, which they procure during their short summer, and dry in the sun, for the winter's supply. Yet another proof of the goodness of Him who tempers the wind to the shorn lamb. Query, would this not be a fit place for our philanthropic missionaries to exercise their ameliorating powers?

From the date of my last remarks until the present

period, the weather has been almost constantly bad ;—
rain, hail and snow almost every day, with a constant gale of wind.   The indians seemed to have had
a knowledge of its approach, as they all left the coast
some days before it set in, and have not been seen
since.

On the 22d inst. the Schooner Sea Gull, Lieutenant Johnson, arrived from the southern cruise, and
brought some curiosities, among which was the skin
of a sea lion, killed at the South Shetlands.

Two days afterward, the Brig Porpoise, Charles
Wilkes, commander in chief, arrived.  He had visited during his cruise, the South Shetlands, Palmer's
Land, and penetrated as far as the sixty-sixth degree
of south latitude, when he was surrounded on all
sides by innumerable icebergs, and field-ice.  About
this time we had another visit from one of the natives,
who remained on board for a considerable time.  He
afforded much amusement for us, and served to beguile the tedious monotony of our hours, in his attempts to imitate and mimic our words and actions.
He seemed to be much pleased with the treatment he
received, but still seemed anxious to get with his old
companions.

At two o'clock, P. M., April 17th all hands were
called to get underway, and we dropped down to
Seapenham Bay, when the wind being light and unfavorable, we again came to anchor, where we lay
but a short time.  During the night all the watch
idlers, and all hands were startled from their slumbers
by the cry of "all hands!" who rushed on deck, and
found that we were close in shore and threatened
with a heavy squall.  It however passed off without

reaching us. At daylight we had a light wind and were just clearing the bay, and in sight of Cape Horn. At four P. M., Cape Horn bore by compass N. sixty-two degrees E., and False Cape Horn twelve degrees W. In a short time we found ourselves in a milder climate, and expected in a few days to be able to reach Valparaiso.

At daylight of the 12th of May, the coast of Chili was in sight, and shortly afterwards the lofty Andes were dimly seen above the eastern horizon, probably not less than fifty miles distant. Those lofty mountains have been seen sometimes at a distance of one hundred and fifty miles, particularly in a clear atmosphere before sunrise. The coast gradually rose into view as we approached it, and on the following day we were near enough to view its irregular form, with pleasing anticipations. As we approached the harbor of Valparaiso, the coast had the high and checkered appearance of some of the bold promontories of New England, though with the aspect of great sterility. When we came up with the Point of Angels, one object after another opened upon us, beginning with a large white house where the Governor occasionally resides for the purpose of inhaling the sea breeze. Then are seen the habitations of the citizens, stretching along above a sand beach, and then higher up the acclivities, almost covering the steep hills, the town is built. The name of the place, the "Valley of Paradise," is calculated to give one lofty expectations and prepare him for disappointment. If such a place is paradise it must be paradise *fallen*; as where the holy pair were expelled by sin.

The soil in the vicinity of Valparaiso, for the most

part, is very poor and the irregular broken country for miles around, has a peculiar desolate appearance, from the most total absence of vegetation and foliage. The long snowy range of the Andes, though so distant as to form a less impressive feature than my imagination had pictured, was still a very fine object, and if it could have been contrasted with any thing like an Italian foreground, would have been far more enchanting. The everlasting snows of the Andes, when viewed in particular lights, would gleam with brilliancy, as if overspread with burnished silver. And as we approached the harbor on the following day, the sombre interest of the scene was heightened by the chiming of bells for vespers, from the gloomy monasteries of the town.

As soon as we had come to anchor, and every thing was secured, the letter bag was brought on deck and its contents emptied on the Quarter. This was an anxious and interesting time,—every one waiting in suspense for his name to be called for a letter. Many of us had not heard from home since leaving the United States. Many were doomed to disappointment, and myself among the number.

A few days after our arrival, I obtained permission to visit the shore in company with a number of my ship-mates. We landed at a pier which had been recently built. This is the only place where a boat can land without being in danger of being dashed to pieces against the rocks, from the violence of the surf which every where beats along the shore.

We were met on the pier by a motley set, principally *Choloes*, or country people, dressed in their large *ponchos*, which very much resemble horse

blankets, with a hole in the middle through which
the head is thrust, so that the ends hang down behind and before. The women of the lower order
were variously habited in dirty calico frocks, and
shawls of coarse baize, either green or crimson. A
short walk made me pretty well acquainted with the
town. It has one large street and one or two small
ones, and in common with most Spanish towns, has
its *plaza*, or public square, with the government
house and a range of houses on the opposite side. I
looked in vain, as I passed along the street, for something interesting among the inhabitants.

Mount Alegre is an eminence which rises abruptly
from the centre of the town, and, in fact, nearly overhangs it. This is the residence of many of the
wealthy foreigners, merchants, doing business in the
towns. From here the view is delightful; the harbor, with all the shipping and the surrounding country, affords a beautiful prospect, seldom surpassed.
There are several inns or taverns in the town, and
among the number two English and one French.
Those houses kept by Chilians seem to be naturally
dirty, as it is a characteristic peculiar to them. But
this is not the case with the houses of the old Spaniards here, which are very clean and tidy. There is
no taste in the building of the town. The houses are
made chiefly of sun-burnt bricks, plastered outside,
and only one or two stories high, with red tiled roofs.
The bricks are generally two feet long, and one wide,
and very coarse. From what I observed, I should
judge their manner of making them might have been
similar to that practiced in Egypt by the Jews, in the
time of Moses.

5

The ladies of Valparaiso—and they form but a small portion of the whole in my estimation—are dress entirely different from those of the lower order; but none of them wear any hat or head dress, on ordinary occasions. Their ringlets or curls hang down the back in two long plaits, in some instances, nearly reaching to the ground.

The public buildings in Valparaiso, are very few, —a custom-house, a town-house, and a court-house are the principal ones. Their places of amusement consist of a theatre, poorly fitted up, and another old building where they hold their "chingonoa dances." This is one of the most ludicrous amusements that can be imagined, and I believe only the most abandoned portion resort there. Decency will not permit me to describe the scenes that may be here witnessed. *Seraglios* are numerous, and may be found in almost any part of the city. According to the number of inhabitants, I never saw so many "courtesans" in any place in my life; still they all pretend to be devoted Catholics. The people appear generally, hospitable and kind to strangers. It is quite amusing to see the country people coming in to market on their asses and mules, with their feet reaching almost to the ground, when, ever and anon, they would scourge the poor animals with a long pole which they invariably carry. The stirrups are made of wood, and almost as large as a peck measure,—even these seemed to be a load for the little animals.

The climate in Chili is very fine in summer, but in winter is subject to heavy rains, and also very severe gales of wind; ships are driven from their moorings and stranded on the beach. Among the most prevailing diseases are fevers. There are no slaves in the Republic of Chili.

The navy has increased considerably in a very short time. A squadron is now at Callao consisting of two frigates, two sloops of war, and several smaller vessels. This force has been recently employed against Peru, in which rencounter they were victorious.

During some of my subsequent visits on shore I strolled out to the burying ground, situated on a high hill which overlooks the town. On my way I passed several crosses, erected, as I was informed, for the purpose of eliciting prayers for souls in purgatory. The grounds are enclosed by two mud walls; one of those was appropriated to Catholics, or natives, and the other to persons of a different faith. Attached to the burying ground is a charnel house, which is literally a place of skulls. The dead are laid with their heads to the west, in shallow graves, and for the most part without either coffin or shroud. They are at first only covered with a small quantity of earth, which is beaten upon them with a billet of wood. When the graves are filled, a wooden cross, in place of a stone, is placed at the head to mark the spot. But the bodies are very often left so much exposed as to be nearly visible. The adjacent "Protestant Burying Ground" presented quite a different aspect. Many of the graves were marked, as in our country, with neat marble slabs, bearing appropiate inscriptions. Yet we were greatly shocked to learn that the Protestant graves have been repeatedly violated, either from malice or for plunder. I picked up several coffin plates marked with names and dates, and

I was assured on good authority, that one of my countrymen, who had been buried here, had been taken up and treated with great indignity.

There is but one road here, which leads to the city of Santiago, the capital of Chili, situated about sixty miles in the interior from Valparaiso. Several important roads have been projected, but the face of the country presents many obstacles, and improvements of this nature must necessarily be gradual. This country has enjoyed more peace than any of the new Republics, and the natives are generally considered superior to the Peruvians.

The government is a Central Republic. There are no inferior sovereignties, like our States, or Mexico and La Plata. The salary of the President is twelve thousand dollars, and that of the Prime Minister three thousand dollars. The people are in a prosperous condition, and far more contented than they were while under the oppressive colonial system of old Spain. Education is in its infancy, but some attention has been bestowed upon it, and the first rudiments of knowledge are pretty generally taught to the young.

On our arrival here, we learned that the storeship arrived at this harbor on the 13th of April, and lay off and on for several days before she could come into port, for want of anchors. She lost all her anchors and chains in a violent gale of wind off Noir Islands, where she came near being lost. The Peacock arrived here a little time before us, from her Antarctic cruise. The Brig Porpoise and Schooner Flying Fish came in with us; but the Schooner Sea Gull is still absent from the Squadron, and fears are entertained for her safety, as, when she was last seen by her consort, the Flying Fish, she was supposed to be in a dangerous situation on a lee-shore, off Cape Horn. She had on board a crew of thirteen men and two officers. Passed Midshipman E. J. Reid and Mr. Baker, were the two officers attached to her. Lieutenant Thomas T. Craven was to remain here, to take charge of the Sea Gull in case she should get here in safety, if not, to go in search of her.

On the 5th of June, we got underway and stood out, bound to sea. The Peacock and Brig Porpoise sailed a few days since for the same port. Nothing worthy of particularizing happened on our passage, which was performed in fifteen days. On the 20th June we came to anchor in the harbor of Callao under the Island of San Lorenzo. We found the U. S. S. ship Relief, Peacock, Porpoise and Schooner Flying Fish all at anchor here, also the U. S. S. Lexicon, the Chilian Squadron, and one English and one French frigate, besides a number of merchant vessels. No news yet from the Sea Gull.

5*

# CHAPTER IV.

San Lorenzo—Epitaphs—Appearance of Natives and Soldiers—
" Glorious Fourth "—Funeral of one of our number—Discovery of several Islands.

> " Saved from the perils of the stormy wave,
> And faint with toil, the wanderer of the main,
>   But just escaped from shipwreck's billowy grave,
> Trembles to hear its horrors named again.
>   How warm his vow, that ocean's fairest mien
> No more shall lure him from the smiles of home,
>   Yet soon forgetting each terrific scene,
> Once more he turns, o'er boundless deeps to roam."

The prospect where we now lay was truly interesting. We had a full view of the town and fortress of Callao, an indistinct view of the spires and churches of Lima and eight miles to the rear of Callao, and to the rear of all, a lofty chain of the Andes, the lofty tops of which were lost amid the clouds. The Island of San Lorenzo, where we then lay, was formed by the earthquakes of 1740, which destroyed the whole city of Callao. It is a large mound or heap of sand and stones, with no sign of vegetation. It is the burying place of foreign seamen, who are not of the Catholic faith, who die in this port. In the course of my rambles on shore I copied some of the most striking epitaphs.

"In memory of William Price, seaman;—on board United States Brig Boxer, who died September 25th, 1830.

> A mother's eye will look,—but look in vain,—
> For her lov'd son returning from the main;
> He left his home to tempt the fickle wave,
> And now reposes in a foreign grave.
> Peace to his soul, an everlasting peace,
> Where troubles come not, and pleasures never cease. "

"To the memory of Bryce Gringle, who departed this life February 27th, 1837, on board United States Brig Boxer.

> Short was the summons to the dreary tomb
> Of him who sleeps beneath this dreary sod,
> The friend* he trusted crushed his early bloom
> And sent him unprepared to meet his God.
> No kindred wept above his youthful bier,
> And stranger hands have placed this tribute here."

"To the memory of Thomas Hedrick, of the United States Ship of the Line North Carolina, who departed this life at Callao on the 13th, 1838, æt sixteen years.

> In vain had youth its flight impeded,
> And hope its passage had delayed;
> Death's mandate all has superseded,—
> The latest order Tom obeyed."

---

* He was murdered in his hammock by his best friend, his traveling companion. He was an Italian, and in a fit of jealousy, perpetrated the foul deed. His friend had given his " rations " to another, and his exasperation could be quenched only by the murder of his companion. Comment is unnecessary.

"Sacred to the memory of James Lawrence, late seaman on board H. B. M. ship President, who departed this life February 8th, 1838.

> A worthy shipmate and a friend sincere,
> In the cold, silent grave now resteth here;
> His warning was but short,—think of his fate,
> Prepare for death before it is too late."

"Sacred to the memory of William Edwards, late of the Royal Marines, on board H. B. M. ship Harrin, who departed this life at Callao, November 29th, 1839.

> I'm here at rest from busy scenes;
> I once belonged to the Royal Marines;
> I'm now confined within these borders,
> Remaining here for further orders."

New Callao, though the sea port of Lima, is, without any exception, the most miserable looking place I ever saw. The principal street, following the curvature of the beach, is miserably paved, which renders walking disagreeable. The rest, excepting the one leading into the road to Lima, are narrow, dirty lanes. The houses are generally of one story, constructed of reeds, plastered with mud, and white-washed both inside and out;—furnished with clumsy wooden verandas and flag staff. The roofs are flat and covered with the same kind of materials, which form the walls; but instead of being preserved for promenades, they are receptacles of all kinds of rubbish, such as rags, broken bottles, demijohns tumblers, old baskets, rams' horns, remnants of bedding, and old boots and shoes. There are very few decent houses in the place. The one occupied by the captain of the port makes the best external appearance. The interior of the dwellings are generally filthy. When passing by the door of the port surgeon, I was struck with astonishment at its appearance;—a hen and chickens were sitting in one corner of the office, where he was writing prescriptions for invalids. It seems to be a natural disposition for all classes of them to live in filth. The women belonging to the higher order are at their toilette about five o'clock in the afternoon, after which they either thumb the guitar or sally forth for a *pasio*, or walk. In passing their houses at any other time of the day, you see them with their dress hanging negligently about their persons, opened behind or exposing their bosom in front, with their feet perched upon the rounds of a chair, and perhaps swinging, or gazing upon the passing stranger. Before the door of many houses, may be seen, exposed for sale by orange women, setting in *dishabelle* on the pavements, the different kinds of fruit peculiar to the climate; some mending their clothes, while their naked children are playing with the fruit.

It is not uncommon to see persons examining each other's heads in the immediate vicinity, if not over the articles they have for sale. The multitude of lazy, idle soldiers, consisting of indians, negroes and mulattoes, lounging about the streets in every direction, fill the stranger with the most unfavorable impressions. A few are stationed on the quay near the landing;—the remainder sauntering about wherever they choose. Their uniform is ridiculous. It usually consists of a coat, and pantaloons of coarse, unbleached canvas, trimmed with black cord; sometimes the pantaloons are made of coarse red flannel, with narrow strips of black and yellow, extending down the outward seam. They have a cartridge box, a bayonet and sometimes a gun, but are often without the latter. A heavy leather bell-crowned hat, or cap, enclosed in a case of white cotton, with a band of black ribbon, completes the list of articles. The Peruvian officers wear a rich uniform. They make a great display of epaulettes and gold lace.

The contrast between the inhabitants of Peru and the United States, was truly striking, and led me to reflect with pleasure upon the superior advantages enjoyed by the citizens of enlightened countries for the cultivation of all those social enjoyments that tend to refine society, and exalt the human mind.

I regretted very much that I did not have an opportunity of visiting Lima, the famed city of the "Five Kings;" however I had my curiosity satisfied with regard to their " bello sexo," for I have had an opportunity of seeing them frequently in Callao. Those which struck my particular attention were dressed in the Saya y Manta, one of the most novel and unique dress I ever saw worn. The universal walking dresses of the ladies of Lima, is the Saya y Manta. It is confined to this and a few other cities in South America. The Manta probably had its origin from the moors in Spain. The Saya consists of an elastic petticoat, made generally of satin or velvet, of black or cinnamon color, plaited up and down in very small folds, and so shaped as to fit very closely, allowing the wearer merely room for walking with a short step. The Manta is a hood of black silk, drawn round the waist, and carried over the head so as to cover the whole upper part of the person. The ladies usually wear it so closely as to expose only one eye. Hence it becomes impossible to recognize an intimate acquaintance when enveloped in the *Saya y Manta*.

To these two garments are added a fine shawl, with silk stockings and satin shoes, while a rose is held in the hand. Some of the ladies on an evening promenade, are seen in the English dress, with a shawl thrown over their heads, but never with any thing like a bonnet or hat. Within the city, the castles, which are two, are the only public buildings of note.

There are no schools in Callao and but few in Lima, and but little thirst for acquiring knowledge is manifested by any of the native Peruvians. Revolution after revolution has kept the country in a constant state of excitement, and prevents them from having any settled government. Anarchy reigns throughout the whole country of Peru.

On the 24th of June all the crew of the Relief, except the invalids, were transferred to this ship, and their places filled by invalids and superannuated seamen from the different vessels of the Squadron, who are to be sent home.

July 4th. "Peruvian dew" prevails extensively. It never rains here, but at this season of the year the atmosphere is very humid, and sometimes the air is so damp as to wet through thick cloth in a very short time.

The ship was dressed on the 4th, commemorative of the "declaration of independence." At twelve,

A. M. a salute was fired on board the Falmouth, and immediately the English ship Samorang answered it. "The glorious fourth" was not forgotten, though we were far from the land that gave us birth,—the land that we love as the home of the free, and the asylum of the oppressed. The associations of home are seldom forgotten, especially when those associations are of a thrilling nature, like those that marked the struggle of our fathers for freedom.

In the afternoon of the 8th, Benjamin Holden, late marine on board United States store-ship Relief, attached to the Exploring Expedition, who departed this life yesterday, on board the Peacock, to which ship he had been transferred as Purser's Steward, was conveyed to the Island of San Lorenzo for interment. The funeral obsequies were performed by Mr. Elliot, our chaplain. The corpse was accompanied to the place of sepulture, by a guard of marines and two or three officers.

All things being ready, at five o'clock, July 13th, we got underway and stood out to sea, all the squadron in company. On the following day, the Commander in Chief's general order was read on the quarter-deck, in the presence of all the officers and crew, respecting their conduct towards the natives of the savage islands which we were about to visit. I anticipated this to be the pleasantest part of our cruise, for we expected to visit many strange islands and have much intercourse with their inhabitants.

After leaving Callao, we had delightful weather, passing through the most pleasant climate in the world. For days together not a cloud was visible; the atmosphere was as clear as a crystal and the stars were shining brilliantly. A combination of such rare beauty and sublimity was sufficient to inspire the mind with awe and veneration.

At half past 12, Aug. 1st, Alexander Ogle, corporal of marines, breathed his last. He had been sick only a few days, with an affection of the brain. At three o'clock, P. M. all hands were called to bury the dead, having been previously ordered to appear in white mustering clothes. This was the first time many on board had witnessed a burial at sea. It was a melancholy and imposing sight. A canvas hammock both served for a coffin and a shroud. The body was inclosed in it in connection with two thirty-two pound shots placed at the feet, and a rough plank was the only bier, while an ensign was the pall. The corpse was borne to the lee gangway by the messmates of the deceased. All was still. The chaplain stationed himself near the corpse, and commenced the beautiful and impressive burial service of the Episcopal church. At the words, "We therefore commit his body to the deep," we heard the plunge, and a momentary silence, and an expression of solemnity was apparent among the crew. The rite of sepulchre ended, silence pervaded the ship for a little space of time, and then all was again bustle and confusion.

On the 13th, we made Mount Tenin Island. During the day we were engaged in surveying it. This island is low and composed of corals, with a coral reef surrounding it. The surface of the island is covered with low shrubbery and high grass. Some of our scientific gentlemen, by dint of swimming through a strong surf, succeeded in reaching the shore, where some specimens of shell, coral, &c. were obtained.

6

No natives were seen at this time, but as there had
been evident signs of natives seen the day before, and
our party not knowing their disposition, desisted from
venturing far into the bushes, fearing a rencounter
with them.

On the following day Captain Wilkes, accompanied by several officers and scientific gentlemen, with
a strong party of armed men, left the ship with the intention of visiting the shore, and, if a landing could
be effected, to examine the interior of the island, and
have intercourse with the natives. For the further-
ance of this object he had provided himself with
some presents for the natives in order to gain their
esteem and confidence. As the boats approached the
shore they found that the natives had assembled to
the number of a hundred or more, and posted themselves along the beach, armed with spears, clubs, and
bows and arrows; and indicated their intention to
attack them should they presume to land. They
were evidently savages in the wildest state, and from
their movements, we were induced to believe that
they never had seen white men before. Captain
Wilkes endeavored to make them understand the intention of his visit and his friendly disposition toward
them, but all to no purpose. They persisted in their
determination to resist, and oppose our landing.
They were all perfectly naked, men, women and
children indiscriminately. Our party thinking to in-
timidate them, fired several of their pieces loaded
with small shot among them; this, instead of having
the desired effect, only served to irritate them more.
The effect produced by the small shot was very
slight, probably not entering the skin; it only made a

smarting sensation for a few moments. They retreated to the bushes for a short time, and then returned, manifesting their anger in loud yells and
hideous grimaces. Captain Wilkes finding it impossible to reconcile the natives, and not wishing to shed
innocent blood, gave up the idea of forcing a landing,
and therefore soon after returned to the ship.

On the following day we made the Island of Hon-
den, and at dark, hove to for the night. In the morning we commenced the survey of it. This island is
small and unimportant, except as it lays in the track
of vessels bound to more important islands. It was
surveyed by Captain Wilkes, and its position correctly laid down on the chart. The bearings of the most
important points were taken, and the soundings
about the reefs ascertained. We caught three large
turtles, a species that grows very large; some arrive
to an enormous size. Those that we caught weighed
about two hundred pounds. Some specimens of
beche-le-mer were obtained and cured for the government.

At meridian, on the 22d inst. we discovered another island, and at five o'clock came up with it. A
white flag was flying on shore, an emblem of peace
among the islands. At dark, tacked ship and stood
on and off during the night. In the morning boats
were sent to survey it, which was completed by ten
o'clock, and we stood on our course.

On the 24th August, made Disappointment Island,
one of the islands belonging to the Dangerous Archipelago. At three o'clock a canoe came along, filled
with natives, but we could not prevail on any of
them to come on board, although presents were offer-

ed them. They were shy, but offered no signs of hostility. In their external appearance they much resemble the Clearmont Island natives. They were stout looking men, well proportioned in all respects, and the most of them were young, but very dirty. They wore their hair long, which was coarse and black, and hung down the back. They were in a perfectly denuded state, except a piece of dirty *tappa* passed round the waist. At twelve a boat was sent on shore with presents for them in charge of an officer. When on shore the natives showed no signs of fear, as they did while alongside of the ship in their canoes. They accepted the presents and seemed to be very thankful. In return, they sent on board some specimens of shells and a few of pearl. Next morning we left Disappointment Island; and at meridian on the same day, discovered King's Island, so called after the look-out man, who discovered it. It is a small island, about four or five miles in circumference, and in breadth not more than one. Its rise from the water to the most elevated spot, is not more than twenty feet. Its shores are every where marked with general sterility. The most remarkable spot is a lagoon of fresh water, which runs through nearly the whole extent of the island. A small aperture runs into the south end, by which the congregated waters of the laguna are poured into the sea. This laguna abounds in fish of a great variety; some were caught, and found to be extremely well flavored. They made quite an agreeable change, after having lived upon "salt junk" for two months. This island was surveyed, and the bearings of some of the most remarkable points taken.

On the following day, 31st August, we made Rara-ka Island, and about nine o'clock came up with it. At ten, Captain Wilkes went on shore, and returned shortly after, bringing with him three natives, one of whom was a chief. The chief was an old man,—I should judge, about sixty years of age.

On the 1st of September, we made and passed a chain of low islands called the Dangerous Archipelago. At four o'clock, we came up with a small island, which, not being found on any chart, Capt. Wilkes called "Vincennes Island," after the name of the ship. It is situated in the latitude of 15 deg. 48 min. south, and, like its neighbors, is very low. It is of coral formation, and surrounded by a coral reef. None of these islands afford any anchorage for vessels of the smallest size, and no safe landing even for boats.

At 9 o'clock, Sept. 3d, came up with Karlshoff Island. Lowered a boat and sent ashore, which soon returned with three natives, who informed the captain that hogs, fowls and cocoa-nuts might be obtained at this island. In the evening a boat was sent on shore for the purpose of obtaining a supply of water. She returned with about five hundred gallons of very excellent water. This was found in a lagoon in the middle of the island. The water was good for present use, but will not keep long at sea, owing to its being impregnated with animalcules, which putrify and cause it to be decomposed. On this island we found a partial supply of cocoa-nuts and breadfruit, which, together with the fish, constitute the principal food of the natives.

At 9 o'clock, Sept. 8th, came up with Fly Island.

6*

Two canoes came off, bringing with them a present of shells for the Expedition. This island is small, and rises gradually from the sea to sixty or seventy feet, in the centre. It is thickly covered with bread-fruit and lofty cocoa-nut trees. The acclivities of the rising ground were handsomely variegated with shrubbery and green verdure.

———◆———

## CHAPTER V.

Island of Matavai—Visit of the Consul—Expedition—Sermon by Rev. Mr. Wilson—Conduct of the American Consul—Treaty—Interview with the Natives—Description of the Islands—Traits of the Inhabitants—Effects of Missionary labor.

> " Unmixed with aught of meaner tone,
> Here nature's voice is heard alone ;
> When the loud storm, in wrathful hour,
> Is rushing on its wings of power,
> And spirits of the deep awake,
> And surges foam, and billows break,
> And rocks and ocean-caves around,
> Reverberate each awful sound ;
> That mighty voice, with all its dread control,
> To loftiest thought shall wake thy thrilling soul."
>
> *Mrs. Hemans.*

At 9 o'clock, Sept. 9, the high and rugged peaks of Matavai Island were seen to emerge from ocean, and as we approached them, became more and more visible, while the surrounding objects were becoming more and more interesting until the mountain tops were seen above the clouds. This island is exceedingly fertile, producing lofty cocoa-nut trees, and the sides of the mountain are covered with dense vegetation, extending down the acclivity nearly reaching the water's edge. It affords, as one approaches it, one of the most beautiful, picturesque and romantic landscapes that we have yet met with any where among the islands.

At 10 o'clock we anchored, and commenced surveying it. We saw two beautiful villages along the coast, only a mile or two apart. These villages are embowered in breadfruit trees, which protect them from the scorching sun of a tropical climate, and supply the natives with food, which they have only to pluck from the trees overhanging their habitations. There are several missionaries, natives of Otaheite, residing here, who, by their influence and example, have done much to convert them to the Christian religion. In each village they have a neat little chapel. Deciding to leave at 5 o'clock, we made sail and stood for Otaheite, distant about fifty miles.

On Tuesday, 10th Sept., after a pleasant voyage, we came to anchor in Matavai Bay, off Point Venus. The island of Otaheite is the most important one of the Georgian Group. We had scarcely come to anchor when the ship was plentifully furnished with necessary supplies from the canoes which literally surrounded us.

Shortly after our arrival at this island, we were joined by the Peacock, with which we had parted some days previous. We were all busily engaged in making preparations for our contemplated observations, and also in fitting up temporary accommodations for the sick of the squadron.  The queen kindly offered the use of a fine airy house on Point Venus for this purpose.  This is the place where the celebrated English circumnavigator, Capt. James Cook, observed the transit of Venus, and since that time, in honor of the circumstance, it has been designated by that name.

On the 12th, an expedition for an exploration of the interior of the island, consisting of the following persons, was projected :—Dr. Pickering, Naturalist; Mr. Peal, Zoologist; Mr. Breckenridge, Horticulturist; Dr. Guillon, Meteorologist; Lieut. Emmons, Hydrographer; Serg't Stearns, Ass't Naturalist Dep't; Samuel Sutton, seaman, Taxedermist; John Brooks, seaman of the Vincennes, and one seaman from the Brig Porpoise; Mr. Lewis, resident at Papiete, as interpreter and guide; and eight natives, to carry baggage.

The object of the expedition, as far as I could learn, was as follows.  First, to visit the lake, situated on the most elevated part of the island, and then, if possible, to reach the highest extremity of the mountain; ascertain the productions of the country,—vegetable, marine, mineral, and animal.  Also, to visit all places celebrated in history, learn something of their inhabitants, former mode of worshiping places; obtain all natural and artificial curiosities worthy of notice; survey the lake, and make specific and general observations on the manners and customs of the islanders.

As we approached the land we were delighted with the verdure, luxuriance and beauty of the landscape, opening to us a beautiful, fertile country, and a handsomely built native church.  The land about the beach to the southward and westward, is very low, while that to the northward and eastward is moderately high. The bay is about two miles wide and one deep, perfectly safe and easy of access. The country is beautifully sprinkled with trees of lofty cocoa-nut growing so near the beach that their roots are denuded by the surf; and a little back from the shore are to be seen breadfruit, pananas, and *ti*, and handsomely variegated with shrubbery and parasitical plants of the richest foliage. Cocoa-nuts here are very abundant, and afford a very grateful beverage to the weary traveler, and is an excellent drink in a hot day. The land begins to rise a few miles back from the village, and continues its rise for fifteen or twenty miles, extending to a thick wood, encircling Obreno. The beach is covered with varied vegetation.

The mission-house is pleasantly situated about one hundred yards from the beach, obscured from our view by a skirt of wood, growing on a small stream which runs parallel with the beach, embowered in the branches of the wide-spreading breadfruit trees, the fruit of which overhangs their habitations, where they have only to go out of their houses and pluck it as they want it for use. The chapel is situated a few hundred yards from the beach, and about the same distance from the mission-house. It is a building capable of holding one thousand persons. Mr. Wilson is the missionary here, and the oldest one on the islands. He was among the number who visited this island in 1812, and was sent out by the London Missionary Society.

I had the curiosity to visit the chapel a few days since, and was much amused at the vocal performance. The chapel is a large, airy building, but in rather a dilapidated state. I was told that the audience was not as numerous as on ordinary occasions, numbering only about four hundred. They all behaved in a very becoming manner, and gave unusual attention to the remarks of the preacher. The natives were better clad, generally, than I expected to find them; and some of the females manifested considerable taste in their dress. Mr. Wilson, so far as I was able to judge in listening to his sermon in an unknown tongue, is a good preacher; at least he is a good orator. At the close of the service, great regularity was observed in leaving the house; the people waited for each other till all could leisurely retire. Captains Wilkes and Hudson, and many of the officers, were present. The hymns which they sung were all set to English tunes.

There was something peculiarly touching in this, however trifling the circumstance may seem to the reader. Imagine the peculiarity—not to say awkwardness of our position—while listening with apparent interest to a sermon of which we could not understand a syllable, not even able to determine whether it was the promulgation of divine truth, or pagan superstitions, from any thing that we could detect. As the service advances, the hymn is announced, read in the same Babel-like language, and as its measured strains fall upon the ear, we detect the harmony of "Old Hundred," "Mear," or "St. Martin's," which, perchance, have greeted our dawn of existence, and quieted us in the restlessness of childhood! Who will wonder that *such* music has power to call up pleasing associations? Who will wonder that our attention was riveted upon that native choir, while the cherished events of other days came crowding thick around us ?

Mr. Murenhaut, now French Consul, but formerly American Consul, visited us during our stay in this place. About twelve months ago his wife was murdered, and he came near being killed, by a Peruvian whom they had in their employ. It appeared that it was his intention to rob the house, after he had finished his atrocious deed. The blow that killed his wife was intended for him ; when she saw it aimed at him, she interposed herself between the murderer and her husband, and received the blow, which caused her death almost instantaneously. The murderer was apprehended, tried and convicted for it, and suffered death ten days after the sentence was passed on him. He was hanged. This is the first execution that has taken place on this island for some years.

About twelve months since, two French Catholic priests arrived on this island, and, without the consent of the government, commenced to teach the Catholic religion to the poor natives. But as soon as the Queen was informed of it she strenuously opposed their proceedings ; of course she was advised by the Protestant clergy to discountenance the religion,—telling her that they worshiped idols and images, and would in a few years be masters of the island. She ordered them to depart from her dominions by the first opportunity ; but they heeded her not, and delayed their departure when an opportunity offered, until they worried the patience of the Queen. Finding that the mild and persuasive orders were not noticed, she determined to force them away. Accordingly she called a council of chiefs, and her adviser,

Mr. Pritchard. It was agreed that a small vessel should be chartered for that purpose, and in her they should be sent to South America, where the Catholic religion was tolerated. The priests when hearing that they were to be forced away, moved to the house of Mr. Murenhaut, the American consul; he had previously promised them protection under the American flag. The authorities of the island sent and had them forcibly taken away, and conveyed on board the vessel, which was destined to take them away, and they were conveyed in safety to the coast of South America, at the expense of the Tahitian government.

For this act of self-preservation and right, the king of the French sent a Frigate, and extorted from them two thousand dollars. On account of this affair, the President of the United States turned Mr. Murenhaut out of office. He was shortly afterwards appointed consul for the French.

While at this place a council was held at the village of Papiete for the purpose of forming a commercial treaty between the United States and the government of the Society Islands. Queen Pomarri could not attend on account of indisposition, and therefore sent her representative. Most of the officers of the squadron were present, dressed in full uniform, cocked hats, swords and epaulettes. The treaty was formed and signed by both parties, and I believe proved satisfactory to all.

Having finished the survey of the harbor, and completed the series of observations at the observatory on Point Venus, we got underway and proceeded to Papiete, the principal village on the island, situated about five miles from Matavai Bay, where we arrived

on the same evening. The harbor of Papiete is safe, commodious, and easy of access. There were then lying here three American whale ships, one missionary brig and one trading brig. The harbor is protected from the violence of the waves by a coral reef. As you enter the harbor, you pass on the right side of an old mud fort, in a dilapidated state. The land in the vicinity of Papiete is much higher, and rises more abruptly than at Matavai Bay. The shores are generally clothed in green verdure, extending within a few yards of the water's edge. It has a beautiful and rich appearance; the village is a neat one, situated about the middle of the curvature of the beach. It is composed of several wooden buildings, built and owned by foreigners, one native church, and a neat seamen's chapel, built near the water. The native houses are about two hundred in number, built of bamboo, in the shape of our hay stacks at home, leaving both ends open. All the furniture they possess, is a few folds of *tappa*, and one or two mats on which to lie, with a block of wood for a pillow. The missionaries have a flourishing village here, and have the principal control of the island.

At 11 o'clock, Mr. Pritchard, English consul, and formerly principal missionary to this island, preached on board. He was accompanied by his lady, and two interesting little girls. Many of the foreign residents, and two of the chiefs were present. Mr. Pritchard is the Queen's adviser ;—is consulted on all occasions of importance, and what he decides upon, she never refuses to sanction. Mr. Pritchard sometimes preaches in the seamen's chapel, as there is no seamen's chaplain here. This is a great resort for our whalemen,

7

who come here for the purpose of recruiting, and sometimes for repairs.

During our stay we were honored by a visit from the principal chiefs, and two Tahitian princesses, sisters to Queen Pomarri,—also by the English and American consuls, the English consul acting as interpreter. The two princesses were neatly attired in light frocks, made after the European fashion, with pink waist, ribbons and straw bonnets, and shoes, with silk stockings. Some of the principal chiefs were neatly dressed in plain citizen's clothes, made also after the European fashion, but the inferior chiefs and attendants wore nothing but *tappa* wrapped round the waist, serving for trowsers; while some of them wore nothing but shirts. The two princesses behaved very modestly, but appeared quite at their ease. After partaking of a sumptuous entertainment, which was prepared for them in the cabin, they visited the different parts of the ship, attended by the officers. At almost every step something attracted their attention, on which they would stop and gaze till they were invited to look at something else. After visiting the different parts of the ship they retired on shore; but before leaving, Capt. Wilkes made them some handsome presents, and also some presents to their attendants. Among the presents to the two princesses was a musical box to each, with which they were highly delighted.

The Island of Tahiti, and all the Society Islands are under the jurisdiction of Queen Pomarri, and from her the power and charge of the different governors and chiefs of districts are derived. The royal residence was once in this village, but since her troubles with the French priests, she has changed it to the west side of the island, where she lives a more retired life, and considers herself more safe from the encroachment of her enemies.

*Common People.* This class constitutes all that portion who are not ranked with the chiefs and land-holders, which is about two thirds of the whole; the latter are an entirely different people in their manners and external appearance. Their labor is not exten-sive, for the spontaneous productions of the islands are enough for their support at all seasons of the year; hence it is to be expected that they live a very indo-lent life. The universal dress for the females of the common order, is a piece of *tappa*, calico, or cotton cloth, fastened loosely around the waist, and covers the whole of the lower portion of the body as far down as the knees; the chest and shoulders are always left bare, which they take great pride in exhibiting to the public. Some few of the common class may be seen dressed in frocks. Shoes are a luxury that but few of the fair sex aspire to; however, for comfort, their climate is so mild that they do not require them. The men have their hair cut short on the top of the head, and some, shaved quite closely.

The whole mass of the native population may be called merely nominal Christians, although the whole of them profess Christianity. Missionaries have at length found out their mistake in regard to the reli-gious principles and actions of the natives. The fe-males are generally extremely salacious, much more so than the men. Polygamy is not allowed to be practiced openly, but adultery prevails secretly to an unknown extent. There is no doubt but prostitution is carried to a greater length now, than when they were in a state of pagan darkness. The inquirer would say, what is the cause of this? I would answer, they have more wants to supply, since they have become acquainted with the civilized world; luxuries they never dreamed of when in their natural state. And they have no means of obtaining them in any other way. Consequently you will find men prostituting their own daughters, and very often the wife, for a dollar. Precocity exists here among the females in an eminent degree, and is manifest to a greater extent than in any place I have yet visited. It is not an uncommon thing to see mothers at the age of twelve, and old women at the age of twenty-four.

Sept. 25th. At daylight we weighed anchor, and stood over for the beautiful and romantic little Island of Eimeo, distant about fifteen miles from Papiete. At 1 o'clock we came to anchor close in shore, and near the principal village and missionary station. The harbor of Eimeo is open and exposed to the westerly winds; however, it seldom blows with such violence as to do any damage to shipping.

The natural productions of this island are nearly the same as at Otaheite. There are some very high mountains on this island; some rise abruptly from the sea to the height of twelve hundred feet. The coast is composed of lofty, craggy peaks, overhanging the surf-beaten shore. When approaching this island, from the first view, it presents a sterile aspect; but on a nearer approach, one finds the appearance changed, and the prospect more lively and animating; and when you enter the mouth of the harbor, you perceive the acclivities of the mountains clothed in

green verdure and dense vegetation. Then the valleys open to your view, presenting lofty cocoa-nut
trees, breadfruit trees, and ornamented with a variety
of fruit trees. Oranges, limes and pine apples were
ripe, and in great abundance.

The missionaries here have a beautiful station, and
fine field for the exercise of their labors. They have
two schools, and a printing press in full operation.
Messrs. Simpson and Scott are the Missionaries who
reside here. It is said to be the birth-place of the
husband of the present Queen, and when she married
him, he was only a common native. I noticed a disease among these islands, which appears to be more
common here. It is "Elephantiases," which the natives call *Fe*. This disease has its principal action
on the lower extremities, and extends upwards, sometimes till the whole thigh is affected; but I have never
seen more than one limb affected at a time. I saw
one so swollen that it measured thirty-six inches in
circumference.

After having completed the survey of the bay, on
the 27th Sept., got underway and proceeded to sea,
steering W. N. W. At sunset passed the Island of
Herniene, another of the Georgian Group. This
island is small and unimportant. On the 28th, we
passed a number of the Georgian Group, all of which
were small, but covered with vegetation.

On the 9th of Oct., we arrived at the Island of
Opoun, and the surveyers and scientific gentlemen
commenced their respective duties immediately.
There was but little of importance on this island.

During the evening a number of canoes came alongside, with natives; bringing cocoa-nuts and other

7*

fruit, for trade. On rounding the point of islands we discovered Toufon and Leon, two small islands west of Opoun. These islands form a group called the Tomalooah Islands; the natives are the same in all respects as those of the Navigator Islands. We engaged in surveying, in the meantime carrying on a brisk trade with the natives for fruit and specimens of shells, giving them tobacco and fish-hooks in exchange. Powder they were very anxious to get, but this we would not let them have, fearing serious consequences. We were informed that a destructive war had been raging between these two islands, which caused the extermination of one half of the natives of both islands.

There were several white men living on the island to which the natives belonged, who were alongside. They appeared to be abandoned, runaway sailors, who had deserted from whale ships that had touched here for supplies of fresh provisions. They informed us that the natives treated them well; they had land given them, but would not allow them to intermarry.

After leaving Opoun, we next directed our course to Tutuilla, one of the Navigator Islands, and anchored in Pango Pango Bay, on the south side. All was still and quiet on shore, from the fact—as we afterwards learned—that it was their Sabbath. Religious services were performed on board of the ship, on the following day, by our Chaplain, in accordance with our custom during the Expedition. Indeed, we have not met with any natives, however degraded, who had not some vague views, at least, of a Power superior to themselves. And it is questioned whether such can be found.

The natives of the Navigators resemble those of the Society Islands in their complexion and features, but there is a great difference in their language. Their huts are built in the same shape and constructed of the same materials. I saw some females engaged in their domestic occupations, such as making mats, *tappa*, fishing nets, &c. They appear more industrious than the females of Tahiti. In some parts of the island polygamy is still practiced, but at this village it is openly discountenanced by all the chiefs and the people. No man, of whatever rank he may be, is allowed to have more than one wife. The missionaries should have the credit of abolishing this practice. By their laws the crime of adultery is punished with death ; this rigid law causes their chastity to be preserved inviolate. Seldom indeed does a case of adultery occur; but when it does, if the offenders are detected, they never fail to suffer the penalty of the law. The females are very reserved in their manners. I was struck with admiration and astonishment at the conduct of these females, on all occasions. They never suffer any liberties to be taken with them, and seem particularly cautious in their intercourse with foreigners. Salaciousness does not exist here, with the females, in such a high degree as at many other islands which we have visited, and particularly Otaheite ; neither is precocity so common.

The whole mass of the natives on this part of the island, where the influence of the missionaries is felt, seems to be fast advancing to a state of civilization. They manifest a kind disposition, and have a mind susceptible of cultivation, and a thirst for knowledge is universal among them ; especially

at this village.  The missionaries have wrought a
great change in the morals of these people in a very
short time.  Mr. Murray is the missionary who has
charge of this station, and a polished gentleman he is
too.  He is devoted to the missionary cause, and in-
defatigable in his labors to cultivate and sow the seeds
of the Christian religion in this once benighted land
of Pagan darkness.  He has two flourishing schools
here, in each about three hundred scholars.  He is
assisted by native teachers, whom he has instructed
in the common rudiments of knowledge, and implant-
ed the true religion in their hearts.  Mrs. Murray, his
wife, is equally interested in the missionary cause,
and is also at the head of a female seminary, where
she teaches the native women the mode of manufacturing their own clothes and making straw bonnets,
in which some of them have become quite proficient.
I saw many of her pupils dressed very neatly in their
own manufacture.  They present quite a pleasing
contrast to their neighbors, the "devil tribe " who reside only a short distance from them.  This tribe has
refused to be instructed by the missionary, and still
remains in their primitive state ; and though only a
few miles off, never visit their Christian neighbors.

On the following Sunday after our arrival, Mr.
Murray preached on board this ship ; he was accompanied by his wife, and one or two missionaries from
other stations on the island.

We again joined our consort, the Peacock, at Apia,
and also the missionary Brig Campden, which had
been in company with us at Otaheite.  This is the
most fertile and by far the handsomest island in the
whole group.  The land rises gradually from the sea-

shore; it breaks into mountains and ridges that are covered with rich foliage and green verdure almost to their summit. The shore abounds in tracts of table land, beautifully sprinkled and variegated with clumps, groves and single trees of the breadfruit, pandanas, and cocoa-nut trees, forming thick and deeply shaded bowers, overhanging the habitations of the natives. Several villages are scattered along the coast, with here and there the residence of a missionary, and a missionary chapel.

## CHAPTER VI.

Visit of the Christian party—Appointments of the Consul—The Samoa Group—Trial of a Native—Embarking of the Squadron—Wallace Island—Arrival at New Holland—Inhabitants.

> " O, when no more the sea-winds rave,
> When peace is brooding on the wave,
> No sounds but plaintive melodies ;
> Soothed by their softly mingling swell,
> As daylight bids the world farewell,
> The rustling wood, the dying breeze,
> The faint, low rippling of the seas,
> A tender calm shall steal upon thy breast,
> A gleam reflected from the realms of rest."

On the following day we were visited by the principal chief of the Christian party, who was accompanied by his wife and two interesting little daughters, together with a number of inferior chiefs and at-

tendants. The principal chief is a man of about
thirty years of age, and of copper color. He was
attired in a round-about jacket, made of blue cloth,
with pantaloons of the same, a white vest, white
shirt, fur hat, and shoes, which constituted the whole
of his wearing apparel. His wife was dressed in a
calico frock, straw bonnet, but wore no shoes. Her
husband looked like a boy by her side, in consequence
of her unusual corpulence. The two daughters were
more gaily attired; they wore gingham frocks with
waist ribbons, straw bonnets and morocco shoes.
The inferior chiefs and attendants wore nothing but
their native *tappa*, wrapped around the waist so as
to cover all the lower portion of the person. They
behaved themselves with much more propriety than
might have been expected from beings who have so
lately emerged from Pagan darkness. After visiting
the different parts of the ship, they were entertained
in the ward-room, where a sumptuous collation had
been provided for the occasion. They ate heartily,
but drank very sparingly of wine. On the following
day the principal chief, attended by a number of his
inferior chiefs, dined in the cabin. They were attended by Mr. Williams, junior, as interpreter. During his stay on board several large guns were fired,
which somewhat alarmed him at the first fire, when
he came immediately on deck, and seemed to be in
much confusion; but was soon reconciled by Mr.
Williams, who assured him that no harm was intended him.

After dinner Captain Wilkes and Captain Hudson,
with most of the officers, accompanied the King and
chiefs on shore to the mission-house, where from one

to two thousand natives had assembled to witness the exercise of small arms of a party of our marines and seamen, who had been sent on shore for that purpose. I was astonished to see such an assemblage of natives, mostly dressed in the native costume, wearing no clothing but a piece of *tappa* around the waist. They were doubtless as much astonished and amused at seeing us perform our military evolutions. At first they crowded around us very eagerly, but at a signal from the old chief, they retreated, and took up their position at a sufficient distance to allow us room for exercising, marching, firing, &c. Several rounds of blank cartridge were fired, which much pleased the natives.

On the same evening Mr. Williams, junior, was appointed American consul, or agent for the Samoa Group, and the American flag hoisted at his house.

### GENERAL REMARKS AND OBSERVATIONS ON THE SAMOA GROUP.

This extensive and populous group is situated in the South Pacific Ocean, and extends four degrees east and west. It was discovered on the 4th of May, 1678, by the French circumnavigator, Bougamville, who gave it the name it now bears, probably on account of the superior construction of their canoes, and their surprising dexterity in the water. The group is called by the natives Samoa, and consist of eight islands,—Manua, Orogangi, Ofu, Tutuilla, Upolu, Mauona, Aborima, and Savaii. In addition to these, there are several small islands off the coast of Tutuilla and Upolu. In the year 1788 this group was visited by the unfortunate La Parouse, whose colleague, M. de

Langley and a number of his men, lost their lives by being barbarously murdered by the natives. This tragical act conveyed such an impression of their treachery and ferocity as deterred subsequent voyagers from venturing among them. And for many years they appear not to have been visited by any vessel from the civilized world until a very late period, when a missionary station was established here, and the Rev. Mr. Williams was among the number who first filled this station. Tutuilla, the first of the Navigator islands where we visited, is about fifteen miles west from Orogangi, in 171 deg. west longitude, and 14 deg. 20 min. south latitude. This is a fine romantic Island, of from eighty to one hundred miles in circumference. It was here that the unfortunate M. de Langley lost his life; and on this account the bay in which he was murdered received the name of Massacre Bay. In passing down the coast you pass some fine bays,—the most conspicuous and important is Pango Pango, in which our squadron rendezvoused for a few days, whilst engaged in surveying the islands. Into this bay vessels of almost any class may run, and anchor in perfect safety, except during a strong south gale.

Opolu, the next island, in circumference is about seventy miles. The mountains on this island are very high, and in clear weather may be seen fifty or sixty miles. These are richly covered with verdure to their summit, and in the north-east part of the island, they present a variety in their form and character, which in some instances renders their appearance romantic and sublime; in others, soft, luxuriant and beautiful. It has been stated that there were no har-

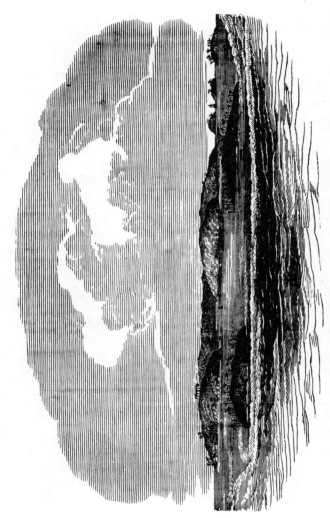

Wallace Island—View taken on the spot.

bors in this group, but at this island alone, we found them and surveyed them. The one at Apia, in which we anchored, is commodious, spacious and safe; and as it faces to the north, it admits, with the prevailing trade winds, of easy ingress and egress. The bottom is sandy, and at twenty-five yards from the beach there are about five fathoms of water. A river runs into the bay, so that any quantity of fresh water may be obtained of an excellent quality.

A council of chiefs was held on board the Peacock for the trial of a native who had been accused of the murder of an American citizen, about twelve months before. On the arrival of the Peacock the accused was delivered up to Capt. Hudson, and since that time has been in double irons on board that vessel. He was found guilty by the council, and sentenced to be executed, but through the influence of Captains Wilkes and Hudson, his sentence was commuted to banishment for life to Wallace Island, and the Peacock was deputed to convey him to his exile home.

At 11 o'clock on the 11th, a signal was made for the squadron to get underway, and by 2, our sails were spread to the breeze of heaven, and we shortly after lost sight of the beautiful coast of Upolu. Favored with a strong breeze we made rapid progress on our course, and at 4, P. M., on the 12th, we came up with Wallace Island for the purpose of landing the prisoner whom we had brought from Apia. A number of canoes came off to us, and in one was a chief, to whom the prisoner was given in charge, with strict injunctions that he should not be killed, or suffered to escape.

From the view I had of Wallace Island, I should

8

say it was very fertile, and capable of much improvement. The Island seemed to abound in breadfruit and cocoa-nut trees, with a thickly covered surface of vegetation. The natives are a savage-looking race, and are said to be very barbarous.

November 15th. We were in the eastern hemisphere. Since leaving the United States, we had gained a day by our time, which is always the case when vessels double Cape Horn, but when coming round the East Cape they always lose a day. On the 18th, we passed Mathew's Island. It is a small barren island of about one or two hundred yards in circumference, of a circular form, and is about 400 feet above the surface of the water. It is situated in the latitude of 22 deg. 30 min. south, longitude 172 deg. east.

After a short passage we discovered a light, which proved to be that of Sydney, New Holland, where we came to an anchor on the following day. In the morning the citizens were not a little surprised to see a "Yankee Squadron" anchored close under one of their principal batteries. And they were still more astonished that we should escape the sight of their supposed vigilant pilots. They have hitherto considered themselves perfectly secure from silent intruders, as no vessel had ever entered there, either by day or by night, without the assistance of a pilot.

We were visited, on the morning after our arrival, by Mr. Williams, American Consul. He informed us that the Relief had sailed from here ten days previous to our arrival, bound to the United States, whither she had been ordered. During the day several English officers visited the ship, to exchange civilities with the officers.

We soon commenced our accustomed survey and collection, which were among the more prominent objects of the Expedition. In the mean time ample repairs were made, with necessary arrangements, preparatory to our voyage to the southern hemisphere, where we might expect to combat the rigors of the elements in their rudest aspects.

I visited the shore, and in my rambles met with some of the aborigines,—the most miserable beings I ever saw. They more resemble baboons than human beings. Those natives are so little known in our part of the world, that I have availed myself of the opportunity of getting information concerning them from different sources, all of which will be found interesting.

The following account is from Mr. F. Armstrong, Botanist, who has traveled much among them and understands their language, and probably knows more of their character than any other man.

None of the tribes with whom the interpreter has had communication, seems to have any just idea of a God. He has very often attempted to convey to them the idea of a Supreme Being, the creator of themselves and every object of their senses, present every where and at all times,—watching the actions of all men; adding, that good men, at death, ascend to him in the sky, but that bad men (instancing those who spear and murder others) are, when they die, banished from his presence forever. Their answer has generally been, "But how will God get us up to him in the sky? Will he let down a long rope for us? What shall we live upon there? Is there plenty of flour there?· Are there earth and trees there?" He has endeavored to meet this difficulty by describing the Deity as a being of infinite power, capable of doing any thing that appears quite impossible to man.

They have but little idea of a future state of rewards and punishments, as the result of their conduct in a prior existence. They believe that the spirit, or "goor de mit" of deceased persons passes immediately after death through the bosom of the ocean, to some unknown and distant land, which becomes henceforth their eternal residence. But in this respect, the arrival among them of the whites has led to a total change of creed. For they very soon recognize among their new visitors many of their deceased relatives and friends—a delusion which exists to this day as strong as ever. They confidently recognize several hundreds of the colonists by their countenances, voices and former scars of wounds.

They are quite positive that the reëmbodied spirits of Yogan, who was shot along with another, are already returned in the shape of two soldiers of the 21st regiment. The obstinacy with which they persist in this conviction, that the whites are all incarnations of the spirits of some departed relations or friends, is so great, that, notwithstanding the great confidence that they usually place in the interpreter, he has never been able to persuade them to the contrary ; at least the old persons,—but the young ones begin to have their faith shaken on this point. The names generally applied to the whites, when speaking among themselves, is "*diango,*" or the dead.

They have shown some curiosity to know what sort of a place the land of the dead is, but not as much as might be expected. They have asked the interpreter to sit down and tell them the names of such of their relatives as he saw there, and have often asked after particular individuals, whether the interpreter knew him or her, or whether he is soon coming back. He has never been asked whether the state of the dead was that of happiness or misery. They have often asked on what the spirits live, whether they have plenty of flour, whether the flour brought by us is dug out of the earth there? They have seen wheat ground into meal in the colony, but they will not believe that the settlers have the power of changing that brown mixture into the same white flour that the ships bring here. What animals, trees, &c., there are in that country? Whether the country was too small for us, or what other cause brought us here; whether we were not very sorry to leave our friends there?

They consider the Malays, Lascars, &c., whom they have seen here, to be, like the whites, returned spirits of some of their ancestors or friends, but who, from some unaccountable cause, have returned still black, and are regarded by them with evident dislike. They attribute the change of complexion in the whites to their ghosts having passed through so much water on their trip through the ocean. They consider each settler to be a resident on the district of that tribe to which, in his former state of existence, he belonged. On being asked how they came to spear the settlers if they considered them as their ancestors or friends, they have answered, that upon the whole, they consider they have treated the settlers well, for that, if any stranger had attempted to settle among them in the same way, they would have done all

8*

in their power to destroy them. With respect to the change thus wrought in their views of a future state, many of them look forward to death as a positive gain, which will enable them to come back with guns, ammunition and provision. They firmly believe in the existence of evil spirits, called by them "*Metagong*," which prowl about at night and catch hold of them, if they go away by themselves from the fire where the rest of the party sleep, as to bring water from the well, &c., by throwing its arms around them. The interpreter has met with several, who say they have experienced it, but he has never heard, though he has put many questions on the subject, that any injury has been the consequence. Yet they certainly stand in great awe of it. They represent it to be occasionally visible, of human shape, of immense size and of such prodigious strength as to render resistance vain. The night-bird which the settlers call cuckoo, and the natives "*pogomit*," is regarded by the latter as the cause of all boils and eruptions on their bodies, which they believe it to produce by piercing them with its beak in the night time, while they are asleep. The "*waugal*" is an aquatic monster, whose haunt is in deep waters. They describe it as having very long arms, long teeth and large eyes, and assert it to have destroyed many lives. They give a confused account of its shape, but from what they have said to the interpreter, their conception appears to be of a creature like an immense alligator. It inhabits deep waters, salt or fresh, and almost every lake or pool is haunted by one or more of such monsters. It is quite certain that they do not mean the shark, for which they have a different name,

and of which they have a superstitious dread; and
besides, it is never seen in the fresh water lakes.

There are certain round stones in different parts of
the island which they believe to be eggs laid by the
" *waugal.*" In passing such stones, they are in the
habit of stopping and making a bed for them of leaves,
but with what precise object, has never been ascertained. They believe most sincerely, that certain individuals among them possess the power, by magic or en-
chantment, of healing any sores, severe wounds, pains
or diseases; and also of effecting at their pleasure,
any malady or distemper, of which rheumatism, ul-
cers, and sores are the most common. These sorcerers are further supposed to have the power of raising
the wind, and of conducting the thunder to strike
their enemies. But they do not know whether this
is an acquired faculty, or natural endowment. The
ceremonies used by the sorcerers in exerting their
magic powers, are blowing, snorting, making hideous
grimaces, and loud ejaculations. Allied to this magic
power is another, which they attribute to some among
them, whom they think has the power to doom, or
devote others to a sudden death. This is believed to
be inflicted by the person having the power of doom,
creeping on his victims like a snake, and pressing the
victim's throat between his two thumbs and fingers :
the death may not be for some time, but the spell has
not the less deadly effect. They have several minor
superstitions, viz., that a fire must not be lighted at
night, or stirred with a crooked stick, or otherwise
some young child will surely die; to burn the blood of
a wounded person, makes the sufferer worse and en-
dangers others. The *mungite*, or flower of the honey

suckle, must not be eaten too soon in the season, or bad weather will surely follow. The relatives of a deceased person will not sleep on the spot where his blood was shed for months afterwards, nor until a victim has been sacrificed to appease his shade ; and the same avenging ceremony takes place in all cases, whether the deceased died a natural death or not. They pretend, however, to say that this intimation to the deceased of having been avenged must be thrown away, according to another of their superstitions already mentioned, by which he must be on his passage through or across the ocean. In one case, in which the body of a deceased European was opened at Pearth by his medical attendants, and as bad weather immediately came on, the change was confidently attributed to that operation ; and they continued to speak in terms of great horror at such treatment of the dead.

There are certain hills, which they consider unlucky to pass over, and all that pass over them will surely die. They have some wild and fabulous traditions of their own origin. They believe their earliest progenitors to have sprung from Emus, or been brought to this country upon the back of crows, but from where, the legend does not add. It is invariably believed that their women conceive in consequence of the infant being conveyed by some unknown agency into the womb of the mother from somewhere across the sea. When a person is asleep or in a deep slumber the interpreter has heard them say of him, "now he is away over the water," meaning as he has collected from them, that the spirit or

mind which had come here an infant, had gone back
to its own country.

A tradition is also current among them that the
whole native population of this country in distant
ages, was confined to the mountains; that the different tribes now occupying the plain between the
mountain and the sea, are the descendants of a very
few families, who migrated into the country's plain
at a comparatively late period; but when asked if
any rumor had been handed to them of their plain
having been covered with the sea before that migra-
tion, they have laughed at it.

They assert, too, that the language of the mountain
tribes, which now differs considerably from that of
the tribes of the plain, was at one time their universal language, and that their own dialect is derived
from the former. It is a remarkable fact that the
mountain dialect is still invariably preferred and used
for all purposes of a public nature or general interest,
—such as their formal public worship or discussions,
chanted narratives of battles and hunting matches.

It is a known fact that there is no trace of civil
government among those with whom the settlers
have come in contact. There is no supreme authority in peace or war, vested either in any individual as
a chief or any body of individuals. A family is the
largest association that appears to be actuated by
common motives or interest. They recognize the
right of property among them, both as to land and as
to their movable effects; but they are by no means
scrupulous in appropriating to their own use, any lost
property which they happen to find. In such cases
they make no inquiry about the owners, but take

some pains to conceal what they have found. The only mode of enforcing their proprietary rights in cases of trespass by hunting or theft, is an appeal to arms; in such cases however the thief stands on an equal footing, and is not bound to give the aggrieved any advantage as in certain other cases.

---

# CHAPTER VII.

Murder of Rev. John Williams—Sydney—New South Wales—Embarkation—Gale—Dangers of Southern Latitudes.

> " Muttering, the winds at eve, with blunted point,
> Blow hollow-blustering from the south.   Subdued,
> The frost resolves into a trickling thaw.
>                         Those sullen seas,
> That wash th' ungenial pole, will rest no more
> Beneath the shackles of the mighty south ;
> Ill fares the bark with trembling wretches charged,
> That tossed amid the floating fragments, moors
> Beneath the shelter of an icy isle,
> While night o'erwhelms the sea, and horror looks
> More horrible.
> The roar of winds and waves, the crush of ice,
> Now ceasing, now renewed with louder rage,
> And in dire echoes bellowing round the main."
>
> *Thomson.*

December 2d, the Missionary Brig Campden arrived, bringing intelligence of a melancholy occurrence which took place last month at Eramanga, one of the New Hebride Islands; and in which the Reverend John Williams, who resided here a short time since, and a Mr. Harris, lost their lives. The following account is given by the English vice consul for the Samoa Islands, Mr. Cunningham, who was passenger on board the Campden, and narrowly escaped, by running for his life to the boat.

On the 19th of last month, we had communication with the natives of Tanna, one of the New Hebride Islands. Finding the natives willing to receive instruction from our teachers, we proceeded to the Island of Eramanga, expecting to find a similar reception, but the result has fatally proved the reverse. We intended making the S. W. side of the island, but it was late in the evening before we came up with Dillon's Bay. We therefore rounded to for the night, and in the morning we found ourselves a little to the windward of Dillon's Bay. It was the only apparent place on the island where a landing could be effected, the whole of which island is with this one exception, a complete iron-bound coast, without the least appearance of culture. The natives are a barbarous race of beings, approaching to the African negro: they are also a different race, but the hair, although curly, is not of that wooly description which the African negroes have, being long and straight. They are a dirty race of savages.

Wednesday morning, November 30th, we sent the ship's boat ashore, containing Mr. Williams, Missionary; Mr. Cunningham, H. B. M. Vice Consul; Captain Morgan and Mr. Harris, who joined the Campden at Otaheite for the purpose of proceeding to this port, to take his passage for England, with a view of arranging his affairs there previous to his return to the Marquesas, as a missionary. As the boat ap-

proached the beach, we could distinctly see that the
natives were averse to holding any communication
with us on friendly terms.  Mr. Williams made them
presents of knives, scissors and some trinkets, for the
purpose of gaining their esteem, but without effect.
Mr. Williams now proposed giving up the idea of
having any intercourse with them, and had made up
his mind to proceed to some other island, where his
services might be required.  Mr. Harris then asked
permission to leave the boat, for the purpose of proceeding among the natives.  Mr. Harris was followed
by Mr. Williams; and when Mr. Cunningham had
reached the summit of the beach, he perceived Mr.
Harris running down towards the boat, followed by
a party of natives armed with clubs, spears, bows
and arrows.  Mr. Harris fell the first victim, for as
soon as one knocked him down, the remainder speared him through.  Mr. Cunningham saw him running,
he turned and made for the boat, and called to Mr.
Williams to run, for the natives had killed Mr. Harris; Mr. Williams unfortunately stopped to look a
moment for Mr. Harris; he made afterwards for the
boat and reached the water,—the boat laying off to
keep her afloat; but in the hurry he stumbled and
fell, when the natives immediately took advantage of
this circumstance and struck him four blows on the
head with their club.  By this time Captain Morgan
and Mr. Cunningham having gained the boat and
pushed off, after Mr. Williams had fallen; another
party of natives, numbering about sixteen or seventeen, speared him through, although our informant
thinks he was dead when they arrived.  The children threw missiles and stones at the corpse.  Neither

of the bodies could be procured, though attempted.
They made an attempt and were attacked by the natives, and part of one of their arrows is now to be
seen, stuck fast in the boat of the Campden. Captain Morgan intended beating the vessel up to windward, and under the cover of her guns to attempt the
rescue of the bodies; but on approaching the beach,
found the natives had carried off Mr. Harris, and Mr.
Williams's body they saw nothing of. Captain Morgan finding all attempts to rescue the bodies useless,
immediately bore away for Sydney, direct. Had the
party in the boat been possessed of a single musket,
the life of the Reverend Mr. Williams would doubtless have been saved, as he was followed to the beach
by one native only.

Sydney, New South Wales, Dec. 4th. Since our
arrival we have had almost daily visits from our consul, who is very attentive to us, in affording every fa-
cility in his power towards our outfits for the contemplated arduous antarctic cruise. We have been visited by several Englishmen, both naval and military,
besides the civil authorities. Governor Gipps kindly
tendered to Capt. Wilkes the use of the Fort for his
scientific instruments, and in which he had the observatory established. Almost every evening a party
was given to our officers on shore by the officers here,
or our officers gave a party to them. Capt. Wilkes
gave a dinner party at the Fort, to which his Excel-
lency, Governor Gipps, and the principal officers of
the colony were invited guests; also, all the English
naval and military officers on the station were present.

As soon as I found it convenient after our arrival
9

there, I visited the shore and had a ramble among
some of the principal streets. The first thing that
struck my attention on landing, was a thick-lipped negro man, black as charcoal, walking arm in arm with
a beautiful young white woman of about sixteen. I
had often before heard of this custom of amalgamation
among the English damsels, but never before saw
such an unusual sight. There was something in it
which to me appeared *so* unnatural, that I could not
resist the temptation of stopping in the middle of the
street to gaze on the sight. I had not proceeded far
before I found this scene to be no novelty, for many
similar ones presented themselves.

The next thing in which I was particularly interested was the convicts, who were seen in every direction, some with shackles on the legs,—some with a
ball and chain dragging after them,—others chained
together, two and two, and again at a little distance
were seen four or five together, escorted by a guard of
soldiers. All the public work here is done by them,
as among them mechanics of all kinds may be found.
Government is compelled to keep one or two regiments
here, and a strong mounted police, to keep the convicts in subjection. Many of the convicts on their arrival are allotted to different settlers, for whom they
work during the term of their transportation, or until
the sentence is mitigated, which very often happens
after serving faithfully half of their time. A ticket of
leave is then granted to them, which allows them to
work for themselves during the balance of their time,
but they have to report themselves once every week
to the Governor, or some person appointed to superin-
tend the convicts. If any new crime of importance is

committed by them, they are sent to Norfolk Island, where they have to work in chains, without any chance of commutation.

Others, again, retire to the bushes, and murder, rob and steal, all that comes within their reach. They are then denominated "bushrangers, or highway-men;" hence they are accounted outlaws, and may be shot wherever they are found. Fourteen of these "desperadoes" have been convicted and hanged. Some few of the convicts become good citizens,— very wealthy; one died a short time since, whose estate was valued at one hundred thousand pounds ster-ling. I met with several New Hollanders, who are the ugliest and the most deformed of any human beings I ever saw.

Sir George Gipps is the present Governor, and Sir Maurice O'Conner commander of the forces.

Dec. 25th. This was quite a dull Christmas with us, in respect to amusements; but with regard to work, there was plenty—for we were busily engaged in preparing the ship for sea, and hourly expected to sail.

What a contrast was my present situation to what I fancied was that of my friends at home, sitting round their cheerful fires, enjoying, as I confidently and sincerely hoped, the blessings of health and hap-piness!

Our voyage was commenced under favorable aus-pices, but we had not been out long when the sudden fall of the barometer, and the fluctuations of the ther-mometer, indicated a change—a gale. In this we were not deceived, as the sequel plainly, but sadly revealed to us. It came on squally at 10 o'clock, and continued to blow at intervals with great violence. All hands were called, and the topsails close-reefed, and every thing made ready to meet the fury of the coming storm. In the evening the gale increased so much that we hove the ship to, and sent down top-gallant and royal-yards. At 10, P. M., a thick fog set in, and continued through the night. During this time we parted company with the Peacock, and schr. Flying Fish. On the 6th of Jan., we had advanced as far south as 53 deg. S. latitude. A number of whales were seen, and some "kelp birds" were our constant companions, and the only new object which served to beguile the tediousness of our hours. We amused ourselves sometimes by catching them with a hook and line; we found the plumage of these birds extremely rich and delicate. We perceived the weather to grow cool very rapidly as we advanced south; but this is somewhat compensated for by our increase of day-light. We have fifteen hours day out of the twenty-four, and the balance of the time is light enough to see to read on the spar-deck.

Last night I witnessed to the southward a brilliant display of the Aurora Australis. It afforded a variety of light and colors, seldom surpassed in any exhibition of fireworks. I could but gaze with intense delight, while my thoughts were absorbed in contemplating the wonderful works of nature. The "Aurora Borea-lis," in point of brilliancy and interest, cannot com-pare with this. The whole southern horizon, the broad extent, reaching as far as the zenith, was beaming with vivid magnificence,—as when the first tints of morn burst from the east; ever changing, from mod-est hues to deeper vividness, and from twinklings to the dazzling blaze of far-reaching splendor and sub-limity. Arch crowded on arch, wave succeeded wave, blaze shot across wave like lightning's fitful glare—figure blended with figure—and anon the pointed shaft—arrow like—peered above the horizon, extending far up the illumined concave, as if some mighty volcano had belched forth, from her fiery bow-els, a blazing herald, sent on a message of death. Now the wide expanse, from the zenith to horizon, glowed with an almost unearthly flame, as if about to "melt with fervent heat,"—and now it slowly subsides, like the half extinguished taper, and all is as placid as a summer evening's twilight.

As we proceeded south, from latitude 60 deg. we saw but little of comparative interest. The first iceberg that we discovered, was after leaving that parallel. It was flat on the top, having the appearance of hav-ing been hewn off. Whales were quite abundant in this latitude, and large numbers of seals surrounded us, apparently on their way farther south. The tem-perature was rapidly changing, and the weather be-coming more and more disagreeable. Storms were becoming more and more frequent and severe. At 10 o'clock, A. M., Jan. 10th, we were surrounded by ice-bergs, which rendered it impossible to pursue our reg-ular course, but were obliged to change to avoid these immense floating islands. A thick gloom had appa-rently settled upon every thing around. The weather was fast becoming cold and severe. Fires were kept burning in various parts of the ship, to render it as comfortable as possible. The water had now assumed a dark pea-green color, and icebergs were seen in every direction, as far as the eye could reach. On

9*

the 12th, we were obliged to heave to, in consequence of having run into a bay of ice, which, apparently was about to prevent our farther progress south.   Yet in all of this desolation, we were attended by animate creation.   Sperm whales were sporting around us, now presenting their huge bodies at the surface of the water, heaving and raging, and sending far upward its icy spray, and now plunging down into ocean's depths, far from the wandering gaze of man.   How illustrative of the power and goodness of Him, whose dominion is from " sea to sea, and from the rivers to the ends of the earth," to adapt the constitution of every living, sentient being, not only to the element in which it is to exist, but to all of the varieties of climate, from pole to pole!

We lost sight, in latitude 64 deg., of the Porpoise, while surrounded by a thick fog.   The weather was cold and disagreeable in the extreme.   Wore ship and stood to the westward in order to find an opening into the sea.   Here we saw large flocks of penguins upon the ice, with a number of cape pigeons, and some large white albatrosses, resembling those seen off Cape Horn.   Hot coffee was made every night during this cold weather, and served to the men when going on deck, and also the watch when coming below.

We continued working to the windward, urging our course with much difficulty.   Large pieces of fucus were floating in every direction, in this vicinity. On the 16th, we saw at a distance the Peacock.   She seemed to be employed in the ice, and to appearance, had suffered much.   The water all this day was of an unusual dirty green.   Hundreds of icebergs were in every direction, some two, and even three hundred feet in height, with conical forms, and others with perpendicular sides and flat tops, as smooth as glass. Many had the most beautiful arches I ever beheld, or fancy could devise, formed by the washing of the waves. We were now in 65 deg. 26 min. south longitude, 157 deg. 43 min. east. The sea during this day was enlivened by animalcules, but owing to a heavy swell, none could be procured, though attempted by our scientific gentlemen.

January 17th. The loom of land was plain in the horizon. The water had a dirty green color, but much clearer than yesterday. Thousands of birds, seals and whales, were all around us. Among the feathered tribe, I noticed the "Mother Cary's chicken," and many cape pigeons.

18th. Every indication of land. We observed last night that all the birds, penguins and seals, went due south, and the first that were seen this morning were coming from that direction, and standing north. I saw to-day some very large sperm whales. They were so large, and covered with so many barnacles, that they looked like huge rocks, when coming up to blow. The weather was extremely cold; good fires were kept constantly in the stoves, one on the quarter deck, the other forward of the fore hatch; and also fire was kept in the galley range, below, and the berth-deck, where the men dried their clothes. Hot coffee and toddy were served to each watch when going on deck, and those "turning in." Extra warm clothing was served out to the men—the hammocks remained below in their berths for several days for the men to rest themselves. The water, a light pea green, and filled with animalcules, and a species of fucus of an enormous length.  At 12 o'clock, our latitude by observation, was 55 deg. 45 min. 62 sec. S., longitude, 156 deg. 67 min. 23 sec. E.

19th.  This morning at 6 o'clock, land was reported from the mast-head, and at 8 it was plainly visible from the deck, stretching from the south and east as far as the eye could extend, with a towering top some two and three thousand feet on a level.  Here we had got fairly into the *rookery* of penguins, albatrosses and seals.  The water a dark green color—it was also full of small animalcules.  The Peacock was seen to-day to the south of us.  We continued to stand toward the land until the afternoon, when we came rudely against an impenetrable barrier of ice, preventing our nearer approach to it.  Our latitude at noon, to-day, was 66 deg. 20 min. south, and long. 154 deg. 27 min. 45 sec. east.  Stood to the eastward in order to find a more eligible place to land.

20th.  Strong winds and cold weather.  Thermometer between decks, from 28 to 34 degrees.  Land in sight.  All attempts to approach nearer to it, proved fruitless.  This day penguins in abundance, and whales seen in all directions.  Land was still in sight all day, and we were anxiously looking for an entrance into it.  At 12 o'clock we were in lat. 66 deg. 07 min. S., long. 151 deg. 26 min. 30 sec. E.  The weather extremely cold.  Thermometer between decks 23 degrees.

22d.  During this day we have fallen in with a number of icebergs of an enormous size.  A large number of penguins were captured upon the ice.  I opened one, and found in his stomach twenty-two pieces quartz and granite, with a quantity of crustacia,

among which were the Hexacherus. At 12 o'clock
our latitude was 66 deg. 12 min. 26 sec. S., longitude
149 deg. 44 min. E. We tried at several places to
effect a landing or entrance, but all to no purpose; an
impenetrable barrier defied all our efforts.

From 22d Jan. to the 25th, we were seeking an
entrance to the land, but without success. This
morning, 25th, we entered a deep bay formed by ice.
Here we examined every point, in the hope of finding
an entrance to the land, but without success. We
hauled the ship alongside of an iceberg, passed a
hawser round it, so that we could hoist it on board,
and in consequence of the calm weather, succeeded in
filling all of our water tanks with ice. On a level ice-
burg near, the captain took a number of scientific instruments, and the dipping needle. It gave 87 deg.
30 min. for the dip. The compasses became useless
in this bay. They all pointed differently, and none
were correct. The captain placed abaft the compass,
Burlow's Plate, to remedy the evil, but it was all to
no purpose, they would not work. They were then
placed in different parts of the ship, but it was all the
same. I observed a number of *Madus* to-day, and
one was caught of a deep brown color, in which I
found a live hyperia.

There were innumerable small crustacia moving
around the sides of the ice island, but they swam so
deep that we could catch none of them. At 12 o'clock
to-day, the lat. was 67 deg. 04 min. S., long. 147 deg.
30 min. E. This bay, Capt. Wilkes called "Disappointment Bay," as all attempts hitherto had been
abortive; and this one seemed to put an end to all
future hope of progressing further south.

27th.  This day we fell in with the Porpoise.  She had come near being imbedded in ice, and suffered considerably in working her way out.  After finding all w'll on board, she made sail and stood on the other tack.  The weather was extremely cold and disagreeable.  Good fires were kept day and night in both stoves on the gun deck, and in the galley range, on the berth deck.  Since our entrance among the ice, and in the bad weather, all hands were mustered at quarters, morning and evening, and the state of their clothing examined by the divisional officers, and reported to Capt. Wilkes.  Every precaution was taken that could be thought of, or suggested, by Capt. Wilkes, to render the situation of the men as agreeable as possible, and prevent sickness.  An abundance of good provisions, sour krout, dried apples, cranberries, and other anti-scorbutics were served out; besides, we had eighteen months provisions on board. At 12 o'clock, latitude by observation 64 deg. 54 min. 21 sec. S., longitude 142 deg. 50 min. 08 sec. E.

28th.  At 5 A. M., we discovered high land to the south, covered with snow.  At noon the land was seen extending from S. E. by E., to W. S. W.  At 9, sounded and found bottom in thirty fathoms water; coarse black sand came up on the drawing of the lead. This was a tolerable good bay, but a gale was setting in, and the ice to windward closing upon us just as we were getting ready to anchor.  To the leeward of us, and forming a side to this bay, was a long ledge of rocks, at the distance of 3½ miles from us, with a strong appearance of volcanic smoke to the south.  At 12 M., our latitude was 66 deg. 32 min. 43 sec. S., longitude 140 deg. 24 min. 43 sec. E.  We were compelled to retrace our course by the way we came, in consequence of the sudden setting in of the gale; and before we had passed it, it set in so thick that we could not see five hundred yards ahead, with rain, hail and snow. This was the thirteenth time that we attempted to effect a landing, but without success, and in an hour from the time we left it, the wind had increased to a violent gale. From our perilous situation we were compelled to keep all hands upon deck all night, the ship passing through a very narrow passage with a tremendous heavy sea running, which caused her to roll so deep that she was near being on her beam ends several times. The decks were covered with ice and sleet, which rendered walking difficult, and even dangerous. Several men were thrown from the weather side to the leeward. Mr. Williamson, gunner, was seriously injured, having three of his ribs broken. The men who were on the maintopsail yard became so benumbed with cold, that they could not get off the yard, and had to be slung and sent down from aloft. The barometer stood at 28,70, and a more furious gale I never experienced in any part of the world; the sea washing against the sides of the icebergs, and the dashing of the waves in arches, made a noise like distant cannon.

29th. All this day a gale and a dreadful sea. At 12 o'clock, latitude 65 deg. 28 min. S., longitude 140 deg. 45 min. E. Land at a distance, nothing but ice! ice!! ice!!!

30th. This day the gale abated and we made sail and stood for the land, it being in sight. We tried to return by the same rout, to regain the bay which we were in on the 28th, but did not succeed, as we fell several miles westward.  We approached near enough to get soundings in forty fathoms.  In winding our way back, we saw what indescribable dangers we had passed through during the gale.

31st.  All this day coasting along the barrier, looking for an entrance through it to the land.

I have been thus minute, and perhaps tedious, in giving the reader some idea,—though vague it must necessarily be, of our peculiar situation, while tossed and driven among the icebergs of that desolate and unexplored field of gloom and exposure.  None but those present on that eventful Expedition, can have any adequate conception of the dreariness of the scenery.  It might be called with comparative propriety, a "waste of waters," a term usually applied improperly to the ocean, in all its sublimity and grandeur.

# CHAPTER VIII.

Attempts to Land continued—Reflections—Return to the North.

" Meanwhile the mountain-billows, to the clouds
In dreadful tumult swelled, surge above surge
Burst into chaos with tremendous roar,
And anchored navies from their station drive,
Wild as the winds across the howling waste
Of mighty waters : now th' inflated wave
Straining the scale, and now impetuous shoot
Into the secret chambers of the deep."
*Thomson.*

February 1st. We again stood in for the land;
having seen it so often in different situations and approached it so near, Captain Wilkes named it the
" Antarctic Continent." We saw again a number of
Mother Cary's chickens, appearing to be as regardless
of the climate here as if they were in the tropics.
We observed to-day a school of porpoises singularly
marked, having a faint yellow band over the nose,
crossing the jaws and running under the neck; a
second band crossing the dorsal fin, and ending by
running parallel with the tail. They appeared very
rapid in their movements through the water, much
swifter than our common porpoise. Means were
used to capture one, but they were unsuccessful.

We again made the land about sixty miles to the
westward of the point first visited. Here we found
the coast thickly defended with large cliffs of ice,
forming the most singular looking barrier that we

10

had seen, which prevented us from reaching the land in any way. And at this very point there was a tongue of land running close to the water, so low that, to all appearances, one might have stepped out of the boat upon it. Our sick list was daily increasing almost to an alarming extent; the number reported was fifteen. Most of these cases were consequent upon the extreme hardships and exposure which the men had undergone during the late gales, when the ship was surrounded with ice. In the surgeon's report he says—"This number is not large, but he feels it necessary to state that the general health of the crew is in his opinion decidedly affected; and that under ordinary circumstances the list would be very much increased; while the men under present exigencies, actuated by a laudable desire to do their duty to the last, refrain from presenting themselves as applicants for the list." And he further says—"Under these circumstances, he feels it his duty to state, that, in his opinion, a few days more of such exposure as they have already undergone, would reduce the number of the crew, by sickness, to such an extent as to hazard the safety of the ship and the lives of all on board."

February 3d, latitude observed at 12 o'clock, 65 deg. 1 min. 10 sec. South, longitude 135 deg. 42 min. 30 sec. East. We fished up some live crustacia, among which was a *euphansia*. This day set in with a regular gale of wind from the S. E., with thick weather. Snow, rain and hail again forced us to stand from the land, often placing us in dangerous positions, from the great number of icebergs, and thick weather. The ship in this gale labored dreadfully; every timber groaned under the pressure of the storm.

This weather continued until the 7th February, when it was clear enough to see the land. We made more sail and stood for it, and was soon up with a perpendicular barrier of ice, similar to that which we had previously seen attached to land. The ice here appeared to be much thicker, and to extend to a great distance. We could not effect an entrance, and were compelled to stand off. Numerous large whales, seals and penguins were in sight. The water was much discolored. We coasted to the westward about seventy miles, when we were stopped by the barrier, which trended to the southward. We could not penetrate any farther south in consequence of a thick barrier of field ice. Here in this critical place, Captain Wilkes remained for twenty-four hours in examining the various places where there was the least sign of an opening, but with no better success than before. So he continued to coast to the westward, beset on all sides with huge icebergs.

Soon after, the weather became more favorable. The sun shone out quite brilliantly for some considerable time. At night we were favored with a beautiful display of the Aurora Australis. The Doctor was busily employed in making observations with the photometer on the density of light. This was one of the most sublime sights that I ever witnessed, and lasted nearly the whole night.

We still coasted to the westward in order to find an entrance through the barrier, to the land, but did not succeed. The weather was very fine for the southern hemisphere, where we had experienced so much severity and exposure. We continued coasting to the westward, close to the barrier, in the hope of finding a passage through it. In the afternoon of the 11th, we came to a part of the barrier where there were immense islands of ice extending farther off, and running parallel with the land. A number of whales were in sight from the mast-head, some of them of an enormous size. The sun rose this morning at a quarter before three o'clock, and set at half past eight. During the remaining part of the time it was so light that we could see to read with considerable ease.

We had another sight of the land on the 12th, but at a distance, with no better prospect of success in reaching it than the first time we saw it. Here the barrier appeared to be seven or eight miles in breadth.

We again succeeded in reaching an opening, which led us to believe that we might approach the land nearer than we had at any other point, as it was distinctly visible, and the shore appeared not more than five or six miles off; but in this we were soon stopped by coming in contact with a quantity of drift ice. We put about and tried to effect a nearer approach to the land, but did not approach within fifteen miles. Not meeting with success we hauled off for the night, with no prospect of landing.

At 8 o'clock, A. M., on the 14th, we stood in for the land, to effect an entrance at another point that appeared clearer, but without success. The breeze was light and we did not reach the point so much desired. A long line of land was in sight, extending from south-west to north-west.

We continued to force our way through the drift
ice trending to the west, and a line of icebergs to the
leeward, extending from north-west to south-east.
We made more sail, and at ten o'clock stood in for
the land, through a passage just wide enough to admit the ship. Captain Wilkes continued to force her
through the ice in the hope of reaching the land. In
a short time, however, the ice became so thick as to
render it impossible to penetrate any farther. The
large pieces of ice began to settle down on us so fast,
and the passage became so very narrow, that the
captain thought it prudent to put the helm up and
make our way through the passage. So narrow was
it at this time as almost to touch the yards of the
ship, which were closely braced up. After we had
gained an opening, we found a great many ice islands opposite to us, and one in particular, which seemed to be aground, from the rock that we saw under it
when the water had washed it clear at the surface.
Upon this island of ice, large quantities of earth and
some pieces of rock were found.

Four boats left the ship for this iceberg, and in one
I took passage with Lieutenant Alden. We soon
effected a landing upon it. Mr. Waldron, purser,
landed on the other side of the island, and both parties met in the centre. Here all hands were busily
employed in collecting sand and sandstone, quartz
and sand. Some of the pieces weighed upwards of
one hundred pounds. Several curious shells were
found, entirely new, so far as our knowledge was
concerned. The French books were examined, but
nothing in them was figured resembling these specimens. It was found to be between a cone and an

10*

olive. The collection of specimens obtained on this island is no doubt more than we should have been able to have got on the land, if we had been so fortunate as to have landed; for the surface of the earth on the land must be covered with ice, many feet deep.

During the afternoon, from three to five hundred gallons of fresh water were collected from the pool on the iceberg. Captain Wilkes took the magnetic instruments on the ice and made observations. He took the bearing and distance of the land, after which, hoisted the flag number one, and at the foot of the flag-staff left a bottle with sealed instructions for the Peacock and Porpoise, in case they should reach this point. From this iceberg there were upwards of sixty miles of coast in sight; bearing the same as that we had seen the preceding day. After all the boats returned, we hoisted up, and commenced selecting our way out for an opening. During the night it was very clear and cold.

We still continued to coast to the westward, in the expectation of an opening to the land; but a long time was spent in vain endeavors. Land was in sight at a distance, yet so far as we were concerned, it might have been beyond the reach of human vision. Several icebergs were seen drifting by, with specimens of sand and stones imbedded in them. On one an enormous sea lion was observed; a boat was immediately despatched with guns to kill him, but he outgeneraled all of them, with a new move in military tactics, unknown to all of our soldiers. He made quite a flare up before he left; leaving our gentlemen to judge of his abilities as a water inhabitant of the antarctic region. During the encounter, several oth-

ers were seen near, which seemed disposed to come
to his rescue. At several times they swam to the
edge and rested their heads upon projecting parts of
the island, but none succeeded in getting upon it. In
his exasperation he would approach us, as if intent
upon our destruction, yet not quite willing to grapple
with us. At last finding himself in danger of being
captured he wisely plunged into his native element,
leaving us to conduct our assault as might best suit
our convenience.

The sea lion is a species of the seal, sometimes
called the mammoth seal. He is of the larger kind,
and has an extensive *mane*, from which circumstance
he derives his name.

We afterward ventured to pass somewhat nearer
to the barrier, which brought us in contact with huge
quantities of *fucus pyriformes*, among which we saw
several seals, feeding on the *lepas anatifera*, in which
this fucus abounds.

Though far removed from the more favored climes,
these animals are still cared for by their Creator, who
adapts conditions to circumstances, and suffers not
the most insignificant creature which he has made,
to perish unpitied or unprovided for.

On the 17th, with much regret, we found ourselves
closely embayed, and unable to proceed any farther
to the westward. There was no alternative for us,
but to retrace our way back as soon as possible, for
the weather had a threatening appearance, and the
small space we had to work ship in would have placed
us in a dangerous situation. We were now in latitude 64 deg. 00 min. 15 sec., longitude 97 deg. 44
min. E.

As we could proceed no further and finding the barrier to the northward and eastward, being surrounded on all sides with an impenetrable mass of ice, we put about and commenced beating up its northern shore to get out.

All of the 18th we were beating along the northern shore of the barrier, in order to effect our escape. A number of whales were seen sporting in their native element, heeding not the rigors of the polar, wintry blasts, and untrammeled by icy barriers. The night passed off with threatening weather and appearances of snow. All of the following day we were still beating, to effect an escape from the barrier, as we had much fear of being embayed in it. The reader can have but vague ideas of the prospect before us. Immense fields of ice were crowding around us, and when once the aperture should become closed, and the masses adhered, the hope of a deliverance might have been exceedingly precarious.

There was a great quantity of animalcules and crustacia in the water; some were caught, among which was *Talitius,* and another was procured before from the stomach of a penguin. At sunset (ten o'clock at night,) on the 20th, the extreme northern end of the barrier was in sight, to the great joy of all on board. We had thus far, in our last critical situation, been favored with tolerably good weather, though it looked very threatening, and if a gale had come on while we were in this situation, we must have been embedded, and no doubt would have caused our destruction. We certainly had great reason to be thankful to the All Merciful Almighty, for this safe deliverance from our perilous situation. We were particularly blessed on this arduous cruise, from the fact that no accident of any kind happened to us.

At 7 o'clock, P. M., 21st, all hands were called to muster, when Captain Wilkes told them that he was happy to inform them that the cruise south had terminated, and that he intended to proceed to the north. He, in a very handsome and brief manner, thanked the officers and men for the very able manner in which they had performed their duty, while engaged in this arduous service. He assured all hands that he should represent their conduct in the most favorable light possible, to the government, and. he had no doubt that a generous people would grant to all a suitable reward for their past services; after which he ordered the "main-brace spliced," that is, an extra allowance of grog to all hands, when there was a general buzz throughout the ship. Hot coffee and refreshments had been served out every night to the different watches, up to this.

This commences a new era in the history of our cruise. Since our departure we have seen almost every variety of climate and scenery. We have been where the tropical sun pours his torrid rays upon a weak and effeminate race of men, in all of the intensity of equatorial heat; in a latitude where spicy gales are wafted from isle to isle, and where blossoms and delicious fruit ever luxuriate;—and we had been in cold, gloomy, sterile, and uninviting regions, where not a leaf or shrub was seen,—not even a trace of a human being could be detected. It is not probable that human footstep ever impressed that sterile, frigid continent. If so, we may be allowed to conjecture that they are a race totally distinct from ours, obtain-

ing a livelihood, not from a culture of the soil,—for
that seemed deep imbedded beneath an enormous
mantle of ice and snow,—but by means entirely distinct from that of any race with which we are acquainted.  We had been more than fifty days in a
bleak latitude, and during most of that time, at an
unpleasant proximity to the continent, with a towering, impenetrable icy barrier preventing our nearer
approach, and often threatening to close in upon us;
thus shutting us out from all communication with our
fellow men.  A portion of that time we were almost
enclosed by this far-reaching field of ice, now rising
to an almost incredible height above us, leaving only
a narrow channel through which we could make our
escape, and now disparted, tumbling and rolling and
chafing in fury, as the rude polar blasts came sweeping by, dashing island upon island, and mass upon
mass, with tremendous crash!  It was a scene that
to be appreciated, must be witnessed.  It will not surprise the reader to learn that we often thought of our
homes, thousands of miles distant, where we once
shared the friendship and confidence of kindred and
friends, interchanged kindly salutations, and recipro-
cated each expression of regard or affection.  There
were times in which the prospect of a return to our
quiet homes was not the most flattering, but when we
were liable at almost any moment to make our bed in
that great receptacle of ocean's sons, uncoffined and
unshrouded, save by the ever-restless wave and massive icebergs, with no requiem, save the deep voice of
ocean's " thunder-gong," pealing in all of its wild
sublimity.  Like the dove of ancient time, or some
lone wanderer bewildered and exhausted, we long

sought for a resting-place, but found none. The haven was within sight, but inaccessible.

After despairing of effecting a landing, we directed our course northward. Our speed was unparalleled in a sea of ice like this, and probably no other man in the world would have made such a cruise in the ice, and tried to effect an entrance in such dangerous situations. He is certainly the most persevering man I ever saw.

As we made our progress toward the north, the weather became more mild and agreeable. The sick were improving, and those men who had been frozen on the yards, on the night of the 29th January, had all so far recovered as to go about the decks.

We parted company with the squadron, and have not seen the schooner since the 3d January, the Peacock on the 19th, and the Porpoise on the 27th.

# CHAPTER IX.

Arrival at New Holland—Singular coincidence—Arrival at New Zealand—" War Dance "—Description of the Islands—Inhabitants—The New Zealanders and New Hollanders contrasted.

> " Ocean, unequal pressed, with broken tide
> And blind commotion heaves ; while from the shore,
> Eat into caverns by the restless wave,
> And forest-rustling mountain comes a voice,
> That solemn sounding bids the world prepare !
>
> Then issues forth the storm with sudden burst,
> And hurls the whole precipitated air
> Down in a torrent.  On the passive main
> Descends the etherial force, and with strong gust
> Turns from its bottom the discolored deep."

On the 5th of March we made the coast of New Holland, to the southward of Botany Bay.  In passing this spot, memorable for being the first place in New Holland which was visited and named by Captain Cook, where convicts are sent, and the last place where the unfortunate La Parouse was heard from, we could but be interested in these associations.  It is a deep bay, and from appearances without the entrance, is between two high head lands, called Cape Banks and Solander.  It makes into two bays, but neither affords good anchorage for vessels of a large size.  It is sufficiently commodious as a place of retreat for small ones, wind-bound, destined to different parts of the coast.  It was ascertained, on the evening of the 27th December, that we had on board a boy

belonging to the 50th regiment, which is stationed at Sydney. He was sick nearly the whole cruise south. He was aware that Capt. Wilkes would give him up. I felt sorry for him; I knew his feelings must be torturing.

At half past 1 o'clock, the telegraph on Sydney Heads, made signal of our approach, and in about half an hour we saw the pilot coming out to us. He soon boarded us, and we learned from him that the U. S. Ship Peacock had arrived at that place on the 22d February in a sinking condition, having carried away her rudder and all her cut-water, and also all of her bulwarks and timbers, from the starboard gangway to the tafrail, and that she was then in Mormon's cove, repairing. This was rather unwelcome news to us, as we only expected to remain in Sydney long enough to get water; but we found, now, that we should be detained with the Peacock for some time. At half past 2 o'clock we came to anchor in "Farmer's Cove," near H. B. M. Transport Ship Buffalo, Capt. Wood. This ship had just arrived with the Canadian convicts, among whom, we were informed, were several citizens of the United States. They must have looked at the American flag with feelings differing widely from those which animated their bosoms when some of them left their homes under its protection, to violate the laws of a country with which we were on terms of friendship. If it had been for the pure love of liberty, I should have pitied them from the bottom of my heart, but this was not the case; it was for self-gratification, and nothing more.

The people of Sydney appeared to be as glad to see

11

us as if it had been our homes. We heard, while here, of the arrival of the two French discovery ships at Hobart Town; and what is more remarkable, they also discovered land on the same day, 19th January, in the evening, being only 1800 miles in longitude from each other. It is one of those remarkable circumstances that sometimes happens.

The French commander has published quite an elaborate report of his discoveries while south. He had been very unfortunate in the loss of his officers and men, among whom was his artist, N. Ernest Goupel. The French Commodore lost, from the 3d Nov. 1839, to the 2d January, 1840, four officers and twenty-seven men.

Every thing being completed on our part, we left the Peacock to join us at Tongataboo. We made sail for the Bay of Islands, New Zealand, on the 29th March. As we passed along, we found the water remarkably full of phosphorescence. We discovered a sail; it proved to be the French whale ship Ville de Bordeux, from New Zealand, bound to Sydney. Her crew were sickly, and the surgeon of this ship went on board and prescribed for them. Her provisions being short we gave her a barrel of beef, and one of pork, and a number of tin cases with roast beef and preserved soup for the sick; after which we parted company.

At 10 o'clock, P. M., March 30th, we came to anchor in the Bay of Islands, New Zealand, in five fathoms water. We found here at anchor the brig Porpoise, and schr. Flying Fish, and a number of English and American whale ships.

We were visited by Bomarri, the principal chief at

the place, with all of his under chiefs, and a number
of his people,—from three to five hundred. Many
presents were distributed to him and his people. He
invited Captain Wilkes and the officers of this ship to
attend, to-morrow, on shore, when he would have a
grand " war dance" performed for them, at the residence of the American consul. On the next day,
hundreds of the natives were seen coming down the
river in their canoes to the consul's wharf, to engage
in the dance. At the appointed time, Capt. Wilkes
and officers went on shore to witness the savage ceremony. One hundred pounds of sugar, two bags of
rice, fifty pounds of tobacco, and several small trinkets were sent ashore, in charge of Mr. Dyes for Bomarri and his people. At 12, the war dance commenced on two hills near the consul's store—the two
parties representing themselves as enemies to each
other. They all had firearms, clubs and spears;
they commenced stamping, and making hideous faces
and loud ejaculations, showing themselves off in a
general perturbation and maddened frenzy. When
they had arrived at the height of their wrath, they
frothed at the mouth, and stamped the ground with
such force, as seemingly to make it tremble. During
the dance they kept moving down the sides of the
hills, facing each other, and at a certain yell, they ran
together with tremendous force, as if they intended to
tear each other in pieces; and as they were all together in this confusion, with arms extended in the
air, they continued to discharge their pieces, and yell
so as to make the elements resound with their noise.
They then in this confusion started off in a full gallop,
making the earth tremble with their noise, as if so

many horses were running at full speed, until they reached the third hill, on which is situated the consul's house. Here they commenced running backward and forward for about 700 yards, coming in contact with a fence, when they would in very good order discharge all of their pieces, then arrange themselves into two phalanges and commence another dance. After finishing this novel amusement, they commenced another dance, which they called "entertaining strangers;" then a speech was made, in which the speaker exhibited considerable taste. This being completed, a number of New Zealand girls were arranged in an angle to perform a "love dance."

This bore some resemblance to the "war dance," though less boisterous. They were arranged in parties—as in the preceding dance—and performed many unique gestures. These consisted in the raising and falling of the hands and feet alternately, sometimes singly and sometimes in pairs. Those of my readers who have seen the ceremonies of the Shakers, may form some idea of a part of these antics. I am not prepared to say which party should claim *originality* in this matter, the Shakers or the Islanders. It is not probable, however, that these simple natives, from the nature of the case, ever saw such exercises among civilized nations.

The group of islands, known under the general name of New Zealand, is situated a little to the westward of the 180th deg. of longitude, and between the 34th and 48th parallel of S. latitude—extending from north to south upwards of 800 geographical miles, with an average breadth of 100 miles, and containing an extent of surface equal to that of the British Islands. The coast line, following the various indentations of the land, extends upwards of 3000 miles, and comprises a greater number of eligible islands, harbors, bays and roadsteads, than is to be found along an equal extent of coast in any other part of the world.

The Bay of Islands, a name derived from the number of rocks with which it is studded, is a remarkably fine and capacious harbor, and affords shelter in all seasons, and all weathers, to a large number of vessels. Its width, from head to head, is about eleven miles, affording sufficient room for vessels to beat in. A great number of European and American vessels touch at this harbor for supplies of fresh provisions and vegetables; most of them are upwards of 300 tons. This bay has been surveyed with great care and correctness by two French ships, La Coquilla, in 1824, and La Astrolobe, in 1830, 1, 2 and 3. Its anchorages are various, namely:—Tepuna, a roadstead on the northern side of the bay, opposite the missionary station of that name, and the native village of Rangihoua Paroa, a deep bay on the south side of the islands, a snug and capacious harbor, affording shelter from all winds, and is the anchorage which the whaling vessels formerly made use of.

The anchorages now generally used, are the Bay of Kororareka and the River Kawakawa. The former is used by vessels wanting a slight refitting, or for procuring water and refreshments;—the Kawakawa, when repairs to any extent are necessary, or the replacing of the masts, being more secured, and having the shores nearer them, from which they procure the greater portion of their supplies, with the excep-

11*

tion of provisions. Both these anchorage grounds possess sufficient water for ships of the greatest tonnage.

There fall into this bay the Rivers Kidi Kidi, in which, at the distance of about two miles from the mission, are the magnificent falls of *Wani Wani*, or " waters of the *Rain Bow ;*" the Warooa, with its falls; the Manganeri; the Palconda, the Kawakawa, and many minor streams; their banks and the interior of the country presenting one of the richest soils of the whole island, yielding crops when cultivated, of every kind known in the country, in the greatest abundance. It is nearly equally divided by Cook's Straits. The islands abound in fine timber, and most of the European vegetables grow in the greatest abundance. We did not visit any other part but the Bay of Islands. The village of Kororareka, the principal village at the Bay of Islands, stands on the west side, as you pass up, and is the principal anchorage for ships. On the opposite shore is the missionary station of the Rev. Mr. Williams, at Paikia. Kororareka is filled with convicts from New South Wales, and, as is natural to suppose, are corrupt in the extreme, there being no laws to restrain them in their evil practices. The natives are exceedingly vicious, and how can we blame them, when they have had such powerful examples set them by their teachers? It appears that these have been here teaching the natives since the year 1814; and instead of sowing the seeds of virtue and morality, are disseminating vices of all kinds, drunkenness, licentiousness and other abominable crimes.

And here let it not be supposed that I would censure the enterprise of civilizing and Christianizing these benighted natives; far from it. Yet it really seems that, in this one instance, these labors have not been productive of as much good as we have a right to expect from the introduction of the truths of Christianity among heathen nations. It is not my province to assign reasons, but simply to state the facts as I have been able to collect them. It is possible that the *counteracting* influences of vicious seamen and others visiting these islands,—as is too often true,— have done much to prevent the *natural* reformatory results of the introduction of the Christian religion.

### NEW ZEALANDERS.

The natives of this island are, on the whole, a fine looking set of men. They are about the common stature of Europeans generally, though I saw some seven feet and some inches. Their general color is a dark olive, but there is considerable difference among some of them, from a light yellow to a deep copper color. Most of them appear black about the face from the deep punctures, caused by tattooing and the insinuating of a dark liquid into the punctures. This is not confined to the face, but extends to the hips, loins, posteriors, thighs, legs, ankles and feet; and in some instances, the individual, when naked, looks as if clothed in a coat of mail. Their faces are round and well proportioned; they have fine proportioned noses, generally full at the point, with well formed mouths. Their lips are full; they have fine white teeth, well set; their eyes are large and strong; the *white* looks of a greyish cast, as if affected with the jaundice. Their hair is jet black, straight, coarse and strong; they wear it cut short, with a bunch upon the top of the head. The women are smaller than the men; they are ugly, and generally perform all the labor out of doors. They, as well as the men, tattoo, but in different parts of the body,—the mouth and *labia pudendi* are the parts which, according to their custom, must be tattooed before they are considered elegible to the matrimonial state.

The beauty and symmetry of the New Zealanders, probably, are owing mainly to their habits. They are accustomed to much exercise and have generally vigorous and athletic constitutions, seldom or never afflicted with those maladies which *seem* to be the necessary attendants upon civilization, though there can be no doubt that they are the result of gross abuses. Deformity is almost entirely unknown. Some of those of modern days, in this age of intelligence and refinement, would be regarded in New Zealand as prodigies, and would surprise those simple and comparatively consistent people. They have but few wants for the body, and these are supplied without much aid from culinary art. Their food is taken from the bosom of the earth, spontaneously supplied in the form of bulbous roots, &c.

In their simplicity, they present to the world forms which the civilized might envy, and a vigor of body and mind, which gives them a preëminence over many of their savage neighbors of different habits. Though active and energetic, they are not,—like some others.—warlike and brutal, but blend muscular strength and vivacity with comparative docility. They are the antipodes of those of New Holland, in about the same latitude, who, in their degradation, feast upon the carcases of dead whales, which by chance float upon their shores. Both are savages, but the one is intellectual, active and *man-like*, the other corrupt, deformed physically and mentally, degraded and *brutal.*

I shall not here enter into a description of their teachers, as the limits of my book will not allow it; for if all their crimes were recorded, they would fill a large volume.

We left New Zealand on the 6th of April, accompanied by all of the squadron, except the Peacock. Our passage was quite pleasant, the wind favoring— a striking contrast with the scenes through which we had passed while on the coast of the newly discovered continent. In a few days after our departure, we passed Sunday Island, but without stopping. The water, during this part of our cruise, wore a very phosphorescent appearance, giving it an enlivened aspect. As we passed along, several islands were in sight, but our particular commission did not require a stay at them. This part of our passage was not signalized by any remarkable occurrences. We were, however, somewhat startled by the violent crash of our vessel, as she struck a rock while passing through a narrow channel. She "heeled down" considerably for a time, but soon passed over it without any very serious damage. On the 23d we made the west point of the Tongataboo Island, where we were to make observations.

The Island of Tongataboo is flat and sandy, and covered with cocoa-nut trees. A destructive war was raging between the heathen and Christian party of this island. It occurred to me that the missionaries were placed in a dangerous situation, but they seemed to make themselves quite easy and place implicit confidence in their proselytes to protect them. Tongataboo, though nearly one hundred miles in circumference, is perfectly flat and rises only a few feet above the level of the sea.

The only elevated spot is a small hill, which is not, I think, more than one hundred feet in height; whether natural or artificial, I did not ascertain, as I had but few opportunities of visiting the shore; and then it was only for a few moments at a time. On the top of this is a fort, where all the people of the district concentrate when driven to extremities, in time of war. This hill is particularly memorable in the annals of Tonga warfare, from the circumstance of its having been the first place where the inhabitants felt the effects and deadly power of the cannon ball. The Christian part of the Tonga army was then encamped upon the top of this hill, expecting every moment to be attacked by their enemies. On the top of the hill is erected a strong reed fence, entrenched around by a deep ditch. Inside of the fortification, they have several pieces of cannon of small calibre. The principal chief of the Christian party is named by the missionaries "King George," after the King of England: his native name I have not learned.

The day after our arrival the belligerent parties met and had a skirmishing engagement, but nothing on either side was effected.

It having been agreed by both parties that the island on which we had our observatory should be considered as neutral ground, and nothing should be molested, and also that no native should go there

without Captain Wilkes's order or permission, we
had but little concern with this war. On the 23d
April the Porpoise arrived, and came to anchor near
us. In the afternoon, the Vincennes, Brig Porpoise
and Schooner Flying Fish stood over for the village,
the brig and schooner running upon a reef. Boats
were sent from the ship to their assistance; they were
both soon got off, however, and came to anchor off the
village near us. A rather singular incident occurred
on the morning of the 4th. It was discovered that
during the night, two females, natives of the Fiji
Islands, had swum to the schooner, and were admitted on board. Their intention was to get a passage
back to the Fijis; they were sent to the Peacock, and
from her to this ship, and were sent on shore with the
pilot when he left the ship.

The reason why these women left and swam this
distance of *ten miles*, was to escape from the cruel
treatment which was inflicted on them by the natives
of this village. They had been tied up by the wrist
for forty-eight hours, and in such a position that their
toes nearly touched the ground. This, as may be
supposed, would cause any person to leave such a
class of people. They were, in my opinion, better
than any of their more enlightened neighbors, for I
candidly believe there is not a philanthropist among
them.

Intemperance rages here to a great extent among
some classes of natives. The first thing the native
pilot asked for, on boarding us, was a bottle of rum.

From this island we proceeded to the Fiji Islands,
for the purpose of examining and surveying them.
Nothing of importance happened on the passage, and

we arrived off the Island of Ovalau on the 6th May, and on the following morning, stood into the harbor and came to anchor near the village of Laboaka, Island of Ovalau.

On coming to anchor we were boarded by some white men from a little trading schooner which came out to meet us; the chief mate of the American trading ship Leonidas was the commander. His name is Wynn, and has traded a great deal among these islands.

Thousands of natives assembled on the beach to witness the operation of furling the sails; and when the men went aloft and lay out on the yards, the natives on shore raised the loudest shout that I ever heard. Shortly after our arrival the principal chief of the village paid us a visit, with a number of white men who reside on shore. The natives flocked in great numbers alongside with yams, fish and other things of this kind to trade, and in a few moments a brisk business was underway. Our South Sea pilot and interpreter was overwhelmed in business, and the jargon he used, and that of the natives, might with propriety vie with that of Babel. In some of the canoes were women and children as naked as our first parents, when inhabitants of the garden of Eden. Yet many of the females seemed quite modest and sensible of their destitute situation. The men wore a *mara*, that is. a strip of *tappa* passed over the loins.

The schooner Flying Fish arrived on the 11th, having been ashore on a coral reef, and carried away a portion of her false keel. This morning the Launch and first cutter sailed in charge of Lieutenant Alden and Sailing Master Knox, to make surveys among the various islands and reefs. The next morning the Peacock's first sea cutter sailed in charge of Passed Mid. Simon F. Blunt, and also the Peacock's launch, in charge of Lieutenant Emmons, sailed on a surveying excursion to operate with the other boats which had sailed the preceding day.

———

# CHAPTER X.

General Remarks—Fiji Islands—Cannibalism—A Convict Exile—Death of a Shipmate—Encounter with the Natives—Visit at Muthwater—A Fatal Contest with the Natives.

> " The natives, while the ship departs the land,
> Ashore with admiration, gazing stand.
> Majestically slow, before the breeze,
> In silent pomp she marches on the seas ;
> Her milk-white bottom cast a softer gleam,
> While trembling through the green, translucent stream,
> Thus the rich vessel moves in trim array,
> Like some fair virgin on her bridal day.
> Thus like a swan she cleaves the watery plain,
> The pride and wonder of the mighty main."
>
> *Falconer.*

## GENERAL REMARKS AND OBSERVATIONS ON THE FIJI ISLANDS.

The Fiji Islands are a numerous group between the parallels of 15 deg. 05 min. and 19 deg. south latitude, and extends from about 177 deg. to 182 deg. east longitude. They were discovered by Abel Jansz Lansman in 1643, after his discovery of Tongataboo,

12

although never made known to the public by the
Dutch Government, until after they were generally
known to Europe.    Captain James Cook, while at
Tongataboo in 1773, learned that there was a large
island by the name of the Fijis, situated N. W. by
W., about three days sail from Tongataboo.    Capt.
James Bligh, of the Bounty, fell in with the eastern
part of the Fiji Group, in long. 178 deg. west, and in
19 deg. 50 min. south lat., in 1791, on his passage in the
Launch of the ship to the Straits of Timore.    Captain
Wilson, in the ship Duff, visited these islands, to land
missionaries, as early as 1797, but was prevented,
from the great difficulty he experienced in the navigation among them, and the hostile appearance of the
natives.

The Fiji, or Viji Islands, may be divided into three
divisions.    1st.    The weather, or eastern group, com-
prising Lakemba and the surrounding islands; 2d.
The Viji Levu, or great Viji, and its neighboring islands; and 3d.    Tarkanava, or North Islands, and
those adjacent.

These divisions contain a group, said by the natives
to amount to 200 in number.    Viji Levu possesses the
largest river, and is navigable for many miles, as well
as other islands which have rivers, for canoes, for
twenty or thirty miles in the interior.    Two of these
islands, Viji Levu, Venna Leva, possess such a vast
interior, that the inhabitants have never seen the sea,
and speak a different language from those residing on
the seaboard.    There has not, as yet, been any information obtained of their number, manners and customs of the natives.    The natives told us that many
of the districts in the interior contained more inhabi-

tants than the island of Tongataboo.  Most of the islands are covered with trees and shrubbery corresponding to the islands in the South Pacific Ocean. The formation of the Fiji Islands varies much; they are, no doubt, of volcanic origin.  From what I saw, I should say that it is not many years since some of them were in full and active eruption.  Their geological structure, as far as my observations extended, is as follows :—Ovalauh as large beds of ferruginous marl, and is conglomerated, showing plainly that it has not been a very long time since it experienced a greater convulsion of the earth; it is very mountainous, and has a beautiful appearance.  Viji Levu abounds in rock of a hexagonal form, apparently composed of a basaltes bau, and appears to be indurated clay—the clay containing nodules of grit. Banga appears to have been a vast volcano, for there have been found at the height of eighty-six feet, large excavations caused by heat, and was covered with scoria; and the harbor, which is said to be a beautiful one, was formed by a crater, once in active operation. All the islands, and passages between them, in this group, are surrounded with coral reefs, and require the greatest attention in navigating them.  The islands are generally destitute of good bays or harbors, only so far as this is compensated for by reefs, which sweep around, so as to form good breakwaters, and afford protection from the violence of the ocean.  I think it would be unsafe for any person to attempt to navigate these passages without a good pilot, and I believe these may be procured at Ovalau, as there is a large number of white men residing at Labouka, who are always cruising and trading among these islands. They are quite well acquainted with all the difficult and dangerous reefs, passages, &c. Most of the coral reefs are thickly covered with the evergreen mangrove tree, for miles along the shores, which forms an impenetrable barrier to large boats, and at the same time, forming an ambuscade for the natives. On many of the islands, I am told, are large forest trees, in great variety. Some, I have no doubt, would answer for ship building, and also for houses. Our Botanist obtained some new specimens of plants, of considerable value.

The climate, at the time that we were there, was remarkably fine, though it was the winter months among the islands. The wind is said to blow in gusts from the south, several days in each month; during these gusts it is cold and chilly—little, or no dew at night. The thermometer ranged, during our stay here, from 70 deg. to 87 deg.; blankets were acceptable at night. The soil is rich and productive, and requires but little labor. The inhabitants are naturally indolent, and depend mostly upon the spontaneous productions of the islands for a subsistence. All kinds of tropical productions and fruits, grow spontaneously in great abundance. These islands have some fine specimens of birds; some of them wear the richest plumage I ever saw—particularly the parrot tribe. The quadrupeds are mostly introduced by foreigners; cattle, hogs, and turkeys thrive well. The rat is the only wild animal that they have. Of reptiles, there are but few—the lizard and snake were all I have seen; one snake, in particular, "a water snake," was worshiped as a spirit.

In 1835, two Wesleyan missionaries came to the

Fiji Islands from Tongataboo, and since that time there has been a reinforcement of them, but their prospects are rather discouraging. Whether it is from the nature of the people they have to deal with, or from other causes, I am not able to determine. One thing is certain, however, which is, that comparatively little has yet been accomplished. In reference to their education, a *beginning* simply has been made. An alphabet has been formed, a grammar and dictionary have been printed, together with a few tracts.

Polygamy is common among all the islands; the chiefs buy as many wives as they wish, or the wives and daughters of their enemies, when taken, are kept as wives, or slaves. The females are very robust, and female children, I observed, are very numerous. The whole population of this numerous group of islands has been estimated by residents of long standing among them, at 200,000. Women are in great demand at many of the islands, and most of the wars are occasioned for, and about women; and yet they are treated in a very brutal manner, in most cases worse than the slaves of Brazil, and obliged to perform most of the labor, both in and out of doors, for the support of the family. The chiefs—and there are many of different ranks among them—do not always succeed the father in his rank.

The houses of the natives are built throughout all the islands on the same plan, and generally constructed of the same materials; a foundation of stone or coral is first laid, and then the timber for sill and corner posts, then the rafters,—all of which are nicely fastened together with cinct, and done with such regularity as to be very neat and beautiful, when there

12*

is a variety of colors displayed. Then comes small
rods lashed to the rafters, on which the grass is
thatched from the top to the bottom. They have one
or two doors, very small. One end of the floor is
raised and covered with mats of several thicknesses;
this is generally screened off with mats, and used as
their sleeping apartments; and at the other end is a
place in which they cook, having a pit dug and lined
with stones, which will contain from two to three
cooking jars; over this is a swinging rack, where
they keep most of their cooking utensils.

The *Bure*, or spirit house, is constructed with great
pains, and besides, there is a temple which answers
the double purpose of a town-house for public meetings, and to entertain strangers, who may be present.
Many of the chiefs pass the greater part of their time
in the Bure. All the property of the god to which
the house has been dedicated, is kept here; this consists of presents from the chiefs, and others, who have
made vows to the gods for recovering from sickness,
success in war, and destruction of their enemies.
These presents are generally made use of by the
priest, or *numbatal*, who look well to their own interests, as a natural consequence. One of their most revolting traits of character is Cannibalism; these natives, on all occasions, prefer human flesh to that of
other animals. The priest of Overlau told me that it
was not for revenge that they kill their men to eat,
but merely from choice. They kill them either by
strangling, or knock their brains out; they are then
bled, after which the intestines are taken out and
washed. A large pit is dug, and the stones, wood
and banana leaves, are all brought; after the whole

has become ignited, and the pit sufficiently heated, the operation of cutting up the body is commenced, which is generally performed by the one who kills him. The limbs are taken off according to certain rules,—first the right foot and left hand, dismembering alternately, until the whole is completely cut up. The bones and limbs are then wrapped carefully in banana leaves, put into the pit and hot stones put over them, and then the whole is covered with earth, there remaining for eight or ten hours, and if it is a white man, he is not eaten until the next day. I was told by a white man who has resided many years among them, that he has seen on the island of Bau six hundred human victims cooked and eaten in one day, after a battle.

Natives of the Fijis, or Viji Islands, taken together, are a wild, ferocious people, and to judge from physiognomy, that, " *Vultus est index animæ,*" you would set them down as a villanous set of beings. There is considerable variety in their color, from the mulatto to the negro; their hair is curly, hard and crisp. They are generally tall and well formed. Their heads are well moulded, have high foreheads, large eyes, wide mouths, fine teeth, and most of them have pleasing countenances, when in the presence of strangers. I have never seen a corpulent Fiji man or an obese woman; the men are spare, on account of their roving disposition, and the women, from having to do all the laboring work, and besides, living principally upon a vegetable diet. It is uncommon to see many of them who have lived to a good old age, for they often destroy their old and infirm, for the purpose of avoiding an increase of labor and trouble!

On the 13th of May, the Peacock sailed for an adjacent island, for the purpose of surveying it, and to endeavor to capture a chief, who had caused the murder of the chief mate, and part of the crew of the brig Charles Doggett, in 1832.

We received a visit from a white man, who informed us that he had been among these islands for nearly forty years. He is a native of Ireland, by the name of O'Connell. He stated that he was sent to Port Jackson in 1800, as a convict, and by some mysterious means contrived to make his escape, and at which time he joined a privateer which touched at one of these islands; from this he deserted, and has remained here an exile from home ever since. He was in a perfect state of nudity, except, like the natives, he wore a piece of *tappa* about the loins. He wore his hair long, and also his beard, hanging down on the breast; upon the whole he was a miserable looking object.

In a short time after his departure, we received information that Captain Hudson, in the Peacock, had captured the chief, who was the cause of the beforementioned murder. From a respectable source, Capt. Wilkes learned that an attack on the observatory was contemplated by the natives of the island, to which the captured chief belonged. The object of the natives was to secure Capt. Wilkes, and by that means make an exchange of prisoners. He immediately moved on board the ship, leaving the observatory in charge of Lieut. Perry and Passed Midshipman. Eld. A reinforcement of marines was sent on shore with twenty seamen, armed and equipped for any emergency. The ship was hauled in opposite to the observatory and placed with springs on her cables so as to bring the guns to bear on each side of it. At night the guns were all loaded, the tompkins left out, the battle lanterns lighted and placed between the guns, and no hammocks allowed to hang near the battery. The night passed without any disturbance, except by a false alarm, caused by the accidental discharge of the musket of one of the sentinels.

On the 18th June, David Bateman, formerly a marine belonging to the Brig Porpoise, breathed his last, and his spirit winged its way to unknown regions above. He had been suffering some time with phithisis pulmonalis, and was, when removed to this ship, very weak and emaciated. The day after our arrival here he was removed to comfortable quarters on shore, where he could enjoy more quiet. Every thing had been done for him that could be thought of by the surgeon; but alas! all availed nothing. A post mortem examination proved that his disease would have baffled the skill of the most experienced surgeon, and that too, under any circumstances, however favorable. The same evening his remains were deposited in the place of sepulchre, in a small garden which had been enclosed by Mr. Breckenridge. The corpse was followed to the place of interment by the marine guard and a party of seamen, also several of the officers. The beautiful and impressive burial service of the Meth. Episcopal church was read by Mr Waldron, purser; and the body was deposited in its final resting-place. He was buried with the honors of war. Three volleys of musketry were fired over the grave by the marines; the earth was then thrown on and the grave filled up, which closed the melancholy scene.

On the morning of the 28th, the observatory was broken up, and all the instruments removed on board, preparatory to leaving the island. At 10 o'clock, all things being ready, we hove up our anchor and bade adieu to our friends the natives of Ovalau, schooner in company.

On the same evening we came to anchor in the harbor of Protection Island, a small, uninhabited island. This island is situated about twenty-five miles from Ovalau, is about ten miles in circumference, and rises in some places almost perpendicularly from the sea shore. This harbor, like that of Laboaka, is formed by a coral reef, which makes out from the island, and sweeps around in a curved direction, leaving a narrow, but safe passage. The island is thickly covered with wood, and the acclivities of the hills richly variegated with shrubbery and vegetation.

On the following day, we got underway and proceeded to *Saba Saba*, at which place we did not arrive until the 1st of July, though the distance is only sixteen miles : this was owing to a strong head current and light wind. We anchored outside of the reef, the wind being too light to venture through the passage, which is very narrow, and has a strong current. During the evening and night we caught some very fine fish, among which were found one or two new specimens.

The next morning we got underway and stood in through the narrow passage, and anchored in the inner harbor, about one mile from the celebrated "boiling springs." Captain Wilkes allowed all of the men to visit these springs; accordingly, on the 4th of July, all the men that could be spared out of the ship improved the proffered recreation. These springs are eleven in number, situated on a level plain near the beach, with a rivulet running through, which is not at all affected by the heat from the springs;—the water in the rivulet being perfectly cool and of an excellent quality. The formation of these springs is certainly volcanic, and confirms me in the belief that all these islands are of that origin. The surface of the earth every where in the neighborhood of the springs was so hot, that we could not walk on it with bare feet. The temperature of the water was 212 degrees. The natives come from all parts of the island to visit these springs, particularly when any great feast is to be held; they there cook their food in them. One of them is considered sacred, and is used only for cooking human flesh. The surface of the ground in the neighborhood is strewed with the bleached bones of these victims.

July 12th. Our Launch returned from a surveying cruise among the islands, in charge of Lieut. Perry. He brought with him Mr. Knox and Mid. Thompson and the crew of 1st cutter; also two chiefs whom they had taken as prisoners. The 1st cutter got ashore on a reef off the island of Sour Laib, and was captured by the natives of that island; and the officers and crew were obliged to flee to the Launch for safety, which was only a short distance from them. In consequence of a strong gale which was blowing at that time, and the dampness of the ammunition, they were unable to prevent the capture of the cutter. Luckily for the crew, however,

the natives busied themselves so much in removing
the plunder, that they did not interfere with their escape, and by this means they passed unmolested to
the Launch.

Captain Wilkes immediately made preparations for
punishing the savages.  He had the schooner Flying
Fish fitted out and manned, together with the launch
and six or eight small boats, with the 1st cutter of
the Peacock, all armed and manned.   At 4 o'clock the
same evening, all those who were to take part in the
expedition were mustered in boats, and Captain
Wilkes joined the schooner; shortly after, all made
sail for Sour Laib, a distance of about sixteen miles.
The wind being contrary, they did not arrive at their
place of destination until 10 o'clock of the next day.
On the arrival of the party, Captain Wilkes went on
shore with a party of armed men, met the chief, and
by means of an interpreter held a parley with him, in
which he demanded the boat and all of the property
that had been stolen from it.   The chief replied, "that
it was a tradition among them that when a boat or
canoe was cast away on their island, that they had a
right to take possession of it in the name of their gods,
to whom it belonged."  Captain Wilkes endeavored
to explain to him the impropriety of such conduct,
and tried to make him understand how he should act
in such cases; but to this he seemed to pay but little
attention, and gave the Captain but little satisfaction.
He told the chief that if the property was not immediately delivered up, he should commence hostilities
against them and endeavor to desolate the island.
To this the chief replied very carelessly, "that it was
not in his power to restore the property, as it was

scattered over the whole island," and seemed to intimate that he should not try, but said that he was willing to give up the boat. This did not satisfy Captain Wilkes; therefore he ordered the men to repair to the schooner, get some refreshments and rest a short time, for they were much fatigued, not having rested, eaten or slept during the night. This news was received with enthusiastic applause, as they wished to show their superiority to the savages.

Accordingly, after partaking of the necessary refreshment, and taking a few moments' repose, they all left the schooner, to the number of eighty men. Capt. Wilkes lay off in his gig, so that he might see the destruction as it progressed. The party on shore was commanded by Capt. Hudson, of the Peacock. On the approach of the men, the natives retreated, and continued to recede as the men advanced toward the village, until they took up their position about three hundred yards from the village, and did not offer the slightest resistance to the destruction of their property.

At the village the work of destruction commenced by setting fire to their houses, destroying their *tarro* beds, killing their hogs, burning up their yams and yam houses, breaking up their war canoes, and in fact destroying every thing that fell in their way. The natives during this time fired a few random shots from the bushes and jungles, but no injury was the consequence. Several ventured to peep from their hiding places, but no sooner did they show their faces than they felt the deadly power of our rifles. Skyrockets were thrown in among them, but their position was so secure that it did no other harm than to frighten them. This it did effectually, which was in-

13

dicated by their loud yells, and their cry of *"curlew!
curlew!! curlew!!!"* spirits! spirits!! spirits!!!

After seeing the town burnt down and the work of
destruction completed, they all returned to their boats,
and on the way burned another small town. When
the men had all embarked, the natives ventured from
their hiding places, came within a short distance of
the boats, and fired a few random shots. But they
were not sufficiently near to be able to do any damage.

The Launch did not arrive in time to partake in
the affray, she having got aground on a coral reef,
and did not get off until late in the evening. The
party ventured to the ship about midnight. The
next morning the chief of Sandal Wood Bay came on
board, and asked for the two prisoners whom the
Launch had taken at Sour Laib, saying that they
wanted to eat them, as they were their prisoners. His
request, however, was not granted.

Sandal Wood Bay, or Miambore Bay, is a well protected place of anchorage. The natives are rather
more diminutive than those of Ovalau, and of a more
ferocious nature. They have a custom of circumci-
sion, similar to that of the ancient Jews, and none
are eligible to marry until they have passed this or-
deal. This operation is performed at the death of
some favorite chief, to manifest their grief at his loss.
Another of their horrible customs is that of putting to
death a number of the favorite wives of the deceased,
and a number of the male relatives. Some of the
chiefs have twenty wives, and those who are his fa-
vorites in this world, are the ones chosen to accompany him on his passage to the other world. I am

told that so great is their desire to accompany him, that disputes often arise between them to know who has the best right to this preferment.

On the 22d, a melancholy event occurred in the death of the third mate of the trading ship Leonidas, who came to an untimely end in the most shocking manner. While the Peacock was engaged in surveying the harbor of Muthwater, the Leonidas was there at anchor; she being an armed vessel, Captain Hudson requested her commander to assist with her guns in firing to measure distances. It was accordingly assented to, and it was during one of these discharges that the accident happened. The second mate, acting in the capacity of a gunner, and being unacquainted with gunnery, neglected to sponge the gun— consequently, when the cylinder was put in and rammed home, when in the act of priming, the powder which he was pouring in, communicated with a spark that had been inadvertently left in the chamber, and immediately exploded, at the same time catching fire to a cylinder in his bosom, which ignited at the same instant. The explosion was so great that he was literally burned from head to foot,—even the hair was completely burned from his head. In this situation he was removed to the Peacock, where all that surgical skill could do was done for him. He lingered in this state for twenty days, most of the time deprived of reason, and suffering the most excruciating pain. He was interred during the evening, on a point near the harbor. A stone was placed at his head to mark the spot, upon which a suitable epitaph was engraved.

After finishing our survey at this place, we embarked, intending next to visit the Island of Muth-water.

In consequence of adverse winds, we were induced to make a short stay at Tevia, a small island about midway between Muthwater and the island from which we had just embarked. Here we recruited, and became acquainted, to some extent, with the na-tives.

The natives of this island are very numerous and warlike, and possess more canoes than any island we had visited among the Fiji group. Hogs, yams and poultry are plenty here. We saw here the remains of the beche-le-mer house which Captain Eckelson, of the ship Leonidas, had erected, while engaged here in curing that article. This is also remarkable as the place where the chevalier Dillon had an engage-ment with the natives, and defeated them with only a few men. When the Peacock was here in June last, a canoe came alongside, having in it the whole body of a roasted man, of which they were eating with great avidity. Some of the flesh was procured by the officers and saved in spirits as a specimen, also the skull and thigh bones were procured.

On the following day we left this island, and pro-ceeded to Muthwater, where we arrived in the even-ing. The Peacock had reached this harbor before us.

The town of Muthwater is very large, and is bet-ter protected than any island among this vast group. The town is built on a level plain at the foot of a very high hill, and is quite near the sea shore. These natives possess, in an eminent degree, the art of pil-fering, and are by no means scrupulous in converting to their own use any property they may happen to find; and in such cases, they make no inquiry about the owner, but are careful to conceal what they have found. Several flags belonging to the Peacock had been stolen from the reefs in the harbor, where they were placed for the purpose of surveying. Captain Hudson demanded of Tuembooa, the king of Muthwater, the immediate restoration of the stolen property; and in case they were not returned or satisfaction given, he would burn his town. This very much frightened Tuembooa, for he had already heard of our doings at Sour Laib, and had learned the deadly power of our guns. He promised to do all in his power to obtain them, and if he could not, he would pay double the value of them in any produce which the island afforded. He also stated that it was not the natives of his town who had committed the theft, but the mountaineers, over whom, he assured Capt. Hudson, he had no control.

July 31st. Our boats, and those of the Peacock, returned from a surveying cruise among the leeward islands, and while the incidents of the cruise are fresh in my memory, I hasten to give an account of them.

On the eventful morning of the 24th inst., at daylight, we sent a party on shore to cook a few yams for breakfast, being all the provisions we had left. The brig and schooner, not being in sight, we wished to procure a hostage of note among the cannibals, to hold in our possession, while we went up to the town to trade; we knew that the savages here were of the most warlike character, and were the dread of all the neighboring islands. While some of the men were cooking the yams, Mr. Underwood and myself went along the beach in search of shells. Mr. U. had

13*

a rifle, and I had a trade hatchet.   We walked about half a mile from the place where the men were cooking the yams, when we were surprised by about forty warriors, led by the eldest son of the king of Malolo.   Mr. U. commenced a conversation with the chief, and meantime I listened to the remarks of the natives, as I could then understand some of their language, though they were not aware of the fact.   One said that he would have my shirt, another, my pants, a third, my hands, and all expected some part of my body for supper.

After some conversation with Mr. U., relative to his becoming a hostage, the chief left him for a few moments, to consult with his men, and, selecting two large warriors, told them what Mr. U. wanted of him. He remarked to them that he should consent to go, at the same time saying that I, probably, should be ordered to conduct him to the boat.   He instructed them to kill me, and take Mr. U. prisoner—whom they supposed to be a chief among us—and by that means they should be able to secure our numerous articles of trade, in exchange for him.   Knowing the fact that they never fight after their chief is slain, I had but little doubt in reference to his safe arrival at the boat, should he be delivered into my hands.

He then turned to Mr. U., saying that he was ready to go, and I was ordered to conduct him.   Taking his right hand in my left, we started for the boat.   On our way I showed him my hatchet, and assured him that if he should go peaceably to the boat, I would present it to him after our arrival, and if he did not, *I would give it to him* BEFORE !   I asked him if he understood me, and learned that he did.    He added that we white men were bad fellows.

We had not traveled more than half the distance, when I heard a low voice from behind, informing the chief that all was ready.    I was not at a loss to divine their intentions.    A moment had scarcely elapsed ere I had prostrated the chief, and, placing my foot upon his neck, threatened his life, should he refuse to drive them back.    After some hesitation, and finding that I was resolute, he yielded, and was permitted to rise and continue the walk to the boat.    He soon, however, manifested a disposition to release his hand from my grasp—which, as I was aware of his intentions, might have been too *cordial* to be *particularly* agreeable.

When remonstrated with for his apparent treachery, he said that he was a good man, and intended to go to the boat.    I replied that *I* was a good man, *too*, and that I intended that he *should* go, at the same time increasing the " sailor grasp," until he was satisfied that he could not release himself.

We then hurried to the boat.    I gave him up to Mr. Alden, and was then sent for Mr. U., and we returned together to the boat.    The men soon after came off with our breakfast, and at the same time the Peacock's first cutter, under Lieut. Emmons, joined us.    At 9 o'clock, A. M., we got underway in the Leopard, taking the hostage into our boat, and rowed up for the town ; the natives came round us as we struck on the reef connecting Malolo Lib and Malolo Lili, and every mark of treachery was apparent in their countenances.

As soon as the boat struck, we jumped out, leaving

two men and the officer to guard the hostage; the natives came rushing round us with a shout of triumph, and filled the boat to its utmost capacity. We attempted to draw the boat over the reef, but our efforts were unavailing. Knowing that they were fond of music, we commenced one of the songs that are frequently sung in the merchant service, while hoisting heavy freight, to produce uniformity of movement by the aid of the music. This was a beautiful exemplification of the fact, that "music hath charms to soothe the savage breast;" for no sooner had we entered into the spirit of the music, than they, one by one, joined us, and ere they were aware, we were again on our loved element. How great must have been their chagrin, when they saw that they had been disappointed in their repast upon human flesh!

In accordance with their tradition in reference to such as are so unfortunate as to get upon their reefs, they had marked us as their victims. So great was the effect of the music, that they not only *permitted* us to escape, but literally aided us by grasping the rope, and attempting to sing with us, although their tune differed as widely from ours as did their words. As soon as the boat was afloat, some of us reëntered, and induced such as were willing to do so, to jump overboard; and such as were not, we "hove" over, and taking in our own men, we went around to the town to buy our provisions. We anchored more than a quarter of a mile from the beach.

A wide flat makes out from the beach, and the tide being low, we could get no nearer in the boat. Mr. Underwood had a brace of pistols, and three men had rifles; one man went without arms, to carry the box of trade. The natives were sitting under the shade of a tree, and to its branches they had hung all their arms; they had also tied two pigs to it.

The king was fishing when we reached there, and we were obliged to wait for him before we could commence a trade, as he allowed no one else to trade with white men. When he came we found him a surly old man, apparently about fifty-five years of age. His eyes were sore, and he wore a white cap on his head, which he drew partly over his eyes to protect them from the sun. His whole appearance was morose and vicious, and he wanted four times as much for the pigs as we had been in the habit of giving any where else, and said he did not care whether we took them or not. Provisions we must get somewhere, and Mr U. agreed to give him his price. Knowing that the natives were fond of music, I sang some lively airs for the king, with which he seemed much pleased, and it was the only time I saw him smile.

One of the pieces sung, was a song called " All in the Tonga Islands," which contains the following couplet :—

> " They said they'd cut me up like pork,
> And eat me without knife or fork."

The king having obtained some knowledge of the language, by trading with whalemen, turned to some of his men, and said, " He knows that we are going to eat him. But I determined to spoil *his* appetite if possible, before he sat down to the "mess," should he attack us.

Mr. Alden took the hostage out of our boat into his

own, as soon as he anchored, and Mr. Henry, a brave and excellent young midshipman, came on shore from the Launch, armed with a bowie knife and pistol; when he came up to us, the king sent several men into the town for some yams and fowls, as he said. Shortly after, the hostage treacherously jumped out of the Launch and dashed through the shallow water for the shore. With a well-meant, but unappreciated forbearance, a shot was fired over him, to induce him to come back. This seemed the signal for the work of death to commence; two Indians seized my rifle, and attempted to take it from me. I drew my knife, and asked Mr. Underwood if I should give it up or fight; he answered, "fight." I instantly stabbed one, and he knocked the other senseless with a blow on the head with his pistol. John Dunnock shot another. As this was going on, I saw as many as forty more joining the throng on the beach from the town; among them was a man with a large scar under the left eye, and I knew him to be one of the men whom the king had sent to the town for yams and fowls. Some of the men fled to the boat on the first attack; others fired their rifles, and finding it impossible to load again, followed them. Mr. Underwood, Mr. Henry and myself, were all that remained to fight at least ninety men. The air around our heads was literally filled with clubs and spears. Hearing an Indian shouting *Turanga, Turanga,* I knew that he was hailing Mr. Underwood, and turned to see what he wanted. He was within fifteen feet of us, and his spear was quivering in his hand; the next moment Mr. Underwood would have been transfixed by it. As I raised my rifle to fire at him, an Indian

sprang out with a musket from behind a tree, and I
let the chief throw his spear, thinking I could parry
it off with my rifle, and then shoot the man who had
the musket. The chief again poised his spear and
darted it; my ignorance of the force of these missiles
very nearly cost me my life. It came like a flash of
lightning, struck me full in the face, tearing my upper
lip into three pieces, loosening my upper fore teeth,
and glancing out of my mouth, passed through the
left arm of Mr. U. I shot him through the head, and
attempted to reload my rifle, when a man ran up behind me and knocked me senseless, for the moment,
into the water. This wet all my powder, and rendered my rifle useless for further service; falling on
my face the water instantly brought me to my senses
again. A few moments after Mr. Henry was knocked
down by a blow from a club on the back of the head.
I saw him struggling under water, and tried to get to
him, but had not fought half way, when I was
knocked down again, and as I rose, I received another
heavy blow between the shoulders. Looking round,
I saw Mr. Underwood lying on his left side, resting
on his left hand in the water, and holding up his right
to parry off the blows of a club, which a gigantic savage was flourishing over his head; the blood was
streaming from his mouth, nose and ears. I sprang
up behind the Indian and caught him by the throat,
and plunged my knife three times into his bosom. I
then stooped down and tried to lift Mr. Underwood out
of the water. He spoke once distinctly :—" Tell her,"
said he, "that I loved her until the last moment."
This was said, probably, in reference to his wife, to
whom he had been married but two weeks before sail-

ing.  Soon after this, his eyes flashed, and he seemed for a moment to recover himself,—his countenance gleaming in all the fierceness of the war spirit; he tried to speak, but his mouth was so filled with blood that I could not understand what he wished to say. He probably saw the stealthy approach of a savage, who was about to aim a blow at my head, and giving *him* that keen, piercing look of defiance, in the last agonies of death, he wished to warn me of my danger—for the next moment I experienced a sensation similar to that produced by the report of a cannon near one's head.  I recollect this distinctly, and remember no more, as I fell senseless into the water.

How long I remained in that situation I do not know ; but when my senses *did* return, the noise and bustle of the fight was over.  I do not know when or how I reached the boat, nor did I know any thing for several days afterward.  On recovering my senses, I learned the following particulars.  Soon after, the first cutter opened a fire upon them, and several being killed, they all retreated to the bushes.  The boats then pulled in, and took possession of the bodies of Lieut. Underwood, and Wilkes Henry, midshipman ; they had been stripped entirely naked, and dragged some distance on the beach, with the expectation, no doubt, of making a hearty meal from them.

They clubbed and speared us until they supposed that there could be no life in us.  I afterward arose upon my feet—being perfectly delirious—and walked among them, talking, laughing and singing, which convinced them that I was a spirit.  In consequence of their superstitious dread of spirits, they offered me no further violence. In this condition I was taken into the boat by Lieut. Alden.

Since the above was written, I have been favored with an interview with a gentleman who visited the island about nine months afterward. He states that during his stay there he heard the natives singing a song which was composed in consequence of this melancholy encounter. In this they refer to some one as a "spirit man" who conducted quite singularly after having been slain. They affirm that they cut off my head, which of itself resumed its former place, and that I went around and gathered up my hands and feet which had been severed from my body, and adjusted them properly, where they soon became as fixed and permanent as they were previous to their dismemberment, and afterward laughed at them.

During this time I had been placed in the "stern sheets" of the boat, and covered with the American Flag, to protect me from the scorching heat of the vertical sun. My wounds were so numerous and severe that no one expected me to survive but a short time. But why I was thus almost miraculously preserved, is known only to the great Disposer of events.

They had not proceeded far when the schooner was seen at anchor. When coming so near to the schooner that the boat's ensigns could be seen, they were set at half mast in token of some accident having befallen them. The signal was no sooner perceived from the schooner than she was got underway and stood down to meet them. Capt. Wilkes and Passed Midshipman Eld were on shore at the time, making observations; and perceiving the schooner underway, and shortly afterwards the boats coming with their

14

ensigns at half mast, they immediately struck their tent and pulled for the schooner, where they arrived a little before the boats. When the boats came alongside, Captain Wilkes anxiously inquired what the matter was, and when informed that Lieut. Underwood and Mid. Wilkes Henry had been murdered, he sprang toward the bodies and fainted. He was taken in this state to the cabin of the schooner, and remained in this senseless condition for fifteen minutes, before he was resuscitated. In the mean time, the bodies were removed from the boat, and placed on the quarter, under the cover of tarpaulins, while I was taken to the berth deck. By this time Capt. Wilkes recovered a little and returned upon deck, but no sooner saw the bodies, than he fell in the same state from which he had just before recovered. On coming to again, he cried and moaned in the most pitiable and melancholy manner.

Mr. Henry was his nephew and the only son of a widowed sister, and from whom he had taken him away. The bodies were kept until the following day, during which time Mr. Agate, artist, succeeded in getting a very correct likeness of them both for their friends at home. After which they were sewed up in separate hammocks, and taken on shore to a small uninhabited island, where both of them were interred in the same grave. "They were lovely and pleasant in their lives, and in death they were not divided," 2d Samuel 1 : 23.

# CHAPTER XI.

The Punishment for the Murders—Funeral Services of the Murdered—Departure—Gardener's Island—Recollections of Home—Arrival at the Sandwich Islands—Honolulu—Common People.

> " E'en the favored isles,
> So lately found, although the constant sun
> Cheers all their seasons with a grateful smile,
> Can boast but little virtue ; and, inert
> Through plenty, lose in morals what they gain
> In manners—victims to luxurious ease."

Captain Wilkes named this island " Henry's Island" and " Underwood's Group." Three volleys of musketry were then fired over the grave, which closed the scene ; after which they all returned to the schooner to premeditate on the means to be adopted for the revenge of their deaths. The plan was arranged in the following manner. The boats were sent to row a guard around the island to prevent the escape of any of the natives, and to stop any from joining them from other islands.

They cruised all that night, until light the next morning, when three large canoes were seen making for the island. Lieutenant Emmons in the Peacock's 1st cutter, made sail and went in chase of them ; when coming within gun shot, he gave them a broadside, each canoe in succession, which soon stopped their headway. All the canoes were destroyed and the natives killed, except two, one man and one woman ; the man was taken prisoner, but the woman was allowed to swim ashore.  The same morning the men were landed from the brig Porpoise (she having joined them the day before) the men of the boats and schooner amounting to nearly one hundred.  On landing, they were divided in three divisions; Capt. Ringgold commanded the whole party and led the 1st in person.  The 2d division was under Lieut. Johnson, and the 3d under Lieut. Maury.  After destroying the plantations of bananas, tarro and yam beds, breaking up their war canoes and literally destroying every thing that fell in their way, and having arrived within sight of their principal towns, the 2d and 3d divisions halted, while the division under Captain Ringgold marched forward to reconnoiter the town.  On their arrival they found the town much larger than they expected and better fortified, and appeared to be strongly defended.  The principal chief came out armed with a spear, and drew himself up in all the pride of self consequence, and gave himself a thousand savage ostentatious airs.  He challenged our little party to proceed, he was ready for them, and he intended to have a white man for his supper. This consequential savage little dreamed that a reinforcement of the enemy was so near at hand, and knew but little of the effects and deadly power of the enemy's weapons, that were so shortly to be brought against them.

The town was fortified by upright posts sunk in the ground, and the bottom part walled in with stones; and between the posts in the top part, spaces were left open, through which to shoot their arrows and throw their clubs.  The whole was entrenched around with a ditch eight feet wide and five or six deep, in the bottom of which were an abundance of spears. Behind this fortification they had defied all the combined Fiji armies, and had been many times attacked by their enemies, but had always come off victorious, which circumstance inspired them with much confidence in their own strength and prowess. After the chief had come out and delivered his challenge, he returned behind the fortification and commenced making vigorous efforts to defend the town by filling up the interstices that would admit ingress. Capt. Ringgold, seeing the strength and determination of the enemy which he had to contend against, made signals for the two remaining divisions to join him.

After the force had concentrated, they formed a line, and marched up to the entrenchment in good order, under a heavy shower of arrows. The natives continued to throw out the spears and arrows in great profusion, but with little judgment. Two of our men were slightly wounded, one in the thigh and the other in the leg. The natives labored under a disadvantage which rendered their breast-work almost useless; they could not throw their spears without exposing the whole upper portion of their bodies, and in such cases almost instantly met their fate from our rifles. Several rockets were thrown in at the onset with the hope of setting fire to their town, but they did not take effect. A volley of musketry was fired at them by each division in succession; this had good effect, upwards of fifteen falling at each volley. The natives having become more bold, showed themselves in greater numbers above the breastwork, but after this deadly fire they became more intimidated, and

14*

retreated behind their houses. Rockets were again thrown in, but with no better success than at the former attempt. The contest had been kept up for more than an hour, when the " *Turanga Laib*," principal chief, was killed by a rifle ball, which circumstance struck a panic through them immediately, and what few there were remaining, fled to the back part of the town; some few made their escape, while many were shot in their retreat. They left their dead and wounded behind, to be consumed in the flames. At this time another rocket was thrown in and lodged upon the top of one of their thatched houses, which soon ignited, and in a short time the whole village was wrapped in flames; and only a few moments elapsed before the village was burned to the ground.

After the flames had sufficiently subsided, a party of our men entered, but found nothing save the dead and wounded. The number killed could not be correctly ascertained—as many had been buried in the flames and were consumed—but the number must have been considerably large. The men refreshed themselves with cocoa-nuts and cocoa-nut milk, and rested a few moments, after which they marched over the hills to the back of the island, where there was another small town;—but on their arrival they found that Captain Wilkes, with his boat's crew, had burnt it early in the morning. The whole party then embarked and proceeded to the brig and schooner, where a comfortable night's repose was very acceptable, following as it did, a day of fatigue, slaughter and bloodshed. The next morning a woman came to the beach and hailed the vessel, holding up a pistol and

Mr. Underwood's cap and a rifle. Capt. Wilkes went on shore, taking with him the interpreter, and had some conversation with her. She stated that the few warriors who were left alive on the island had sent her to treat for peace on any terms he might think proper to propose, and in their name she solicited his forgiveness. Captain Wilkes told her to tell them to assemble on the hill at 10 o'clock, and that he would meet them and hear what they had to say.

Accordingly, at the appointed time Captain Wilkes, taking with him all the men who had been on shore the previous day, embarked in the boats and proceeded to the shore. On landing, the men were formed into a hollow square, for the purpose of receiving the vanquished warriors. They did not come at the appointed time, however, and Captain Wilkes sent the prisoner, who had been taken by Mr. Emmons, in the boat, to tell them to come immediately or he would renew hostilities and destroy the remaining portion. In a few moments they were seen moving slowly up the acclivity of the hill, crawling on their hands and knees; when, coming up where our men were stationed, they prostrated themselves at their feet in open submission. Thus were these treacherous savages brought low, and made to know their own weakness. They brought as an offering to Captain Wilkes three girls, from the ages of 12 to 16, as they said,—the handsomest that could be found on the island; these were intended as an offering of peace. This offer, of course, was refused, but the Captain told them he wished to let them know the impropriety of their conduct, and that the terms on which he should make peace were, that they should promise never to be guilty of another like act. To this the chief of the party replied, that they knew they were placed in the same position with guilty ones, but they assured the captain that none of the party then present was engaged in the murder of the two officers, and all that were, were killed in the fight, or perished in the flames of the town. When they were informed that not one of our men was killed, or seriously injured in the fight, they were much surprised, and exclaimed in a loud voice, "Curlew, curlew, curlew!" meaning, as I afterwards learnt, that we were all spirits.

After the treaty was concluded the men were all discharged, and returned to the brig and schooner, where they all remained until the following day, when they returned by the boats to their respective ships.

Captain Wilkes remained in the schooner with the intention of visiting Somo Somo and Cartab, and from thence to join the ship Vincennes at Muthwater.

The same boats brought information of the demise of William Smith, seaman, who came to an untimely end in a mysterious manner.

The officers had been on shore, leaving the vessel in the charge of two seamen, one of whom was Smith. Soon after their departure Smith proposed to go into the cabin and pilfer some of the spirits which the officers had in charge. To this, however, his companion did not consent. When Smith was assured that the theft would not be divulged by his shipmate, he went alone and drank a large quantity, by which he was much intoxicated. During the watch on the following night, Smith was unable to attend to the duties assigned him, and was found asleep by one of the officers. He was reproved for this conduct, and while under the influence of the dram, he attacked the officer, when a scuffle ensued, and both fell overboard. The officer recovered himself and regained the deck, but Smith could not be rescued.

The foregoing facts were not made known at the time of his decease, and there was an air of mystery connected with his sudden death. I have since obtained them from one who was on board at the time of the fatal encounter. I am not aware that any blame can be attached to the officer.

On the morning of Aug. 2d, the king of Muthwater, Tuembooa, sent us some hogs and yams as a compensation for the whole number of flags stolen from the reefs by the natives. At the same time he informed Captain Hudson that he had endeavored to recover the flags, but found it utterly impossible; he expected that they had been destroyed.

A signal was made, on the morning of the 10th, for all the officers and men that could be spared from each ship, to repair to the Vincennes, to attend the funeral service of Lieut. Underwood and Mid. Wilkes Henry, who were so treacherously murdered by the natives of Malolo. At half past 10 o'clock the service commenced. All was hushed and still; a death-like silence pervaded the ship throughout, and a deep melancholy seemed apparently visible on the countenances of all, particularly among the officers; and all, both men and officers, listened with an unusual attention to the solemn and impressive service. The chaplain took for his text :—" Boast not thyself of to-morrow, for thou knowest not what a day may bring forth," Prov. 27 : 1. "It is even as a vapor that appeareth for a little time and then vanishes away," James 4 : 14. After he had finished the sermon, he delivered a very flattering eulogium on the lives and character of the two officers.

In the afternoon a signal was made to get underway, and proceed to Mali, a distance of about twelve miles. We came to anchor about three miles from the village, which we found deserted and the canoes all hauled up and hid among the bushes. The natives were getting very shy of us since the news of the destruction of Soui Laib and Malolo had spread among the islands.

The land here rises to a moderate height, and the ground presents every where a rich soil. The shore is handsomely variegated with different kinds of shrubbery and plants. At a little distance from the shore may be seen groves of cocoa-nut trees and breadfruit, among which the habitations of the natives are tastefully erected, under the wide-spreading branches of the trees. The houses are constructed in the same manner as those of the neighboring islands. In the middle of the village stands conspicuous, a building of a spiral shape, much larger than any of the rest, and handsomely decorated with shells of different kinds and colors. This is their *Buri*, or spirit house, in which they hold all their public meetings and Cannibal feasts ; and also entertain strangers, besides perform their religious ceremonies. We had no communication with the natives of this village, owing to their shyness.

The formation of the island is a complete mass of

coral, with little or no vegetation. Great numbers of birds of the aquatic species were found upon it; and so tame were they, as to be captured with clubs. After having completed the survey on this island, we hoisted up the boats and made sail,—steering to the southward, for the purpose of trying the dipping needle.

At meridian, on the 20th of August, we discovered another island, or sand bank. This is claimed as a discovery by Capt. Wilkes, as it is not found on any chart,—and named by him McKean's Island, after the man who discovered it.

Our stay at Gardener's Island was very short, as it was also at several less important islands which we made on our passage to the Sandwich Islands. This fact was interesting to many of us, in consequence of the approach of the expiration of our term of service. Many cherished the fond anticipation that on our arrival at Oahee, they should be sent to their loved homes. *Home!* there is a magic charm in that word, appreciated only by those who have been long removed, far, far from its hallowed associations. And if I mistake not, the young man,—his bosom throbbing in all the glow of youthful buoyancy and vivacity, cradled on the heaving bosom of the mighty ocean—can respond to ennobling sentiments as its remembrances pass in review. His bosom beats with a quicker pulsation, as fancy recalls the prayers of a fond, unchanging mother, or the warm affection of a sister. Indeed, I have but little hope of the sailor who loves not the very place that gave him birth, with the sunny recollections of childhood's home. There is but little hope of reform, when the friends of one's

youth are spurned, his home avoided, and the remembrance of the hallowed scenes of the family altar,
where morning and evening a sacred incense arose to
high heaven, from a humble group bowed in rever-
ence; when *such* scenes, I say, are ridiculed, the probability of a return from the paths of vice is extremely
precarious.

At 6 o'clock, A. M., Sept. 20th, we made the Island
of Onehow, one of the Sandwich Islands, about ten
leagues distant. By the 24th, we had succeeded in
beating up to the bar off Honolúlu, and came to
anchor about 6 o'clock in the morning. We were
visited by Mr. Reynolds, P. A. Brinsmaide, Esq.,
American consul, and several other American residents here. We lay here until the following morning,
when a number of boats from the shore, and several
from whale ships in the harbor, came out to assist in
towing us over the bar, and up to the town, according
to a general custom here. By 8 o'clock, we had the
ship hauled close into the Consul's wharf, and safely
moored.

In the afternoon, all hands were called aft under
the half deck, when Captain Wilkes informed them
that he wished to reënter them for eighteen months
longer, and at the same time saying, that it was impossible to get through with the work sooner. Those
who chose to remain were to have three months' pay
and two weeks' liberty; those who did not, should
have only three days' liberty. Those who reëntered
were to have one quarter more pay. Very few seemed
willing to make any change in their plans on this occasion, but on the following day they commenced putting their names down, and taking the liberty.

The Bay of Honolulu is not more than half a mile long, and a quarter broad, but deep, and perfectly safe. Its western side is lined by marshes and fish ponds of artificial workmanship, stretching northward, till they reach a small river at the head of the harbor, by which the congregated waters from the mountains are poured into the sea. The town of Honolulu lies on a point formed by the eastern side of this river, and the curvature of the beach, as it sweeps again towards the sea, and presents to the view some tolerably well built houses near the beach. The first is the consul's, a building of coral and mud, and several wooden buildings in the same enclosures, used as warehouses; the first is used as a store, and the place of his office. The consul's residence is in the middle of the village. It is a wooden building of a moderate size, with covered verandas and venetian blinds. To it is attached a beautiful yard, covered with green grass, and richly variegated with shrubbery,—the whole enclosed with a mud wall. In the same yard is another respectable building, used as an apothecary shop below, and a billiard room above. Immediately behind and around these buildings, are to be seen the thickly crowded and irregularly built huts of mud and straw—the habitations of a population of about five thousand natives; and beyond, are the beautiful, cultivated valleys of the interior, enclosed by mountains of great height and wildness.

Diamond Hill, as you enter the bay, has a beautiful, majestic and romantic appearance; it is the principal point on the south side of the island. It is the crater of an extinguished volcano, the mere shell of a decapitated mountain, whose bowels have been ex-

15

hausted by fire.   It is of a circular form, and rises almost perpendiculaly several hundred feet.   Its sides
every where look like seared walls, and are fluted
and furrowed from top to bottom by the washing of
water courses, as if by artificial workmanship.   They
also are surrounded in many places by a kind of
moulding of equally singular formation, and again,
by blocks and piles of jagged lava, having in their elevation, the appearance of the parapets and battle-
ments of a dilapidated castle.   A more unique object
can scarcely be imagined.

Honolulu is the Kanaka name of the seaport town
of the Island of Oahu, and is an excellent and convenient harbor for ships bound to and from the East
Indies round Cape Horn.   It affords, also, a convenient recruiting station for whalemen while prosecuting
the arduous duties of their useful and lucrative business among the monsters of the great deep, in the
boundless expanse of the Pacific.   This island is, like
all the rest of the group, evidently of volcanic origin.
Several craters, now dormant, are in the immediate
vicinity of Honolulu.   An extensive tract of table land
stretches along this side of the island, for several miles
in length, and about a mile in width.   This tract is
cultivated, and produces an abundance of tarro and
sweet potatoes.   All kinds of melons are growing
spontaneously on the high land, back of the plain.
Here and there are small groves of cocoa-nut trees.
A few hamlets of the thatched houses of the natives
are also rising among the herbage, resembling hay-
stacks in their appearance, and occasionally the resi-
dences of the missionaries are seen situated in the
midst of beautiful gardens, and shaded with such trees

as are best adapted to shade. Some of the missionaries cultivate a large tract of land by native labor, which no doubt is of the first importance to them, as they can there learn the art of agriculture, in the knowledge of which there is a very great deficiency among the islanders.

The Rev. Mr. Cook, whose residence is located on the banks of Pearl River, a few miles from its mouth, is one of these farming missionaries, and from what I saw, I should judge he was very much beloved by the natives.

The banks of Pearl River, about one mile from the sea, is a mass of fossils. Among the collection of shells, are to be found large quantities of oyster shells, like those of our own country, but none of the species are to be found in any part of the group. At what period these oysters grew here, is not known.

To the mind of the candid traveler, the town of Honolulu exhibits in its appearance much that is interesting. One may see a plain delineation of the effects of the missionary labor there. The people in their dwellings, their manners and their dress, are living epistles of the good effects of missionary labor. Those who have had the longest residence in the town, live on Main Street, in fine, large, framed houses, painted white, many of them with green blinds, enclosed in neat picket fences. The occupants of these buildings dress like Americans or Europeans, and some of them exhibit much polish in their manners, and have a very tolerable classical education. This street occupies a place near the harbor. The next street farther back is occupied by those whose residence in town is of more recent date. The buildings are thatched, roof and sides, the most of them,—a few have the walls boarded, with roofs thatched. They have glass windows and framed doors; and are enclosed with walls of bricks dried in the sun, and white washed. The women of this class are clad in part with foreign manufacture, and a part in the bark cloth, which they call "Tappa." Their garments are made in good form, and they exhibit all the marks of rapid advancement in the scale of civilization and refinement.

The next street has a perfect representation of the semi-barbarous state, in its buildings and inhabitants. The houses are rudely fashioned, and thatched, enclosed in a palisade of sticks and vines, or of half formed, sun-dried bricks. The males are clad, some of them in trowsers and hat, and no shirt or shoes; others with shirts and minus the trowsers; and one I saw with hat and shoes, and without either shirt or pants. The ladies of this class wore a garment of the bark cloth, made like a long bag, with a hole in the bottom, without sleeves. This is drawn over the body until the head is thrust out of the end, and the arms appear from places in the side, left open for that purpose. This garment reaches as low down as the ankles, and they look all the same size from the shoulders to the feet.

Back of this street, you see a collection of the mud huts that once formed the only habitations of the Sandwich Islanders. The natives of this class come dressed in the garb of the heathen, which is no more than a narrow strip of tappa tied around the loins, and a dirty blanket of the same material, thrown corner-wise over the left shoulder, coming up under the right arm, and tied in a large knot on the chest.

These individuals have just caught the sound of the gospel, and have come to settle near the place where they can enjoy the privilege of hearing and learning the doctrines of the Bible. One of this class exhibited the most ludicrous view of the vanity of pride that I ever witnessed, and I could not well help drawing a lesson from it. He had felt evidently a desire for the finery that those enjoyed who had lived longer in the town, and in his zeal he had made an effort to jump at once from barbarism to refinement, and no doubt, in his own estimation, had made a masterly stride towards the accomplishment of his object. But his position was convincing every one that saw him, that he would be more happy and comfortable in the condition of the heathen. This individual had upon his left foot the remains of what once had been a shoe. All the outer sole was worn away to the instep, and the inner sole was dragged along the street, as he stepped, like the tongue of a dog. On his right leg, he had the top of a boot, altogether minus the soles, and the crown of a hat, without top or brim, was drawn on his head, which he could only keep off his neck by crowding into one side a large roll of grass. In this finery he was perambulating the streets. He had left his tappa blanket at home, and every one that saw him was laughing at his ridiculous appearance. So it is often with boys. The same spirit that led this man leads many boys. They see others wise, rich and great, and make an effort to jump into just such a condition, over all the labor and study by which the truly wise and great became so,

15*

and instead of labor and study, they institute lying and theft, and thus dispossess themselves of good character as the native did his blanket, and appear ten times worse in the estimation of the world than the man who has rested satisfied with his poverty and ignorance.

On Sabbath day, I saw the natives going in great numbers to the place "where prayer was wont to be made." They were neatly dressed, and the most profound seriousness rested on every face; no noisy mirth was heard among them. The loud laugh that speaks the thoughtless mind was hushed, and silently and solemnly the heathen journeyed to the sanctuary, to hear of the mercy and merits of that Saviour, of whom but a few years since, many of them were entirely ignorant. The little girls looked like butterflies in their tappa dresses, which are fancifully stained with bright red, yellow and jet. About thirty from our ship, all man-of-wars-men, followed along to the church, and stood around the doors to see and hear. The missionary who was to officiate that day, was the Rev. Mr. Bingham. He read a hymn in the native language, but when the native choir began to sing, the effect upon our party was electrical. They began to sing the hymn to the tune of old "Greenville." Before the first verse was finished, our party were all seated under the shade of the house, and took off their hats, and many a tar that was insensible to fear in dangers and death, wet the corners of his neck handkerchief with tears, that were called from their fountains by the recollections of childhood, friends and home, which were brought upon their minds in connection with that old tune; and when at length the sermon commenced in the native tongue, we started to go away, I saw some with their shoes in their hands, and others on tiptoe, lest they should make a noise and disturb the worshipers.

In external manners and habits of life, the common people or Kanakas, present a strong contrast to the chiefs; and indeed are wretched people, subject, not only to blindness of heart and mind, but also the most abject poverty. Their condition is as bad, if not worse, than many slaves in the U. S. If the former are an object of interest, the latter should be of a compassion that should almost border on agony.

The greatest wealth of which some of the less enlightened can boast, consists of a mat on which to lie, a few folds of tappa to cover them, one calabash for water and another for *poi*, a rude implement or two for the cultivation of their ground, and the instruments used in their simple manufactures. Tarro, potatoes and suet, with occasionally a fish, constitute their general food; while all else they raise, or take, and every result of their labor, goes to meet the exorbitant taxes levied by the king and his governors, and their own respective chiefs and landlords. The spontaneous production is very scarce, and labor at all seasons of the year is necessary to the support of life. In this respect this group differs widely from the Society and other Islands in the South Pacific Ocean, which we have visited, where eight months in the year, the natives have only to pluck their food, principally breadfruit, from the trees overhanging their habitations. The growth of the breadfruit here is confined to a few districts on one or two islands, and where found, yields a very partial supply at any season.

*Tarro*, an article which I have frequently mentioned, is the principal food of the Sandwich Islanders, and to the whole nation, answers the double purpose of bread and vegetables. The plant to which it belongs, is the Arum, a root growing in many parts of America, and particularly in the West India Islands; and sometimes known by the name of the wild indian turnip. Tarro is the *Arum Esculentum* of the botanist, and is used in many other warm climates as a vegetable. It here occupies the most of the cultivated ground, especially such as is capable of being overflown by water; and the planting, irrigation and necessary care of it, form the most laborious part of native farming. The islanders have arrived at great skill in the cultivation of this plant, and perhaps their mode of growing it, considering the general face of the country, scarcely admits of improvement, unless it be in the implements with which they work. The beds in which the tarro stands, are generally square or oblong, of various sizes, from that of a few yards to half of an acre. The natives prepare it for use, by baking it in the only manner practiced among them. This is by digging a hole in the ground, one or two feet deep and five or six in circumference, and placing a layer of stones upon the bottom, upon which wood is placed and a fire kindled; other stones are laid on the fire, and by the burning of the wood the whole becomes ignited; those on the top are drawn off, and the tarro, dog, pig, or fish,—closely wrapped in the leaves of the *ti*,—is laid on the hearth of stones still remaining on the bottom, and hastily covered with the rest; a little water is poured on to create a steam, and the whole is then covered with earth,—by which the heat and steam are kept from escaping—and the article in the *umaii*, or oven, becomes cooked. The tarro thus baked, is in the next place made into their favorite poi. The process is very simple, though so laborious as to be performed by the men;—it is simply by beating the *tarro* upon a short plank of hard wood, slightly hollowed in the middle, like a tray, with a stone something in the shape of a clumsy pestle, wetting it occasionally with water, like dough. It is then put into a calabash, diluted with water and set aside for fermentation. This soon takes place and the pot is fit for use in a day or two, though preferred when four or five days old.

It is eaten by thrusting the fore finger into the mess and securing as much as will adhere to it in passing it to the mouth. Next to *tarro*, the sweet potato is the principal article of cultivation. The yam also is grown, but chiefly at the leeward islands. I saw none here. Indian corn has been introduced, but is very little used as an article of diet. Esculent plants, such as cabbages, squashes, water-melons, musk-melons, pumpkins, cucumbers and beans,—the seeds of which have been introduced by the missionaries and foreigners,—are becoming abundant; they are cultivated principally for ships, and the table of foreign residents.

These islands were discovered in the year 1778, by Captain James Cook, of the British navy, and from him, in honor of the Earl of Sandwich, then the first Lord of the Admiralty, received the name by which they are at present designated. The tragical

event, and lamented death of this celebrated navigator at Hawaii, in the succeeding year, caused their
existence to be made known to the civilized world
with an excitement of feeling that deeply stamped the
event on the public mind.

## CHAPTER XII.

Visit of a Native Chief—Sentence of death passed upon two Natives for the murder of a Female Chief—Departure—Arrival
at Hawaii—Expedition—Visit to the Volcano—Mouna Roa.

> " Deep midnight now involves the lurid skies,
> While infant breezes from the shore arise,
> The waning moon, behind a watery shroud,
> Pale glimmered o'er the long-protracted cloud.
> A mighty ring around her silver throne,
> With parting meteors crossed, portentous shone ;
> This in the troubled sky full oft prevails,—
> Oft deemed a signal for tempestuous gales."

On the 27th of Sept., Governor Tekooanoa visited
the ship, and was received with military honors.
During the day the English, American, and French
consuls also visited us, with a portion of the mission
and foreign residents.

In a short time afterward the news of the death of
Commodore D. T. Patterson was received, and read
to all hands on the quarter deck, and the officers ordered to wear crape on the left arm for thirty days, in

testimony of respect for the deceased. All the American vessels in the harbor, as well as the foreign vessels and the fort on shore, had their colors at half mast. On the 28th inst. the king of the Sandwich Islands arrived in his yacht from Maui, on which occasion the fort fired a salute of 21 guns. On the 29th the Peacock arrived off the bar and came to anchor, she having separated from us several days before our arrival here.

The sentence of death was published on the 5th, for the murder of a female on the 28th of Sept. The following is the sentence.

Eia ka pai palu a ua' bi i palupalu i ia Kamanawa laua o Lonopuakau, ike mai na Kanaka a pan. E Kamanawa a me Lonopuakau. E like me ka olelo hoo hewa in olua, e maki, i hoo holoin' ii kula 30 o Sepatemabu, ke hai aku rei molama, i ka hora ii Pomaikai olua, ke mihi i oleed i keia marr la, e kaluin mai ai i ko olua hewn nui e Jesu.

KAMEHAMEHA iii
KEKAULUOHI.

*Honolulu, Okatobu 4th*, 1840.

### TRANSLATION.

*Sentence of the Chiefs, sent in writing to Kamanawa and Lonopuaka, published for the information of all persons.*

To KAMANAWA AND LONOPUAKA.—In accordance with the sentence of death, passed upon you on the 30th Sept., we hereby notify you that the day of your execution will be the 20th day of the present month, at 11 o'clock, A. M. Happy indeed will you be, should you improve the present few days by repentance, that your heinous crimes may be forgiven through Jesus Christ.

KAMEHAMEHA iii
KEKAULUOHI.

*Honolulu,* Oct. 5th, 1840.

While here, the Commander in Chief of the Expedition and officers paid their respects to his Hawaiian majesty.  They were received with due respect, and treated very courteously during their stay.  There was some of the " pomp and circumstance " of princely grandeur and consequence, which are usually seen in more enlightened portions of the world.  Truly,

> " Feeble man
> Clothed with a little brief authority,
> Plays such fantastic tricks before high heaven,
> As make the angels weep."

On the 20th, the day previously appointed for the execution, at 11 o'clock the chief Kamanawa and the native Lonopuakau, were both hanged by the neck upon the ramparts of the fort, before an immense crowd of spectators.  The Rev. Messrs. Armstrong and Smith addressed the throne of grace in their behalf.  About eight hundred natives, under arms, were assembled, and passed behind them, two and two, with arms reversed, until the whole was concluded. As they dropped, the colors were half-masted, the bell tolled, and there was a general yell and weeping throughout the village.  The chief died a very hard death.

At 10 o'clock, Dec. 3d, Mr. Alex. Adams, pilot, came on board for the purpose of conducting us out of the harbor, but in consequence of some difficulty with the captain, was ordered ashore. After dispensing with the services of the pilot, boats were sent out with signals, to point out the passage, which compensated for the sudden ejection of the pilot. We received P. A. Brinsmaide, Esq., American consul, and Dr. J. P. Judd, physician to the mission, who came on board to take passage to Hawaii.

Our passage out of this dangerous harbor was not only safe but pleasant, nothing of particular importance occurring to mar the harmony of our company, which had become considerably changed, from the fact that many who had been with us from the commencement of the expedition, had already embarked for their native shores, and their places had been supplied by a corresponding number of natives. A few days brought us in sight of the beautiful Island of Hawaii. We came to an anchor on the 9th, in Hilo Bay.

Hawaii or Owhyhee is the most southerly island of this group, and on account of its great elevation is generally the first land seen from the ship on approaching the Sandwich Islands. No other spot in the boundless expanse of North and South Pacific exhibits so much of beauty and sublimity, as is displayed to the traveler in approaching this island. Along the sea-shore in the vicinity of the bay, the hills and valleys, covered with a rich soil, are heavily laden with crops of tarro, sugar, and various tropical fruits; sweet potatoes grow well, and the arrow root is also an article of export from this island, and ginger is the spontaneous production of the soil. Its origin is volcanic. Several craters, now dormant, are found in various parts of the island, some of which

16

are filled up with earth and covered over with a luxuriant growth of grass and herbage.  Cattle, horses
and sheep eat and sleep where once the volcano roar-
ed and vomited forth its stores of liquid fire, and
where, doubtless, now at no great depth beneath them,
broad streams of perpetual fire are furiously coursing,
flashing, sparkling, madly driven by the power of the
gas as it careers along by the guidance of Omnipotence, to the safety valves that the God of nature has
provided for its escape.

This bay is large and commodious, sufficiently so
for ships of any size to come in and anchor.  On approaching the land, we were delighted with the verdure, luxuriance and beauty of the landscape, opening
to us the village of Hilo and its neighborhood.  The
land rises gradually from the beach, to a distance of
fifteen or twenty miles, bordering upon a heavy wood,
encircling Mouna Roa.  Though the country is but
partially cultivated, this large district has all the
appearance of cultivation, and of having been laid
out by artificial workmanship,—being an open country, covered with grass, and beautifully studded and
sprinkled with clumps and groves and single trees,
with here and there a patch of sugar-cane, after the
manner of park scenery, with a cottage here and there
peeping from the rich foliage.  The summits of the
two great mountains of Mouna Roa and Mouaked are,
most of the time, covered with snow, with a belt of
clouds hanging below, which gives to the scene, in
that direction, quite a gloomy aspect, but it is by no
means a sterile country.  The channel is formed by a
cliff on the right hand side, and on the left a sunken
coral reef, the point of which comes within a short

distance of the shore, making it necessary for ships to
pass so near the breakers as to appear in a dangerous
situation; seamen, however, think it perfectly safe.
The reefs run in a curved direction, to a point in the
channel about half a mile to westward, where it joins
a romantic little islet, covered with cocoa-nut trees.
Near this place our observatory was situated, together
with two or three small thatched houses, which were
built by the king's order for our accommodation, some
time previous to our arrival. A small channel runs
between this and the main land, which is low, and
sweeps round to the western cliffs in a beautifully
curved sandy beach of about three miles, making the
form of the bay that of a flattened horse-shoe. The
beach is covered with varied vegetation, and ornamented by clumps, groves and single trees of lofty
cocoa-nut, among which the habitations of the natives
are to be seen;—not in a village, but scattered every
where among the plantations, like farm-houses in a
thickly settled country. The mission houses are
pleasantly situated about three hundred yards from
the water's edge, and in full view from our ship in
the middle of the curvature of the beach, forming the
head of the bay. They look like so many palaces,
when compared with the wigwams of the natives.
At a very short distance from the beach, the breadfruit trees are to be seen in every direction, intersected with the pandanas, *tutui*, or candle tree, the hybis-
cus and acacia, &c. The tops of these rise gradually
one above another, as the country ascends gently towards the mountains in the interior, for twenty or
thirty miles in the S. E., presenting a delightful forest

scene, totally different from any thing that I have seen among the islands.

Soon after our arrival, Capt. Wilkes was busily employed in preparing the instruments, &c., for an expedition to Mouna Roa, the most elevated volcano of this group, and said to be second in height to none in the world, the summit of which, although within the tropics, is glistening with the ice and snow of perpetual winter. One hundred and fifty natives were engaged to carry the instruments and baggage, portable houses, tents, etc., and six seamen were selected from the crew to accompany the officers appointed to the management of the affair, the commodore in person commanding the whole party. Having separated the natives into parties in numbers proportionate to the burden assigned to each, we got them loaded, and we started from the observatory about three o'clock in the afternoon, and it was really interesting to see the whole cavalcade winding along the hills and valleys on their way to the volcano.

After following the banks of a river about a mile, we traveled in a south-westerly direction. The soil of this highly interesting island, where we could see it, was fertile, and in many places well cultivated, producing sugar, tarro, breadfruit, yams, potatoes, and an abundance of bananas, and other tropical fruits. But by far the larger portion of land over which we traveled, was perfectly encrusted with lava, probably the work of other volcanoes now extinct; several craters were to be seen in different parts of the island, one of which was in plain sight from the ship. In many places the lava is covered with a rich soil, which furnishes roots to a variety of handsomely flowered

shrubbery. We encamped about 6 o'clock, P. M., having traveled eight miles to a small town called Tuoro,
until the moon should rise to give us sufficient light,
which was not until midnight, at which time we
again resumed our journey, and traveled to another
town called Winla; here we again encamped about
10 o'clock, A. M. We took breakfast, and again resumed our journey. The path began to grow more
and more rugged and our progress, of course, slower.
At 4 o'clock, P. M., we encamped at a town called
Kappaohee. The country here presents a more sterile
aspect; the masses of lava were more prominent and
were cleft in many places by convulsions of the earth.
Some of these chasms were three or four feet in width
and of immense depth.

At 8 o'clock on the morning of the 16th, we left
Kappaohee and arrived at the volcano at 2 o'clock,
P. M. As we approached the crater, the soil continued to grow more barren, and the only productions
are a few trees, called in the native tongue, *Ohea* and
*Koa*, a gigantic growth of fern and brake. The road,
owing to the crumbled state of the lava, was much
more even and smooth than I expected to find it.
The natives who carried the instruments had become
lame, fatigued, and their shoulders much swolen and
sore, although the commodore had treated them kindly—had never hurried them in the least, and they
were well supplied with provisions.

At 7 P. M., a party of seamen went from the tents
to witness the great exhibition of the powers of nature's God. The encampment was about 200 yards
from the crater.

Our object was to get round to that side of the cra-
*16

ter that commanded a view of the largest fire; and we had to climb over several precipices of almost perpendicular masses of scoria. It was a moonless night, and the attempt was made still more dangerous by wide and deep chasms that frequently crossed the path. Some of these were three or four miles in length, and as many feet wide, and of immeasurable depth, and we were enabled to find our way over them only by the light of the fires below. We approached the crater from the south-east, and when seated on the brink of the frightful chasm, nothing can exceed the grandeur and soul-thrilling sublimity of the scene. Here we had a full view of all the fires. I do not expect my pen can give any thing like an adequate description of this place, nor do I believe it in the power of any thing finite to do so; on the contrary, the awfully grand and sublime display of the wisdom and goodness, as well as the power of God, is infinitely beyond description.

In order to give my readers a faint description of the scene, they must imagine a chasm eleven miles in circumference, by three in diameter, and over one thousand feet deep. The walls are of solid scoria, and perpendicular with several boiling lakes of liquid fire, the bottom of which is at least a mile in circumference; the stupendous walls of the crater were illuminated by the strong light of the fire; the gas which rushed up to escape from its confinement in the fiery depths, was throwing up a thousand streams at once into the air seventy-five or one hundred feet, with a monotonous sound as of heavy surf breaking on a rock-bound shore, combined with the hissing, rushing roar of a vast conflagration, while a huge column of smoke, which seemed to be converted into flame by the light of the fire, rising a thousand feet above the crater, and which is seen in a clear night at least fifty miles, added to the imposing effect of the scene, and I have never had my nerves put to such a test, as they were while seated on the brink of this frightful abyss, with my feet hanging over the edge, surveying this magnificent display of Almighty Power. Compared with this, what are the proudest works of art. Man may look on his cities, his catacombs, his machinery, but let the man most famed for wisdom and power, be seated for ten minutes on the brink of this fiery abyss, and a sense of his nothingness will thrill through every part of his little soul. And yet, while almost breathless by the intensity of the feelings awakened by this scene, it dwindled into nothing as I thought of that day fixed by the eternal fiat of Omnipotence, when this whole world, its continents and islands, its oceans and seas, should be exhibited to a congregated world in the same state as the fiery gulf below.

The commodore immediately ordered us away from our fearful proximity to the crater, where in our recklessness we had perched ourselves, and we all sat together for some hours in inexpressible admiration and wonder. The night was dark, and the aspect of the whole scene was more imposing on that account; and while we were sitting there, a new place opened on the side of the crater, opposite to us, and a stream of liquid fire ran down into the bottom of the abyss, winding its way along among the cones and spires of scoria with serpentine course, beautifully marked by its own light, now turning some corner in a narrow stream, now widening out into a lake as it filled up some hollow in its bed, until at length it emptied itself into the great sea of fire. It was not until after midnight that we reached the encampment.

On the 17th, the natives complained of their fatigue and lameness so much, that Capt. Wilkes concluded to remain at the volcano until the day following. We spent the day in walking about, and going down into the crater. Mr. Budd, Mr. Eld and myself missed our path, and walked so far out of the way, that we did not get back in season to go to the bottom; we were descending into the crater, when we met the commodore and his attendants coming out. One of the natives who attended the commodore could speak a little English tolerably well, and he told Mr. Eld, with his usual quaintness of expression, "that if he went to the bottom it would be dark before he would get out, and that he would fall into some of the holes and *kill his neck*."

This evening I was again at the place that commanded a full view of the largest fire, and it evidently seemed much larger than it was the night before, and we saw that it was rapidly increasing; several new places had opened about the bottom, and the noise was much louder. The lava was spouting very high at the northern end of the molten sea, and a rapid current was flowing to the southward and westward. The commodore, Mr. Brinsmaide, Dr. Judd, Mr. Budd, and Mr. Eld joined the party of seamen about 8 o'clock, and it was the opinion of us all, that in a few days the whole bottom of this vast crater would be one sea of liquid fire.

Next morning early we struck our tents, and, as

soon as possible, resumed our journey towards the summit of Mouna Roa. The base of this mountain is about twelve miles from the volcano in a direct line, but to follow the path the distance is much greater. The road during this day was much more rugged and uncomfortable, leading over an extensive bed of rough lava. A few dwarfish trees and shrubs, for miles, were the only productions to be met with. After passing this we passed over some uneven prairie land, and encamped about 3 P. M. on the summit of a lofty hill. The natives came up to us one after another, and as they arrived, immediately set to work building their huts for the night, and in two hours we had an encampment of seven tents and forty-five huts. The natives displayed more ingenuity and celerity in the art of hut building than I have seen among them in any other way. Each hut had a large fire before it, and when the night set in, the scene was highly interesting; the huts were built in a circle around the tents, and the whole encampment made quite an imposing village. Our elevation was 4500 feet above the level of the sea.

The next morning, Dec. 19th, we resumed our journey and traveled about eight miles, and again encamped on the side of the mountain. The lava here had a much more ancient appearance, the shrubbery and herbage more sickly and sallow. Elevation 6000 feet. Therometer 48 degrees, Fahrenheit.

This part of the country is dry, and persons traveling here are often obliged to go several days without water. The whole of this vast mountain is perforated with caves, so numerous, indeed, that we visited five in one day, some of them of unknown extent.

One of them was carved and finished in a style that bore a close resemblance to the works of art. A projection ran along on both sides, elegantly moulded, about three feet high, and perfectly smooth,— making a splendid seat nearly 300 feet in length. The floor was smooth, and the whole cave bore evident marks of having been, at some period, a subterraneous passage, leading from some crater, through which had flowed a stream of boiling lava, and probably it is through such passages as this that the lava has flowed, which has so completely inundated the whole island.

Having followed the passage nearly half a mile, we came to an opening in the floor, and getting down on the fragments of lava which lay underneath, we found a second passage as spacious as the first, running parallel with it  having followed this second passage about half a mile, we came to another opening, and looking down, we saw another passage leading under this.   How far it extended we did not ascertain. Being disappointed in our search for water, we concluded to go no further ;  the water was dripping from the roof in a thousand places, but the floor was too porous to retain it.   The roof was beautifully coated with stalactite, resembling stucco work.   This is formed, probably, from particles of lime and salt, which are dissolved by the water that passes through this cave, and is admitted through the overhanging arch ;—these are pendant like icicles, and some of them acquire the length of three or four feet.

In two of the caves we visited, we found water; being thoroughly filtered by its passage through the lava, it was as clear as a crystal, extremely cold, and very sweet. In a distant part of one of the caves we found the bones of some birds, and the remains of a human skeleton. The bones were much decayed, but enough of them remained to show that they belonged to the human species.

On Monday morning, Dec. 21st, we again struck our tents and resumed our journey up the mountain. The road was precipitous, and our ascent tiresome; the whole mountain seemed to be a mass of lava. There are some craters on the summit, and it is probable that the whole of this vast mountain has been ejected from them and their outlets.

From the appearance of this island, so far as I am able to judge, it might with great propriety be termed "Terra del Fuego," which signifies, in English, the land of fire. Judging from the quantities of lava now on the surface, and the quantities that must have run into the sea, there must be an immense vacuum under this island. Nothing here relieves the dreary grey of the lava, excepting here and there a small tuft of stunted shrubbery, which takes root in the crevices of the rock. I saw no birds or animals at this place, or any thing living, except what belonged to the party. The air is sensibly colder; the clouds were then rolling below us, and their appearance was often grand and majestic. We were now about fifty miles inland, but from this height we can see the surf of the ocean breaking on the beach. Our elevation on the evening of the 21st, was 9000 feet. Thermometer 40 deg. At sunrise on the morning of the 22d, the weather was much colder. Thermometer 37 deg. The natives were mostly naked, and the cold seemed to frighten them. Dr. Judd, Serg. Stearns, and one of the seamen went on, when the party encamped, to the summit, and returned at sunset, bringing some ice and snow with them. When the natives saw it, they all shouted "*oury miti,*"—meaning, not good.

About 9 A. M., the commodore and some of the seamen, together with as many of the natives as were able to go up, started for the summit, with some of the instruments, the portable house, and some of the tents. Lieut. Budd, Dr. Pickering, Mr. Eld and three seamen, remained at the encampment, to send on the natives as they arrived with such instruments as were wanted. At 4 P. M., some of the officers returned from the summit, and brought information that one of the seamen had been taken sick, and was lying on the rocks, unable to get up. No compensation could induce the natives to venture in search of him. I started alone, just at dark, but could not find him. The night shut in dark and rainy, and our tent was but a poor protection from the inclemency of the weather. A number of natives were comfortably lodged in the tents, but no inducement could get them out, to assist in getting some articles which we wanted to make our shelter better.

Dr. Judd, Mr. Eld and Dr. Pickering, went up the mountain on the 23d, accompanied by as many natives as could be hired to ascend. Mr. Eld went in search of William Longley, the man who was sick, and returned with information at sunset, that he was better, and had gone up the mountain. At 10 o'clock, fifty seamen arrived from the ship, under Lieut. Alden, and remained with us until the next morning.

During the 24th, the weather was in unison with the face of the country. The clouds, which had been collecting round the foot of the mountain, rose towards noon, and enveloped us in a misty veil, with occasionally drizzling showers of rain. The tents were insufficient to hold us all, and a party of the seamen repaired to an adjacent cave, and slept very comfortably. About 7 o'clock, a few natives came down from the summit to the cave, and informed us that Longley had not been found, and that general fears were entertained that he was dead; the night being excessively dark and foggy, further search was deferred until the next morning. At 7 A. M., the seamen were sent to the summit with the large pendulum, and journeyman clocks, and other instruments. At 11 o'clock, thirty-four natives arrived from the ship with provisions for the men and officers. At 3 o'clock, I was suddenly seized with a violent pain in the head; several others of the seamen, and some of the officers, were affected in the same way. It was attributed to the rarity of the air at so great an elevation.

At sunset the scouts returned, but brought no intelligence of Longley. All the seamen were employed in carrying up the instruments,—most of the natives having become discouraged at an elevation of 9000 feet, and returned home. Their clothing consisted of a narrow strip of *tappa* tied round the loins, and a scanty blanket of the same material over the shoulders—leaving the body, arms and legs, entirely naked and exposed. Such apparel could not be comfortable where the thermometer falls to 37 deg., particularly to those, who, from childhood, had been accustomed to a temperature of from 70 to 80 degrees.

At sunset, one of the residents returned from the summit, and informed us that Longley had been found,

17

crawling on his hands and knees over the rocks. He said he had been lying near the track, and that he had frequently seen people passing and repassing close to him, but that he was unable to travel, and consequently had been exposed to the cold and rain for three days and nights.

———◆———

# CHAPTER XIII.

Ascent of the Mountain continued—The Lava—Fatigue and Exposure of the Journey—Descent into the Crater—The Basin—Severity of the Weather—Return to the Ship—Visit of the Chief.

> " Pleasing were many scenes, but most to me,
> The solitude of vast extent, untouched
> By the hand of art, where nature sowed herself,
> And reaped her crops ;—whose garments were the clouds,
> Whose organ-choir, the voice of many waters ;
> Whose banquets, morning dews ; whose lovers, flowers ;
> Whose orators, the thunderbolts of God ;
> Whose palaces, the everlasting hills ;
> Whose ceiling, heaven's unfathomable blue ;
> And from whose rocky turrets, battled high,
> Prospects immense spread out on all sides around,
> Lost now between the welkin and the main,
> Now walled with the hills that slept above the storm."

The road above our encampment grew more precipitous and uneven, and as we passed up the mountain, the weather grew rapidly colder. We stopped at Longley's tent, and found him slowly improving; af-

terward we proceeded to the middle station, under
Lieut. Alden. From here we went to the last encampment of the seamen, visiting on our way a spacious cave, containing a large pond of water. This
pond was frozen over, the ice of which was two or
three feet thick, while large icicles were hanging from
the roof. It was here that we first discovered snow;
it had drifted into the crevices of the lava, giving it a
peculiar aspect of fleecy whiteness.

The more prominent parts of the lava were bare.
When we reached the last encampment of the seamen,
the weather and mountains were alike wintry and
dreary; the black masses of lava were contrasted
with the drifts of snow, and a strong, piercing wind
from the westward, sweeping along the sides of the
mountain, howled among the spires and cones of lava,
like Boreas among the shorn branches of a forest in a
North American winter. In many places the lava
was piled in detached masses, bearing an exact resemblance to the cinders from a blacksmith's forge.
Sometimes these fields of *climpers*, as they are called,
are bare to the extent of several miles. When we
left the encampment of the seamen, we were obliged
to travel over a field of them, at least a mile and a quarter in extent. We arrived at head quarters about 3
o'clock, P. M., when the wind was so strong that we
all commenced building a strong wall as high as we
could reach, with these climpers, to protect the tents
from the force of the wind. The commodore and
Mr. Eld worked with us, and as hard as the best of
us. The markee of the commodore was pitched within thirty yards of the largest crater, on the summit.
This crater was then dormant; no fire was visible

about it, but through several fissures in and about it, there were constantly emitted streams of sulphurous smoke and hot ashes, a positive proof of the fiery state of the regions below, sooner or later to burst forth in eruptions from this crater.   It is nine miles in circumference, by three in diameter, and about 1000 feet deep.   The bottom is rough and black; the sloping sides, nearly to the bottom, are covered with snow. At night, one of the tents made of new cotton canvas, was rent several feet by the force of the tempest above, notwithstanding the protection of the wall.   It was not a steady breeze, but would one minute blew a living gale, and the next a perfect calm ensued.

At sunrise, on the morning of the 29th, I left headquarters and returned to the lower station, under Lieut. Budd, at which time Longley was ordered to be brought down to our encampment.   In consequence of the peculiar state of the weather, the sudden transition from a mild climate to that of great severity, together with our extraordinary fatigue and exposure, there was considerable sickness among our number. One after another had fallen victims, and the sick list was presenting a fearful aspect.   We had found the natives of little service to us, after reaching that part of the mountain where the cold was sensibly increased.   Our labors had necessarily become very arduous.

The ascent, owing to the rough surface of the lava, was certain destruction to shoe leather.   We often wore out one pair of shoes per week; in consequence of this, several of the seamen, being entirely destitute of shoes, were ordered by the commodore to remain until shoes should arrive from the ship.   Ninety-five natives arrived on the 30th, from the ship, with provisions. On the same day, orders came down from the commodore, to break up the middle station. Lieut. Alden, who had command there, was ordered to the lower station, and Lieut. Budd of the latter, was ordered to the summit. We immediately began to move the provisions from the lower station up to the summit, with the stores which were in the possession of Mr. Budd, who remained at the middle station until the next morning. Our elevation was 11,500 feet at this time.

We struck the tents at the middle station, and removed them to the summit on the following day. The instruments were then taken up, and the day was passed in setting them up, and pitching our tents. We had then reached an elevation of 13,000 feet. Here the weather was excessively cold, yet there was a clear and invigorating atmosphere. We were forcibly reminded of the propriety of making immediate improvements around our tents, preparatory to an exposure to the rigors of the wintry weather, and chilling blasts of our elevated position.

At 9 o'clock, A. M., two seamen went down into the crater, and at half past 11, two more of us followed them. The path down leads over beds of climpers, and the innumerable wide and deep gaps told most plainly the violent convulsions of the earth, while in the act of emitting from its bosom its stores of liquid fire. After descending the first precipice, of a height little less than two hundred feet, we traveled over an extensive bed of lava, composed of beautiful colors, and in every shape that the imagination can conjecture;—sometimes like the ruffled bosom of the ocean,

17*

sometimes rising in cones, and at other times piled up in rugged and uneven masses, but every where rent by wide and deep gaps. We traveled about two miles, when we approached the brink of the crater at the south-west corner. The descent was extremely dangerous on this side; the bank was sloping, but very steep, and composed of loose masses of broken lava, in color resembling the granite of Massachusetts. The height of this part above the bottom of the crater, was at least eight hundred feet, and gave some idea of the danger of the ascent. I suppose that in descending this eight hundred feet, the base would not exceed two hundred feet from a perpendicular. To start one of these loose stones would have been inevitable destruction to the adventurer, but we had started to go to the bottom, and we did not intend to relinquish our plan. We began the descent, and in half an hour were safely landed at the bottom of the crater. As we descended, the experiment was made still more dangerous by patches of snow that covered many chasms, and by shelving over the larger masses of lava, would have deceived the traveler to his inevitable destruction, but for our constant and extreme caution.

Having accomplished about two thirds of the descent, we came upon a fissure in the bank, from which a column of hot steam was constantly emitted; the snow around this was discolored as it fell by the heat of the steam, and under its protection a beautiful crop of green herbs and lovely flowers was growing, singularly contrasted with snow and the grey appearance of the rocks around it. About 150 feet below this little plat of verdure, we came upon a small round hole about three inches in diameter, from which issued a strong current of hot air without steam, but bringing with it a large quantity of hot ashes. The fire had burst from the sides of the crater, within two hundred yards of the top, during the last eruption, and poured its floods of liquid fire into the crater, overleaping in its descent, a precipice of at least 200 feet perpendicular, into a basin of about one acre in extent. When the basin filled, it flowed down into the bottom of the crater. The lava in this basin was a beautiful shining olive color, but it was brittle, and in walking over a heap of charcoal when we reached the bottom, the scene was awfully grand and majestic. From the surface, the bottom looked even and smooth, but when we stood on the bottom nothing could exceed the wildness and sublimity of the scene, and we saw a good illustration of the awful power of the subterraneous fires. Rocks weighing 5000 or 6000 tons were tossed one on the other fifty or sixty feet, with apparently the same ease that a pettish child would toss its toys about. The bottom, like the surface, was full of fissures and chasms, from which the steam was rushing with a hissing sound, like a huge engine letting off its steam, and which, to men in our situation, was not altogether pleasing.

We spent about an hour in collecting specimens of different colored lava. When we were coming out I trod on a piece of lava, which at first sounded hollow, then crushed beneath my weight ; on removing some of the pieces, I found there was a large space filled with glauber salts and sulphur. These drugs abound in great quantities in these craters. At half past 4 o'clock we reached the encampment.

On the 4th of Jan. the weather was colder than it had been previously; the thermometer had fallen to 18 degrees. We hastened our observations as much as circumstances would permit, so that our stay might not be unnecessarily protracted. The elevation of this mountain has long been the subject of dispute; the English admeasurements run from 13 to 17000 feet,—by ours the height is established at something over 13,000 above the level of the sea.

There were indications of a change in the weather; it became rather thick and hazy, while the severity of the cold had somewhat diminished. Another crater was found which was in a south-westerly direction from the principal one. Preparations were immediately made for its measurement, but from the unfavorableness of the weather our operations were considerably retarded. We had an occasional fall of sleet, and a slight snow storm.

A party of seamen came up from the lower station with provisions, wood and fruit. The weather being too cold for the pendulum, the commodore ordered the pendulum house thatched with long grass from the prairie. This house had a heavy "fearnaught" cover over it, and a tent of best cotton canvas over that; the thatching was to go between the "fearnaught" and the house.

It is impossible to place a sailor in a situation that will deprive him of his mirth and jolity; exposed as he is to the most sudden extremes of climate, yet no heat can scorch, or cold congeal the ardor of his temperament; he meets with every kind of danger with the utmost coolness. I have seen the orders of Commodore Wilkes while in the greatest emergency, amid

ice and snow of the Antarctic, obeyed with the same
cheerful alacrity as if the ship, at that time, had been
lying becalmed within the tropics. Nor is it on the
ocean alone that the sailor can be useful; here at
Owhyhee, where the men who had been all their lives
on shore, at an elevation of 9000 feet, the seamen
came up the mountain, "fisted" the instruments—as
"jack" has it—and "walked" them up to the summit, laughing, singing and joking each other with as
much contempt of the toil as if the whole band had
been sent on a party of pleasure; and I think that
very few of our American farmers would take these
rugged *climpers* and lay more uniform or more permanent walls than those which the seamen built
round the encampment on the summit of Mouna Roa.

The whole encampment was covered with snow on
the morning of the 8th. After sunrise, however, being quite clear and pleasant, this soon disappeared,
and we were able to continue our observations. At
night the weather became more unfavorable; it was
wintry, dark and tempestuous, while a strong wind
blew from the south-west. During this time, our
house had blown down and the snow was falling
rapidly. The morning of the 9th the sun arose clear
and bright; the wind had died away and the clouds
looked like a vast field of wool, for below us every
thing was tranquil and pleasant. Some of the tents
were injured during the night, and a barometer and
several thermometers were destroyed by the force of
the tempest.

During our stay upon this lofty and desolate
mountain, we were exposed to many hardships, and
were subject to frequent and sudden changes of tem-

perature. The winds were cold and boisterous, often tempestuous. The pelting storms of mingled snow and sleet rendered our situation exceedingly unpleasant. The snow was carried high in the air by the furious blasts which howled among those bleak, craggy peaks and frightful chasms, giving to the scenery a gloom and dreariness which cannot be easily appreciated. Our tents were fluttering in the strong winds, and our instrument houses were scarcely repaired ere they were rudely scattered among the rocks and fissures of the summit.

Aside from the toils and dangers of our situation, some of its features were somewhat ludicrous. The breeze was "cutting fantastic capers" with us, and fragments of our houses were hurled furiously into the air, falling far down the rough and romantic sides of the mountain. Several acres were literally besprinkled with them, while the "star spangled banner" was proudly waving far above this scene of desolation, on the brink of the crater.

As soon as the necessary survey was completed, we made preparations to break up the encampment, and return to a more congenial climate. Accordingly, the instruments were packed, and the remnant of our tents, houses and furniture, was collected and carried down by the natives and seamen.

When the last of the seamen got outside of the wall, Mr. Budd gave orders to "stand by" the colors; we then gave three cheers, which were echoed back by the crater, and from the walls of the encampment. With the last cheer, one of our number raised the flag staff, and returned our salute; we gave him the answering cheer, which he received with a grateful

flourish of the colors, and then bore the starry standard of Columbia from Pendulum Peak, and probably
from the greatest elevation over which it had ever
waved. At half past 3 o'clock, we had reached the
lower station under Lieut. Alden, which had formerly
been the station of Mr. Budd,—ten miles from the
summit. At 8 o'clock on the morning of the 17th of
January, we left Mr. Alden's tent, and at sunset
reached the volcano of Keluare, having traveled over
a serpentine and rugged road of at least thirty miles.
This distance, to a landsman on a good road, would
not be hard, but let a party of landsmen be accustomed to the narrow limits of a ship's decks for two
or three years, and then let them take forty or forty-
five pounds on their shoulders and attempt to walk
over these *climpers* for thirty miles in eight hours, and
I am sure, unless they possessed the enterprise and
perseverance of the sailor, they would not accomplish
half the distance.

The weather continued cool, and our accommodations were still insufficient to protect us from the severity of the season. The natives were unable to
descend at an equal rate with the seamen, in consequence of which our tents did not all arrive in season
for the night. Some of our number took shelter with
the natives, in huts previously constructed.

On the morning of the 18th, the wind was strong
from the northward, and while cooking breakfast one
of the huts caught fire, and for a few moments threatened the destruction of the whole encampment. It
was really interesting to see the manoeuvres of the
seamen at that moment; some were darting through
the flames, rescuing the property of their shipmates;—

some stationed themselves between the huts and the commodore's tent, ready to tear down the huts in case the fire could not be extinguished before it reached that point, and others tore down the burning building, and stopped the progress of the flames. The fire was soon extinguished and but little damage was done.

The commodore, Mr. Budd and Mr. Eld, with a party of seamen, went down into the crater to examine the largest fire. Mr. Budd, with six seamen, went down to the bottom of the crater, where we ventured within ten feet of one of the boiling lakes; here the surface of the dry lava was so hot that any wood would ignite in a very short time. Dr. Judd, on the preceding day, ventured still nearer, and dipped a frying pan full of the boiling lava, but the crust on which he stood bent like thin ice, and he was only saved by the prompt assistance of an attending native.

From this station several parties were sent in advance to the ship. At Kappaohee we overtook a party that had been previously despatched. We made a short tarry at Paoli, situated on the route from Kappaohee to the ship.

This town is beautifully situated in a wood; the clearing may be about 150 or 200 acres in extent, highly fertile, producing sugar cane, tarro, breadfruit and potatoes; all kinds of fruit and ginger are spontaneous productions of the soil. At night we arrived at Wyakea. This town is the largest on this side of the island; it is built at the head of Byron's Bay. Next morning we reached the ship.

In a short time afterward, the remaining part of our company arrived, having followed the track of the lava, as it coursed its way from the boiling crater down the sides of the mountain and emptied itself at last into the ocean. Several boats were constantly employed in surveying the harbor, and gleaning necessary information. A partial survey had been made by Lord Byron during the year 1825, while in the Frigate Blonde.

Having completed the survey of the harbor, and made such observations and researches in the island as were thought necessary, we got underway and stood to sea, bound to Lahaina, island of Maui, the residence of the king and royal family. The wind during the day was very light, therefore our progress was slow; but as the evening shades appeared, enveloping the surrounding mountains in obscurity, a gentle breeze sprung up, and on the following morning by sunrise, the wild mountains which overhang the district of Lahaina were in distinct view, and by the aid of a propitious breeze and a favorable current, we advanced rapidly to the anchorage, where we arrived about 2 o'clock. The place is far more beautiful than any we had visited among the islands, and is rendered doubly interesting from the fact that it is the royal residence, and also the headquarters of the mission. The entire district, stretching nearly three miles along the sea-side, is covered with luxuriant groves, not only of the cocoa-nut, but also of the breadfruit and of the koa, an ornamental tree, resembling, at a distance, a large and flourishing full-topped apple tree;—while banana, plantain and sugar-cane are abundant, and extend almost to the beach, on which a fine surf constantly rolls. The view here presented was pure indian in all its features, from the

18

bare and lofty trunks of the cocoa-nut, with their tuft-
ed summits, nodding like plumes in the breeze, to the
thatching of a rude hut, here and there peeping from
the broad leaves of the plantain, and the richness of
more lowly growth.

Lahaina, Maui, March 8th, 1841. This day commenced with great preparations to receive his Hawaiian Majesty on his official visit to our ship. Life
lines were put on the yards on the preceding day,
and the men stationed for manning the yards.
There was a great display of epaulettes and gold lace,
swords, and cocked hats. His Royal Highness made
his appearance at 1 o'clock, and when he entered on
board, all were anxious to catch a glimpse of the royal
personage. The king's retinue was not as numerous
as it was in former times, but presented a great contrast in the manners and external appearance of its
members. The king was splendidly dressed in full
uniform, with cocked hat epaulettes, sword and a
gold star on his breast, while the distinguished chief-
tains wore rich military uniforms.

Our marine corps was paraded on the quarter deck,
and went through several evolutions of the manual
exercise for the amusement of His Royal Highness,
and our band, such as it was, played several fine
airs. The king's retinue was composed of fine looking men, who conducted themselves with much propriety, like well-bred gentlemen. The king was
then about twenty-five or six years of age, had a
commanding figure, appeared graceful and much at
his ease. He was entertained in the cabin by Capt.
Wilkes, where a sumptuous dinner had been prepared
for the occasion.

When he made his appearance over the gangway the yards were manned, and again when he left, and at the same time the men on the yards gave him three cheers, which he acknowledged by waving his cocked hat. Before sitting down to dinner, he and his suit were conducted to the different parts of the ship, accompanied by Captain Wilkes and most of the officers. When taken on the berth deck, it was lighted fore and aft, and the tin ware of the messes was burnished bright, and set out in front of the dispensary ; the yeoman's store-room was fitted up with unusual splendor and all the officers' rooms on the berth deck lighted up brilliantly ;—the whole, no doubt made quite an interesting scene to him.

He returned on shore at 5 o'clock, P. M., in the captain's gig. A few days after, he was invited to dine in the ward room, on which occasion he was not dressed in uniform. He was attended by the same noble personages who were with him on his official visit. It is said that he makes free use of wine and ardent spirits, but on these occasions he drank very sparingly.

### MAUI.

Lahaina, the principal town on the island, and residence of the king and royal family, is considered the most healthy island in the group. Lahaina is quite a respectable looking town for the Sandwich Islands, considering the rude state of barbarism from which they have so lately emerged. It is on a semi-circle, covering a handsome plain, which recedes to some distance, where the land rises abruptly and breaks into gulleys and broken, romantic peaks. The *Roads*, in which is the only anchorage, I should consider unsafe for vessels to lie at anchor, particularly in the winter season, when the gusts of wind are very violent and frequent; there is also a strong current between Mauri and Ranai. The bottom is sandy and very deep, and vessels are often liable to drag by the change of the current. Lahaua-Luna may be termed the seat of knowledge among the islands. The high school is a very worthy institution and is well conducted. The scholars who have been regularly taught in all the branches here, are smart men, when contrasted with the other natives, and worthy of the nation to which they belong. There were admitted from the first of June to the 1st Jan. 1841, fifty-five—two of whom had completed their studies. The different branches taught, are reading, writing, arithmetic, natural theology, scriptural history, geography and mathematics.

The building is large and capacious. The spacious hall in the second story is used for the chapel; the third story is the library or lecture room, containing an apparatus to explain natural history, chemistry, &c. There are fine collections of minerals and curiosities, obtained from different parts of the world, with a tolerably good skeleton, and one of their ancient gods, placed behind the door as you enter the room.

In one of my subsequent visits on shore, I had the satisfaction of visiting the palace of Kamhameha. I felt much anxiety to see it, simply because it had the name of a palace. I saw four tolerably well finished oil paintings, representing Alexander the Great, field marshal Blucher, Tamehameha ii. and his wife, who died in England.

We shipped several men out of the fort, who had been confined here for several months to hard labor. This is one of the wise(?) laws enacted by Mr. Richards, the king's secretary and adviser, and approved by the king. If one half of the stories respecting Mr. Richards be true, and if there is any law to punish men for crimes, it is highly probable that if he had not come to the Sandwich Islands, he might have had an opportunity to serve a portion of his time in the State Prison, or to labor in chains.

---

## CHAPTER XIV.

Visit of the Missionaries—Survey of the Harbor—Embarkation—Arrival at the Columbia River—Description—Arrival at Protection Island—Survey—Natives—Admiralty Inlet—Meteor—Observance of the " 4th "—Accident.

> " As yet, amid this elemental war
> That scatters desolation from afar,
> Nor toil, nor hazard, nor distress appear
> To sink the seamen with unmanly fear.
> Though their firm hearts no pageant honor boasts,
> They *scorn* the *wretch* that trembles at his post ;
> Who from the face of danger strives to turn,
> Indignant from the social hour they spurn.
> No future ills unknown, their souls appal,
> They know no danger, or they scorn it all !
> A short repose alone their thoughts implore,
> Their harassed powers by slumber to restore."

On the 12th of March, we were favored with a visit, which differed essentially from many former

18*

ones, in which the pomp and display of "crowned heads" formed some of the more prominent features. Our visitors on this occasion, were the missionaries and their families. We could but observe the contrast. In one case, there was a gaudy display of glittering toys,—indexes of the degree of refinement and taste of the wearers—and in the other, a "crown of righteousness" was possessed, whose beauty shall never fade away. One governed by force of arms, physical superiority, the other moulded the soul, bringing all into subservience to the "law of love."

During our stay here, the surveys were commenced as usual. On one of these excursions the Leopard was lost; the crew were rescued, though they very narrowly escaped a watery grave. These were soon completed, and preparations were made to embark. At 8 o'clock, A. M., on the 16th, we got underway, and directed our course to the Columbia River. The services of Mr. Edwin Butler, an American, had been secured as a pilot, previously to leaving the island. The first few days of our voyage passed off very pleasantly; the weather was decidedly fine. In a short time, however, it gradually grew cooler, rendering extra clothing necessary. The only objects to beguile the tedious monotony of the hours, were the blue sky above, and the ocean beneath, through which we were ploughing, and now and then a lonely bird of the aquatic species, flying over our vessel, to let us know we were not alone. Some days after our embarkation, all hands were called to muster, and the rules and regulations of the Exploring Expedition were read, for the information of those men who shipped at Oahee, and such as probably never heard them before.

At daylight on the morning of the 28th, we heard the cheerful cry of " land ho ! " from the mast head. We had a fine breeze, and every prospect of reaching our intended haven, but

" Disappointments lurk in many a prize,
As bees in honey ; that sting with surprise. "

At 10 o'clock, we entered a strong tide rip, and soon after came within sight of the Columbia River. The wind was then moderate, but had been blowing very fresh the day previous; when standing close in we found the bar breaking furiously entirely across it. Capt. Wilkes consulted Mr. Butler, the pilot, who advised him to stand off, for he considered it unsafe at that time to attempt an entrance.

The river enters the Pacific between two points of land, one on the north called Cape Disappointment, or Cape Hancock, in lat. 46 deg. 18 min. ; the other is called Point Adams, which is seven miles southeast from the former. From each of these points, a sand bar runs into the water, above which the waves of the Pacific, on the one side, and the torrents of the Columbia on the other, meet with terrific violence, producing a most formidable line of breakers. These circumstances render the entrance and departure of vessels hazardous at all seasons, and almost impossible when the winds are high. The depth of water between the bars, is thirty feet at the lowest ; no vessel drawing more than fourteen feet, can, however, proceed far up the river, on account of the irregularities of the channel.   The river, like others in North America, is said to abound in fish, particularly in salmon, which ascend all its branches, even up to the Blue Mountains, affording the principal means of subsistence to all the natives along the coast; many from the interior also repair to this river in the fishing season, for the purpose of procuring their winter's supply.

The land about the sea-coast is moderately high, but at a short distance in the interior it is very mountainous; from the appearance of the gigantic trees, however, I am of the opinion that the soil must be good.

On the following day, April 29th, we squared away for Puget Sound, distant 120 miles north-east from Columbia River.   We proceeded on our course with a fine breeze, but had thick weather until 11 o'clock, when we were suddenly arrested by the cry of "breakers on the lee bow!"   It was reported to Capt. Wilkes, who lost no time in getting upon deck, at which time all the studding sails were taken in, and the ship hauled "close on a wind;" shortly after, we sounded, and found that we were in five fathoms of water.   At this time we passed the points of rocks not more than a stone's throw distant.   Had we continued our course for five minutes longer, we must have been dashed in pieces against the rocks, and as the result of such a circumstance, inevitable death must have been the consequence.

On the morning of the 30th, the weather was still foggy, so much so indeed, that we could not venture to run in for the land.   We saw an abundance of geese and ducks flying in every direction.   At 10 o'clock, the weather clearing up a little, we made sail and stood in for Puget Sound. At 4 o'clock we passed Cape Flattery and entered the Straits of Juan de Fuca. The shores are composed of low sandy cliffs, overhanging beaches of sand or stones; from them the land ascends gradually to the foot of the mountain, which rises abruptly to a great height within a few miles. The country here is thickly wooded, but affords but little variety in its growth, being principally cedar and spruce, some of which are very lofty.

During the evening several canoes passed near us with indians in them, who seemed very anxious that we should heave to for them; several attempted to catch hold of the ship, but were unsuccessful. Their dress consisted of a skin, thrown over the shoulders and fastened round the neck, leaving the lower extremities bare.

We continued to beat in this sound with a head wind until the 2d of May, when we were favored with a fine wind; we made sail and at 8 o'clock passed Protection Island, and in about an hour afterward, came to anchor in thirty fathoms of water in the harbor of Port Discovery. This is the only harbor immediately on the Straits of Juan de Fuca, and is situated near the south-east angle. It is safe for ships of any size; it runs southward from the straits into the land and is defended from the violence of the waves by Protection Island, which stretches partly across its entrance on the north. Vancouver says in his book, "when he was engaged in surveying these straits, that he never had occasion to anchor, but always hauled close in to the banks and made fast to a tree."

Soon after coming to anchor we were visited by a canoe having in it two indians; one of them came up the gangway and asked, in broken English, if we were from Boston. This led us to believe that the first American vessel trading here, was from that place, as the indians seemed to know of no other place in the United States. They called all of us Bostonians, while they called the English King George.

On the morning of May 3d, at daylight, several boats were sent on surveying duty. The land every where in the neighborhood is moderately high, very broken and thickly covered with wood. The mountains in the interior are very high, and present quite a variety in their shape and appearance; the tops of some are seen above the clouds, which are covered with everlasting snow, and afford a striking contrast to the valleys near the sea, which are covered with verdure, and trees in full bloom.

We were at this time on our native continent, although more than three thousand miles from the place of our birth, yet I could not resist the sensations kindled by the remembrance of "dear home;" all the emotions incident to natural attachment and early prejudices played around my heart.

We had been literally surrounded with canoes all the morning; most of them were loaded with a variety of fish, venison and bears' meat, all of which they bartered at very moderate prices, in exchange for knives, fishhooks, old clothes and files, the principal articles for which they seemed anxious. They particularly valued our files; for one we could purchase a salmon weighing upwards of forty pounds.

These natives are a meagre, dirty race of savages; they have no fixed habitations, but, like a snail, carry their houses with them, and seldom stop more than two days in a place. They all have their heads flattened by compression in infancy, which disfigures them to such a degree that they look more like monsters than human beings. They have small eyes, flat noses and wear their hair long, both men and women.

Our stay at this place was not of long continuance. At dawn, May 6th, we made necessary preparations, and sailed, beating out of the harbor. After clearing the point which forms the harbor, we changed our course and ran down the coast to the eastward, a distance of about twelve miles from Protection Island, from which point we entered Admiralty Inlet, which penetrates the continent southward from the straits more than ninety miles, terminating near the forty-seventh degree of latitude, in a bay named by Vancouver, Puget Sound. Hood's canal is a branch of this inlet, nearly opposite which we came to anchor, the wind and tide being against us.

The country surrounding Admiralty Inlet is beautiful, fertile, and in every respect agreeable; and the bay, with its numerous arms stretching into the interior, must offer great advantages for commercial intercourse hereafter. The country here is extensively covered with trees of a gigantic growth, and from their appearance, I think some are well adapted to ship and house building. We anchored opposite a piece of table land about two miles in circumference, the most beautiful spot I ever beheld. It was perfectly level, as if made so by artificial workmanship, covered with green grass about two feet high, and variegated with different kinds of shrubbery, and fringed with a variety of vegetation. It affords a delightful prospect, especially in this high latitude, and would make a neat location for a village or city, and probably, at some future period, will become a flourishing settlement.

We got underway the next day, and commenced beating up the bay for Nasqually, and on the 11th of May, came to anchor off Nasqually, at the head of Puget Sound. Soon after coming to anchor, we were visited by Mr. Anderson, agent for the "Hudson's Bay Company," at this station. Capt. McNeal, commander of the company's steam boat Beaver; Mr. Wilson of the American Mission to the Oregon Territory, and Doct. Richmond, physician to the mission, comprised the whole number of residents here, except some of the half-breed race, and a few Canadians, servants of the "Hudson's Bay Company."

On the 17th, the expedition of boats under Lieut. Case, left the ship on a surveying cruise. Also an expedition to the interior of Oregon Territory was projected,—composed of the following gentlemen, viz. Lieut. Johnson, Doct. Pickering, Naturalist, Mr. Breckenridge, Horticulturist, Mr. Waldron, and T. A. Stearns, Q. M. G. The most satisfactory results were anticipated from these competent gentlemen, in every department of science. On the following day, Capt. Wilkes, accompanied by Mr. Drayton and purser Waldron, left the ship for the Columbia River.

At ten minutes past 8 o'clock, on the 31st, a meteor of immense magnitude and brilliancy shot across the heavens in a north-west direction, illuminating the heavens to such an extent that there was a resemblance to a sheet of fire, till it nearly reached the horizon, when it exploded, sending off myriads of corruscations in every direction. When it first commenced its flight, it was exceedingly slow in its descent, but as it increased its distance towards the horizon, it increased its velocity considerably, until it burst. Many old seamen on board never witnessed a meteor half so large, nor one whose light remained so long visible. From the time it was first seen until it entirely disappeared, was *one hour and twenty-five minutes.*

On our arrival at this place we were expecting to join the Peacock and Schooner, but in this we were disappointed; they parted from us some time before, and were to be at the Columbia River two months previous to that time. Fears were entertained in reference to their safety. From the importance of this position it was decided to make critical surveys of the harbor and its vicinity. Accordingly, temporary houses were erected for that purpose, and other necessary arrangements made. The carpenter deposited a sealed bottle under the corner of one of the houses, containing a piece of paper with the following inscription :—

" Though far from our homes, yet still in our land
True yankee enterprise will ever expand,
And publish to all each side of the main,
We triumphed once and can do it again.
A problem, a problem, oh ! hear great and small,
The true owners of the country are still on the soil,

19

While Jonathan and John Bull are growling together
For land which by right belongs not to either.
Let philosophers listen, and solve the question
Which has troubled the statesmen of each nation,
By what right the " Big Bull " claims sustenance here,
While he has plenty of pasturage elsewhere."

Lines written by R. P. R.

*Observatory of the U. S. Ship Vincennes, Charles Wilkes, Esq.,
Commander in Chief of the U. S. S. S. and Exploring Expedition, by Amos Chick, of Portland, Maine, Carpenter of the U.
S. S. Vincennes, June, 1841.*

Mr. Dyes, assistant to the scientific corps, deposited
in the same bottle two pieces of American coin,—one
a cent coined in 1817, and the other a dime coined
in 1838. The paper was enclosed in parchment
and well secured in the bottle.

On the 12th of June, Thomas Harden, officers'
cook, and John McKean, ship's cook, having been
three days lost in the woods, were found by a white
and some indians who were sent in search of them.
When found they were so exhausted as not to be able
to walk to the ship;—horses were procured for them.
They had eaten nothing since leaving the ship.

July 4th coming on Sunday, we celebrated the 5th,
commencing in the morning with a national salute of
twenty-six guns, which were fired at the observatory
on shore. Capt. Wilkes gave a dinner and invited the
officers to it. An ox was roasted whole for the crew,
on a plain about one mile from the ship. At 9 o'clock,
every man and officer was ordered on shore, except
Mr. Vanderford, who was left in charge of the ship.
On landing, the men proceeded up the hill to the ob-

servatory, where Capt. Wilkes was residing, there to await his orders. At 10 o'clock the procession was formed and marched in order, the starboard watch in advance, the marines in the centre, and the larboard watch bringing up the rear. We proceeded through a narrow strip of wood about half a mile, when we came to the company's fort; there we halted and formed in front of it, and gave three cheers, which were returned by the people in the fort, and answered by us. The procession was again formed and marched as before, about one mile further, when we came to a deep valley,—crossing which we came to a plain several miles in circumference, in which Doct. Richmond's house is situated.

Here was the place intended for the exhibitions of the day; various kinds of amusements were proposed, in which Capt. Wilkes took an active part. Every thing went on well for a time, and bade fair for a day of recreation and pleasure, but soon an accident occurred, which could not but disturb the feelings of all. At 12 o'clock, when firing a salute, Daniel Whitehorn Jr., gunner, while loading one of the guns, it accidently discharged, and lacerated his forearm very seriously. All the integuments, from midway of the forearm to the wrist, were blown off—the carpal extremity of the ulna exposed for about two inches upon the outer face. All the tendons for about three inches from the carpus were much torn. The surgeon having thoroughly examined the wound, decided that it was his duty to recommend the removal of the limb. At the time the accident happened, the weather was quite warm, and tetanus was to be apprehended. All the large blood vessels were either carried away entirely, or much injured, and the consequences of an attempt to save the arm were much to be dreaded. Dr. Richmond, physician to the mission family, was called upon, who agreed in opinion with our surgeon, that amputation was the only means to insure life. The doctors then stated to the patient their views of the case, and recommended an operation. He declined for the present, and chose to risk an attempt to save the limb.

The amusements proceeded, but not with that spirit with which they were commenced ; a deep melancholy seemed to mark the countenance of many. Whitehorn was much esteemed by all his shipmates.

Such events, the sailor is often called upon to witness. Perils and death often surround him. Disease may make a stealthy approach, when far away from the comforts and endearments of home, and the last throes of expiring nature are witnessed by tearful shipmates, and the departed is consigned to his deep, coral bed, unhonored by the respects of sympathizing survivors in the land of his nativity, and the last tokens of affection, by kindred hearts. A boom may strike, a yard break, and a struggling victim is hurled into the foaming waves, to sink beneath its restless waters, with no solacing word of comfort or hope, in the hour of conflict. By the frequent occurrence of such painful incidents, his sympathies are ever awakened, and his better nature constantly developed. He almost instinctively is taught to " Rejoice with those that rejoice, and weep with those that weep."

# CHAPTER XV.

General Remarks on Nasqually, &c.—Return to Columbia River — Point Dungeness — Indian Settlement — Natives — San Francisco—Inhabitants.

" Ungrateful task ! for no asylum traced,
A passage opened from the watery waste.
Fate seemed to guard with adamantine mound,
The path to every friendly port around.
On deck the watchful helmsman cries aloud,
' Secure your lives—grasp every man a shroud !'
Roused from his trance he mounts with eyes aghast,
When o'er the ship in undulation vast,
A giant surge, down rushes from on high,
And fore and aft, dissevered ruins lie."

## GENERAL OBSERVATIONS AND REMARKS ON NASQUALLY, PUGET SOUND.

Situated about half a mile from the sound is a fort or trading post, belonging to the Hudson's Bay Company, composed of upright posts eight or ten feet high, secured with trunnels at top and bottom. At the corner, is a sentry-box or house, large enough to hold fifteen or twenty persons, perforated with holes large enough to admit the muzzle of a musket.

Within this stockade is a number of wooden houses, serving as dwellings, store-houses, magazines and workshops, and also one or two small buildings occupied by the laborers and servants. The nature of the country in this region of the Oregon Territory, will not admit of extensive cultivation, and seems to be best adapted to a pastoral life, especially in the imme-

*19

diate vicinity of the streams and mountains; irrigation must be resorted to, if a large population is to be supported in it. This country, which affords little prospect for the tiller of the soil, is, perhaps, one of the best in the world for grazing.

Every where, in this part of the country, the prairies open wide, covered with a low grass of a most nutritious kind, which remains good throughout the year. In September there are slight rains, at which time the grass commences a luxuriant growth, and in October and November, there is an abundance of green grass, which remains until the ensuing summer; about June, it is ripe in the lower plains, and, drying without being wet, is like our hay in New England; in this state, it remains until the Autumn rains begin to revive it.

The Hudson's Bay Company has here about one thousand sheep, six or eight hundreds of cattle—all of which are in a thriving condition. Wolves are very numerous in this region of the Oregon Territory, and are very destructive to the sheep when they get among them, but the shepherd uses great caution in protecting the sheep from the ravages of these ferocious animals. Upwards of one hundred have been killed by them within the last three years. These animals when pressed with hunger, often attack horses, and I was told that seven were eaten by them in a single night, in this immediate neighborhood. Foxes, deer, and bears are common, but not so numerous as they are in Upper California.

On the evening of the 17th of July, having completed the survey of Puget Sound, and its multifarious arms and bays, and completed the series of observa-

tions, we got underway and left our anchorage off
Nasqually, and commenced beating down the bay for
Columbia River. A surveying party was sent over
land to meet us at the mouth of the river, composed
of the following persons. Passed Midshipman Eld,
in charge of the party, passed Midshipman Colvoco-
ressis, Mr. Breckenridge, Horticulturist, Simeon A.
Stearns, Q. M. S., to assist in the surveys, with two
marines and two seamen. At 9 o'clock on the same
evening we came to anchor, the wind and tide being
against us. On the following morning we got underway and proceeded on our voyage.

At 2 o'clock, P. M. of the 22d, we came to anchor
off Point Dungeness, in 12 fathoms of water. Immediately on coming to anchor, three boats were got
ready, and were sent on surveying duty for three
days. Here we met with the Brig Porpoise. She
had been engaged in surveying this part of the sound,
and Hood's Canal, for two months.

Another accident happened at this time with powder. Samuel Williams, gunner's mate, was firing a
four pounder, for the purpose of measuring a base line
by sound ; a spark had remained in the gun after its
discharge, which communicated with the horn containing about four pounds of powder, while in the act
of priming. A terrific explosion followed, but, as if
by some miraculous interposition, no very serious injury was done. His hands and arms were burned,
though not badly, as the cuticle only was destroyed.

At this anchorage our anchor was scarcely gone,
before we were literally surrounded with canoes,
bringing salmon, codfish, and venison to sell, which
are taken here in great abundance.

On Point Dungeness, is one of the most remarkable
settlements of indians seen any where on the sound.
They have a stockade of considerable size, in which
they retreat when driven to extremities in time of
war.   Such a retreat is rendered necessary from the
frequency of their wars ; and since the most of them
have obtained guns and ammunition, they are very
destructive to each belligerent party.   Their prisoners
taken in war, they do not murder as many savages
do, but keep them as slaves, and make them perform
all the more laborious work.

At each corner of this stockade is erected a bust of
some of their most distinguished chiefs, roughly
carved and constructed of wood ; these are venerated
and worshiped by the indians.   In this place they
also deposited their dead, the chiefs always having a
separate place allotted to them.   Their *Bouri*, or
spirit house, is also here.

We remained at this anchorage for six days, during
which time we were plentifully supplied with salmon,
venison, &c., by the indians.

On the 28th of July, we got underway and proceeded down the Straits of Juan de Fuca, bound to Columbia River.   On the 2d of August we were off Cape
Flattery.   After beating with light and head winds
for four days, we succeeded in reaching the outer extremity of the straits, opening into the North Pacific,
and were then nearly opposite Clausette Harbor, so
named after a tribe of indians inhabiting this part of
the coast.   At 9 o'clock, a canoe came off to us, bringing fish, &c., for trade.   In this party was a chief of
some distinction, who stood erect in the canoe, no
doubt to render himself more conspicuous.   When he

came alongside, Capt. Wilkes asked him if he wished
to come on board, to which he replied in broken English in the affirmative; and accordingly he was permitted to come on board. Afterwards several others
were permitted to come on board. One or two of
them spoke a little English; the chief in particular,
spoke many words quite distinctly. The chief informed Capt. Wilkes that opposite to us there was a
good harbor, and invited him to go in and anchor.

The stature of these people, like most on this coast,
is much below the general standard. The height of
an old man who came on board, and who was rather
bent with age, was about four feet ten inches, and
that of the others was about five feet. Their faces
are flat and broad, but quite plump in the young individuals; their skin is smooth,—complexion not very
dark, except in some who were smeared with charcoal; their teeth were very white, nose flat and broad,
hair black, straight and glossy, and their hands and
feet extremely diminutive. The adult females are
quite as tall as the men, being from four feet eleven
inches to five feet. The features of the children were
regular, their complexion clear and by no means
dark, their eyes small, and although the form of their
faces is flat, their countenances might perhaps be
considered pleasing, according to the ideas of beauty
which habit has taught us to entertain.

Their hair, which is jet black and very long, hangs
loosely about their shoulders, a part of it on each side,
being carelessly plaited and sometimes rolled up into
an awkward bunch, instead of being neatly tied up
on the top of the head. Some of the younger females
seem to have much bashfulness and timidity, and

differ very materially from the women in the South Sea Islands, in not being tattooed. The chief was very decently dressed for an indian, and was the only one in the party who was. He was attired in a thin coat which had been originally white, but was then rather worse for wear, and also a little dingy,—blue cloth pantaloons, with a red sash around the waist, and over that a sash belt, composed of different colored beads; also in each ear a string of beads was suspended. He was quite loquacious, and spoke to the captain on many interesting subjects relative to the different tribes of indians with which he was acquainted.

At 3 o'clock we came to anchor in Clausette Harbor;—the first ship, no doubt, that ever anchored here. It has never been properly surveyed, and but little has been known even to the fur traders, probably on account of the savage disposition of the natives, with whom they trade very cautiously; they never trust more than half a dozen on their decks at a time. Capt. Wilkes deemed it important that it should be accurately surveyed, and a chart of it made; therefore two days were occupied in its completion. The harbor is small, but safe for vessels to enter, and will doubtless prove a very useful retreat for vessels trading on the coast when it becomes generally known. On the following day, after completing the survey, we got underway and stood out to sea.

At 8 o'clock on the morning of the 6th, we made the land near the mouth of Columbia River. We fired a signal and shortly afterwards perceived the schooner Flying Fish coming out from the river to meet us. Another ship was also standing in for the harbor at the same time. When the schooner was coming out, Mr. Knox, commander, saw that the ship was approaching the wrong passage, and immediately fired a shot across his bows, which made him heave to; he then ran along side and informed the captain of his imminent danger. In a few moments more she would have shared the fate of the Peacock, as she was in the same track. She proved to be the American whale ship Orozembo, bound into port for the purpose of recruiting her men. She was supplied from our ship with preserved meats and antiscorbutics. At 10 o'clock we were boarded by Capt. Hudson, who came out in the schooner. We then had the news of the wreck of the Peacock confirmed, which happened on Sunday, the 17th of July, while attempting to cross the bar at Columbia River.

Captain Wilkes, learning the fate of the Peacock, declined venturing over the bar with his vessel, and in the evening joined the brig Porpoise, in which vessel he proceeded over the bar, intending to survey Columbia River,—leaving orders for us to stand off and on until the Schooner should return on the following day.

After an unusual delay, in consequence of bad weather, the Schooner arrived, bringing twenty of the Peacock's crew, and also Captain Ringgold, of the Brig Porpoise, who was to take charge of our ship in the absence of Capt. Wilkes. At twelve o'clock all hands were called to muster, when Capt. Ringgold informed them that he was about to take command of them for a short time, and hoped that their conduct would merit a favorable report to Capt. Wilkes on his joining us at San Francisco. The broad pendant was hauled down and the coach-whip hoisted in its place.

Shortly after we made sail and squared with a fair wind for Port San Francisco, upper California, where Captain Wilkes intended to join us in about two months.

On the 12th August we stood in for the land and took a view of the land about Cape Blanco, situated in lat. 38 deg. north. The coast every where presents a dreary prospect; and is composed of rocky cliffs and overhanging beaches of stones and sand; from them the land ascends abruptly until it breaks into mountains and ridges, clothed in absolute sterility.

The rains of heaven are often withheld from here for eight and ten months at a time, at which time the sources of vegetation are dried up in most places, except in some valleys which are watered by streams; owing to this circumstance no prospect is here offered to the adventurous husbandman.

On the 14th of August, we were near Port San Francisco, and at 2 o'clock crossed the bar at the entrance of the harbor, in five fathoms of water. We had a fine breeze and glided rapidly and beautifully along. We proceeded up the bay a distance of ten miles, and came to anchor opposite the Spanish settlement of Yerba Bueno, a settlement so called by the Romish missionaries who settled it. There were at anchor also two American ships, and two brigs, one American, and the other Mexican.

Shortly after coming to anchor, we were visited by Capt. Phelps, of the ship Alert of Boston, who informed us of the death of William H. Harrison, President of the United States, which occurred one month after taking the Presidential chair.

We remained at this anchorage until the 16th, when we got underway and beat over to Sansantito or Whaler's harbor, a distance of about five miles, where a supply of fresh water could be obtained, and also fresh provisions. We had been plentifully supplied with fresh beef, but vegetables were scarce and very dear; the Spaniards here, like the indians, are too lazy to cultivate the soil.

A short description of this region of America, probably, may be somewhat interesting.

San Francisco, Upper California, is a deep bay making into the land on the west coast, and is one of the discoveries of Sir Francis Drake in 1579, while running along the coast of America. He, however, did not examine it, but merely mentions that there is such a place. There is no doubt but that the Spaniards knew of its existence long before Drake ever sailed in the Pacific, for while colonizing this country, this place was taken up as one of their early missionary stations, to civilize and christianize the natives; and even to this day there are many remains of the different missionary stations existing. To what extent these missionaries succeeded is not known to any part of the civilized world, except Spain, whose interest it was to keep every thing of this nature a profound secret; this was also their policy in reference to their discoveries and interior researches, fearing that some other country might supersede them, and reap the benefits.

Whether this part of the coast was ever thickly inhabited by the aborigines or not, I am unprepared to

20

say, but such is the fact, that for many miles in the interior, there is scarcely a native to be seen now, except an inmate of some Spanish dwelling. The appearance of the land in the vicinity of this bay is mountainous and much broken, possessing an exceedingly sterile appearance. This, however, is owing, in part, to the severe drought which had prevailed for the last two years. The interior is more fertile and productive; wheat, rye, barley, indian corn and beans, grow in great abundance when cultivated; all kinds of garden vegetables thrive, and particularly onions, which grow very large. Those vegetables, in most cases, for the last two years have to be watered by means of irrigation.

The entrance into the bay is somewhat narrow; the land being high on both sides and much broken, renders the scenery rather of a romantic appearance, when contrasting the white sand beach with the sterile hills. On the right hand, and at a commanding distance, is a battery, situated on an elevated rock, which, if properly fortified and commanded, would be able to bid defiance to any number of vessels that might attempt an entrance. A little beyond, on the same side in a valley, is the barracks for the men and officers, belonging to the same. Within the bay and before you arrive at the port, as it is termed, are several small islands, together with the mouth of the Rio Sacremento, which empties its waters among these variegated islands, and gives the whole an appearance somewhat romantic. As you advance, you suddenly round a projecting point, which terminates in a peak, and forms a small indenture where vessels anchor. This little bay is of a semicircular form, the land receding in many places abruptly, at the bottom of which there are a few houses, built in the European style, with here and there a "*rancho*," or country seat.

Just back of this place, at a distance of about nine miles, is one of those missions, which generally supplies the port with vegetables. During the time in which this country was subject to Spain its ports were closed against all foreign intercourse, but since it has changed its masters, its ports, with certain restrictions, have been open to the commercial world. From the immense number of wild cattle which roam in the vast plains of California, and which have been killed for their hides and tallow only, of late many vessels from the United States have visited the different parts annually to procure hides. Their tallow and jerked beef are exported by land, along the coast, and even to many parts of Europe. Consequently, this country, from this scource alone, receives an immense revenue; and at that time there were two American vessels at anchor there, engaged in that trade, with those of Columbia and Mexico, collecting hides and tallow. From some mysterious cause no meat of any kind can be cured here with salt, or in any other way except by drying it in the sun; however, this can be effectually accomplished, from the fact that the climate is so fine and the air so salubrous.

I am of the opinion that this region of California is very healthy for invalids in pulmonary diseases. I have been informed by a long resident in this country that there is no one disease peculiar to it or in any way common.

The inhabitants are Spaniards or their descendants,

generally mixed with the natives of the country by intermarriage, until there is scarcely a Spanish feature to be seen among them. The aborigines of the country are a diminutive race, much below the common stature of Europeans, and are smaller than those inhabiting the region of Oregon, about Juan de Fuca. Another striking peculiarity in the feature of the country, is the extreme diminutiveness of all kinds of vegetables, compared with those that we saw in Nasqually. The trees here are mere dwarfs and sink into insignificance in the comparison.

The country abounds in all kinds of game. Deer are so plentiful that we saw fifteen and twenty in a drove, playing on the declivities of the hills, in sight of our anchorage. Birds of various kinds were seen in great abundance, and in the interior were so tame as to allow themselves to be captured with clubs. The seine was hauled once and the fish caught were of an excellent quality, but not in any great abundance, though embracing several species. There were many venomous reptiles to be found every where in the country; the rattlesnake is common, also an animal about the size of a rat, whose bite is said to cause instant death.

The preceding remarks are applicable more particularly to that part of California which borders on the coast. As you recede, the soil becomes more fertile, and the country more interesting. The greater part of the entire territory is exceedingly fertile, though its excellencies are not appreciated by its badly governed inhabitants. Though republicanism—self-styled— had been long talked of, yet but little of the pure genius of freedom has ever dawned upon this beautiful country. The officer of government has been here, but nothing like a system has ever existed. The unalienable rights of free suffrage are neither generally understood, nor practised. Popular elections are entirely unknown.

Yankee enterprise, and the "spirit and principles of the pilgrims," might make this the "garden of America." Its physical resources are almost unbounded. The soil is rich and deep, varying from three to four or five feet in depth. Nor is this confined—as is often the case—to valleys and meadows, but extends to the "table land" and mountains, whose variegated acclivities are clad in a thick garment of verdure and luxuriance, for the greater part of the year. The various kinds of grain may be raised here in profusion, not only from the fertility of the soil, but from the fact that more than one crop may be harvested in the year. There is a freshness and luxuriance in the vegetable kingdom that give this place a decided preeminence.

This country has superior facilities for the culture of the grape, &c. Could fruit of this nature be properly cultivated, the time would not be far distant when this country, and indeed this continent, would not be dependent upon the eastern world for fruit. There are, however, several vineyards to be found among the more wealthy Spaniards, which produce fruit of an excellent quality, but all are but poorly cultivated. We can only infer from *these* what would be the result if the vine should be cultivated here, as elsewhere.

The numerous herds of cattle upon the many hillsides and verdant plains, give ample evidence of its

20*

qualities as a grazing country. Thousands of them may be seen quietly grazing, unscared by the ordinary labors of the husbandman, for the native is too indolent to cultivate the soil to any considerable extent. When the calls of nature demand food, he has simply to select a bullock from some of these extensive herds and capture his prize as may best suit his convenience. The lasso is often used for this purpose. While beef can be obtained so easily, they make but little effort to obtain the fruits of the earth by culture. Though grain may be raised with comparative ease flour can not ordinarily be obtained' without about four times its expense in New England. They are emphatically a beef-eating people.

The New England farmer, who prides himself in his beautiful horses, his fine oxen, &c., his improvements in his stock in general, would be surprised to see the beauty and symmetry of these large herds, which are simply *permitted* to grow, without any effort to improve their quality. They would gladly dispense with their "imported specimens of perfection," and furnish themselves from those fertile plains, where nature is seen in her simplicity.

In fine, few places, probably, can vie with this in almost every thing that pertains to agriculture. Superadded to a rich soil, animate nature seems to conspire to lend her influence to give a charm to this important avocation. The plains and "table lands" are checkered with unnumbered cattle, the forests resound with the music of numerous birds of rare beauty of plumage, and every lake, river and smaller body of water teems with the finny tribe, some of the most delicious flavor.

In a commercial point of view, it has many facilities of no ordinary description. Nearly surrounded on the one hand by the broad Pacific, and on the other by its deep and beautiful gulf,—to say nothing of its rivers,—it has a line of sea-coast that may, at some future day, be whitened by the sails of the world. Indeed this cannot long remain unnoticed and unoccupied by an enterprising people. It is not too much to predict that many years will not elapse, ere the shrill whistle will echo through these verdant glens and deep ravines, as the car thunders along the plains of California to its metropolis on its western borders. The steam-ship may ascend its gulf and be moored at the mouth of the Colorado freighted with the production of the East Indies, China, or the British Isles. Works of art may soon gild these hill-sides, where now the grazing herds bear undisputed sway ;—fortifications may rise along these almost uninhabited shores, and Loreto and San Diego become to western California, what Boston and New York are to the Eastern States.

On the 8th, a large party of Spanish ladies, by invitation, paid a visit to the ship; the quarter deck was decorated with a profusion of the flags of almost every country in the civilized world, and a regular "fandango" commenced at half past twelve o'clock, which was continued until ten at night. It appeared to be the desire of all the officers to render the ladies' time as agreeable as possible, although there were only one or two who could speak the language. The ladies performed many dances peculiar to the country, such as the old gentleman teased to death by a young girl whom he had promised to marry, but afterwards found her inconstant, and finally makes up with her and they get married. Another dance was performed solely by the ladies, which was *gracefully* executed, personating a "bull dance," or rather a *bull bait*. This was something new to me, and it will not be surprising that I was somewhat interested, however ludicrous it may have been. Both men and women retired to the shore with a good stock of wine on board.

A boat with Passed Midshipman Davis and three marines was sent to capture some of the runaway crew of the whale ship Orozembo, supposed to be secreted somewhere about the Rio Sacremento.

They succeeded in securing the deserters who had foolishly left us. In reference to the reasonableness of the dissatisfaction on the part of such as left the whaler, I am not prepared to decide. Those of our number, however, had not, in my estimation, sufficient reason for the course pursued by them. Capt. Wilkes and our officers were uniformly kind, and did much to subserve the welfare and comfort of the crew.

It is true, however, that seamen are often, very often, improperly treated, yet it is also true that they are sometimes inclined to a spirit of insubordination, and entail upon themselves many evils.

In extenuation of the conduct of the above deserters, it should be stated that they had been long from home, and probably a recollection of their birthplace and the many associations of childhood's home, had much influence in producing these sad results. The love of home probably is among the strongest sentiments of the human mind ; nor can it be lamented that such the case. Yet when such misfortunes result in a non-fulfilment of previous engagements, it is to be deprecated.

Captain Salter, from the Rio Sacremento, formerly a captain in Bonaparte's army, made a visit to the ship in company with the Russian Governor ; several other distinguished visitors called about the same time. We learned that Captain Salter had purchased the Russian settlement at Port Diego for thirty thousand dollars, and that the Governor and all the Russians were to leave for their settlement in North America by the first opportunity.

During the afternoon another regular "Spanish set-to" took place on board; all the Spanish ladies around in the vicinity came on board and dined, after which they commenced waltzing, and a fandango closed the evening's entertainment. They were "quite blue," and returned under the shades of the evening. This was the second bacchanalian feast held on board during our stay there.

On the 20th, the United States Brig Oregon, Capt. Hudson, arrived from Columbia River. This vessel was the late Thomas Perkins, and was purchased by Captain Wilkes for the purpose of taking the officers and crew of the Peacock home. The Peacock, it will be recollected, was wrecked in passing a bar off Columbia River. The crew were to be transferred to the brig.

On the evening of the 24th, the Launch arrived with a portion of the officers, scientific gentlemen and men, who had been on a land expedition from Columbia River to California. A number of these suffered very much on the route from intermittent fever, and some were quite exhausted. The distance traveled by

them was about six hundred miles; during most of
the time, they were compelled to be constantly on
their guard against the indians, some of whom were
of the most savage character. However, the party
mustered too strong for them to risk an attack, and
they suffered them to pass unmolested.

The launch and first cutter were hoisted in, and the
tents on shore, with some of the instruments, removed
on board. Things now began to look like going to
sea. In a short time all things were ready and we
were about to take our leave of this place. This was
acceptable news to most of us, as we were getting
somewhat fatigued with the monotony of our duties,
more especially for a few weeks immediately preceding that time. We felt that leaving this place was
nearly allied to an embarkation for home.

At 3 o'clock, P. M., all hands were called to get
underway, and by half past 2 o'clock the anchor was
up, and we were passing slowly from our anchorage,
with a very light wind, bound to sea,—Brigs Porpoise
and Oregon in company. At 7 o'clock the wind died
away perfectly calm, at which time we were immediately on the bar, and meeting a flood tide were compelled to anchor, to avoid being drifted back and
probably on shore, as the ship was at that time entirely unmanageable. In this situation we were compelled to lie all night, and a more disagreeable time I
never experienced. When the tide set in strong, the
breakers on the bar were tremendous; the waters of
the Rio Sacremento meeting those of the Pacific,
created a formidable line of breakers which at times
rolled in with fearful violence over the bar.

The Rio Sacremento is a river of considerable size,

and rising as it does in lakes at some distance from the coast, it pours a mighty mass of waters into the ocean at this place. Its turbid current enlarges in its course toward its ocean home, becoming more and more precipitous as it urges its way along the mountainous region, until its chafing tide reaches the inrushing waters of the Pacific. Here then is a mighty contest. The mingling masses rise high in air as they meet, and foam, and lash each other with tremendous power. They roll, and dash, and heave in the wildness of ocean scenery, crest meeting crest, current opposing current, billow overleaping billow, while a far-reaching spray is sent up, which distinctly marks the place of the "warring element." Its roar is heard at a distance, especially when the Sacremento is swollen, and a strong breeze from the south and west drives the approaching tide toward this projecting bar with doubly accelerated force.

It is at such times that the sailor, who is so unfortunate as to be on this bar, is reminded of the frantic storm, "wild in its madness," in mid ocean, when the Creator of the "sea and the dry land" stretches forth his mighty hand, and the "winds and waves obey him;" when it is lashed into fury by the tornado's fearful power, raging, rolling, and uplifting in stupendous grandeur.

During the night, we were in constant danger of being overwhelmed by the billows that were breaking around us. In the gloom of darkness a formidable roller came in and struck the ship, which inundated the deck, and floated several of the officers out of their state-rooms.

But little sleep could be obtained by any one during

this tedious night, in consequence of the motion of the ship, and the noise made by different articles that were rolling about the deck.  The morning came, but with it, but little hope of being relieved from a disagreeable and dangerous situation.  The calm still continued, and the rollers still came in at intervals, roaring like distant thunder for a mile or more before they made their appearance, while we were expecting every moment to hear our chain part, from the sudden jerks of the ship while rising over the rollers.  At 4 o'clock a tremendous roller came in and struck us violently on the larboard bow, carrying away the nettings as far as the after part of the fore rigging, flooding all the decks, and breaking the boats and spare spars on the main deck.

At this time, Joseph Aushouse, marine, was going upon deck to the head previous to going on post, and was killed by the rupture of the "*vena cava abdominalis*." This accident happened by a blow against the abdomen, with a spare spar which was thrown against the unfortunate man.  He died almost immediately, and his body was opened by the surgeon, with the above results.  The extent of the injury was such as to have rendered all medical assistance useless under any circumstances, even by the most skillful physicians.  At 8 o'clock we were favored with a fair wind, but it was light, however; we took the first opportunity to extricate ourselves from this disagreeable situation, and got underway, and as Providence favored us, we succeeded in clearing the bar; afterward, the wind dying away, we were compelled to come to anchor in the stream in twelve fathoms of water.  At half past 1 o'clock all hands were called

to "bury the dead." The seamen had been previously dressed in their uniform, white frocks and blue
pantaloons, and the marines in clean fatigues. The
body was brought on deck by the mess-mates of the
deceased, and conveyed to the lee gangway; an ensign was the pall and a rough plank the *bier*. The
funeral obsequies were performed by Capt. Hudson,
who took his station near the corpse, and read the
burial service of the Methodist Episcopal Church.
For a time all was hushed and still,—a death-like
silence pervaded the ship throughout. At the words
we "therefore commit the body to the deep," a plunge
was heard, and a momentary melancholy seemed to
impress the minds of all; but it was soon over, and
the usual pleasantry and mirth were soon commenced.
Three volleys of musketry were fired by the marine
guard over the ocean grave of the dead, and the sound
of the boatswain and his mate's whistle, announcing
that all was over, closed the awful scene.

At three o'clock the wind again favored us, when
we hove up the stream anchor and made sail.

On the morning of Nov. 2d, land was discovered,
which proved to be Monterey. The appearance of
this land is very mountainous and much broken and
diversified; the prospect was sterile, with no sign of
vegetation any where visible on the seaboard. We
stood within four or five miles of the anchorage, and
sent the Porpoise in with the letter bag intended for
Mazatland.

We were at this time favored with fine breezes,
and were making rapid progress toward the place of
our destination. Our hearts were beating high with

21

hope and buoyancy, and the "lights" of the sailor life were quite discernible.

The true sailor remembers his hardships but a short time. Storms may gather wildly above him, thunders roar, and lightnings play around his devoted head ; a single plank of a noble wreck may buoy him above a deep, dark, ocean grave, yet when the placid sun again shines upon him, as the mutterings of the thunder are heard only in the distance, a smile lights up his countenance, and he is the same joyous, fun-loving creature as in more favorable circumstances. His solemn vows are forgotten, thoughts of land are dismissed and danger is thought of, only as connected with the past. The probability of a recurrence of scenes of toil and peril, apparently is seldom suggested to him, save by moaning winds or overcast sky, ominous of the approaching tempest.

---

# CHAPTER XVI.

Arrival at the Sandwich Islands—Incident at Oahu—Departure —A meditated attack of the Natives—Arrival at Singapore.

> The dim horizon lowering vapors shroud,
> And blot the sun, yet struggling in the cloud ;
> Through the wide atmosphere, condensed with haze,
> His glaring orb emits a sanguine blaze.
> The pilots now their rules of art supply,
> The mystic needle's devious aim to try.

It would be no easy matter to delineate to my readers our feelings, as we " filled away " the main topsail, when we were about to leave the continent. We could look abroad over the wide expanse of waters which surrounded us, while the vast foaming fields of the Pacific, China Sea, Indian and Atlantic Oceans were stretching, as an almost unlimited barrier, between us and our loved homes, that mysterious place, of all others the most sacred. Notwithstanding the immense extent of this great "highway of nations," every heart seemed elated with a secret joy, as the waters went gurgling by, sparkling and foaming under our bow, while the Vincennes was plowing her way toward the setting sun. We were not, however, to pass immediately to that cherished spot, but were now bound for the Sandwich Islands. This fact compensated, in a measure, for a longer detention from the place which calls up, as from the grave, the scenes and associations of childhood.

Our previous visit at the islands had been of a very interesting character, and we had formed many pleasing acquaintances, more especially with those connected with the missions. Their uniform kindness to us on our previous acquaintance, had left a deep impression upon us, and it was a source of gratification that we were again to witness the almost miraculous effects of the introduction of Christianity among these islands, so lately in the darkness of barbarism.

Nothing of particular interest occurred during our departure from the continent, until we arrived at the Island of Oahu, and once more dropped our anchor in the harbor of Honolulu. Our friends and acquaintances received us with every mark of respect and esteem, and every thing seemed to wear an additional charm, as we were reminded, by these tokens of kindness, of those endeared to us by the ties of affection, toward whom we were urging our way as fast as circumstances would permit. Our greetings were scarcely over, and few necessary preparations made, ere we were ordered to be in readiness to embark, preparatory to a cruise to the East Indies.

An incident occurred on the eve of our departure, to relate which, I must beg leave to deviate somewhat from the general tenor of the narrative. While we were at Oahu at the previous time, we were furnished with an "advance" of three months, together with about two weeks for innocent recreation. And as if to render the circumstances still more ruinous, a plentiful supply of " grog money " was added, amounting, probably, to some hundreds and even thousands of dollars. There were but few, if any, of the crew, who had not at least fifty dollars, when they left the ship. One week had not elapsed, however, before the landlords—who much resemble those of other parts of the world—had stripped them of nearly the entire amount. It is not necessary to say whether, indeed, they received any thing in exchange; those acquainted with that part of creation denominated " land sharks," will be able to make their own inferences.

The Commodore had foreseen this result, and knowing quite well that they would not be content with this amount, but would induce many to enlarge their bills, looking to him for the liquidation, caused notices to be issued, forbidding such a course. In direct violation of this order, however, they pursued the course anticipated, swelling a bill of some $1500 or more. When the Commodore remonstrated with them for their treachery, they acknowledged that they saw his notices. They were asked if they wished him to falsify his word, and readily replied that they did not. He then reminded them of the fact that they knew, while granting the credit, that they must lose it or he must be guilty of a falsehood, and as they did not wish him to be thus guilty, they of course must lose it. They were earnest and boisterous in their complaints against the measure, while the Commodore listened with much apparent attention to their arguments, from which they inferred that they had very much softened him in regard to his resolution. In this they were mistaken.

After they closed their arguments, he said that he "was very sorry indeed, and that his sorrow was still greater that the bill was not $10,000 instead of $2,000, not that he believed they had had half the amount of their bill, but if it was the $10,000, he would not suffer one cent to be paid, and that they could go ashore as soon as they chose." At this they were exceedingly exasperated, and were very profuse of their threats, at the same time intimating their design of sending their bills to the United States for collection. Commodore Wilkes had encountered many dangers during his eventful life, and was not much alarmed at this "tempest in a tea-pot." The threats of rum-loving extortioners could not move him at this advanced period of life, and the bills were "squared by the foretop-sails," as jack has it; there are thousands beside these soulless landlords, who will long have occasion to remember the United States Exploring Expedition. No ship had ever visited these islands, connected with which there were so many marked incidents, or so great an amount of money left. After completing all

21*

necessary preparations, we took a final leave of our
friends on these islands, and embarked. It was, indeed, a scene of thrilling interest, to see our ship swiftly gliding through her watery way, as the dim outline of this interesting spot faded from our view; she
was a rapid sailer, and we felt that every mile was
an additional evidence of the speedy termination of
our long and eventful cruise.

We touched at no islands of much importance until
we reached Manilla, which port we made after a
pleasant passage of several days. My opportunities
for observation at this time were somewhat limited,
from the fact that our stay was short; consequently I
shall be able to give but a vague description of the
manners, customs, &c., of the inhabitants. Manilla is
the capital of the Philippine Islands, and is a place of
considerable importance. It is by far the most commercial city of the Archipelago, and contains, probably, about 14,000 inhabitants. Its exports are somewhat extensive, and are seen throughout the civilized
world. It is a Spanish port, and has the usual characteristics of Spanish towns,—narrow streets, low
buildings and misshapen verandas.

The Philippine Islands, embracing four in number,
are remarkably fertile; the climate is hot and in some
parts unhealthy, though the extensive ranges of
mountains, which rise far above the blue, foaming
waters of their shores, tend to mitigate the fervid heat
of the tropics. The luxuriant soil produces an excellent quality of rice, sugar, some of the spices and
gums, though but few of the usual aromatics of the
tropics; the various grains are abundant, while minerals are found to some extent.

Manilla.

When we left Manilla, our course was through the Sooloo Sea. This part of the ocean world had been but little known to navigators, although some of the more adventurous and enterprising had passed through this sea; the navigation is exceedingly dangerous on account of the innumerable coral reefs and sunken rocks which often present themselves, while there is no accurate chart to warn of their existence. Disasters had attended the imperfect surveys that had been projected, and few that had been so unfortunate as to be wrecked on the reefs, had ever survived to relate the horrors of their fate. On the one hand were the dangers of the ocean, and on the other, the ferocity of the natives who inhabited the islands which intersperse this part of the Pacific; they were treacherous and warlike, and delighted in blood and plunder. They were Malays, and truly their "habitations were filled with cruelty." They were far more barbarous than most of the inhabitants of the islands which we had visited during our cruise in the Pacific.

An incident occurred while we were surveying on their coast, which very aptly illustrated the character of the inhabitants. While our boats were engaged in "measuring base," by firing muskets, &c., the Malays mistook us for a ship's company in distress, and supposed that our guns were designed as a signal for assistance; they filled several of their largest prows with men, armed with shields, spears, crises, &c., and came down with full speed to attack us. One of the boats, under the command of Lieut. Perry, was at the head of the bay, while the others were stationed around the reefs; the pirates ran into the bay, landed, and began to brandish their spears, and commenced surrounding the men, who were immediately ordered to the boat. By the coolness and address of the officers and men, the natives hesitated a moment, during which time the men had succeeded in reaching the boat, carrying with them the *eprovet ;* they had an abundance of small arms in the boat, and the natives somewhat suspicious of our movements, probably distrusted their own strength. Mr. Budd, who commanded the cutter, the boat to which I belonged, seeing the apparent intentions of the natives, immediately weighed anchor and ran down to render assistance, if it was required. When the Malays saw us coming, they hurried back into their prows, and hoisted a white flag in token of peace. We sailed up to them, and after some conversation with them, through an interpreter that we had taken from Manilla for that purpose, they were induced to relinquish their designs of plunder. After they were shown our arms, and became acquainted with our strength, they made sail and returned, while we continued our survey unmolested. Had we been the crews of stranded merchantmen, there can be but little doubt but that we should have been plundered, and murdered or enslaved.

From the best information that I have been able to obtain from those who have jeoparded their lives in navigating the Sooloo Sea, all vessels that make this voyage should be well provided with the means of defence, should they be so unfortunate as to be wrecked on these shores. Even now, it would be fortunate if vessels should be able to pass without coming in contact with the reefs that so thickly lie along the passage. In addition to these dangers, the Sooloo Isl-

ands have a regular system of organized piracy in
their employ, as it is supposed, four hundred vessels,
with an ample quota of desperadoes, which are engaged in committing depredations upon defenceless
vessels that may chance to fall into their power.

The Malays, who are found at many of the islands
visited by us, are a treacherous, passionate and reckless class of barbarians, and seem to attach but little
value to human life. It is not unfrequently the case
that in a fit of rash and feverish excitement, they dis-
card all restraint and sacrifice their own lives to their
baser passions. One of the most usual methods, is
called "running Amok." When self-destruction is
premeditated, the victim prepares himself by some
means of intoxication, more generally by chewing
*opium, assumes a more frightful aspect, while his
long, black, disheveled hair is dangling carelessly,
giving a fearful appearance to the self-constituted ma-
niac. In this attitude he unsheaths his murderous
crise, and rushes forth with deadly intent; he attacks
such as may chance to fall into his power, vocifera-
ting "kill! kill!" with terriffic madness. This
slaughter is continued until he is overcome, and falls
a victim to his unhallowed passions.

We next made a harbor at Singapore, in lat. 3 deg.
N. and long. 105 deg. E., off the southern coast of Asia.
Singapore is an English island, but the majority of the
inhabitants are Chinese and Malays, by whom the
greatest part of the business is performed. We were
about discontinuing our surveys, and were to sail directly for our native land. Store ships, armaments,
&c., were to be of but trifling importance to us during
the remaining part of the cruise. At this port, the Fly-

ing Fish, which had been our companion through the
cruise thus far, was disposed of, as unnecessary for us
after completing our surveys.  She had been our associate in toils and dangers, and when she passed us
with a strange commander and crew, with a foreign
pennon streaming in the fragrant gales of this balmy
spot, an involuntary sadness filled every bosom on
board.  There seemed to be something in the nature
of· our enterprise which strengthened the bonds of
sympathy, extending even to inanimate nature.  Her
companion, the Sea Gull, had probably been lost off
the coast of Terra Del Fuego, and her crew found a
deep watery grave.  The Peacock had been stranded at the mouth of the Columbia River, the Relief
had been sent home from New Holland, and the Vincennes and Porpoise were all that remained of the
original fleet, which were to return to the United
States.

Singapore produces the finest pine apples that I
ever saw, and in the greatest abundance.  We had a
fine illustration of this fact at the Consul's, whose
plantation I visited; he had several acres of his
grounds covered with a most luxuriant growth.  He
kindly offered us as many as we might choose to accept; we accordingly filled our boat about half full,
and took them to the ship.  When perfectly ripe, and
plucked fresh from the stalk, they are decidedly
healthy, and they constituted a feast for us, for which
we felt grateful to the kind-hearted consul.

The Chinese, at this place, have a beautiful temple,
ornamented with some of the finest specimens of their
famed ingenuity; the whole fabric is indescribable,
from the innumerable figures that adorn its unique

structure. It produces, while gazing at it, just such feelings in the beholder, as one has while listening to the recital of their mysterious views of God and a future state of existence. One might feel at a loss to classify this singular edifice, as it is totally unlike any thing recognized in the "likeness of things in heaven above, the earth beneath, or in the waters under the earth," that has ever come under my observation. In examining this temple, I could but regard it as a tangible index of the solitary characteristics of that highly cultivated, yet semi-barbarous people. Claiming a great antiquity, they can boast of but little progress.

Preparatory to our final departure for home, our ship was put in proper condition for the cruise. We left Singapore after a stay of a few days, passing down through the Straits of Banca, and entered the Java Sea, and through the Straits of Sunda into the Indian Ocean. All was now life and hilarity, while bright visions were flitting before us. The wind was favorable, the weather fine, and our noble ship was making rapid progress toward our destined haven; for six days in succession, we were averaging thirteen and a half miles per hour. We passed directly for the Cape of Good Hope, but were detained two days in consequence of head winds. This is always unpleasant, but doubly so under the present circumstances. The sailor dreads the calm; he choses rather to see the ocean foaming, heaving and tossed, lashed by the fearful tornado's power. There is too much tameness and quiet about it to harmonize with the energy and vivacity of his temperament.

After doubling the Cape, we sailed for the Island of

St. Helena. It is impossible for me to gaze on this desolate, barren isle, without sad reflections upon the singular fate and probable feelings of that great man, who signalized this gloomy rock, and clustered around it associations which will run parallel with the flight of time, and be vividly impressed upon the great mind of a world, until this barren waste shall mingle in chaotic confusion with a melting universe, when the angel shall "stand with one foot upon the sea and the other upon the dry land," and shall put a period to all earthly things!

Great men not unfrequently give character to the age in which they live, and mark the spot in which they were born or closed life's career, with an imperishable fame. Such is St. Helena, the tomb of one of the greatest warriors of his own or any other age; and his confinement on this isolated "rock of the sea," has called forth expressions of different feelings from different minds, and while I would not approve his faults, I would not depreciate his virtues, and the *close* of his eventful life awakens in his behalf much sympathy.

I visited the Longwood residence of this illustrious Emperor, and found that it had been converted into a stable for horses; the "dew-drooping willow" is still "leaning over" what had once been his grave. I found but little satisfaction in my visit to this prison rock, and was happy to arrive on board where the "stars and stripes" of my own happy country waved over my head in triumph.

After a stay of two days, the word "all hands up anchor for the United States!" was given, ringing through the various parts of the ship, producing quicker and more joyous pulsations in every bosom; the capstan was manned, the anchor "walked up to the bows," sail was made, and but a few moments elapsed before the ship was underway, to tarry no more until she should arrive at New York. And now followed a time for thought, retrospect, and future arrangements; all were filled with plans for future action; a thousand different schemes were originated by which the schemer seemed confident that he might obtain a compensation on shore.

All on board had been schooled in all the mysteries of the sailor boarding-house system, and were particular to caution each other against the treachery and fraud of landlords; each seemed fully determined to take special care of himself and his money, but, poor fellows, they knew but little of the tempter's power; they knew but little of those artful stratagems which were so soon to be thrown around them, which they had neither the moral courage nor firmness to resist.

Day after day, our ship continued to urge her way onward with rapid strides, while nothing of moment occurred to mar our happiness, or elate us with joy, save the prospect before us. Of the feelings which agitate the bosom of the sailor on an occasion like this, the landsman can know but little. Hope, perchance, speaks of kindly greetings, a reunion of those long sundered by time and space, the consummation of the fancies of childhood's sunny hours, or Fear may marshal a dread train of forbodings, veiling the countenance in a pall of sorrow. Four long years! how great and heart-rending the changes which that time may have effected. How many loved ones had terminated all earthly scenes, riven all the ties of af-

22

fection, and left naught behind save their virtues, and a dying blessing, to console the wanderer, as he nears the cherished spot of early life.  Perchance a mother, whose prayers, fervent, heart-breathed and effectual, which arose to heaven for a departing son, may have joined that vast congregation which has gone before us; a father's voice, so often heard in friendly counsels, may be hushed in death; loved associates, a brother, or a sister, whose memories may be cherished as a sacred treasure, to be relinquished only at death, may greet us no more.  As scene after scene comes up as a memento of the past; as spot after spot is revisited, how frequent may be the evidence that some kindred spirit chants above.

Some who had left home with the same joyous hopes as ourselves, mingled not with us as we were about to step again upon our native soil.  One after another had been committed to a deep, dark, coral bed, surrounded by ocean's treasures, to slumber until the trump of God shall summon the " sea to give up her dead."  The Sea Gull's crew, bound together by endearing ties of friendship, had not been separated in the hour of dissolution, but had sunk together, to remain until this " mortal shall put on immortality." Some who left the paternal roof, hand in hand with ourselves, could not accompany us in our return. Our approach was to cause many a bosom to swell with joy or heave with anguish, as the sad tidings of the death of loved ones should fall upon the ear, as the mournful knell of departed hopes.

On the 10th of June, 1842, the faint outlines of the highlands of Nevisink peered in view, pointing us to our place of destination.  As we approached the

land, the wind died gradually away, and it was
thought advisable to come to an anchor and wait for
a steamer to tow us in. In a short time the boat arrived, and took us to the quarantine ground, when
the health officer boarded us; after a very short detention we passed rapidly up the bay to the city. As we
came abreast of the North Carolina, we fired a salute
of twenty-six guns, at the last of which the broad
pendant which the Commodore had honored for more
than four years, was hauled down and the command
of the ship was committed to Captain Hudson of the
Peacock, who then proceeded toward the navy yard,
and came to a final anchor. A steam boat was soon
along side, and the joy with which we passed our
bags and hammocks, on board, can be better imagined by the reader, than expressed by myself. In the
short space of two hours we were all ashore in the
land of our nativity,—the toils and dangers of a long
and eventful cruise ended, and we were again free
men, in " the home of the free."

As it is probable that this volume will be read by
many a brother sailor, it may not be inappropriate to
recur to incidents connected with landlords, and some,
I am sorry to say, are not only *lordly*, but perfidious.
To those who have had fewer facilities of judging of
the character of the " land sharks " than myself; who
have observed less of their intrigues and stratagems,
it may be serviceable as a means of avoiding the
tyrants' power. All may be aware of the fact that as
the hardy sailor returns from a long voyage, with his
hard-earned wages, this class of men—if the term is
appropriate—is ever ready to defraud such as may
come within their iron grasp, but by what means this

is effected, some may yet be ignorant. They are, apparently, unmoved by the tears and moans of kindred, as they see loved ones drawn into the vortex of dissipation and licentiousness, indifferent to the common claims of humanity. Money they wish and money they will have, though they wade through seas of blood to accomplish their ends; though the widowed mother toils in sorrow and wastes her ebbing energies as the direct consequence, or orphan children supplicate a meager pittance from a frigid, heartless world. Is this severe language? I would that it were untrue, that it were the fitful imaginations of a disordered brain, but many, ah! too many can sadly vouch for its truthfulness.

Those employed in our naval service, are far more in danger from this source than other seamen; they are longer from the hallowed influences of home, and the refining, reclaiming tendencies of fireside associations. They are also more exposed to the hardships, dangers and unfavorable influences of a marine life, and consequently have an almost irresistible desire to " enjoy themselves " (what *enjoyments !*) by throwing off all restraint and plunging into a senseless hilarity and inebriation. Again, they ordinarily have larger amounts of money when they come on shore, and, as a natural consequence, soon come within the contaminating grasp of these modern *harpies,* and they seldom escape from their talons until their funds are gone, and they are plunged low in the depths of degradation and ruin, by this arch enemy,— for such he must be, however artful his pretended friendship may be. This apparent friendship seems very carefully graduated by the amount of remaining funds, and its last impulse dies away, as the last cent falls into his misery-filled coffers.

The "vilest of the vile," of both sexes, are brought into requisition, when a man-of-war is reported, and a great many *new* boarding houses are opened for the occasion. The whole fraternity of conspirators now form their plans, and the whole wharf in the vicinity of the ship is crowded with landlords and runners, and as often as a sailor raises his head above the netting, he is hailed with "mess-mate," "ship-mate," with other familar appellations which are most coaxingly applied to him, while their countenances and hearts are living exemplifications of the sentiment expressed by Shakspeare, "A man may smile and smile, and be a villain;" but as the sailor is a stranger to this clan of *new* boarding masters, and as he is too frank and honest himself to suspect their insincerity, they often succeed in decoying large numbers of them into their dens of infamy. The result is, that the fruit of years of toil is dissipated in about as many days, and their pleasant homes(?) are soon transformed into very forbidding ones, and the victims, for whom they expressed so much regard, are required to find *new* quarters. The purse being empty, the bags and chests are next rifled, and not a vestige of decent clothing remains which can become available. Exorbitant and imaginary bills, with downright robbery for the climax, soon terminate the sailor's tarry on shore. Diseased, degraded and dispirited, he is soon obliged to ship—or perhaps this is done for him by his ever-watchful *gaurdian*, and his advance secured, and when he is reinstated on the deck of the receiving

22*

ship, he is cared as little for by the landlords as the
brutes that are slaughtered for his convenience.

These things were once transacted openly, but now
more cunning and management are requisite; they
have recourse to every plot which they can devise, to
facilitate the accomplishment of their unworthy designs.   Draymen are bribed to obtain their clothes,
hammocks, &c., under pretence of conveying them to
houses of good reputation, but instead of this, they are
carried where the premeditated plunder is effected.

New York abounds in just such places, and sailors,
on coming into port, must be exceedingly careful how
they select a boarding place, especially if they design
to visit their friends, and devote their earnings to
more consistent objects.   They must be continually
on the alert, lest they are robbed while sober, but if
they can be induced to quaff the fatal cup, they may
bid adieu to pleasing associations with friends, and
the sweets of domestic life.

These secret plans are skillfully digested, and faithfully executed.   Runners and accomplices are employed and bountifully compensated, making it a regular business to underrate all respectable "homes," and
temperance boarding houses; intoxicating drink is an
important agent in the work of destruction.   These
emissaries will distinguish themselves by their coarse
imprecations, profane curses and vulgar epithets;
nothing appears too harsh that can be said respecting
such homes for the sailor, as, they are well aware, tend
directly to abridge their nefarious business.   Their
mental powers, it would seem, are taxed to concoct
falsehoods which shall be sufficiently libelous to prejudice seamen against such places, where they know

that they will be beyond their reach. Should these fabrications fail, their next resort, perchance, is to get their baggage into the hands of some bribed coachman, under the pretext of conveying it to a temperance house, and a liberal fee will ensure the safe arrival at some degraded and degrading den of infamy, and before the sailor is aware of the character of the place, his things are under the control of an intriguing landlord, and it is with the utmost difficulty that he can recover his property, without a legal interference, during which delay, should not his pockets or his chest be rifled, he may regard himself as fortunate. An individual who will be guilty of such cowardly and contemptible intrigue, will not be very scrupulous when he has his victim within his grasp; what he fails to get by permission, he will take by force.

Another stratagem is to employ some shrewd individual to commence the work of destruction while at sea, who under the garb of a shipmate can practice his deception and be credited, however much he might traduce respectable establishments, and discolor the merits of other resorts, of which he is a base hireling and utters falsehoods for the same reason that he engages in his ordinary employments.

It is ordinarily true, that the payment on board of a man-of-war does not occur until some days after their arrival at port; of this circumstance, the landlord is fully aware, and soon avails himself of this advantage. His agent is furnished with funds, and very generously—as it might seem—supplies their present wants by loaning money or otherwise, but is particularly careful to be present at the time of payment, and receives the check from the purser, of course losing nothing by his investment.

The last, though not the least of these arts which are devised to defraud the mariner, of which I shall make mention, is performed by woman,—*woman* did I say? I will not thus dishonor that name, ever dear to the virtuous. Degraded and unprincipled females, by feigned smiles and hypocritical and specious graces, insinuate themselves into favor with the unsuspecting sailor, extorting from him valuable presents, or otherwise making large draughts upon his funds,—often relinquishing their victim only when the last dollar is transferred to their hands, with not even an apology for an equivalent. These individuals know well the frankness, kind-heartedness and generosity of the sailor, and effect his ruin when other efforts less facinating, might fail. Numerous instances of this kind have come under my own observation, but a few will suffice to illustrate the effects of such devices to extort presents by abusing the sailor's generosity, and the consequent treatment. Two seamen with whom I was acquainted, had returned from a cruise up the Mediterranean, one receiving $280, and the other $310. The landlord had a wife and daughters who were adepts in this kind of robbery. I was shown a valuable silk dress, beside a considerable amount of jewelry which had been presented by these seamen. These were given on Monday; on Thursday they were driven from the house, and on Friday, while I was standing with them, these females passed us, arm in arm with seamen who had more recently returned, who might have shared a similar fate at the next arrival. As they passed us on the sidewalk, the same beautiful and rich dress was drawn aside, that it might not come in *contact with that of the donor*, while the remark was distinctly heard, "*I wish these filthy scamps would keep clear of the sidewalks, and not spoil people's nice clothes.*" This occurred in *eight days* after their arrival, and what became of the $590, I will leave the reader to infer.

This is but one of *many* similar incidents, and those who have long been familiar with this subject, will, I think, sustain me in the assertion that " not one half has been told." They know well that the daughters and wife of the landlord, richly attired, promenade the public resorts, displaying the fruits of toil on the " mountain wave," the lavish gifts of the afterwards despised sailor.

Lastly, I will mention one other means of ensnaring the sailor. Many landlords, for the purpose of the more effectually deceiving, remove the bar, while liquors are kept secretly, and every effort is employed to induce men to purchase it. In this way a far greater number is drawn into such places only to be robbed, than less hypocritical persons, who make no pretension to temperance can obtain. Others again do not keep spirits of any kind, yet quite as effectually filch the sailor, while they preserve the appearances of respectability, and unfurl the banner of temperance as a " false beacon." Two facts of this nature were divulged by a sailor landlord, by way of boasting, which I will insert. I well recollect of hearing the same landlord censuring Mr. Morris, a Bethel preacher, because he did not refer to his house in his prayers, as well as the " Sailor's Home," a house of the first respectability.

A sailor who had been paid off from a man-of-war, knowing that he would be in danger of being robbed of his earnings, and wishing to remain on shore as long as possible, paid this landlord for one year's board in advance.  In a short time afterward the sailor had been deprived of the remainder, and being unable to find employment on shore, went to the landlord for a portion of his funds, as he was compelled to go to sea again, and was in want of clothes.  He was refused, and was obliged to go to sea with the few articles that could be purchased with a month's advance, and leave his money behind him.  The landlord soon afterward removed to the state of Maine.

Another man boarded with him at the same time, who deposited fifty dollars with the landlady for safe keeping, offering her enough of it to purchase a dress, for her trouble.  On the next day, when he asked her for a few dollars, he was informed that she had used it all for her dress, and the poor fellow was left penniless, nor did he ever recover one cent of his investment.  This is one of the temperance boarding houses, of which every sailor should beware.  It is not a specimen of temperance houses, nor should such assume the name.  There are many homes for the sailor, where temperance principles are strictly adhered to, and where the welfare of boarders is conscientiously regarded.  A list of these houses will be found in each number of the Sailor's Magazine, published by the American Seamen's Friend Society.

This is but a system of miniature piracy, and it is presumed that in no fraudulent enterprise is there more concert of action, more deeply laid plans, or more success in pilfering, when the amount of funds and the extent of the field of action are taken into the account. True or false colors are raised, as may best suit convenience, or best promote the objects. As the wages are nearly exhausted the attentions become less and less; the Mr. is forgotten, and "jack" is substituted; pointed remarks in reference to "long stays on shore" become more frequent; after, neglect ensues, and should this fail, he is thrust into the streets to lie scorned and maltreated until he becomes awake to the sadness of his situation, leaving behind him, perhaps, the last cent of his wages and advance. He has no other alternative but to rush from the scenes of his degradation, a disconsolate, misery-stricken mortal.

Happy would it be if *one* misfortune of this kind were sufficient to serve as a beacon for the remainder of life; but not so. The snare is laid in new and ever-varying forms, victim after victim is entangled, involving them deeper and deeper in misery and ruin.

It is a painful fact that our fears in reference to our own crew, were sadly realized. As toilsome as had been our cruise; though dangers had crowded thickly around us, yet they were literally increased as we greeted familiar faces in this great emporium of commerce. But a few days had elapsed before some who had been long associated with us, and who were endeared to us by lasting bonds, were groveling in pollution and drunkenness. Before the expiration of one week, many had been placed on board the receiving ship, the earnings of the entire cruise exhausted, some never having seen the checks which had been transferred to the grasping landlords. Many who had had bright hopes of pleasing intercourse with their kindred, were denied that sacred privilege, and instead of a few weeks of recreation and exemption from the dangers of an ocean life, were soon to commence another cruise of years, probably to react the same scenes of vice and dissipation.

Others, again, had departed in different directions, and were soon revisiting the homes of their childhood, where four years before they had pressed the parting hand.

The events of the Expedition can not but awaken peculiarly lively emotions in all who participated in its deeply interesting incidents. Five hundred men had left Norfolk to visit bleak and untraversed parts of the world, in which cruise a deep, dark uncertainty necessarily enshrouded our undertakings. The sequel proved it to be such; of the five hundred, but two hundred and thirty-six reached the shore at that time. A portion of the remainder arrived at different times, and some slept in coral beds, to obey the summons of Omnipotence, when the unnumbered millions of ocean's children shall rise above its troubled bosom an august assemblage, and join the vast universe of created intelligences.

The remote results of this Expedition cannot easily be predicted. Though the continent discovered may not be, and perhaps may never be capable of being peopled, its discovery was an acquisition to science which may not be easily appreciated. We had visited unknown nooks of the globe, navigated unexplored seas, and surveyed many islands of which there was no previous knowledge. Hidden rocks and dangerous reefs had been laid down upon charts, that future adventurers may not hazard life and property, while extending the conquests of commerce and enterprise.

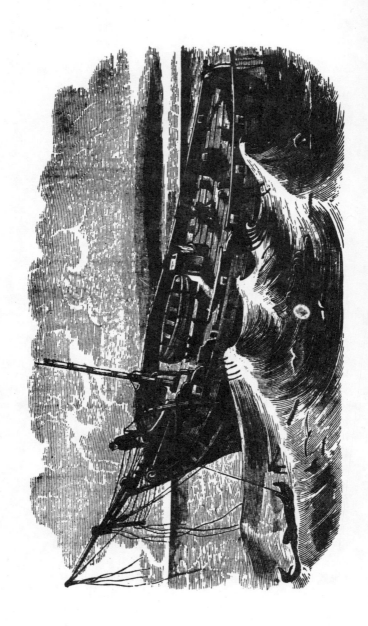

# REMINISCENCES.

## WRECK OF THE PEACOCK.

The sailor's life is emphatically one of toil and danger. He braves the tempest's rage, the tornado's power, the lightning's glare, the attack of pirates,— not only on shipboard, but on the shore. He is liable at any and every moment to be roused from his slumbers, to defend himself and that committed to his charge, against the attacks of the ruthless bravado, or to struggle with the warring elements. This fact is very aptly illustrated in an eventful cruise of the United States Ship Peacock from the Island of Zanzibar to the coast of Arabia. This was commenced in the month of September; the weather was delightful, and the smiles of heaven and earth combined, seemed to augur a safe and speedy voyage to the abode of Ishmael's descendants. The thermometer ranged from 80 deg. to 85 deg., except on the 12th, when it arose to 90 deg., at which time we crossed the equator. On the following day we had the most magnificent display of light and colors which the eye of man has ever witnessed. At 4 o'clock the wind died away,— not a breath gave the least ripple to the glassy surface

23

of the ocean; not even a fluttering of the royals was discernible.  As the sun neared the western horizon, a curtain of fleecy white clouds that lay outspread like a spacious mantle, extending from the north-east to the far south, began to be tinged with a faint yellow, which continued to deepen through gold, orange and scarlet, to the richest, deepest crimson; the sun seemed to go down swelling with pride, as it waded through this flood of glory to his western retreat.

The colors were presented with a brilliancy so dazzling, so indescribably magnificent, that any attempt to give an adequate idea of their grandeur would be ineffectual.  The ocean too, as if to lend its aid, presented a broad expanse of a mirror-like surface, reflecting the glittering glories of the heavens, and adding a tenfold splendor and sublimity to the scene.  All on board came upon deck, and so intensely were all absorbed in the gorgeousness of the display, that not a sound was heard for a considerable time, save some involuntary ejaculations of astonishment and admiration.

About ten minutes after sunset, a faint breeze began to wave the lighter sails, and the commanding voice of the officer, giving the order,—"Lay aft to the braces," was the first sound that broke the stillness of that beautiful evening.  The order was followed by the rattling of blocks and cordage, and the hasty tread of seamen about the decks.  The sails were trimmed, and the breeze continued to freshen until daylight, when we were dashing through the brine at the rate of nine "knots."  We were rapidly leaving that beautiful spot, yet I dare predict that not a man will ever forget that sunset scene in the Indian Ocean.

We passed on gaily and quietly, nothing of note oc-
curing until the 20th, when a train of circumstances,
following closely in the "wake" of each other, gave
us an additional illustration of the "lights and shadows" of a sailor's life. Every thing had borne an encouraging aspect, and all were cheered with the bright
prospect of soon reaching Arabia, and partaking the
delicacies which that fertile soil so abundantly produces, and where we might become acquainted with
the manners, customs, costumes and matters of general
interest among this singular class of people, but how
illustrative of the fact that we "know not what a day
may bring forth." Between "five and six bells,"* on
the night of the 20th, while the watch below were se-
curely sleeping in their hammocks, the ship struck
with great violence upon a reef of coral rocks. In an
instant every thing was bustle and confusion;—all
hands rushed on deck. The ship continued to urge
her way among the rocks, until her collision with
them produced a continuous sound, resembling the
rumbling of thunder, and before the studding sails
could be taken in, and lighter sails furled, the ship
had forced her way about one mile and a half among
the rocks of the reef. It was nearly a half hour before the ship was fairly stopped, and from that time
until daylight, she continued to strike violently, so
that no one could stand upon deck without attaching
himself to the rigging. As soon as it became sufficiently light to distinguish objects at a distance, we
discovered a low sand beach, nearly encircling us at a
considerable distance. There was also some higher

---

* From half past 5 to 6 o'clock.

land near, which proved to be an island. To add to
our distress, we found that we had run on the reef at
high water, at the height of the spring tide. Orders
were immediately given to "break out" the spare
spars, booms, &c., lower all the boats as soon as possible. The yards and topmasts were sent down, and
every effort made to ease the ship, but still she continued to strike heavily. Soon afterward the tide began to ebb, and the ship began to careen so much
that it was necessary to set a spar on the reef, to partially prevent it. The spare spars were then thrown
overboard and formed into a raft, upon which fifty or
sixty barrels of beef and pork were placed; ten thousand gallons of fresh water were discharged, large
quantities of grape and canister, &c., were thrown
overboard for the purpose of lightening the ship.

During the day we saw several *proads* or *prows*,
filled with men, sailing around us occasionally, and
intently watching our movements. The captain, pilot,
and passed midshipman, and several seamen left the
ship for the purpose of speaking them, but they
avoided them, brandishing their swords and sailing
toward a point of land near, where they anchored.
We had but little doubt of their character, and had
reason to expect an intended attack at night. Accordingly we made all necessary preparations to receive them in a soldier-like manner, with the "honors
of war." Every officer and man slept with cutlases,
pistols, muskets, pike or battle axes at hand, but we
were not disturbed at this time.

On the next morning a boat was sent out for the
purpose of sounding; it was found that there was not
as much water astern of the ship as on the day of the

collision, though it was high water. After taking refreshments—raw pork and bread—we continued to
lighten the ship by throwing over two chain cables,
several hundred fathoms of hawser, after having buoy-
ed them. At noon we succeeded in taking an observation, and ascertained that the high land was the
small Island of Muceiva, in latitude 20 deg., and
longitude 58 deg. east, and almost fifteen miles from
Arabia Felix, or Happy Arabia. About this time the
pirates had considerably increased, having some eight
or nine *prows*, containing from twenty to sixty men
each; they ran down near us and anchored, forming
themselves into a line of battle,—a position very unfavorable to us, as the situation of our ship gave such an
elevation to our guns that we could not dislodge them.
All hands were called to quarters and furnished with
small arms, preparatory to the expected encounter.
The warlike appearance of our ship, and the sight of
some of our men, who inadvertently arose above the
netting, probably deprived us of an opportunity of
teaching them an important lesson in military tactics,
and the futility of attacking a yankee man-of-war,
though in distress. The chiefs of the different *prows*
assembled in one of the savage vessels and held a consultation, and afterward two of them jumped into the
sea and approached the ship. A rope was thrown to
them to assist them in coming on board, but they looked terribly frightened when they saw themselves in
the presence of two hundred men, armed with all the
implements of naval warfare.

We had, while at Zanzibar, become acquainted
with a Polish officer, who had taken passage with us.
This man was the only one on board who could

23*

speak the Arabian language, and was employed as
our interpreter. They had not been on board but a
few moments, before they had the hardihood to ask
how much money, and how many men we had on
board; they were answered that we had an abundance of both. The interpreter was then directed to
ascertain their terms upon which they would carry a
message to the Sultan at Muscat, returning the reply.
Although the distance was not more than might have
been traveled in one day, they refused to go for less
than $1000! In a short time they left us, made sail
and did not trouble us farther for the day.

On the next morning six men volunteered to go in
an open boat to Muscat, for the purpose of carrying
Mr. Roberts, Minister to the East Indian and Asiatic
Courts, and Mr. Rogers Taylor, a passed midshipman,
a most excellent and brave gentleman, a native of
Newport, R. I. The next morning at daylight, they
left the ship to perform their arduous journey. It
was soon observed that the pirates had concerted an
attack upon them, and were in hot pursuit.

Preparations were continued on board the ship, to
effect an escape from the reef if possible. The stream
anchor was dropped astern, with one hundred fathoms
of cable, and the capstan manned, but without moving the ship. At last, finding that she would not
float at high tide, we were driven to the painful necessity of throwing a portion of our guns overboard;
she then "righted," and by means of the anchor, we
succeeded in starting from our unpleasant position.
The fifer commenced that soul-thrilling air of the sail-
or, "The girl I left behind me," the men marching in
time with the music, with hearts as buoyant as if

nothing had befallen us, while the ship was rapidly moving from her dangerous moorings. It was amusing to witness the ardor with which the men performed their circuit; when the fifer was unable, from fatigue, to give us music, the sailors were not at a loss to supply that deficiency, by substituting songs of their own, making *some* music, but more jargon. A colored man rendered very important services on this joyous occasion, by a sudden peal of a favorite air, commencing with, "I wish I was in yankee town," in which he was joined by about two hundred stentorian voices, and when the chorus—" 'Tis time for us to go," was struck, it might remind one of an earthquake in miniature. The scene, though animating, was really ludicrous.

Whether attributable to the power of music or otherwise, one thing is certain, which is, that the capstan was rapidly revolving and the ship was grating harshly over the coral bed, and was soon beyond the reach of danger. We again felt free, had less to fear from attacks of the pirates, though their number should be much increased. Though disabled and deprived of many of our guns and other necessary implements. we were afloat on our loved element, and felt that we could cope with a similar force, should circumstances require it.

During this time we had been obliged to leave our raft, provisions, &c., at the place where we commenced lightening. This had been observed by the eagle-eyed pirates, and they determined to avail themselves of an opportunity to plunder us before the ship could be in readiness to pursue them. At 12 o'clock, while we were refreshing ourselves, an alarm was given; the marines were immediately mustered, and a volley of musketry was discharged from the quarter deck, but the distance was so great that it did no execution. Lieut. Gordon sprang into the boat, followed by Messrs. Darlington and Caldwell, and twenty seamen; we made all possible speed to the windward of the *prow* which had stolen our provisions. The pirates kept close in under the land, following the curvature of the beach, in order to avoid an attack from the ship. As soon as they arrived at a position in which the guns could be brought to bear upon them, they opened a broad-side upon the prows, but did not reach them, as they were some three or four miles distant.

It was an exciting time for us in the boat; we were laboring at the oars with our full strength, while the roaring of the thirty-two pounders, and the rushing of the shot, hissing and yelling over our heads, as they were sent on an errand of vengeance to the freebooters, together with the expectation of grappling with them, though at least three times as numerous as ourselves, gave a zest to our enterprise which should be experienced to be appreciated. Fortunately for them, we broke two of our oars, which materially diminished our strength.

By this time the chief seemed confident of his ability to outsail us, and, jumping into the bow of his boat, brandished his *creece* in defiance, while it glittered and sparkled in the sunbeams. This was too much for us. I raised my musket, and suddenly leveled it at him, when he dropped his *creece* and fell into the bottom of the boat. This was followed by a general discharge from all in the launch. How many were destroyed we were unable to ascertain; it was certain, however, that a large number was wounded. They succeeded in passing in about a half musket shot in the advance of us, carrying off some of our spars and one or two barrels of provisions. We gave up the chase and returned to the ship, highly incensed at the conduct of these base marauders, who could thus plunder us while in distress.

The next tide we worked the ship still farther from the reef, and at night, slept with our arms by our sides. On the following morning, at daylight, we learned that the enemy had very much increased their number, and were again standing down for us, probably elated with their success on the preceding day. We were well aware of their intentions, and made preparations to welcome them. We had now "righted," and had eleven thirty-two pounders on deck, with which we could have met a very much greater number. It was the universal desire that they should attack us during the day. In the mean time our labors were continued as usual. We parted one of our hawsers, and lost our stream cable and anchor. The Commodore's gig was laying off, and several boats, with grapplings, were busily engaged in attempting to secure them. While our boats were thus engaged, the pirates attempted to run between them and the ship, so that an attack upon *them* would endanger the lives of our men. They were carefully watched and their manoeuvres perfectly understood. When they had approached sufficiently near, we poured a broad-side of grape and canister upon them. The shot went whistling among them, carrying away their masts, tearing their sails and dashing large quantities of water among the affrighted desperadoes.

No sooner did they learn their mistake than they "tacked ship," and attempted to escape from our destructive fire, but it was no easy matter; we continued a constant fire as long as they were within reach of us, much to their chagrin, no doubt. It is impossible to determine with any accuracy what their loss was, but judging from the hideous yells that arose from all their boats, it was evident that the work of destruction had been extensive. The principal regret on our part, seemed to have been that we were not able to give them "a little more grape."

They were a wandering tribe of Arabs, inhabiting the desert and known by the name of Bedouins; they have no established government, and live by plundering such as may be so unfortunate as to be wrecked on their coast, while they carry the captured crews into the desert, and subject them to the most abject slavery. They are regarded by the Sultan, as pirates are with us, and are executed, when captured, without trial by jury. They probably learned a lesson in this instance, that will make them somewhat reluctant to attack a yankee man-of-war, though stranded on their coast.

That afternoon we worked the ship into about five fathoms, after which all hands were called to "splice the main brace," as an expression of commendation (a ruinous practice, by the way.) It was found necessary to keep a quarter watch at the pumps, as the ship was making fifteen inches of water per hour; half of her false keel had been torn off, the copper displaced to some extent, and what other damage, we could not determine. The ship was put in as good condition as circumstances would allow, preparatory to making sail for Muscat, which occurred on the 27th.

On the morning of the 28th, while on our passage, we saw a ship approaching us; she continued to bear down for us until within about three miles, when she "rounded to," fired a gun and raised Arabian colors. Finding that we did not notice her, she approached nearer and fired again; this was answered by us, at the same time hoisting our colors. When she was within one mile of us we saw a few men on the fore-castle, dressed in the style of American seamen. She hoisted out her boat which was soon along side, bringing, beside her own crew, Mr. Taylor and the crew of our 2d cutter. A smile of satisfaction animated the faces of all on board, while the cordial grasp indicated the warmth of attachment which existed among the crew. Dangers, distress and trials bind hearts together more firmly than prosperity and pleasures can, and the recent events that we had encountered, strengthened more and more the bonds of attachment that had previously bound us together.

We soon learned the results of the expedition of our 2d cutter, which had been previously despatched to Muscat. Finding that the pirates would overtake them, they steered broad off to sea. They followed them nearly out of sight of the land, but, having no compass, did not dare follow them farther. That night they encountered a severe gale, in which the boat came near being swamped, off the Island of Maceiva; they nailed tarpaulins over the boat, leaving apertures through which the head of the oarsman could be thrust, and by dint of toil at the oars and bailing, they succeeded in keeping afloat, until the gale was over, when they sailed for Muscat, where they arrived in safety after four days' sail. As they rounded the point, and entered the harbor, they hoisted the boat's ensign and made for the city. The Sultan's palace stands at the head of the bay, close to the water. He discovered the boat, and as soon as he observed the American colors, he sent an officer to meet them, and came himself to welcome them. He had had an acquaintance with Mr. Roberts; the meeting was one of thrilling interest to all who saw it. When he learned that our ship was in distress on his coast, the finer feelings of his nature were aroused, and he deeply sympathized with us in our misfortunes. He immediately ordered a sloop of war, then lying at the harbor, to be fitted up and to be placed in our service, together with the crew. He also ordered his general to detach 400 of his best men, to march immediately over land to the place of disaster, to assist and protect us, were we obliged to abandon the ship. The detachment left the same night, marching under American colors, and hastened on their errand of mercy. The sloop was soon in readiness, and was freighted with sheep, goats, buffaloes, fruit and water, to supply us, should they meet us on the passage. This was the vessel that we had met, under the charge of Mr. Taylor, whose appointment was ratified by the Commodore, when he came on board. Our ship was soon filled with Arabian fruit, which was a most welcome gift to us at that time, after so long a season of incessant toil. The fruit consisted principally of grapes, fresh and preserved dates, pomegranates, and melons of various kinds. The pomegranates were a rare fruit, having never seen them before. They are of about the size of a quince, of a light green color; they are enclosed in a hard and brittle shell or rind. On opening, the whole inside is filled with detached parts or berries, like our currants, very much resembling them in taste. Fresh figs just plucked from the trees were also very abundant.

Our passage was very slow at this time, owing, in part, to head winds, calms, &c., and to the shattered condition of our vessel. On the morning of the 29th, however, an incident occurred which relieved us of some of our difficulties. We ran into a large shoal of sun-fish, bearing some resemblance to the sea animalcules, only larger, and of a transparent jelly. This shoal extended for several miles, and while the ship was passing them, they were pressed with great force into the bottom, nearly stopping the leak, very much to our satisfaction.

On the 28th, we were passing Cape Rosalgat, about eighty miles from Muscat. Every day after the sloop met us, the Sultan's barge came down to us, loaded deeply with cattle, fruits and vegetables. We were now making rapid progress toward the haven.

As soon as we rounded the point, coming in sight of the forts, they commenced an incessant firing, at the same time hoisting the American flag. So dense was the smoke and so continuous the firing, that little could be seen save a thick cloud of smoke, curling far above and around the fort; few sounds were heard but those of the deep-toned cannon, belching forth its emblems of destruction. In about thirty minutes the fort ceased, and we raised the Arabian ensign, returning a salute of twenty-seven guns. Immediately after our arrival, we were visited by several gentlemen

24

from the shore, who gave us a very cordial reception.
Our decks were well stored with fruits, provisions, &c.,
and there was a nearer resemblance to Fulton Market
than to a yankee man-of-war.   The Sultan had sent
off hundreds of fowls, droves of cattle and sheep, &c.,
all of which blending their croaking, bellowing, bleat-
ing and cackling, produced a jargon that might remind one of the "confusion of languages."

During the entire day we were surrounded with
boats, loaded with cakes, milk, butter, melons and
fruits, offered for sale.   And here it is but just that I
should say something of the honesty of the Arabs, in
their dealings among themselves, and also with
strangers.   When their articles were presented for
sale, the absence of money seemed no hindrance to
the purchase.   When told that we wished for their
articles but had no money, they were quite willing to
adopt the "credit system."   Dialogues like the following, frequently occurred.   "You want?"   Yes.
"You got no money?"   None.   "You pay by and
by, John?"   Yes.   "Take."   At their visit on the
following day, they would usually ask, "You got no
money to-day, John?"   No.   "You want bread,
butter, fruit, milk, cheese?   Take what you like."
The inhabitants of civilized society might learn some
important lessons of humanity and honesty from this
class of Arabians.

Capt. California, commander of the Arabian navy,
is one of the handsomest men that I ever saw; he
speaks excellent English.   At his visit on the 4th, he
brought some ten or fifteen divers with him.   These
divers, after having prepared a split stick, and fastened it upon the nose, to prevent the admission of water,

would sink and remain about two minutes under the vessel. They reported that the copper was nearly off, and brought up some of the loose sheets, and quantities of the sheathing, assuring us that there were large holes, filled with weeds and sun-fish.

Capt. California's son was with him, a lad of about 10 years of age; he exhibited clearly a praiseworthy sense of honor, so characteristic of the Arabians. He had brought his gun on board for the purpose of having it repaired; he wore a cartridge-box, containing twenty silver cases for powder, each case having a high-wrought silver cover. In addition to this, he wore an Arabian dirk, silver-mounted, very highly burnished, and worth, at least, fifty dollars. Lieut. Gordon proposed to fill his cases with powder in exchange for his dirk, for the purpose of testing his honesty. To this he immediately assented, drawing his dirk and presenting it. It was placed where he could take it, should he choose to do so, but he seemed satisfied with the exchange, notwithstanding the contrast of the respective values. It was then taken from his presence, and placed in the ward-room; of this he seemed to take no notice. At last, finding that he did not intend to regain his favorite weapon, it was produced, as he was about to leave the ship, and offered to him, but he refused to receive it. It was urged upon him, but he firmly refused to accept it, asserting that it had been bought and paid for, and that it would not be *right* to accept it. Finally, finding that all our efforts would prove ineffectual, his father took it and replaced it in his belt; at this his eyes filled with tears, and raising his hand and looking mournfully into his father's face, he said, " Allah knows that I don't want it." I could but think that there are many boys even in the United States, who *should* come within the reclaiming influence of our civil, literary and religious institutions, who might with much propriety emulate the example of this lad, though surrounded with the gloom of barbarism, and moral darkness of Mohammedanism.

During our stay, the young prince, son of the Sultan, was married, on which occasion the officers were invited to be present; a salute of seventeen guns was fired, which was responded to by the vessel in the harbor, and by the fort.

Muscat is a small city, containing about 10,000 inhabitants, situated at the head of Muscat Cove, and is surrounded on all sides but that bordering on the bay, by massive, craggy rocks, which rise from 800 to 1000 feet above the town. The streets are narrow, and the buildings do not exhibit much taste in their arrangement. The people are very cleanly in their persons and dress; the merchants are gentlemen of highly cultivated manners, and many of them were excellent scholars. The art of penmanship seemed to have received an unusual degree of attention; some of them wrote the most beautiful hand that I ever saw.

On the day following the wedding, the Sultan and his son, together with Capt. California and some of the principal men of the realm, came on board and honored us with a visit. He is a tall, spare man, apparently about 60 years of age. His dress was in accordance with Arabian customs. He appeared in a loose flowing gown, of black silk, with pantaloons of white linen, cut after the Turkish style, a vest of yellow satin; he wore also tasty sandals of superior workmanship, wrought with gold wire, and a neat turban upon his head, in imitation of the Turks. He addressed the officers with much politeness, though not the kind ordinarily taught in the northern seminary, where this branch is learned like arithmetic, geography or the languages, but it was the graceful politeness of simple nature, every movement and expression carrying with it the conviction that he felt all the friendship, kindness and benevolence that he expressed verbally. As he came on board we gave him a salute, while the Arabian colors were waving above him. He visited the various parts of the ship, examined all matters of interest, and afterward partook of refreshment in the cabin, prepared for the occasion. When he took leave of us, we gave an honorary salute, which was seconded by the frigates and forts.

On the next day we made preparations to sail. Notwithstanding the shattered state of the ship, the commander ventured an attempt to cross the sea of Arabia; accordingly on the 9th, we unmoored, and made ready for sea, after having concluded a commercial treaty with the Arabian government. The treaty secures a free trade between the two governments, for the term of one hundred years; this act promises much to the Arabian government, and may be the means of restoring them to the high and important position which they once sustained in relation to the neighboring nations of Asia and Africa. By a consistent course of political economy, they may yet regain their former strength and military prowess, as

24*

well as their previous attainments in science and the arts.

Our next place of destination was Bombay, in Hindostan. One morning during our passage, about midway between the two ports, probably 500 miles from the nearest point of land, a large flock of land birds visited the ship, such as owls, sparrows, black-birds &c.; they had been blown to sea, probably, by some severe gale of wind, and in their fatigue, were induced to alight wherever they could find a resting place. They perched themselves upon the rigging and various parts of the ship, and were exceedingly tame; they descended among the "messes," and it was with some difficulty that they were kept out of the dishes. They suffered themselves to be handled, would share our "mess" with us, and expressed their gratitude by singing happy strains, while seated on our hands, head, or shoulders. Some of them prolonged their stay with us for two or three days and then left, probably to perish at sea.

This occurrence developed some of the nobler characteristics of the sailor. Though he has a rough exterior, he has a heart keenly alive to the sufferings of his fellows, and even of the brute creation. Not a bird was injured, but were treated with great tenderness, and might have remained any length of time, a welcome guest, and shared his simple fare.

The commodore's cat, however, was not quite as kind, but caught one of the number. She was not permitted, by the more humane seamen, to retain her ill-gotten prey, but was robbed of it as soon as she could be secured. In the genuine spirit of tenderness and sincerity, a weight was attached to the victim and he was sunk deep in the sailor's grave, where so many lie entombed, whose bosoms were once warmed by the same overflowing sympathy that dictated this simple act of respect to a mere bird. Not so with the cat. Severe but suppressed murmurings were heard at the time, but no violence was offered. On the next morning diligent search was made for poor "tabitha," but it was in vain. It was conjectured that she had followed the murdered songster, though not with the same ceremony and respect that attended the former burial. The circumstance may seem trivial to the reader, but it is introduced to illustrate this important principle.

We arrived at Bombay after a delightful passage of twenty-one days, where we found our consort, the Enterprise. Our ship was immediately taken into the dry-dock, there to undergo thorough repairs.

Bombay is the western capital of British India, and contains about 220,000 inhabitants. The city is strongly fortified, and is surrounded by three deep ditches and the same number of strong, high walls, which are mounted with heavy artillery. There are many things in and about the city that would be exceedingly interesting to the attentive observer, though he might not select it as a permanent residence. An extensive plain lies in the rear of the city, which is used as the parade ground of the English soldiery; beyond this is a large town called the "Suburbs."

Bombay is one of several very populous cities of Hindostan. In point of population, it ranks next to China, and has been the theatre of many important events in the history of Asia. It has long been celebrated for its civilzation, and the richness of its articles of commerce. The soil is exceedingly fertile, and produces an abundance of sugar, cotton, indigo, opium and rice, the last of which forms the principal article of diet. In color, the people very much resemble the Africans, but in features are more European ; they are courteous and quite polished in their manners, and display much taste in their works of art.

Yet with all of their comparative intellectual culture, they are still accustomed to some of the most revolting practices of paganism. Even the burning of widows on the pyre of her husband, was practiced until 1830, when it was abolished by the British government. Nor has the influence of resident Europeans, now numbering about 50,000, been sufficient to radically change the popular feeling in reference to their cruel customs. The most revolting one now remaining, probably, is the self-torture consequent upon " losing caste." They are divided into four castes or classes ; these castes have certain rules by which they are respectively governed, and are not allowed to mingle with those of another class. As a penalty for the violation of any of these rules, the offender is spurned from society as unworthy of existence among his former associates. These outcasts are called *Pariahs*, and can be restored to the caste only by the most excruciating self-infliction.

While here I was shown one of these wretched victims of their degrading superstition. This individual is known to travelers as the " flower-pot-man," and is suffering the penalty of his disloyalty to his caste. I found him in an old hovel, situated at the termination of a spacious arch which leads from the street to the rear ; he was seated on a rude bench. His hair was white as snow, hanging around his cheeks and neck in long matted locks; his beard, which was twelve inches or more in length, was made to turn upward and adhere to his face, by white clay. His cheeks were hollow, his cheek bone remarkably prominent, and his eyes deeply sunken in their sockets; his dress consisted of a pair of tattered thin pants, that came down a little below his knees, and a thin, dirty mantle thrown over his shoulders and partly wrapped around his body. In his hand he held a flower-pot.

He had violated the principles of his religion, or in some way displeased the priest, and had presented himself before him for restoration, after having suffered the penalty which the priest might choose to impose. After mature deliberation it was decided that the term of *twenty-one* years might be sufficient time to expiate his crimes. Some terms have been considerably longer than this, depending upon the turpitude of the crime. He had already served fifteen years of his penance. The flesh of the arm had gradually perished, until but little remained save bone and withered muscle. His nails had grown to the length of a foot or more, and had assumed an ill-formed, spiral shape. It also sometimes occurs that the fleshy parts of the fingers become elongated, giving to the hand a very unnatural and revolting appearance.

The pot was made of willow, weighing about a pound and a half, and contained three kinds of sacred flowers,—the "rose," two or three small stalks of the "marigold," and a tuft of "ladies' delight." I requested our guide to ask him how he had contrived to sleep, and whether he had never let it fall. He informed me that at first he was obliged to employ boys, provided with long reeds, loaded with pointed metalic substances, to goad him whenever he slept so soundly as to suffer his arm to be depressed. After a short time, he was able to sleep and still retain the position of his arm. During the first two or three years, he felt much pain in that arm and side, which gradually diminished, resolving itself into the sensation which would naturally be produced by piercing those parts with needles; this slowly disappeared, and for some years he had been entirely destitute of pain, and even of sensation. It had been for some time immovably fixed in one position. These devotees are objects of charity, and not unfrequently amass considerable fortunes.

To those who are unacquainted with the Hindoos, this may seem too horrid to merit credence, but I can assure such, that *this* is a mere trifle, when compared with some of their schemes of torture. We know but little of the sacrifice and devotion of heathenism and false religion. The Christian might well emulate their adherence to their dogmas, and the cheerfulness with which they voluntarily endure the most excruciating tortures, for the vain purpose of appeasing the wrath of dumb idols.

When we remember that millions of our fellow men are suffering thousands of tortures, simply from a want of a knowledge of divine things; that they, by nature, are on an equality with those of the most favored climes; when we reflect also, that we owe all our superiority to the Bible, how vaguely do we estimate its value, and how little do we think of one of its plainest injunctions, which says,—"Go ye into all the world and preach the gospel to every creature!"

In the harbor of Bombay there is a remarkable island, called "Elephanti," which is regarded as one of the "seven wonders of the world;" it contains a cave which seems to have been cut out of solid stone. As one enters the cave, directly in front of the opening is the exact figure of an elephant of the usual size; there are, also, several other animals, together with human beings, all of which are cut from solid rock. Some of these were intended to represent kings and queens,—all beautifully sculptured, but have a very ancient appearance. We broke off some small pieces, such as hands, feet, &c., from the more remote parts of the cave, for preservation. At what period these were wrought or by whom, must ever remain a matter of speculation.

After a stay of some weeks at Bombay,—which time was spent in making necessary repairs,—we made preparations to sail; other guns had been substituted for those lost on the coast of Arabia, by a loan from the English Admiral, Sir Charles Macomber, and we were about in readiness to buffet the dangers of the raging ocean, or meet again a more ruthless foe. While on the eve of our departure, we discovered a vessel in the offing, coming into port; as she approached, we saw Arabian colors flying, and did not sail until after her arrival. In a short time a boat was sent along side, in which we recognized some of our Arabian friends, with whom we had formed so agreeable an acquaintance at Muscat. From them we learned that the Sultan had sent out a party of men, immediately after our departure, in search of the guns, anchors, cables, &c., which were sunk at the place of disaster. They had succeeded in grappling them and the vessel was chartered to restore them to us. Our borrowed ones were soon dismounted, and those that had been our companions in trouble, and had lain in a deep coral bed where unknown treasures have long been entombed, were placed in their former stations, where they soon gave but little evidence of having been so long imbedded beneath the wave. My feeble pen can not do justice to this noble-minded Sultan, in consideration of his generosity toward us while in distress. We could but mark the contrast between our treatment while on the reef, by the wanderers of the desert, and that of the Sultan at Muscat.

After leaving Bombay, we sailed down the eastern coast of Hindostan, bound to Ceylon, thence through the East Indies. This part of our cruise was not as eventful as the preceding had been, but not without interest. Nor indeed can it be, to the attentive observer of creation's wonders, who can appreciate the wildly-grand, the magnificent and sublime. The ocean presents these in their ever-varying forms. The wild grows wilder, the sublime becomes awful, the terrific quickly changes to more terrible and overwhelming, as nature puts on her wilder aspects, or is quietly lulled to rest, the beautiful softening in the lovely, as the tempests cease their rude blasts, and threatening clouds disappear. The monsters of the deep are ever around, raising their huge sides above the restless surface, regardless of these innovators of their vast domain.

## SAILOR INFLUENCE.

Among seamen, as in all classes of society, may be found a diversity of circumstances and characters. While all possess some of the more striking characteristics, the effects produced upon the inhabitants of the uncivilized parts of the world are widely dissimilar. The gloom of heathenism may be made more visible and appalling by vicious seamen who are mingling with them as representatives of civilization, or a gleam of light and hope may be radiated by the more virtuous. The natives may be exasperated and prejudiced more and more against all innovators, or the barriers may be removed and the influences of Christianity be disseminated, by an association and intercourse with our less favored fellow men. The two classes are already in the field, whose influences are, and must be, antagonistic. The elevation of seamen is among the cardinal means of pouring light into the dark portions of the earth.

This may be more distinctly seen in intercourse with the natives of the Lagoon Islands. They had been visited by French whalemen, who had abused their confidence, and trampled upon their rights. Natural results followed; they were incensed against all foreigners, and had leagued themselves to murder such as should visit them.

While engaged in the Expedition we had occasion to visit these islands, and necessarily encountered these difficulties. When we arrived off these isles, the different vessels were stationed at given points, and

25

commenced measuring base lines by means of guns fired from each station in succession, noting the time between the flash and report. The natives, hearing our guns, came down to the beach and watched our movements with apparent interest and concern. Having finished our admeasurements, obtained the necessary angles by the sextant, the boats were lowered and we attempted to land; the natives, however, forbade this, and by signs indicated their desire for our departure. We continued to approach slowly, at the same time throwing presents to them; these were thrown back to us, refusing to receive any thing from us. Some of them threw stones into the water, very much bespattering us, which we thought proper to bear patiently. The fact that we did not retaliate, seemed to convince them that we were intimidated, and they commenced throwing stones into our boats, mistaking our forbearance for fear. One of our number, who was injured by one of these stones, raised a musket and discharged a quantity of mustard-seed shot among them; the distance was so great that it simply produced a smarting sensation, without penetrating the surface. No sooner was the musket discharged than the whole party began jumping in the most ludicrous manner, talking, picking and rubbing themselves, as if they had been suddenly attacked with some annoying cutaneous disease. They moved off in company up the beach, where they seated themselves and indulged in an unintelligible jargon. We were soon after ordered on board, as we did not choose to land unless it could be effected peaceably. It was decided to visit another of the same group lying near, which we did on our return to the ship. Our object was to reconcile them to us if possible. While we were considering our adventure, one of our number volunteered to visit the natives of the island to which we were destined, singly, and negotiate conditions of peace, as he was acquainted with their language, having visited the island on former occasions.

These islands are of a coral formation, and as there are many matters of interest, it may not be amiss, briefly, to advert to them. Coral is the production of a very minute animalcule; though invisible of itself, its constructure is of astonishing magnitude. It may give the reader some vague idea of the vastness of this little creature's operations to say that we sounded, or attempted to, within a few yards of the reef, sinking the lead eleven hundred fathoms, ( 6600 feet ) but did not find bottom; these little invisibles had reared their fabric to this surprising height, and how much below that, formed the foundation, I am unable to determine. This stupendous wall is about one half a mile in thickness, is built in a circular form, the inside resembling a huge chimney; this has a diameter of some eight or ten miles, while others are somewhat larger. The land describes a circle, which forms around the inner edge of the wall about one fourth of a mile, on some of them, but much less on the major part of them. At first you land on the coral that is submerged at all times for some distance in from the outer edge; then succeeds a part of the reef that is above the surface during a portion of the time; afterward a sand beach, then shrubs, trees, bearing various tropical fruits, then shrubs again as one approaches the water's edge of the lagoon in the centre. This lagoon occupies the greater part of the space contained be-

tween the visible portion of the coral as we approach
this singularly formed island, and sends up its waves
towards those that are rolling upon the beach from
the surrounding ocean.  By this process substances
have been thrown up by opposite forces, forming a
perimeter of land, so that the island is surrounded by
water externally and *internally.* This stupendous
*basin* contains salt water, but whether in direct communication with the ocean, can not be ascertained.
We were unable to find a bottom, though we sank
our lead some five or six hundred fathoms.  Near the
inner shore of this lagoon, an abundance of the pearl
oyster is found, which are sought for the beautiful
pearls taken from them.

A rather novel incident occurred while we were on
this island, which it may not be inappropriate to my
design in delineating characters.  As the man approached the shore, it was evident that the natives
did not wish for any intercourse.  He had provided
himself with a variety of articles to serve as presents,
threw himself into the surge, and was carried, by one
of the rollers which are continually breaking on shore,
safely to the reef.  As he reached the reef, he was in
the immediate vicinity of the natives, who began to
approach, making various signs by holding their
hands over their heads, and afterward bringing them
behind them.  He attempted to communicate with
them, but was not understood, and retreated, assuring
us that they were hostile, and that it would be useless to attempt to make peace with them.  I did not
like the idea of thus relinquishing our plan, and immediately volunteered to make an effort myself.  I

took a bag of old iron hoop which I had broken into pieces of some two or three inches in length, knowing that iron was of much value here; as soon as I plunged into the w· ter, the natives commenced throwing stones, but did me no injury, and I was soon standing erect upon the island. I immediately approached them; they seemed satisfied that I was not afraid of them, and began to repeat their signs. I knew not, nor did I much care what their gestures were intended for, but imitated their manoeuvres, meaning war or peace, as they might choose to construe it. They gazed at me a moment and then brought their hands behind them, which I followed, at the same time slowly advancing toward them. As they receded before my advance, they came to a natural wall of coral, situated about one fourth of a mile from the beach, in which there was a small opening. This wall extended along this side of the island, and in front of the town, and was about three and a half feet in height. At this place they seemed inclined to enter into a parley with me, the chief placing the men, some on one, and some on the other side of the pass, behind the wall; some were armed with bows and arrows, stationed in the front of the opening, while the chief posted himself at the pass.

He was an old grey-bearded man, and had a very venerable appearance; he held his spear in his left hand, while the right was presented toward the iron which I held before him; he seemed disinclined to change his position, while I advanced, offering him the iron. As soon as his finger came in contact with it he suddenly withdrew it, as if severely burned by

25*

it. At length, after various attempts, he ventured to receive it, tasting, smelling, and rubbing it, for the purpose of judging of its quality. When he saw that it was good iron, he seemed very much pleased, and approaching me, he placed his right arm around my neck, holding his spear in the other. Wishing to reciprocate his affection, I placed my left arm around his neck; he commenced drawing me toward him until our faces were nearly in contact; inferring that he was about to kiss me, I prepared for such an event. Not certainly knowing his intentions, I grasped my sheath knife, knowing that if his embrace should prove too cordial, I could easily disengage myself. He then brought our noses in contact, rubbing his three times across mine. After releasing me, he danced about with much apparent happiness. But the worst was not over; the same ceremony was to be performed with the entire party, who were generally besmeared with cocoa-nut oil and charcoal, and I found myself thoroughly bedaubed by their filthy persons.

I afterward took the chief by the hand and led him down toward the boat, but met the Commodore, with all of the men save two left in each boat, who were coming up to ascertain the result of our interview. Afterward this ceremony was repeated, until our company, from the Commodore to the boys, effected a reconciliation with these natives, at the close of which we were nearly as black as the natives themselves. They then escorted us up to their houses, assisted us in collecting all the specimens in natural history that could be found on the island. They gave us fish and every thing that could convince us of their friendship, and requested us to invite other white men to visit them. We made trifling presents to the whole number, completly overcoming their prejudice against all white men. From this is easily seen the importance of having virtuous sailors, to go into all parts of the world to meet and counteract the pernicious influences of too large a portion of our 2,000,000 of seamen, who are scattering the seeds of vice and licentiousness in the dark portions of the earth. These effects, to be fully appreciated, must be witnessed; the intoxicated sailor should be traced as he mingles with the benighted pagan, regardless of all the restraints of that Christianity under which he has been nurtured, and which, to the mind of the pagan, he represents. Such sad consequences can only be averted by counter efforts from the same *Omnipresent* source; that as Jesus, the Lamb of God, assumed the title and some of the characteristics of the lion (" the lion of the tribe of Judah,") to be able to meet the "roaring lion that goeth about, seeking whom he may devour," so the sailor of Zion must meet those in the service of Satan, and establish the superiority of the kingdom of grace over that of the prince of darkness.

Other unfavorable results, affecting seamen and the natives of other climes, are produced by a custom which prevails far too extensively. I refer to an unwarranted sailing on the Sabbath. Perhaps no transgression of equal magnitude is committed with so little remorse of conscience, as the custom of sailing from port on the Sabbath. The excuses which are urged to hush the voice of conscience, and to oppose such as present scriptural objections to this course, are wholly selfish, and consequently futile; such practices must necessarily be a violation of the plainest requisitions of God, and must entail upon the transgressor the penalties threatened against such disregard of divine requirements.

By the way of illustration of natural consequences, I insert a brief description of three attempts to get under way during a voyage of eight months. Some may have sailed without any regard to these obligations, and apparently may have been successful, yet there may generally have been a connection between disasters and an improper time of sailing. I record the events just as they transpired, and leave the reader to make his own conclusions. The incidents to which I refer, occurred on board the bark Southerner of Boston. At the commencement of these singular providences, we were lying at Lisbon.

At twelve o'clock on Saturday night, we were called to get under way. This was displeasing to myself and to many on board. It was painful to us to commence the holy Sabbath under such circumstances, and we could but feel that it was not only displeasing to God, but that nothing was really gained in a temporal view. A train of circumstances followed each other in quick succession, which exemplified the futility of an attempt to wholly disregard the established laws of the Creator.

The windlass was manned and we began to heave up our anchor just as the Sabbath commenced, apparently to devote to secular purposes every moment of

a day designed for more sacred employments; when
it was within about six fathoms of the surface, the
chain "surged" upon the windlass and sank again
to the botton and became entangled with the cable of
a Portuguese brig, lying near us. With the greatest
difficulty, after nearly an hour of incessant effort, we
succeeded in getting the anchor above the water, and
at about 4 o'clock, A. M., we had it in its proper place,
—having labored four hours with all our strength to
perform what might ordinarily have been accomplished in thirty minutes. Having "hove short," we set
the top sails and returned to the windlass, ready to
get the anchor, but scarcely was it in motion, before
the chain again surged, and sixty fathoms of cable
ran out like lightning. At 10 o'clock of the same
day we got under way, but the wind soon died away
and we were unable to proceed. We drifted about
five miles, when we again anchored, where we lay
until the following morning. On the next morning
we again attempted to sail, but it soon commenced to
rain rapidly, while the deep-toned thunder was heard
above and around us, so that our departure was considerably delayed. During the forenoon the word
" up anchor " was given, but before the order could
be obeyed, we were reminded of the danger which
might attend it; a dense black cloud was seen rolling
in from the sea with a threatening aspect; we were
satisfied that it would be madness to leave our moorings before the squall should have passed, and immediately made preparations to meet its fury. I never
before saw a storm advance in such awful majesty;
the forked lightning glared in startling wildness as it

leaped, unshackled, from cloud to cloud, now sending a broad, bold sheet of livid fire across the blackening vault of heaven, rendering the succeeding blackness far more visible; now shooting *upward*, as cloud over-hung cloud; and now dashing franticly to the earth, leaving a pale, quivering light behind, to mark its zig-zag course. The scene was awfully grand; the sub-lime was deepened into the terrible, and the quickly succeeding flashes were as if element warred with element, and contending foemen rushed to the deadly conflict. The ship shook like the tempest-beaten leaf, as the deafening thunder rolled and muttered around us, and spoke in tones that could not easily be mis-understood.

The mate was standing on the quarter deck as the storm approached, leaning upon the iron railing, when he received a violent electric shock, which left his right arm strengthless. The storm now burst upon us in all its fury, and the waters foamed and dashed on every side of us. A shower of huge hail stones was dashed upon the deck in the strength of the tem-pest, while the ceaseless howlings of the wind through the shrouds and spars, added to the terrors of the scene. We rode in safety through this tempest, how-ever, without any very serious incidents.

When the storm was over, we made ready to set sail; at this time two brigs, whose masters could not consent to sail on the Sabbath, now came down from the city, and passing us, went out without any diffi-culty. Just as we had nearly reached the bar at the mouth of the Tagus, the wind left us and the flood tide began to set in, and our only alternative was to go back to our anchorage in the harbor, to anchor until the wind and tide should again favor us. We were here at anchor about 12 o'clock, within one mile from the place that we had left on the preceding morning. We once more weighed anchor with the utmost difficulty, while no one could account for such a series of disasters, though all seemed satisfied that there was something peculiarly mysterious. As the anchor arose to the surface it was ascertained that it had become attached to a broken one, which had been lost or abandoned previously. After excessive toil, we succeeded in getting all things in readiness, and at sunset we sailed out, bound to sea.

On the 1st of November, the ship came to an anchor at the quarantine ground, in the bay of Rio Janeiro; our arrival was on Saturday, and we had hoped that the incidents at Lisbon might prove effectual; that the lesson there learned, might prevent our captain from making a second attempt to violate the sanctity of the Sabbath. Yet, early on Sabbath morning, as on the former occasion, we were called from our slumbers, to get under way. I could but feel surprised and grieved, that the captain would be so utterly reckless in this matter. I at that time remarked to the crew, that in my opinion God would punish him for his impiety, previous to the expiration of the voyage. We got under way without the least trouble at this time, and ran up to the other shipping. The harbor master came along side and gave us directions where to anchor. In getting to our anchorage we were obliged to pass between several other vessels. While passing some of the last, the captain

was giving his orders with an air of much self-confi-
dence, apparently cherishing the idea that he was
able to contend successfully with his God, and trample
upon his laws with impunity.  He seemed very much
inclined to hazard the consequences, but a "haughty
spirit goeth before a fall."  While he was exhibiting
his seamanship, and working his vessel with much
skill among the other shipping, the end of our main
yard came in contact with the fore-top-gallant stay of
the beautiful bark Daniel Webster, of Boston, carrying away her fore and main-top-gallant masts, beside
doing other very serious damage.  This misfortune
was somewhat enhanced by the circumstance that the
injuries could be repaired in this place, only with
much difficulty.

We remained here for some few weeks, and after
completing our arrangements, we were again destined
to witness the exemplification of the relations of transgression and natural results.  On the first Sabbath in
December, the captain made his third attempt to des-
ecrate the day by leaving port unnecessarily.  Our
work was accomplished in season to have left some
time previous.  A portion of the preceding day was
spent in scenes of amusements, and it could but be
inferred that this day was deliberately selected, but
for what purpose I leave the reader to form his own
opinions.  The order was given to get under way,
but this was instantly prevented by a most singular
circumstance; no sooner was the order given to "man
the windlass," than the captain was suddenly surprised by a violent attack, the cause of which could
not be satisfactorily accounted for.  A boat was sent

to the shore with all despatch, to obtain a physician.
On his arrival, he was unable to divine this attack,
or, indeed, to decide in regard to its nature. Its severity, however, did not long continue, yet before we
were able to leave, a strong easterly wind commenced
blowing, which afterward prevented our departure.
In consequence of this, we were detained here until
the 12th of the month, anxiously waiting for an opportunity to escape from a place which seemed almost
identified with disaster.

After the change of the wind, we made ready to
leave the harbor. This occasion was fraught with
incidents of a most thrilling nature. Judgment and
mercy were most singularly blended, and while we
were filled with awe and almost overwhelmed with
our peculiarly hazardous situation, we could but recognize the merciful hand of Him who " commandeth
and raiseth the stormy winds, and lifteth up the waves
thereof;—who maketh the storm a calm, so that the
waves thereof are still." Having waited for a considerable time for the officer to bring the countersign,
without which no ship could pass Santa Cruz, the
captain decided to go on shore in quest of him, as he
was anxious to improve the ebb tide and land breeze,
which blows in this place during only four hours in
the morning. After our arrival at Fort Glorio, we
ascertained that the officer had gone among the shipping, and it was not until we had followed him from
ship to ship, that we at last met him along side of our
own vessel. He arrived about 7 o'clock, A. M., after
which we weighed our anchor preparatory to the welcome departure. Before we had made any considera-

26

ble progress the wind died away, and we drifted for
about one half mile in this fine harbor.  As we passed
along, we saw that we were in danger of coming in
contact with a brig which was anchored near us.
Our only means of avoiding this collision was to anchor again, as the ship was now wholly unmanageable.  At this time the Josephine, of New York, swept
swiftly by, borne along by the current, and was
carried by several vessels, toward the Sugar-Loaf, a
huge rock that stands at the entrance of the bay, on
the southern shore.  As she passed along, a favoring
wind gradually sprang up, while she and several
other vessels which had remained with us windbound,
passed out of the harbor with a fine breeze, leaving
us behind.

About 10 o'clock, we again weighed anchor and
made an attempt to follow them.  At the place where
we lay there was not sufficient wind to fill the sails,
in consequence of high eminences which intercepted
the land-breeze which was then blowing briskly within one-fourth of a mile of us.  A boat, well manned,
had already been ordered out to tow us along, but
they were not able to counteract the strength of the
current; we were carried along rapidly, notwithstanding all efforts to give the ship a different direction.
We were fearfully nearing a group of rocks, upon
which the Brazilians had erected a strong fortification, known as "Square Fort," from the peculiarity
of its form.  The Sugar-Loaf was towering high
above the clouds, and from the peculiarity of our position, it was impossible to have a current of wind
which could serve us at this important juncture.

There were, indeed, occasional gusts, sweeping down the sides of the mountain, fitful in their occurrence and irregular in their direction, while the current, which was rushing with much force between the rock and land, was rapidly sweeping us on toward the rocks. The officers and men were whirling the yards to catch every breath of air that might occasionally favor us in our critical position. Yet, with all the efforts of those on board, together with the most vigorous efforts of the oarsmen, we were still drifting on to apparent destruction. The boat was now ordered along side, and we anchored as soon as possible, but here again we failed; the ship continued to drag her anchor among the rocks, while the cable was " veered away," as long as a fathom remained. She at last swung around to the anchor, and her stern was not twenty-five feet from the rocks! At this time, very fortunately for us, and as it might seem, providentially, the steamer Brazilia was passing us, on her return from Montevideo; the captain took his trumpet and hailed her, requesting her commander to come to our rescue, but with an utter disregard of our perilous situation—unlike the majority of commanders—he refused, and directed us to a government boat that had just passed us. That boat, however, had already seen our distress, and had put about for the purpose of coming to our relief. The officers at the fort were anxiously watching us, and when they saw the Brazilia passing by without rendering necessary assistance, the stern voice of the commander thundered through a huge trumpet, repeating the request of Capt. Hallet, but this was also disregarded. We

were still drifting fearfully along toward these shelving, craggy rocks, and a heavy sea was rolling in with
tremendous force, while that loud, monotonous and
dismal roar with which every sailor is acquainted,
who has been where the surf breaks on an iron-bound
shore, and which has been the sad requiem of many a
sailor, was deepening the gloom and anxiety which
our situation naturally produced.  As the sea retired,
we could distinctly see the sharp, ragged shelf of
rocks, projecting from the main body of the ledge,
against which the sea was dashing and foaming furiously, sending up a thick, humid spray, and against
which, in all human probability, we were to be dashed.

The officers and soldiers of the fort had seen the
crash of many a noble vessel in the same spot; had
seen plank part from plank, massive cordage rent
asunder like the frail spider's web; the ship disman-
tled, crushed as a thing of naught, and perchance, the
last struggles of ill-fated crews, as they contended
against the might of overwhelming waves.  As they
saw the noble ship floating on to inevitable destruction, they seemed to appreciate our feelings and sym-
pathize with us while in our distress.

No sooner did the commander see his orders disregarded, than he stepped from the embrasure and a
stream of smoke and flame burst from a piece of
heavy artillery, while the deep-toned thunderings
came booming over the waters, a signal that could
not be misinterpreted.  It had a magical effect upon
the seamen; the wheels stopped instantly, and she
returned to us with all possible speed.  Another moment, and the standard of Brazil fell " a' half mast,"

another gun thundered from the port, and the news of a ship in distress flew with that sound in every part of the harbor. Fort Gloria, a fortification that stands on the same side with the city, passed the signal by the discharge of artillery, and, "half masted" her colors, while fort Santa Cruz hurried along the mandate by a similar course. This was the work of a moment, but in that time the ship had approached so near the rock that she could swing to the current no more. I felt that it was a time that the sailor must act the man. We had done all that we could do, and much alarm was manifested on board. The mate was very much excited and called to the captain to observe the rapid progress which he supposed the ship was making toward the rocks. I saw the tendency of such remarks to disconcert the entire crew, and remonstrated with him, assuring him that in my opinion he was mistaken in reference to our progress, and spoke encouragingly of our rescue. By this time a boat from the steamer was under our bows, and I passed a hawser into it; she hurried back to the boat, and in one half minute the steamer was under, way. At the same moment, a boat filled with men from the government boat, came along side, and assisted in manning the windlass, and if ever I sang "yeo heave ho" at the top of my voice, it was at this moment. The steamer soon drew the hawser taught, and our ship, which had been acquiring such a fearful proximity to that disastrous spot, was moving slowly away, and in fifteen minutes we were riding safely at anchor, one mile from the scene of danger. The colors were brought again to the mast head, an-

26*

nouncing to thousands of anxious spectators, that the
ship was safe. The sullen roar of the surf had died
gradually away, and we were now permitted to indulge in gratitude for our almost miraculous deliverance.

At the time that the boat took us in tow, we were
only about ten feet from the rock, and the mighty
swelling of the waves was lifting us some six or
eight feet, and had we struck a projection, we must
have been dashed in pieces, and sunk to that deep
bed where so many had been plunged in the hour of
extremity. The ship was loaded very deep, and but
a few moments could have elapsed after the first concussion, before she would have sunk, and the circling
waves of the accompanying vortex would have closed
sadly over us, and another crew would have been
carried by the strength of the current among those
fearful rocks, which are as a mighty monument of the
multitude who sleep beneath those troubled waters.

We lay at anchor until the next morning, at which
time we succeeded in getting out, after an unnecessary
detention of about two weeks, and a wonderful escape
from a watery grave.

I am not disposed to indulge in any thing like superstition in reference to this eventful voyage, but
simply give the facts as they occurred. I know that
it is often affirmed that seamen are inclined to a sentiment of marvelousness, which predisposes them to a
firm belief in supernatural agencies. I will admit that
this may be true to some extent; probably the nature
of the profession may tend to the production of such
a peculiarity. These, above all other men, " see God's

wonders in the deep," and are naturally more impressed with his more immediate agency in the affairs of
men. Disclaiming all "heathen notions," I can but
adopt the language of a commander on a similar occasion after the *wreck* of his vessel, and "believe
that there was a connection between the result, and
sailing on the Sabbath." He who has said " *Remember* the Sabbath day to *keep it holy*," and affixed penalties to all transgression, will not be unmindful of
such flagrant disregard of his righteous requirements.
He who commanded the Israelite to be put to death,
who had offended his Maker by " picking sticks on
the Sabbath day;" he who followed the offending
Egyptians and engulfed them in the Red Sea, of
whom it was said, "he hath triumphed gloriously;
the horse and his rider hath he thrown into the sea,"
will not now "let the wicked go unpunished," though
thousands of years may have passed away since the
command was issued, and the summary punishment
was inflicted.

Again,—to say nothing of its relations to the great
law of Eternal justice,—it has other important bearings, to which I will briefly advert. From the established relation of things, and from the example of
nature's great Architect, there is ample evidence that
periodic rest is designed for "man and beast." Indeed, were inspiration silent upon this point, we
might learn from our own constitutions, that such an
arrangement is *absolutely necessary*. This privilege,
landsmen claim, not as a moral right alone, but as a
*natural* right. Indeed, all experiments which have
related only to secular economy, have established the
propriety of the divine command.

Seamen, as a class, labor a much greater proportion of the time than the great mass of men, and for a compensation widely disproportioned to the amount of labor performed, and the hazards endured. It has been justly remarked that "There are no Sabbaths or nights on the ocean." The sailor has no time in which he can feel perfectly exempt from care and toil. This often follows from the nature of his employment; while at sea, he is liable at any moment to be called to the post of duty, though exhausted nature may require rest. In the gale, the efforts of all on board are requisite. All necessary assistance, under such circumstances, the sailor renders cheerfully. The safety of human life, and the faithful discharge of the obligation entrusted to him, require such a sacrifice at his hands.

To this necessary relation of things, is attributable, probably, the premature death of a large portion of seamen. A careful investigation of facts has resulted in the conclusion, that in no branch of business is there so great a mortality as in this,—not even in the army. Nor is this referable alone to losses by shipwreck, when hundreds sink into one common grave. However great this may be, it forms but an inconsiderable item in the great result. Excessive and long-continued labor, exposure to the ever-varying vicissitudes of climate, with various other improprieties, are the active agents of this sad destruction. It is a pleasing consideration that some of these evils are removed by the genius of reform, which is effecting the more prominent enterprises of the day. It can not be doubted but that the incipient stages of malignant

disease are seen in, and are traceable to improperly constructed forecastles. Many of them, in former times
—and too many still exist—were dark, damp and
confined, in which poisonous exhalations could escape
only with much difficulty, but remained to be inhaled
by the large number who are crowded into them, until insinuating diseases are immovably fixed. Were
it not for the comparative exemption of the luxuries
of more fashionable life, and their active habits, &c.,
probably a far greater number would fall early victims to these imprudences.

While, therefore, there are so many active agencies
that are calculated in their nature to make sad inroads
into the constitution, and people that spacious receptacle of ocean's sons, it is lamentable that men should
conspire to increase unnecessarily these causes of untimely dissolution, by wresting unjustly a portion of
time that inalienably belongs to every freeman.

It is not contended that a vessel should *never* sail
on the Sabbath; this would be impracticable. It is
against *leaving* port designedly on that day, that these
remarks are urged. All that is asked, is, that the
customs by which seamen are governed should corres-
pond to those of landsmen; in other words, that men
shall have but *one* code of morality, whether on the
ocean or on shore. No class of men, ordinarily, select
the Sabbath as an appropriate day to commence a
journey, or engage in any important enterprise upon
the land, yet those who would *shrink in horror* from
such a palpable outrage, do not hesitate to commence
the most hazardous enterprises by sailing on this
day, professedly dear to them while associated with,

and exposed to the gaze of their fellows. This is altogether irreconcilable with consistency of character.

While in mid ocean, there can be no doubt, probably, of the propr.ety of *continuing* the voyage. It is doubtful whether there could be any material diminution of labor, should the attempt be made. They have simply to be wafted on, by the favoring breezes of heaven, unattended by the ordinary labors of leaving or arriving at port. During the longer voyages, which must necessarily require several Sabbaths, there may not, indeed, be the necessity for additional seasons of rest; such voyages are not usually attended with any considerable amount of fatigue in the discharge of the ordinary duties on ship-board.

It is not my wish to produce a spirit of insubordination, or even that of dissatisfaction, only so far as good will result from it, among those who have selected a marine life, yet a reform is really demanded. The spirit of the age in which we live requires it. Reform is the watch-word, and society must feel its influence to its remotest limit. Men are asserting their *manhood*, and while the genius of true liberty survives, individual aggression can not long survive. The power of popular feeling will be felt, and ship owners and masters will be obliged to grant to seamen some of the privileges which they claim for themselves. More especially will this be true, when the unjust requsition conflicts with the claims of *conscience*. Enlightened men will not long submit to such tyrannical injustice. As the great mass becomes more and more acquainted with the grievances of seamen; more and more interested in their welfare, a radical change must be effected. Encouraged by popular sympathy the sailor can assert his natural right, and such proceedings, though sanctioned by those occupying important positions in society, must soon become comparatively rare.

When seamen shall feel their relative importance in the great operations of the country, and indeed of the world, when they shall recover in a measure from the effects of their former degradation, it will be clearly seen that there are freemen alike in the forecastle and the cabin, each having their appropriate duties and spheres of action.

Indeed, this is the only healthful feeling that can exist. The interests of the two great classes,—officers and seamen,—are identified, and when the harmony of this relation is marred, disastrous consequences immediately follow. Yet when this friendly relation can not exist without a sacrifice of principle; when necessary discipline is attained, or power ensured only be a degradation of the governed; when his rights as a social and accountable being are wrested from him, a recourse to the only alternative may be justifiable. The association of 2,000,000 of seamen, inspired by a love of republicanism, enlightened, and acting in harmonious concert, may effect a revolution which shall distinctly mark the age in which it occurs, as an era in the history of the marine enterprise.

The indications of the present age are exceedingly cheering in this respect. The first dawnings of a brighter day for the sons of the ocean are already visible, and we dare predict, that the time is not far distant, when some of their fondly-cherished hopes

will be realized; when the sacred endearments of social life, when family ties will not be riven; when the
exercises of the sanctuary will not be abridged for the
purpose of engaging in the pressing duties of the departure, and exchanging the melody of songs of praise
for the boisterous confusion and hilarity of the ship.

In this change there will necessarily be less of the
compulsory features, less apparent necessity to be removed from the more endeared relations of life,—those
influences which soften the asperities of our nature
and make men wiser and happier; less of the feeling
of dependence and degradation which attends one
when he feels that he must implicitly obey the will
of another, and less of the recklessness and vice
which materially influences such as feel that they
have but little to lose, and can aspire to nothing beyond present attainments.

# REFLECTIONS.

## THE MURDERS AT MALOLO.

Various reports have been circulated through the community, relative to the causes which led to this most painfully afflictive event, and I feel myself called upon as an act of justice to the gallant dead, to give the sad details, and leave a candid community to make candid inferences. I am still more impressed with a sense of duty in this matter, since some imputations have been urged, perhaps by evil disposed persons, in reference to the official character of Mr. Underwood.

Lieut. J. A. Underwood was a citizen of Pawtucket, Mass.; his parents and family connections rank with the first society of the state. At an early period in life, he was distinguished for a brilliancy of intellect, a generosity and manliness of character, combined with a high sense of honor, which won the respect of, and endeared him to, all with whom he was associated. He entered the navy when he had arrived at manhood, and distinguished himself there by his gentlemanly deportment; the rapidity with which he ac-

27

quired a knowledge of his profession, together with his good sense and coolness in the various emergencies incident upon the life of the sailor, gave him the confidence of those around him, as well as of the Hon. D. Webster, and others of his friends, who were instrumental in securing his appointment. In 1838 he was married to the beautiful and accomplished daughter of Dr. J. E. Stevens of Boston, and left the object of his affections in a few days after his union, to participate in the eventful incidents of this cruise, which to him proved to be his last, long voyage. At this time he ranked as passed midshipman; early in the cruise he was promoted to that of lieutenant, and was zealous, active and efficient in that capacity, and his services were very valuable in the various departments of scientific research.

I have penned this obituary notice of him, not so much as a memoir, but for the purpose of introducing him to the public as he was, and by the light of his own character, to eradicate imputations that may have gained some credence in the community.

We left the ship, then lying at Sandal-Wood Bay, on the 16th of July, 1840, with six days' provisions in the boat, with orders to join the brig and schooner at Malolo, on the 22d, three boats in company,—the Leopard, under Lieut. Underwood, the launch of the Peacock, Lieut. George F. Emmons, and the 2d cutter of the Vincennes, Lieut. Alden. On the evening of the 22d, the boats of the Vincennes arrived at the island; the brig and schooner were not in sight at that time. We landed at the Island of Great Malolo, called by them, Malolo Laib—ascended some of the hills, to look for the vessels. At noon we finished our stock

of provisions, and were obliged to retire that night sup-
perless. On the morning of the eventful 24th, we
were joined by Lieut. Emmons, from whom we had
been separated three days, who was also without provisions. It was thought advisable to venture up to
the town for provisions, though we regarded it as hazardous; it devolved upon Lieut. U. and his crew to
perform this perilous duty, as his boat was the smallest. That morning Mr. U. and myself procured the
hostage, knowing that while we retained him there
could be no danger. When we succeeded in getting
off the reef, we left the hostage in the charge of two
seamen, in whose care he was perfectly safe. We
then landed with a sufficient force to have repulsed
the armies of the entire island, had we obeyed the orders of our officers. We numbered eleven men on
shore, armed with four rifles and three pistols, at the
time of the attack. Here the reader may see the true
cause of the disastrous events which have made many,
many a heart to bleed from wounds which time can
never fully heal.

Some of the prominent causes of the disaster were,—
First, the want of provisions, which rendered it necessary that we should go on shore;—Secondly, the over-
sight of Mr. Alden, in permitting the hostage to escape
from his boat, after he had taken him from those with
whom Mr. Underwood had entrusted him;—and Lastly, the want of judgment and presence of mind on the
part of some of the men who were on shore; this is attributable to the suddenness of the attack, and the vast
superiority in point of numbers. Mr. Underwood's first
order was, "Keep together men, we can fight our way
to the boat." Had this order been obeyed, we might

have repulsed them until the boats could have come to our rescue.

There was one other circumstance which had much to do with this sad adventure; I refer to the fact that we had not a sufficient number of weapons to furnish all of our men. When we left the ship, we had a rifle, a cutlass and a pistol each, but the last time that we were with the Brig Porpoise, the cutlases, pistols, and more than half of the rifles were taken from the boat. By whose order, or for what purpose this was done, I am not prepared to say. I remonstrated by every argument that I could urge against it, and I well recollect that it was repugnant to the wishes and feelings of Mr. Underwood; I remember, however, that he said it was the order, because they were getting rusty in the boat. The men that had no weapons started for the boat first, and this had its influence upon those who were supplied. John Dunnock and John McKean, were the only men beside the officers and myself, who fired, and neither of those attempted to reload. I observed William J. Lester, a Virginian who carried the box of trade, in an encounter with some of the natives, fighting them as best he could, as he was without weapons. I was knocked down, and as I looked for him when I arose, he had disappeared; whether he had escaped, or had been slain, I could not then determine, but afterward learned that he succeeded in reaching the boat.

These are the facts relative to the murder of the officers, as I learned them from sad experience. Here I leave the subject so far as Mr. Underwood is concerned, and ask the reader to make his own inferences. It was an event in which I felt a deep interest, and shared largely in its perils. I felt, in the loss of Mr. Underwood, that I had lost a most valuable friend, and one for whom I felt all the strength of attachment that a sailor can feel, and while I regret that the tongue of slander or " green-eyed " envy should assail the reputation of a friend, it gives me pleasure to clearly disprove all that has been urged against an officer, whose real merits the nation will never be able to appreciate.

Mr. Henry was an officer of much merit, and was esteemed in the squadron; he possessed a greater share of the esteem of the crews than any other midshipman. In addition to personal beauty, he was possessed of an amiability of disposition and gentlemanly carriage, which made him a peculiar favorite, for the sailor always loves the *gentleman*. Nature had endowed him with the necessary qualifications for an officer, and had his life been spared, in my estimation, he would have been one of the brightest ornaments in the American navy. What an exemplification of the truthfulness of the remark of the poet, that " Death loves a shining mark ! "

The sentiments which I entertained for Mr. Henry are contained in the following stanzas, which were written while I was recovering from my wounds, and presented to the Commodore. I insert them, not as a specimen of poetry, but as a testimony to the talents and worth of the young officer. " He was the only son of his mother, and she was a widow,"—a sister of Commodore Wilkes; his death was a deep affliction to his mother, who could be sustained under her afflictions only by Divine grace.

27*

He went to the home where his kind mother dwelt,
To tell her the squadron was ready to sail,
And merry the heart of the young sailor felt,
For bright was the morning and fair was the gale.

In vain were his efforts her tears to restrain,
By reciting the hopes that inspired him with joy,
For she secretly felt,—O how keen was the pain,—
That this was the last she would see of her boy.

The hand of his mother he grasped in his own,
And bade her " farewell " as he rose to depart;
She could breathe no response, for to her 'twas the tone
Of the death-knell of all that was dear to her heart.

He hastened on board and the anchors were " home;"
The wide canvas spread, his ship started from shore,
But ah! who can tell of the evil to come,—
He had left her indeed, to behold her no more!

To the Isle of Malolo, the lonely abode
Of a Cannibal King and his murderous train,
The youth in the path of his duty had trod,—
Was attacked by the natives and treacherously slain.

I saw from his eye flash the heroic fire
Of a brave and true heart that was formed to command;
He could not advance, and he would not retire,
But he stood, fought and fell with his knife in his hand.

To a desolate island his body we bore,
And laid his remains with his comrades to rest;
That island ne'er held such a treasure before,
As the jewels we buried so deep in its breast.

Dear youth! he has gone to his rest with the brave,
To the source whence true glory, true happiness springs;
The tears of his countrymen sprinkled his grave,
And the blue, rolling ocean his requiem sings.

In closing this work, having given my testimony to the illustrious dead, I feel that it is but duty to give my views of the living, and having had eight years experience in the U. S. navy, I am prepared to say that it only needs an opportunity, to exhibit as much real and active talent as has ever characterized our navy at any previous time in its history. As a general principle, the naval officers of the United States are gentlemen, who would not suffer by a comparison with those of any country in the world; and being mostly inducted into sea life in their boyhood, they grow up in their business, and at the expiration of their minority, are as capable of managing a ship under any circumstances, as many officers whose heads are sprinkled o'er with age. I have heard foreigners urge as an objection to the efficiency of our navy, the extreme youth of many of our lieutenants; but I feel satisfied that the glory of the American navy will never be tarnished from this cause. On the contrary, there are many decided advantages arising from the youth of our officers. The great experience of those who are now past the middle age, and who, in the ordinary course of nature, will be active and efficient commanders long after our young lieutenants will be flying their own pennants, is one of these advantages.

But there are two sources of evil that may be easily closed,—one by the government, and the other by the commanders of the different ships, from which an influence is expanding that must ultimately tarnish American naval glory. The very common practice of promoting foreigners to places of extra emolument and trust among the grades denominated petty officers, has the effect to fill our navy with the sailors of

other countries, while American seamen are becoming
disgusted with the service, by being compelled to submit to the authority of those who, with or without pro-
vocation, will abuse the country, curse the flag of the
United States every day; and if in the indulgence of
those patriotic feelings which give spirit to the navy,
the American sailor should resent the insult, he would
be sure to receive the degrading penalty of one or two
dozen lashes from the "cat-o'-nine-tails" on his naked back.   This practice, in time of war, will be productive of the most pernicious consequences;—an illustration was furnished in the late war with England.   In that unfortunate affair of the Chesapeake,
a Portuguese boatswain's mate was heard to say, on
going below after the battle, "So much for not pay-
ing men their prize money!"—plainly intimating that
he had purposely neglected his duty because he had
no interest in the engagement beyond the expectation
of prize money and wages.   The practice, then, of
filling all such offices with foreigners, must appear, to
the mind of every officer who knows the importance
of such stations in war, highly deleterious both to the
honor and efficiency of our navy.

The other source of deterioration, and one from
which unnumbered evils emanate, opening the flood-
gates of iniquity, is the serving of the "grog rations."
Probably, an officer cannot be found, who could not
honestly testify that nine tenths of the insurrections,
desertions, and indeed the whole catalogue of crimes
which curse the navy, are attributable to this pernicious practice.   And yet government, knowing the
legitimate effects of this course, still persist in dealing
out destruction, wo and misery.   By this custom the

seamen are degraded, ill-treated, brutalized, and in many cases probably remain so, from a kind of necessity; after having lost all self-respect, they have but little inducement to mingle in decent society on shore.

How inconsistent! The sailor is tempted, virtually compelled to disobey,—by presenting him with the intoxicating bowl, while his appetite is almost ungovernable—and then is flogged for his disobedience! He is crushed, hurled to the depths of dissipation and pollution, and is subject to discipline for his degradation! In fine, almost insuperable barriers to his promotion, and even to respectability are interposed, and perchance it is deeply lamented that the sailor does not become *eminent* in his profession. From the same treasury the draught is drawn to defray the expenses of the Chaplain, and to purchase "liquid fire" to counteract the most benign influences! "Oh shame where is thy blush!"

No man is a greater friend to discipline than I am. I think I understand the necessity of having strict discipline rigidly enforced. The navy cannot be governed without the aid of corporal punishment, so long as the inducement is held out to make our men of war the great receptac of the besotted sailors of all nations, who, by their excesses, have been rendered incapable of doing their duty in the merchant service, and seek for the gratification of a depraved appetite in the service of the American government. I have been flogged in the navy, through the effects of rum, not drank by myself however, but by others; for I never was drunk in my life. But though unjustly flogged, I would give my voice decidedly against the banishment of the "cats" from the navy so long as

the grog ration is served there, as this is the only efficient restraint the commander can impose upon the
appetite of young sailors.

When the time arrives in which Congress shall
cease to encourage drunkenness and rebellion, our
own seamen, patriotic and responsible, will take their
stations, and do honor to the navy of their country.
Corporal punishment, with all its degrading attendants, will then be abolished, and respectable officers
will be able to secure respectable men.   And here I
am happy to add my testimony to the character of
Captains Wilkes and Hudson.   They are both temperance men and *officers*, and probably no two naval
officers are held in higher estimation, as men of judgment and energy and decision of character.   They
have seen the sad effects of intoxication, and I have
heard them both advocate the abolition of the "spirit
rations."

The officers of the expedition were generally young
men, most of the lieutenants acting by the appointment of the Commodore ; the voyage was long, exceeding four years to most of us.   Its duties were arduous, and many of them hazardous in the extreme,
but by the skill and perseverance of the commanders,
the active and efficient coöperation of the younger officers, together with the fidelity and zeal of the seamen,
the most satisfactory result accrued from the cruise.
The most sanguine expectations of its projectors were
realized, and indeed much more than was originally
designed, was accomplished by our observations.   We
had even here, ample demonstration of the fact that
more of the evils, and less of the benefits resulted
from the "grog tub" than from all other causes combined.

# INDEX.

———

### CHAPTER I.

### CHAPTER II.

### CHAPTER III.

### CHAPTER IV.

### CHAPTER V.

### CHAPTER VI.

### CHAPTER VII.

### CHAPTER VIII.

ENVIRONMENTAL RESEARCH ADVANCES SERIES

# ADVANCES IN ENVIRONMENTAL MODELING AND MEASUREMENTS

# ENVIRONMENTAL RESEARCH ADVANCES SERIES

**A True Tale of Science and Discovery**
*Lawrence A. Curtis*
2010. ISBN: 978-1-60876-595-9

**Amazon Basin: Plant Life, Wildlife and Environment**
*Nicolas Rojás and Rafael Prieto (Editors)*
2010. ISBN: 978-1-60741-463-6

**Handbook of Environmental Research**
*Aurel Edelstein and Dagmar Bär (Editors)*
2010. ISBN: 978-1-60741-492-6

**Behavioral and Chemical Ecology**
*Wen Zhang and Hong Liu (Editors)*
2010 ISBN: 978-1-60741-099-7

**Advances in Environmental Modeling and Measurements**
*Dragutin T. Mihailović and Branislava Lalić (Editors)*
2010. ISBN: 978-1-60876-599-7

# ADVANCES IN ENVIRONMENTAL MODELING AND MEASUREMENTS

## DRAGUTIN T. MIHAILOVIĆ
### AND
## BRANISLAVA LALIĆ
### EDITORS

**Nova Science Publishers, Inc.**
*New York*

**NOTICE TO THE READER**

The Publisher has taken reasonable care in the preparation of this book, but makes no expressed or implied warranty of any kind and assumes no responsibility for any errors or omissions. No liability is assumed for incidental or consequential damages in connection with or arising out of information contained in this book. The Publisher shall not be liable for any special, consequential, or exemplary damages resulting, in whole or in part, from the readers' use of, or reliance upon, this material.

Independent verification should be sought for any data, advice or recommendations contained in this book. In addition, no responsibility is assumed by the publisher for any injury and/or damage to persons or property arising from any methods, products, instructions, ideas or otherwise contained in this publication.

This publication is designed to provide accurate and authoritative information with regard to the subject matter covered herein. It is sold with the clear understanding that the Publisher is not engaged in rendering legal or any other professional services. If legal or any other expert assistance is required, the services of a competent person should be sought. FROM A DECLARATION OF PARTICIPANTS JOINTLY ADOPTED BY A COMMITTEE OF THE AMERICAN BAR ASSOCIATION AND A COMMITTEE OF PUBLISHERS.

LIBRARY OF CONGRESS CATALOGING-IN-PUBLICATION DATA

Advances in environmental modeling and measurements / editors, Dragutin T. Mihailovic and Branislava Lalic.
    p. cm.
 Includes index.
 ISBN 978-1-60876-599-7 (hardcover)
 1. Environmental sciences--Mathematical models. 2. Environmental monitoring. 3. Environmental sciences--Research--European Union countries. I. Mihailovic, Dragutin T. II. Lalic, Branislava.
 GE45.M37.A38 2010
 628.01'5118--dc22
            2009040479

*Published by Nova Science Publishers, Inc.* + *New York*

# CONTENTS

# PREFACE

Awareness of how our world is changing inevitably introduces an anxiety defined by the following question: can humanity preserve the existing world for the future of its children? To achieve this preservation, we must all strive for sustainable development and progress that meets the developmental needs of society without introducing threats to life and property. Human security is an essential ingredient of sustainability, and it is increasingly being threatened by extreme events, both natural and man-made. The environment is increasingly endangered as humans encroach upon and modify fragile environments. So why are environmental problems in the limelight at this particular time? One possible answer can be found in a hierarchy of the most significant scientific problems for the 21$^{st}$ century, as compiled by a community of physicists, biologists, chemistries, engineers and sociologists. According to them, in the 21$^{st}$ century, the scientific community will be preoccupied by the environmental problems that are primarily linked to climate change and related issues; these questions are concerned with the survival of human beings on Earth. This is the first time in the history of science that environmental problems take the place at the forefront of science, from fundamentals to applications. Environmental science can be defined from various points of view from many science disciplines. However, we follow the Random House Dictionary (2006) definition because it implicated the interdisciplinary nature of the science: "the branch of science concerned with the physical, chemical, and biological conditions of the environment and their effect on organisms".

Environmental science encompasses issues such as climate change, biodiversity, water quality, groundwater contamination, soil contamination, use of natural resources, waste management, sustainable development, disaster reduction, air pollution, and noise pollution. Its core disciplines are atmospheric sciences, ecology, environmental chemistry, and geosciences. Atmospheric sciences examine the phenomenology of the Earth's gaseous outer layer, emphasizing its interrelation with other systems, and include meteorological studies (atmospheric chemistry and atmospheric physics), greenhouse gas phenomena, atmospheric dispersion modeling of airborne contaminants, sound propagation phenomena related to noise pollution, and, most recently, light pollution. Ecological studies typically analyze the dynamics between biological populations and some aspect of their environment. These studies address such topics as endangered species, predator/prey interactions, habitat integrity, the effects of environmental contaminants on populations, and impact analyses of proposed land development on species viability. Such studies may also include interdisciplinary analyses of ecological systems being impacted by one or more stressors, incorporating other related environmental science fields, like water pollution. Environmental chemistry investigates chemical alterations in the environment, including such focus areas as soil contamination and water pollution, and studies problems like chemical degradation in the environment, multi-phase chemical transport, and chemical effects upon biota. Geosciences include environmental geology, environmental soil science, volcanic phenomena, and evolution of the Earth's crust; in some classification systems, it can also include hydrology studies, including oceanography.

The European Union recently invested significant effort and financial resources toward solving environmental problems on fundamental and applied levels. Part of this effort involved establishing the Center for Meteorology and Environmental Predictions (http://cmep-serbia.if.ns.ac.yu), in the Department of Physics, Faculty of Sciences at University of Novi Sad (Serbia), as an R&D Center of Excellence. This center is a part of the FP6 project entitled "Reinforcement of the Research Potential in Center for Meteorology and Environmental Predictions", founded by the European Commission for the period January 1, 2007 – September 30, 2009. Its official logo depicts the Earth with a removed rectangular piece, which symbolizes the fine balance between man and nature. The blue and brown colors symbolize the water and land, respectively, while green is a symbol of all life, particularly that which covers the planet. Our center is devoted primarily to physics and modeling of environmental processes and the interface between them. We are not, however, concerned with every type of physical and biological interaction, only with a few primary processes that characterize the world in which we live. The following subjects are areas of primary focus: numerical simulations, agricultural modeling, air pollution modeling, UV radiation modeling and measurement, and non-linear dynamics. The center's major accomplishment achieved during the FP6 project period was the "Workshop on Modeling and Measuring Aspects of Some Environmental Issues in European Union and National Projects", which took place on 27-29 April 2009, at the University of Novi Sad, Serbia.

The objective of this workshop, and of this book, was to bring together scientists and engineers working at research institutions and universities, who are engaged in theoretical, modeling, measurement, and software studies of environmental and related sciences. The intent was to provide a forum for participants to obtain the most current information on the topics at hand, and to exchange new ideas and expertise through presentations on recent achievements from projects throughout the European Union. A variety of professionals from a wide spectrum of fields created a broad spectrum of unique viewpoints of environmental theoretical modeling and experimental approaches, including the issues of software design and measurements.

This book is organized into four sections: Introduction, Environmental Fluid Mechanics Issues (Part One), Air Pollution, Ionizing and Non-Ionizing Radiation and Turbulent Energy Exchange Issues (Part Two) and Climate Change Impact on Agriculture (Part Three). The introduction includes two chapters that cover the fundamentals of the European partnership for international scientific and technological cooperation in the $21^{st}$ century, and the major features of policy framework used to foster centers of excellence. Part One has seven chapters covering various theoretical and modeling aspects of environmental fluid mechanics, such as regional climate modeling, transverse turbulent mixing in a shallow flow, albedo of different surface geometries, the impact of canyon geometry albedo on surface temperature calculations, forest-atmosphere interaction modeling, local interactions and functional robustness modeling in living systems, and the synchronization in coupled interactions of natural complex systems. Part Two spends seven chapters addressing a broad range of subjects, including ionizing and non-ionizing radiation, air pollution and turbulent energy exchange issues (such as spectral solar UV radiation measurements, monitoring of solar UV radiation, modeling of non-local diffusion, and vertical mixing schemes for use in chemical and air quality control models), numerical treatment of the advection term in equations for motion, atmospheric deposition of heavy metals, and airborne radionuclides using the moss biomonitoring technique, concentration gradient measurements of atmospheric ammonia over grasslands, and  measurement of evaporation under field experiment conditions. Part Three is comprised of seven chapters dealing with climate change impacts on the following: European winter wheat and maize, Tuscan durum wheat quality, the appearance of small grain diseases in the Vojvodina region (Serbia), agriculture in North-West Russia. Adaptation options for climate change impacts are also considered with respect to European agriculture, the agro-climatic potential of the landscape under climate change conditions in Slovakia, and climate indicators used by viticultural researchers.

The introduction begins with a chapter by A. Beuf describing the growing power of the EU, particularly in fields of science and technology, emphasizing that researchers in political sciences believe that the European Union will dominate the 21$^{st}$ century. The EU's sphere of influence is continuously growing through emerging European common policies. The international cooperation efforts of EU treaties have been and remain a powerful tool to develop its relationships with all regions of the world. Finally, some statistical parameters about number of projects are presented to illustrate the high level of cooperation between Europe and other countries. Following this, the chapter by A. Belić and A. Bogojević presents a bottom-up procedure for developing a national policy framework conducive to promoting R&D excellence. This procedure is based on the EU Framework Program priorities, and is initiated by identifying and reinforcing R&D centers of excellence. The capacity of these centers to impact national R&D policy is then enhanced by the development of recommendations for policy makers to foster the growth of research excellence in a rapidly changing and competitive environment.

Part One begins with a chapter by V. Djurdjević and B. Rajković whose work presents the EBU-POM coupled regional climate model along with some results from climate change time-slice experiments using a two-way regional coupled model, with an Eta/NCEP limited area model for its atmospheric portion and Princeton Ocean Model for its ocean portion. The authors performed climate integration for the base period of 1961-1990 and an analysis of an A1B climate change scenario experiment, focusing on changes in seasonal mean surface temperature and precipitation patterns. Following this, the chapter by C. Gualtieri deals with modeling transverse turbulent mixing via an eddy viscosity approach. Results are presented from a numerical study simulating the transverse mixing of a steady-state point source of a tracer in two-dimensional rectangular geometry. An approach based on the Reynolds Averaged Navier-Stokes (RANS) equations was applied wherein the closure problem was solved using turbulent viscosity concept. Two methods were then applied to the model results to evaluate the turbulent transverse mixing coefficient. Finally, the author compared and studied the effect on transverse mixing of two different grids located upstream in the area of the tracer source, confirming that the RANS-approach may provide acceptable results. The next chapter, by A.M. Ćirišan, D.T. Mihailović and D.V. Kapor, is devoted to calculating the albedo over heterogeneous interfaces for different geometries. The authors offer a new approach for calculating the flux of the short-wave radiation lost due to the absorption on the vertical lateral boundaries of higher-level surfaces. This approach used analytical and numerical (Monte Carlo "ray tracing") methods to elaborate this effect for different geometries. Finally, the authors compared the expression derived for the albedo of the specifically designed grid-cell with the conventional approach. In the next chapter by D.V. Kapor, D.T. Mihailović, and A.M. Ćirišan, the authors studied impacts of canyon geometry albedo on the calculation of surface temperature. The albedo of this system was calculated using a new approach that takes into account the geometrical effect of losing the short-wave radiation flux laterally. Further, this aggregated albedo is then introduced into the land-atmosphere parameterization scheme for calculating the surface temperature. The following chapter by B. Lalić, D.T. Mihailović, B. Rajković, and D. Kapor considers an approach for parameterizing the wind speed profile, realistically describing turbulent momentum transport inside the forest canopy and showing that a forest canopy can be treated as a space consisting of a large number of homogeneous vegetation and air elements. Accordingly, all relevant processes could be described as a combination of single processes representing homogenous vegetation and air space. Finally, the authors compared wind profile data measured in the Amazonian Forest (Reserva Jaru, Brazil) and in the Shasta Experimental Forest (California, USA). In the next chapter, I. Balaz and D.T. Mihailovic address local interactions and functional robustness in living systems. After theoretical analysis, the authors use category theory to construct a model of spatio-temporal locality of functional elements in an abstract living system.   They then analyze the formal consequences of the model, including: observation based generation of equivalence classes, system stability in situations when operating rules are local and temporally restricted, and the difference between external and internal rules (or a priori and ad hoc rules, respectively). In the last chapter of Part One, D. T. Mihailović, M. Budinčević, I. Balaz and D. Perišić consider the emergence of chaos and synchronization in coupled interactions at environmental interfaces regarded as biophysically complex systems. The authors consider energy and substance exchanges, describing them in terms of the dynamics of driven coupled oscillators. In particular, this was done through dynamics of two coupled maps representing the exchange processes between two biophysical entities. Finally, they identified relatively small regions wherein system synchronization is allowed.

Part Two begins with a chapter by S. Simic, M. Fitzka, P. Weihs, and H. Kromp-Kolb, who monitored spectral UV radiation in Austria via measurements from two stations that have met high quality standards since 1994. The authors focus on quantitatively understanding the influence of clouds, ozone, and surface albedo on spectral UV radiation. From the Sonnblick observatory, they also examined continuous spectral UV irradiance measurements alongside model calculations from a one-dimensional radiation transfer model. Finally, they analyzed long-term trends in UV irradiance based on clear-sky measurements using non-parametric trend tests. Results indicated significant downward trends for several combinations of solar zenith angle and wavelength; these trends are apparently caused by a seasonal increase in sunshine duration during periods of high total column ozone. The next chapter, by Z. Mijatović, S. Milićević, D. V. Kapor, D. T. Mihailović, I. Arsenić and Z. Podraščanin, presents pioneering work in UV radiation measurement and modeling in Serbia, carried out at the University of Novi Sad. The authors compared model outputs with measured values, based on directly measured ozone layer thickness and aerosol optical thickness that were taken from satellite measurements. The following chapter is authored by D.T. Mihailović, Á. Bordás, and K. Alapaty and offers a short overview of vertical mixing schemes for air quality and environmental model applications. Specific applications included description of atmospheric boundary layer (ABL) characteristics and comprehension of complex boundary layer interactions and their proper parameterization; these are important for air quality as well as many other environmental models. Simple single-column vertical mixing models are comprehensive enough to describe ABL characteristics; therefore, they can be employed to illustrate basic concepts of boundary layer processes and to represent tools appropriate for boundary layer measurements. When coupled to 3D models, single-column models can provide detailed and accurate simulations of the ABL structure and mixing processes. The authors offer a short overview of non-local mixing schemes and combined non-local schemes for vertical diffusion, and of non-local mixing schemes (developed in the last two decades) for vertical mixing during convective conditions in the ABL. The overview is supported with illustrative 1D and 3D model outputs. The next chapter, by I. Arsenić, D.T. Mihailović and B. Rajković, presents a contemporary numerical treatment of passive advection. They designed a new advection scheme consisting of two components; the first is pure Lagrangian advection, while the second is an interpolation procedure for obtaining the Lagrangian values on the Eulerian grid. The authors performed numerical tests comparing the proposed scheme against piecewise parabolic Eulerian and Semi-Lagrangian schemes. The tests indicated that this new approach has definite advantages in terms of increased accuracy and decreased computational time. The following chapter, by M. Krmar, D. Radnović, M.V. Frontasyeva, S.S. Pavlov, and Y.S. Pankratova, considers atmospheric deposition of heavy metals and airborne radionuclides studied by moss biomonitoring. This work is the continuation of a systematic atmospheric pollution study regarding heavy metals, based on moss analysis in northern Serbia beginning in 2000. The authors investigated possible variations in radionuclide atmospheric deposition over a large area, considering temporal variation in $^7$Be, $^{210}$Pb, and $^{137}$Cs in moss samples over a 14-month period, as continuously measured at a single fixed sampling site. Additionally, they measured the duration and amount of precipitation and subsequently considered their influences on the activity concentrations determined in moss samples. The next chapter, by T. Weidinger, A. Pogány, L. Horváth, A. Machon, Z. Bozóki, Á. Mohácsi, K. Pintér, Z. Nagy, A.Z. Gyöngyösi, Z. Istenes, and Á. Bordás, presents concentration gradient measurements and flux calculations of atmospheric ammonia over grasslands (Bugac-puszta, Hungary). The authors discuss results of ammonia flux measurements as continuously monitored since July 2008 at the 'Bugac-puszta' Hungarian NitroEurope site. Measurements were taken in semi-natural grasslands in the Kiskunság National Park (Great Hungarian Plain) using instrumentation developed at the University of Szeged. Furthermore, they compared the daily mean ammonia concentrations at the Bugac-puszta site to data measured 20 km away at the Hungarian background air quality monitoring station (K-puszta). The two data sets corroborated one another to an acceptable degree. At the end of this chapter, turbulent ammonia flux is calculated with a similarity theory using eddy covariance data regarding friction velocity ($u_*$) and the Monin-Obukhov length scale. Part Two concludes with a chapter by J. Eitzinger, T. Gerersdorfer, H. Schume, W. Laube, F. Holawe, and T. Orfanus claiming that the accurate estimation of evapotranspiration is a crucial issue for many agrometeorology applications. This is due to the influences of many parameters in this complex mass flux process, which impede the establishment of a robust method for estimating representative evapotranspiration values, both potential and actual. In order to compare direct potential evapotranspiration measurement methods by different types of evaporimeters with indirect calculation methods from hourly to daily potential evapotranspiration estimates, the authors analyzed experimental results from the Marchfeld region of Austria, that compared with evapotranspiration calculated by empirical equations. These results should highlight the respective application potential of evaporimeters, their accuracy, and their response to calculated evapotranspiration values.

Part Three begins with a chapter by V. A. Alexandrov that considers the impacts of climate variability and change on agricultural production in Europe, which is perhaps the most sensitive and vulnerable region. Although agriculture in Europe only accounts for a small part of GDP, and the vulnerability in the overall economy to changes affecting agriculture is therefore low, the local societal effects may be significant. The author shows some model results of climate change impacts on selected crops across Europe, using ATEAM climate data for the period 1991-2000, climate change HADCM3 scenarios for the $21^{st}$ century, and the RoIMPEL crop model to simulate changes in phenological dates and the crop yields of winter wheat and maize. The next chapter, by S. Orlandini, D. Grifoni, F. Natali, M. Mancini and A. Dalla Marta, analyzes the relationship between meteorological conditions and the quality of durum wheat (*Triticum turgidum* L. var. durum) in terms of protein content, in the Tuscany region of Central Italy, on the basis of current meteo-climatic variability. The authors found significant relationships between meteorological conditions and wheat quality. In addition, they also analyzed teleconnections between quality data and 500 hPa geopotential height, sea surface temperature, sea level pressure, and NAO index for the potential development of wheat-quality forecasting tools. The chapter by R. Jevtić, M. Telečki, B. Lalić, D.T. Mihailović, and M. Malešević considers a case in the Vojvodina region (Serbia) where climate change impacts prevalence of small grains diseases, causing significant yield losses. They show that climate changes have resulted in the dominance of pathogens that either require higher temperatures for their development or are better able to adapt to drought conditions (*Septoria* spp., *Pyrenophora tritici-repentis*, *P. teres*, *Rhynchosporium secalis*). Finally, they emphasized that small grain cultivars for planting should be adapted and chosen based on resistance to abiotic and biotic factors, while the breeding strategy should be oriented towards developing genotypes adapted to stress factors. The next chapter, by M.V. Nikolaev, presents the potential climate change impact on agriculture in northwestern Russia in the coming decades, based simulation results from a general circulation models For analysis, the author uses input data including such climatic indicators as "winter severity" and "winter wetness" indices, effective temperature sums, and soil moisture content, as well as agronomical/technological parameters that include regular dates of sowing and optimum fertilization. Assessment results provided evidence of opportunities for cultivating more productive crops based on increased fertilizer efficiency; on the other hand, opportunities for deteriorating winter crops in regions with mild/moderate winters, and the potential acclimatization of some insect pest species in the more northern parts of northwestern Russia. At the end, the author suggests adaptation measures and strategies. Following this, the chapter by J. Eitzinger, G. Kubu, S. Thaler, J. Glauninger, V. Alexandrov, A. Utset, D.T. Mihailovic, B. Lalic, M. Trnka, Z. Zalud, D. Semeradova, D. Ventrella, D.P. Anastasiou, M. Medany, S. Altaher, J. Olejnik, J. Leśny, N. Nemeshko, M. Nikolaev, C. Simota, and G. Cojocaru highlights the main results of the ADAGIO project, which was designed to focus on regional studies and uncover regional specific problems. In this context, the bottom-up approach is used, in addition to the top-down approach of using scientific studies, by involving regional experts and farmers in the evaluation of potential regional vulnerabilities and adaptation options. Results of the regional studies and feedback gathered from experts and farmers show that, in general, increasing drought and heat are the primary factors affecting agricultural vulnerability, not only in the Mediterranean region but also in Central and Eastern Europe. Another important aspect is that the increasing risk of pests and disease may play a more important role for agricultural vulnerability than previously assumed; however, until now this field has rarely been investigated in Europe. Another key point is that there are increasing regional differences in the European crop production potentials due to climate change. Positively or negatively impacted agricultural systems can vary within a relatively small spatial scale, depending on the specific limiting environmental conditions, such as climate or soil conditions (especially in complex terrain). Although dominant risks such as increasing drought and/or heat are common to most regions, the specific vulnerabilities in different regions are very much influenced by characteristics of the dominant agroecosystems and prevailing socio-economic conditions. The authors emphasized that the most important adaptation options in Europe concern changes in crop and soil management, pest and disease management, and land use options at different scales. The feasibility of many adaptation options, however, is strongly influenced by regional socio-economic conditions, which can vary significantly within regions and countries in Europe. In the chapter by B. Šiška, J. Takáč and P. Nejedlík, the authors emphasized that current GCMs for Central Europe show an increase in air temperature, changes in precipitation distribution, and a decrease in water balance. As the growing season continues, rising air temperature will probably cause a significant increase in the productive potential. The precipitation regime will change, and a higher drought frequency will be the most significant characteristic influencing the crop production. Precipitation and potential evapotranspiration balance out between 550 m a.s.l. and 700 m a.s.l. This fact, along with the increase in air temperature, will likely affect both the zonality of growing areas of some crops (especially maize) and crop rotation. Slovak territory belongs to one of the European watersheds and its precipitation values represent the only water coming to this territory. According to the authors, keeping water in the country will become an urgent issue in the near future. The last chapter in Part Three, contributed by M. Ladányi, considers the fact that if the probability of extremely high grapevine production has increased as a result of climate change in Hungary, the risk of production quantity and quality has also considerably increased. On the basis of international and national literature and practice, the author gleaned some weather indicators that may significantly define grapevine production from quality and/or quantity aspects. In addition, based on RegCM scenarios as well as specially generated weather data, the expected change of the plant specific weather indicators in the future are defined. Finally, the author described the possible impacts of changing indicators on production quality and quantity, and formulated some important conclusions for Hungary that can be built into the national climate change prevention and adaptation strategy.

Not all papers represent a new and original contribution, but they are interesting in the context of scientific review and they offer appropriate approaches for understanding the problems considered here in a comprehensive and critical way. We are particularly proud that young researchers took part in the workshop, contributing their first papers and giving valuable contributions and insight.

The editors wish to thank all the chapter authors for their continuous and dedicated efforts, which made possible the realization of this book. We are especially grateful to Miss Ana Firanj, who invested a great deal of effort in the creation of this book. The editors also thank the anonymous reviewers of the project for their thoughtful and detailed suggestions, which have improved both the content and presentation of this book. Finally, the editors gratefully acknowledge the assistance of the Nova Science Publishers Editorial Office.

Dragutin T. Mihailović
Branislava Lalić

# DEDICATION

*To Mihailo Luković from Čačak*

In: Advances in Environmental Modeling and Measurements        ISBN: 978-1-60876-599-7
Editors: D. T. Mihailović, B. Lalić, pp. 1-11            © 2010 Nova Science Publishers, Inc.

*Chapter 1*

# ENHANCING EUROPEAN PARTNERSHIPS FOR INTERNATIONAL SCIENTIFIC AND TECHNOLOGICAL COOPERATION

## *A. Beuf*[*][≠]

European Commission, Brussels, Belgium

## ABSTRACT

Researchers in political science believe that the European Union will dominate the 21st century  (Leonard Mark Why Europe will run the 21st century Fourth Estate publishers London 2005). The sphere of influence of the EU is continuously growing in various ways: through the development of European common policies, the European single market, the European monetary system, S and T agreements, bilateral and bi-regional policy dialogues, and ongoing pre-accession schemes.

Based on EU treaties, the international cooperation activities of the EU have been and remain a powerful tool that can be used to extend its relationships with all regions of the world, including major industrialized countries (USA, the Russian Federation, Japan), emerging countries (Brazil, China, India, and Southeast Asian countries), Central Asian countries, African, Caribbean and Pacific countries, associate candidate countries, and Mediterranean partner countries. In 2007, 95 strategies and 92 annual programs were adopted in the field of EU foreign policy. Concerning international scientific and technological cooperation, 32 agreements were signed and enforced; 17 agreements were signed on the basis of the EC and 15 on the basis of the Euratom treaty. In 2007, 12 countries, including all western Balkans countries, were associated with the 7th research framework program.

---

[*] Corresponding author: E-mail address: Armand.Beuf@ec.europa.eu, Phone: + 322 2965170
[≠] The author is Principal Scientific Officer working with the European Union. His views and opinions, as expressed in his introduction, do not represent either the European Commission or any other European Institution.

# 1. INTRODUCTION

During the last decade, the EU and its Member States defined significant economic and political goals:

- The establishment of the Lisbon agenda for creating the most competitive and knowledge-based economy in the world by 2010;
- The definition of the Barcelona objectives for increasing research and technological development (RTD) investment in the European Union to approximately 3% of gross domestic product (GDP) by 2010;
- The European Council (EC) affirmed its enlargement strategy, its full support for the European perspective on the Western Balkans, and embarked on a new European neighborhood policy;
- The choice of multilateralism at the world level, adopted by the EU, leading to joint action with multilateral bodies in many geographical areas of cooperation (Central Asia, ACP countries) in order to tackle global issues such as climate change.

The European Parliament and the Council of Ministers co-decided EU research framework programs FP6 (2002-2006) and FP7 (2007-2013). FP6 explicitly addressed the concept of the European research area (ERA), with an emphasis on actions integrating, structuring and strengthening its foundations.

In 2008, the European Council passed a resolution to develop an ERA vision for 2020, stipulating that in 2020, all actors will benefit from the "fifth freedom": the free circulation of researchers, knowledge and technology. Additionally, the European Commission proposed a new strategic European framework for international science and technology cooperation (Com 588 final of 24/09/2008).The Council of the European Union endorsed it and invited the Member States and the Commission to form a European partnership in the field of international scientific and technological cooperation ('S&T cooperation') with a view toward implementing this European strategy [1].

## 1.1. Pursuing a Strong Collaborative Research Based on European Excellence

The bulk of EU research funding associated with FP6 and FP7 goes toward collaborative research, with the objective of establishing excellent research projects and networks able to attract researchers and investments from Europe and around the world. This is to be achieved through a range of funding schemes, including collaborative projects, networks of excellence, co-ordination/support actions, etc.

Further to any call for proposals, the selection of projects is based at first on criteria of excellence. A very large range of successful projects in many areas might be mentioned; for example, in the SPACE domain, the IMPRESS project [2] instituted under FP6 investigates new space-age materials. This project will make Europe a leader in the strategically important area of materials science and has already made a major contribution to Europe's ability to meet the Kyoto Protocol targets for reductions to the amount of carbon dioxide and nitrogen oxides released into the atmosphere. In the CLIMATE CHANGE domain, the EPICA project, [3] also instituted under FP6, has revealed how levels of greenhouse gases, thought to be major contributors to climate change, have progressed over time, so that we can predict temperature shifts and start to prepare scenarios to tackle climate change. The ADAM project [4] has developed a policy appraisal framework that will engage policy communities within Europe and allow policy advisors to examine and explore the effectiveness of different policy options with respect to contrasting criteria. Finally, the RRP CMEP project [5] provides a solid grounding for prospects in nations of the Western Balkans and beyond. In the INFRASTRUCTURES domain, the ESFRI project [6] has produced the first-ever European Roadmap for Research Infrastructures, which outlines 35 research projects identified as vital to the development of science and innovation in Europe. In REGIONAL POLICY IMPLEMENTATION, the Pro-Act project, [7] undertaken under FP6, has brought together four established and four new EU member states to create a best-practices approach to managing the way regional development policies are implemented. The project is aimed at identifying the links between regional research needs and the policies that need to be put in place to support them. For USE OF EXPERTISE IN POLICYMAKING, the SYNAPSE e-network [8], another project funded under FP6, aims to make better use of expertise in policy-making and to link experts in the scientific community with public authorities. For the COORDINATION OF POLICIES, the Open Method of Coordination [9] provides the Member States with an opportunity to learn from each other, exchange experiences, and identify good practices. The Open Method Coordination research policy is supervised by CREST, which has published a report on the coordinated use of the EU's Framework Research and Structural Fund programs, both of which provide significant financial resources for R&D.

Many international collaboration research projects have been launched under FP6. Based on a regional approach, specific research priorities and eligibility criteria requiring Third World countries' participation, the INCO program was designed to address research needs identified according to the specific socio-economic context of the partner regions, while serving mutual interests and securing benefits for both the EU and the targeted Third World countries. The dual mandate given to INCO implies a commitment not only to striving for scientific excellence, but also to responding to institutional needs, such as support for external policies and research capacity-building in partner countries, as well as ensuring access for European researchers and companies to knowledge systems in other parts of the world.

The three programs used for international cooperation with partner regions were the Specific Targeted Research Projects (STREPs), Coordination Actions (CA), and Specific Support Actions (SSA). STREPs were meant to address challenges to European competitiveness and to meet the needs of society and the community in the targeted geographic areas. CA projects were concerned with the networking and coordination of research and innovation actions. SSA projects supported the implementation of FP6 INCO and Thematic Priorities, contributed to the preparation of future framework programs and stimulated, encouraged, and facilitated cooperation.

The costs of implementation of FP6-INCO amounted to 309.9 million EUR, through 387 projects with 2 729 partners involved, 48% of which were from INCO partner countries. Of these, 144 projects were STREPs, with 244.4 million EUR allocated, 23 were CA projects, with 22.8 million EUR allocated, and 220 were SSA projects, with 34.8 million EUR.

Project participants' self-assessments indicated that opinions regarding the capacity of INCO to strengthen capacity and knowledge are overwhelmingly positive. When analyzing the answers from INCO-targeted countries only, it can be seen that the project's achievements are assessed more positively by participants in the INCO program than by participants in the Thematic Priorities program, especially with regard to networks and access to knowledge and facilities.

Members of the Advisory Group and members of the Program Committee of the INCO program have also mentioned network-building and access to knowledge and capacity development as the main achievements of the INCO program.

## 1.2. Towards a European Partnership in the Field of International Scientific and Technological Cooperation

As mentioned, the Council of the European Union has recently invited Member States and the European Commission to form a European Partnership in the field of international scientific and technological cooperation and has invited both parties to coordinate activities and positions vis-à-vis Third countries and within international forums [1].

Moreover, the Commission's stakeholder consultation, conducted on the future of European research, revealed strong support for increased coordination of national research programs from all categories of contributors. The 7$^{th}$ Framework Program will support two main tools to encourage the restructuring of the ERA. Together, they should reduce its fragmentation in several national and regional research programs by favoring the development of joint calls, joint programs, and actions supported by both Member States and the European Commission.

## 2. USE OF ERA-NET SCHEME

ERA-NET scheme aims to develop and strengthen the coordination of national and regional research programs in two ways:

- By providing a framework for actors implementing public research programs to improve coordination through new ERA-NETs or by broadening and deepening existing ERA-NETs.
- By providing, in a limited number of cases, additional EU financial support to participants who create a common fund for the purpose of joint calls for research proposals from national and regional programs ('ERA-NET PLUS').

In terms of global achievements, the FP6 and FP7 framework programs have helped to create a stimulating pace for the ERA and to reinforce national research potential.

Under FP6 (2002-2006), 71 geographic and thematic ERA-NETS were launched, involving more than 1000 participations and 450 participants. More than 30 ERA-NETs are still running as of 2009 (ERA-NETs on stage; Annual event 31/03/09 and 01/04/09 Brussels; [10]). Over 40 countries are involved, primarily from the EU15. The main rationale for participation was to create and support transnational projects. Participants originated mainly from governmental organizations and not-for-profit private organizations. The majority of these organizations are involved in 1 to 5 ERA-NETs (ERA- NETs on-stage; idem)

The range of activities performed was in line with the initial rationale for participation and included:

1) An action plan taking up common strategic issues and preparing joint activities (75% of participants); Benchmarking and common schemes for monitoring and evaluation (67% of participants); Coordination/Clustering of ongoing nationally funded research projects (59% of participants); Multinational evaluation procedures (55% of participants); Schemes for joint training activities (49% of participants); Specific cooperation agreements arrangements (43% of participants); Schemes for joint opening of facilities and laboratories (20% of participants).

2) Two examples of ERA-NETs will be detailed in order to illustrate the political context, the specific tasks, and the expected impact of such tools.

## 2.1. The "ERA ARD" NET: Coordination Action for Deepening Agricultural Research Development

### 2.1.1. Background

For many historical, socio-economic, and cultural reasons, European Member States have developed unique field-based scientific expertise in Agricultural Research for Development (ARD) and have enjoyed support directly or indirectly from their bilateral and multilateral programs. For the past 25 years, Europe has provided continuous financial support to the international agricultural research centers of the CGIAR. In 2003, this financial contribution amounted to 140 million EUR, of which 22 million EUR came directly from the European Commission. It has also taken the lead, on behalf of Europe, in supporting the emerging regional and sub-regional agricultural research organizations, such as the Forum for Agricultural Research in Africa (FARA), the Association for Strengthening Agricultural Research in Eastern and Central Africa (ASARECA) and the Conseil Ouest and Centre Africain pour la Recherche et le Développement Agricoles (CORAF/WECARD). In the context of 6th framework programs, the European Commission has launched a series of bi-regional dialogues on Scientific and Technological Cooperation with the developing regions, and is funding a number of ARD projects through the INCO DEV instrument. In addition, in the context of the accompanying measures of INCO DEV, the European Commission provided 1.5 million EUR for the development of a European ARD information system. This information system is currently named EARD-InfoSys. It provides a very useful tool for scientific exchange related to ARD [11,12].

### 2.1.2. Strategic Objectives

ARD ERA-NET was created under the auspices of FP6 with two strategic objectives:

1) Improving synergies between the European national ARD programs by increasing the effectiveness and efficiency of European research planning, funding and

implementation to fight poverty and hunger and to support more rapid and sustainable development in the poorest countries in the world.

2) Improving cooperation and coordination of national ARD programs by strengthening Europe's contribution to, and impact on, regional and global ARD systems. The ERA-ARD project assists the European Union in fulfilling important commitments made at the international level by encouraging greater efficiency and coherence among the European national ARD programs. Commitments include the achievement of the Millennium Development goals and increasing the support for more rapid and sustainable development of the world's poorest countries (WTO Doha Development Round, World Summit on Sustainable Development, World Food Summit). In addition, through its strong international dimension and its focus on problem solving in partner countries, the ERA ARD will contribute to improving the ways food safety and security issues are addressed in Europe.

### 2.1.3. Impact

In addition to these contributions to the general European and international agendas, the ERA ARD will have three more specific types of impact:

1) Impact on the European Research Area through overall improvements to the efficiency and effectiveness of the European ARD sector. Given that 11 countries are involved, as are several ministries (Research, Agriculture and Food Foreign Affairs) and agencies (CIRAD, IAO, SDC), the project has achieved a critical mass to contribute to the strengthening and greater coherence of the European "ARD offerings" and its contribution to regional and international ARD systems.

2) Impact on national ARD programs through assistance in structuring, harmonizing and integrating the 11 national ARD programs. This will be achieved by the development of common insights into the content and management of the programs, the exchange of good practices in terms of governance, the development of common approaches and standards for planning, monitoring, evaluation, and impact assessment, and the planning and funding of joint and transnational activities.

3) Impact on ARD stakeholders and public awareness. The ERA ARD program decision-makers and managers, by sharing and exchanging best practices, will develop a common understanding of strategic issues and a shared vision of ARD. It could favor the emergence of new partnerships to implement joint and transnational activities. ERA ARD also contributes to public awareness through a better understanding of development-related problems in Europe and to the increased mobilization of resources to address them.

## 2.2. The "NEW INDIGO" ERA-NET: Initiative for the Development and Integration of Indian and European Research

### 2.2.1. Background And Objectives

India has become a prominent country in Asia and beyond from economic and political points of view but also from the scientific point of view. It has been designated a strategic target country by the European Commission. Since the ratification of the Europe-India Science and Technology Agreement in November 2001 [13], a Joint Action Plan has been drawn up and EU-India summits in S&T have been held in order to promote this cooperation. It was quoted in the India-EU Joint Statement on 30th November 2007 that efforts should be concentrated towards the creation of joint infrastructure for advanced research and funding systems for symmetric programs that promote S&T collaboration. It was also stated that leaders would welcome strengthened partnership initiatives, such as joint projects with the co-investment of resources in selected fields of mutual priority. Additionally, longstanding scientific cooperation between India and certain European countries, especially France, Germany and the UK, is vigorous and fruitful. Despite these facts, relationships with India in R&D have not yet been harmonized at a European level. There is little multilateral S&T cooperation between the European Union and India, and there is no dedicated program of cooperation between these two large scientific communities.

The aim of New INDIGO is to help fill these gaps and to ultimately provide the most relevant framework possible, allowing the Indian scientific community and Indian institutions access to the European Research Area, and allowing the Euro-Indian S&T cooperation to fully benefit from the new networking tools that have been set up, notably the FP7.

### 2.2.2. Overall Strategy

New INDIGO presents itself as an initiative for the development and the integration of Indian and European research, building an extended web of partnership to ultimately launch European programs in conjunction with India. This will allow New INDIGO to achieve the following strategic objectives:

- Structuring the international dimension of the ERA through the exchange of information, expertise, and best practices and through the design of common databases;
- Positioning a strategic partnership with India;
- Implementing a Networking Pilot Program (NPP);
- Following up on the NPP;
- Paving the way for long-term scientific cooperation between Europe and India.

### 2.2.3. Implementation and Dissemination Activities

The 15 partners and 8 observers will contribute actively to the implementation of the NEW INDIGO project.

All partners will fulfill the following tasks in order to reach the challenging objectives of the new network:

- Building a efficient model for the NPP;
- Setting up the platform at the core of NEW INDIGO, defining its management structure, and also gathering financial allocations from EU Member States, Associate Countries, and India in order to fund common projects;
- Identifying relevant fields within science and technology to be eligible for the NPP;
- Launching joint calls for proposals, evaluating of proposals submitted, and monitoring of NPP-selected projects;

- Conducting a policy foresight study by implementing a scenario-based Delphi process with policy-makers and program creators in order to assess the potential future of how science and technology relationships and cluster-building processes between the EU and India can be organized.

All partners will aim to contribute actively to raising awareness about S&T potential with a view to boosting the cooperation between EU and India.

One of main strategic objectives will be to create the appropriate supports for the dissemination of such material based on the perspective that this activity in itself should have a positive impact on the networking of research players in EU and India. A specific action directed towards thematic ERA NET will be launched in order to help integrate India into the ERA networks.

Such an exchange of information may involve international cooperation geared toward S&T and bi-regional activities, using seminars and workshops where justified. In particular, for the sake of optimal use of resources, the process of disseminating S&T cooperation between the EU and India should take advantage of initiatives implemented independently of New INDIGO. To meet this objective, it will be necessary to conduct careful follow-ups regarding relevant cooperation activities being jointly undertaken by India and EU.

Events promoted by NEW INDIGO itself, solely for the purpose of raising awareness regarding research and collaboration opportunities and disseminating the results of the project, could take place either in Europe or in India.

Moreover, the main activities under the direct EU-India agreement and the ones related to International Cooperation in the FP7 should be tackled, followed by NEW INDIGO and disseminated where justified. For this purpose, the website should be maintained [14], supported, and updated with relevant information; this will be one of the main challenges of the project in general. In order to allow the monitoring of efficient dissemination, a structured and efficient Dissemination Action Plan will be set up and constantly updated throughout the implementation of New INDIGO.

### 2.2.4. Expected Impact

New Indigo, launched in January 2009, will significantly contribute to the coordination of high-quality research between India and the European Union. The processes are listed below.

1. The identification of research hotspots in Europe and in India from the point of view of common scientific interest and complementary expertise is of the utmost importance.
2. The calls for research projects and their evaluation and follow-up by a committee of highly qualified scientists will help to structure high-quality collaborative research. The aim is not only to identify and support such projects, but also to provide the frameworks for future extended programs and actions directed towards international cooperation of European and Indian scientists.
3. Sharing experience with other geographic ERA-NETs and comparing their respective outputs will strengthen national and international standards of S&T programming and program management and, therefore, will contribute to the quality of coordinated research projects.

These three processes will converge in working toward the same goal of enhancing European-Indian research collaboration; their results, however, will go beyond this goal. From the European perspective, it will provide a new means of identifying and enhancing the coordination of high-quality research, while the same is also true from the Indian perspective.

## 2. USE OF INCO NET SCHEME

Many INCO NETS have been launched, including: "WBC INCO NET" for the Western Balkans, "EECA" for Eastern Europe and Central Asia, "MIRA" for the Mediterranean Partner Countries, "CAAST NET for sub-Saharan Africa, "EULARINET" for Latin America and "SEA-EU-NET" INCO NET for South Asia [15-20]. The last INCONET, detailed hereafter, will provide the reader with a sense of the main components of the mechanism.

### 2.1. Background Objective

"SEA EU NET" facilitates the Bi-Regional EU-ASEAN Science and Technology Dialogue. It aims to integrate key research institutions from Southeast Asia into the European Research Area. The international scientific community is well aware of the potential of the ASEAN countries with regards to specific fields of S&T, notably in ICT, environmental and sustainable development, human resources development, health, and biotechnology. These research fields are also priority fields to be supported by the EU FP7 (2007-2013). Thus, the new Framework Program provides increased opportunities for collaboration with the international scientific community as well as the ASEAN member countries. Such collaboration under the Specific International Cooperation Actions (SICAs) of FP7 (the "Peoples"-program and the "core activities") needs to be developed for topics of mutual interest to the EU MS/AS and SEA regions. Additionally it will be necessary to establish EU info-points within the SEA region in order to create and foster better collaboration between scientists from academia and the industries of the two regions. Toward that end, a bi-regional policy dialogue platform has been built up and 6 work packages have been defined, as shown below (Fig. 1).

## 3. USE OF BILATERAL S AND T COOPERATION PARTNERSHIPS

The objective is to strengthen the cooperative partnership between the EU and countries that have created an S&T cooperation agreement or are in the process of negotiating one. The EU has recently created such bilateral platforms with the Ukraine, launched in 2008, [21] and India (EUINEC), launched in 2008 [22].

The core activities of partners are:

- Improving the exchange of information on programs and funding designed to promote cooperation between Europe and Third countries;
- Developing national information platforms;

- Reinforcing promotion and awareness activities;
- Sharing best practices for venues such as workshops and presenting the state of the art and the prospects for cooperation in particular fields;
- Assistance in forming research partnership.

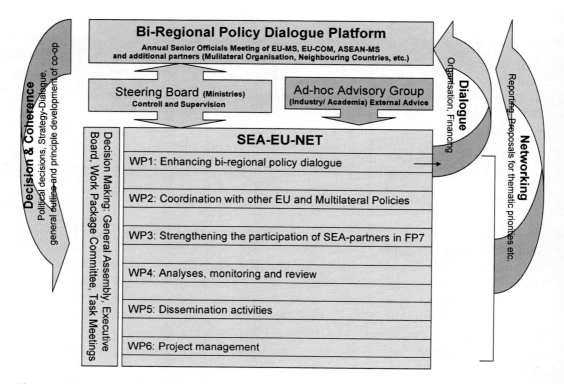

Figure 1. Bi regional policy dialogue platform.

## 3.1. Towards a European Partnership for International Scientific and Technological Cooperation and Investment Framework within the Western Balkan Countries

Regarding western Balkan countries (WBC) in particular, the integration of the region into the growing European Research Area has benefited greatly from the EU-Western Balkans Action Plan in Science and Technology, which was launched in June 2003 by the Greek EU Presidency. Additional momentum was provided during the Austrian EU Presidency in 2006, by the initiation of the Steering Platform on Research for the WBC as a joint initiative of the EU member states strongly supported by the EU Commission. The context of the significant added value of the South East European Area (SEE-ERA-NET) lies in its enhancement of the cooperation between WBC and EU member states through the development and implementation of scenarios for coordinating bilateral S&T programs among these countries. Furthermore, the INCO NET for the WBCs [15], launched in 2008, is designed to become a major strategic project to support cooperation in the field of S&T between the EU, the countries associated with FP7, and WBCs.

The overall potential of Research, Development and Innovation in the WBC region and of each country individually could be optimized using a strategic combination of national capacities, EU instruments like Research Framework Programs and Competitiveness and Innovation Programs [23], intergovernmental schemes such as EUREKA (1984) and COST (1970) and multilateral programs. The European Commission, taking into account the tangible results of policy measures taken at the national and regional levels, has decided to move towards establishing a Western Balkans Investment Framework by 2010 as agreed with the European Investment Bank, the European Bank for Reconstruction and Development and the Council of Europe Bank (COM 2008 (674) final of 5/11/2008).

## REFERENCES

[1]    *Official Journal of the European Union* C 18, pp. 11-13.
[2]    *http://www.spaceflight.esa.int/impress/*
[3]    *http://www.esf.org/index.php?id=855*
[4]    *http://www.adamproject.eu/*
[5]    *http://cmep-serbia.if.ns.ac.yu/*
[6]    *http://www.cordis.europa.eu/esfri*
[7]    *http://www.cetim.org/apps/pub.asp?Q=2107&T=Research*
[8]    *http://www.eusynapse.mpg.de/*
[9]    *http://www.eu-newgov.org/datalists/project_detail.asp?Project_ID=02*
[10]   *http://netwatch.jrc.ec.europa.eu/static/*
[11]   *http://www.era-ard.org*
[12]   *http://www.infosysplus.org*
[13]   *http://www.new-indigo.eu*
[14]   *Official Journal of the European Union* L 213, pp. 30-37.
[15]   *http://www.wbc-inco.net*
[16]   *http://www.ico-eeca.net*
[17]   *http://www.miraproject.eu*
[18]   *http://www.caast-net.org*
[19]   *http://www.S21lat.eu/eularinet*
[20]   *http://www.sea.eu.net*
[21]   *http://www.bilat-ukr.eu*
[22]   *http://www.euinec.org*
[23]   *Official Journal of the European Union* L 310, pp. 15-40.

In: Advances in Environmental Modeling and Measurements     ISBN: 978-1-60876-599-7
Editors: D. T. Mihailović, B. Lalić, pp. 13-19     © 2010 Nova Science Publishers, Inc.

*Chapter 2*

# POLICY FRAMEWORK FOR FOSTERING CENTERS OF EXCELLENCE

## *A. Belić\* and A. Bogojević*

Institute of Physics Belgrade, Belgrade, Serbia

## ABSTRACT

We present a bottom-up procedure for developing a national policy framework conducive to the promoting of R&D excellence. The procedure is based on the priorities of the EU Framework Programme, and is set in motion by identifying and reinforcing R&D Centres of Excellence with the added capacity to impact national R&D policy by developing recommendations for policy makers for fostering growth of research excellence in a rapidly changing and competitive environment. The key points in the process are: (a) development of specific benchmark procedures for quality assessment; (b) implementation of the first round of quality assessments; (c) development of detailed proposal to serve as a basis for the development of a national strategy of long term sustainable growth of research excellence in a transition environment; (d) maintaining of continued communication with relevant policy makers at all levels. The above procedure is illustrated in detail on the case of Serbia and the policy framework developed through the CX-CMCS project.

## 1. INTRODUCTION

Scientific research, technology development and innovation are universally acknowledged as the principal pillars supporting strong and sustainable economic growth. While all countries benefit from developing and implementing new technologies, the strongest relative gain is in countries in transition which have only recently made the first foothold in this competitive arena.

The governments of countries in transition see the long- and medium-term benefit of developing competitive new technologies, however, the very nature of the transition process

---

\* Corresponding author: E-mail address: abelic@phy.bg.ac.yu, Phone: +381 11 13162067, Fax: +381 11 13162190

is such that they are faced with simultaneously managing a large number of burning short-term problems. This makes it extremely difficult for them to set up a top-down procedure for developing and putting in place a national policy framework for promoting R&D excellence. Another problem with the top-down approach is to define sensible national developmental priorities conducive to the creation of a competitive R&D sector. Researchers within a competitive R&D system are more flexible, tuning their effort to the ever changing topography at the forefront of research. In transition countries the situation is generally more static. This leads to the possibility of a negative feedback loop – the less developed system could enhance its relative performance were it more dynamic, but it is not, and so instead of narrowing the gap it may in fact increase it.

There are in principle two ways a country could approach the upgrade of its R&D sector. One way would be to continually upgrade research quality by morphing the existing effort into a globally competitive one. This must necessarily be a top-down approach, it is slow, and requires the input of substantial new funds. The other way to proceed is to set up a new and parallel R&D effort to coexist (briefly) with the old one. This can be implemented by combining the strengths of top-down approaches led by policy makers with bottom-up approaches flowing from the R&D sector itself. This approach is more flexible, faster, and it does not rely on substantial funds. On the other hand, it depends crucially on the existence of a critical number of competitive R&D units, as well as the continued and in depth communication between them and relevant policy makers at all levels.

In the following section we outline an iterative three step bottom-up procedure for setting up quality R&D in transition countries, grounded on the thematic priorities of the EU Framework Programme. The first step builds on the existing strengths of a transition country's research, identifying and strengthening Centres of Excellence as the first seed points of a new R&D effort. The second step extends this process to the level of R&D institutions with capacity to influence the national R&D sector. The third and final step in the upgrade process goes from strong R&D to a truly integrated national R&D&I sector (Research and Development and Innovation) capable of conducting competitive applied research, developing new technologies, and transferring them into innovative new products.

## 2. EU ROLE IN UPGRADING R&D IN TRANSITION COUNTRIES

The starting point for a policy framework designed to set up a competitive national R&D sector is a set of well defined developmental goals. Countries in transition in general do not have such explicated goals, and often not even the capacity to create them *ab initio*. Even if such goals are created they then have to be successfully integrated into a wider European setting, as the national R&D effort cannot be globally competitive if it is only loosely integrated into the European Research Area (ERA). Of central importance for transition countries like Serbia is the existence of precise EU developmental goals from which follow the thematic priorities of the Framework Programme, Europe's principle instrument for boosting the competitiveness of its R&D sector. The fine tuning of these priorities into a national context is a relatively simple process, and this way of proceeding guarantees integration into ERA. For this reason the entry into the Framework Programme is a crucial time for a transition country.

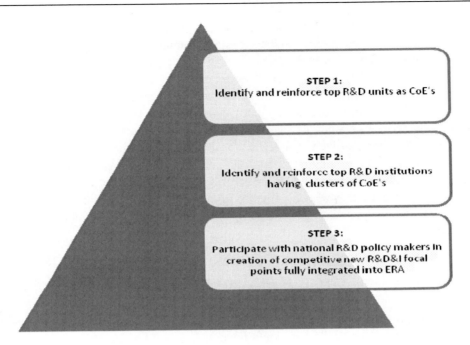

Figure 1. EU role in upgrading national R&D capacity.

The role of EU and the Framework Programme in bolstering R&D competitiveness of transition countries can be seen as a three step process. The first step consists of identifying and reinforcing top R&D units as Centres of Excellence (CoE). By so doing one forms the basis of the country's future competitive sector. The successful R&D units already show that they have the capacity to conduct quality research in priority areas, and that they can be competitive in a wider European arena. The distribution and clustering of CoE's, as well as of other R&D units participating in the Framework Programme, gives national policy makers crucial input regarding the most competitive part of their R&D sector. For example, the clustering in terms of thematic priorities is in fact a way how a country can, from the bottom-up, determine where its core competencies lie, and, conversely, in which directions it should focus its developmental goals.

R&D units are usually groups of 10 to 20 researchers. Their relatively small size makes them ideal for the above outlined first step of identifying quality focal points. That size, however, also limits their potential effect on the wider R&D effort at the national level. For this reason the second step in our process focuses on identifying and reinforcing top R&D institutions (typically consisting of a hundred or several hundred researchers), i.e. marked clusters of CoE's and other R&D units that have successfully participated in the Framework Programme. The institutions are strengthened though: increasing internal coherence and interdependency of effort of individual CoE's making up the cluster; strategic planning (institution mission, vision and hierarchy of objectives; conducting of a SWOT analysis based on those objectives; formulating, implementing and controlling actions and processes that need to be taken to achieve the objectives); upgrading and bringing into the cluster of the institution's remaining R&D units. The result of step 2 is the creation of one or more globally competitive R&D institutions in the country that are fully integrated into ERA and have the critical mass to transform the national R&D sector. Much of what needs to be undertaken in this step has already been initiated in the first step, although on a smaller scale.

Just as high quality scientific research does not directly translate into a viable R&D effort, so a competitive national R&D sector does not automatically lead to strong and sustainable economic growth. One needs to put in place an integrated R&D&I system translating ideas into technologies into innovative products. To do this step three initiates an in-depth joint process between EU and national policy makers whose goal is the creation of the country's first competitive new R&D&I focal points whose mandate is not only to narrow the intra-European technology gap, but also to make Europe as a whole globally more competitive in a specific priority areas. Such focal points are not planned at the national or European level. Rather they appear naturally from the initiated procedure through the process of clustering and complementing of the competitive R&D institutions obtained in step two of the process.

# 3. UPGRADE OF R&D IN SERBIA

The previous section gave a general outline of the iterative process for upgrading R&D in transition countries. To a very large extent the details depend on specificities of each country undergoing the process. The common thread is the division into three distinct phases. As always, the devil is in the details. For this reason in this section we focus on Serbia, and analyze the results of its recent completion of the first step in the above process.

Serbia entered the Framework Programme in FP6 (2002-2006) in which it had third country status. This status gives limited access to project calls, which is best illustrated by the fact that the participants from 116 countries belonging to this category obtained only 1.9% of the FP6 16.7 billion EUR budget, the bulk of which went to participants from 25 member countries (EU-25) and 10 associate countries [1]. Irrespective of this limited access, Serbian R&D made an successful entry into the Framework Programme. With 135 participants and EU funding of 14.9 million EUR Serbia emerged as a leader among nations with third country status [1]. A comparison of top performing nations with third country status in FP6 is given in Tab. 1.

**Table 1. FP6: top performing nations with third country status.**

| Rank | Country | Participants | EU funding (M EUR) | % of third country funding |
|------|---------|--------------|--------------------|----------------------------|
| 1 | Russia | 454 | 49.8 | 15.4b% |
| 2 | Serbia | 135 | 14.9 | 4.6b% |
| 3 | Brazil | 155 | 14.4 | 4.5b% |
| 4 | South Africa | 125 | 14.4 | 4.5b% |
| 5 | USA | 426 | 12.5 | 3.9b% |

Serbia's performance indicates that its R&D sector has at its centre a globally competitive core of "critical mass", making it viable candidate for the R&D upgrade discussed in this chapter. Similar reasoning lead the EC Research Directorate to open up two special calls towards the end of FP6 specifically targeted to stabilize and reinforce research potential in West Balkan Countries through the creation of CoE's [2,3]. The calls reinforced

30 CoE's in the region, 16 of these went to Serbia forming the aforementioned core of quality R&D units. In effect, these two calls initiated step 1 of the upgrading of Serbia's research capacity, a process completed by the end of FP6.

The substantial amount of data on FP6 makes it possible to analyze the results of step 1 in the case of Serbia. The strongest performance was focused on two priorities: Information society, and Nanotechnology and new materials. Serbian R&D was also competitive in the priorities of Food safety, and Life sciences and biotechnology. Fig. 2 depicts the quality core of Serbian R&D across these two important groups of thematic priorities. Darker circles indicate CoE's, lighter circles participants in other FP6 projects across these priorities. The figure illustrates the size of the competitive core at the centre of Serbia's R&D sector, indicating that it has the "critical mass" needed to sustain an iterative upgrade process like the one presented in this chapter. The figure also shows that, at least in the directions of these two groups of thematic priorities, there is already in place a clustering of excellence, both at the level of R&D units (dashed circles), and several R&D institutions (solid circles). This is precisely the kind of clustering that is necessary in order to make step two of the outlined national R&D upgrade possible. From the figure we see that 3 CoE's have demonstrated sustainability of effort already during FP6 by participating in other FP6 projects. Two of these are located at the Institute of Physics Belgrade (IPB), an institution whose four CoE's make it the country's principal competitive R&D cluster. Not surprisingly, the highest scoring project in the two calls for Centre's of Excellence from WBC countries (circled in red), the CX-CMCS project, is itself located at IPB in its Scientific Computing Laboratory [4]. The foremost candidates for the institution-level reinforcing envisaged in step two of the presented upgrade procedure are IPB in the field of physical sciences and technologies, and the Faculty of Agriculture of the University of Belgrade in the field of life sciences and technologies. An exceptionally positive sign of cooperation at the level of institutions is indicate by the solid lines linking R&D units in different institutions, an indication that, if step two upgrade is put in place, Serbia's leading R&D institutions may have the capacity to initiate substantial institutional clustering needed for step three.

Step two (reinforcing of top R&D institutions) builds on the existing internal coherence and interdependency of effort of its individual R&D units, particularly its CoE's. For step two to be viable, however, it is also necessary that step one has created a basis for the initiating of the bottom-up process of the setting up of a national policy framework for building a R&D sector based on excellence. In addition, it is necessary that at this point the institutions that are to apply for reinforcing have at least initiated a strategic planning procedure explicating in detail their current state (mission), where they plan to be (vision), and a hierarchy of measurable objectives consistent with that vision. These form the basis for a institutional SWOT (Strengths-Weaknesses-Opportunities-Threats) analysis. The results of the SWOT analysis in turn make it possible to formulate the processes that need to be taken to achieve the institutions objectives, as well as to determine how those actions are to be implemented, monitored, and controlled.

CX-CMCS (Centre of Excellence for Computer Modelling of Complex Systems) has played a key role in both setting up the basis of a national policy framework of R&D excellence, as well as initiating the process of strategic planning at the IPB. In this direction it has already created the following deliverables [5] in the first two years of the three year project:

- Career development plan for newly employed researchers;
- Mobility and training plan;
- Benchmark procedures for quality assessment of RTD centres of excellence;
- SCL research quality assessment.
- By completion of the CX-CMCS project its researchers will produce and make publically available the following detailed studies:
- Strategy of long term sustainable growth of research excellence in transition (an overview of this is strategy is given in the present chapter);
- High performance computing landscape of Serbia;
- Strategic plan of the Institute of Physics Belgrade (2010-2014).

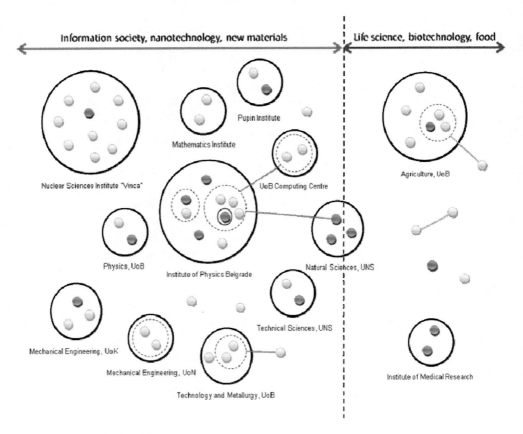

Figure 2. Quality core of Serbian R&D.

In order to successfully impact national R&D, and in particular make possible step two of the wider national R&D reinforcing envisaged by the proposed bottom-up procedure, these policy documents need to be made available to other R&D units and institutions, as well as to relevant policy makers at all levels. CX-CMCS has for this reason put strong emphasis on project visibility through:

- Playing an active role in strengthening national and regional R&D sectors (training researchers to participate in Framework Programmes);

- Enhanced interaction with R&D centres throughout ERA [6,7];
- Setting up and maintain of strong two-way dialogue with R&D policy makers at all levels;
- Enhanced relations with industry;
- Increased visibility in the media and general public.

## 4. CONCLUSION

An overview is given of a three step iterative process based on the Framework Programme for the long term sustainable growth of research excellence in transition. The first step in this process was completed by Serbia during FP6. Results indicate that this process can be extremely successfully implemented on transition countries like Serbia, whose R&D effort has a globally competitive core of "critical mass" existing within a wider sector that is starved for funds. We end by present the crucial contribution of the CX-CMCS project to this process.

## REFERENCES

[1]  FP6 *Final Review: Subscription, Implementation, Participation, EC, Brussels*, June 2008

[2]  *Evaluation of the Sixth Framework Programmes for Research and Technological Development* 2002-2006, Report of the expert group, February 2009

[3]  *Calls FP6-2004-INCO-WBC/SSA-3 and FP6-2005-INCO-WBC/SSA-3*

[4]  Scientific Computing Laboratory web site: *http://www.scl.rs*

[5]  CX-CMCS project web site: *http://cx-cmcs.phy.bg.ac.rs*

[6]  *International projects:* CX-CMCS, SEE-GRID, EGEE II, SEE-GRID-2 (in FP6); EGEE III, SEE-GRID-SCI, PRACE (in FP7); LEARNIG@ATLAS; COST action P10; NATO reintegration grant ESCCM; and bilateral projects with Slovenia, France and Germany.

[7]  *Visits to the Scientific Computing Laboratory*, IPB: EU Commissioner Potocnik (start of CX-CMCS), Minster of Science Popovic, Minister of Finance Dinkic (launch of National Investment Plan), Director General JRC Schenkel, Deputy Prime Minister Djelic (launch of National Supercomputing Initiative); regular meetings at Ministry of Science.

# PART ONE – ENVIRONMENTAL FLUID MECHANICS ISSUES

In: Advances in Environmental Modeling and Measurements      ISBN: 978-1-60876-599-7
Editors: D. T. Mihailović, B. Lalić, pp. 23-32      © 2010 Nova Science Publishers, Inc.

Chapter 3

# DEVELOPMENT OF THE EBU-POM COUPLED REGIONAL CLIMATE MODEL AND RESULTS FROM CLIMATE CHANGE EXPERIMENTS

## V. Djurdjević* and B. Rajković

University of Belgrade, Belgrade, Serbia

## ABSTRACT

This work presents a coupled regional climate model (CRCM) and some results from climate change time-slice experiments. EBU-POM is a two-way regional coupled model, with Eta/NCEP limited area model as its atmospheric part and Princeton Ocean Model as its ocean part. Both models are well known and have been extensively verified, Eta was operational model in NCEP for many years and POM is one of most used models for scientific investigations but also for operational ocean forecasts. Exchanges of atmosphere fluxes and sea surface temperature (SST) between the two components are done interactively, during integration, using specially designed coupler software. In every physical time step of the atmospheric model (360 seconds), surface atmosphere fluxes, needed for the ocean forcing, are transferred to ocean model grid, and after that SST is transferred back onto atmosphere model grid, serving as the new bottom boundary condition. In this study CRCM domain covers Europe region. Atmospheric model horizontal resolution was 0.25° and ocean model horizontal resolution was 0.2°. Two-way coupled scheme was only applied over the Mediterranean Sea. For other water bodies (Atlantic Ocean and the Black sea) we have used SST from the global model integrations. Here we will present verification of present climate integration for base period 1961-1990 and an analysis of A1B climate change scenario experiment. CRCM was nested within integrations of atmospheric ocean global circulation model SX-G. Focus will be on changes of seasonal mean surface temperature and precipitation patterns.

* Corresponding author: E-mail address: vdj@ff.bg.ac.rs, Phone: +381 11 2625981, Fax: +381 11 2634975

# 1. INTRODUCTION

Since the early nineties, starting with work of Giorgi [1] and later followed by series of papers [2-8] and by other numerous authors [9-11], high resolution limited domain models have been nested into low resolutions global models. Such models become known as Regional Climate Models (RCM). The idea was that regional models with much higher resolution will improve global results by improving at least forcing at the surface-atmosphere interface. Beside that, a regional model may have improved parameterizations of various physical processes in comparison with the respective parameterizations of the global circulation model (GCM). The biggest differences are in representations of the topography, land-sea contrast and surface characteristics of the land, such as soil types and soil vegetation. Since we know that large part of the climate forcing comes from the land-sea-air interactions we expect that this, higher horizontal resolution, will improve RCM simulations in comparison with the global ones. Of course there are obvious limits in these improvements. If GCM has a large bias in representing the large scale fields, on horizontal scales larger than the domain of the RCM, then that cannot be corrected by the RCM. On the other hand where forcing is local we do hope to improve possible biases of the GCM simulations. In our case improvement could be expected from the new sea/ocean SST since GCM ocean part has low resolution in the Mediterranean Sea, the main sea that influences the Italy and Balkan region.

# 2. THE MODEL

The regional climate model that was used is a combination of two limited area models one for the atmosphere and the other one for the ocean [12,13]. The reason for the inclusion of the ocean model into RCM is that our integration domain was the region of the southern Europe, Italy and Balkan Peninsula. Both are surrounded by the Mediterranean Sea and presumably influenced by it. The atmospheric component was the limited area model developed by Janjić. The model has two versions of the vertical coordinate system. The original σ, orography following system and η, quasi-horizontal coordinate system introduced by Mesinger [14]. In our simulations we kept the η choice of the vertical coordinate (Eta in the further text), for details of the model please see papers by Janjić [15-20] and Mesinger [21].

To insure good representation of the geostrophic adjustment process, model is on the E-grid, [22,23] nomenclature. Its dynamic core has conservative advection scheme for all variables and efficient time stepping through splitting of the fast processes (geostrophic adjustment etc.) and slower ones advection and physics in general. The physics package consists of surface scheme, radiation scheme [24], turbulence closure sub model, viscous sublayer and convection parameterization. The centre of atmospheric model was at 16 E, 42.5 N and the horizontal resolution were 0.25 degrees. In vertical direction model had 32 levels, with first level at 20 meters, while the top was at 100 mb. The standard radiation scheme assumes that the composition of the atmosphere is constant with several possibilities of the amount of $CO_2$. In our runs profiles of the greenhouse gasses was as in the A1B scenario, which means changing of the $CO_2$ amount from the present value to roughly $2 \times CO_2$. So we took another radiation scheme that was kindly provided to us by Dr Carlos Pérez from the

Barcelona Supercomputing Center, and Dr Slobodan Nickovic, [24] which had the option of variable content of the greenhouse gasses. We have improved its part that does connection between radiation and clouds. After some adjustment we were relatively satisfied with its performance.

The ocean component is the Princeton ocean model (POM), a three-dimensional, primitive equation, numerical model, developed by Blumberg and Mellor [25]. A comprehensive description of POM can be found in [26]. Its principal attributes are: horizontal grid is on the C-grid (Arakawa and Wininghoff nomenclature), vertical coordinate is σ coordinate, efficient time differencing (explicit in horizontal and implicit in vertical), free surface, complete thermodynamic and has imbedded second order turbulence closure Mellor-Yamada 2.5 [27].

Important part of every coupled model is method of exchange of data between its two components. Due to very different geometries of the two components of the model special care was taken in design of this coupling module. Beside different positions of the corresponding points there is difference in horizontal resolution. Roughly, the atmospheric component had four times coarser resolution. That led to different land-sea masks two components with slightly different distributions of sea and land. A same point can be seen as a land point and for the atmospheric component and ocean point by the ocean model. Then, due to large differences in heat and momentum fluxes over land and sea, energy and momentum exchange between sea and atmosphere will be wrong. To avoid such situation ocean points are separated in two categories. The first category consists of the points that are seen as ocean points in both atmosphere and ocean component. The ocean points, which are seen as land points by the atmosphere component, are the second category. Fluxes at such points were computed in the following way. First we assign the value of the average flux, averaging done over all points in the first category. In order to avoid possible jumps, at the edge of the two sets of points, laplacian smoothing is applied over the second set of points. Relative positions of the both models are shown in Fig. 1 with atmospheric model domain (Eta) light blue and the POM domain dark blue. This system we will call CRCM in the further text. Models exchange fluxes and SST every physical time step of the atmospheric model, which was in these runs 360 seconds. While the whole Mediterranean Sea was inside of POM's domain, Black Sea and parts of the Atlantic were not. The SST of those water bodies were the one from the GCM. Our Mediterranean Sea was closed on both Gibraltar and Dardanelles

The global modeling data employed in this work are time series obtained from climate simulations carried out with the SX-G coupled atmosphere-ocean general circulation model (AOGCM), which is an evolution of the SINTEX and SINTEX-F models [28-33]. The ocean model component is the reference version 8.2 of the Ocean Parallelise (OPA) [34] with the ORCA2 configuration. The model longitude- latitude resolution is 2°x2° cosine (latitude) with increased meridional resolutions to 0.5° near the equator. The model has 31 vertical levels, ten of which lie in the upper 100 meters of the ocean. For more details about the ocean model and its performance, readers are referred to online web-site http://www.lodyc.jussieu.fr/opa/. The evolution of the sea ice is described by the LIM (Louvain-La-Neuve sea ice model) and the atmospheric model component is the latest version of ECHAM-4 [35]. The horizontal resolution was T106, corresponding to a Gaussian grid of about 1.12°x1.12°. In the pantheon of long coupled climate simulations, this is a considerably high horizontal resolution. A hybrid sigma-pressure vertical coordinate is used with 19 vertical levels.

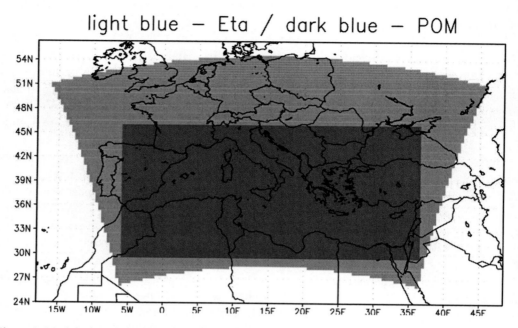

Figure 1. Models domains. Light blue area represent Eta model domain and dark blue rectangle represent POM model domain.

## 3. THE REFERENCE DATA

The simulated climate of the Euro-Mediterranean region and the main features of its variability are evaluated comparing the model results with observational data sets. Specifically, we use data from the NCEP Re-Analysis, and the observed precipitation and air surface temperature from the Climate Research Unit (CRU) data set [36]. For the sake of simplicity, in the rest of the paper we will refer to all of these data as observations. We have performed two time slice integrations, the present climate (1960-1990) and the end of the 21st century (2070-2100). The initial fields for the atmosphere were obtained from the global runs as well as the boundary conditions. Updating at the boundaries was done every 6 hours according to the boundary conditions of the Eta model. If the flow was entering the domain, at the first row of points values are read in. In the second row of points we had diagonal averaging between the points of the first row and the points of the third row where model did calculate. If the boundary point is an out flow point model had the upstream advection from its inside over boundary 4-5 points. The ocean points were initialized with the MODB (Mediterranean Ocean Data Base) data set [37] the monthly climatology of the Mediterranean Sea. Over Atlantic and Black Sea SST was initialized interpolating it from the SST of the global model. In the case of the future climate both atmosphere and ocean were initialized from the global model.

## 4. ANALYSIS OF THE 20TH CENTURY SIMULATION

The first step in establishing the quality of a climate model is comparison of it's simulations with the observed climatology. To do that we present seasonal means over period 1961-1990 for the winter season, December-January-February and summer season, Jun-July-August (DJF and JJA in the further text) from our CRCM and corresponding fields from the CRU data set.

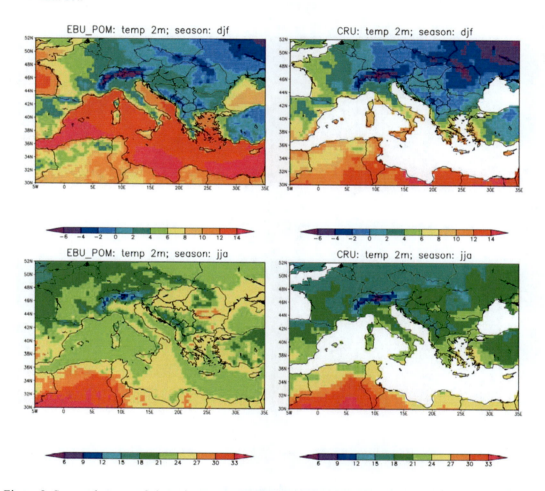

Figure 2. Seasonal means of air surface temperature, for DJF season, upper panels and for JJA season, lower panels. Results from model are presented on left side and CRU data set on right.

On the Fig. 2 we present two meter temperature (T2m in the further text) for the DFJ season, with left panel showing temperature from the CRCM, right the same from the CRU data set. First we can say that there is a general agreement between CRCM and CRU except in the North-east part where CRCM has larger T2m. Going from region to region we see that North Africa is captured very well and similar for Spain. Italy, north and central are well captured with Sicily slightly cooler by 1 degree. The western Balkan and Albania shows quite good resemblance. Going to the Northeast situation gets worse, as mentioned at the beginning. To the South, Greece and Turkey, we are back to the previous level of accuracy.

Alps are still the region with the strongest signal. Due to the smaller scale mountains like Primes and Carpathians are less prominent. Italy is warmer at least 1-3 degrees increasing going to the South. Over Balkans agreement is relatively good having in mind the differences in the horizontal resolutions. Turkey similarly is captured well while Greece is slightly warmer, more to the South. In numbers bias score is -0.21, mae is 1.88 and rmese is 2.15, numbers quite similar to the one reported in literature. On same figure, Fig. 2, we show results for the summer season in the same order of panels.

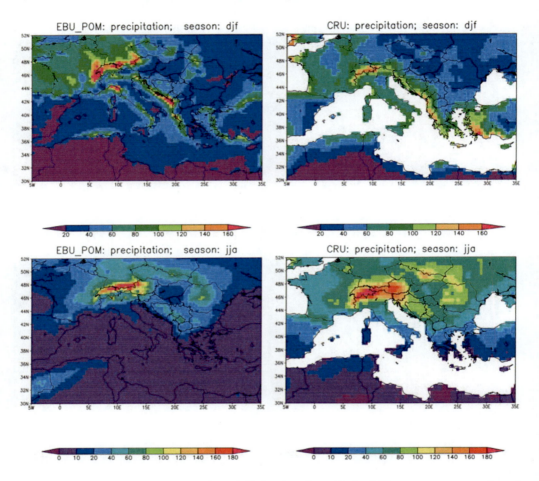

Figure 3. Seasonal means of accumulated precipitation (mm/month), for DJF season, upper panels and for JJA season, lower panels. Results from model are presented on left side and CRU data set on right.

CRCM simulations are warmer than the verification but general resemblance is present. Again west is better then the east. Actually the shape of the T2m fields from CRCM and CRU scale quite well. This is also visible from the scores, which are worse than fore the winter season but still quite acceptable for the climate simulations.

The summer results, presented in Fig. 2 show clearly the excessive warming in the eastern part of the. Next we turn to the precipitation verifications. Fig. 3 have winter and summer seasonal averages of the precipitations. Positions of the extreme precipitation over Alps and on the Eastern Adriatic coast is captured but the values are larger in the CRCM simulations then the observed. In general one should not "argue" with the observations but in this case, of the precipitation, maybe the CRCM results are closer to the reality then the CRU data set. In particular the Montenegro coast maximum looks reasonable since we know that we have the Europe maximum in precipitation in the winter season. On the other hand the south Turkish coast maximum is missing in the CRCM results. Also the North Africa, coast of Allegers has to narrow precipitation zone, which is missing in the eastern Libya coastal region. For the summer season we get reduction of the precipitation thought the integration region, which is consistent with the higher T2m temperatures earlier documented. Maximum over Alps is present but is narrower and weaker then in the observations. To the east of Alps there is even larger decrease particularly over Hungary and over Carpathians as well. Unfortunately the CRU data set has only land measurements so we cannot verify precipitation over sea.

## 5. COMPARISON BETWEEN 20TH CENTURY AND A1B SCENARIO OF THE 21ST CENTURY

The results from climate simulations are presented as differences of 30 years means between future climate (2071-2100) and present climate (1961-1990). The 30 year means should be able to capture 75% of the variance of the true signal according to, [38] as well as statistically significant changes in extreme precipitation. We present these differences for DJF and JJA seasons for two main parameters, air surface temperature and precipitation.

We start with T2m fields. In Fig. 4, top panel, present differences from the CRCM simulations, with the DJF season on the left and JJA season on the right. For the CRCM simulations the range of changes is between 1.2-3.5 degrees for the DJF season while for the JJA season are larger and are in the range of 1.8-4.2 degrees. Larger values are connected either to the local topography, Alps, Pyrenees, Balkan Mountains, and Apennines or like for the Italy with both topography as land-sea line. The same holds in the case of the southern edge of the Turkish Plato. Two maximums with strongest warming, for the DJF, occur over the Alps region, with almost 3.5 degrees, and northeastern region of the southern Alger n corner of the domain. The weakest warming is over Aegean Sea and in Africa in Sahara around 30 degrees North and 5 degrees East. Looking at the temperature over the Mediterranean Sea, the Aegean Sea shows the smallest while northwestern Mediterranean has the largest increase. In the rest of the domain variations are from about 1.5 to 2.2 degrees. Several warmer spots are in Spain, over Prokletije Mountains in the northern Albania and in the western Morocco.

On bottom, in Fig. 4, we present differences in precipitation. On left we present simulations for the DJF, and on right for the JJA season. The bottom panels have global results, for the winter to the left, and summer to the right. Fields are relative differences in accumulated precipitation in percents. For the DJF season, CRCM has almost every where decrease with variable amount, going from -50-0%. There is a small part of the domain, the south-center and the southeastern part with increase between 10-40%. The largest differences are Saharan part of Algiers and Morocco.

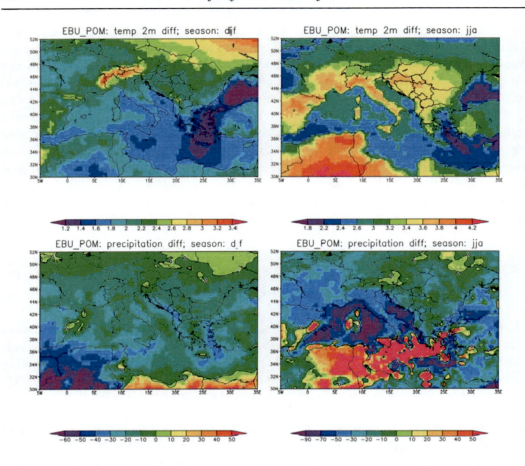

Figure 4. Changes in seasonal mean air surface temperature, for seasons DJF and JJA over period 2071-2100 compared to base period 1961-1990 following A1B scenario (upper panels) and changes in seasonal accumulated precipitations for same periods and seasons (lower panels).

For the JJA season and land part of the domain, we have similar results with slightly larger decrease of precipitation over France and Northern Italy. Much larger are differences over the sea. Decrease in precipitation is from 10-50%, over the Mediterranean Sea but quite variable from region to region. The western Mediterranean, central and southern Adriatic show the largest decrease while central and eastern Mediterranean have increase of precipitation up to 40-50%. Similarly Algiers and Tunisia have increase in precipitation of 20-50% while north d northwestern parts cf the domain have the smallest changes in both seasons. Very ear Gibraltar; we get even larger decease of about 40-50%.

# 4. CONCLUSION

The climate of the Euro-Mediterranean region and the main features of its variations are evaluated by coupled regional climate model; the model results are also compared to observational data sets. In addiction both models, after some preliminary simulations with increasing greenhouse gases (GHGs) concentrations, have been used to simulate the possible climate changes induced by GHGs by applying the climate scenario A1B from IPCC. The main scientific conclusions regarding the possible climate change at the end of the 21$^{st}$ century.

Summarizing, the results from the climate regional model for the end of 21$^{st}$ century, following A1B scenario, show overall increase in surface air temperature and decrease in precipitation over the Euro-Mediterranean region. High increase in surface air temperature has been found during summer season (June-July-August), close to 4 °C, over both Italy and Serbia. Decrease in precipitation is also amplified during summer season with maximum over Italian costal zone. In some areas the decrease of precipitation is about 70% respect to 1961-1990 period. These results are in agreement with results obtained with other regional climate models (e.g., IPCC-AR4 2007, Chapter 11, Regional Climate Projections). Finally, this approach has confirmed that using an advanced high resolution global climate model along with an advanced high resolution regional climate model connected through dynamical downscaling is a successful approach in order to capture many small-scale processes in the atmosphere and the ocean. This is due to better representation (more detailed structure) of some characteristics of climate system (topography, soil and vegetation types, land-sea coastline, etc.). These high resolutions climate data can be used for climate change impact models of the in order to investigate small-scale phenomena, like sediment transport in coastal areas, hydrological cycles over smaller river basins and hydropower production.

## ACKNOWLEDGMENTS

This research was financed through SINTA project, supported by Italian Ministry for the Environment, Land and Sea.

## REFERENCES

[1]     F. Giorgi, and G.T. Bates, *Mon. Wea. Rev.*, 117 (1989).

[2]     F. Giorgi, *J. Clim.*, 3, 941-963 (1990).

[3]     F. Giorgi and L.O. Mearns, *Rev. Geophy.*, 29, 191-216 (1991).

[4]     F. Giorgi, M.R. Marinucci, G. De Canio, G. T. Bates, *Mon. Wea. Rev.*, 121, 2811-2832 (1993).

[5]     F. Giorgi, M.R. Marinucci, G. T. Bates, *Mon. Wea. Rev.*, 121, 2794-2813 (1993).

[6]     F. Giorgi, C. Shields Brodeur, G. T. Bates, *J. Clim.*, 7, 375-399 (1994).

[7]     F. Giorgi, X. Bi and J. Pal, *Clim. Dynam.*, 23, 839–858 (2004).

[8]     F. Giorgi, X. Bi and J. Pal, *Clim. Dynam.*, 22, 733–756 (2004).

[9]     R. G. Jones, J.M. Murphy, M. Noguer, M. Keen, *Q. J. R. Meteoral. Soc.,* 123, 265–292 (1997).

[10]   M. L. Ekman and H. Rodhe, *Clim. Dynam.*, 21, 1–10 (2003).

[11]   J. Räisänen, U. Hansson, A. Ullerstig, R. Döscher, L. P. Graham, C. Jones, H. E. M. Meier, P. Samuelsson, U. Willen, *Clim. Dynam.*, 22, 13–31 (2004).

[12]   V. Djurdjevic and B. Rajkovic, *Ann. Geophysics,* 26, 1935–1954, (2008).

[13]  S. Gualdi, B Rajkovic., V. Djurdjevic., S. Castellari, E. Scoccimarro, A. Navarra. M. Dacic,*http://www.earthprints.org/bitstream/2122/4675/1/SINTA_FInal%20Science%20 Report%20_October%202008.pdf*, (2008).

[14]  F. Mesinger, *Riv. Meteor. Aeronaut.*, 44, 95-202 (1984).

[15]  Z. I. Janjić, *Contrib. Atmos. Phys.* 50, 186–199 (1977).

[16]  Z. I. Janjić, *Contrib. Atmos. Phys.*, 52, 69–84 (1979).

[17]  Z. I. Janjić, *Mon. Wea. Rev.*, 112, 1234–1245 (1984).

[18]  Z. I. Janjić, *Mon. Wea. Rev.*, 118, 429–1443 (1990).

[19]  Z. I. Janjić, *Mon. Wea. Rev.*, 122, 927-945 (1994).

[20]  Z. I. Janjić, *WMO, Geneva, CAS/C WGNE*, p. 4.16–4.17 (1996).

[21]  F. Mesinger, Z. Janjić, S. Nicković, D. Gavrilov, D. Daven, *Mon. Wea. Rev.*, 116, 1493–1518 (1988).

[22]  F. J.Winninghoff, *Ph.D. Thesis, UCLA* (1968).

[23]  Arakawa, and V. Lamb, *Met. Comput. Phy.*, 17, 174–265 (1977).

[24]  Pérez, S. Ničković, G. Pejanović  J. M. Baldasano, E. Özsoy, *J.Geophy.Res.*, 111, D16206, doi:10.1029/2005JD006717 (2006).

[25]  Blumberg, G. Mellor, *Three-Dimensional Coastal Ocean Models*, edited by N. Heaps, 4, pp. 208 (1987).

[26]  G. L. Mellor, *Program in Atmospheric and Oceanic Sciences*, Princeton University, Princeton, NJ 08544-0710 (2002).

[27]  G. L. Mellor , T. Yamada, *Rev. Geophys and Space Phys.*, 20(4), 851–875 (1982).

[28]  S. Gualdi, A. Navarra, E. Guilyardi, P. Delecluse, *Ann. Geophysics*, 46, 1–26 (2003).

[29]  S. Gualdi, E. Guilyardi, A. Navarra, S. Masina, *Clim. Dynam.*, 20, 567–582 (2003)

[30]  E. Guilyardi, P. Delecluse, S. Gualdi, A. Navarra, *J. Clim.*16, 1141–1158 (2003).

[31]  J. J. Luo, S. Masson, S. Behera, P. Delecluse, S. Gualdi, A. Navarra, T. Yamagata, *Geophys. Res. Lett.*, 30, 2250, doi:10.1029/2003GL018649 (2003).

[32]  S Masson., *Geophys. Res. Lett.* 32, doi:10.1029/2004GL021980 (2005).

[33]  S. K. Behera, J. J. Luo, S. Masson, P. Delecluse, S. Gualdi, A. Navarra, T. Yamagata, 2005: *J. Clim.*, 18, 4514–4530 (2005).

[34]  G. Madec, P. Delecluse, M. Imbard, C. Levy, *Internal Rep.* 11, Inst. Pierre-Simon Laplace, Paris, France (1999).

[35]  E. Roeckner, and Coauthors, *Max-Planck-Institut fur Meteorologie, Rep.* 218, (1996)

[36]  P. D. Jones, D.E. Parker, T.J. Osborn, K.R. Briffa, *A Compendium of Data on Global Change.* Carbon Dioxide Information Analysis Center, Oak Ridg National Laboratory, U.S. Department of Energy, (2006).

[37]  P. Brasseur, J. M. Brankart, R. Shomnenauen, J. M. Beckers, *Deep-Sea Res.*, 43, 159-192 (1996).

[38]  Huntingford, R. G. Jones, C. Prudhomme, R. Lamb, J. H. C. Gash, *Q. J. R. Meteorol. Soc.*, 129, 1607-1621 (2003).

In: Advances in Environmental Modeling and Measurements    ISBN: 978-1-60876-599-7
Editors: D. T. Mihailović, B. Lalić, pp. 33-46    © 2010 Nova Science Publishers, Inc.

*Chapter 4*

# MODELING TRANSVERSE TURBULENT MIXING BY USING AN EDDY VISCOSITY APPROACH

## *C.Gualtieri*[*]

University of Naples "Federico II", Naples, Italy

## ABSTRACT

Although transverse mixing is a significant process in river engineering when dealing with the discharge of pollutants from point sources or the mixing of tributary inflows, no theoretical basis exists for the prediction of its rate, which is indeed based upon the results of experimental works carried on in laboratory channels or in streams and rivers. The chapter presents the results of a numerical study undertaken to simulate the transverse mixing of a steady-state point source of a tracer in a two-dimensional rectangular geometry. This geometry is that of Lau and Krishnappan, who collected turbulent mixing data for a shallow flow. In the numerical study an approach based on the Reynolds Averaged Navier-Stokes (RANS) equations was applied, where the closure problem was solved by using turbulent viscosity concept. Particularly, the classical two-equations k-ε model was used. Two methods were applied to the model results to evaluate the turbulent transverse mixing coefficient. The effect on transverse mixing of two different grids located upstream and in the section of the tracer source was also compared and studied, confirming that RANS-approach may provide acceptable results.

## 1. INTRODUCTION

Although transverse mixing process is of significant importance when dealing with wastewater treatment plants discharges, cooling water returns and the mixing of tributary inflows, this process has received less attention by the researchers than longitudinal mixing [1,2]. In such situations, since steady-state conditions are approximated, that is temporal concentration gradients are small, the spreading across the channel is important and accurate modeling and prediction of transverse mixing is required [3]. Also, it is well known that

* Corresponding author: E-mail address:carlo.gualtieri@unina.it, Phone: + 39 081 7683433, Fax: + 39 081 5561909

transverse mixing is important in determining the rate of longitudinal mixing because it tends to control the exchange between regions of different longitudinal velocity. Particularly, transverse mixing and longitudinal mixing are inversely proportional. A strong transverse mixing tends to erase the effect of differential longitudinal advection and pollutants particles migrate across the velocity profile so fast that they essentially all move at the mean speed of the flow, causing only a weak longitudinal spreading. On the other hand, a weak transverse mixing implies a long time for differential advection to take effect, so the pollutants patch is highly distorted while it diffuses moderately in the transverse direction and longitudinal mixing is large [4]. Despite its importance, no established theory exists to predict transverse mixing rates, turbulent diffusion coefficient and its dependence on the various flow parameters must be determined from experimental works.

This chapter presents the results of a numerical study undertaken to simulate the transverse mixing of a steady-state point source of a tracer in a 2D rectangular geometry, which is expected to reproduce a shallow flow. A shallow flow can be defined as a predominantly horizontal flow in a fluid domain for which the two horizontal dimensions greatly exceed the vertical dimension [5]. The considered geometry is that of Lau and Krishnappan [6], who collected transverse turbulent mixing data in a rectangular channel. Two methods were applied to the results obtained with Multiphysics 3.5a™, a commercial modeling environment [7], to evaluate the transverse turbulent mixing coefficient. Numerical results were compared to estimate the effect on transverse mixing of two different grids inserted upstream and in the section of the point of injection. Finally, they were compared with previous numerical results.

## 2. TRANSVERSE TURBULENT MIXING. LITERATURE REVIEW

It is believed that transverse or lateral mixing is due to following causes [1,8,9]:

- turbulence generated by the channel boundaries, which involves many eddies of various sizes and intensities, all embedded in one another [10]. These eddies are responsible for both momentum and mass transfer, according the Reynolds analogy [11] resulting in a contaminants mixing far exceeding that occurring in the molecular scale. Also it could be expected that in a turbulent flow the largest eddies regulate the rate of turbulent diffusion. In a river, lateral mixing is due to the transverse eddies that rotate horizontally, about a vertical axis;
- vertical variations in the transverse velocity (velocity shear), which are significant in the vicinity of channel banks and further contribute to transverse spreading of contaminants;
- secondary currents, which causes contaminants to move in opposite directions at different depths increasing the rate of mixing [2,12,13].

However, since in the field observations it is difficult to distinguish their own effects on contaminants spreading in the lateral direction, the effect of these processes is usually combined into a single mixing coefficient for convenience, that is $D_{t-y}$ [1]. However, in some conditions, it is possible to argue that one process would be more important than the other one. Also, the effects of the secondary currents may play their role. For example, at bends of natural channels there are strong secondary currents which carry solute sideways in different directions at different depths increasing significantly the transverse mixing process [1]. On the other hand, in straight rectangular laboratory channels, the flow does not depart significantly from plane shear flow and transverse dispersion is negligibly small. Thus, in these conditions mixing is mainly due to turbulent diffusion even if secondary currents could occur increasing the rate of mixing in the channel. Nevertheless, since no established theory exists to predict transverse mixing rates even in those channels, turbulent diffusion coefficient and its dependence on the various flow parameters must be determined from experimental works. A good number of experimental works are available in the literature [1,6,8,9,14].

As previously recalled a theoretical model for the transverse turbulent diffusion does not yet exist. Prandtl mixing length hypothesis relates vertical turbulent diffusivity $D_{t-z}$ with vertical gradient of longitudinal velocity [9]

$$D_{t-z} = L_m^2 \left| \frac{\partial \langle u \rangle}{\partial z} \right| ,$$

(1)

where $z$ is the vertical distance, $D_{t-z}$ is the vertical turbulent diffusion coefficient, $\langle u \rangle$ is the ensemble mean longitudinal velocity and $L_m$ is the mixing length, that is a turbulent length scale. Drawing an analogy for the transverse turbulent mixing process yields

$$D_{t-y} = L_m^2 \left| \frac{\partial \langle u \rangle}{\partial y} \right| .$$

(2)

However, in a plane shear flow, ensemble mean of $u$ does not vary across the channel which implies that $D_{t-y}$ vanishes in disagreement with experimental findings [1]. Eq. (2) may be applied near the banks where there is a strong transverse velocity shear but in the thalweg that equation cannot be used. Nevertheless, the first part of Prandtl theory could be still considered because from dimensional reasoning it relates turbulent mixing coefficient to a turbulent length and velocity scales, $L_T$ and $U_T$, respectively, as

$$D_{t-y} = L_T U_T .$$

(3)

In a plane shear flow turbulence is generated by vertical velocity shear which arises as a result of bed friction [1]. Since shear velocity $u^*$ is a measure of bed friction, it could be selected as velocity length scale in Eq. (3). This is also consistent with literature for vertical diffusivity and longitudinal dispersion coefficient [1]. There is indeed something of controversy about the proper length scale to be used in Eq. (3). It is very common to assume flow depth $h$ as length scale for transverse diffusivity too, that is $h=L_T$, since this parameter controls the largest vertical eddies. However, it may be argued that the maximum length scale of transverse eddies, which are responsible for transverse turbulent mixing, cannot be restricted to the water depth [1]. Thus, although it is not clear how vertical eddies generated by bed friction undergo rotation and become transverse eddies, it was also suggested to apply channel width $W$ as characteristic turbulent length scale for $D_{t\text{-}y}$ [6].

Gualtieri and Mucherino re-analyzed a 217 literature data set collected in straight rectangular laboratory channels [15]. The data set was obtained bringing together 139 data collected by Rutherford [1] from different investigators and 78 experimental data more recently collected by Chau in a 4.0 m width laboratory channel [14]. This data set is believed to be the largest ever prepared. The analysis of these data confirmed that a linear relationship holds between $D_{t\text{-}y}$ and $hu^*$ [15]

$$D_{t\text{-}y} = 0.166\,h\,u^*\,. \tag{4}$$

Note that Fischer et al. [16] from the review of several studies proposed:

$$D_{t\text{-}y} = 0.15\,h\,u^*\,, \tag{5}$$

where there is the possibility of an error of $\pm 50\%$. On the other hand, Rutherford stated that the most likely value of the transverse diffusivity in plane shear flow is for 0.13 [1]. Therefore, Eq. (4) provides a larger value for $D_{t\text{-}y}$ than previous literature equations.

# 3. NUMERICAL SIMULATIONS

As above outlined, a shallow flow can be defined as having a lateral extent greater than its vertical confinement, as is the case in natural rivers, estuaries, stratified layers in lakes, the upper ocean and even for large scale motions in the oceans [5,17]. In a shallow flow the turbulent field can be considered as homogeneous and stationary in the horizontal plane and mixing is governed by two-dimensional coherent structures [17]. Therefore, as a first approximation two-dimensional or depth-averaged models may be applied to describe hydrodynamics and mass-transfer processes. Since the flow is turbulent, mass conservation equation and the Navier-Stokes equations of motion must be averaged over a small time increment applying Reynolds decomposition, where flow quantities are decomposed in a temporal mean and a fluctuating component. The fluctuations include all the turbulent motions. The application of such decomposition results in the Reynolds-averaged Navier-Stokes equations (RANS), where the effect of turbulence appears as a number of terms representing the interaction between the fluctuating velocities and termed Reynolds stresses. These equations provide the simplest level of modeling a turbulent flow. They introduce closure problem, which can be solved, in analogy with the viscous stresses in laminar flow, by using an eddy viscosity or turbulent viscosity concept [18]. By analogy with the molecular viscosity of a fluid, the eddy viscosity can also be expressed as a product of the characteristic turbulent length and velocity scales. Hence, dimensional reasoning provides for eddy viscosity an equation like Eq. (3). Different approaches can be used to derive these scales. The most popular approach is that uses the turbulent kinetic energy $k$ and its rate of dissipation $\varepsilon$, resulting in the $k$-$\varepsilon$ turbulence model. This model and its variation are the most widely used turbulence models and this is largely due to their ease in implementation, economy in computation and, most importantly, being able to obtain reasonable accurate solution with the available computer power [19]. Despite some shortcomings inherent in RANS background, recent studies demonstrated that for simplified cases, where mean velocities and bulk mixing properties are needed, RANS-modeling of shallow flows is still appropriate [20]. For a planar, incompressible flow RANS equations are

$$\frac{\partial \overline{u}}{\partial x} + \frac{\partial \overline{v}}{\partial y} = 0 ,$$  (6)

$$\overline{\rho}\left( \frac{\partial \overline{u}}{\partial t} + \overline{u}\frac{\partial \overline{u}}{\partial x} + \overline{v}\frac{\partial \overline{u}}{\partial y} \right) = \overline{\rho}\, g_x - \frac{\partial \overline{p}}{\partial x} + \left(\mu + \rho\, v_t\right)\nabla^2 \overline{u}$$

$$\overline{\rho}\left( \frac{\partial \overline{v}}{\partial t} + \overline{u}\frac{\partial \overline{v}}{\partial x} + \overline{v}\frac{\partial \overline{v}}{\partial y} \right) = \overline{\rho}\, g_y - \frac{\partial \overline{p}}{\partial y} + \left(\mu + \rho\, v_t\right)\nabla^2 \overline{v}$$  (7)

where $\rho$ and $\mu$ are the fluid density and viscosity, $p$ is the fluid pressure and $u$, $v$ are velocity components in the $x$ and $y$ directions, respectively. The overbar indicates time-averaged quantities. Notably, in Eq. (7) there is the eddy kinematic viscosity $v_t$, that in the above assumption of isotropic turbulence could be estimated as

$$v_t = \frac{C_\mu k^2}{\varepsilon} ,$$  (8)

where $k$ and $\varepsilon$ are the turbulent kinetic energy per mass unit and its dissipation rate, respectively, and $C_\mu = 0.09$. To estimate these parameters the two-equations of standard $k$-$\varepsilon$ model are [7]

$$\rho\frac{\partial k}{\partial t} + \rho \overline{\overline{V}} \cdot \nabla k = \nabla \cdot \left[ \left( \frac{\mu + \mu_t}{\sigma_k} \right)\nabla k \right] + \frac{1}{2}\mu_t\left( \nabla \overline{\overline{V}} + \left( \nabla \overline{\overline{V}} \right)^T \right)^2 - \rho\varepsilon ,$$  (9)

$$\rho\frac{\partial \varepsilon}{\partial t} + \rho \overline{\overline{V}} \cdot \nabla \varepsilon = \nabla \cdot \left[ \left( \frac{\mu + \mu_t}{\sigma_\varepsilon} \right)\nabla \varepsilon \right] + \frac{1}{2}C_{1\varepsilon}\frac{\varepsilon}{k}\mu_t\left( \nabla \overline{\overline{V}} + \left( \nabla \overline{\overline{V}} \right)^T \right)^2 - \rho C_{2\varepsilon}\frac{\varepsilon^2}{k} ,$$  (10)

where $\mu_t$ is the dynamic eddy viscosity, whereas $C_\mu$, $\sigma_k$, $\sigma_\varepsilon$, $C_{1\varepsilon}$ and $C_{2\varepsilon}$ are constants and their values are listed in Tab. 1.

**Table 1. Values of the constants of the standard $k$-□ model.**

| $C_\mu$ | $\sigma_k$ | $\sigma_\varepsilon$ | $C_{1\varepsilon}$ | $C_{2\varepsilon}$ |
|---|---|---|---|---|
| 0.09 | 1.00 | 1.30 | 1.44 | 1.92 |

The transport of solutes in the rectangular geometry was modelled by using the 2D advection-diffusion equation for isotropic turbulence [7]

$$\frac{\partial \overline{C}}{\partial t} + \overline{u}\,\frac{\partial \overline{C}}{\partial x} + \overline{v}\,\frac{\partial \overline{C}}{\partial y} = \frac{\partial}{\partial x}\left( D_t\,\frac{\partial \overline{C}}{\partial x}\right) + \frac{\partial}{\partial y}\left( D_t\,\frac{\partial \overline{C}}{\partial y}\right),$$
(11)

where molecular diffusion was neglected, $D_t$ is the turbulent diffusivity and $\overline{C}$ is the solute concentration. Turbulent diffusivity was derived from turbulent viscosity following Reynolds analogy [4]. Their ratio is the turbulent Schmidt number $Sc_t$

$$Sc_t = \frac{v_t}{D_t}\ ,$$
(12)

which is analogous to the classical Schmidt number $Sc = v/D_m$, ratio of kinematic viscosity to molecular diffusivity. In open channel flows, $Sc_t$ is usually in the range from 0.3 to 1.0 [1]. For the simulations, $Sc_t = 1.00$ was applied.

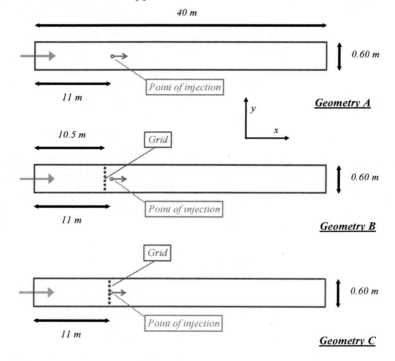

Figure 1. Sketch of the simulated 2D geometries.

These equations were solved by using Multiphysics 3.5a™ modeling package, which solves for the same flow domain both motion and advection-diffusion equations. The model provides as outputs the velocity components $\overline{u}$ and $\overline{v}$, $k$-$\varepsilon$ model parameters, solute concentration $\overline{C}$ and many others [7]. Multiphysics 3.5a™ was applied to the three rectangular 2D geometries presented in Fig.1. They are the view from above, i.e. in the $x$-$y$ plan, of the channel used by Lau and Krishnappan in their experimental works on turbulent transverse mixing [6]. However, in Geometry B there was a grid formed by 6 squares elements, each with dimension 0.02·0.02 m, with a center-to-center spacing $d$=0.06 m . The grid was located 0.5 m upstream the point of injection. In Geometry C, the same grid was located in the section of the tracer source. In Geometry A the square grid was absent. Note that Multiphysics 3.4™ was already applied to both Geometry A and Geometry B applying different model settings and boundary conditions [21].

Lau and Krishnappan [6] conducted their experiments in a rectangular flume 30.7 m long and 0.60 m wide. Flume bed roughness was varied by using sands of different sizes. In addition, some experiments were made with a smooth coverings on the bottom flume. The flow depth varied from 0.013 m to 0.050 m, whereas mean flow velocities were kept approximately constant at 0.20 m s$^{-1}$ for most of the experiments. Mixing measurements were made using salt solution as the tracer. The solution was continuously discharged from a constant head injection apparatus into the middle of the flume at approximately mid-depth. Injections were made 11 m downstream from the beginning of the flume to ensure fully developed boundary layers for all the experiments. The tracer concentrations were measured at mid-depth at 8 or more stations downstream the injection point, where vertical mixing was completed [6].

For the simulations water with density $\rho$=999.05 kg m$^{-3}$ and molecular viscosity $\mu$=1.14·10$^{-3}$ kg m$^{-1}$ s$^{-1}$, was selected as fluid. Inflow velocity was 0.20 m s$^{-1}$. For the $k$-$\varepsilon$ model, boundary conditions were assigned at the inlet, the outlet and at the walls:

- at the inlet, an inflow type boundary condition was applied, with uniform velocity profile. Also inlet turbulent intensity and length scale were assigned. Turbulent intensity was set up to 5%, which corresponds to fully turbulent flows. The turbulent length scale is a physical quantity related to the size of the large eddies that contain the energy in turbulent flows. Also it is a measure of the size of the turbulent eddies that are not resolved [7]. For fully developed channel flows, this parameter can be approximately derived as 0.07·$W$, where $W$ is the channel width;
- at the outlet, a zero pressure type condition was assigned;
- at the walls and at the square elements, logarithmic law of the wall boundary condition was applied. It is well-known that turbulent flows are significantly affected by the presence of walls. The classical $k$-$\varepsilon$ model due to its basic hypothesis of isotropy needs to be modified to account for the effect of the walls on the local structure of turbulence [22]. Thus, a logarithmic wall function was applied. It assumes that the computational domain begins a distance $\delta_w$ from the real wall, the flow is parallel to the wall and the velocity can be described by

$$u^+ = \frac{u}{u*} = \frac{1}{\kappa} ln\left(\frac{\delta_w u*}{v}\right) + C_1,$$  (13)

where $\kappa$ is the von Kármán constant, which is equal to 0.42, and $C_1$ is the universal constant for smooth walls equal to 5.5 . Note that the ratio of the kinematic viscosity to the friction velocity, $v/u*$ is the viscous length scale. Moreover, the term in the round brackets is $\delta_w^+$ and the logarithmic wall functions are formally valid for values of between 30 and 100. Multiphysics 3.5a™ allows to select $\delta_w^+$ value, which was assigned equal to 30. In a previous simulation of the same geometry it was applied $\delta_w^+$=100 [21].

In all the geometries, for the advection-diffusion equation, boundary conditions were assigned at the inlet, the outlet, at the walls and in the injection point:

- at the inlet, a concentration type boundary condition was applied, assuming zero concentration entering the domain;
- at the outlet, an advective flux type condition was assigned;
- at the walls, an insulation type condition was applied. This condition means that the solute cannot cross the walls;
- at the injection point, a flux type boundary condition was applied, assuming herein a constant flux equal to 30 mol m$^{-2}$ s$^{-1}$.

For all the geometries, different values for the maximum element size were selected for the geometry upstream and downstream the point of injection. Finer values were selected downstream of this point to better capture transverse mixing. Maximum element sizes were 0.1 and 0.05 m in the upstream region and in the downstream region, respectively. Also, for all the geometries, at the walls, maximum element size was 0.05 m, whereas, at the square elements in Geometry B and C, maximum element size was 0.01 m. Thus, the mesh for Geometry A, B and C has 35104, 37284 and 25815 triangular elements, respectively.

Stationary segregated solver with non-linear system solver was used, where the relative tolerance and the maximum number of segregated iterations were set to $1.0 \cdot 10^{-4}$ and 100, respectively. The segregated solver allows to save both memory and assembly time by splitting the solution steps into substeps. These are defined by grouping solution components together. Three groups were considered, namely velocity components $\bar{u}$ and $\bar{v}$ and pressure $\bar{p}$, turbulence model parameters $k$ and $\varepsilon$, and the solute concentration $\bar{C}$.

## 4. DATA POST-PROCESSING. TRANSVERSE MIXING COEFFICIENT ESTIMATION

Data resulting from numerical simulations were later post-processed to estimate the overall transverse mixing coefficient. Starting point were the simulated cross-stream concentration distributions of the tracer. Two methods were applied to derive $D_{t-y}$ for the whole geometry:

- the method of moments, where the transverse mixing coefficient is derived from the rate of change of spatial variance of the tracer transverse profile [1]

$$D_{t-y} = \frac{1}{2}\frac{d}{dt}\left(\sigma_y^2\right), \tag{14}$$

where $t$ is the time of travel and the transverse variance is given by [1]

$$\sigma_y^2 = \frac{\displaystyle\int_{y=0}^{W}(y-\tilde{y})\overline{C}(x,y)\,dy}{\displaystyle\int_{y=0}^{W}\overline{C}(x,y)\,dy}, \tag{15}$$

and the centroid of tracer distribution is [1]

$$\tilde{y} = \frac{\int\limits_{y=0}^{W} y\,\overline{C}(x,y)\,dy}{\int\limits_{y=0}^{W} \overline{C}(x,y)\,dy} \; . \tag{16}$$

Eqs. (14)-(16) can be applied provided that four conditions are accomplished, as explained by Rutherford [1]. First, tracer mixing must obey Fick's law with a constant mixing coefficient. Second, the tracer must not impinge on the channel banks. Third, the tracer source must be steady. Fourth, the channel must be uniform so that the plume does not expand and contract along the transverse cross-section and its velocity is constant. Therefore, Eq. (14) can be approximated by the finite difference form [1]

$$D_{t\text{-}y} = \frac{u}{2}\,\frac{\sigma_y^2(x_2) - \sigma_y^2(x_1)}{x_2 - x_1} \, , \tag{17}$$

where $u$ is the average flow velocity, which is assumed to be constant. The cross-sectional values of $D_{t\text{-}y}$ were later averaged over the geometry. In a Fickian process, transverse turbulent mixing coefficient $D_{t\text{-}y}$ and transverse variance are related as [1]

$$\sigma_y^2 = 2\,D_{t\text{-}y}\,t \, , \tag{18}$$

which may allow to derive another estimation of the average transverse mixing coefficient $D_{t\text{-}y}$ in each cross-section;

- the method based on the transverse profile of turbulent kinematic viscosity $v_t$, which provides a local value of the turbulent diffusivity. Note that $v_t$ values were obtained from Eq. (8). The average value for each transverse profile provides the value of $D_{t\text{-}y}$ for that cross-section. In turn, averaging cross-sectional $D_{t\text{-}y}$ values along the geometry provides again the value for the whole geometry.

## 5. ANALYSIS OF NUMERICAL RESULTS. DISCUSSION

Numerical simulations provided field velocity and pressure, $k$ and $\varepsilon$, kinematic viscosity $v_t$ values throughout the flow domain of the three considered geometries. Fig. 3(a,b,c) present the concentration field from $x=10.2$ m to $x=13.0$ m in the Geometry A, B and C, respectively. Note that the injection point was at $x=11.0$ m and the grids were located at $x=10.5$ m and $x=11.00$ for Geometry B and C, respectively. The plume width was larger in the grid geometries than in Geometry A.

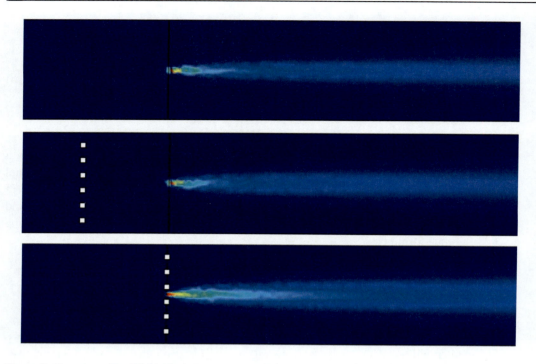

Figure 2. Concentration field in (up) Geometry A. (mid) Geometry B. (down) Geometry C.

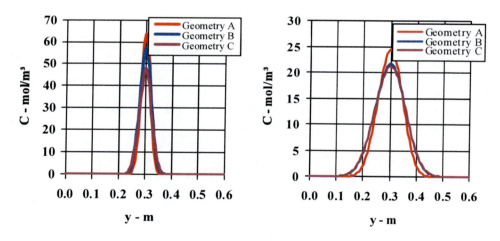

Figure 3. Concentration transverse distribution at (left) $x$=11.125. (right) $x$=12.00.

Tab. 2 lists the locations of the cross-section where simulated cross-section tracer concentration distributions were collected. For each cross-section 120 points were considered. Also, the maximum value of concentration in those locations is presented for the three geometries. Values for Geometry A are the highest, whereas values for the Geometry B are always larger than those for Geometry C, i.e. the grid located in the injection section provides an enhanced turbulent mixing respect to the upstream grid. This increased mixing is larger closer to the injection section and decreased downstream in the geometry. Also, plume width was larger in the grid geometries.

**Table 2. Peak values of cross-section tracer concentration distributions.**

| Reach | $x$ - m | $\Delta x$ - m | Geometry A $\overline{C}_{max}$ – mol m⁻³ | Geometry B $\overline{C}_{max}$ – mol m⁻³ | Geometry C $\overline{C}_{max}$ – mol m⁻³ |
|---|---|---|---|---|---|
| 1 | 11.125 | | 63.41 | 57.44 | 48.25 |
| 2 | 11.25 | 0.125 | 46.57 | 41.17 | 38.54 |
| 3 | 11.50 | 0.25 | 33.76 | 30.01 | 29.24 |
| 4 | 11.75 | 0.25 | 27.99 | 24.80 | 24.31 |
| 5 | 12.00 | 0.25 | 24.47 | 21.69 | 21.18 |
| 6 | 12.25 | 0.25 | 22.00 | 19.51 | 19.10 |
| 7 | 12.50 | 0.25 | 20.21 | 17.93 | 17.58 |
| 8 | 12.75 | 0.25 | 18.82 | 16.68 | 16.38 |
| 9 | 13.00 | 0.25 | 17.69 | 15.67 | 15.40 |
| 10 | 13.50 | 0.50 | 15.98 | 14.12 | 13.90 |
| 11 | 15.00 | 1.50 | 12.98 | 11.35 | 11.21 |
| 12 | 15.50 | 0.50 | 12.34 | 10.75 | 10.63 |
| 13 | 17.50 | 2.00 | 10.53 | 9.11 | 9.02 |
| 14 | 20.00 | 2.50 | 9.10 | 7.96 | 7.88 |
| 15 | 25.00 | 5.00 | 7.29 | 6.81 | 6.74 |
| 16 | 30.00 | 5.00 | 6.23 | 6.21 | 6.15 |
| 17 | 35.00 | 5.00 | 5.65 | 5.77 | 5.72 |
| 18 | 40.00 | 5.00 | 5.34 | 5.44 | 5.40 |

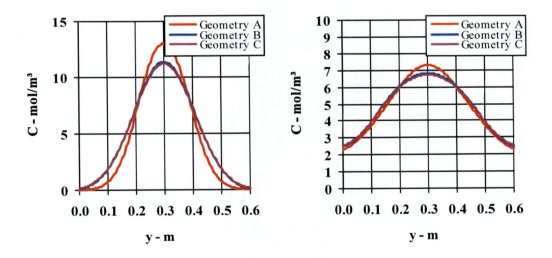

Figure 4. Concentration transverse distribution at (left) x=15.00. (right) x=25.00.

Fig. 3 shows the cross-section tracer concentration distributions at $x$=11.125 m (left) and $x$=12.00 m (right). Fig. 4 presents the cross-section tracer concentration distributions at $x$=15.00 m (left) and $x$=25.00 m (right), where peak value for Geometry B and Geometry C was similar. In the final cross-section, i.e. $x$=40 m, for all the cases the tracer was almost completely mixed in the geometry width and its maximum concentration was around 10% of the initial maximum concentration.

**Table 3. Values of transverse mixing coefficient $D_{t\text{-}y}$ in $m^2\,s^{-1}$.**

| Reach | $x-m$ | Geometry A Eq. (17) | Eq. (8) | Geometry B Eq. (17) | Eq. (8) | Geometry C Eq. (17) | Eq. (8) |
|---|---|---|---|---|---|---|---|
| 1 | 11.125 | --- | $1.54{\cdot}10^{-4}$ | --- | $2.81{\cdot}10^{-4}$ | --- | $2.49{\cdot}10^{-4}$ |
| 2 | 11.25 | $2.14{\cdot}10^{-4}$ | $1.54{\cdot}10^{-4}$ | $3.43{\cdot}10^{-4}$ | $2.76{\cdot}10^{-4}$ | $3.30{\cdot}10^{-4}$ | $2.83{\cdot}10^{-4}$ |
| 3 | 11.50 | $2.20{\cdot}10^{-4}$ | $1.54{\cdot}10^{-4}$ | $3.33{\cdot}10^{-4}$ | $2.66{\cdot}10^{-4}$ | $3.32{\cdot}10^{-4}$ | $2.82{\cdot}10^{-4}$ |
| 4 | 11.75 | $2.09{\cdot}10^{-4}$ | $1.53{\cdot}10^{-4}$ | $3.20{\cdot}10^{-4}$ | $2.58{\cdot}10^{-4}$ | $3.39{\cdot}10^{-4}$ | $2.71{\cdot}10^{-4}$ |
| 5 | 12.00 | $2.05{\cdot}10^{-4}$ | $1.53{\cdot}10^{-4}$ | $3.09{\cdot}10^{-4}$ | $2.52{\cdot}10^{-4}$ | $3.23{\cdot}10^{-4}$ | $2.62{\cdot}10^{-4}$ |
| 6 | 12.25 | $1.94{\cdot}10^{-4}$ | $1.52{\cdot}10^{-4}$ | $2.99{\cdot}10^{-4}$ | $2.46{\cdot}10^{-4}$ | $3.10{\cdot}10^{-4}$ | $2.54{\cdot}10^{-4}$ |
| 7 | 12.50 | $1.88{\cdot}10^{-4}$ | $1.52{\cdot}10^{-4}$ | $2.88{\cdot}10^{-4}$ | $2.41{\cdot}10^{-4}$ | $2.98{\cdot}10^{-4}$ | $2.47{\cdot}10^{-4}$ |
| 8 | 12.75 | $1.84{\cdot}10^{-4}$ | $1.52{\cdot}10^{-4}$ | $2.79{\cdot}10^{-4}$ | $2.36{\cdot}10^{-4}$ | $2.87{\cdot}10^{-4}$ | $2.42{\cdot}10^{-4}$ |
| 9 | 13.00 | $1.82{\cdot}10^{-4}$ | $1.52{\cdot}10^{-4}$ | $2.70{\cdot}10^{-4}$ | $2.31{\cdot}10^{-4}$ | $2.77{\cdot}10^{-4}$ | $2.36{\cdot}10^{-4}$ |
| 10 | 13.50 | $1.77{\cdot}10^{-4}$ | $1.51{\cdot}10^{-4}$ | $2.58{\cdot}10^{-4}$ | $2.23{\cdot}10^{-4}$ | $2.64{\cdot}10^{-4}$ | $2.27{\cdot}10^{-4}$ |
| 11 | 15.00 | $\mathbf{1.73{\cdot}10^{-4}}$ | $1.51{\cdot}10^{-4}$ | $\mathbf{2.29{\cdot}10^{-4}}$ | $2.02{\cdot}10^{-4}$ | $\mathbf{2.34{\cdot}10^{-4}}$ | $2.05{\cdot}10^{-4}$ |
| 12 | 15.50 | $\mathbf{1.73{\cdot}10^{-4}}$ | $1.52{\cdot}10^{-4}$ | $\mathbf{2.02{\cdot}10^{-4}}$ | $1.96{\cdot}10^{-4}$ | $\mathbf{2.06{\cdot}10^{-4}}$ | $1.99{\cdot}10^{-4}$ |
| 13 | 17.50 | $\mathbf{1.75{\cdot}10^{-4}}$ | $1.55{\cdot}10^{-4}$ | $\mathbf{1.72{\cdot}10^{-4}}$ | $1.78{\cdot}10^{-4}$ | $\mathbf{1.76{\cdot}10^{-4}}$ | $1.80{\cdot}10^{-4}$ |
| 14 | 20.00 | $\mathbf{1.70{\cdot}10^{-4}}$ | $1.62{\cdot}10^{-4}$ | $\mathbf{1.33{\cdot}10^{-4}}$ | $1.63{\cdot}10^{-4}$ | $\mathbf{1.34{\cdot}10^{-4}}$ | $1.64{\cdot}10^{-4}$ |
| 15 | 25.00 | $\mathbf{1.38{\cdot}10^{-4}}$ | $1.81{\cdot}10^{-4}$ | $\mathbf{9.50{\cdot}10^{-5}}$ | $1.50{\cdot}10^{-4}$ | $\mathbf{9.47{\cdot}10^{-5}}$ | $1.50{\cdot}10^{-4}$ |
| 16 | 30.00 | $\mathbf{8.87{\cdot}10^{-5}}$ | $1.97{\cdot}10^{-4}$ | $\mathbf{6.50{\cdot}10^{-5}}$ | $1.54{\cdot}10^{-4}$ | $\mathbf{6.42{\cdot}10^{-5}}$ | $1.54{\cdot}10^{-4}$ |
| 17 | 35.00 | $\mathbf{5.10{\cdot}10^{-5}}$ | $2.05{\cdot}10^{-4}$ | $\mathbf{4.40{\cdot}10^{-5}}$ | $1.70{\cdot}10^{-4}$ | $\mathbf{4.34{\cdot}10^{-5}}$ | $1.70{\cdot}10^{-4}$ |
| 18 | 40.00 | $\mathbf{2.78{\cdot}10^{-5}}$ | $2.07{\cdot}0^{-4}$ | $\mathbf{2.83{\cdot}10^{-5}}$ | $1.88{\cdot}10^{-4}$ | $\mathbf{2.77{\cdot}10^{-5}}$ | $1.88{\cdot}10^{-4}$ |
| Average | --- | $\mathbf{1.84{\cdot}10^{-4}}$ | $1.52{\cdot}10^{-4}$ | $\mathbf{2.93{\cdot}10^{-4}}$ | $2.24{\cdot}10^{-4}$ | $\mathbf{3.01{\cdot}10^{-4}}$ | $2.30{\cdot}10^{-4}$ |

In all the geometries transverse variance was increasing with the distance from the injection point as expected. Moreover, both variance and plume width values in Geometry B and C were in average higher of about 17% and 18% than those in the Geometry A, reflecting an enhanced degree of turbulent mixing due to the grids. Tab. 3 lists the values of the transverse mixing coefficient $D_{t\text{-}y}$ for the geometries deriving from the application of the methods of moments, that is Eq. (17), and from the transverse profile of turbulent kinematic viscosity $v_t$, that is Eq. (8). Note that from reach n.13 and 11, in Geometry A and in both Geometry B and C, respectively, the method of moments cannot be properly applied because the plume impinged the walls of the geometry. The data listed in Tab. 2 were averaged to derive one value for each geometry. The values were weighted using the length of each reach. Also, both for the method of moments and the method based on turbulent kinematic viscosity, the average value was obtained by using only the values up to reach n.13 and n.11 for Geometry A and in both Geometry B and C, respectively. A comparison showed that $D_{t\text{-}y}$ values in the geometries with the grid, i.e. Geometry B and C, were generally larger. Second, the average values derived from method of moments for Geometry B and C were about 59% and 63% larger than that for Geometry A. Third, the average $D_{t\text{-}y}$ values derived from turbulent kinematic viscosity were always lower than those obtained from Eq. (17).

Finally, these results were compared with those from previous numerical simulations, where Multiphysics 3.4™ was already applied only to Geometry A and Geometry B applying different model settings and boundary conditions [21]. Particularly, $\delta_w{}^+=100$ and a concentration boundary condition in the injection point were applied [21]. With these settings, the values of $D_{t\text{-}y}$ from the method of moments were larger, i.e. $1.99{\cdot}10^{-4}$ $m^2\,s^{-1}$ and $2.98{\cdot}10^{-4}$ $m^2\,s^{-1}$ for Geometry A and B, respectively [21]. The values from turbulent kinematic viscosity were also larger, i.e. $1.70 \cdot 10^{-4}$ m$^2$ s$^{-1}$ and $2.48 \cdot 10^{-4}$ m$^2$ s$^{-1}$ for Geometry A and B, respectively [21]. Note that the maximum experimental value collected by Lau and Krishnappan in same geometry without grid was $1.41 \cdot 10^{-4}$ m$^2$ s$^{-1}$. Therefore, the application of the current model settings provided a better agreement with the experimental data.

# 4. CONCLUSION

The Chapter presented the results of a numerical study undertaken to simulate the transverse mixing of a steady-state point source of a tracer in a two-dimensional rectangular geometry, which is expected to reproduce a shallow flow. An approach based on the Reynolds Averaged Navier-Stokes equations (RANS) was applied, where the closure problem was solved by using a turbulent viscosity concept. Particularly, the classical $k$-$\varepsilon$ model was used since it is the easiest to implement and the most economical in computation. Numerical values of the transverse turbulent rate of mixing were obtained by using the method of moments and the values of kinematic viscosity predicted by the model. Comparison between the results without and with a grid located upstream and in the section of injection demonstrated an enhanced mixing due to the grid. The highest level of mixing was in the case of the grid inserted in the section of injection. A comparison with the previous numerical results obtained with different model settings demonstrated a better agreement of the present simulations with literature experimental data available for the geometry without the grid.

# REFERENCES

[1]    J.C. Rutherford, *River Mixing*, John Wiley & Sons, Chichester, U.K., pp. 348, (1994).

[2]    C. Gualtieri, *Environmental Hydraulics*, Lecture notes (in Italian), CUEN Editore, Napoli, Italy, pp. 410, (2006).

[3]    J.B. Boxall, I. Guymer, *J. Hyd. Eng.*, 129, n.2, 129-139 (2003).

[4]    B. Cushman-Roisin, *Environmental fate and transport*, Lecture Notes, Thayer School of Engineering, Dartmouth College, NH, USA (2007).

[5]    G.H. Jirka, *J. Hyd. Res.*, 39, 6, 567-573 (2001).

[6]    Y.L. Lau, B.G. Krishnappan, *J. Hydr. Div. ASCE*, 103, HY10, 1173-1189 (1977).

[7]    Multiphysics 3.5a *User's Guide*, ComSol AB. Sweden (2009).

[8]    G. Webel, M. Schatzmann, *J. Hyd. Eng.*, 110, n.4, 423-435 (1984).

[9]    R.I. Nokes, I.R. Wood I.R., *J. Fluid Mech.*, 187, 373-394 (1988).

[10]   S.B. Pope, *Turbulent flows*, Cambridge University Press, Cambridge, U.K. (2000).

[11]   H. Schlichting, *Boundary layer theory*, McGraw Hill Book, New York, NY, USA, pp. 818, (1979).

[12]   F.M. Henderson, *Open channel flow*, Macmillan Series in Civil Engineering, New York, NY, USA, pp.522, (1966).

[13]   H. Chanson H., *Environmental hydraulics of open channel flows*, Elsevier Butterworth-Heinemann, Burlington, MA, USA pp.430, (2004).

[14]   K.W. Chau, *Adv. Environ. Res.*, 4, 287-294, (2000).

[15] C. Gualtieri, C. Mucherino, *Proceedings of 5th International Symposium on Environmental Hydraulics (ISEH 2007)*, Tempe (USA), December 4-7, (2007).

[16] H.B. Fischer, E.J. List, R.C.Y. Koh, J. Imberger, N.H. Brook, *Mixing in inland and coastal waters* Academic Press, New York, NY, USA, pp.484, (1979).

[17] A.C. Rummel, S.A. Socolofsky, C.F. v.Carmer, G.H. Jirka, *Physics of Fluids*, 17, 075105-1-12, 2005.

[18] P.K. Kundu, I.M. Cohen, *Fluid Mechanic*s, Elsevier Academic Press, San Diego, CA, USA 2004, pp.760.

[19] D.B. Ingham, L. Ma, *Computational Fluid Dynamics. Applications in Environmental Hydraulics,* edited by P.D. Bates, S.N. Lane & R.I. Ferguson, John Wiley & Sons, Chichester, England, 2005, pp.534.

[20] B.C. Van Prooijen, W.S.J. Uijttewaal, *Water Quality Hazards and Dispersion of Pollutants*, edited by W. Czernuszenko & P. Rowinski, Springer Science+Business Inc., New York, NY, USA, 2005, pp.250.

[21] C. Gualtieri, *Environ. Fluid Mech.*, DOI 10.1007/s10652-009-9119-6, in press.

[22] F. Sotiropoulos, *Computational Fluid Dynamics. Applications in Environmental Hydraulics,* edited by P.D. Bates, S.N. Lane, R.I. Ferguson, John Wiley & Sons, Chichester, England, 2005, pp. 534.

In: Advances in Environmental Modeling and Measurements    ISBN: 978-1-60876-599-7
Editors: D. T. Mihailović, B. Lalić, pp. 47-55    © 2010 Nova Science Publishers, Inc.

*Chapter 5*

# IMPLEMENTATION OF A NEW APPROACH TO ALBEDO CALCULATION OVER HETEROGENEOUS INTERFACES FOR DIFFERENT GEOMETRIES

*A.M. Ćirišan*[*1], *D.T. Mihailović*[2], *and D.V. Kapor*[2]

[1]Institute of Physics, Belgrade, Serbia
[2]University of Novi Sad, Novi Sad, Serbia

## ABSTRACT

Most environmental studies today focus on calculations and modeling of important parameters over non-homogenous interfaces. The parameter analyzed in the present study is the albedo of the surface, a fundamentally important parameter for calculating radiation fluxes. In order to determine the aggregated albedo over a heterogeneous surface, various approaches have been developed. One of the most commonly used is the method of parameter aggregation, defining area-averaged parameters in environmental models for land surfaces with mesoscale heterogeneity. Scientists from the University of Novi Sad have found that the geometrical factor plays an important role in albedo calculations. They have offered a new approach for calculating the flux that is lost due to absorption on the vertical lateral borders of surfaces lying on a higher level. The results obtained using analytical and numerical (Monte Carlo "ray tracing"- MCRT) approaches to elaborate this effect for different geometries are presented in this paper. The derived expression for the albedo of the particularly designed grid-cell is compared with the conventional approach, using a common parameterization of albedo as defined by Delage et al. Their values are then implemented in the LAPS parameterization scheme to analyze the effect of this new approach on dependent physical parameters.

[*] Corresponding author: E-mail address: anacirisan@yahoo.com, Phone: +381 21 6350552, Fax: +381 21 6350552

# 1. INTRODUCTION

The fraction of incoming solar radiation that is reflected by the land surface, integrated over the whole viewing angle, is defined as surface albedo. It is a parameter of great importance in the environmental sciences. As albedo influences the energy budget of the Earth, especially radiative transfer, it is a crucial variable in parameterising land-surface processes.

Determining albedo over heterogeneous land surfaces is a key component to sufficiently capturing the complexities of land-atmosphere interactions. However, assessing albedo over heterogenous surfaces presents practical problems. For a long time, this problem was avoided using simple arithmetic averaging to determine albedo as the average of a grid cell. It is an approach commonly used by numerical modelers in grid-based environmental models. Recently, physics-based analysis has shown significant deviations in albedo from that calculated by simple averaging.

A new approach for calculating albedo over heterogeneous interfaces has been proposed by scientists at the University of Novi Sad, Serbia [1-3]. It is related both to a geometric effect resulting from different heights of the underlying surfaces and to the type of the surfaces present in a given grid-cell. In order to avoid complicated analytic solutions in a case of complex geometries, the so called ray-tracing Monte Carlo approach is used as an efficient numerical procedure.

Further achievements of the presented approach will be discussed in this chapter. In the previous papers, simpler geometries were analyzed where the border of a surface lying on a higher level was completely vertical and parallel with the edge of the grid-cell. Here, we consider cases which represent a generalization of this problem – the geometry of a trilateral prism, with a vertical border made by a higher surface not parallel to the edge of the grid-cell and with incidence geometry such that the surface of the higher patch is not horizontal but sloped under some angle.

# 2. PHYSICAL BASIS OF THE NEW APPROACH

The general idea of the new proposed approach is based on the fact that the light, after it was reflected from the surface, is completely absorbed by the lateral sides of the surface lying on a higher level. It is assumed that the reflected light is diffuse, homogeneous and single-scattered, neglecting the dependence of the albedo on the zenith angle of the incident radiation. Computing the amount of radiation lost is based on the solid angle under which the lateral sides, on which the reflected radiation falls, are seen from any point of the lower surface.

A flux that is lost due to absorption on the vertical lateral boundaries is defined as a "loss coefficient", coinciding with Oke's sky-view factor [4] for some ideal urban geometries. Otherwise, the concept of determining the loss coefficient has been used in some models of urban areas, where the flux of ongoing long-wave radiation is calculated over the urban canyon, with a certain amount of radiation loss within the canyon [5-10]. Since the flux of radiation that reaches the vertical boundary surface is completely lost, the contribution of the radiation reflected from the lateral surface is neglected.

The loss coefficient is calculated as a ratio of a part of total energy coming from the lower horizontal surface towards the lateral one and the amount of flux emitted from the lower surface into the upper space. The expression to calculate the radiant energy flux $dE/dt$ was taken following Liou [11].

After obtaining the value of the loss coefficient $k$, we can calculate the average albedo over a heterogeneous grid-cell, where the albedo $\alpha_1$ of the surface from which the radiation is reflected is decreased by the factor $k\alpha_1$. The value of the aggregated albedo, calculated using the new approach, is then compared to the simple, arithmetically-averaged albedo value, an approach commonly used for albedo derivation over heterogeneous grid-cells in most atmospheric models. Decreasing the albedo of the underlying surface will highly influence the effective surface temperature over that area, increasing its value for several degrees, as will be shown further in this chapter.

## 3. ANALYZED GEOMETRIES

In order to get closer to reality, we applied the new albedo approach for a number of complex geometries. In the first case, we analyzed albedo for a geometry with an elevated corner area and a triangular base, the so-called trilateral prism geometry. In the second case, slope geometry is introduced: in addition to the reflection from the lower, horizontal surface, there is also a reflection from light reaching first the sloped surface, reflecting from it, and falling on the horizontal area. This reflected light should be also taken into the calculation of the loss coefficient, which will decrease the albedo value.

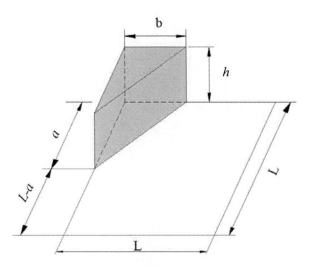

Figure 1. Schematic representation of "trilateral prism" geometry.

Let us now give a more detailed description of the analyzed geometries. In a square grid-cell, in the top left corner, there is an elevated surface at height $h$ with respect to the rest of the grid (Fig. 1). This triangular area has dimensions $a \times b$, where $a$ is the length of the fixed arm, exactly half of the length of the cell, while the arm $b$ varies in length depending on the angle of the incidence surface.

In the case of slope, the horizontal axis is divided into two parts. The first part corresponds to the visible horizontal surface marked $l_1$, while $l_2'$ is a base of the sloped surface (Fig. 2). The slope of the incident surface is determined by the angle $\beta$, with respect to the horizontal surface, and the height $h$ of the surface. Assuming the loss coefficient calculation, it is necessary to find two values of the coefficient, and a final value for $k$ is obtained by their sum. The first value of the coefficient relates to the reflected light from the lower horizontal surface onto the sloped surface, and the other value addresses light reflected from the slope to the horizontal.

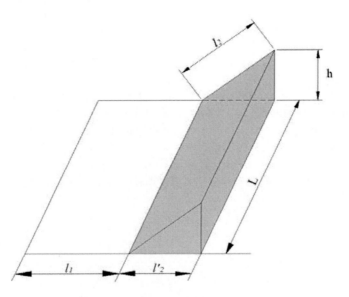

Figure 2. Schematic representation of the "sloped" geometry.

The analytical solution to this complex geometry was too complicated to be found, so a direct system simulation using a well-known "ray tracing" Monte Carlo method was used to retrace a ray destiny and determine the loss coefficient needed for calculating the average albedo. By using random inputs, the appropriately chosen ray of light is followed after it has been single-scattered from the lower surface of the grid-cell. After a large number of numerical experiments, the result is obtained by averaging the observed behavior over a large number of followed light paths. The "loss-coefficient" is estimated as a ratio of the number of cases that were positive for absorption to the number of conducted numerical experiments.

In Fig. 3(a,b), the value of the loss coefficient calculated by the MCRT method is presented for different values of the reduced length and height of the surface lying on a higher level. The reduced dimensionless quantities $\hat{b} = b/L$ (in the case of trilateral prism geometry) and $\hat{l}_1 = l_1/L$ (in the case of sloped geometry) and $\hat{h} = h/L$ were introduced for simplicity of the loss coefficient calculation, where $L \times L$ is the area of the grid-cell. In order to confirm the accuracy of the MCRT method, a standard numerical integration procedure is used to obtain the results of the loss coefficient for both geometries. As can be seen, there is quite a good match between them.

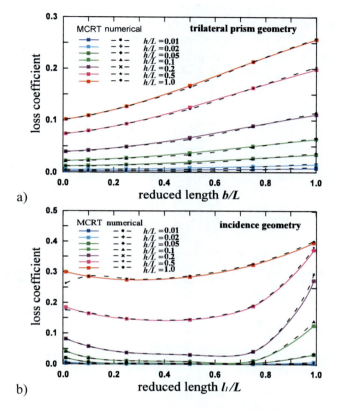

a)

b)

Figure 3. Dependence of the loss coefficient of the relative length calculated by standard numerical integration and the MCRT method: (a) trilateral prism geometry and (b) sloped incidence geometry.

In the case of trilateral prism geometry, for all values of reduced height there is constant, approximately linear growth of the loss coefficient. The sloped geometry indicates the existence of a minimum loss, which varies depending on the reduced height, while the maximum values of coefficient of loss occur with maximum relative length.

## 3. DISCUSSION OF THE RESULTS

Albedo is one of the critical surface parameters in the land surface schemes to determine radiative balance and the turbulent exchange regime. It has a large impact on surface fluxes and thus indirectly on temperature. We analyzed variation in the effective surface temperature over the heterogeneous grid-cell calculated using the new albedo aggregation approach and the conventional one, where albedo was obtained by simple arithmetic averaging. Temperature values were calculated using the LAPS (Land Air Parameterization Scheme) surface scheme [12], implementing the albedo value in the prognostic equation for evolution of the effective surface temperature over heterogeneous grid cells. More details about the calculation procedure can be found in Kapor et al. [2].

The goal of the experiment was to examine differences in the daily cycle of effective surface temperature over a heterogeneous grid-cell between the new approach of aggregated albedo calculation and the conventional approach, as well as to determine the sensitivity of the scheme to changes in the geometry of the grid-cell. Simulations were done for a two-patch grid-cell of size 100 m × 100 m with different horizontal dimensions and heights and for different surface types (grass, forest or concrete having albedo values of 0.20, 0.15 and 0.30, respectively).

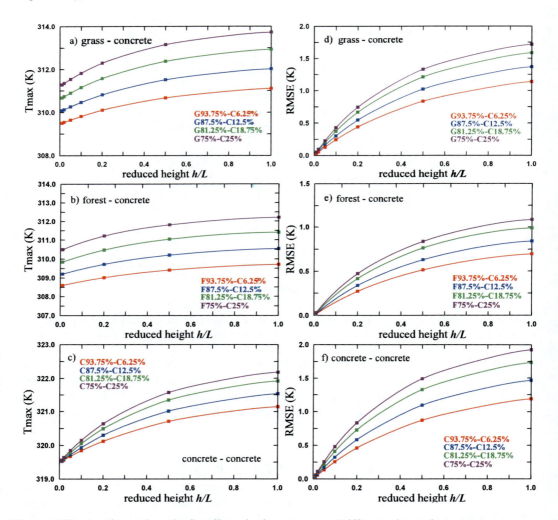

Figure 4. The experimental results for trilateral prism geometry. Difference in maximum temperature obtained by the new approach of albedo calculation and the conventional one for different values of reduced height and fractional cover of each patch [(a) (b) and (c)] and the root mean square error between the temperature values calculated by both approaches of albedo derivation as a function of reduced height [(d) (e) and (f)].

Fig. 4(a,b,c) shows the difference in maximum temperature obtained by the new approach for albedo calculation and the conventional one at different values of reduced height and the fractional cover of each patch, in the case of trilateral prism geometry. When the cell is covered with grass and concrete or if all of the grid-cell is covered with concrete, the increase in the maximum temperature is about 1.5 K to 2.5 K. In a forest-concrete case, there is an increase of 1 K when the cell is more covered with forest and 2 K when a larger part of the cell is covered with concrete. Considering the RMSE (Fig. 4(d,e,f)), the case when the whole cell area is covered in concrete gives the largest difference between the temperature obtained from the new and traditional methods of calculating albedo. As the area of the surface lying on a higher level is larger, it increases the RMSE value for the observed case.

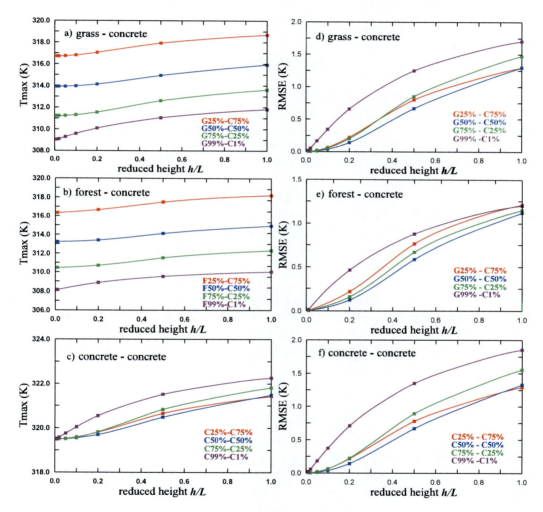

Figure 5. The experimental results for sloped geometry. The difference in maximum temperature obtained by the new approach of albedo calculation and the conventional one for different values of reduced height and fractional cover of each patch [(a) (b) and (c)] and the root mean square error between the temperature values calculated by both approaches of albedo derivation as a function of reduced height [(d) (e) and (f)].

What happens when the sloped surface is introduced? The smallest deviation from the classical approach of albedo calculation appears in the case when the grid-cell is equally covered with both patches, while the largest in the case with nearly the whole cell covered by the horizontal surface. For the grass-concrete and whole cell concrete case, maximum temperature increase goes from 2 K to 3 K, while in the forest-concrete case it is 2 K in all variations of different fractional cover (Fig. 5(a,b,c)). The RMSE is dramatically larger in the case of 99% horizontal surface coverage (Fig. 5(d,e,f)), which is understandable since in that situation we have reflection and absorption from the largest part of the surface and therefore the largest decrease in albedo. When the horizontal and sloped surfaces cover the same area of the cell, there is the least loss of albedo in all three cases considered. This causes the minimum temperature profile difference obtained using both methods of albedo calculation in relation to the other considered variants.

## 4. CONCLUSION

In this chapter, we discussed the effect of the trilateral prism and sloped geometry on the value of albedo for the simplest case of grid-cell area coverage with only two patches of different dimensions and characteristics. It is shown that the influence of different surface geometries that occupy the grid-cell area can lead to a significant decrease in values of albedo and cause more consequences, like a change in the effective surface temperature, as shown in this chapter.

The factor that dominates in the trilateral prism geometry is the size of the absorbing area on which the reflected radiation falls. Increasing that area decreases the albedo value because of a greater absorption of the reflected radiation. In the case of sloped geometry, the smallest difference between the albedo calculated by new and classical approach is evident when we have equal coverage of both patches, while largest when the sloped surface is almost under a right angle.

The main conclusion taken from this research is that variation in the size of the observed surfaces of the grid-cell, their height and the type of surface can drastically reduce albedo in relation to the classical approach. As a result, a significant increase in the surface temperature is obtained, depending on the properties of the surface, which points to the importance of a geometric factor in calculating albedo.

## ACKNOWLEDGMENTS

The research presented in this chapter has been funded by the Serbian Ministry of Science and Environmental Protection under the project "Modelling and numerical simulations of complex physical systems", No. OI141035 for 2006-2010.

## REFERENCES

[1]    D. Kapor, D.T. Mihailovic, T. Tosic, S.T. Rao, C. Hogrefe, *Proceedings of iEMSs*, 2, 389-394 (2002).

[2]    D.V. Kapor, A.M. Cirisan, D.T. Mihailovic, *Proceedings of iEMSs*, 1, 114–121 (2008).

[3]   D.T. Mihailovic, D. Kapor, C. Hogrefe, J. Lazic, T. Tosic, *Environ. Fluid. Mech.*, 4(1), 57-77 (2004).

[4]   T.R. Oke, *Boundary Layer Climates*, 2-nd edition, Methuen, 1987.

[5]   K. Fortuniak, *Theor. Appl. Climatol.*, 91(1-4), 245-258 (2007).

[6]   I.N. Harman, M.J Best, S.E. Belcher, *Bound.-Lay. Meteorol.*, 110, 301-316 (2004).

[7]   M. Kanda, T. Kawai, K. Nakagawa, *Bound.-Lay. Meteorol.*, 114, 71-90 (2005).

[8]   V. Masson, *Bound.-Lay. Meteorol.*, 94, 357-397 (2000).

[9]   T.R. Oke, *Q. J. Roy. Meteor. Soc.*, 108, 1-24 (1982).

[10]  D.J. Sailor, H. Fan, *Atmos. Environ.*, 36, 713-725 (2002).

[11]  K. N. Liou, *An Introduction to Atmospheric Radiation*, 2-nd edition, Academic Press Inc., 2002.

[12]  D.T. Mihailovic, *Global Planet. Change.*, 13, 207-215 (1996).

In: Advances in Environmental Modeling and Measurements       ISBN: 978-1-60876-599-7
Editors: D. T. Mihailović, B. Lalić, pp. 57-65       © 2010 Nova Science Publishers, Inc.

*Chapter 6*

# AGGREGATION OF CANYON ALBEDO IN SURFACE MODELS

## *D.V. Kapor[*1], D.T. Mihailović[1] and A.M. Ćirišan[2]*
[1]University of Novi Sad, Novi Sad, Serbia
[2]Institute of Physics, Belgrade, Serbia

## ABSTRACT

As a preliminary study for the biosphere of mountains, we performed a simulation of a system consisting of a plane bounded with two slopes—a kind of moderate canyon. We calculated the albedo of this system using a new approach that takes into account the geometrical effect of lateral sides on the loss of flux. This aggregated albedo was then introduced into the land-surface scheme in order to calculate the surface temperature. We assumed that the plane and the slopes would initially be covered with grass or forest, then later covered by concrete or some other building material. The results are relevant by themselves, but it is also important to compare them to results obtained using the standard, arithmetically-averaged albedo.

## 1. INTRODUCTION

Mountains with "untouched" nature, i.e., forests and meadows, are becoming rather rare, even in countries where urbanization has not yet reached its peak. These regions are often, in principle, protected as natural reserves or national parks. But in countries in transition, like Serbia, even these regions are being urbanized in a rather unplanned manner, mostly due to lack of institutional control.

There are many arguments in favor of the aforementioned activities. Many arguments defending the development of tourism are often based on rather unrealistic assumptions, while arguments against such activity are often quite qualitative and usually cannot beat the

---

[*] Corresponding author: E-mail address: dvk@if.ns.ac.yu, Phone: +381 21 485 2809, Fax: +381 21 459 367

"affirmative" arguments in any public discussion. The subject of this study was inspired by the lack of quantitative arguments against the urbanization of mountain regions.

We wish to offer such arguments using a rather simple model that will be clear to everyone and that will provide us with clear numbers. The model consists of a "canyon," or, more precisely, two mountain slopes with a valley between them. We shall assume that these slopes and the valley are covered with forest or meadows. We will then observe what happens when this is "substituted" by asphalt or concrete.

First we will use a recently developed technique for the evaluation of aggregated albedo of surfaces that are geometrically inhomogeneous [1,2,3]. Then, we will use this albedo in one of the possible schemes describing the interaction of land and atmosphere in order to check the change of surface temperature. This is a parameter that will definitively demonstrate the changes induced by urbanization, even in such a simple model.

## 2. THE MODEL

Albedo is a very important factor in understanding the interaction of radiation balance and climate and vegetation dynamics. However, it is also a significant source of uncertainty in radiation computation in general. As Rowntree [4] has pointed out, many climate simulations have shown that small deviations in the values of albedo or surface roughness can produce significant changes in atmospheric circulation. Since it gives a strong feedback effect, knowledge of albedo is important in determining weather conditions and characteristics of atmospheric boundary layers.

In recent years, the consideration of a terrain's geometry in urban area albedo modeling, especially that of slanted surfaces, has become an important application in mesoscale modeling. This approach has shown that a loss of albedo occurs when reflected radiation is absorbed from surrounding surface areas that lie at a higher altitude. Our proposed method of albedo aggregation is based on this approach.

Our research also concentrates on the incorporation of heterogeneous areas in models of different applications (such as those used for numerical weather forecasts, chemical models, air quality control, predicting the development of the environment, and so on). For simplicity, our simulations considered a grid cell covered with two different surface characteristics. Each of these areas had a different albedo. We then analyzed the differences in results obtained by our approach compared to the standard approach, where arithmetically averaged albedo over the heterogeneous grid cell is calculated.

Let us first describe and analyze the geometry we consider in this chapter; it is one of the most complicated geometries we have analyzed within our studies. As previously mentioned, two mountain slopes with a valley between them formed the shape of our canyon (Fig. 1). A grid cell had a rectangular base, covering an area of $L \cdot \left(L + l_2'\right)$. The horizontal dimension of the valley was $l_1$ with width $L$, while the base length of both slanted surfaces was $l_2' = L - l_1$. These surfaces were sloped under the angle $\beta$, having height $h$. This geometry is specific because the reflection of incident radiation occurs from the horizontal surface, as well as from the surfaces under a certain angle, which affects the further reduction of albedo values. Simulations were made for several values of reduced length (0.01, 0.10, 0.25, 0.50,

0.75 and 0.99) of the visible horizontal surface $\hat{l}_1 = l_1 / L$, where the reduced base value of a slanted surface was determined to be $\hat{l}_2' = 1 - l_1/L$. In addition, the value of reduced height $\hat{h} = h / L$ was considered to have the following values: 0.01, 0.02, 0.05, 0.1, 0.2, 0.5 and 1.0. The fractional cover of the horizontal area was calculated as $\sigma_1 = \hat{l}_1 / (1 + \hat{l}_2')$, while, for the rest of the surface, it was calculated as $\sigma_2 = \hat{l}_2' / (1 + \hat{l}_2')$.

   Before continuing with our representation and analyses of the results from these simulations, a brief review of our approach in aggregated albedo calculation will be presented.

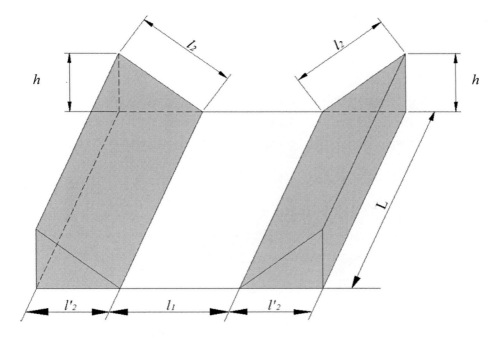

Figure 1. Schematic representation of "canyon" geometry.

## 3. AGGREGATED ALBEDO

   Our approach relies on the fact that part of the radiation reflected from a lower surface is absorbed by the lateral sides of a surface lying at a higher level. The ratio of the reflected energy lost is obtained by calculating the solid angle in which these lateral sides are seen from each point of the lower surface. We assumed here that the incoming radiation from a given surface is diffuse and homogeneous, discounting the multiple scattering effects and the dependence of albedo on the zenithal angle.

   In order to define the flux that is lost due to absorption, we introduced a "loss coefficient" $k_l$, determined by a radiant energy flux ratio. Following Liou [5], the basic expression for calculating the radiant energy flux is $dE/dt$

$$(dE / dt) = I \, dS \, \cos \theta \, d\Omega , \tag{1}$$

where $I$ is the total intensity of radiation obtained from the monochromatic intensity by integration over the entire range of the spectrum, $dS$ is the infinitesimal element of surface on which radiation comes or reflects from, $\cos \theta$ gives the direction of the radiation stream and $d\Omega$ is the element of the solid angle, within which the infinitesimal amount of radiant flux emitted from the infinitesimal surface element $dxdy$ is confined. The amount of flux emitted from the lower horizontal surface into the upper space is $(dE/dt)_h = IS_1 \pi$, where $S_1$ is the area from which the radiation is emitted. The total energy coming from the lower horizontal surface towards the lateral surface is $(dE/dt)_l$ and is derived using the following expression

$$(dE / dt )_l = I \iint_S dxdy \int_{\varphi_l(\vec{r})}^{\varphi_u(\vec{r})} d\varphi \int_{\theta_l(\vec{r},\varphi)}^{\theta_u(\vec{r},\varphi)} \cos \theta \sin \theta \, d\theta \quad , \tag{2}$$

where the boundaries of the integration for a given point are determined over the local azimuthal $(\varphi_l,\varphi_u)$ and zenithal $(\theta_l,\theta_u)$ angles in terms of the $x\,y$ coordinates.

The ratios shown in Eqs. (1) and (2) give the loss coefficient evaluation formula

$$k_l = (dE/dt)_l / (dE/dt)_h . \tag{3}$$

If we assume that the grid-cell of area $S$ is divided into two subregions having the areas $S_1$ and $S_2$, with corresponding albedos $\alpha_1$ and $\alpha_2$, respectively, the average albedo over the grid-cell, following the standard (conventional) approach, is

$$\overline{\alpha}_c = \alpha_1 \sigma_1 + \alpha_2 \sigma_2 , \tag{4}$$

where $\sigma_i$ is the fractional cover, calculated as a ratio of a patch's area $S_i$ and total grid cell area $S(\sigma_i = S_i / S, i = 1,2)$. Introducing the loss coefficient, the average albedo is then calculated as

$$\overline{\alpha}_n = (1-k)\alpha_1 \sigma_1 + \alpha_2 \sigma_2 . \tag{5}$$

The loss coefficient definition is conceptually analogous to the sky-view factor introduced by Oke [6].

Since an analytical expression for the "canyon" geometry was too complicated to be found, it was necessary to apply a technique for estimating the solution by performing statistical sampling experiments. We used an efficient numerical method—the so-called Monte Carlo ray tracing approach (MCRT)—in order to calculate the loss coefficient. This method is usually used in order to obtain numerical solutions to problems that are too complicated to be solved analytically. The MCRT method had reproduced analytic results to a high level of precision in a case of simpler geometries [1,2,3]. Using a set of random numbers as inputs, uniformly distributed in the interval (0, 1), a point of interception between the lower surface and the incoming beam was found. To simulate the propagation of light in landscape, a random direction in the upper-half space was chosen. The case was positive for absorption if the diffusively scattered beam reached the vertical boundary. The loss coefficient was determined by averaging the observed behavior over a large number of followed light paths $N = 10^6$

$$k_l = N_a / N \,, \tag{6}$$

where $N_a$ is the number of cases that were positive for absorption and $N$ is the number of conducted numerical experiments.

The value of loss coefficient varied with different values of reduced length $l_1/L$ and reduced height $h/L$, as is shown in Fig. 2. As we can see, for heights of sloped areas less than 10 m, when the distance between them was lower than 75 m, there was not a significant loss coefficient value. Nevertheless, upon increasing the height, remarkable values of $k_l$ were obtained, especially for the values of reduced length $l_1/L$ larger than 0.75.

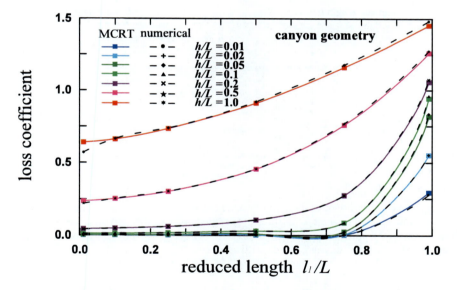

Figure 2. Dependence of "loss-coefficient" on reduced length $l_1/L$ and height h/L obtained by the MCRT method and compared with results of a standard numerical integration procedure.

In order to see how these values influence the aggregated albedo, the following graphics Fig. 3(a,b,c,d,e) present the albedos calculated by our approach in three different scenarios. First, there is a case in which the whole canyon area is covered with meadow or forest. We then present a case in which the valley between the sloped areas is covered with concrete. Finally, we present a case in which the whole area is covered with concrete.

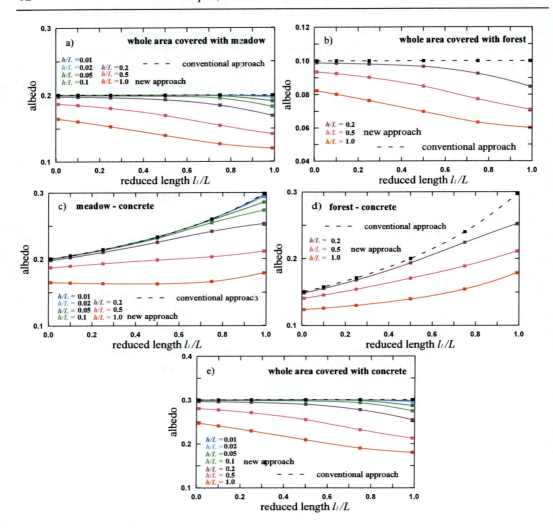

Figure 3. Aggregated albedo values for different kinds of surfaces: (a) whole canyon covered with meadow, (b) whole canyon covered with forest, (c) sloped areas of the canyon covered with meadow and valley covered with concrete, (d) sloped areas of the canyon covered with forest and valley covered with concrete and (e) whole canyon covered with concrete.

# 4. TEMPERATURE CHANGES

Since albedo has a great influence on the radiation and energy balance of the Earth, leading to significant changes in the interactions of land and atmosphere, a proposed approach for calculating the albedo over heterogeneous surfaces was recently included in the LAPS radiation module. A Land Air Parameterization Scheme (LAPS) is an SVAT scheme, which is designed to describe mass, energy and momentum transfer between land surface and atmosphere. Further details about this scheme, and the parameterization procedures for radiation components, can be found in Mihailovic [7] and Mihailovic et al. [8-10].

In order to demonstrate the changes induced by urbanization, we analyzed the influence of a new albedo approach on so-called effective surface temperature, calculated over a heterogeneous surface. Using a combination of parameter and flux aggregation methods, the mean values of the necessary parameters were obtained and, together with the average value of albedo, utilized in the prognostic equation concerning the evolution of the effective surface temperature.

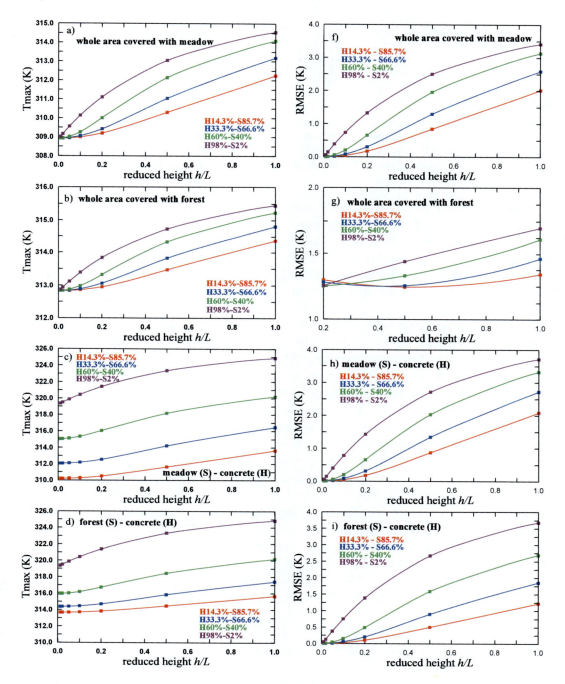

Figure 4. (continued)

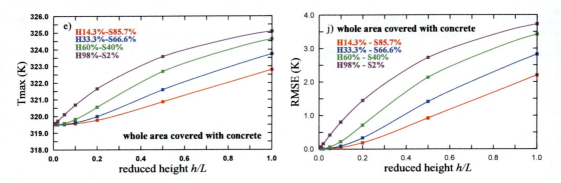

Figure 4. Differences in maximum temperature obtained using the new approach of albedo calculation and the conventional approach for different values of reduced height and fractional cover of each patch [(a), (b), (c), (d) and (e)]. Also shown are differences in the root mean square error between temperature values calculated by both approaches of albedo derivation as a function of the reduced height of sloped areas [(f), (g), (h), (i) and (j)].

We performed several simulations, using the forcing data for July 17, 1999 over the Baxter site in Philadelphia, PA. In the absence of representative monitoring, it was necessary to make measurement corrections from a height of 10 m in order to represent the state of the atmosphere at an altitude of 150 m [11-13]. Since the simulations were made for the assumed surface, the results could not be verified. We analyzed only the differences between temperature profiles obtained by the aggregated and conventional approach, as is shown in Fig. 4(a,b,c,d,e,f,g,h,i,j).

The maximum temperature difference between the values calculated by the new and the conventional approach, show a larger deviation with increasing values of reduced height and fractional coverage of the horizontal area. When the whole area is covered with meadow or with concrete, there is a similar increase in temperature of 3.5 K to 5.5 K for the largest reduced heights of the sloped areas. As can be seen, differences exist only in the temperature values, with approximately 10 K higher temperature values in the concrete scenario. In a meadow-concrete case, there is an even larger deviation in maximum temperature values for the different fractional cover of patches—from about 4 K to 6 K for the largest values of reduced height. When the canyon is completely covered with forest, there is a smaller increase in temperature values, from 1.5 K to 2.5 K, while values range from 1 K to 5 K in the forest-concrete scenario. In order to more precisely determine the difference between temperature profiles obtained by the aggregated and conventional approaches, the root mean square error (RMSE) was determined. Very similar values of RMSE (2 K-4 K) were found in the meadow-concrete situation, as well as when the whole grid-cell was covered either with meadow or concrete. In the scenario in which the sloped areas were covered with forest, the RMSE values were about 1.3 K to 3.7 K for the largest values of reduced height, and from 1 K to 1.5 K when the whole canyon area was covered with forest.

## 5. CONCLUSION

In order to analyze the importance of a terrain's geometry in albedo modeling of urban areas or slanted surfaces, we presented, in this chapter, achievements related to the new approach of albedo aggregation over the heterogeneous grid cell. We performed this analysis in a case of highly complicated "canyon" geometry. We assumed that the plane and the slopes were initially covered with meadow or forest and subsequently covered by concrete or some other building material, thus demonstrating the changes induced by urbanization. The results show that the decrease of albedo can be significant. The effective surface temperature is highly affected, since its value depends on albedo deviations; but it is also influenced by the fractional cover of grid-cell patches with different types of surfaces. In addition, increasing the canyon depth strongly affects the amount of energy flux that is lost due to the absorption of reflected light from the opposite surface. These results indicate one of the main reasons for opposing the urbanization of mountain regions, as it is an important contributing factor to the stabilization or reduction of global warming effects.

## ACKNOWLEDGMENTS

The research presented in this chapter has been funded by the Serbian Ministry of Science and Technological Development under the project "Modelling and numerical simulations of complex physical systems", No. OI141035 for 2006-2010.

## REFERENCES

[1]   D. Kapor, D.T. Mihailovic, T. Tosic, S.T. Rao, C. Hogrefe, *Proceedings of iEMSs*, 2, 389-394 (2002).

[2]   D.V. Kapor, A.M. Cirisan, D.T. Mihailovic, *Proceedings of iEMSs*, 1, 114–121 (2008).

[3]   D.T. Mihailovic, D. Kapor, C. Hogrefe, J. Lazic, T. Tosic, *Environ. Fluid. Mech.*, 4(1), 57-77 (2004a).

[4]   K.M.Rowntree, *S. Afr. J. Aquat. Sci.*, 17, 28-43(1991).

[5]   K. N. Liou, *An introduction to atmospheric radiation*, 2-nd edition, Academic Press Inc., 2002.

[6]   T.R. Oke, *Boundary Layer Climates*, 2-nd edition, Methuen, 1987.

[7]   D.T. Mihailovic, *Global Planet. Change.*, 13, 207-215 (1996).

[8]   D.T. Mihailovic, S.T. Rao, K. Alapaty, J.Y. Ku, *Abstracts of Scientific Conference on EMEP: Linking Science and Policy*, Albany, New York, USA, 39 (2001).

[9]   D.T. Mihailovic, K. Alapaty, B. Lalic, I. Arsenic, B. Rajkovic, S. Malinovic, *J. Appl. Meteorol.*, 43(10), 1498-1512 (2004b).

[10]  D.T. Mihailovic, S.T. Rao, K. Alapaty, J.Y. Ku, I. Arsenic, B. Lalic, *Environ. Modell. Softw.*, 20(6), 705-714 (2005).

[11]  Y. Delage, L. Wen, J.M. Belanger, *Atmos. Ocean.*, 37, 157-178 (1999).

[12]  S. Dupont, E. Guilloteau, P.G. Mestayer, *Proceedings of the AMS 3rd Symposium on Urban Environment*, 149-150 (2000).

[13]  J. Lazic, D.T. Mihailovic, B. Lalic, I. Arsenic, C. Hogrefe, *Proceedings of IEMSS*, 448–453(2002).

In: Advances in Environmental Modeling and Measurements    ISBN: 978-1-60876-599-7
Editors: D. T. Mihailović, B. Lalić, pp. 67-76    © 2010 Nova Science Publishers, Inc.

*Chapter 7*

# AN APPROACH TO FOREST-ATMOSPHERE INTERACTION MODELLING: IMPLICATIONS OF MOMENTUM TURBULENT TRANSPORT WITHIN THE FOREST

## *B. Lalić[*1], D.T. Mihailović[1], B. Rajković[2] and D.V. Kapor[1]*
[1]University of Novi Sad, Novi Sad, Serbia
[2]University of Belgrade, Belgrade, Serbia

## ABSTRACT

Despite the process of rapid deforestation, nearly one quarter of the Earth's surface is still covered by forest. Consequently, forest is a surface frequently encountered in environmental models of different scales. The amount of leaves and stems in a forest, and their architecture and spatial distribution, play a crucial role in interactions between the forest canopy and the atmosphere. The current approaches commonly used in their parameterization like, for example, either a single vegetation layer or a "sandwich" layer, are not good enough in the case of forest.

Experimentally observed wind speed values within the forest are often found to be below wind speeds indicated by the profile proposed by Cowan [1]. That profile, based on the single layer vegetation approach, has been used for a long time as a standard by numerical modellers. To avoid the drawbacks of this method, we offer an approach for parameterising the wind speed profile that more realistically describes forest-atmosphere interactions. We supposed that the forest leaf area density is not a constant, but is rather function of height. In this case, the forest canopy can be treated as a space that consists of a large number of homogeneous vegetation and air elements. Accordingly, all relevant processes could be described as a combination of single processes that represent homogenous vegetation and air space.

To check the validity of the new approach, we applied to turbulent transfer of momentum within a forest canopy, supposing that shear is the dominant mechanism of eddy production. Shear stress that describes the intensity of a turbulence source was calculated as a linear combination of shear stresses above the leaf surface and in the

* Corresponding author: E-mail address: branka@polj.ns.ac.yu, Phone: +381 21 4853204, Fax: +381 21 6350552

canopy air space. Solving a commonly used approximation for the zonal component of the equation of motion for the canopy air space, we obtained the vertical distribution of the zonal wind speed component. The horizontal component of the pressure gradient force that is usually neglected below the crown was also taken into account because it is comparable to other terms in the equation of motion. Calculated wind profiles were compared with (i) the ABRACOS data measured in the Amazonian forest Reserva Jaru (Brazil) and (ii) data measured in the Shasta Experimental Forest (California, USA).

# 1. INTRODUCTION

During the last century, many research projects and assessment studies have been devoted to the investigation of processes describing forest-atmosphere interactions, as comprehensively elaborated in [2]. This subject is equally important for forest managers, physiologists, physicist, meteorologists and environmental scientists [3]. Variation of wind speed, water vapour, temperature and gas or particle concentration within the forest canopy has been considered to result from physical and physiological processes representing this interaction. Depending on the level of knowledge available and the needs and possibilities of specific research, the forest, as a complex physical system, and its representative processes have been treated with varying levels of complexity. This system was considered using approaches ranging from (1) a big leaf model [4] to a sophisticated multilayer model [5] and (2) simplified fluid dynamics above a rough surface to a very complex parameterisation of turbulent transfer above and within the forest using different techniques [6-12].

If we take the point of view of boundary layer modelling, the air layer above and within any environment consisting of large roughness elements is strongly affected by turbulent motion at scales that are large relative to the height of the roughness elements. The intermittent character of turbulent eddies imposes difficulties in simulating processes that describe exchanges between a forest and the lower atmosphere [13,14,2]. The majority of attempts to model turbulent exchange between the atmosphere and tall vegetation involve closure schemes that are based on ensemble-averaged statistics, using one- or two-layer forest models [15,16,8]. In a limited number of studies, a multilayer model has been used [5], where the forest is also considered to be a layer of porous material on the Earth's surface with a strongly defined boundary at the top of the forest, at height $h$. This approach implies two strictly separated domains of parameterisation: above ($z > h$) and below ($z \leq h$) the top of the forest with coupling that comes from mathematical reasons (continuity conditions) rather than from physical ones (turbulent exchange of physical quantities).

Deviations between calculated and observed profiles (above and within the forest) could be addressed by the existence of large downbursts [17], inappropriate parameterisation of vegetation and improper treatment of edges and the distribution open space in the forest canopy [18]. Recently, the authors, either implicitly or explicitly, have agreed that for further advances in simulating interactions between forests and the atmosphere we should highly revise the current understanding of the physical processes that govern production of canopy turbulent eddies.

The main intention of this chapter is to offer a new consideration of processes of turbulent exchange at the forest-atmosphere boundary and, further, to give a more physical picture of production and dissipation of turbulent eddies within the forest canopy. First, this approach was applied to parameterisation of momentum transfer within the forest using the first order closure model. The commonly used "K- theory" was modified to provide deeper insight into the physical nature of phenomena by accounting for the influence of forest structure on the mixing length of eddies. Second, the results obtained were compared with observed values of wind speed profiles and bulk canopy resistance to assess the correctness of the suggested approach. Observed data were obtained from micrometeorological experiments performed in the Shasta experimental pine forest (California, USA) [19] and the Amazonian rain forest during the ABRACOS experiment (Reserva Jaru, Ji Parana, Brazil) [20].

## 2. A New Approach to Turbulence Parameterisation within The Forest

### 2.1. Canopy Effect

For environmental models of different scales, a forest can be considered to be a non-homogeneous, porous medium covering Earth's surface. Much evidence indicates that in the vicinity of the top of the forest canopy, a volume element of that environment is almost completely occupied by air while leaves are present only in traces. This implies the need to re-evaluate recent modelling approaches that are based on the assumption that through the whole environment within the forest, there is a unique mechanism of turbulent production and dissipation. However, as the ground approaches, air becomes more "occupied" by the forest biomass. Consequently, we have no free-air-only produced turbulence, as turbulence is now shifted towards direct production by the forest elements. Visualisation of this "picture" of turbulence is seen in Fig. 1, where "a" denotes turbulent eddies generated in the free atmosphere, while "c" denotes eddies that come from air-plant interactions [21]. The dimension of an eddy is proportional to its scale.

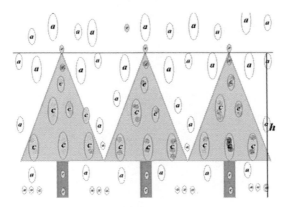

Figure 1. A plausible representation of turbulent eddies produced within the forest environment.

To put the presented picture of turbulence in a forest-atmosphere interaction perspective, it is essential to know the spatial distribution of plant elements. Even the assumption of canopy homogeneity is broadly applied; in the real world, it is often unrealistic to a degree that can produce significant errors. An efficient way to overcome the previously described problems is to describe canopy structure using the leaf area density distribution $L(z)$. An empirical relationship describing $L(z)$ for different types of forests has been suggested by Lalić and Mihailović [22] in the form and where the following notation is used: $h$ is the tree height, $L_m$ is the maximum value of leaf area density and $z_m$ is the height corresponding to $L_m$.

$$L(z) = L_m \left( \frac{h - z_m}{h - z} \right)^n \exp\left[ n \cdot \left( 1 - \frac{h - z_m}{h - z} \right) \right], \text{ where } n = \begin{cases} 6 & 0 \le z < z_m \\ 1/2 & z_m \le z \le h \end{cases}, \tag{1}$$

All of the above assumptions give a more realistic physical picture of the forest canopy but, at the same time, capture some very important features of within-canopy turbulence. For example, the mixing length of turbulent eddies produced within the canopy is strongly affected by the canopy structure. A comprehensive approach to parameterisation of mixing length within the forest has been elaborated by Watanabe and Kondo [23]. On the basis of the probability of eddy dissipation on the leaf surface, they derived an expression for mixing length within the canopy, $l_{mc}$, in the form

$$l_{mc}(z) = k \int_0^z \left[ r \exp\left( -\int_0^r \mu(z - t)dt \right) \mu(z - r)dr \right] + z \exp\left( -\int_0^z \mu(z - t)dt \right), \tag{2}$$

where $k$ is the von Karman's constant and $\mu(z)$ is the function describing the distribution of roughness elements in the form $\mu(z) = BC_dL(z)$, where $B$ is the empirical constant and $C_d$ is a drag coefficient of leaves. Using Eq. (2), for the case of a deciduous tree forest described in the paper by Watanabe and Kondo [23], we calculated mixing length profiles for (i) a homogenous canopy model ($L(z)$ = const.) and (ii) a forest model with leaf area distribution given by Eq. (1). Obtained values were compared with measured data, following the original paper by Watanabe and Kondo [23] (Fig. 2). When the non-uniform forest model is considered, with its leaf area distribution given by Eq. (1), the approximation supports a realistic treatment of turbulent eddy diffusion within the canopy.

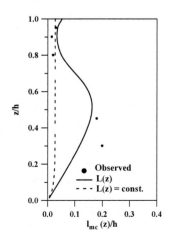

Figure 2. Mixing length profile within deciduous forest observed (•) and calculated using uniform (---) and non-uniform approximations ( — ) for $L(z)$.

## 2.2. Flow within the Canopy

The full governing equation for the zonal velocity component, $u$, of the air motion within the canopy can be written in the form

$$\frac{\partial u}{\partial t} + u\frac{\partial u}{\partial x} + v\frac{\partial u}{\partial y} + w\frac{\partial u}{\partial z} = -\frac{1}{\rho}\frac{\partial p}{\partial x} + g\frac{\theta}{\theta_0}\sin\alpha + fv - \frac{\partial \overline{u'w'}}{\partial z} - C_d L(z)u^2, \tag{3}$$

where $\rho$ is the air density, $p$ is the atmospheric pressure, $g$ is the gravitational acceleration, $\alpha$ is the terrain slope, $f$ is the Coriolis parameter, $\overline{u'w'}$ is the Reynolds stress in the $z$ direction, and $\theta$ and $\theta_0$ are perturbed and background potential temperatures [24]. Assuming steady-state, horizontally homogeneous one-dimensional flow over flat terrain and ignoring the Coriolis force within the canopy, Eq. (3) can be reduced to a balance between the vertical divergence of Reynolds stress, the canopy drag force and the pressure gradient force, which has been shown to be important [12]

$$\frac{1}{\rho}\frac{\partial p}{\partial x} + \frac{\partial \overline{u'w'}}{\partial z} + C_d L(z)u^2 = 0. \tag{4}$$

Namely, even for typical values of the pressure gradient (0.01-0.03 h Pa km$^{-1}$), far away from the forest edge, the pressure gradient force is still sufficient to cause the secondary wind speed maximum [18].

Stabler and Fitzjarrald [25] pointed to that difficulty, which had been previously recognised, that mixing inside the canopy is often provided by penetration of large eddies produced in the shear layer just above the canopy. As a result of that penetration, a frequently observed feature is a secondary wind maximum that occurs in certain types of forest [26] and which cannot be reproduced by the commonly-used Cowan's profile [1]. It seems that a more physical model of forest-atmosphere interactions can be obtained if we follow this evidence. To introduce the influence of the turbulence produced just above the canopy with the non-uniform leaf area density distribution, let us suppose that friction is the dominant mechanism of turbulent eddy production within the canopy and that shear stress $\tau(z)$ at height $z$ within the forest can be defined as a linear combination of shear stresses produced by friction on the leaf surface, $\tau_b$ and shear stress produced in the free atmosphere above a rough surface, $\tau_a$ [21,27]

$$\tau = \frac{L(z)}{L_m}\tau_b + \left(1 - \frac{L(z)}{L_m}\right)\tau_a. \tag{5}$$

Further, if we include that momentum turbulent flux is proportional to shear stress ($\overline{u'w'} = \tau/\rho$), and if we substitute Eq. (5) into Eq. (4), this equation becomes

$$\frac{1}{\rho}\frac{\partial p}{\partial x} - \frac{1}{\rho}\frac{d}{dz}\left[\frac{L(z)}{L_m}\tau_B + \left(1 - \frac{L(z)}{L_m}\right)\tau_a\right] + C_d L(z)u^2 = 0, \tag{6}$$

which is general enough for different parameterisations of shear stress above and within the canopy. One simple way of parameterising is to (i) apply K theory within the forest ($\tau_b = \rho K_{mcl}\, du/dz$) and (ii) assume constant shear stress above it ($\tau_a = \rho\, u_*^2$). After we apply this parameterisation, Eq. (6) becomes

$$\frac{1}{\rho}\frac{\partial p}{\partial x} - \frac{d}{dz}\left[\frac{L(z)}{L_m}K_{mc1}\frac{du}{dz} + \left(1 - \frac{L(z)}{L_m}\right)u_*^2\right] + C_d L(z)u^2 = 0 ,\tag{7}$$

where $K_{mcl}$ is the turbulent transfer coefficient within the fully planted volume element and $u_*$ is the friction velocity used to be constant. The physical meaning of coefficient $K_{mcl}$ is usually refered to eddy viscosity and supposed to be proportional to wind speed, $u$ ($K_{mcl} = \sigma u$), where $\sigma$ is a scaling factor that has to be parameterised. After some manipulations, Eq (7) can be written in the form

$$\frac{d^2 u^2}{dz^2} + f_2(z)\frac{du^2}{dz} + g_2 u^2 + h_2(z) = 0 ,\tag{8}$$

where the following replacements are made

$$f_2(z) = \frac{1}{L(z)}\frac{dL(z)}{dz} ,\tag{9}$$

$$g_2 = \frac{-2\, L_m C_d}{\sigma} ,\tag{10}$$

and

$$h_2(z) = -\frac{2\, u_*^2}{\sigma}f_2(z) - \frac{2\, L_m}{L(z)\sigma}\frac{1}{\rho}\frac{\partial p}{\partial x} .\tag{11}$$

In order to solve Eq. (8), we used that the leaf area density profile is defined by Eq. (1), while for the preasure gradient force was assumed a constant value in $z$ direction. Due to form of functions $f_2(z)$, $g_2(z)$ and $h_2(z)$, obtained using the latest assumptions, Eq. (8) has to be solved using a numerical procedure. Because of singularity problem for $z = h$ we supposed that $L(z)$ profile can be applied in the infinitesimaly small distance from the level $z = h$. If we still remain in the "K- theory workspace", an equivalent canopy turbulent transfer coefficient $K_{mc}$ is parameterised as

$$K_{mc} = \frac{\dfrac{L(z)}{L_m}\tau_b + \left(1 - \dfrac{L(z)}{L_m}\right)\tau_a}{\rho\left|\dfrac{du}{dz}\right|} ,\tag{12}$$

and finally, after using expressions for $\tau_a$ and $\tau_b$, Eq. (12) becomes

$$K_{mc} = \frac{L(z)}{L_m}\sigma\, u(z) + \left(1 - \frac{L(z)}{L_m}\right)\frac{u_*^2}{\left|\dfrac{du}{dz}\right|}\,,$$
(13)

while expression for the bulk canopy resistance, $r_b$, Sellers et al. [28] takes the form

$$r_b = \int_0^h \frac{1}{\dfrac{L(z)}{L_m}\sigma\, u(z) + \left(1 - \dfrac{L(z)}{L_m}\right)\dfrac{u_*^2}{\left|\dfrac{du}{dz}\right|}}\,dz\,.$$
(14)

## 3. DISCUSSION OF THE RESULTS

To verify the correctness of the approach presented, wind speed profiles were calculated using Eq. (8) (NP in further text) and Cowan's equation (CP), within the Shasta experimental forest (USA) and the tropical rain forest in Reserva Jaru (Brasil), which is part of the ABRACOS experiment site network. In the absence of observed pressure gradient data, the value of 0.02 h Pa km$^{-1}$ was used in calculations [18]. Bulk boundary resistance was calculated only for Reserva Jaru forest, for which measured values were available. All calculated results were compared with observations from the sites (Figs. 3-4). Continuity conditions on the canopy top were provided using a standard logarithmic wind profile above vegetation [29] in the case of Cowan's profile and the new logarithmic profile [27] for the new wind profile within vegetation.

The presented results (Fig. 3) suggest the superiority of the new parameterisation of within-canopy turbulence in reproducing the wind profile, particularly in the top canopy layer and in the area where the second wind speed maximum occurs. A huge difference in the morphological characteristics of pine forest and Amazonian rain forest produce substantial differences in the wind speed gradient under the same initial value at the canopy top. It could be a source of deviation between observed wind speed and values obtained using the new profile in Reserva Jaru. This is because the dense canopy so strongly attenuates wind momentum that at levels below the crown, the wind speed tends to be less than 0.3 m s$^{-1}$. In contrast to Cowan's profile, the new profile demonstrates a high level of sophistication and capability to introduce these differences into a wind profile calculations.

Fig. 4 demonstrates that bulk resistance of forest canopy calculated using new wind profile (white diamond) deviates less from observed values for each of eight profiles than do results obtained using standard Cowan's profile (black diamond).

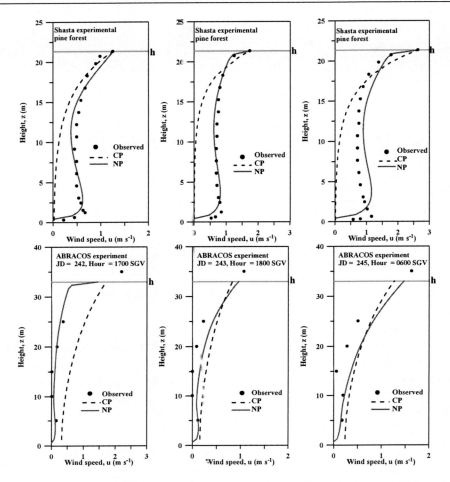

Figure 3. Cowan's (CP) and new (NP) wind profiles within the Shasta and ABRACOS experimental forests.

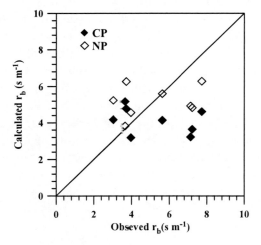

Figure 4. Bulk resistance of the forest canopy calculated using Cowan's (CP) and new (NP) wind profiles.

# 4. CONCLUSION

This chapter presents a new approach to modelling turbulence production and diffusivity within the forest, taking into account the vertical structure of the canopy. Shear stress within the canopy, as a dominant mechanism of eddy production, was considered to be a linear combination of shear stresses produced (a) by friction on the leaf surface and (b) in the free atmosphere above a rough surface. A new wind speed profile within the forest was obtained using the foregoing assumptions and, together with the classical Cowan's profile, was compared with empirical data. For the purpose of this study, three profiles from the pine forest and three from the Amazonian rain forest were selected. In contrast to Cowan's profile, the new wind profile agrees well with observations and demonstrates the ability of the new profile to reproduce secondary wind maxima in the lower portion of the forest canopy. This feature may be due to including in the calculations the vertical distribution of friction elements and the influence of pressure gradient forces.

Additionally, the turbulent transfer coefficient inside the forest was considered, bearing in mind its importance for calculations of temperature, humidity and air pollution deposition. Bulk resistance, as the integral of its reciprocal value, was calculated and compared with values observed in the Amazonian rain forest and calculated using Cowan's profile. The new wind profile agreed more closely with observations than did Cowan's profile.

To demonstrate the impact of forest vertical structure on turbulent field characteristics, a mixing length was calculated for turbulent eddies within the canopy using uniform and non-uniform approximations for the leaf area density profile. The results obtained using the suggested empirical relationship to describe non-uniform distributions of leaf area density within the canopy show excellent agreement with observations.

The results of the present work show the capability of these concepts to better represent the physical processes that describe forest-atmosphere interactions. This will allow for more reliable calculations of all wind-flow related scalar gradients within the forest and significantly improve modelling of forests as a source and sink of atmospheric pollution.

## ACKNOWLEDGMENTS

The authors are grateful to Prof. J.H.C. Gash for providing the results of the ABRACOS field experiments. This research is supported by the Ministry of Science and Technology of the Republic of Serbia under contract OI141035.

## REFERENCES

[1]  I.R. Cowan, *Quart. J. Roy. Meteorol. Soc.*, 94, 523–544 (1968).
[2]  J.J. Finnigan, *Annu. Rev. Fluid Mech.*, 32, 519–571 (2000).
[3]  D.G. Fox, *Handbook of applied meteorology,* edited by: D. Houghton, New York: A Wiley Interscience Publication, John Wiley & Sons, USA, 605-666, 1985.
[4]  J.L. Monteith, *Vegetation and atmosphere II*, London: Academic Press, pp 343, 1976.

[5]   J. Goudriaan, *Wageningen Center for Agricultural Publishing and Documentation*, pp. 249, 1977.

[6]   N.R. Wilson, R.H. Shaw, *J. Appl. Meteorol.*, 11, 1197–1205 (1977).

[7]   T.P. Meyers, K.T. Paw U, *Boundary-Layer Meteorol.*, 37, 297–311 (1986).

[8]   T.P. Meyers, K.T. Paw U, *Agric. For. Meteorol.*, 41, 143–163 (1987).

[9]   J.D. Wilson, *Boundary-Layer Meteorol.*, 42, 371–392 (1988).

[10]  W.J. Massman, J.C. Weil, *Boundary-Layer Meteorol.*, 91, 81–107 (1999).

[11]  G.G. Katul, L. Mahrt, D. Poggi, C. Sanz, *Boundary-Layer Meteorol.*, 113, 81–109 (2004).

[12]  H.B. Su, H.P. Schmid, C.S. Vogel, P.S. Curtis, *Agric. For. Meteorol.*, 148, 862–882 (2008).

[13]  J.J. Finnigan, *Boundary-Layer Meteorol.*, 16, 223–236 (1979).

[14]  O.T. Denmead, E.F. Bradley, *The Forest-Atmosphere Interaction*, edited by: B.A. Hutchinson, B.B. Hicks, Dordrecht: D. Reidel Publishing Co., 1985, pp. 421-442.

[15]  P. Zeng, H. Takahashi, *Agricultural and Forest Meteorology*, 103, 3, 301-313 (2000).

[16]  Z. Li, D.R.Miller, J.D. Lin, *Boundary-Layer Meteorol.*, 33, 77–83 (1985)

[17]  R.H. Shaw, U. Schumann, *Boundary Layer Meteorol.*, 61, 47-64 (1992).

[18]  X. Lee, *Forest Ecologya and Managament*, 135, 3-18 (2000).

[19]  W.L. Fons, *J. Forestry*, 38, 481-487 (1940).

[20]  O.M.R. Cabral, A.L.C. McWilliam, J.M. Roberts, *Amazonian Rainforest and Climate*, edited by: J.H.C. Gash, C.A. Nobre, J.M. Roberts and R.L. Victoria, Chichester: John Wiley, 1996, pp. 207– 220.

[21]  B. Lalic, *Abstracts of Fifth Annual Meeting of the European Meteorological Society (EMS)*, ISSN 1812-7053 (2005).

[22]  B. Lalic, D.T. Mihailovic, *J. Appl. Meteorol.*, 43, No. 4: 641–645 (2004).

[23]  T. Watanabe, J. Kondo, *Jour. Met. Soc. of Japan*, 68, No. 2, 227–235 (1990).

[24]  L. Mahrt, *J. Atmos. Sci.*, 39, 2701–2711 (1982).

[25]  R.M. Staebler, D.R. Fitzjarrald, *J. Appl. Meteorol.*, 44, 1161-1179 (2005).

[26]  R.H. Shaw, *J. Appl. Meteorol.*, 16, 514–521 (1977).

[27]  B. Lalic, PhD Thesis, University of Novi Sad, pp. 139, 2006.

[28]  P.J Sellers, Y. Mintz, Y.C. Sud, A. Dalcher, *J. Atmos. Sci.*, 43, No. 6, 505–530 (1986).

[29]  U. Hogstrom, *J. Atmos. Sci.*, 42, 263-270 (1985).

In: Advances in Environmental Modeling and Measurements    ISBN: 978-1-60876-599-7
Editors: D. T. Mihailović, B. Lalić, pp. 77-87    © 2010 Nova Science Publishers, Inc.

*Chapter 8*

# A SHORT ESSAY ABOUT MODELING OF LOCAL INTERACTIONS AND FUNCTIONAL ROBUSTNESS IN LIVING SYSTEMS

## *I. Balaz*[*1] *and D.T. Mihailović*[2]

[1]Institute of Physics, Belgrade, Serbia
[2] University of Novi Sad, Novi Sad, Serbia

## ABSTRACT

One of distinguishing characteristics of living systems is their ability to autonomously adapt to changes in their environment, thus achieving a great deal of robustness. Such adaptations can be sorted into two groups: evolutive and physiological adaptations. In this chapter, we will deal with the latter group. It means that we will consider only adaptations performed within given fixed boundaries. Also, we will not consider adaptive mechanisms that are specific to some organisms. We will focus our attention on general mechanisms that enable intracellular shifts in running processes. This focus insures that interruptions, changes of parameters or changes in controlling signals at any stage of the process cannot lead to a collapse of the whole system. We propose that the main mechanisms for achieving robustness in living systems are spatio-temporal locality of functional elements along with functional parallelism. Combining a relatively short lifespan with two aspects of spatial locality (reduced mobility due to intracellular crowding and observer-based locality) results in the emergence of a weak compartmentalization of the functional space, which is further facilitated by the continuous existence of multiple copies of each functional element.

In this chapter, after theoretical analysis, we will construct a model of spatio-temporal locality of functional elements in abstract living system using category theory and analyze its formal consequences including: (i) observation-based generation of equivalence classes, (ii) system's stability in situations where operating rules are local and temporally restricted, (iii) difference between external and internal rules (or *a priori* and *ad hoc* rules, respectively).

---

[*] Corresponding author: E-mail address: ibalaz@polj.ns.ac.yu, Phone: +381 21 4853290, Fax: +381 21 6350552

# 1. INTRODUCTION

The functions of living systems and details of their processes from the micro- to macro-scale are the focus of many scientific disciplines. However, despite all of these efforts, there is a noticeable lack of general and precise theories for the organization of living systems embedded into an appropriate formalism, as is usual in physics. Rather, descriptions of the organization or cells or organisms are formulated as collections of the descriptions of particular processes, with all available data thrown together. There are objective reasons for using this method. In a number of cases, the molecular details of metabolic processes have only been revealed recently, or they are still unknown. Among various groups of organisms there is great variability in the regulation of particular processes and diversity in the molecular entities that participate in them. Moreover, some concepts that initially seemed clear and straightforward became gradually more complicated as further discoveries took place, such as the concept of a gene or the function of genetic regulatory networks. As a consequence, there are only a limited number of formulations of the general principles of cellular organization [1-4].

In this manuscript, we consider only one part of the problem: the spontaneous emergence of functional organization among different agents and the consequences of functional robustness. By spontaneous emergence, we imply the appearance of ordering in a set of interacting agents, without any external force to shape or govern the final outcome. The term functional indicates the existence of relations between two or more agents such that the input values of one are a result of the output values of the other.

In contrast to the usual representations of metabolism as a predefined set of algorithmic processes, our starting point is that the flow of transformations in living systems are generated during life and that decisions about the next step are always local and actual. In this view, establishing control and arranging particular processes into organized metabolic pathways is achieved only through the resolution of local conflicts between subsystems with their own tendencies of assimilations. This picture is much more consistent with the available experimental results about protein turnover and protein dynamics [5,6]. Since the crucial notion here is the emergence out of local interactions, we have investigated the notion of locality in further detail and used these findings to construct the formal treatment.

In this discourse, locality could be functional (observer based), spatial and temporal. When modeling living systems, none of these aspects should be neglected because they have distinct and important consequences. All of them are inherent at both the intracellular and intercellular/interorganismic level, so the development of a formal treatment can be applied to the emergence of metabolic functional processes and the emergence of colonies or other types of structured populations.

Functional locality is based on the ability of each agent to translate vast diversity of external physical and/or chemical changes into an "understandable" signal, or a set of signals in the case of cells or organisms. The existence of such a translation can be generalized by the notion of observers that reside within the universe. By summarizing available considerations [7,8,9] on the topic, we can derive following postulates:

a)   each individual is considered as an observer that resides within some environment;

b) observation is an act of assimilating a segment of external changes with an appropriate set of internal operations in order to produce a reaction.

We extend these with more specific postulates, derived from general patterns of functioning of living systems:

c) operational environment is defined from the perspective of an individual, so that external changes functionally exist for an individual only if they can be observed;
d) the environment is divided (schematized) into operative segments, functional, spatial and temporal, only by observing;
e) schematization models are the same endogenous factors that determine internal functioning of the individual;

The whole process, described in these five postulates, will be called "operative assimilation," and it gives rise to functional locality where, by definition, assimilation can be performed only within the scope of the agent. However, if we maintain a focus only at that level of consideration, then each observable entity can be treated immediately. In other words, there are no spatial relations that could prevent materialization of some reactions. Therefore, both agents and their environment should be embedded into uniformly applicable metrics. Finally, in living systems, the life spans of agents are also limited. This means that patterns of operative assimilation are not fixed to some part of space and the structure of functional relations is invariable. Also, referring to absolute time flow in living systems is highly problematic since the internal mechanisms for uniform measurement and comparison of temporal sequences do not exist. Therefore, we will introduce only local chronologies as a representative of time.

In order to formally represent all of the described aspects of locality and to investigate its functions, we start with a basic representation of relations between two finite sets. They will be regarded as both objects in the space and mappings. Collections of these sets will be embedded into a metrizable Euclidean topology over a derived index set. We will observe emergence of partial ordering in topologies and their temporal development, as well as embodiment of these structures into categories.

## 2. EMERGENCE OF FUNCTIONALITY FROM LOCAL INTERACTIONS

In simplified terms, a metabolic space can be represented as a collection of proteins and substrates, and population can be seen as a collection of cells/organisms within some environment. In both cases, we deal with sets of mappings residing within a more complex environment than either domain of any single mapping or the domain of the set of all available mappings. Also, the behavior of the mappings is somewhat dependent on the environment. Therefore, central points in setting up the frame are determining the domain/codomain and the dual character of mappings that behave both as mappings and objects.

**Definition 1** (*Relations*). If we denote $M = \{f, g, h, ...\}$ as a set of proteins/cells/organisms, and $U = \{a, b, c, ...\}$ as a set of environmental objects, then relations within $U$ can be represented as

$$R = (U, G(R)),$$ (1)

where $G(R): U_1 \times ... \times U_k \big| U_1, ..., U_j, ..., U_k \subset U$ is determined by $M$ (in a given context, the internal determination of $G(R)$ by $U$ is not important) such that

$$aG(R)b \big| a, b \in U, G(R) \equiv f \in M.$$ (2)

All $a \in U$ are called the domains of the relation $R$ and are denoted as **dom**$f$, while all $b \in U$ are called the codomains of the relation $R$ and are denoted as **cod**$f$. Since relation $R$ is structure preserving, it can be called morphism. Relation $G(R)$ is:

- irreflexive: $\neg aG(R)a$ ;
- symmetric: $aG(R)b \Rightarrow bG(R)a$ ;
- nontransitive: $aG(R)b \wedge bG(R)c \Rightarrow \neg aG(R)c$ ;
- with a unique resultant: $aG(R)b \wedge aG(R)c \Rightarrow b = c$ .

**Definition 2** (*Composition of Relations*). If $G(R): U_i \times U_j \big| U_i, U_j \subset U$ and $G(S): U_j \times U_k \big| U_j, U_k \subset U$ are relations defined over a set $U$, then their composition $G(S) \circ G(R)$ is defined as

$$G(S) \circ G(R) = \{(u_i, u_k) \in U_i \times U_k \big| \exists u_j \in U_j : (u_i, u_j) \in G(R) \wedge (u_j, u_k) \in G(S)\} \subset U_i \times U_k$$ (3)

Therefore, the composition $G(S) \circ G(R)$ can be defined iff there is a $u_j \in U_j$ such that $u_i G(R) u_j G(S) u_k$.

**Definition 3** (*Metric Space*). If for a set, $C$ we specify a real valued function $d$, such that for $a, b \in C$ :

i) $d(a, b) \geq 0$ ;
ii) $d(a, b) = 0 \Leftrightarrow a = b$ ;
iii) $d(a, b) = d(b, a)$ ;
iv) $d(a, c) \leq d(a, b) + d(b, c)$ for all $a, b, c \in C$ ;

then, $d$ is a metric on $C$, denoted as $(C, d)$.

**Definition 4** (*Mapping into Shared Metric Space*). If both sets, $M$ and $U$, can be mapped into $(C,d)$

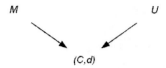

$$M \qquad\qquad U$$

$$(C,d)$$

such that $C \equiv M \oplus U = \{(1,m)|m \in M\} \cup \{(1,u)|u \in U\}$ and $t_1(m) = (2,m)$, $t_2(u) = (2,u)$ then $C$ is a coproduct of $M$ and $U$, while $(C,d)$ is shared metric space over $M$ and $U$.

**Definition 5** (*Attributes*). If we define a set of many-valued attributes $P = \{p, q, r, ...\} | \forall p \in P, p = \{p_1, p_2, p_3, ..., p_n\}$, and each $a \in U$ and $f \in M$ are associated with the $P_n^\wedge$, where $n \in \{M \cup U\}$, $P_n \subseteq P$, and $P_n^\wedge$ is a strictly ordered set $(P_n, <)$, where the ordering relation is determined in accordance to the underlying structure of $a \in U$ and $f \in M$, and $a = b$ ($f = g$) iff $P_a = P_b$ ($P_f = P_g$), then members of both $M$ and $U$ are divided into disjoint classes of equivalence with respect to $P$.

**Definition 6** (*Domain Determination*). For **dom**$f$, $a \in \mathbf{dom}f$ iff there exists an $a \in U$ such that:

- $P_a^\wedge \subseteq (P_f^\wedge)^{\sqcap OP}$ where $(P_f^\wedge)^{\sqcap OP}$ is given by the composition $G \circ F$ of functions $F: p \to p^{OP}$ (defined for all $p$ whose cardinalities are $|p| = 2$ and

$$p^{OP} = \begin{cases} p_1 \text{ for } p = p_2 \\ p_2 \text{ for } p = p_1 \end{cases}$$) and $G: (P_f, <) \to (P_f^{OP}, <)$;

- $d(f,a) = 1$ for $d(f,a) = \begin{cases} 0, & \text{if } |f-a| > |(f \pm 1/2\, p_f^r) - (a \pm 1/2\, p_a^r)| \\ 1, & \text{if } |f-a| \le |(f \pm 1/2\, p_f^r) - (a \pm 1/2\, p_a^r)| \end{cases}$ where $p_f^r$ and $p_a^r$

are denoted as the "activity radius" values for $f$ and $a$, respectively, and are determined by their corresponding attribute values.

In other words, the element of the environment must be within the scope of protein/cell/organism in order to be recognized by that observer. All of the elements recognized in such a manner are collected into an equivalence class $[a]_{\mathbf{dom}f}$.

**Definition 7** (*Codomain Determination*). Codomain is determined in accordance to the structure of $f$ in two phases:

- part of sequence $P_f^\wedge$ is a **cod**$f$ generator if it is in the neighborhood of the segment for which $(P_f^\wedge)^{\sqcap OP}$ is determined, where the neighborhood is $\pm n$ places from the segment ($n \in \square$ and is fixed in accordance to the model) and if the set of $p$ within the neighborhood is clustered into prevailing and non-canceling attributes;

- $a$ can be transformed into **cod**$f$ if the $P_a^\wedge$ segment is non-canceling compared to the **cod**$f$ generator sequence.

All of the details about the exact structure of the mappings in Definitions 6 and 7 are dependent on a chosen set of attributes, and their mutual relations. Therefore, we give only most general guidelines, independent of constructed models.

**Definition 8** (*Topology Based on Observations*). If the metrical radius $R(f)$ for **dom**$f$, is defined as $R(f) = \{a, b \mid a \in \mathbf{dom}f, b \in \mathbf{cod}f \wedge d(a, f) = 1, d(b, f) = 1\}$, then the collection of all $R(f)$ for a given metric space $(C, d)$ is a basis for topology $T$ on $C$. Therefore, a subset $N$ of $C$ is in $T$ (is an open set) iff it is a union of members of the collection of all $R(f)$. Such a topology $T$ is induced by the metric $d$ and $(C, T)$ is the induced topological space. It should be emphasized that each open set is defined with respect to a particular $f \in M$.

**Definition 9** (*Emergence of Functional Closure and Boundaries*). In order to describe functional relations induced by the operative assimilations, we will focus on the emergence of closure and boundaries for open sets in the induced topological space:

- for $R(f)$, a point $a \in C$ is defined as the limit point of $R(f)$ if every open set of induced topology containing $a$ contains a point of $R(f)$ different from $a$. The set of all limit points of $R(f)$ is denoted as $R(f)'$. Then, $R(f) \cup R(f)'$ is called the closure of $R(f)$, denoted as $\overline{R(f)}$. Within the given framework, $\overline{R(f)}$ signifies the emergence of metabolic processes/interacting populations;
- for an open set $R(f)$, the interior, denoted as **int**$(R(f))$, is the largest open set contained in $R(f)$. In other words, **int**$(R(f))$ is $R(f)$ itself. All of the points in the closure of $R(f)$ not belonging to **int**$(R(f))$ define a boundary on $R(f)$, denoted as **bd**$R(f)$. An element of the boundary of $R(f)$ is called a boundary point of $R(f)$. Less formally, the boundary points of $R(f)$ are those points that can be approached both from $R(f)$ and from the outside of $R(f)$. Within the given framework, **bd**$R(f)$ signifies points of possible divergence or differentiation of emerging metabolic processes/interacting populations.

**Definition 10** (*Operations over $R(f)$*). Each element of $R(f)$ defined by **dom**$f$ is subject to transformation into **cod**$f$, and *vice versa*. As stated in Definition 8, newly produced elements remains within the "activity radius" values given for $f$.

To be ordering, a relation over the set has to be transitive and asymmetric. However, in Definition 1, it is stated that relations induced by proteins, cells or organisms are nontransitive and symmetric. Therefore, it is clear that one relation determined by $f \in M$ cannot induce ordering over the environment. Instead, we need to introduce a relation that would naturally follow from existence of a number of different members of the set $M$ within range of each other.

**Definition 11** *(Ordering).* If $a \in (\mathbf{bd}R(f) \wedge \mathbf{bd}R(g))$ and $b \in (\mathbf{bd}R(g) \wedge \mathbf{bd}R(h))$ then a causal influence is established between $a, b$ with respect to $\overline{R(M)} | M = \{f, g, h, ...\}$, denoted as $<_{\overline{R(M)}}$, which is transitive and asymmetric.

**Definition 12** *(Chronology).* If $a, b \in \bigcup \mathbf{bd}R(M) | M = \{f, g, h, ...\}$ ordered by the relation $<_{\overline{R(M)}}$, are mapped into a finite indexed set $I$ such that $I = \{i, j, k, ...\} | I \subset \square$ , and $*$ is a strict partial ordering over $I$, then we can define chronology over closure. This chronology is not imposed onto the structure but emerges from the bottom as a consequence of established causal relations.

**Definition 13** *(Locality of Chronology).* The chronology defined by the relation $<_{\overline{R(M)}}$ is local in the sense that Definitions 6 – 9 dictate that it is applicable only to:

- structures determined by the observable subset of $U$ , and
- metrics determined by the observable subset of $U$ .

Therefore, it is globally nonlinear in the sense of Robb's axiom, [10] which says that "For every element $x$, there is another element $y$ such that neither $x > y$ nor $y > x$," and its strengthened form: $(\forall x)(\forall y)(\exists z)(y \prec x \quad z \prec x \wedge \neg(z = y \vee z \prec y \vee y \prec z))$, given by [11], if we try to broaden our scope beyond $\overline{R(M)}$ over which $<_{\overline{R(M)}}$ is established. However, within the closure, both are invalid.

By these definitions, we have formalized the establishment of local interactions between observers within a shared metric space, and identified some of their topological properties and the emergence of local chronologies. However, since one of distinguishing characteristics of proteins, cells and organisms is their temporal locality, (periodic disappearance of existing ones as well as the periodic appearance of new ones) we should focus on global properties of transformations induced by observer turnover.

**Definition 14** (*Category Based on Observations*). If we take that:

- a collection of closures of $R(M) | M = \{f, g, h, ...\}$ for a given topology is a basis for collections of objects such that each object consists of a quadruplet $G = (A, O, \partial_0, \partial_1)$, where $A$ is a set of directed edges defined by Eqs.(1), (2) and (3), $O$ is a set of objects whose members are equivalence classes $[a]_{\mathbf{dom}M}$, $[b]_{\mathbf{cod}M}$ where $M = \{f, g, h, ...\}$ and mappings $\partial_i (i = 0, 1)$ from $A$ to $O$, such that $\partial_0$ is a source map that sends each directed edge to its source and $\partial_1$ is a target map that sends each directed edge to its target;

- the homomorphisms between objects $G$ such that if $D : G \to G'$, where $G = (A, O, \partial_0, \partial_1)$ and $G' = (A', O', \partial_0', \partial_1')$, then $D$ consists of two maps $D(A) : A \to A'$ and $D(O) : O \to O'$ such that the following diagram commutes:

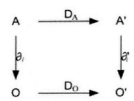

- to each object is assigned an arrow $\mathrm{id}_G : G \to G$ called the identity on $G$;
- the composition of homomorphisms is defined as an associative operation assigned to pairs of morphisms such that for $D : G \to G'$ and $E : G' \to G''$, a map $E \circ D : G \to G''$ is defined by $(E \circ D)(G) = E(D(G))$,

then the category $\Gamma$ of graphs and their homomorphisms is defined over interacting agents residing within a subjective environment. $\Gamma$ is subcategory of the *Graph* category but it does not place any constraints on our framework since each finite category can be represented in the category *Graph* (Corollary 4.23 in [12]).

**Definition 15** *(Subobjects)*. Subobjects $S$ of any object $G$ can be defined as a structure $S$ together with an inclusion map $S \overset{i}{\longrightarrow} G$ such that for any object, $T$, and for any pair of mappings, $T \overset{s_1}{\underset{s_2}{\longrightarrow}} S$, $i \circ s_1 = i \circ s_2$ imply $s_1 = s_2$, and the mapping $i$ determines the structure preserving process of relation between $S$ and $G$. Therefore, if in category $\Gamma$ we have an object $G$, then we can form category $\Gamma / G$ where:

- objects are mappings from $\Gamma$ for which $G$ is codomain ($\alpha : A_0 \to G, \beta : A_1 \to G, ...$)
- mappings $f, g$ are given by the following diagram

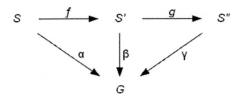

Here, $\alpha, \beta, \chi$ are inclusion maps from $G$ and consequently objects in $\Gamma / G$ are subobjects of $G$ in $\Gamma$.

In category theory, a forgetful functor is defined as a functor that "forgets" some or all of the structure of an algebraic object. For example $U : Grp \to Set$ assigns to each element of $G \in Grp$ its underlying set and to each morphism $D : G \to G'$ the same function regarded as a function between sets. Since in our framework, the structure of an object is defined as a collection of closures determined by $R(M)|M = \{f, g, h, ...\}$, a function that "forgets" any $f$ and corresponding interior of $R(f)$ will accurately represent events such as protein turnover, and will simultaneously cause reorganization to the structure of the subjective environment.

**Definition 16** *(Forgetful Function).* For an object $G = (A, O, \partial_0, \partial_1)|G \in \Gamma$, we define a forgetful function, $\Phi$, as a homomorphism such that in the mapping $\Phi : (A, O, \partial_0, \partial_1) \rightarrow (A', O', \partial_0', \partial_0')$ one or more $R(M)|M = \{f, g, h, ...\}$ are ignored. In $G'$ equivalence classes $[a]_{\mathrm{dom}M}$, $[b]_{\mathrm{cod}M}$ are changed and the according structure of $G'$ is reconfigured.

# 3. DISCUSSION

In our framework, interacting agents have a twofold role. They are the basis for generating functional boundaries by performing operative assimilation, and are simultaneously susceptible to assimilation and subsequent transformation, reflected here through use of the forgetful function (Definition 16). Along with a direct establishment of spatial locality, such a configuration also influences chronological stability. As can be seen from Definitions 11-13, chronology is always local and actual (in the sense that it can only exist if causal influence is established). By introducing categories, these chronologies are enclosed into objects. Object morphisms induce changes in the current structure of closures, which causes the same effect on local chronology. In living systems, it is represented by events such as protein turnover. In such situations, the influences on system stability are very complex. In a system theoretical approach [13,14] or in an agent-based approach to functioning of living systems [15], emphasis was placed on the vertical arrangement of subsystems by externally given rules or on a fixed base of rules consisting of $N$ condition-action rules. In both of these approaches, in order to achieve functionality, a great part of system architecture should be explicitly and *a priori* given. Different models can be constructed by assigning sets of internal (*ad hoc*) rules in order to perform specific tasks. In our model, the order was reversed. If a set of mappings is externally given (*a priori*), then the system architecture will be build around them, exclusively for a given set (*ad hoc*). In this way, we obtain greater flexibility in the possible configurations, which achieves a much higher level of functional robustness. By the local emergence of closures, which are only weakly connected by weakly interacting local determinations, and the introduction of forgetful functions, we embedded the possibility of interruptions, changes of parameters or changes in controlling signals into the internal description of the system, such that their presence at any stage of the process cannot collapse the whole system. Robustness of the system is additionally strengthened by patching the environment into equivalence classes, thus avoiding external dynamics that are not important for the system.

It is clear that in the given framework, the emergence of functionality is allowed but not unavoidable. There are number of conditions that should be fulfilled in order to observe the emergence of local closures. However, once established, the architecture is composed such that it can hardly be disturbed in a way that would lead to a collapse of the system.

# 4. CONCLUSION

We have given a formal treatment to the emergence of organization induced by observers with the following properties: (i) they are able to perform operative assimilations giving rise to functional locality, (ii) they have limited spatial range and (iii) they are susceptible to turnover, which creates temporal locality. Based on these properties, which closely reflects the empirically identified characteristics of living systems and their functional parts, we have investigated the structure of the resulting mathematical objects. We found that the closure and boundaries of topological spaces play a crucial part in the emergence of functional relations, since they create foundations for naturally introducing local ordering and local chronologies. By using category theory, we have further represented higher levels of transformations (between closures), with special focus on the turnover of observers.

Finally, it should be emphasized that in order to fully represent a single organism in terms of category theory, it is required to be in the Cartesian closed category. In other words, the category must have all finite products, and for every pair of objects, $A, B$ there must exist a map object $A^B$, the collection of all maps $B \rightarrow A$. This will ensure that our model is closed with respect to efficient causation [4]. Implementing these changes remains a task for future work.

## ACKNOWLEDGMENTS

This research was funded by the Serbian Ministry of Science and Technology under the project "Modeling and numerical simulations of complex physical systems," No. OI141035 for 2006-2010.

## REFERENCES

[1]    Y.P. Gunji, T. Haruna, K. Sawa, *Phys. D*, 219, 152-167 (2006)
[2]    R. Rosen, *Life Itself: A Comprehensive Inquiry Into the Nature, Origin, and Fabrication of Life.* (New York: Columbia University Press, 1991), pp. 285.
[3]    F.J. Varela, H.R. Maturana, R. Uribe, *Biosystems* 5, 187–196 (1974)
[4]    O. Wolkenhauer, J.-H.S. Hofmeyr, *J.Theor.Biol.* 246, 461-476 (2007)
[5]    D. Finley, A. Ciechanover, A. Varshavsky, *Cell* 116, S29-S34 (2004)
[6]    H. Sumi, *J. Mol. Liq.* 90, 185-194 (2001)
[7]    Atkin., *Peirce's Theory of Signs*, In The Stanford Encyclopedia of Philosophy (ed. Zalta, E.N.), URL = http://plato.stanford.edu/entries/peirce-semiotics/, 2006.
[8]    J. Hoffmeyer, *Eur. J. Sem. Stud.*, 9, 355-376 (1997)
[9]    O.E. Rössler, *Endophysics : The World As an Interface.* (Singapore: World Scientific Pub Co, 1998)
[10]  A.A.Robb, *The Absolute Relations of Time and Space.* (Cambridge: Cambridge University Press, 1921) pp. 80.
[11]  J.R. Lucas, *The Conceptual Roots of Mathematics: An essay on the philosophy of mathematics.* (New York: Routledge, 2002), pp. 471.

[12] P. Hell, J. *Nešetřil, Graphs and Homomorphisms.* (New York: Oxford University Press, 2004) pp. 256.

[13] M.D.Mesarovic, *Trends in General Systems Theory* (ed. Klir, G.J.), (New York: Willey-Interscience, 1972), pp. 462.

[14] M.D. Mesarovic, D. Macko, Y. Takahara, *Theory of Hierarchical, Multilevel, Systems.* (London: Academic Press, Inc., 1970), pp. 294.

[15] J.H. Holland, A*daptation in natural and artificial systems: an introductory analysis with applications to biology, control, artificial intelligence,* (The MIT Press, 1992), pp. 228.

In: Advances in Environmental Modeling and Measurements        ISBN: 978-1-60876-599-7
Editors: D. T. Mihailović, B. Lalić, pp. 89-100        © 2010 Nova Science Publishers, Inc.

*Chapter 9*

# EMERGENCE OF CHAOS AND SYNCHRONIZATION IN COUPLED INTERACTIONS IN ENVIRONMENTAL INTERFACES REGARDED AS BIOPHYSICAL COMPLEX SYSTEMS

**D.T. Mihailović[*1], M. Budinčević[1], I. Balaz[2], and D. Perišić[1]**

[1]University of Novi Sad, Novi Sad, Serbia
[2]Institute of Physics, Belgrade, Serbia

## ABSTRACT

In modeling environmental interfaces regarded as biophysical complex systems, one of the main tasks is to create an operative interface with the external environment. The interface should provide a robust and prompt translation of the vast diversity of external physical and/or chemical changes into a set of signals that are "understandable" for an organism. Although the organization of any system is of crucial importance for its functioning, it should not be forgotten that in biophysical systems we deal with real-life problems where a number of other conditions must be satisfied in order to put the system to work. One of them is the proper supply of the system with energy and necessary substances. Their exchange in biophysical systems can be described by the dynamics of driven coupled oscillators. In order to study their behavior, we consider the dynamics of two coupled maps representing exchange processes between two biophysical entities. Starting with the vector mapping $\mathbf{X}_{n+1} = \mathbf{F}(\mathbf{X}_n)$, $\mathbf{X}_n = (x_n, y_n)$ and its $n$-th iterate $\mathbf{F}^n(X) = \mathbf{F}(\mathbf{F}^{n-1}(\mathbf{X}))$, where $\mathbf{F}(\mathbf{X}) = (rx(1-x), \ ry(1-y)) + \mathbf{P}(\mathbf{X}, \varepsilon, p)$, we describe the substance exchange between biophysical entities in their surrounding environment where $\mathbf{P}$ represents the influences of various perturbations. Further, we investigate the behavior of the Lyapunov exponent as a measure of how rapidly two nearby orbits converge or diverge (the emergence of synchronization in coupled interactions of environmental interfaces regarded as biophysical complex systems). For different combinations of the perturbation parameters $p, \varepsilon$, and $r$ ranging for calculation of Lyapunov exponent bifurcation diagrams are obtained. We also show that for the appropriate values of

[*] Corresponding author: E-mail address: guto@uns.ac.rs; Phone: +381 21 485 3203, Fax: +381 21 6350 552

$p, \varepsilon, r$ , almost all points $(x, y)$ except those on the diagonal $(x = y)$ are vanishing. In other words, in investigating the multidimensional state-space of coupled interactions of biophysical complex systems within given settings, we determined relatively small regions where the synchronization of systems is allowed.

# 1. INTRODUCTION

A complex system is a system composed of interacting parts that, as a whole, exhibit novel features that are usually referred to as emergent properties. A system may display one of two forms of complexity: disorganized complexity and organized complexity [1]. In disorganized complexity, the number of variables is very large and their rules of behavior are largely unknown, while organized complexity shows the essential feature of organization. Examples of complex systems include climate, populations (from simple bacterial colonies to sophisticated ant colonies), life systems and their components (e.g., the nervous system or the immune system), as well as various social structures including the economy, infrastructures, and the internet. Complex systems are studied by many areas of natural sciences, mathematics and social sciences, motivating a number of interdisciplinary investigations from diverse fields such as ecology, epidemiology, cybernetics, sociology and economics [2].

Until now, there has been no commonly accepted taxonomy of complex systems, but most can be classified into the following categories. (1) Chaotic systems are dynamic systems characterized by the following properties: (i) they must be sensitive to initial conditions, (ii) they must be topologically mixing, and (iii) their periodic orbits must be dense. Sensitivity to initial conditions means that each point in such a system is arbitrarily closely approximated by other points with significantly different future trajectories. Thus, an arbitrarily small perturbation of the current trajectory may lead to a significantly different future behavior. (2) Complex adaptive systems are special cases of complex systems. They are complex in the sense that they are diverse and made up of multiple interconnected elements, and adaptive in that they have the capacity to change and learn from experience. Examples of complex adaptive systems include the stock market, social insect and ant or bacterial colonies, the biosphere and the ecosystem, the brain and the immune system, cells, development and manufacturing businesses and any human social group-based endeavors within a cultural or social system such as political parties or communities. (3) A nonlinear system is one whose behavior is not subject to the principle of superposition.

Can life be considered as a complex system? Obviously, life is complex, but does that mean that it is a complex system? In order to answer this question, at least two aspects need to be considered: (i) the physical/mathematical aspect and (ii) the biological aspect. These two aspects have points of overlap, but also significant differences. Let us consider the physical/mathematical aspect. As mentioned above, a complex system is a system of interacting elements whose collective behavior cannot be described as the simple sum of the behaviors of the elements. Hence many systems studied in physics are in this sense not complex. The meaning of the word complex in our context is not the same as complicated. For example, microprocessors are difficult to design and their functioning is difficult to understand, but their behavior is easy to understand. In contrast, a double pendulum linked by rubber bands is easy to design and understand in terms of its function. However, it is very difficult to understand its behavior. An essential ingredient of complex systems is their built-in non-linearity. In a "linear" world, a difference keeps increasing, while in a "non-linear" one a difference can increase, but can also decrease. Complex systems often exhibit the following characteristics: robustness, self-organization and adaptability. Next, let us investigate whether some of the characteristics of a complex physical system can be found in living systems. Clearly, life is "built" by combining many elements at many levels: phospholipids → cell walls, cell (intra) → DNA (made of base-pairs), cell (inter) → multi-cellular organisms, etc. Within these levels, a cell behaves very differently from its components; for instance, DNA is by itself static, while the cell is alive. Thus, if we look back at our definition we can see that a complex system is a system of interacting elements whose collective behavior cannot be described as the simple sum of the individual elements' behaviors. It can clearly be seen that cells posses the following qualities: robustness, self-organization and adaptability. In summary, we can say that physical and biological systems have (i) common points (elements, collective behavior, robustness, self-organization, adaptability) and (ii) differing points (the underlying equations are not available in the life sciences, and biosystems are not deterministic (at least not in the same way)).

The field of environmental sciences is abundant with various interfaces and is a good place for the application of new fundamental approaches leading to a better understanding of environmental phenomena. We define the environmental interface as an interface between two abiotic or biotic environments that are in relative motion, exchanging energy through biophysical and chemical processes and fluctuating temporally and spatially regardless of the space and time scales [3]. This definition broadly covers the unavoidable multidisciplinary approach in environmental sciences and also includes the traditional approaches in the sciences that deal with an ambient environmental space. The environmental interface as a complex system is a suitable area for the occurrence of irregularities in temporal variations of physical or biological quantities describing their interactions [4-9]. For example, such an interface can be placed between cells, human or animal bodies and the surrounding environment, aquatic species and the water and air around them, and natural or artificially built surfaces and the atmosphere. Environmental interfaces, regarded as complex biophysical systems, are open and hierarchically organized, and the interactions between their parts are nonlinear, while their interaction with the surrounding environment is noisy.

In recent years, the study of deterministic mathematical models of complex biophysical systems has clearly revealed a large variety of phenomena, ranging from deterministic chaos to the presence of spatial organization. The chaos in higher dimensional systems is one of the focal subjects of physics today. Along with the approach starting from modeling physical systems with many degrees of freedom, there has emerged a new approach, developed by Kaneko [10], in which many one-dimensional maps are coupled to study the behavior of the system as a whole. However, this model can only be applied to study the dynamics of a single medium, such as pattern formation in a fluid. What happens if two media border on each other, as at an environmental interface? One may naturally be led to a model based on coupled logistic maps with different logistic parameters. Even two logistic maps coupled to each other may serve as the dynamic model of driven coupled oscillators [11]. It has been found that two identical coupled maps possess several characteristic features that are typical of higher dimensional chaos. This model of coupling can be applied, for example, to the modeling of the energy exchange between two interacting environmental interfaces [12]. In modeling processes occurring at environmental interfaces, we should keep in mind that in such interacting biophysical systems hierarchical relationships are always established.

Practically, this means that we cannot directly compare interactions from different hierarchical levels. Their mutual relationships are always mediated through particular segments of the underlying processes, which serve as inputs/outputs for functional regulation. In order to formally represent this, we cannot use standard tools from mathematical analysis. Instead we need to use a more general algebraic approach under which we can construct subsystems with different local rules [13].

In this chapter, we will address an illustrative issue important for the modeling of biophysical systems represented as interacting environmental interfaces, i.e., substance or information exchange between biophysical entities and their surrounding environment. In the following section, we will investigate the mathematical properties of a particular system of coupled one-dimensional maps. After that, the results obtained will be interpreted within the framework of interaction of bacterial cells as an example of interacting environmental interfaces.

# 2. MODEL OF COUPLED MAPS REPRESENTING EXCHANGE PROCESSES BETWEEN TWO BIOPHYSICAL ENTITIES

## 2.1. Model Background

Following the approach introduced by Kaneko [10], we investigate the behaviors of two interacting biophysical entities, representing environmental interfaces regarded as complex systems, when they stimulate each other in the presence of perturbations. In biological terms, this can be interpreted, for example, as the situation during the formation of bacterial colonies, e.g., the aggregation and proliferation of bacterial cells induced by quorum sensing. As has recently been shown [14-16] the underlying mechanism of altruistic behavior in bacteria is based on information exchange (in the form of specific signaling molecules) between cells, which activates the so called "biofilm phenotype". This includes many metabolic changes, but two of the most obvious ones for the formation of the colony are the synthesis and extraction of the polysaccharide matrix and the beginning of rapid cell multiplication. In order to initiate such phenotypic changes, several important factors must be fulfilled: (i) the concentration of signaling molecules must reach a certain threshold, which is denoted as quorum sensing, (ii) the supply of nutrients must be uninterrupted, (iii) the turbulence of the surrounding medium must be minimal, and (iv) an appropriate surface for the formation of a colony must exist.

If we denote the existence of a suitable surface as a necessary precondition that is either present or absent in the observed situation, then the other requisite points can be easily interpreted in terms of coupled logistic equations. Before proceeding with the model description, let us note that the logistic equation [17,18] often fails to describe the evolution of realistic populations and exchange processes (the reasons are many and related to the particular model used, e.g., the heterogeneity of the environment, the fact that dispersal may not increase linearly with density or that there may be a time delay in the operation of dispersal and/or competition, and time delays can occur in structured populations when density affects vital power at particular sizes or ages, as the random collision of individuals assumed in the logistic equation, etc.). However, the aforementioned processes can still be successfully interpreted by this equation due to its general character, which is not bound to a particular model.

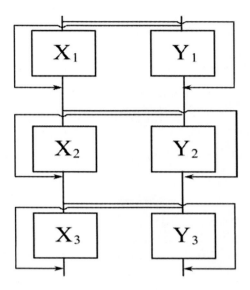

Figure 1. Graphic depiction of a system of two coupled maps representing mutual positive influences between two interacting biophysical entities that exchange substances.

In order to study the model of substance exchange between two biophysical entities, we consider the dynamics of two coupled maps belonging to the same universality class as the oscillators. The system of difference equations to be investigated is of the form

$$\mathbf{X}_{n+1} = \mathbf{F}(\mathbf{X}_n) \equiv \mathbf{L}(\mathbf{X}_n) + \mathbf{P}(\mathbf{X}_n),$$        (1)

where

$$\mathbf{L}(\mathbf{X}_n) = (rx_n(1-x_n), ry_n(1-y_n)), \mathbf{P}(\mathbf{X}_n) = (\varepsilon y_n^p, \varepsilon x_n^p),$$        (2)

and $\mathbf{X}_n = (x_n, y_n)$ is a vector. For the so-called logistic parameter $r$, which in the logistic difference equation determines an suitability of the environment to a given population and exchange processes, we set the range from 0 to 4, and $\varepsilon$ is a positive number in the interval $(0,1]$. $\mathbf{P}(\mathbf{X}_n)$ represents the stimulative coupling influence of members of the system, which is here restricted only to positive numbers in the interval $(0,1)$. The starting point $\mathbf{X}_0$ is determined such that $0 < x_0, y_0 < 1$. Such a choice of $\varepsilon$ defines a model in which the mutual stimulation of growth of populations and exchange processes is obvious ($\varepsilon < 0$ would cause the reverse effect). In [19], $\mathbf{P}(\mathbf{X}_n)$ has the form $(\varepsilon(y_n - x_n), \varepsilon(x_n - y_n))$, with the effect that the larger population and exchange processes stimulate the growth of the smaller one, and *vice versa*. Some other forms of $\mathbf{P}(\mathbf{X}_n)$ can be found in [20]. The set $\{(x,y): 0 < x, y < 1\}$ we denote as $D \in R^2$, while the symmetral of the first quadrant will be denoted as $\Delta$. Since

$\mathbf{F(X)} = (f(x,y), g(x,y))$, where $f(x,y) = rx(1-x) + \varepsilon y^p$, $g(x,y) = ry(1-y) + \varepsilon x^p$, it is obvious that

$$g(y,x) = f(x,y).\tag{3}$$

We denote as $d(x)$ the restriction of the function $\mathbf{F}$ to $\Delta$, $x_{n+1} = rx_n(1-x_n) + \varepsilon x_n^p \equiv d(x_n)$. If $\mathbf{X}_0 \in D$, then $\mathbf{X}_1 = \mathbf{F}(\mathbf{X}_0)$ belongs to the first quadrant; moreover, by (3), it leads to $\mathbf{X}_1^s = \mathbf{F}(\mathbf{X}_0^s)$, where $\mathbf{X}^s$ is the point symmetric to the point $\mathbf{X}$ with respect to $\Delta$. In order to determine when $F(D) \subset D$ holds, it is enough, by (3), to choose a family of curves $C \therefore x = x_0, y = t, 0 < x_0 < 1, 0 < t < 1$ and find their mappings. As $F(C)$ is a family of curves $F(C) \therefore x = rx_0(1-x_0) + \varepsilon t^p, y = rt(1-t) + \varepsilon x_0^p$, it follows that $x < r/4 + \varepsilon$, $y < r/4 + \varepsilon x_0^p < r/4 + \varepsilon$. Therefore, the condition $r/4 + \varepsilon \le 1$ implies that $F(D) \subset D$. Note that this restriction is independent of $p$.

It is clear that for the starting system as well as for its restriction on $\Delta$, only a few analytical results can be obtained and the main burden of investigation lies in numerical analysis.

## 3. ANALYTICAL AND NUMERICAL ANALYSIS

### 3.1. Analytical Considerations

Let us consider the starting system as $p \to \infty$. Then, it becomes

$$x_{n+1} = rx_n(1-x_n),\tag{4a}$$

$$y_{n+1} = ry_n(1-y_n),\tag{4b}$$

because $x^p, y^p \to 0$ for all $0 < x, y < 1$. In that case, there is no stimulation between the two interacting biophysical entities and they behave according to the law of the logistic difference equation.

In the opposite case, as $p \to 0$, the starting system becomes

$$x_{n+1} = rx_n(1-x_n) + \varepsilon,\tag{5a}$$

$$y_{n+1} = ry_n(1-y_n) + \varepsilon,\tag{5b}$$

since $x^p, y^p \to 1$ for all $0 < x, y \le 1$. Again, there is no interaction between the two interacting biophysical entities and again they behave according to the law of logistic equation even on the larger interval $(-\delta, 1+\delta)$, where $\delta = (\sqrt{(r-1)^2 - 4r\varepsilon} - r + 1)/2r > 0$, which is mapped onto itself under the condition $r/4 + \varepsilon < 1+\delta$. Comparing with the standard logistic equation

$$x_{n+1} = \rho x_n (1 - x_n),\tag{6}$$

we now have $\rho = (r + 4\varepsilon + 4\delta)/(1 + 2\delta)$.

Equation $x_{n+1} = d(x_n)$ for $p = 1$ becomes the logistic equation

$$x_{n+1} = x_n (r + \varepsilon - rx_n),\tag{7}$$

on the interval $(0, 1 + \varepsilon/r)$, while for $p = 2$,

$$x_{n+1} = x_n (r - x_n (r - \varepsilon)),\tag{8}$$

which is also logistic, but now on the interval $(0, r/(r-\varepsilon))$. All of the information regarding bifurcations and chaotic behavior for Eqs. (7) and (8) is again obtained by comparing those equations with equation (6), taking $\rho = r + \varepsilon$ and $\rho = r$, respectively.

For the starting system, for $p = 1$ and $p = 2$ we obtain analytic expressions for fixed points and a periodic point of period two, as well as the conditions under which they are attractive. If a fixed point is in $D$, then it must be on the diagonal. The mapping can also have fixed points off of the diagonal, but in that case, they do not belong to $D$. Periodic points with period two that belong to $D$ are either on the diagonal or symmetric with respect to the diagonal.

## 3.2. Analysis of the Orbits

The orbit of the point $\mathbf{X}_0$ is the sequence $\mathbf{X}_0, \mathbf{F}(\mathbf{X}_0), ..., \mathbf{F}^n(\mathbf{X}_0), ...$ where $\mathbf{F}^0(\mathbf{X}_0) \equiv \mathbf{X}_0$ and for $n \geq 1$, $\mathbf{F}^n(\mathbf{X}_0) = \mathbf{F}(\mathbf{F}^{n-1}(\mathbf{X}_0))$. We say that the orbit is periodic with period $k$ if $k$ is the smallest natural number such that $\mathbf{F}^k(\mathbf{X}_0) = \mathbf{X}_0$. If $k = 1$, then the point $\mathbf{X}_0$ is the fixed point. The periodic point $\mathbf{X}_0$ with period $k$ is an attraction point if the norm of the Jacobi matrix for the mapping $F^k(\mathbf{X}) = (f_k(x, y)), (g_k(x, y))$ is less than one, i.e., $\|J^k(\mathbf{X}_0)\| < 1$, where

$$J^k(\mathbf{X}_0) = \begin{bmatrix} \dfrac{\partial f_k}{\partial x} & \dfrac{\partial f_k}{\partial y} \\[2mm] \dfrac{\partial g_k}{\partial x} & \dfrac{\partial g_k}{\partial y} \end{bmatrix}, \quad \mathbf{X} = \mathbf{X}_0.\tag{9}$$

Here, we define $\|J^k(\mathbf{X}_0)\|$ as max $\{|\lambda_1|, |\lambda_2|\}$, where $\lambda_1$ and $\lambda_2$ are the eigenvalues of the matrix. It is worth noting that

$$J^k(\mathbf{X}_k) = J^k(\mathbf{X}_0) = J(\mathbf{X}_{k-1})... \quad J(\mathbf{X}_1)J(\mathbf{X}_0),$$            (10)

where

$$J(X) = \begin{bmatrix} r(1-2x) & \varepsilon py^{p-1} \\ \varepsilon px^{p-1} & r(1-2y) \end{bmatrix}.$$            (11)

In particular, for the scalar equation $x_{n+1} = d(x_n)$ the norm is $|(d^k(x))'|_{x=x_0} = |d'(x_{n-1})...d'(x_1)d'(x_0)|$, where $d'(x) = r(1-2x) + \varepsilon px^{p-1}$.

In order to characterize the asymptotic behavior of the orbits, we need to calculate the largest Lyapunov exponent, which is given for the initial point $\mathbf{X}_o$ in the attracting region by

$$\lambda = \lim_{n \to \infty} \frac{\ln \|\mathbf{J}^n(\mathbf{X}_0)\|}{n}.$$            (12)

With this exponent, we measure how rapidly two nearby orbits in an attracting region converge or diverge. In practice, using (10), we compute the approximate value of $\lambda$ by substituting in (12) successive values from $\mathbf{X}_{n_0}$ to $\mathbf{X}_{n_1}$, for $n_0, n_1$ large enough to eliminate transient behaviors and provide good approximation. If $X_0$ is part of a stable periodic orbit of period $k$, then $\|\mathbf{J}^k(\mathbf{x}_0)\| < 1$ and the exponent $\lambda$ is negative, which characterizes the rate at which small perturbations from the fixed cycle decay, and we can call such a system synchronized. Quasiperiodic behavior is indicated by a zero value of $\lambda$, while $\lambda$ becomes positive when nearby points in the attracting region diverge from each other, indicating chaotic motion. This exponent depends on the initial point of iteration.

### 3.3. Numerical Analysis

In order to further investigate the behavior of the coupled maps, we performed a numerical analysis of the given system. For a fixed $\varepsilon = 0.06$, we calculated the bifurcation diagrams for two values of $p = 0.25$ and $p = 4$ as illustrative extremes representing the influence of perturbations on the occurrence of bifurcation points (Fig. 3). Also, for the same value of $\varepsilon$, $p = 4$ and $r = 3.7$ we found the attractor of the system (Fig. 4). As can be seen from Fig. 2, for $p = 4$, after entering the chaotic regime around $r \approx 3.5$, the appearance of a stable period four cycle can be observed. Comparing with the case $p = 0.25$, where the second appearance of a stable region is not observed, it is obvious that smaller perturbations are more favorable for the expectation of stability in the interacting system. However, this holds only within a relatively narrow range since from Eqs. (4a, and 4b) it follows that lessening the influence of perturbations will eventually lead to two independent oscillators that behave according to the law of the logistic difference equation. From Fig. 2, which was calculated for the same parameter values, we can see that the appearance of a secondary stable period corresponding to negative values of the Lyapunov exponent. This means that within the indicated region, the introduction of small perturbation decays and the system of two interacting entities settles into a synchronized state.

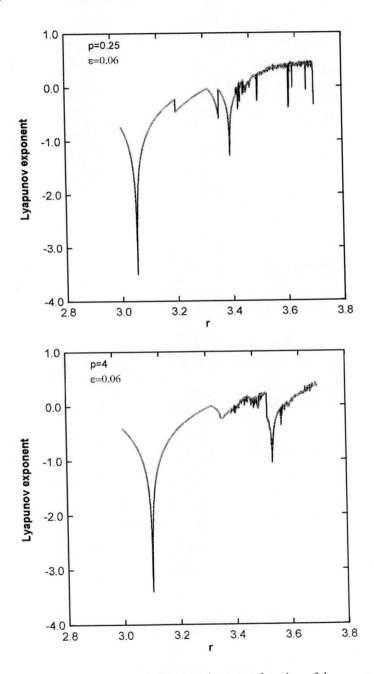

Figure 2. Lyapunov exponent of the coupled maps, given as a function of the parameter $r$ ranging from 3 to 3.75, for two values of the parameter p and a fixed value of $\varepsilon$.

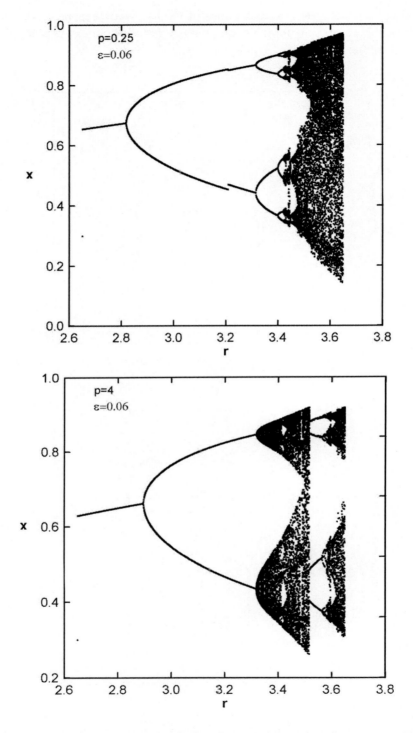

Figure 3. Bifurcation diagrams of the coupled maps as a function of the parameter $r$ ranging from 2.65 to 3.65, for a fixed value of $\varepsilon$ and two given values of the parameter $p$.

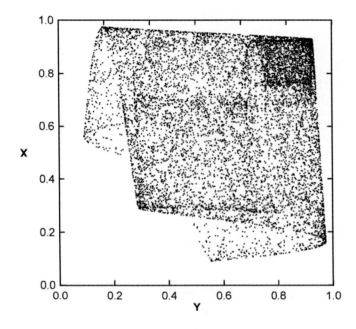

Figure 4. Shape of the attractor of the coupled maps for parameter values $p = 4$, $\varepsilon = 0.06$ and $r = 3.7$.

In our analysis, we chose a situation where the exchange of signals was stimulating and the turbulence of the surrounding medium was minimal. In other words, all requirements for the occurrence of a bacterial colony are met in the model. However, even in this situation, the synchronization of interacting biophysical entities (Lyapunov exponent less than zero) occurs only within a very narrow range of conditions, which is indicated by calculating the Lyapunov exponent (Fig. 2). Also, it should be pointed out that all calculations were done for a fixed value of $\varepsilon$. Keeping this in mind, the observed dislocation of bifurcation points with changes in the parameter $p$ indicates a region of synchronization where the emergence of order is possible.

## 4. CONCLUSION

In this chapter, we used the method of coupling one-dimensional maps to represent the dynamics of a multi-dimensional system. An equation of the form $X_{n+1} = F(X_n) \equiv L(X_n) + P(X_n)$ where there is mutual stimulation between two interacting biophysical systems is interpreted within the context of interacting bacterial cells as the consequent formation of a colony induced by information exchange. The main finding is the observed narrowness of the synchronization region during the interactions. However, in order to specify the full region of synchronization, the influence of the attractor and its basin of attraction on the dynamics and time development in an environment of multiply changing parameters, further investigations are necessary.

## ACKNOWLEDGMENTS

The research described here was funded by the Serbian Ministry of Science and Technology under the projects "Modeling and numerical simulations of complex physical systems", No. OI141035 for 2006-2010 and "Functional analysis, ODEs and PDEs with singularities", No. OI144016 for 2006-2010.

## REFERENCES

[1]   W.Weaver, *Am. Sci.*, 36, 536 (1948)
[2]   N.Boccara, *Modeling Complex Systems* (New York: Springer, 2004), pp. 410.
[3]   D.T.Mihailovic, I.Balaz, *Idojaras,* 111, 209-220 (2007)
[4]   H.R. van der Vaart, *Bull. of Math. Biol.,* 35, 195-211 (1973)
[5]   F.J.Varela, H.R.Maturana, R.Uribe, *Biosystems,* 5, 187–196 (1974)
[6]   R.Rosen, *Life itself: A comprehensive inquiry into the nature, origin, and fabrication of life* (New York: Columbia University Press, 1991), pp. 285.
[7]   A.M.Selvam, S.Fadnavis, *Meteor. Atmos. Phys.*, 66, 87-112 (1998)
[8]   Y.P.Gunji, T.Haruna, K.Sawa, *Phys. D.*, 219, 152-167 (2006)
[9]   Wolkenhauer, J.-H.S.Hofmeyr, *J.Theor.Biol.,* 246, 461-476 (2007)
[10]  K.Kaneko, *Prog. Theor. Phys.* 69, 1427-1442 (1983)
[11]  S.Midorikawa, K.Takayuki, C.Taksu, *Prog. Theor. Phys.*, 94, 571-575 (1995)
[12]  D.T. Mihailovic, *Proceedings of iEMSs 2008,* 134-140 (2008)
[13]  Balaz, D.T.Mihailovic, *Proceedings of iEMSs 2008,* 104-113 (2008)
[14]  G.J.Velicer, *Trends Microbiol.* 11, 330–337 (2003)
[15]  A.S.Griffin, S.A.West, A.Buckling, *Nature,* 430, 1024–1027 (2004)
[16]  M.A.Brockhurst, M.E.Hochberg, T.Bell, A.Buckling, *Curr. Biol.* 16, 2030–2034 (2006)
[17]  B.E.Kendall, *Theor. Popul. Biol.,* 54, 11-37 (1998)
[18]  R.Law, D.J.Murrell, U.Dieckmann, *Ecology,* 84, 252-262 (2003)
[19]  T.Hogg, B.A.Huberman, *Phys.Rev. A.,* 29, 275-281 (1984)
[20]  S.Midorikawa, T.Kubo, T.Cheon, *Prog. Theor. Phys.,* 94, 571-575 (1995)

# PART TWO – AIR POLLUTION, IONIZING AND NON-IONIZING RADIATION AND TURBULENT ENERGY EXCHANGE ISSUES

In: Advances in Environmental Modeling and Measurements ISBN: 978-1-60876-599-7
Editors: D. T. Mihailović, B. Lalić, pp. 103-111 © 2010 Nova Science Publishers, Inc.

*Chapter 10*

# MONITORING OF SPECTRAL UV IN AUSTRIA AND INVESTIGATION OF SHORT- AND LONG-TERM CHANGES

## *S. Simic\*, M. Fitzka, P. Weihs, and H. Kromp-Kolb*

University of Natural Resources and Applied Life Sciences, Vienna, Austria

## ABSTRACT

Monitoring of spectrally resolved UV radiation and total ozone in Austria is continually performed at two stations since 1994, meeting the high quality standards of NDACC (Network for the Detection of Atmospheric Composition Change). Spectral UV measurements at the Sonnblick observatory (47.05°N, 12.95°E; 3,106 m a.s.l.) represent the longest time series available in Austria.

The second station was established in 1998 in the periphery of the capital city Vienna (Großenzersdorf; 48.20°N, 16.57°E; 156 m a.s.l.). The sustained monitoring will continue to deliver high quality data to identify changes in total ozone concentration and spectral UV irradiance.

A national UV-B monitoring network was established in 1996 [1] by the Federal Department of Environment, which now consists of 11 broadband UV-B detectors. The recently measured values are regularly made available on an openly accessible webpage (http://www.uv-index.at).

A goal of current investigations is to quantitatively understand the influence of clouds, ozone and surface albedo on spectral UV radiation. For Sonnblick observatory, continuous spectral UV irradiance measurements are examined alongside model calculations from a one dimensional radiation transfer model.

Additionally, long-term trends in UV irradiance based on clear-sky measurements are investigated using non-parametric trend tests. Results from [2] indicate significant downward trends for several combinations of solar zenith angle and wavelength, which are apparently caused by a seasonal increase in sunshine duration during periods of high total column ozone.

# 1. INTRODUCTION

UV irradiance reaching the earth's surface is influenced by the concentration of stratospheric ozone as well as by further atmospheric parameters, such as clouds, aerosols, and surface albedo. All these parameters are to a certain degree influenced by climate change. Knowledge of spectral UV irradiance, changes in UV irradiance over the past decades and possible future changes is necessary to estimate present and future risks of UV radiation for human health and the whole ecosystem in general.

As a result of the Montreal Protocol for the protection of the ozone layer and the ban on production of CFCs and HCFCs, which was signed 20 years ago, the concentration of ozone depleting substances has already reached its maximum and has now started to decline. However, it remains to be seen how global climate change will affect the stratosphere and hamper or delay the recovery of the ozone layer.

Overexposure of human skin to UV radiation can lead to several reactions, ranging from sunburn to skin cancer. The increasing number of incidences of the malignant melanoma is cause for alarm. A significant increase of new affections was registered worldwide in the past years. During the last two decades an increase in the number of new affections was observed in Austria as well [3].

From 1979 to the mid 1990s the net decrease of stratospheric ozone was about 10-15% over mid latitudes [4]. Consequently, surface UV irradiance continued to increase at rates of a few percent per decade. The observed increases and their significance depend on location, wavelength range, and the period of measurements. The first spectrally resolved routine measurements started in the 1990s, thus studies on long-term changes in spectral UV irradiance are hampered by the limited number of years of available data. High quality time series of spectral UV and total ozone are obtainable from several stations in Austria (major cities, high altitude stations, etc.), some of which are among the longest in Europe.

The investigation of the effects of various influencing parameters such as ozone, clouds, surface albedo and aerosol content on surface UV, the investigation of long-term variations in UV reaching the earth's surface as well as the estimation of health risks for the population due to changing intensities relies on the availability of complete, accurate and high quality measured time series of spectral UV radiation.

# 2. MONITORING OF UV AND OZONE IN AUSTRIA

As opposed to broadband instruments, spectral measurements allow for the calculation of various weighted quantities through the use of the associated action spectra (e.g. UV-Index related to the CIE weighted erythema action spectrum). Multiple weighted spectra can be computed from one single spectral measurement and can be recalculated any time, should the action spectra change (Fig. 1). Additionally, spectral measurements can be used to differentiate the influences of wavelength dependent parameters (e.g. ozone, cloud cover).

* Corresponding author: E-mail address: stana.simic@boku.ac.at, Phone: +43 1 476545630, Fax: +43 1 476545610

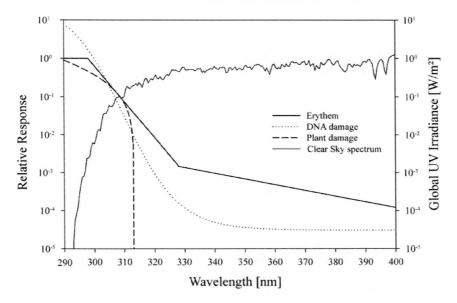

Figure 1. Relative response spectra (aka weighting functions) for Erythema, DNA damage and Plant damage that can be applied to spectral UV measurements. Clear-sky spectrum as acquired at Hoher Sonnblick during summer 2008.

## 2.1. Monitoring of Spectral UV Irradiance and Total Ozone at Hoher Sonnblick and at Groß-Enzersdorf

Monitoring of spectrally resolved UV radiation and total ozone at Hoher Sonnblick (47.05°N, 12.95°E; 3,106 m a.s.l.) meeting the high quality standards of NDACC is continually performed since 1994. This demands very narrow tolerances in absolute accuracy, wavelength resolution, wavelength alignment and calibration uncertainties, ensuring the contribution of high quality, homogenous long-term data series. Time series from the Sonnblick observatory rank among the longest series available in Europe.

Sonnblick observatory is situated on a mountain top in the Austrian Central Alps (Fig. 2). The site is characterized by undisturbed, very clean air with low aerosol content, its high altitude and the complex surrounding topography. The valley adjacent to Sonnblick is 1 300 m lower than the summit. Nearby summits in this region are at approximately at the same altitude. About 16% of the surrounding area are covered with glaciers. During winter, more than 80% of the surface are covered with snow on the assumption that no snow covers the rock faces [5]. Cloud cover below the station occurring frequently because of the station's high altitude encourages multiple reflection of UV radiation between the ground (or clouds below the observatory) and cloud bases. Surface albedo at Hoher Sonnblick is heavily dependent on snow cover and snowline a.s.l.

In 1993, a Brewer Mk IV spectrophotometer (serial number 093) was installed on site. It utilizes two entrance optics: The Teflon diffuser captures global UV irradiance, whereas the entrance optics for direct sun measurements are used for the determination of total ozone at several discreet wavelengths. Wavelength separation is accomplished by a single-monochromator within a range of 290–325 nm with 0.5 nm resolution.

A second instrument for the measurement of spectral UV irradiance based on a Bentham DM150 double-monochromator in CZERNY-TURNER configuration was added in 1996. Usage of a double-monochromator improves stray-light rejection over single-monochromator designs in favor of better wavelength separation and accuracy. The Bentham is used for continuous measurements in the range from 290 up to 500 nm at a wavelength resolution of 0.5 nm. It is fitted with a diffuser by CMS SCHREDER that exhibits a significantly reduced cosine error. The photomultiplier and the monochromator are constantly held at a temperature of 25 °C for improved stability. With its low detection limit and the high measurement accuracy, it allows for the detection of changing surface UV levels due to a change in total ozone column as small as one percent.

The monitoring site Groß-Enzersdorf (48.20 °N, 16.57 °E; 156 m a.s.l.) in the periphery of the capital city Vienna (Fig. 2) was established in 1998. The instrument (Bentham DM150) is to most parts identical with the one at Hoher Sonnblick, except for an additional entrance slit, that can be switched to via a swing-away mirror. Recently, the second entrance has been used for the addition of a 2π-steradian diffuser for actinic flux. Unlike global irradiance, actinic flux is weighted independently from the incident angle (i.e. weighted to the unit sphere) rather than to a horizontal plane, allowing a more direct assessment of UV doses received by individuals.

All instruments are calibrated on a regular basis. The Brewer is compared to a portable 50 W lamp (SCITEC company) and to a self-built portable 1000 W lamp assembly which itself is calibrated to a NIST (National Institute of Standards and Technology) calibrated 1000 W lamp and another 1000 W lamp standardized by PTB (Physikalisch Technische Bundesanstalt, Germany) in the optical laboratory of BOKU-Met. The Bentham spectroradiometer is calibrated to the self-built 1000 W lamp-assembly, as well as to the NIST- and PTB-calibrated lamps.

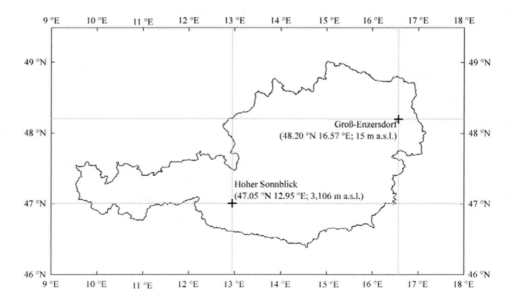

Figure 2. The positions of the monitoring sites in Austria. Groß-Enzersdorf is situated in the flatlands in the vicinity of Vienna. Sonnblick observatory is located in the Austrian Central Alps.

## 2.2. The Austrian UVB Network

The national UV-B monitoring network was established in 1996 [1] by the Federal Department of Environment and is operated by the Division of Biomedical Physics of the Innsbruck Medical University. By now, eleven stations spread all over Austria are contributing data to the network on a regular basis (ca. 10 min). Additional data are supplied from three German and Swiss sites. The stations utilize broadband UV-B detectors, whose wavelength response is modeled after the human skin and closely follows the CIE erythema action spectrum. Each instrument is yearly calibrated to a reference spectroradiometer and further UV biometers.

The UV-Index values are published on an openly accessible webpage (http://www.uv-index.at) as soon as they become available. The overview of surface UV levels over the federal territory given at this site is supposed to act as a source for public information and for quick assessment of the risk of sunburn and skin damage for individuals.

# 3. SHORT- AND LONG-TERM CHANGES

Ozone, clouds, surface albedo and atmospheric aerosols are the major parameters affecting surface UV levels. Following the method of [6] the impact of each single factor on daily and monthly UV variability is estimated for Hoher Sonnblick.

Long-term changes in surface UV levels are investigated for several combinations of wavelength and solar zenith angle in the time series from 1994-2008 under clear-sky conditions. It is attempted to identify trends through the use of regression models (e.g. $R^2$, THEIL-SEN estimate) and assess trend significance using statistical tests.

## 3.1. Data and Method

The analysis of both short- and long-term changes is based on measurements of spectral UV irradiance and total ozone column from the Brewer MkIV #093 spectrophotometer at Sonnblick observatory, available since 1994. The analysis of short-term changes uses additional model calculations of UV irradiance using the radiative transfer model SDISORT. Calculating surface UV also requires information about cloud cover, surface albedo and atmospheric aerosols. Detailed cloud and snow observations are obtained from the Austrian Weather Service (ZAMG). As no measurements of surface albedo exist at Sonnblick observatory, a semi-empirical algorithm based on fresh snow, snow height, time since last snowfall and snowline height a.s.l. was developed and deployed for the reconstruction [7]. Atmospheric aerosols were found to have a negligible influence at the specific site [5], and were therefore excluded from the analysis.

Short-term variability of UV irradiance is calculated using a combination of daily climatological means of input data along with actually measured data that are fed to the model SDISORT. The variation of UV irradiance due to a specific parameter X (e.g. ozone, albedo, clouds) is estimated as the ratio of modeled UV using the actual value of parameter X and climatological data of the remaining variables to modeled UV using climatological data of all variables, including parameter X (Fig. 3). The amplitude is calculated as the spread of ratios divided by the mean ratio on a daily / monthly basis. The amplitude can be regarded as the maximum variability due the specific parameter during a day or a month respectively.

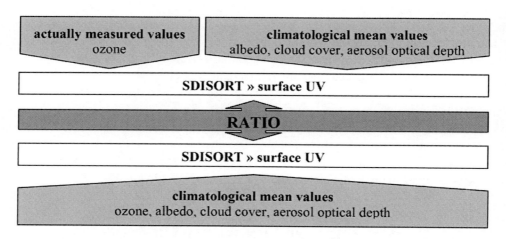

Figure 3. Calculation of the variation in surface UV due to total ozone column for one single measurement, procedure is identical for all other parameters.

Long-term changes were investigated for various combinations of wavelength (e.g. 305 nm, 310 nm, 315 nm) and solar zenith angle (45°, 55° and 65°) in spectra acquired with the Brewer spectrophotometer. Monthly mean values were calculated for each combination of wavelength and solar zenith angle for the period from January 1994 to December 2008. Trends are supposed to be more easily identified in time series of clear-sky measurements [8]. Therefore only measurements under the presence of 3 and less octa cloud cover were selected, virtually removing the influence of clouds from the analysis. Monthly climatological mean values where obtained for the 15-year period, which allow for the calculation of deviations from the long-term mean values for each month. The non-parametric MANN-KENDALL trend test was deployed to assess the level of significance at which the null hypothesis of no trend being present in the data (the time series of deviations from the climatological mean values) can be rejected, if at all. In addition, the method proposed in [9] to determine the minimum length of a given time series to possibly exhibit a linear change at 90% significance level was applied. Finally these time series were fitted with linear trends through the use of regression models to estimate the magnitude of any present long-term change.

## 3.2. Results

Regarding short-time changes, ozone is the dominating parameter influencing surface UV levels throughout the year. On a daily basis, ozone can cause variability of more than 200%. The highest values are found during late winter and spring, which is the period of the strongest variations in stratospheric ozone. Enhanced cumulus convection surpasses the effect of ozone during summer, daily variability of more than 150% can be reached. Cloud influence is notably reduced during the rest of the year. Additionally, due to the station's high altitude, cloud layer thickness is smaller, reducing the influence of clouds compared to lower altitude stations [6,10]. Albedo has its greatest influence in April. This is the period of snow melt, causing the snowline height and therefore albedo to change rapidly. Variability due to albedo can reach a maximum of 32% on a daily basis. On a monthly time scale, despite being significantly reduced in magnitude, variations show the same behavior throughout the year (Fig. 4).

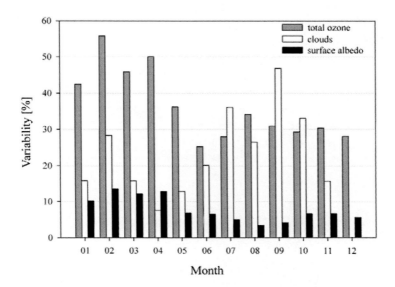

Figure 4. Summary of variability in surface UV levels due to total ozone, clouds and surface albedo on a monthly basis.

As for long-term changes, due to the relatively short time series and the strong variations therein, only few trends could be reliably identified. Most of the significant changes were found at a solar zenith angle of 55°, representing the data selection criteria yielding the greatest number of available measurements. Trends were only found at wavelengths of 305 nm and higher, as variations are distinctly increasing with decreasing wavelength. Unexpectedly, the significant trends display decreases, rather than increases. For the most significant trends, magnitudes lie between -10% per decade and -15%/dec. (Tab. 1) lists all linear trends alongside denotations of the related levels of significance.

**Table 1. Summary Of Linear Regression Slopes ($R^2$) In Percent Per Decade. Symbols Denote Trend Significance (˙: Insignificant, +: Significant, *: Highly Significant).**

| SZA | 305 nm | 310 nm | 315 nm | 324 nm |
|-----|--------|--------|--------|--------|
| 45° | -11.52+ | -11.81* | -10.77* | -11.65* |
| 55° | -15.18* | -15.02* | -13.73* | -13.36* |
| 65° | 0.08˙ | -2.48˙ | -2.66+ | -3.88* |

Decreases in surface UV levels would suggest an increase in stratospheric ozone, but no significant changes were found in the time series starting in 1994. Checking for long term changes in time series of cloud cover and reconstructed albedo to possibly account for the changes in UV irradiance also did not identify significant linear trends over the period 1994–2008: According to the method proposed in [9], the time series of reconstructed albedo would have to extend over more than 50 years for the downward trend of −3.9% per decade to be significant at a level of at least 90%. Likewise, there was no significant change in partitioning of octa cloud cover either. The decreases my therefore be explained by increasing sunshine duration during spring and summer over the period of investigation: At a solar zenith angle of 55°, an increase of about 45% per decade is present in the number of available clear-sky spectra over the whole period. At the same time, the increase during spring exceeds 55%/dec and 50%/dec during summer. This may explain the observed highly significant downward trends, since more measurements of UV irradiance during higher total ozone concentrations (Fig. 5) were included in the later parts of the investigation period. The same behavior was identified at different zenith angles and wavelengths as well as with the inclusion of spectra taken during overcast sky (N>3), although less pronounced and significant. Tab. 1 summarizes the calculated trends.

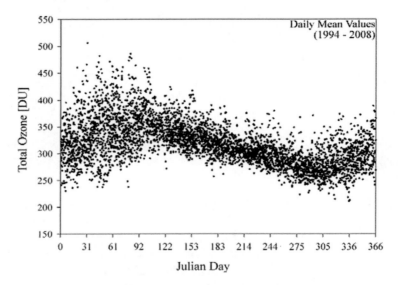

Figure 5. Daily mean values of all total ozone measurements with the Brewer #093 in the period 1994 – 2008. The highest values occur during late winter and spring.

# 4. CONCLUSION

On a daily basis, ozone can cause variability of more than 200% during late winter and spring, followed by a maximum of 150% caused by clouds due to enhanced cumulus convection during summer. Albedo has its greatest influence in April during the period of snowmelt, reaching 32% maximum on a daily basis.

Most investigations focusing on long-term changes in spectral UV radiation are still hampered by the high variations found in the relatively short time series. This study is based on one of the longer time series available today and already allows for some statements regarding actual trends in surface UV levels at a decent level of resilience. The investigated time series exhibit significant downward trends for several combinations of solar zenith angle and wavelength. The significant trends range from -10%/dec to -15%/dec at wavelengths from 305–324 nm. These trends can be explained through an increase in the number of measurements under the influence of high total column ozone over the investigated period.

## ACKNOWLEDGMENTS

This work has been funded by the Austrian Ministry of Agriculture, Forestry, Environment and Water Management and by the Commission of the European Communities, project "Stratosphere-Climate Links with Emphasis on the UTLS, Scout-03".

## REFERENCES

[1]   M. Blumthaler M, *Measurements and trends of terrestrial UVB radiation in Europe,* edited by B.L. Diffey, Milano: OEMF spa, 1996, pp. 31-40.

[2]   S. Simic, P. Weihs, A. Vacek, H. Kromp-Kolb and M. Fitzka, *Atmos. Chem. Phys.*, 8, 7033-7043, ISSN 1680-7324 (2008).

[3]   S. Simic, A. Schmalwieser, H. Moshammer, Final report of StartClim2007.B, 2008, pp. 1-42.

[4]   *World Meteorological Organization, Scientific Assessment of Ozone Depletion*: 2006, Global Ozone Research and Monitoring Project—Report No. 50, Geneva: WMO, 2007.

[5]   P. Weihs, S. Simic, W. Laube, W. Mikielewicz, G. Rengarajan, and M. Mandl, *J. Appl. Meteorol.*, 38(11), 1599–1610 (1999).

[6]   Arola, K. Lakkala, A. Bais, J. Kaurola, C. Meleti and P. Taalas*, J. Geophys. Res.,* 108(17), 9, 1–11 (2003).

[7]   S. Simic, *PhD thesis*, BOKU Vienna, 2006, pp. 1-181.

[8]   M. Glandorf, A. Arola, A. Bais G. and Seckmeyer, *Theor. Appl. Climatol.*, 81, 33–44 (2005).

[9]   E.C. Weatherhead, G.C. Reinsel, G.C. Tiao, X. Meng, D. Choi, W. Cheang, T. Keller, J. DeLuisi, D.J. Wuebbles, J.B. Kerr, A.J. Miller, S.J. Oltmans J.E. and Frederick, *J. Geophys. Res.*, 103, 17.179–17.161 (1998).

[10] M. Blumthaler, W. Ambach, A. Cede J. and Staehelin, *Photochem. Photobiol.*, 63(2), 193–196 (1996).

In: Advances in Environmental Modeling and Measurements    ISBN: 978-1-60876-599-7
Editors: D. T. Mihailović, B. Lalić, pp. 113-119    © 2010 Nova Science Publishers, Inc.

*Chapter 11*

# SOLAR UV RADIATION: MONITORING AND A NEW APPROACH IN MODELING -PIONEERING WORK IN SERBIA

## *Z. Mijatović\*, S. Milićević, D.V. Kapor, D.T. Mihailović, I. Arsenić, and Z. Podraščanin*

University of Novi Sad, Novi Sad, Serbia

## ABSTRACT

We present various steps in the development of UV monitoring activities in Serbia, where pioneering work has been done at the University of Novi Sad. There, a theoretical model for UV index forecasting, NEOPLANTA, was recently developed. Previous comparisons of model outputs with measured values showed quite good agreement, but the input data, including ozone layer thickness and aerosol optical thickness, were taken from satellite measurements. Here, we use data measured on the earth's surface at our institutions. In addition to a detailed explanation of the theoretical background of the NEOPLANTA model, the output results, obtained with both predicted and measured input parameters, are compared with measured UV Index values.

## 1. INTRODUCTION

The detection of the depletion of stratospheric ozone has provoked concern about increased surface UV radiation levels [1]. For that reason, emphasis has been placed on monitoring UV radiation and on developing estimation procedures for doing so (see [2-6]). The World Meteorological Organization (WMO) and World Health Organization (WHO) have proposed the UV index as a quantity for measuring biologically relevant solar UV radiation [7]. The UV index forecast is based on radiative transfer models used in connection with predicted values of the relevant atmospheric parameters.

* Corresponding author: E-mail address: mijat@uns.ac.rs ; Phone: +381 21 4852817; Fax: +381 21 459367

In spite of many general recommendations true UV monitoring in Serbia is still in its infancy Practically all of the pioneering steps made thus far, however, have been undertaken at the University of Novi Sad. The first step was measurement of the UV index (started in 2003), followed by model development. After installing additional equipment, we were able to test the model properly. These tests are the subject of this chapter.

Our team initiated the development of a model for UV index forecasting. The model, "NEOPLANTA," was developed at the University of Novi Sad [8] and is the first model of its kind to originate in Serbia. Spectral irradiance models can be classified into three basic categories: 1) multiple scattering spectral models, which integrate radiance over the whole sky vault [9-11]; 2) fast spectral models, which are analytical simplifications of the radiative transfer equation [12-14]; and 3) empirical models, which compute UV irradiances based on fits of several years of UV observations [3,15]. A comparison among several models belonging to these classes has been performed by Koepke et al. [3]. The "NEOPLANTA" model can be classified as either of the first two types he model was described in detail in our previous paper [16], so we shall summarize it here only briefly.

## 2. DESCRIPTION OF THE MODEL

The numerical model NEOPLANTA computes the solar direct and diffuse UV irradiances under cloud-free conditions for the wavelength range 280-400 nm (with 1-nm resolution), as well as the UV index. The model includes the effects of $O_3$, $SO_2$, $NO_2$, aerosols, and nine different ground surface types (albedo) on UV radiation. In addition to computing instantaneous spectral irradiance for a given solar zenith angle (SZO), the model can also calculate the UV index for the whole day at half-hour intervals from sunrise to sunset.

The model atmosphere is divided into several parallel layers (maximum 40), assumed to be homogeneous, with meteorological parameters set to constant values. The vertical resolution of the model is 1 km for altitudes below 25 km and 5 km above this height. The upper boundary of the highest layer in the model is 100 km. The model uses standard atmosphere meteorological profiles. It also offers an option, however, of including real-time meteorological data profiles from high spatial resolution mesoscale models.

The required input parameters are either the local geographic coordinates and time or the solar zenith angle, plus the altitude, spectral albedo, and the total amount of gases. The model includes its own vertical gas profiles [17] and extinction cross-sections [15,18], extraterrestrial solar irradiance shifted to terrestrial wavelengths [3], aerosol optical properties for 10 different aerosol types [19], and spectral albedos for nine different ground surface types [17]. The output data are the spectral direct, diffuse, and global irradiance divided into the UV-A (320-400 nm) and UV-B (280-320 nm) parts of the spectrum, the biologically active UV irradiance calculated using the erythemal action spectrum described by [20], the UV index, the spectral optical depth, and the spectral transmittance for each atmospheric component. All outputs are computed at the lower boundary of each layer.

As mentioned previously, 10 different aerosol mixtures, which are representative of a boundary layer of certain origin from the Optical Properties of Aerosols and Clouds (OPAC; see [19]) model, are available in the NEOPLANTA model. These aerosol types differ from one another with regard to scattering efficiency, single scattering albedo, and asymmetry factors. The OPAC software package also gives the optical properties of upper-atmosphere aerosols, which are representative of the properties of free troposphere (boundary layer-12 km) and stratospheric (12-36 km) aerosols. OPAC also describes the vertical distribution of aerosol particles by an exponential profile [19]. In estimating the amount of aerosols in the layer on the ground, the NEOPLANTA model provides one of the following options: (i) use of datasets supplied with the averaged amounts of aerosols, provided by the OPAC aerosol model; (ii) use of the turbidity coefficient calculated following Angstrom [21]; (iii) use of the visibility parameter [12,22]; and (iv) use of the aerosol optical depth at 550 nm. The results for UV radiation modeling obtained using these parameters are compared with results obtained using measured values for aerosol optical thickness.

# 3. MODEL EVALUATION

The performance of the model was tested by comparing UVI values of the model outputs with measurements recorded with a Yankee UVB-1 biometer (see [23]). For the test, we selected data from several days, measured in the years 2003, 2004, and 2005, with cloudiness less than 0.2, although every day since the start of UV radiation monitoring is included in the database (April 2003).

The measurement device is located at the Novi Sad University campus (45.33 °N. 19.85 °E: 84 m MSL.). The biometer measures UV radiation every 30 s, but the final outputis an average over a 10-min interval. Several necessary corrections were included [16], so that the estimated maximum error of the measurements is less than 9%.

The UVI was calculated by the model every half hour from sunrise to sunset. In the model calculations, we considered the effects of $O_3$, aerosols, and the ground surface type on UVI. The effects of $SO_2$ and $NO_2$ were not taken into account because of their low impact on UVI [24,25]. The total ozone column in the atmosphere must be known and is used as an input parameter. In the past, the total ozone column over the Novi Sad coordinates for the considered days has been taken from the online database of the Total Ozone Mapping Spectrometer Earth Probe observations [26]. There exist no measurements of aerosol chemical composition and amount in Novi Sad, so we considered aerosol to be the main source of difference between measured and calculated values. Because of a large proportion of soil particles and soot present in the air of the town, the continental averaged aerosol type is assumed. We calculate aerosol extinction by taking visibility data at 1200 UTC from SYNOP data files and using the equation by Koschmieder [22]. For simplicity, ozone and aerosol levels were assumed to be constant over the course of the day. The surface albedo was fixed for each surface type considered. An analysis presented in Malinovic et al. [16] shows that the NEOPLANTA model gives values that are very close to the observations. The amount of the water vapor in the atmosphere was deduced from the standard atmosphere model.

Since August 2007, the ozone layer thickness, aerosol optical depth, and water vapor content have been measured from the same place as UVI. These data are used now as inputs for modeling, and results obtained with these parameters are compared to those calculated using assumed values.

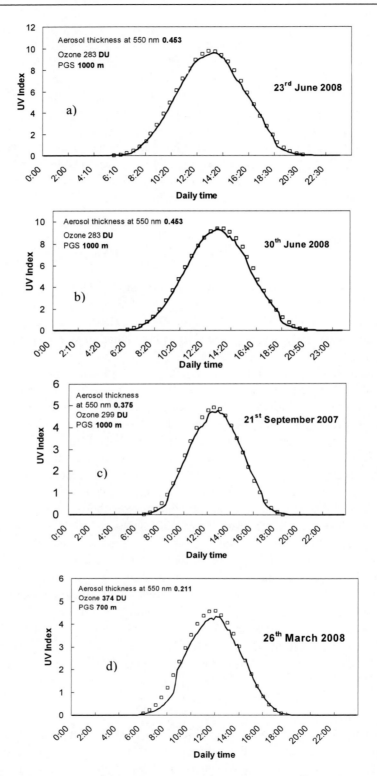

Figure 1. Comparisons between values predicted by the NEOPLANTA model and measured ones. Open squares (□) represent predicted values, while the solid line (—) represents the measurements.

## 4. RECENT DEVELOPMENT

An improvement of each model would allow it to use the values measured at the site rather than someone else's observations. For that reason, the Department of Physics has recently purchased an instrument, the MICROTOPS II, Ozone Monitor & Sunphotometer, Version 2.43, (produced by the Solar Light Company, Inc.), that allows for the direct determination of the ozone layer thickness, the water column content, and aerosol optical thickness at 1020 nm. Since NEOPLANTA model demands values for the aerosol optical thickness at 550 nm, these values must be calculated from both the value measured at 1020 nm and the Angstroem coefficient, obtained from satellite measurements (http://www.icare.univ-lille1.fr/parasol/browse/index.php?date=20081102&args=07#). The measurements of aerosol optical thickness and ozone layer thickness were only performed at noon. We assume that these quantities do not change significantly during the day and use noon values for the whole day's prognosis. The measurements during 2007 and 2008 used in this work were made on cloudless days (more precisely, those with cloudiness less than 0.2). The model predictions were compared with measurements of UV index done by the Yankee UVB-1 biometer. Since 2003, the database of measured UV indices was produced for every day. For the illustration of our results, only a few examples were chosen for presentation in this chapter, but the conclusions drawn from these examples are valid for all other measurements. Examples of comparisons between measured and predicted values of the UV Index are given in Fig. 1(a,b,c,d). In these figures, a comparison of two summer days with high SZA and two days with moderately low SZA (spring and autumn) is presented. Open squares (□) represent predicted values, while a solid line (—) represents the measurements. Within each figure, the dates and the data for ozone layer thickness, aerosol thickness at 550 nm, and PGS that are taken as input parameters in the modeling are given. The chosen days were almost cloudless except for the first half of 26 March, 2008.

As can be seen from the figures, the predicted values are slightly higher than the measured ones, but this difference is between 1% and 6% for the maximal daily values (6% for 26 March, 2008, a day that was not perfectly cloudless). These are typical disagreements for all our results for cloudless days. Of course, for cloudy days, the disagreement between the measured and predicted UV Indices is considerable, but the NEOPLANTA model does not take into account the effects of the clouds.

This fact can be explored through an analysis of Fig. 1d. The first half of this day was slightly cloudy, but with almost homogeneous clouds (resulting in an almost systematic discrepancy between the measured and predicted values). The second half of the day, however, was cloudless, and the agreement between the measured and predicted values is almost perfect.

In Fig. 2 a comparison between the measured and predicted UV indices, using the assumed input data and data taken from our measurements, is presented.

The example presented in Fig. 2 is taken from a spring day with moderately low SZA. The reason for this choice is twofold: the UV index is high enough that the measurement error is inside the limit of a few percent, while, due to the low SZA, the path of a light beam is considerably longer than for high SZA, meaning that ozone layer thickness, water content in atmosphere, and aerosol optical depth have considerable influence on the UV index. As was mentioned previously, the UV indices predicted by the NEOPLANTA model are usually slightly higher than the measured indices. This situation is the case in Fig. 2, when the input parameters were assumed. The difference at local noon is about 10%, which is typical. When the values measured at the site were used, however, much better agreement was obtained. This fact suggests that all input parameters have an important role in determining the final results of UV index prediction. Further investigation should be directed to the particular influence of all input parameters on the final results of UV index predictions.

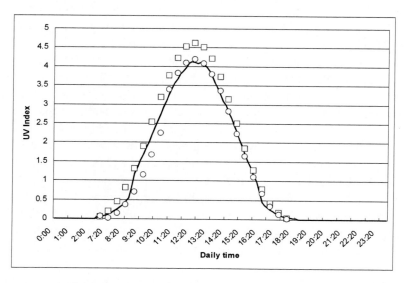

Figure 2. Comparisons between UVI values predicted by the NEOPLANTA model using measured input parameters (circles), assumed input parameters (squares), and the measured input parameters .

## ACKNOWLEDGMENTS

The research work described in this chapter has been funded by the Serbian Ministry of Science and Environmental Protection under the project "Modeling and numerical simulations of complex physical systems." ON141035 for 2006-2010. This work is also partially supported by the Municipal Council for Environmental Protection of City of Novi Sad. The authors thank Mr. Vladimir Skoric for proofreading the chapter.

## REFERENCES

[1]    M. Glandorf, A. Arola, A. Bais and G. Seckmeyer, *Theor. Appl. Climatol.*, 81, 33-44 (2005).

[2]    C. S. Zerefos, *Phys. Chem. Earth*, 27, 455-460 (2002).

[3]    P. Koepke, A. Bias, D. Balis, M. Buchwitz, H. De Backer, X. De Cabo, P. Eckert, P. Eriksen, D. Gillotay, A. Heikkilä, T. Koskela, B. Lapeta, Z. Litynska, J. Lorente, B. Mayer, A. Renaud, A. Ruggaber, G. Schauberger, G. Seckmeyer, P. Seifert, A. Schmalweiser, H. Schwander, K. Vanicek and M. Weber, *Photochem. Photobiol.*, 67, 657-662. (1998).

[4]    S. Madronich, L. O. Björn, M. Ilyas and M. M. Caldwell, *J. Photochem. Photobiol. B*, 46, 5-19 (1998).

[5]    WMO, Scientific assessment of ozone depletion: 2002. *Global Ozone Research and Monitoring Project*, 47 (5), Geneva, Switzerland, 49 pp. (2003).

[6]    R. L. McKenzie, L. O. Hjörn, A. Bais, and M. Ilyasd, *Photochem. Photobiol. Sci.*, 2, 5-15 (2003).

[7]    WMO, *Report of the WMO-WHO meeting of experts on standardization of UV indices and their dissemination to the public.* WMO GAW 127, WMO Tech. Doc. 921, Les Diablerets, 187 pp. (1997).

[8]    S. Malinovic, *M.S. thesis, ACIMSI*, University of Novi Sad, 1–104, (2003).

[9]    V. V. Rozanov, D. Diebel, R. J. D. Spurr and J. P. Burrows, *J. Geophys. Res.*, 102(D14), 16 683-16 695 (1997).

[10]   F. X. Kneizys, E. P. Shettle, L. W. Abreu, J. H. Chetwynd, G. P. Anderson, W. O. Gallery, J. E. A. Selby, and S. A. Clough, , Tech. Rep. AFGL-TR-88-0177, *Environmental Research Papers* 1010, 146 (1988).

[11]   H. Schwander, A. Kaifel, A. Ruggaber and P. Koepke, *Appl. Opt.*, 40, 331-335 (2001).

[12]   C. Gueymard, *Florida Solar Energy Center Tech. Rep.* FSEC-PF-270-95, 78 pp. (1995).

[13]   R. E. Bird, and C. Riordan, *J. Climate Appl. Meteor.*, 25, 87-97 (1986).

[14]   B. L. Diffey, *Phys. Med. Biol.*, 22, 309-316 (1977).

[15]   J. P. Burrows,  A. Richler, A. Dehn, B. Deters, S. Himmelmann, S. Voigt, and J. Orphal, J. Quant. *Spectrosc. Radiat. Transfer*, 61, 509-517 (1999).

[16]   S. Malinovic, D.T. Mihailovic, D. Kapor, Z. Mijatovic, I. Arsenic, *J. App. Met. and Climat.*, 45, 1171–1177 (2006).

[17]   Ruggaber, R. Dlugi and T. Nakajima, *J. Atmos. Chem.*, 18, 171-210 (1994).

[18]   K. Bogumil, J. Orphal and J. P. Burrows, Proc. ERS- ENVISTAT Symp., Gothenburg, Sweden, ESA-ESTEC,; *http://earth.esa.int/ pub/ESA_DOC/ gothenburg/ 099bogum.pdf* 11 pp., (2000)

[19]   M. Hess, P. Koepke and I. Schult, *Bull. Amer. Meteor. Soc.*, 79, 831-844 (1998).

[20]   F. McKinley and B. L. Diffey, *CIE J.*, 6, 17-22 (1987).

[21]   Angstrom, *Tellus* 13, 214 – 231 (1961).

[22]   H. Koschmieder, *Beitr. Phys. Atmos.*, 12, 33-53 (1924).

[23]   Yankee Environmental Systems, Inc., UVB-1 UV Pyranometer, *Installation and User Guide,* version 2.0. 44 pp. (2000).

[24]   P. Forster, K. P. Shine and A. R. Webb, *J. Appl. Meteor.*, 34, 2426-2439 (1995).

[25]   J. Zeng, R. McKenzie, K. Stamnes, M. Wineland, and J. Rosen, *J. Geophys. Res.*, 99 (D11), 23 019-23 030 (1994).

[26]   NASA, cited 2005: Total Ozone Mapping Spectroradiometer. *http://toms.gsfc.nasa.gov/.*

In: Advances in Environmental Modeling and Measurements        ISBN: 978-1-60876-599-7
Editors: D. T. Mihailović, B. Lalić, pp. 121-132        © 2010 Nova Science Publishers, Inc.

*Chapter 12*

# An Overview of Vertical Mixing Schemes for Applications in Air Quality and Environmental Models

### *D.T. Mihailović[*1], Á. Bordás[2], and K. Alapaty[3]*

[1]University of Novi Sad, Novi Sad, Serbia
[2]Eötvös Loránt University, Budapest, Hungary
[3]Department of Energy, Washington, D.C., USA

## Abstract

The description of the atmospheric boundary layer (ABL) characteristics, understanding of complex boundary layer interactions, and their proper parameterization are important for air quality as well as many other environmental models. In that sense, though simple, single-column vertical mixing models are comprehensive enough to describe ABL characteristics. Therefore, they can be employed to illustrate the basic concepts on boundary layer processes and represent serviceable tools in boundary layer investigation. When coupled to 3D models, single-column models can provide detailed and accurate simulations of the ABL structure as well as mixing processes.

Vertical turbulent mixing in the atmosphere is commonly described by different types of local closure formulations, based on the analogy with molecular diffusion. This approach is reasonable during conditions of stable and neutral static stability when the scale of turbulent motion is much smaller than the scale of mean motion. The limitations of the diffusive schemes for representing convective conditions in the ABL are well known and comprehensively elaborated. In the convective boundary layer, much of the mixing is caused by buoyant plumes, which originate in the surface layer, rise up to the top of the boundary layer, and penetrate into the capping inversion. Therefore, during convective conditions in the ABL it is useful to use an asymmetrical convective non-local scheme. However, combined non-local turbulent kinetic energy schemes for vertical diffusion and asymmetrical convective non-local schemes provide a less rapid mass transport out of the surface layer and into other layers during convective and non-convective periods than other schemes that parameterize mixing processes in the ABL.

* Corresponding author: E-mail address: guto@polj.uns.ac.rs; Phone: +381 21 485 3203, Fax: +381 21 6350 552

The aim of this chapter is to offer a short overview of non-local mixing schemes and combined non-local schemes for vertical diffusion, as well as non-local mixing schemes developed in the last two decades, to describe vertical mixing during convective conditions in the ABL. The overview is supported with illustrative 1- D and 3- D model outputs.

# 1. INTRODUCTION

The atmospheric boundary layer is the layer where interactions take place between the Earth's surface and the large-scale atmospheric flow. The formation of the layer is a consequence of the interactions between the atmosphere and its subjacent surface, where almost all human activities take place. Treatment of the ABL and surface processes has important implications for simulations in air quality and chemical transport models, particularly for the pollutants highly affected by them, as well as many other environmental models.

Description of the ABL during convective conditions has long been a major source of uncertainty in the air quality models and chemical transport models. There exist two approaches, local and non-local, for solving the turbulence closure problem. While the local closure assumes that turbulence is analogous to molecular diffusion in the non-local closure, the unknown quantity at one point is parameterized by values of known quantities at many points in space. The simplest, most popular local closure method in Eulerian air quality and chemical transport models is the K-Scheme used both in the boundary layer and the free troposphere. Since it uses local gradients in one point of model grid, K-Scheme can be used only when the scale of turbulent motion is much smaller than the scale of mean flow [1], such as in the case of stable and neutral conditions in the atmosphere in which this scheme is consistent. However, it cannot: (a) describe the effects of large scale eddies that are dominant in the convective boundary layer (CBL) and (b) simulate counter-gradient flows where a turbulent flux flows up to the gradient. Thus, K-Scheme is not recommended in the CBL [1]. Recently, in order to avoid the K-scheme drawbacks, Alapaty [2] and Alapaty and Alapaty [3] suggested a "non-local" TKE scheme based on the K-Scheme that was intensively tested using the EMEP chemical transport model [4,5]. In order to quantify the transport of a passive tracer field in three-dimensional simulations of turbulent convection, the non-local and non-diffusive behavior can be described by a transilient matrix whose elements contain the fractional tracer concentrations moving from one subvolume to another as a function of time. The approach was originally developed for and applied to geophysical flows known as turbulent transilient theory (T3) ([1], ([6,7]), but this formalism was extended and applied in an astrophysical context to three-dimensional simulations of turbulent compressible convection with overshoot into convectively stable bounding regions [8]). The most frequently used non-local closure method is the asymmetrical convective mixing ACM suggested by Pleim and Chang [9]. The design of this model is based on the Blackadar's scheme [10], but takes into account the important fact that, in the CBL, the vertical transport is asymmetrical [11]. Namely, the buoyant plumbs are rather fast and narrow, while downward streams are wide and slow. Accordingly, transport by upward streams should be simulated as non-local and transport by downward streams as local. The concept of this model is that buoyant plumbs rise from the surface layer and transfer air and its properties directly into all layers above. Downward mixing occurs only between adjacent layers in the form of a slow subsidence. The ACM can be used only during convective conditions in the ABL, while stable or neutral regimes for the K-scheme are considered. Although this approach results in a more realistic simulation of vertical transport within the CBL layer, it has some drawbacks that can be elaborated in condensed form: (i) since this method mixes the same amount of mass to every vertical layer in the boundary layer, it has the potential to remove mass much too quickly out of the surface layer and (ii) this method fails to account for the upward mixing in layers higher than the surface layer [12]. Wang [13] has compared three different vertical transport methods: a semi-implicit K-scheme (SIK) with local closure and the ACM and T3 schemes with non-local closure. Of the three schemes, the ACM scheme moved mass more rapidly out of surface layer into other layers than the other two schemes in terms of the rate at which mass was mixed between different layers. Recently, this scheme was modified in two ways: (i) by combining of the non-local scheme of the original ACM with an eddy diffusion scheme (ACM2), which is able to represent both the supergrid- and subgrid-scale components of turbulent transport in the CBL [14] and (ii) with varying upward mixing rates (VUR), where the upward mixing rate changes with the height, providing slower mixing [15]. Except, the aforementioned, widely used schemes are based on the operator splitting method (OSM). The use of the OSM schemes enables us to compare combinations of different local and non-local schemes during the numerical modeling procedure [16].

The aim of this chapter is to offer a short overview of non-local mixing schemes and the combined local scheme for vertical diffusion and non-local vertical mixing schemes developed in the last two decades to describe vertical mixing during convective conditions in the ABL. The overview is supported with 1-D and 3-D illustrative model outputs.


## 2. AN OVERVIEW OF THE VERTICAL MIXING SCHEMES

### 2.1. Non-Local Vertical Mixing Schemes

The non-local vertical mixing schemes were designed to describe the effects of large scale eddies that are dominant in the CBL and to simulate counter-gradient flows where a turbulent flux flows up to the gradient. During convective conditions in the atmosphere, both small-scale subgrid and large-scale super grid eddies are important for vertical transport. In this section, we will consider three different non-local mixing schemes: the Blackadar's scheme [10], the asymmetrical convective model [9] and the scheme with varying upward mixing rates [15].

Transilient turbulence theory [1] (the Latin word *transilient* means to jump over) is a general representation of the turbulent flux exchange processes. In transilient mixing schemes, elements of flux exchange are defined in an $N \times N$ trasilient matrix, where $N$ is the number of vertical layers and mixing occurs not only between adjacent model layers, but also between layers not adjacent to each other. That means that all of the matrix elements are nonzero and that the turbulent mixing in the convective boundary layer can be written as

$$\frac{\partial c_i}{\partial t} = \sum_{j=1}^{N} M_{ij} c_j \,, \tag{1}$$

where $c$ is the concentration of passive tracer, the elements in the mixing matrix $M$ represent mass mixing rates, and $i$ and $j$ refer to two different grid cells in a column of atmosphere. Some models specify mixing concepts with the idea of reducing the number of nonzero elements because of the cost of computational time during integration.

**The Blackadar's scheme** [10] is a simple non-local closure scheme, that is designed to describe convective vertical transport by eddies of varying sizes. The effect of convective plumes is simulated by mixing material directly from the surface layer with every other layer in the convective layer. The schematic representation of vertical mixing simulated by the Blackadar's scheme (BLACK) is presented in Fig. 1. The mixing algorithm can be written for the surface and every other layer as

$$\frac{\partial c_1}{\partial t} = -Muc_1 \sum_{i=2}^{N} \frac{\Delta \xi_i}{\Delta \xi_1} + Mu \sum_{i=2}^{N} c_i \frac{\Delta \xi_1}{\Delta \xi_i} \,, \tag{2}$$

and

$$\frac{\partial c_k}{\partial t} = Muc_1 \frac{\Delta \xi_k}{\Delta \xi_1} - Muc_k \frac{\Delta \xi_1}{\Delta \xi_i} \; (2 < k \le N), \tag{3}$$

respectively, where $Mu$ represents the mixing rate, $\xi$ is the vertical coordinate, and $\Delta \xi$ denotes the layer thickness. The mixing matrix which controls this model is nonzero only for the top row, the left most column, and the diagonal.

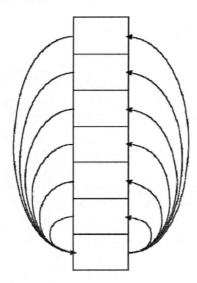

Figure 1. A schematic representation of vertical mixing in a one dimensional column as simulated by the Blackadar's scheme.

**The asymmetrical convective model** [3] is a non-local vertical mixing scheme based on the assumption of the vertical asymmetry of buoyancy-driven turbulence. The concept of this model is that buoyant plumes, according to the Blackadar's scheme, rise from the surface layer to all levels in the convective boundary layer, but downward mixing occurs between adjacent levels only in a cascading manner. The schematic representation of vertical mixing simulated by the ACM is presented in Fig. 2a. The mixing algorithm is driven by equations

$$\frac{\partial c_1}{\partial t} = Md_2 c_2 \frac{\Delta \xi_1}{\Delta \xi_2} - Mu c_1 \sum_{i=2}^{N} \frac{\Delta \xi_i}{\Delta \xi_1}, \tag{4}$$

$$\frac{\partial c_k}{\partial t} = Mu c_1 - Md_k c_2 + Md_{k+1} c_{k+1} \frac{\Delta \xi_{k+1}}{\Delta \xi_k} \ (2 < k < N), \tag{5}$$

and

$$\frac{\partial c_N}{\partial t} = Mu c_1 - Md_N c_N, \tag{6}$$

where $Mu$ and $Md$ are the upward and downward mixing rates, respectively. The downward mixing rate from level $k$ to level $k-1$ is calculated as:

$$Md_k = \frac{\xi_N - \xi_k}{\Delta \xi_k} Mu. \tag{7}$$

The mixing matrix controlling this model is non-zero only for the leftmost column, the diagonal and superdiagonal.

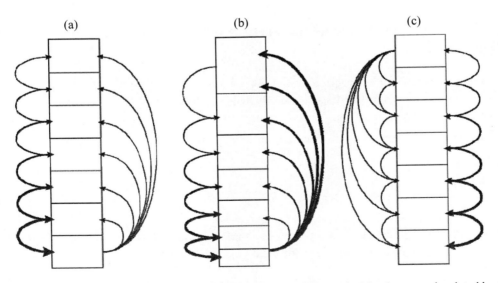

Figure 2. Schematic representation of vertical mixing in a one-dimensional column as simulated by the (a) ACM, (b) VUR scheme and (c) ACM2. Line thicknesses are proportional to mixing rates.

**The scheme with varying upward mixing rates** [15] is a modified version of the ACM, where the upward mixing rate changes with the height, providing slower mixing. The schematic representation of vertical mixing simulated by the scheme is shown in Fig. 2b. The upward mixing rates are scaled with the amount of turbulent kinetic energy in the layer as

$$Mu_k = Mu_1 \frac{e_k \Delta \xi_k}{\sum\limits_{i=1}^{N} e_i \Delta \xi_i}, \tag{8}$$

where $Mu_1$ is the upward mixing rate from surface layer to layer above and $e_k$ denotes the turbulent kinetic energy in the considered layer. The upward mixing rate from surface layer to layer above is parameterized as

$$Mu_1 = \frac{\rho u_*^4 + Hw_*}{h(\rho u_*^3 + H)}, \tag{9}$$

where $\rho$ is the air density and $u_*$ and $w_*$ are the friction and convective velocity, respectively, $H$ represents the sensible heat flux and $h$ is the height of the convective layer. Using the VUR scheme, the mixing algorithm for the lowest layer can be written in the form

$$\frac{\partial c_1}{\partial t} = Md_2 c_2 \frac{\Delta \xi_1}{\Delta \xi_2} - Mu_1 c_1 - \sum_{k=3}^{N} Mu_k c_1 . \tag{10}$$

The algorithm for the other layers is very similar to the ACM algorithm [Eqs. (5) and (6)], with the upward mixing rate $Mu$ substituted with varying upward mixing rates $Mu_k$.

## 2.2. Combined Local Scheme for Vertical Diffusion and Non-Local Vertical Mixing Schemes

**The asymmetrical convective model** [14], the advanced version of the ACM, represents a combination between the local eddy diffusion scheme and the non-local ACM. The schematic representation of the vertical mixing simulated by ACM2 is presented in Fig. 2c. The vertical eddy diffusivity for momentum ($K_z'$) and the upward mixing rate ($Mu'$) are defined as

$$K_z' = K_z(1 - f) \quad \text{and} \quad Mu' = fMu , \tag{11}$$

respectively, where $f$ denotes the weighting factor. It is evident that the weighting factor is the key parameter that controls the degree of local versus non-local behavior. At either extreme

($f = 1$ or $f = 0$), the scheme reverts to either the ACM non-local scheme or the local eddy diffusion scheme. For various proportion of local and non-local components $f = 0.5$ seems to give the most realistic results [14].

**Mixing scheme based on operator splitting method.** Operator splitting method is a widely used procedure in the numerical solution of real-life complex time-dependent phenomena. The basic idea behind the operator splitting method is decomposing the problem according to the different physical processes in the mathematical models. The spatial operator of the global system is divided into a few simpler operators and the corresponding problems are solved one after the other, successively in time. The OSM has some disadvantages (e.g. the portion of the spatial operator is not always natural), and replacing the original problem with split models usually results in a so-called splitting error. The disadvantages and errors of the splitting methods are described in detail in [17]. The use of the OSM enables us to simulate total mixing in the convective layer as [16]

$$\frac{\partial c}{\partial t} = L + N,$$ (12)

where $L$ and $N$ represent operators of local and non-local processes, respectively.

## 3. TESTING OF VERTICAL MIXING SCHMES

In this section, some of the considered schemes are compared in bottom-up and top-down mixing processes using 1-D models and the advantages of the combined schemes are described. To show the performance of the VUR scheme, simulated and measured concentrations of a pollutant ($NO_2$), believed to be one of the most affected ones by the processes in the ABL, were compared for the year 2002. The comparison was made for the whole domain used in simulations performed by the 3-D chemical EMEP Unified model (version UNI-ACID, rv2.0) where the scheme was incorporated.

Assuming that convective mixing in the atmosphere can be viewed as the superposition of bottom-up and top-down diffusion processes [18], the Blackadar's scheme, the ACM, and the OSM scheme were compared using 20 equally spaced vertical layer models. The OSM scheme was assembled using the eddy diffusion model to describe local, and the Blackadar's scheme to simulate non-local mixing processes. Emitting a constant flux of passive tracers from the bottom or top layer during convective conditions, one nondimensional unit of concentration could accumulate in the model layers in the unit of nondimensional time.

Nondimensional concentration and nondimensional time were defined as

$$\frac{c}{c^*} \text{ and } \frac{t}{t^*},$$ (13)

respectively, where $c^* = F/\bar{e}_*$, $t^* = h/\bar{e}_*$, $F$ represents the entrainment flux, $h$ is the height of the boundary layer, and $\bar{e}_*$ denotes the vertically integrated turbulent velocity. The vertically integrated turbulent velocity was estimated as

$$\overline{e}_* = \frac{1}{h}\int\limits_0^h \sqrt{e(\xi)}\,\Psi\left(\xi\right)\mathrm{d}\xi\,, \tag{14}$$

where $e(\xi)$ is the turbulent kinetic energy profile, $\Psi\left(\xi\right)$ is the vertical profile function [2,15] for turbulent kinetic energy as obtained in large-eddy simulation studies, and $\mathrm{d}\xi$ is the layer thickness. Following Zhang et al. [19], the turbulent kinetic energy profile $e(\xi)$ can be expressed as

$$e(\xi) = \frac{1}{2}\left(\frac{L_E}{h}\right)^{2/3}\left[0.4w_*^3 + u_*^3\left(h-\xi\right)\frac{\Phi_m}{\kappa\xi}\right]^{2/3}\,, \tag{15}$$

where, $\Phi_m$ denotes the nondimensional function of momentum [12] $\left[\Phi_m = \left(1-15\xi/L\right)^{-1/4}\right]$, $\kappa$ is the von Kármán constant $\left(\kappa = 0.4\right)$ and $L_E$ characterizes the integral length scale of the dissipation rate. We used $L_E = 2.6h$, which is within the $2.5h - 3.0h$ range suggested by Moeng and Sullivan [20]. The vertical eddy diffusivity for momentum and the upward mixing rate were calculated as

$$Mu = \frac{\overline{e}_*}{h} \text{ and } K_z = \overline{e}_*\kappa z\left(1-\frac{z}{h}\right)^2\,. \tag{16}$$

Starting with an initial condition of zero concentration everywhere in the convective layer, vertical profiles of nondimensional concentration $(c/c^*)$ at $t = 4t^*$ for the bottom-up case and at $t = 6t^*$ for the top-down case were simulated by the BLACK scheme, ACM, and OSM schemes, as presented in Fig. 3a and Fig. 3b, respectively. The BLACK scheme and the ACM produce exactly the same very simple profile for the bottom-up flux case, because they use the same algorithms for upward transport. The concentrations are constant through the CBL layer, with the exception of the lowest layer. The OSM scheme shows a steep negative gradient near the surface, which decreases gradually from about $0.3h$. Above $0.3h$, a slight and nearly constant negative gradient continues to the top of the boundary layer. The profile obtained by the OSM scheme is slightly more realistic than the profile obtained by the BLACK and ACM schemes. Unfortunately, if we work with constant upward mixing rates, the compared models cannot reproduce positive gradients at the top of the boundary layer simulated by the large-eddy simulation profile [14]. In the top-down flux experiment, the ACM fits the large-eddy profile [20] nearly exactly. The gradient of the concentration profile gradually decreases down to around $0.6h$. Below $0.6h$, the profile is approximately linear with a slight positive gradient (see Fig. 3b). The BLACK model simulates a constant profile through all levels except the top and the bottom layer. It is possible to improve the characteristics of this scheme using the OSM scheme, but the ACM describes top-down processes more realistically. Here, we did not perform these tests with the ACM2 scheme since it can be found, in more details, in [14].

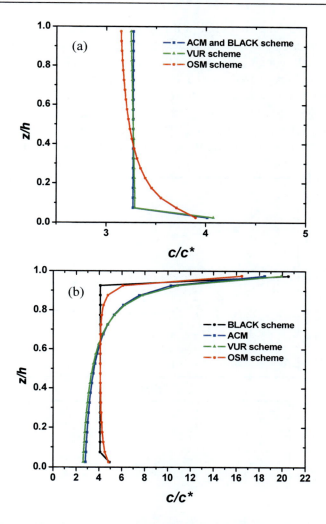

Figure 3. Comparison of the BLACK scheme the ACM and the OSM scheme for (a) the bottom-up flux test and (b) the top-down flux test. We note that the BLACK scheme and the ACM scheme are the same for the bottom-up test.

Using the EMEP Unified model (version UNI-ACID, rv2.0), the VUR scheme and the eddy diffusion scheme (KSC), often used in chemical transport models, were compared. The basic physical formulation of the EMEP model is unchanged from that of [21]. A polar-stereographic projection, true at 60° N and with a grid size of $50 \times 50$ km$^2$, was used. The model domain used in simulation had (101, 91) points covering the area of whole Europe and North Africa. The $\sigma$ terrain-following coordinate was used with 20 levels in the vertical – from the surface to 100 hPa with the lowest level located nearly at 92 m. The horizontal grid of the model is the Arakawa C grid. All other details can be found in [22]. The Unified EMEP model uses 3-hourly resolution meteorological data from the dedicated version of the HIRLAM (HIgh Resolution Limited Area Model) numerical weather prediction model with a parallel architecture [23]. The horizontal and vertical wind components are given on a staggered grid. All other variables are given in the centre of the grid. Linear interpolation between the 3-hourly values is used to calculate values of the meteorological input data at each advection step. The time step used in the simulation was 600 s. In the EMEP Unified model, the eddy diffusion scheme remarkably improved the vertical mixing in the ABL, particularly under stable conditions and conditions approaching free convection, compared with the scheme previously used in the EMEP Unified model. The improvement was particularly pronounced for $NO_2$ [4,24]. However, with reducing the horizontal grid size and increasing the heterogeneity of the underlying surface in the EMEP Unified model, there is a need for the mixing scheme having a higher level of sophistication in the simulation of turbulence in the ABL. It seems that the VUR scheme displays good performance for that.

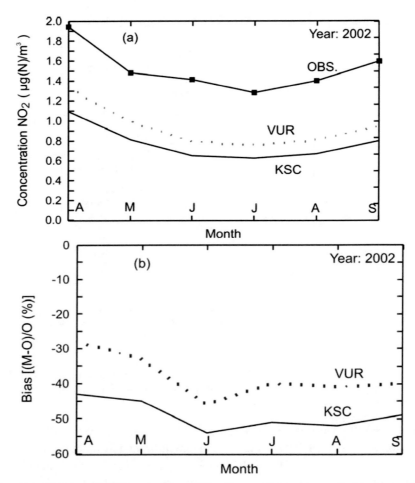

Figure 4. The eddy diffusion (KSC) versus the VUR scheme. Comparison of: (a) the modelled and observed $NO_2$ in air ($\mu g(N)$ $m^{-3}$) concentrations and (b) their biases in the period April-September for the year 2002. $M$ and $O$ denotes modelled and observed value, respectively.

The comparison of the VUR scheme and the eddy diffusion schemes has been performed using simulated and measured concentrations of the pollutant $NO_2$, since it is one of the most affected ones by the processes in the ABL layer. The simulations were done for the year 2002 in the months when the convective processes are dominant in the ABL (April-September). The station recording $NO_2$ in air ($\mu g(N)$ $m^{-3}$) concentration was considered for comparison when measurements were available for at least 75% of days in a year (82 stations). The bias on the monthly basis as $(M-O)/O$ 100%, where $M$ and $O$ denotes the modeled and observed value, respectively, was calculated. The comparison of the modeled and observed $NO_2$ in air ($\mu g(N)$ m$^{-3}$) concentrations between both schemes is shown in Fig. 4. The values used in the calculations were averaged over the whole domain of integration. It can be seen that both schemes underestimate the observations. However, for all considered months, $NO_2$ concentrations calculated with the VUR scheme are in general higher and closer to the observations than those obtained using the eddy diffusion scheme (of the order of 15-20%). Correspondingly, the bias of the VUR scheme is lower than the eddy diffusion scheme.

## 4. SUMMARY

In the ABL during convective conditions, when much of the vertical mixing is driven by buoyant plumes, we cannot properly describe mixing processes using local approach and eddy diffusion schemes. Non-local mixing schemes simulate vertical mixing caused by large-scale eddies, but they neglect small-scale mixing processes. Combined local and non-local schemes designed in the past few years, merging characteristics of local and non-local schemes describe small-scale and large-scale turbulent processes simultaneously. In this chapter, three non-local schemes (the BLACK scheme, the ACM and the VUR scheme) as well as two combined local and non-local schemes (the ACM2 and OSM scheme) for applications in air quality and environmental models are described. The comparison of the BLACK scheme, the ACM and the OSM scheme in bottom-up and top-down flux tests are presented. Finally, the overview is supported with EMEP chemical model outputs obtained for comparison of the VUR scheme and the eddy diffusivity scheme.

## ACKNOWLEDGMENTS

The research work described in this chapter has been funded by the Ministry of Science Republic of Serbia under the project "Modeling and numerical simulations of complex physical systems", No. OI141035 for 2006-2010.

## REFERENCES

[1] R. B. Stull, *An Introduction to Boundary Layer Meteorology*, Dordrecht: Kluwer, 1988.

[2] K. Alapaty, 2003. *Development of two CBL schemes using the turbulence velocity scale.* The 4$^{th}$ WRF Users' workshop, Boulder, Colorado, June 25-27.

[3] K. Alapaty, M. Alapaty, 2001. *Development of a diagnostic TKE schemes for applications in regional and climate models using MM5.* Research Note, MCNC-North Carolina Supercomputing Center, Research Triangle Park, NC, pp. 5

[4] D. T. Mihailovic and K. Alapaty, *Envoiron. Model. Software.*, 22, 1685-1689 (2007).

[5] D.T. Mihailovic, J.E. Jonson, 2005. *Implementation of a TKE scheme in the Unified EMEP model. Air Pollution report* 5/2005, ISSN: 1503-8025. Norwegian Meteorological Institute, Oslo.

[6]   R. B. Stull, A.G.M. Driedonks, *Bound.-Layer Meteor.* 40, 209-239 (1987).

[7]   K. Alapaty, J.E. Pleim, S. Raman, D.S. Niyogi, D.W. Byun, *J. Appl. Meteor.* 36, 214–233 (1997).

[8]   M.S. Miesch, A. Brandenburg, A. Zweibel, E.G. Zweibel, *Phys. Rev. E.* 61, 457–467 (2000).

[9]   J. E. Pleim and J. S. Chang, *Atmos. Environ.*, A26, 965-981 (1992).

[10]  A.K. Blackadar, *Fourth Symp. Atmospheric Turbulence, Diffusion ad Air Quality*, 46-49 (1976).

[11]  J.C. Wyngaard, R.A. Brost, *J. Atmos. Sci.* 41, 102-112 (1984).

[12]  G. Tonnesen, J. Olaguer, M. Bergin, T. Russell, A. Hanna, P. Makar, D. Derwent, Z. Wang, 1998. *Air quality models.* Draft as of 11/26/98, pp. 55.

[13]  Z. Wang, *Proceedings of the photochemical Reactivity Workshop*, U.S. Environmental protection Agency, Durham, NC (1998).

[14]  J. E. Pleim, *J. Appl. Meteor. Climat.*, 46, 1385-395 (2007).

[15]  D.T. Mihailović, K. Alapaty, M. Sakradžija, *Environ. Sci. Pollut. Res.*, 15, 296-302 (2008).

[16]  L. Faragó, *Időjárás*, 110, 379-395 (2006).

[17]  Á. Bordás, *Phys. Scr.*, T123, 014032 (2008).

[18]  J. C. Wyngaard, R. A. Brost, *J. Atmos. Sci.* 41, 102-112 (1984).

[19]  C. Zhang, D.A. Randall, C.H. Moeng, M. Branson, K.A. Moyer and Q. Wang, *Mon. Wea. Rev.*, 124, 2521-2536 (1996).

[20]  C.H. Moeng and P.P. Sullivan, *J. Atmos. Sci.*, 51, 999-1022 (1994).

[21]  E. Berge, H.A. Jacobsen, *Tellus*, 50, 205-223 (1998).

[22]  D. Simpson, H. Fagerli, J.E. Jonson, S. Tsyro, P. Wind, J.P. Tuovinen, *EMEP Status Report,* Oslo: The Norwegian Meteorological Institute, (2003).

[23]  D. Bjorge and R. Skalin, *PARLAM – the Parallel HIRLAM Version of DNMI*, Oslo: The Norwegian Meteorological Institute, (1995).

[24]  H. Fagerly and A. Eliassen, *Modified Parameterizaton of the Vertical Diffusion*, Oslo: The Norwegian Meteorological Institute, (2002).

In: Advances in Environmental Modeling and Measurements    ISBN: 978-1-60876-599-7
Editors: D. T. Mihailović, B. Lalić, pp. 133-146      © 2010 Nova Science Publishers, Inc.

*Chapter 13*

# CONTEMPORARY NUMERICAL TREATMENT OF PASSIVE ADVECTION

## *I. Arsenić*[*1], *D.T. Mihailović*[1], *and B. Rajković*[2]

[1]University of Novi Sad, Novi Sad, Serbia
[2]Belgrade University, Belgrade, Serbia

## ABSTRACT

The interpretation of advection in equations of dynamic meteorology is a key component of different numerical models, particularly numerical weather predictions, and air quality and climate models. As a result, a number of numerical schemes offer solutions to addressing advection calculation problems. These schemes can be classified into two broad groups: Eulerian and Semi-Lagrangian schemes. Advection schemes that use these approaches suffer from several disadvantages such as numerical dispersion, implicit diffusion and violation of mass conservation. In this chapter, we present descriptions of backward and forward Semi-Lagrangian schemes as well as numerical tests designed with these schemes. Recently, we have proposed the application of a pure Lagrangian scheme in numerical modeling of advection. This new advection scheme consists of two components. The first component is pure Lagrangian advection, while the second component is a kind of interpolation procedure to obtain Lagrangian values to the Eulerian grid. Numerical tests performed to compare the proposed scheme against piecewise parabolic Eulerian and Semi-Lagrangian schemes indicate that the new scheme has persuasive advantages in terms of increasing accuracy and saving computational time.

## 1. INTRODUCTION

Modeling atmospheric phenomena such as air pollution transport or integrating equations of motion in numerical weather prediction models require application of the advection equation. There are a number of numerical schemes with different levels of accuracy that

---

[*] Corresponding author: E-mail address: ilija@polj.ns.ac.yu, Phone: +381 21 4853407, Fax: +381 21 6350552

offer a solution to this problem. Analysis of scheme quality requires consideration of three characteristics: stability, accuracy and efficiency. In this chapter, stability of an examined scheme will be considered through production of negative function values in a positive definite field. The production of negative function values are a potential source of instability in numerical models. It is particularly problematic when the results of advection are used as inputs to other parts of models dealing with nonlinear equations such as those used in cloud microphysics or atmospheric chemistry. Briefly, a scheme that produces negative values in a positive definite field will be unstable. Advection schemes can be broadly classified into two groups: Eulerian and Semi-Lagrangian (SL) schemes [1]. In Eulerian approaches, space coordinates are time independent and consequently the grid points are fixed in space during integration. This approach is widely accepted, and most schemes apply this approach for solving advection equations. The most basic advection scheme that utilizes this approach is the well known upstream scheme. However, this scheme suffers from a strong implicit diffusion. The inconvenience of the upstream scheme can be reduced by introducing so called "antidiffusion" processes that have the same intensity as the implicit diffusion does [2,3]. The numerical efficiency of the Eulerian approach is their primary advantage. The occurrence of implicit diffusion can be removed using second or higher order accuracy advection schemes, but in these cases numerical dispersion is produced. The production of numerical dispersion is particularly high in cases of sharp gradients. For example, in cloudy, cold-front boundaries or air pollution transport analyses, where the Fourier spectrum of the advected function consists of a high number of waves with very different wave numbers. Numerical dispersions also result in violations of the positive definite advected quantity, and instability can occur in the whole numerical system. As a source of specified problems, one may find that the aforementioned schemes do not correctly represent the value of the advected physical quantity between two grid points, assuming that this value is a constant. Eulerian schemes can resolve this disadvantage by making interpolations of function between grid points and then advecting the resulting values [4]. This interpolation can be either linear (piecewise linear) or parabolic (piecewise parabolic). Schemes constructed in this way are both positive definite, and they have significantly lower implicit diffusion than schemes including antidiffusion processes. Unfortunately, these schemes are inefficient and time consuming to apply. A common feature of all these schemes is a restricted maximal time step to a value determined by the Courant-Friedrichs-Lewy (CFL) criterion. This disadvantage is particularly important when the advection scheme is applied in climate simulation models.

A completely different approach for numerically solving the advection equation is the Semi-Lagrangian (SL) approach [1]. With this approach, the values of advected physical quantities are distributed regularly in grid points (i.e., Eulerian points) and in current time steps. They are calculated as values of that quantity in irregularly distributed upstream points from the previous time step. The position of departure points are determined by an iterative procedure while function values are determined by interpolation. Such SL schemes are called backward or upstream SL schemes. This method can be applied in such a way that the departure points are distributed regularly, while the arrival points are irregularly distributed as downstream points. In this situation, interpolation should be done between irregularly distributed points. This is more difficult than interpolation between regularly distributed points. These types of schemes are called forward or downstream SL schemes. The distance between departure and arrival points can be a few times greater than the distance between two grid points. In other words, the CFL criterion is not a restriction for these types of schemes.

This characteristic of SL schemes is their most important advantage in comparison to Eulerian schemes. However, two disadvantages of SL schemes are that the interpolation process is inefficient and time consuming and the scheme is not positive definite.

A new passive advection scheme conditionally classified as a pure Lagrangian (PL) scheme is described in Section 2 of this chapter. The proposed scheme is positive definite and computationally efficient, producing no implicit diffusion or numerical dispersion. In Section 3, an interpolation technique, which is the most important use of the scheme, is analyzed. Accuracy and efficiency attributes of the proposed scheme are tested, and the results of the numerical tests are described in Section 4.

## 2. ADVECTION

First, we will explain the basic idea behind the SL method for solving the advection equation. Thus, let us consider passive advection as the simplest case. Passive advection is described by the equation:

$$\frac{dF}{dt} = \frac{\partial F}{\partial t} + \frac{d\vec{r}}{dt}\frac{\partial F}{\partial x} = \frac{\partial F}{\partial t} + \vec{u}\frac{\partial F}{\partial x} = 0 \,, \tag{1}$$

where: $F$ is the scalar property of fluid (e.g., concentration of air pollution or water vapor); $\vec{r}$ is the position vector of concerned fluid particle and $\vec{u}$ is its velocity. This equation means that the scalar property of the fluid is constant along a fluid particle trajectory. The fundamental idea behind the SL method is to determine the fluid particle trajectory, which at the beginning of a time step starts its motion from some upstream point (point A, Fig. 1) and arrives exactly at the node of the regular grid at the end of the time step (point C, Fig. 1). Due to discretization, the position of point A cannot be evaluated directly, so some nearby point will be considered as the start point (point A', Fig. 1). In some schemes, the meaning of the term "close point" is defined as a compromise between desired accuracy and numerical costs of procedures applied for evaluating the position of the point. In SL nomenclature, point A' is referred to as the **departure point** while point C is referred to as the **arrival point**. Because advection is a conservative process, the value of the scalar property, $F$, at the regular grid node C, at time, $t_n + \Delta t$, is exactly the same as the value of the scalar property, $F$, at upstream point A at time level, $t_n$. According to Fig. 1 and equation (1), we can write the basic equation of the SL method as:

$$F(\vec{r}_i, t_{n+1}) = F(\vec{r}_i - 2\vec{\alpha}_i, t_n) \,. \tag{2}$$

To apply of SL method, we have to solve two problems. The first problem requires determination of the position of all departure points at time level, $t_n$. That is, we are required to determine the distance that the particle travels during each time step. This distance is denoted as vector $2\vec{\alpha}_m$ in Fig. 1. This problem can be solved by using an iterative procedure. We apply procedures similar to those proposed by Roberts [5]. In those procedures, the assumption is adopted that particles during time steps travel with constant velocity equal to velocity in points located in the middle of the trajectory (point B in Fig. 1.) at time level, $t_n + \Delta t / 2$. This can be summarized with the following formula:

$$\vec{\alpha}_m^{s+1} = \frac{\Delta t}{2} \vec{V}^* \left( \vec{r}_m - \vec{\alpha}_m^s, t_n + \frac{\Delta t}{2} \right). \tag{3}$$

Here $\vec{\alpha}_m^s$ is the estimated distance in the s'th step of the iteration and $\vec{V}^*$ is the velocity vector at point B. Hence, during an evaluation of particle traveling distance, we need to evaluate velocity at point B at time level, $t_n + \Delta t / 2$. This means that we need to perform time as well as spatial interpolations. Assumptions made here lead us to a kind of time interpolation procedure. In our advection scheme, we have chosen procedures very similar to that proposed by Staniforth and Cote [1] in their review paper discussing backward SL schemes

$$\vec{V}^* \left( \vec{r}_m, t_n + \frac{\Delta t}{2} \right) = \frac{1}{2} \left[ 3 \vec{V} \left( \vec{r}_m, t_n \right) - \vec{V} \left( \vec{r}_m, t_n - \Delta t \right) \right]. \tag{4}$$

Spatial interpolation of velocity, as well as the evaluation of function at departure points, can be solved by an interpolation procedure. We will discuss interpolation in more detail later, but here we need to point out that this interpolation approach is always made between points of the regular grid.

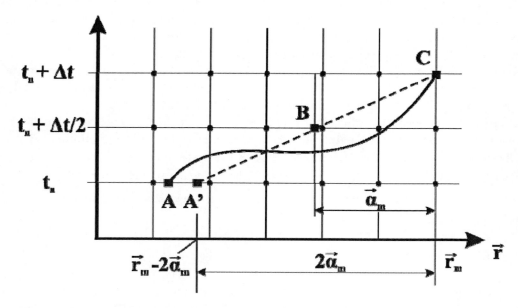

Figure 1. Schematic description of the backward Semi-Lagrangian (SL) scheme.

As previously mentioned, values of F at the time level, $t_n + \Delta t$, in regular grid points are evaluated as values of F in upstream points at time level, $t_n$. Thus, such SL advection schemes are called **upstream** or **backward** SL schemes. In **forward** or **downstream** SL schemes, a fluid particle starts its motion from the regular grid point. In this situation, arrival points will be irregularly distributed in space (point C, Fig. 2).

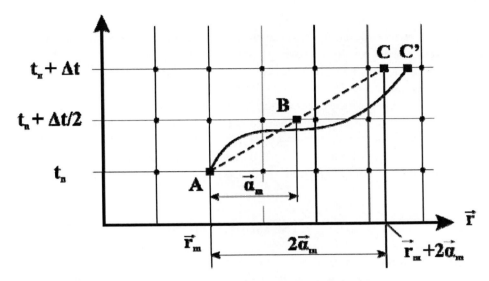

Figure 2. Schematic description of the forward Semi-Lagrangian (SL) scheme.

Based on the above considerations and Fig. 2, we can derive the basic equations of forward (or downstream) SL schemes as follows:

$$F(\vec{r}_m + 2\vec{\alpha}_m, t_n + \Delta t) = F(\vec{r}_m, t_n),$$  (5)

and

$$\vec{\alpha}_m^{s+1} = \frac{\Delta t}{2}\vec{V}^*\left(\vec{r}_m + \vec{\alpha}_m^s, t_n + \frac{\Delta t}{2}\right),$$  (6)

where the symbols used have the same meaning as in previous equations. In these forward (or downstream) SL schemes, interpolation should be done between irregularly distributed points. This approach is much more complicated and numerically costly than when interpolation is applied between regularly distributed points, as in upstream (or backward) SL schemes. This is also the main reason upstream SL schemes are often used in atmospheric models.

Recently, we have developed highly efficient interpolation procedures that can be used between regularly and irregularly distributed points. This enables use of forward algorithms to solve advection equations. Proposed schemes can be classified as SL forward (or downstream) schemes and its governing equations are identified in formulas (5) and (6) with described procedures for solving them.

The origin of the forward (or downstream) SL method is from a PL method. The difference between these two methods lies in fact that in forward (downstream) SL methods, positions of the arrival points (further Lagrangian points) have been overlooked after interpolation is applied. Thus, transition from this class of SL schemes to the PL scheme is relatively straight-forward. Specifically, we only need to save Lagrangian point positions for the following time step. Thus, in PL advection schemes, we deal with two grids— Lagrangian or real grids—where we prepare advection and Eulerian grids that represent convenient pictures of the real (Lagrangian) grid where advection is performed. The purpose of the Eulerian grid is to provide a base for application of other parts of the numerical model (e.g., diffusion, vertical mixing, etc.) where calculation of a gradient is required. Consequently, such numerical models usually work only on regular grids. Increased computer memory use when PL advection schemes are used could be defended because increased accuracy is achieved. Increased accuracy is a result of reducing the introduction errors due to interpolation. Namely, during application of SL methods, either forward or backward, errors due to interpolation are accumulating from time step to time step. In contrast, in PL methods, errors introduced by interpolation from Lagrangian to Eulerian grids at one time step have no implication to Lagrangian fields in the next time step. This characteristic makes it possible to apply some simple interpolation procedures that save considerable computational time.

## 3. INTERPOLATION

Interpolation procedures (in further text interpolation) are widely used in many branches of science and technology. In studies from the literature a variety of different interpolation techniques become apparent. For example, a frequently used interpolation technique is interpolation by polynomials. During the solving of the advective equation with a SL method, a range of examples from the literature can be found regarding the use of different types of interpolation techniques. In early studies, the Lagrangian interpolation polynomial was used nearly exclusively [6-9]. In 1990, Bermeyo [10] successfully applied spline interpolation during the integration of an advective equation. After work by Colella and Woodward [4] to use piecewise parabolic methods, Rančić [11] successfully combined the procedure with a SL approach and then applied it to solving advective equations. Zerroukat has combined a piecewise cubic [12] and a piecewise spline method [13] with the SL approach to solve advective equations.

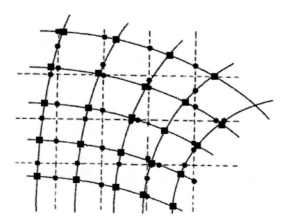

Figure 3. Two steps of the internet interpolation technique: First, function values from Lagrangian points (filled squares) are interpolated toward Lagrangian-Eulerian grid intersection points (filled circles) and second, an interpolation from these points toward nodes of the Eulerian grid is determined.

It is notable that the aforementioned interpolation methods are either unusable or very difficult to use if it becomes necessary to conduct an interpolation of a function with irregularly distributed points to a function with regularly distributed points. The irregular grid appears when applying the forward variants of the SL advective scheme. (For the remainder of the text, the term Lagrangian grid will be used rather than irregular grid.) This is the reason that the backward variant of the SL method is used instead of the more natural forward variant. Wen-Yih and Kao-San [14] have shown one forward SL advective scheme where the interpolation function from irregular to a regular network of points is done by using the so-called internet interpolation procedure. The internet interpolation procedure consists of two steps. During the first step, the interpolation of the function is calculated from a Lagrangian grid (solid lines in the Fig. 3) toward points of intersection on the Lagrangian and Eulerian grids (filled circles in Fig. 3). In the second step, an interpolation from these points is done towards the Eulerian grid (dashed lines in Fig. 3).

Lagrangian interpolation is used in each part of the interpolation with this procedure. However, the procedure is numerically expensive because the Lagrangian interpolation procedure needs to be applied twice at each time step.

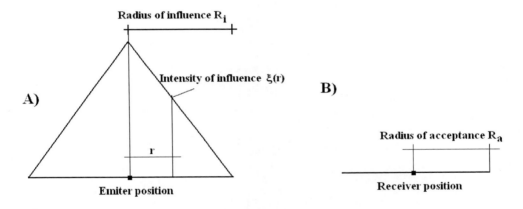

Figure 4. Characteristics of (A) Lagrangian (L) points and (B) Eulerian (E) points.

In more recent interpolation techniques, the grid point from which the interpolation is performed are seen as "emitters" and the grid points where the interpolation is performed are seen as "receivers" of function values. In applying this interpolation procedure in the forward SL scheme or in the PL scheme, the emitters are the Lagrangian points and the receivers are the Eulerian points (or simply the L and E points). (This nomenclature, L and E points, will be used in the remainder of this text.) The L points (Fig. 4a) are described by their positions, embedded function values, influence intensities and radiuses of influence. The influence intensity is a measure of the transmission of function values from the L point to surrounding E points. The radius of influence is the shortest distance from the L point to the point where the intensity equals zero. The function that is describing the change in the influence intensity (described in the remainder of text as the shape of influence) with distance from the emitter must fulfill the following conditions: (1) positively definite to keep the sign or a positive definiteness of the size that is advected; (2) monotonously declining and (3) surface below the function equal to the unit due to mass conservation. The radius of influence and the shape of influence are chosen to be the same for all L points. The E points (Fig. 4b) are described by their position, the value of the function within and the radius of acceptance. The radiance of acceptance is defined as the greatest distance from the same L point from which the E point of interest can still accept the function value. Although the radius of acceptance can have an arbitrary value, it is calculated using the numeric value, dx/2, where dx is the grid step or the distance between E points. The radius of acceptance is the same for all E points.

A part of the function value that the L point will transmit to some E point is equal to the surface below the curve of the influence intensity, dS, that is located within the area of acceptance of the E point. Fig. 5 depicts this with the gray shaded area of the triangle. Transmission between L and E points will be done if their distance is shorter than the sum of the radius of influence and the radius of acceptance. (For the remainder of the text, this sum will be referred to as the radius of transmission.)

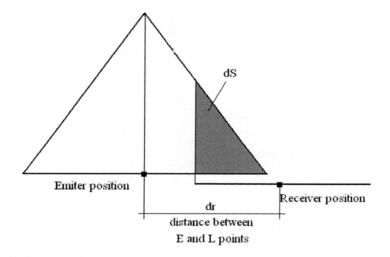

Figure 5. Transmission of the function value between emitter and receiver.

If we choose the shape of influence to be a linear, declining function of the distance, and the radius of acceptance, $R_a$, to be equal to the half grid step, considering that the triangle surface in the figure has a unit of surface, the gray part of the surface, $dS$, can be presented as

$$dS = \frac{(R_a + R_i - dr)^2}{2R_i^2} .$$
(7)

If $F^L$ is the function value in L point, some of that will be transmitted to the E point, $dF^E$, can be calculated as

$$dF^E = dS \cdot F^L .$$
(8)

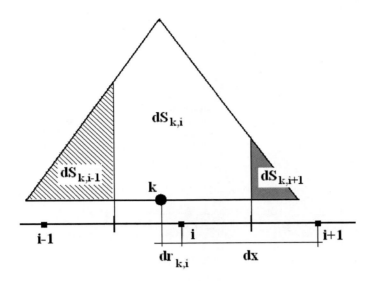

Figure 6. Transmission of the function value between Lagrangian (L) points and all surrounding Eulerian (E) points.

Let us assume now that the i'th E point (filled square in Fig. 6) is the closest E point to the k'$th$ L point (filled circle in Fig. 6), and that their distance, $dr_{ki}$, is shorter than the radius of transmission. In this situation, the k'$th$ L point will transmit the function value to the three E points, to the nearest, i'$th$ to the left (i-1) and value to the right (i+1). Corresponding parts of the function value that are left, right and nearest to the E points that will accept from the L point are proportional to the dashed, gray and blank surfaces in Fig. 4. This relationship can be evaluated with the following formulas

$$dF^E_{i+n} = dS_{k,i+n} \cdot F^L_k ,$$ (9)

where n can use values 1, 0, -1 and $dS_{k,i+n}$ is defined as:

$$dS_{k,i+n} = \begin{cases} \dfrac{(R_a + R_i - dx - ndr_{k,i})^2}{2R_i^2} & n \neq 0 \\ 1 - dS_{k,i-1} - dS_{k,i+1} & n = 0 \end{cases} .$$ (10)

The final function value in an E point is equal to the sum of the contributions of all L points that are closer to it then the radius of transmission is long. Generalizations of this interpolation into two dimensions is relatively straight-forward. First, interpolation from a L point (filled circle in Fig. 7) is made to the nearest points that lie on vertical Eulerian grid lines (points depicted as X in Fig. 7). After this and using the same procedure, interpolation is made from these points to the E points (filled squares in Fig. 7).

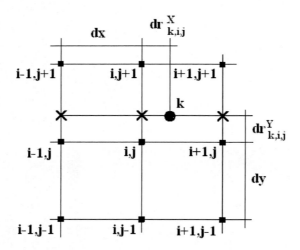

Figure 7. Generalizations of two dimensional interpolation procedure.

One L point transmits its function value to the nine surrounding E points. Each E point accepts parts defined as:

$$dF^E_{i+n,j+m} = dS^X_{k,i+n} dS^Y_{k,j+n} \cdot F^L_k ,$$  (11)

where: $dS^X_{k,i+n}$ and $dS^Y_{k,j+n}$ are defined as in Eq. (10) but use the corresponding distances, $dr^X_{k,i}$ and $dr^Y_{k,j}$, respectively. It has been shown that the same results will be obtained if the first step of interpolation is made on horizontal Eulerian grid lines. A proof of this outcome is omitted here.

# 4. NUMERICAL TESTS

Results of numerical tests where piecewise linear and piecewise parabolic (PWP) advection schemes are compared to Smolarkiewicz's scheme [2]. Upstream and fourth order leap frog advection schemes are presented in [4]. In this study, much higher accuracy of the PWP scheme was achieved in comparison to the other tested schemes. As such, in the present study only comparative numerical tests of the PL scheme against PWP schemes, described as a forward SL scheme and backward SL scheme, were performed. As a representative of backward SL schemes, an upstream two-time level Semi-Lagrangian passive advection scheme [1] has been used, with Lagrangian interpolation polynomial of order 3 (SL3).

In one-dimensional (1D) numerical tests, we applied chosen advection schemes on advection of so called step functions (solid line in Fig. 8). Integration parameters are chosen as follows: integration domain (n)= 1000 points; grid step ($\Delta$x)= 15 m and time step ($\Delta$t)= 1 sec. Step function in initial time step has a value equal to zero except in perturbed area-wide 50 points (indicated by A), where it has a value of 1. Numerical tests of this kind are convenient to apply as a cyclic boundary condition. These tests are convenient because they provide capabilities that perturbation introduced in initial fields after a number of time steps, and can be returned to initial positions and then compared with values or shape of the function at the initial time. Unfortunately, application of a cyclic boundary condition with PL advection schemes introduces additional complications. Namely, case interpolations should be performed between starting and ending points of the integration domain. In order to avoid this inconvenience, constant boundary conditions are used and all calculations with the perturbed part of the function are performed far away from the boundaries of the integration domain. After a specified number of time steps (1 800 time steps in these tests), wind direction is changed to the opposite direction in order to return the perturbation to the starting position. Such cycles can be repeated until effects under study reach sufficiently large values.

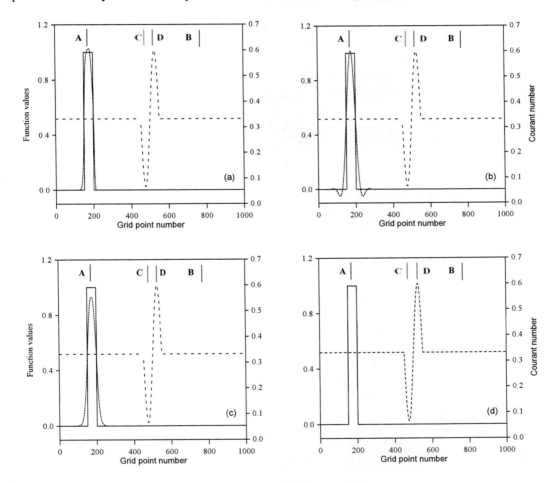

Figure 8. Advection of step function in divergent wind velocity fields.

In our experiment, the shape of the step function before and after advection is analyzed (Fig. 8). In all panels of Fig. 8, the shape of the step function after advection is presented by dotted line while its value is given on the left axis. Courant number is depicted as dashed line and its value is given on the right axis. The x-axis gives the ordinal number of grid points. Step function is advected by wind field, perturbed by a harmonic wave in the vicinity of points C and D, in the right hand side direction until it reaches position B (1 800 time steps).

After this, wind direction is changed to the opposite direction, and the perturbation is returned to the starting position. It is worth noting that symmetry of the velocity perturbation implies that the exact solution is an unchanged step function. This cycle is repeated ten times in all the performed tests to emphasize differences between tested schemes. To establish distinctions between compared schemes, the following statistical parameters are considered: (a) relative efficiency (Re), which is defined as the ratio of time consuming the most efficient advection scheme (upstream scheme) to the time consuming the examined scheme; (b) root mean square error (RMSE) of differences between the initial function values and the function values after ten cycles of advection; and (c) relative mass changes (RMC), which is defined as the ratio between total mass change and total mass in the initial time step. Here, the total mass represents the sum of function values in all the grid points. The results of the comparison between schemes using the above described parameters are given in Tab. 1.

In panel (a) of Fig. 8, results obtained by applying PWP schemes are depicted. Agreement between exact and obtained solutions is high (RMSE = 3.95E-3) while the positive definiteness of function is saved. Furthermore, the mass conservation is highly satisfied (RMC = 5.13E-2%). However, as seen in Table 1, the relative efficiency of the PWP scheme is weak compared to the other schemes (Re = 0.20). Panel (b) of Fig. 8 presents results obtained by applying a SL scheme with a Lagrangian SL3 scheme. The accuracy of the SL3 scheme is weaker (RMSE = 5.97E-3). In addition, this scheme does not satisfy mass conservation when perturbation approaches areas around points C and D. The area of convergence for point C remains only 12% of mass after the beginning of integration. In contrast, in the area of divergence for point D, the mass sum is 31% higher than the correct value. This disadvantage of backward SL schemes can be eliminated by applying some additional correction techniques. Relative efficiency (Re = 0.46) is more than twice as high as that calculated using the PWP scheme. The tested forward SL scheme (panel (c), Fig. 8) introduces considerable error in the model (RMSE = 3.85E-2) but is highly efficient (Re = 0.52) and the mass conservation is well satisfied (RMC = 3.05E-6%). Proposed PL scheme (panel (c), Fig. 8), has remarkably enhanced test characteristics. Specifically, the error is fifty times less than in the PWP scheme (RMSE = 6.25E-5%) with low numerical cost (Re = 0.52) that fully satisfies mass conservation (RMC = 0%).

Table 1. Statistical parameters describing differences between compared schemes in a one-dimensional (1D) experiment. PWP = Piecewise parabolic; SL3 = Semi-Lagrangian, Interpolation polynomial order 3; FSL = Forward Semi-Lagrangian; RMSE = Root Mean Square Error; Re = Relative Efficiency; RMC = Relative Mass Change.

|         | (PWP)    | SL3      | FSL      | L4E      |
|---------|----------|----------|----------|----------|
| RMSE    | 3.95E-3  | 5.97E-3  | 3.85E-2  | 6.25E-5  |
| Re      | 0.20     | 0.46     | 0.52     | 0.51     |
| RMC     | 5.13E-2% | 3.58E-3% | 3.05E-6% | 0        |

Two-dimensional (2D) numerical tests with the advection schemes were performed using the slotted cylinder under the motion of solid-body rotation about the center of the cylinder. The following initial conditions are shown in Fig. 9a: radius of the cylinder was 40 $\Delta x$; the width of the groove was 10 $\Delta x$; the domain was 200×200 points and the amplitude of the distribution was 1. The numerical solution after two revolutions (1 600 time steps and maximal Courant number of 0.7), and obtained using the PWP advection scheme, is depicted in Fig. 9b. This scheme introduces considerable error (RMSE = 9.45E-2) into the model. Fig. 9c presents results of the application of forward SL schemes after two revolutions. This scheme has very weak accuracy (RMSE = 1.55E-1), but its efficiency is many times higher than the efficiency of the PWP scheme. The results depicted in Fig. 9c were obtained using a maximum Courant number of 7. Consequently, this integration required 15 fold less time to complete. Finally, Fig. 9d depicts results obtained using a PL scheme after twenty revolutions (1 600 time step and maximum Courant of 7). This integration consumed two fold less time to complete than when the PWP scheme was applied. The most desirable characteristic achieved with the PL scheme is very high accuracy (RMSE = 2.52E-8).

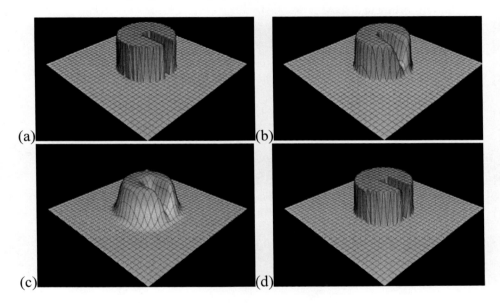

Figure 9. Results of two-dimensional (2D) numerical tests.

# 4. CONCLUSION

A functioning of PL advection scheme in environment of static grid points distributed in regular way is described in this chapter. In order to make Eulerian picture of the field obtained after advection a new efficient interpolation procedure is introduced. Such combination of Lagrangian approach in numerical modeling of advection term and application of economical interpolation procedure provide to the proposed scheme to be a very fast and accurate. Performed numerical tests of comparison PL scheme versus Semi-Lagrangian and Piecewise parabolic schemes proved, in an unambiguous way, the aforementioned advantages of PL scheme. In these tests four characteristics of mentioned schemes: accuracy, efficiency, mass conservation and positive definiteness are examined. In all numerical tests PL scheme shows persuasive advantages compared to all other schemes concerning all above characteristics. PL scheme is positive definite, more accurate, more efficient and completely satisfies the mass conservation law. These advantages are particularly obvious in tests where advection is performed in the divergent wind field. In that case SL3 schemes are not positive definite and even they seriously violate mass conservation law. PWP scheme is positive definite and well conserves mass but it is not efficient as the PL scheme. 2D generalization of PL scheme is tested using the slotted cylinder under the motion of solid-body rotation. These tests approve aforementioned advantages of the PL scheme. On the basis of these speculations L4E scheme can be highly recommended for application in numerical modeling of atmospheric processes that include advection term.

## REFERENCES

[1]    A.N. Staniforth and J. Coté, *Mon. Wea. Rev.*, 119, 2206-2223 (1991).
[2]    P.K. Smolarkiewicz,. *Mon. Wea. Rev.*, 111, 479-486 (1983).
[3]    Z.I. Janjic, *Research Activities in Atmosphericand Oceanic Modelling, WMO, Geneva, CAS/JSC WGNE, 3.14* (1997)
[4]    P. Colella and P. R. Woodward, *J. Comput. Phys.*, 54, 174–201 (1984).
            A.   Robert, *Atmos. Ocean*, 19, 35-46 (1981).
[5]    T.N. Krishnamurti, *J. Appl. Meteor.*, 1, 508-521 (1962)
[6]    C.E. Leith, *Tech. Note No. 66, WMO, Geneva*, 168-176 (1965).
[7]    M.B. Mathur, ,. *Mon. Wea. Rev.*, 98, 214-219 (1970).
[8]    J.R. Bates and A. McDonald, *Mon. Wea. Rev.*, 112, 1831-1842 (1982).
[9]    R. Bermejo, *Mon. Wea. Rev.*, 118, 1615-1627 (1990).
[10]   M. Rančić, *Mon. Wea. Rev.*, 120, 1394-1406 (1992).
[11]   M. Zerroukat, N. Wood & A. Staniforth, *Q.J.R. Meteorol. Soc.,* **128**, 2801□2820 (2002).
[12]   M. Zerroukat, N. Wood & A. Staniforth, *Int. J. Numer. Meth. Fluids*, 51, 1297–1318 (2006).
[13]   W.Y. Sun and K. S. Yeh, *Q.J.R. Meteorol. Soc.,* **123**, 2463–2476 (1997).

In: Advances in Environmental Modeling and Measurements     ISBN: 978-1-60876-599-7
Editors: D. T. Mihailović, B. Lalić, pp. 147-157     © 2010 Nova Science Publishers, Inc.

*Chapter 14*

# ATMOSPHERIC DEPOSITION OF HEAVY METALS AND AIRBORNE RADIONUCLIDES STUDIED BY THE MOSS BIOMONITORING TECHNIQUE

*M. Krmar[*1], D. Radnović[1], M.V. Frontasyeva[2],*
*S.S. Pavlov[2], and Y.S. Pankratova[2]*
[1]Faculty of Sciences, Novi Sad, Serbia
[2]Joint Institute for Nuclear Research, Dubna, Russia

## ABSTRACT

The first systematic study of atmospheric pollution from heavy metals based on moss analysis in the northern part of Serbia was undertaken in 2000. The next moss survey was performed in 2005. Both sets of samples were subject to instrumental neutron activation analysis (INAA) for determination of more than 40 elements. Comparison of the 2005 and 2000 results for the same sites and moss species allowed exploring difference in spatial deposition patterns of several elements of interest. The activities of the $^7$Be, $^{210}$Pb and $^{137}$Cs were measured in the terrestrial moss samples. The objective of study was to investigate possible variation of radionuclide atmospheric deposition over the large area. Temporal variation of $^7$Be, $^{210}$Pb and $^{137}$Cs in moss samples over the 14-month period were continuously measured at one fixed sampling site. Duration and amount of precipitations were measured and their influence on the activity concentrations determined in moss samples was considered

## 1. INTRODUCTION

Studies on atmospheric contamination can be limited by high cost and difficulty of carrying out extensive sampling in time and space. It is a reason of increasing interest in using indirect monitoring methods such as the use bioaccumulators. The moss technique, first

[*] Corresponding author: E-mail address: krmar@im.ns.ac.yu, Phone: +381 21 459 368, Fax: +381 21 455 318

introduced in Scandinavia [1,2], has shown to be very suitable for studying the atmospheric deposition of heavy metals as well as other trace elements.

Terrestrial mosses, growing in different climatic zones, obtain water and most nutrients directly from air by precipitation and dry deposition. The absence or strong reduction of the cuticle and thin leaves allows easy uptake from the atmosphere. Mosses do not have a rooting system, so uptake of the nutrients from the substrate is insignificant. Accumulation of elements taken from the air in measurable concentrations makes mosses a superior sampling medium for heavy metals and other trace elements. Additional advantage of the moss technique is the simplicity of sample collection and possibility that much higher sampling density can be achieved than with the conventional precipitation analysis. Results from moss surveys allow examination of both spatial and temporal trends heavy elements deposition and identification of areas exposed to high deposition of pollutants. Several different analytical techniques were used for determination of heavy metal deposition: atomic absorption spectrometry, inductively coupled plasma spectrometry, fluorescence spectrometry and neutron activation analysis.

Systematic surveys of atmospheric deposition of heavy elements are performed on a regular basis every 5 years since 1990. Currently, the 2005/2006 moss survey is being conducted in 32 countries, analyzing moss samples from over 7000 sites across Europe [3].

The pilot study of air pollution using the moss technique was carried out in the northern part of Serbia in 2000 for the first time [4]. The study was repeated in 2005 and almost all area of Republic Serbia was cowered. During the NATO military action in the spring of 1999 the two largest oil refineries and several chemical plants were damaged. As a consequence of this, large amounts of pollutants were emitted to the atmosphere. Comparison of the 2005 and 2000 results for the same sited and moss species allowed exploring difference in spatial deposition patterns of oil combustion elements [5].

Naturally occurring $^7$Be and $^{210}$Pb together with $^{137}$Cs, after reach the atmosphere, follow identical transport routes and can be used as tracers in investigations of atmospheric processes. Berilium-7 is formed by spallation reaction between cosmic rays and nuclei of oxygen and nitrogen in the stratosphere and upper troposphere. By following the $^7$Be atmospheric deposition, it is possible to investigate stratospheric intrusions in the troposphere, vertical transport in troposphere, horizontal movement of air masses, residence time of aerosol particles in the troposphere, etc. Lead-210 is a member of $^{238}$U chain and comes into atmosphere from the soil. Whereas crust minerals containing $^{238}$U are source of $^{222}$Rn, presence of $^{210}$Pb and other radon daughters depends on geological properties of the ground, distribution of continent and sea areas, general conditions of ground surface layer. However, $^{210}$Pb is also released from industrial processes such as the sintering of ores containing some amount of $^{238}$U, the burning of coal or the production and use of agricultural phosphate fertilizers. The great majority of $^{137}$Cs was released in atmosphere in nuclear accident in Chernobyl and more than 400 atmospheric nuclear weapon tests. Since there were no significant $^{137}$Cs emissions after Chernobyl accident, atmospheric cesium was exposed to physical decay ($T_{1/2} = 30$ years) as well as wet and dry deposition. General trend of $^{17}$Cs concentration in air is decreasing including possible soil resuspension.

Air sampling provides [6] a good way to determine the amount of radionuclides in the air. Sampling stations are usually located near the ground, so temporal variations of activity concentration of some radionuclide in surface air (in Bq m$^{-3}$) can be measured by this technique. Aerosols are removed from atmosphere by dry deposition or wet deposition caused by precipitation scavenging. Deposition samplers usually consist of different size vessels collecting rainwater samples or dry fallout. By means of this technique [7], activity of some radionuclide in fallout (in Bq m$^{-2}$) for selected time interval can be measured. Limited number of precipitation and air sampling stations can not provide satisfying resolution in spatial analysis of airborne radionuclides atmospheric deposition. Widespread occurrence, inexpensive sampling procedure and simple gamma spectroscopy measurement, without preparatory chemical treatment of sample, can establish mosses as a very promising medium in investigation and monitoring of airborne radionuclides deposition.

Some preliminary results of the first study [8], concerning capabilities of mosses to indicate spatial distributions of $^7$Be and $^{137}$Cs deposition showed that activity distributions of both of them in mosses collected over some relatively large area are not uniform. In second study [9] activity concentrations of $^7$Be, $^{210}$Pb and $^{137}$Cs in moss samples taken on the regular time basis (one week sampling frequency) from the very same place during four seasons of year were measured to get (and interpret) time dependence of airborne radionuclide deposition. First results show that temporal variations of moss activity can give information comparable with information acquired by precipitation collector or air sampling technique. It can increase awareness and attempts to establish mosses in time and spatial analysis of atmospheric deposition of airborne radionuclides.

## 2. EXPERIMENT AND RESULTS

Samples of the epigeic moss *Hypnum cupressiforme* for elemental analysis were collected during two periods: in the summer 2000 (first survey), and summer and autumn 2005 (second survey) according to guidelines [10]. In first 2000 survey, moss samples were taken at 92 sampling sites evenly distributed over the north part of Serbia. In second, 2005 survey, the network of sampling locations included 194 sampling sites evenly scattered over the all territory of Republic Serbia, excluding Kosovo, south-west part of state where access was temporary limited.

Details concerning sample preparation are described in reference [4]. The content of elements in the moss samples was determined by instrumental neutron activation analysis (INAA) performed at the IBR-2 reactor in the Frank Laboratory of Neutron Physics. Two different procedures of analysis were done. One is a short irradiation of 3-5 minutes to measure short-lived isotopes (Al, Ca, Cl, I, Mg, Mn, and V). After a decay-period of 5 to 7 minutes the irradiated samples were measured twice, first for 3-5 and then for 10-15 minutes. A long-irradiation of 4-5 days was used to measure long-lived radionuclides. After irradiation the samples were re-packed and measured twice, first after 4-5 days for 40-50 minutes to determine As, Br, K, La, Na, Mo, Sm, U, and W and after 20 days for 2.5-3 hours to determine Ba, Ce, Co, Cr, Cs, Fe, Hf, Ni, Rb, Sb, Sc, Sr, Ta, Tb, Th, Yb, and Zn. The processing of the data and determination of the content of elements were performed using certified reference materials and flux comparators with the help of the software developed in FLNP, JINR [11]. To determine Cd, Cu and Pb in moss samples flame atomic absorption spectrometry technique was used.

The characteristic deposition patterns of Cu and several others associated non-ferrous metals (Zn, As, Se, Mo, Ag, Cd, In, Sb, and Au) were recognized in the both surveys. These elements show high levels at a limited number of sites surrounding the town of Bor, center of copper basin and low levels almost everywhere else, as indicated in the case of Cu in Fig. 1. Iron and several associated elements as Sc, Cr, Co, as well as rare earth elements show similar deposition patterns in both surveys. These elements are all typical of crustal material, and partly reflects contamination of moss samples with soil particles. However, the high levels of these elements predominantly in the highland near the border where Romanian ferrous industry is located indicate that industrial activities may be a more important source.

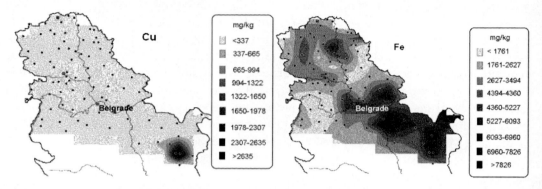

Figure 1. Distribution maps of Cu and Fe in moss samples measured in 2000 survey.

Results of the 2005 survey confirmed that Serbia is characterized with the relative high median for several elements: Cu, Mo, Fe, Cs, As and V. Increase of As and Cl in highly populated region of Belgrade was noticed in 2005 survey. Elevated values in Belgrade region are probably evidence of the chemical industry activities. Good correlation between Ni and V observed in the 2005 survey indicates oil industry. Distribution maps of Ni and As are presented at Fig. 2. Several characteristic statistical values are given in Tab. 1. Some elements, as Cl for example have general lover values in 2005 than in 2000 survey, but the mean value is almost same. Elements characteristic for oil burning processes, as Ni and V in 2000 survey have higher values than the values registered in 2005 survey. Some elements, as Br showed opposite trend. Several elements, as As and other Cu associated elements have much higher maximal values in the first survey than in the second one.

**Table 1. Some characteristic statistical values.**

|       | Cl 2000 | 2005 | Ni 2000 | 2005 | As 2000 | 2005 | Br 2000 | 2005 |
|-------|------|------|------|------|------|------|------|------|
| min   | 131  | 56   | 2.1  | 0.9  | 0.46 | 0.41 | 1.83 | 2.3  |
| max   | 1030 | 793  | 25.7 | 12.2 | 60.8 | 13.7 | 17.6 | 15.9 |
| mean  | 269  | 269  | 6.9  | 4.6  | 3.1  | 2.1  | 5.9  | 6.3  |
| med.  | 235  | 251  | 5.6  | 3.8  | 1.39 | 1.54 | 5.5  | 5.8  |

The comparison of 2000 and 2005 survey results shows significant changes in the depositional pattern of several oil burning elements. Ratios of values measured in the first and the second survey were calculated for all elements. Couple distribution maps of 2000/2005 ratio, presented at Fig. 3 indicate regions with significantly higher emission and deposition of several elements in period before first survey. It can be seen that in the Novi Sad area (signed by arrow) concentrations of characteristic oil burning elements was 3 times higher in the first 2000 survey. It is probably the result of large fires in oil refinery located near Novi Sad town in the 1999 NATO aggression.

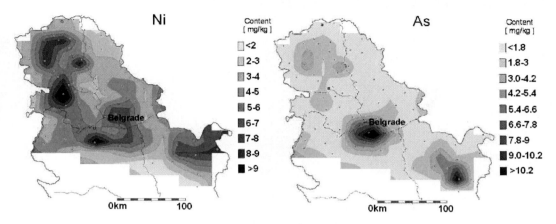

Figure 2. Depositional pattern of Ni and Se measured by the use of moss technique 2005 survey.

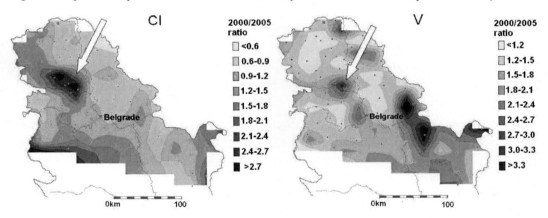

Figure 3. Spatial distribution of calculated 2000/2005 ratio values for Cl and V.

The very first moss-based study concerning uniformity of airborne radionuclide atmospheric deposition was carried out in autumn 2005. Samples of *Hypnum cupressiforme* were collected from 19 sampling sites distributed along the one direction, starting from the northern Serbian province of Voyvodina to the southern border of the Republic Serbia. The altitude smoothly increases from north to south across the sampling line from 80 to 350 m. All samples of fresh plant material were collected in a short time interval, 26th and 27th October 2005. During two days of sampling there was no rain which avoided the complication that some sample could have been exposed to additional precipitation and extra component of airborne radionuclides by washing of the atmosphere. Gamma spectroscopy measurements of moss samples were carried out using high resolution HPGe detector. Experimental details were briefly described in reference [8]. The lowest measured value of $^7$Be activity per unit mass of dry plant material was 195(24) Bq kg$^{-1}$ and the highest one was 560(40) Bq kg$^{-1}$. The spatial distribution of $^7$Be in moss is presented in Fig. 1. Samples taken from two close locations typically have similar values of $^7$Be, within the frame of statistical error, but between distant locations non-uniformity is seen. For example, samples 9-12 taken from a 100-km-long region have significantly lower amounts of $^7$Be than the neighboring samples 6-8 and sample 13. Prominent nonuniformity of $^{137}$Cs concentrations in moss samples was observed too, as can be seen at Fig. 4.

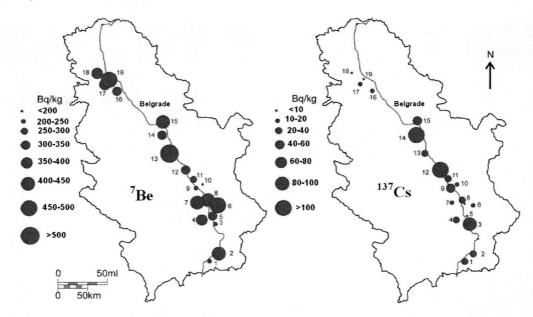

Figure 4. Spatial distribution of $^7$Be and $^{137}$Cs activity measured in mosses.

Second systematic measurement of radionuclides activity in moss samples was taken out to establish temporal variation of $^7$Be, $^{137}$Cs and $^{210}$Pb in mosses collected at same sapling place. Mosses sampling (*Hypnum cupressiforme* only) was made from January 2007 to March 2008 on weekly bases. Entrance roof of the Department of Biology (more than 300 m$^2$), cowered by the thick carpet of natural grooving mosses was sampling place. On the 3.5 m height, roof is directly exposed to the precipitations and mosses had no direct contact with the soil. Experimental details were presented in reference [8]. The daily amount of precipitation and duration of precipitation were taken from the nearest meteorological station Rimski Šančevi, that is in the network of meteorological stations of Hydro-meteorological Institute of the Republic of Serbia.

Average values (simple arithmetic mean of 4 or 5 samples taken in one month) were calculated for all 14 months. Obtained results for $^7$Be and $^{210}$Pb are presented on Fig. 5. It can be seen that $^7$Be activity concentration after almost constant value (about 250 Bq kg$^{-1}$) in first four months of 2007-th year shows increase that begins from the end of spring season. At the beginning of the August 2007 maximal value of 700 Bq kg$^{-1}$ was measured. Observable decreasing trend begins in November. Relatively low values, about 300 Bq kg$^{-1}$ were measured in January and February 2008. At the same time, activity concentration of $^{210}$Pb does not fluctuate significantly. The maximal deviation from the average value of 530 Bq kg$^{-1}$ is about 11%. Values of $^{137}$Cs activity concentrations in moss samples vary from 2.1 Bq kg$^{-1}$ to 19.9 Bq kg$^{-1}$. There is no periodicity or some seasonal variability of $^{137}$Cs concentration.

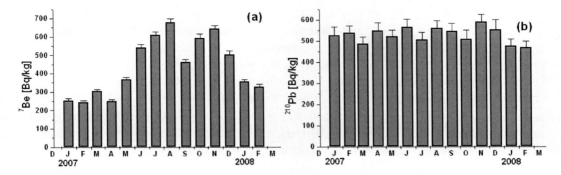

Figure 5. The average monthly data of $^7$Be and $^{210}$Pb activity in moss samples.

Cumulative curve of $^{210}$Pb activity concentration as a function of time is straight line, as can be expected because the activity concentration of $^{210}$Pb is almost constant. Fig. 6 presents the cumulative values of $^7$Be/$^{210}$Pb activity ratio. Three different segments having evidently different slope can be seen. The slope changes in May and December, corresponding to changes of $^7$Be activity concentration ratio presented on Fig. 6.

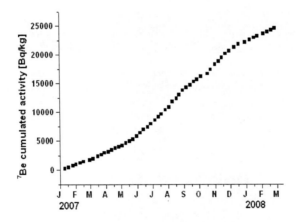

Figure 6. Time dependence of $^7$Be/$^{210}$Pb cumulated activity concentration ratio

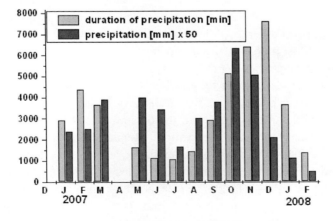

Figure 7. Monthly values of precipitation and duration of precipitation.

The dependence of cumulative activity concentrations on cumulative precipitation and cumulative duration of precipitation have never been analyzed before. Fig. 7 shows integral month amounts of precipitation and duration of precipitation. Measured values of precipitation (in [mm]) were multiplied by factor 50 to fit the graph. The lowest amount of rain and duration of precipitation was in summer season. It is interesting to see that in April 2007 was no precipitation at all. Cumulative $^7$Be and $^{210}$Pb activity concentrations as a function of cumulated precipitation are shown at Fig. 8. The points in the Fig. 8 are grouped in clusters depending on precipitation. Dry deposition aligns points in vertical direction and abundant precipitation tends to decrease the slope of the $^7$Be vs. precipitation line. Dependence of cumulative $^{210}$Pb activity concentrations shows identical behavior, as can be seen on the Fig. 8.

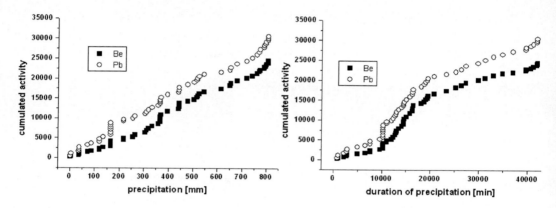

Figure 8. Cumulated activity concentrations of $^7$Be and $^{210}$Pb as a functions of cumulative values of precipitation and cumulative values of duration of precipitation.

# 3. DISCUSSION OF THE RESULTS

Deposition patterns for studied elements show different pollution sources and source categories. An exceptionally clear-cut industrial component, with the very high loadings for Cu, Zn, As, Se, Mo, Ag, Cd, In, Sb, and Au was recognized in both surveys. The main reason for the high pollution in this area is the non-ferrous metal industry in the «Copper Basin» near the Romanian/Bulgarian border. High loadings for Sc, Cr, Fe, Hf, Ta, and they were detected in the both surveys. Most probably, this component reflects (at least in part) contamination of moss samples with soil particles. Vanadium and nickel are normally found in relatively high concentrations in the crude oil, and these elements are, therefore, often used as markers of fuel oil combustion in air pollution studies. Relatively high values of V and Ni measured in 2000 survey at sampling sites not far from the oil industries damaged by the NATO bombs indicated elevated emission and deposition. Repeated measurements in 2005 show significantly lower values of Ni and V at locations near destroyed oil refineries.

The spatial distribution of $^7$Be in moss samples is non-uniform. Difference between minimal and maximal values (factor 2.5) cannot be explained by local variation in $^7$Be production. It can be the result of different atmospheric depositional paths. A non-uniform spatial distribution and higher concentrations of $^{137}$Cs measured in our samples are probably a result of random re-suspension and re-deposition of cesium emitted from Chernobyl accident or a prior aboveground weapons testing.

Seasonal data for $^7$Be deposition fluxes measured by number of authors show a high variability depending on location, local climate, precipitation etc. [11]. The highest deposition fluxes of $^7$Be occurring in the spring and lowest in winter and the late-summer maximum of the $^7$Be activity concentration in air affected by vertical transport from upper troposphere levels into the lower ones during the warm season were reported [12,13,14]. Similar result was obtained in study of wet depositional fluxes in Switzerland [15] where the highest mean concentrations of $^7$Be in precipitation appeared in June, July and August. Mean summer air activity of $^7$Be in air was two times higher than winter one [12,15]. Mean seasonal values of $^7$Be activity concentration measured in our study varied by a factor 2 during the year. At the same time, activity concentration of $^{210}$Pb does not fluctuate significantly. It is shown [8] that different lifetime of $^7$Be and $^{210}$Pb cause very different level of saturation activities. Relatively short half-life of $^7$Be sets saturation activity to the level of about 11 weekly yields. In this simplified approach activity of long living $^{210}$Pb can be accumulated until reach more than 1600 weekly yields. Regarding that green part of moss contains 3–4 annual growth segments; it is very realistic to expect that activity of $^{210}$Pb in mosses can reach activity 130 times higher than average weekly contribution. Even the large variations of depositional fluxes of $^{210}$Pb can not influence significantly level activity of $^{210}$Pb cumulated in mosses during couple years.

It is very interesting to notice that some overall slope of the cumulative $^{210}$Pb or $^7$Be activity concentrations as a function of cumulated precipitation show relatively constant value. Local variations of slope, ranging from vertical to the almost horizontal do not affect seriously general trend of lines presented in Fig. 8. Dependence of the cumulative $^{210}$Pb or $^7$Be activity concentrations do not show apparent segments having different slopes as time dependence of $^7$Be/$^{210}$Pb ratio presented on Fig. 6 do. However, graph presenting cumulated airborne radionuclide activity as a function of cumulated precipitation duration shows three apparent regions having different slope. The first change of the slope occurs at the beginning of May 2007 after long dry period. Increase of the slope corresponds to higher (or constant for $^{210}$Pb) radioisotope deposition in the period of shorter precipitation duration. Another change of slope begins in the middle of November. In this part of graph large value of cumulate duration of precipitation is not followed by proportional increase in cumulated activity concentrations.

# 4. CONCLUSION

From the results obtained in two surveys, it can be concluded that atmospheric deposition of heavy metals is a considerable problem in Serbia even at the current level of industrial activity. The most obvious problems are present in the Bor region, where the maximum deposition levels are observed for elements associated with the extraction of sulfide ores there, and for most elements that are representative of the general composition of the Earth's crust. Some trends possibly associated with the NATO aggression in the spring of 1999 seem to be distinguishable from the data for V and Ni. Comparison of 2000 and 2005 measurements showed significant difference in the oil burning tracer elements deposition in the region of oil refineries.

Mosses could be a good sampling medium for the detection of $^7$Be and other airborne radionuclides accumulated through some period. Moss sampling is a relative simple and inexpensive procedure, and a very dense network of sampling sites can be established to provide excellent spatial resolution. Mosses can be found in broad regions in several climatic zones, so large areas can be covered. The final result can be a detailed spatial distribution of the integral amount of $^7$Be and other airborne radionuclides deposited over the chosen area during some period. The seasonal $^7$Be and other isotope deposition can be achieved by repeating the described measurements. Mapping of $^7$Be activity distribution in moss samples finally can provide information about some regularity of atmospheric deposition over some large area. Preliminary results showed noticeable nonuniformity in $^7$Be content in moss samples taken in 400 km long region.

The relative amplitude of the seasonal pattern of measured $^7$Be activity concentration in mosses is very similar to the relative amplitude of seasonal pattern of $^7$Be air activity or depositional fluxes. It means that mosses can offer results comparable to air sampling or depositional measurements. In potential use of $^7$Be moss activity for mapping of atmospheric deposition over large area, it can be expected that mean values of $^7$Be activity can be about factor 2 higher in summer than in winter season. There are no seasonal variations of accumulated $^{210}$Pb activity concentration in mosses thus potential nonuniformity in $^{210}$Pb distribution can be consequence of diverse deposition only.

Moss technique is already established and widely used in examination of atmospheric transport and deposition of heavy metals and trace elements. Preliminary results of our studies showed that mosses have good potential in examination of atmospheric processes using airborne radionuclides as tracers.

# REFERENCES

[1]  Å. Rühling and G. Tyler, *Botaniska Notiser*, 122, 321-342 (1968).

[2]  Å. Rühling and G. Tyler, *Air and Soil Pollution*, 2, 445–455 (1973).

[3]  *European Atlas: Spatial and temporal trends in heavy metal accumulation in mosses in Europe* (1990-2005), UNECE ICP Vegetation. Edited by H.Harmens, D. Norris, Centre for Ecology & Hydrology, University of Wales Bangor, UK 2008

[4]  M. V. Frontasyeva, T. Ye. Galinskaya, M. Krmar, M. Matavuly, S. S. Pavlov, E. A. Povtoreyko, D. Radnovic, E. Steinnes, *J. Radioanal. Nucl. Chem.*, 259, 141-147 (2004)

[5]  M. Aničić, M.V. Frontasyeva, M. Tomasević, A. Popović, *Environ. Monitor Assess.*, 129, 207-219 (2006)

[6]  S.R. Daish, A.A. Dale, C.J. Dale, R. May, J.E. Rowe, *J. Environ. Radioact.*, 84, 457-467 (2005).

[7]  F. Cannizzaro, G. Greco, M. Raneli, M.C. Spitale, E. Tomarchio, *J. Environ. Radioact.*, 72, 259-271 (2004).

[8]  M. Krmar, D. Radnović, S. Rakić and M. Matavuly, *J. Environ. Radioact.*, 93, 53-61 (2007).

[9] M. Krmar, D. Radnović, D.T. Mihailović, B. Lalić. J. Slivka and I. Bikit, *Appl. Radiat. Isot.*, 67, 1139-1147 (2009).

[10] Å. Rühling and E. Steinnes (Eds), *Atmospheric Heavy Metal Deposition in Europe* 1995-1996. Report Nord 1998:15, Nordic Council of Ministers, Copenhagen, 1998.

[11] M.V. Frontasyeva, S.S. Pavlov, *JINR Preprint*, E14-2000-177, Dubna, (2000).

[12] Kulan, A. Aldahan, G. Possnert, I. Vintersved, *Atmospheric Environment*, 40, 3855–3868 (2006).

[13] Ioannidou, M. Manolopoulou, C. Papastefanou, *Appl. Radiat. Isot.*, 63, 277–284 (2005).

[14] E. Gerasopoulos, C.S. Zerefos, C. Papastefanou, P. Zanis, K. O'Brien, *Atmosph. Environ.*, 37, 1745–1756 (2003).

[15] S. Caillet, P. Arpagaus, F. Monna, J. Dominik, *J. Environ. Radioact*, 53, 241–256 (2001).

In: Advances in Environmental Modeling and Measurements      ISBN: 978-1-60876-599-7
Editors: D. T. Mihailović, B. Lalić, pp. 159-170      © 2010 Nova Science Publishers, Inc.

*Chapter 15*

# CONCENTRATION GRADIENT MEASUREMENTS AND FLUX CALCULATION OF ATMOSPHERIC AMMONIA OVER GRASSLAND (BUGAC-PUSZTA, HUNGARY)

*T. Weidinger[*1], A. Pogány[2], L. Horváth[3], A. Machon[1,4], Z. Bozóki[5], Á. Mohácsi[5], K. Pintér[4], Z. Nagy[4], A.Z. Gyöngyösi[1], Z. Istenes[1] and Á. Bordás[1]*

[1]Eötvös Loránd University, Budapest, Hungary
[2]University of Szeged, Szeged, Hungary
[3]Hungarian Meteorological Service, Budapest, Hungary
[4]Szent István University, Gödöllő, Hungary
[5]Hungarian Academy of Sciences, Szeged, Hungary

## ABSTRACT

Ammonia flux has been monitored continuously since July 2008 over semi-natural grassland at the Hungarian NitroEurope site '*Bugac-puszta*'on the Great Hungarian Plain. Results presented here are based on the data obtained from July to September, i.e., during the vegetation period. The instrument used for ammonia concentration gradient measurement was a novel diode laser based photoacoustic device combined with preconcentration sampling (WaSul-Flux), developed at the University of Szeged. Ammonia concentration measurements were performed at three different levels (0.5 m, 1.3 m and 3 m), on a cc. 30-minute accumulation interval. The three inlets were moved automatically to the same level (1.3 m) twice a week by a remote controlled automated system to check the precision of the measurement.

The turbulent flux of ammonia was calculated using the similarity theory based on eddy covariance data of momentum, heat, water vapor and carbon dioxide fluxes (provided by a CSAT3 sonic anemometer and a LICOR-7500 open path $CO_2/H_2O$ sensor), in view of the friction velocity ($u_*$) and the Monin-Obukhov length scale ($L$). Sensitivity analyseis of ammonia flux calculation as (i) calculation of ammonia gradient,

* Corresponding author: E-mail address: weidi@ludens.elte.hu, Phone: +36 1 3722500/ext. 6612, Fax: +36 1 3722904

(ii) choice of universal function and (iii) application of different gradient and profile techniques, have been investigated.

The diurnal variation of the ammonia concentration and flux has also been investigated. During the studied period the net daytime emission and nocturnal deposition were observed with large deviation exceeding the average flux values both during day and night.

The daily mean ammonia concentrations were compared to data measured at the Hungarian background air quality monitoring station (K-puszta) ~20 km far from the Bugac-puszta site, and fairly good agreement was found between the two datasets.

# 1. INTRODUCTION

The NitroEurope EU Framework 6th Integrated Project aims at a detailed investigation of the biosphere-atmosphere exchange of different nitrogen (N) compounds. The objectives of this international project are (i) to establish robust datasets of N fluxes and net greenhouse-gas exchange (NGE) as a basis to investigate interactions and assess long-term change, (ii) to quantify the effects of past and present global changes (climate, atmospheric composition, land-use/land-management) on C-N cycling and NGE, (iii) to simulate the observed fluxes through refinement of plot-scale models, and (iv) to scale up N and NGE fluxes for terrestrial ecosystems to regional and European levels [1-3]. One of the measurement stations of the NitroEurope network has been established in Central Hungary (*Bugac-puszta*). Four Hungarian institutes are involved in the project: the Forest Research Institute (with an observing system of N fluxes and pools), the Photoacoustic Research Group at the University of Szeged (with the development of photoacoustic ammonia monitoring instruments), the Institute of Botany and Ecophysiology at Szent István University (with a network of manipulation experiments and micrometeorological measurements) and the Department of Meteorology at Eötvös Loránd University (with an observing system of N fluxes and pools, micrometeorology and flux calculations).

The N balance of terrestrial ecosystems is mainly determined by surface-atmosphere exchange processes. This exchange is bi-directional: wet and dry deposition from the atmosphere is a major N input to ecosystems (especially in case of non-treated sites without fertilizer or manure application), while at the same time a significant amount of N compounds is emitted by the biosphere. The net flux is the sum of deposition and emission. Ammonia is emitted mainly by plants through the stomata, while other nitrogen compounds (NO, $N_2O$ and $N_2$) are emitted dominantly by the soil. Soil emission of ammonia can only be observed above alkaline soil (pH > 7).

The timescale of these exchange processes ranges from some hours to several years. To understand the small timescale processes (e.g., plant physiology) on-line ammonia flux measurements (with high time resolution and accuracy) are needed instead of long-term, time averaged flux calculations.

The aim of this chapter is to present the research and technological development to estimate net $NH_3$ flux between the atmosphere and a grassland surface in Central Hungary (*Bugac-puszta*) using a novel method (the combination of diode laser based photoacoustic spectroscopy and preconcentration sampling).

## 2. MEASUREMENT SITE AND INSTRUMENTATION, DATASET AND QUALITY CONTROL

The *Bugac-puszta* site is located on semi natural, semi arid, sandy grassland in the Kiskunság National Park (46°41′ N, 19°36′ E) in the Great Hungarian Plain. The dominant plant species are *Festuca pseudovina*, *Carex stenophylla*, *Salvia pratensis* and *Cynodon dactylon*. The flora is sensitive to external effects, but Hungarian Grey Cattle (*Bos p. hungaricus*) has been grazing for centuries in equilibrium with the grass ecosystem (0.5–0.8 cattle ha$^{-1}$ in the periods of investigation). The landscape is flat, the average altitude is 110 m AMSL. The soil is a Chernozem-like sandy soil (with a mean composition of sand : silt : clay at a ratio of 87 : 8 : 5, in the upper 30 cm layer of the soil). The climate is continental: the annual mean temperature is 10.5 °C and the average precipitation is about 530 mm year$^{-1}$ [4]. Ammonia flux has been monitored continuously since July 2008, while the measurement of basic micrometeorological parameters, radiation, energy budget components and $CO_2$, $N_2O$ fluxes started in 2002 (EU 5[th] Greengrass program) [5]. Determination of nitrogen fluxes and estimation of N balance has been performed since 2006 (EU 6th NitroEurope program, Fig. 1). Continuous NO, $NO_x$ and $O_3$ profile measurements and chamber measurements of NO, $N_2O$, $CH_4$ have also been carried out [6].

The bi-directional flux of $NH_3$ between the atmosphere and the biosphere (including soil emission) has been determined using the photoacoustic method. The photoacoustic effect is based on the absorption of modulated laser light in a photoacoustic cell, which creates an acoustic wave through non-radiative relaxation of the excited molecules. The amplitude of the acoustic wave, which is sampled with a sensitive microphone, is proportional to the concentration of the absorbing component [7-9].

Advantages of this system include: (i) linear response over more than four orders of magnitude, high selectivity (i.e., insensitivity to the presence of other components), relatively short response time (15–45 minutes), high sensitivity (detection limit below 1 ppb) and accuracy in the few percentage range, (ii) simple construction and capability of long-term automatic operation. The performance of the instrument proves that is has a potential to become an alternative of currently used ammonia flux monitoring instruments [10-12].

Ammonia measurements have been performed at three different heights (0.5 m, 1.3 m and 3 m) above canopy level, with a cc. half hour averaging interval. The inlets are moved automatically to the same height twice a week for cross-calibration, and concentration values measured at different heights are corrected according to the results of cross-calibration. The uncertainty of concentration measurement may cause significant uncertainty in flux calculation only in case of low concentrations or concentration gradients. The turbulent flux of ammonia is calculated using the similarity theory based on eddy covariance fluxes of momentum, heat, water vapor and carbon dioxide (measured by a CSAT3 sonic anemometer and LICOR-7500 open path $CO_2/H_2O$ sensor).

Flux calculation and quality control was performed using the methods of the EU 6th CarboEurope program [5, 13], which means omitting data during nocturnal highly stable conditions, during fog or dew formation and during instationarity.

The friction velocity ($u_*$) and the Monin-Obukhov length scale ($L$) were determined from half hourly momentum ($\tau$) and sensible heat flux ($H$) data.

Figure 1. The Bugac-puszta station in the Great Hungarian Plain with the eddy covariance measurement system (CSAT-3 sonic anemometer and LICOR-7500 open path $CO_2/H_2O$ sensor), inlets for NO, $NO_x$, $O_3$ profile measurements, radiation (global, reflected, net, PAR) measurement pole (in background) and dynamic chambers for NO flux calculation (in foreground).

In cases when momentum and sensible heat flux data were not available (due to the measurement error of the latent heat or $CO_2$ flux) for a certain half hour period, they were calculated using regression relationships from raw fluxes, available energy ($A = Rn - G$) and measured wind speed data. The Schotanus correction [14, 15] was performed in all cases for the correction of raw sensible heat fluxes. The friction velocity ($u_*$) was estimated from the measured wind speed.

## 3. AMMONIA FLUX CALCULATION

The ammonia flux was calculated on the base of the similarity theory using the profile method. Based on model calculations, the general form of the universal functions [11, 16] has been chosen in our study and according to Ref. [17] a constant value has been considered in case of highly stable conditions. Several publication report ammonia flux calculations performed with the application of different universal functions [18]. The results are highly similar, which means that the uncertainty of flux calculation is determined mainly by the uncertainty of gradient measurements [19].

Let us consider the main steps of the flux calculation. The turbulent fluxes (covariance) for momentum ($\tau$), sensible heat ($H$) and ammonia ($F_c$), respectively, are described by the following equations:

$$\tau = -\rho_m \overline{w'u'} = \rho_m u_*^2 , \quad H = c_{pm}\rho_m \overline{w'T'} = -c_{pm}\rho_m u_* T_* , \quad F_c = \overline{w'c'} = -u_* c_* , \tag{1}$$

where $\rho_m$ is the density of moist air, $c_{pm}$ is the specific heat capacity of moist air at constant pressure, $T'$, $c'$, $u'$ and $w'$ are fluctuations of temperature, concentration, horizontal wind speed and vertical wind speed, respectively, $u_*$, $T_*$, and $c_*$ denote the friction velocity, the dynamic temperature and dynamic concentration, respectively. The similarity theory provides a flux-profile relationship for the ammonia concentration profile:

$$\frac{\partial c}{\partial z} = \frac{c_*}{\kappa z}\varphi_{Fc}(\zeta), \tag{2}$$

where $\zeta = z/L$ is the non-dimensional stability parameter, $\varphi_{Fc}(\zeta)$ represents the universal function for ammonia flux and $z$ denotes the vertical coordinate. The Monin-Obukhov length scale ($L$) was determined as:

$$L = -\frac{(\tau/\rho_m)^{3/2}}{\kappa\beta(H/c_{pm}\rho_m)} = \frac{u_*^2}{\kappa\beta T_*}, \tag{3}$$

where $\kappa$ is the von Kármán constant, $\beta = g/T$ is the stability parameter and $g$ is the acceleration due to gravity. The process of trace gas (or moisture) transport is similar to the transport of sensible heat, which means that $c_*$ is a passive characteristic of the turbulent motion ($\varphi_H(\zeta) = \varphi_{Fc}(\zeta)$).

The value of the universal function during neutral stratification ($\zeta \approx 0$) is 1 and a logarithmic profile approximation can be used. During stable cases ($\zeta > 0$) the log-linear profile approximation is applied, while during highly stable stratification ($\zeta \geq 1.5$) constant values are used:

$$\varphi_{F_c}(\zeta) = \varphi_H(\zeta) = 1 + 5\zeta, \ \zeta \leq 1.5,$$
$$\varphi_{F_c}(\zeta) = \varphi_H(\zeta) = 7.5, \quad \zeta \geq 1.5. \tag{4}$$

In unstable cases ($\zeta < 0$) the power law approximation is used:

$$\varphi_{F_c}(\zeta) = \varphi_H(\zeta) = (1 - 16\zeta)^{-1/2}. \tag{5}$$

The ammonia concentration profile is calculated with the integration of equation (2) as:

$$c(z_i) - c(z_j) = \frac{c_{*(i,j)}}{\kappa}[\ln(z_i/z_j) + \Psi_{F_c}(\zeta_i) - \Psi_{F_c}(\zeta_j)], \tag{6}$$

where $z_i > z_j$ ($i, j = 1, 2, 3$) are the measurement heights above canopy level.

$$\Psi_{F_c}(\zeta_i) = \int(\varphi_{F_c}(\zeta) - 1)d\ln\zeta, \tag{7}$$

is the integral form of the universal function [17, 20]. The lower boundary of the constant flux layer model is the roughness length height ($z_0$) with the assumption of zero wind speed at that level. The dynamic concentration ($c_*$) has been calculated from concentration differences between the sub-layers (8) with the least-square method as:

$$\min\left(\sum_{\substack{i,j \\ i>j}}\left((c(z_i) - c(z_j)) - \frac{c_*}{\kappa}[\ln(z_i/z_j) + \Psi_{F_c}(\zeta_i) - \Psi_{F_c}(\zeta_j)]\right)^2\right)^{\frac{1}{2}}. \tag{8}$$

Those cases were accepted when the (8) square errors of the differences in the measured and calculated concentrations did not exceed 0.75 ppb in all sub-layers.

## 4. RESULTS AND DISCUSSIONS

Results of ammonia gradient measurements between 2[st] July and 5th October 2008 are summarized in this chapter. 1160 measurements have been made during 96 days, covering about 25% of the studied period and 30% of these data were filtered out during the quality control procedure.

Let us consider the daily mean concentration values first. They have been compared to the continental background air quality monitoring station at K-puszta (~20 km away from Bugac-puszta), where the so-called "three stage filter pack method" (applied in the EMEP network) was used for daily sampling of air, and the samples were analyzed spectrophotometrically (using the indophenol-blue method for ammonia). One of the longest ammonia concentration data series in Europe have been recorded at K-puszta [21, 22]. Data series from the two sites are showing relatively good agreement ($r = 0.38$). Higher concentration at *Bugac-puszta* site may be due to the effect of a farm nearby performing extensive breeding of grey cattle (Fig. 2).

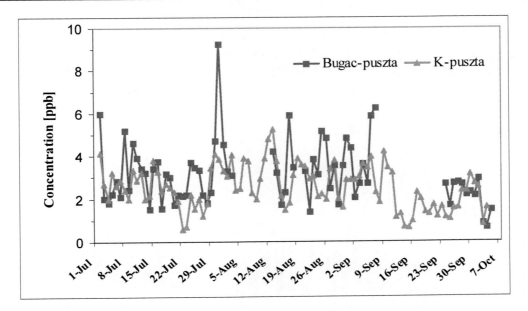

Figure 2. Comparisons of daily mean ammonia concentration data measured using photoacoustic (Bugac-puszta) and filter pack – spectrophotometry (K-puszta) methods at the two measurement sites for a 96-day period (between 2$^{st}$ July and 5$^{th}$ October 2008).

The results for July 2008 are shown below. Half hourly data of the friction velocity ($u_*$) and the sensible heat flux ($H$) are presented in Fig. 3. Flux calculation and quality control methodology (also used in the EU 6$^{th}$ CarboEurope program) have been applied [5, 13] as described in the previous section, while in about 20% of the period (especially during nighttime) gap filling was necessary to fill out missing or inappropriate data using raw fluxes, wind measurement and available energy data. There is a strong correlation ($r = 0.89$) between wind speed ($u$) and friction velocity ($u_*$). The latter is about the tenth (0.08) of wind speed measured at a height of 4 m. According to the daily variations of wind speed, higher values are obtained during the day and lower during the night. This effect has been amplified by strong nocturnal stability – weak mechanical turbulence. The hot dry days at the beginning of July are clearly visible in the course of the sensible heat flux (maximum values exceeding 250 W m$^{-2}$) together with the cloudy, humid days with low maxima.

Half hourly concentration values measured at each level and ammonia flux calculated using the similarity theory are depicted in Fig. 4. The typical daily variation of ammonia concentration is demonstrated: higher values were observed during the day and lower values during nighttime. High concentration episodes showing the effect of advection (e.g. the effect of grazing in the vicinity of the station or the effect of the farm) are also remarkable. During daytime, the measured concentration was decreasing with height (emission) and inverse profile (deposition) is typical during the night, showing the influences of the stomata. The calculated fluxes were higher during the first, warmer and drier period, while they were lower during the second, cooler and more humid period. The overall ammonia flux was positive: total emission exceeds total deposition. Similar results were obtained from recent measurements at Hortobágy (the largest „puszta" or grassland in the Great Hungarian Plain) for the summer months [12].

We note that the simplest model for the estimation of ammonia deposition uses average deposition velocities. The standard value used for estimating ammonia fluxes above Hungarian grass canopy is 0.3 cm s$^{-1}$ [23], and is positive, which would result in deposition instead of emission. This deviation of the theory from the measurement is significant, and is most probably caused by an elevated emission of ammonia at the studied site due to the nearby cattle farm.

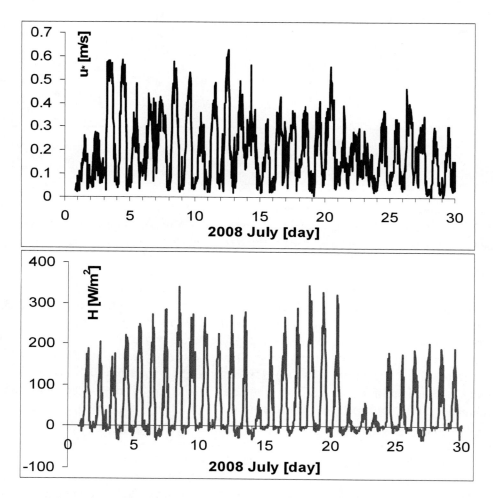

Figure 3. Half hourly values of dynamic velocity ($u*$) and sensible heat flux ($H$) at *Bugac-puszta* in July, 2008.

The average diurnal variation of the ammonia flux during the whole campaign (from 1$^{st}$ July to 4$^{th}$ October 2008, which is the second half of the vegetative period) has also been calculated. Results are presented in Fig. 5. Since each half hour consists of 10 to 25 data that represent less than 20% of the total period, therefore the presented results are only rough estimates. Like in July, ammonia is emitted during the day and deposited during the night, however, the absolute values of the fluxes are relatively small. Large spreads are showing big uncertainty of the estimates: the values of the spreads are exceeding the averages of fluxes both during day and night.

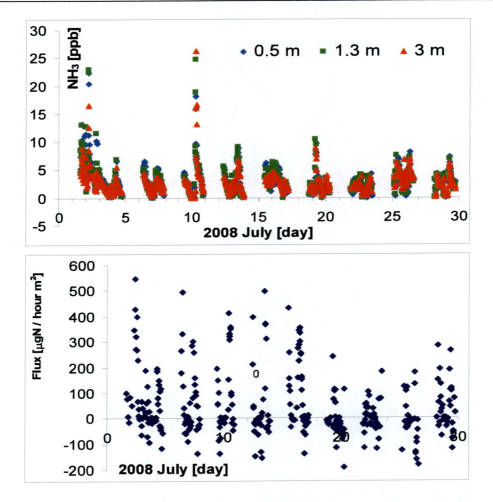

Figure. 4. Measured ammonia concentration (top) at three levels (0.5 m, 1.3 m, 3 m) and the calculated fluxes (bottom) – *Bugac-puszta* in July, 2008.

The mechanism of the biosphere-atmosphere exchange of ammonia is described by the canopy compensation point model [11]. The canopy compensation point concentration, (i.e., the atmospheric concentration of ammonia above which deposition and under which emission occurs) is determined by a couple of the cuticular and stomatal features [12]. The N content of plant tissues is strongly dependent on the N content of the soil. Elevated N content in the soil enhances N uptake by the roots, which induces higher compensation point, as a result of which emission is preferred. Alkaline intracellular pH is also favorable for emission. During nighttime, when the stomata are closed, deposition dominates (see in Fig. 5). During daytime, ammonia emission can occur, especially in the vegetation period (as it was observed using this study), however, over semi-natural grasslands net deposition is expected for a whole year [23].

Generally, yearly ammonia deposition is dominating on fields where there is no grazing or fertilization, while ammonia emission is observed in N loaded areas. Daily ammonia flux depends on soil conditions (available inorganic N), canopy compensation point concentration [12] and the studied period (vegetation or dormant season).

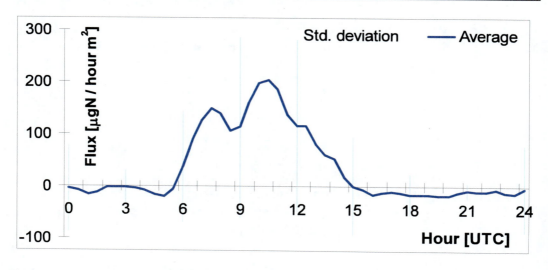

Figure 5. Average daily course of the ammonia flux during the measured period at Bugac-puszta site for a 96-day period (between 1st July and 4th October 2008).


## 5. CONCLUSION

Ammonia concentration and flux measurements play the key role in the better understanding of the N-cycle and for the optimization of agricultural technologies. A micrometeorological measurement setup has been developed for continuous or campaign measurements of ammonia concentration gradient.

The recently developed photoacoustic ammonia gradient monitoring instrument is suitable for continuous monitoring of the bi-directional flux of ammonia. However, at low concentrations and advective situations, the assessment of the concentration gradient is problematic. During the application of our quality control procedure, 30% of the profile measurements had to be filtered out.

During the studied three months overall net ammonia emission has been observed, which implies the reconsideration of ammonia deposition estimates, based on a mean annual positive deposition velocity (+0.3 cm s$^{-1}$). The assessment of the ammonia budget, its spatial extrapolation, and the determination of the accuracy of the newly developed ammonia flux measuring system are the challenges for the near future.


## ACKNOWLEDGMENTS

This work has been supported by the NitroEurope Framework EU 6th IP and the GVOP 6-028-2005 project. The authors are grateful to the Kiskunság National Park for giving the opportunity to perform the measurements in the area of the park.

# REFERENCES

[1]   *http://www.nitroeurope.eu*

[2]   M.A. Sutton, E. Nemitz, J.W. Erisman, C. Beier, K. Butterbach Bahl, P. Cellier, W. de Vries, F. Cotrufo, U. Skiba, C. Di Marco, S. Jones, P. Laville, J.F. Soussana, B. Loubet, M. Twigg, D. Famulari, J. Whitehead, M.W. Gallagher, A. Neftel, C.R. Flechard, B. Herrmann, P.L. Calanca, J.K. Schjoerring, U. Daemmgen, L. Horvath, Y.S. Tang, B.A. Emmett, A. Tietema, J. Peñuelas, M. Kesik, N. Brueggemann, K. Pilegaard, T. Vesala, C.L. Campbell, J.E. Olesen, U. Dragosits, M.R. Theobald, P. Levy, DS.C. Mobbs, R. Milne, N. Viovy, N. Vuichard, J.U. Smith, P. Smith, P. Bergamaschi, D. Fowler and S. Reis, *Environ. Pollut.* 150, 1, 125–139 (2007).

[3]   *Annual European Community greenhouse gas inventory 1990-2007 and inventory report* 2009. Submission to the UNFCCC Secretariat, 2009, European Environment Agency, EEA Technical report, No 4/2008, ISSN 1725–2237.

[4]   L. Horváth, B. Grosz, A. Machon, J. Balogh, K. Pintér and Sz. Czóbel, *Community Ecology* 9 (Suppl.) 75–80 (2008).

[5]   Z. Nagy, K. Pintér, Sz. Czóbel, J. Balogh, L. Horváth, Sz. Fóti, Z. Barcza, T. Weidinger, Zs. Csintalan, N.Q. Dinh, B. Grosz and Z. Tuba, *Agric. Ecosyst. Environ.* 121, 21–29 (2007).

[6]   T. Weidinger, L. Horváth, A. Machon, K. Pintér, Z. Barcza, A.Z. Gyöngyösi, Z. Nagy and Z. Tuba, 2008: *Uncertainties in the calculation of NO–NO$_x$–O$_3$ fluxes by the gradient and the profile methods,* Open Science Conference Reactive Nitrogen and the European Greenhouse Gas Balance. February 20$^{th}$ & 21$^{st}$, 2008, Het Pand, Ghent, Belgium, Edited By the NitroEurope IP Secretariat, pp. 53–54.

[7]   H. Huszár, A. Pogány, Z. Bozóki, Á. Mohácsi, L. Horváth and G. Szabó, *Sens. Actuators B*, 134, 2, 1027–1033 (2008).

[8]   A. Pogány, Á. Mohácsi, L. Horváth, Z. Bozóki, G. Szabó, 2008: A photoacoustic system for measuring ammonia exchange between the biosphere and atmosphere, *Geophysical Research Abstracts,* 10, EGU2008-A-01665, 2008 SRef-ID: 1607-7962/gra/EGU2008-A-01665.

[9]   A. Pogány, Á. Mohácsi, A. Varga, Z. Bozóki, Z. Galbács, L. Horváth and G. Szabó, *Environ. Sci. Technol.,* 43(3), 826–830 (2009).

[10]  M. Norman, C. Spirig, V. Wolff, I. Trebs, C. Flechard, A. Wisthaler, R. Schnitzhofer, A. Hansel and A. Neftel, *Atmos. Chem. Phys. Discuss.*, 8, 19791–19818 (2008).

[11]  E. Nemitz, C. Milford, M.A. Sutton, *Q. J. R. Meteorol. Soc.* 127, 815–833 (2001).

[12]  L. Horváth, M. Asztalos, E. Führer, R. Mészáros and T. Weidinger, *Agr. Forest Meteorol.* 130, 282–298 (2005).

[13]  M. Mauder, T. Foken, C. Bernhofer, R. Clement, J. Elbers, W. Eugster, T. Grünwald, B. Heusinkveld and O. Kolle, *Biogeosciences*, 5, 451–462 (2008).

[14]  P. Schotanus, F.T.M. Nieuwstadt, H.A.R. de Bruin, *Bound.-Lay. Meteorol.*, 26, 1, 81–93 (1983).

[15]  M. Mauder and T. Foken, 2004: Documentation and Instruction Manual of the Eddy Covariance Software Package TK2. UNIVERSITÄT BAYREUTH Abt. Mikrometeorologie, Arbeitsergebnisse Nr. 26. *http://www.bayceer.uni-bayreuth.de/mm/*

[16]  A.J. Dyer, *Bound.-Lay. Meteorol.*, 7, 363–372 (1974).

[17] T. Foken, *Angewandte Meteorologie*, Springer-Verlag Berlin Heidelberg 2006, pp. 325.

[18] T. Weidinger, J. Pinto and L. Horváth, *Meteorol. Z.*, 9, 3, 139–154 (2000).

[19] T. Weidinger, Á. Bordás, D.T. Mihailovic, A.Z. Gyöngyösi, A. Machon, K. Pintér and L. Horváth, 2007: Uncertainties in surface layer flux calculations using gradient and profile methods, *First Serbian Congress on Theoretical and Applied Mechanics*, Kopaonik, Serbia, April 10-13, 2007. Proceedings, edited by D. Sumarac and D. Kuzmanovic pp. 267–274.

[20] H.N. Lee, *J. Appl. Meteorol.*, 36, 1416–1423 (1997).

[21] L. Horváth and M.A. Sutton, *Atmos. Environ.*, 32, 3, 339–344 (1998).

[22] L. Horváth, H. Fagerdi, and M.A. Suttom, Long-term record (1981-2005) of Ammonia and Ammonium concentrations at K-puszta Hungary and the effect of Sulphur Dioxide emission change on measured and modeled concentrations. *Atmospheric Ammonia* edited by M.S. Sutton, S. Reis and S. Baker, Springer 2008, pp. 181–186.

[23] Machon, L. Horváth, B. Grosz, T. Weidinger, K. Pintér and Z. Tuba, 2008: *Measurtement and modelling of fluxes of nitrogen compounds above a semi-natural grassland ecosystem in Hungary*, Open Science Conference Reactive Nitrogen and the European Greenhouse Gas Balance. February 20th & 21st, 2008, Het Pand, Ghent, Belgium, edited by the NitroEurope IP Secretariat, pp. 65–66.

In: Advances in Environmental Modeling and Measurements    ISBN: 978-1-60876-599-7
Editors: D. T. Mihailović, B. Lalić, pp. 171-180    © 2010 Nova Science Publishers, Inc.

*Chapter 16*

# COMPARISON OF EVAPORIMETERS WITH EVAPOTRANSPIRATION EQUATIONS

*J. Eitzinger*[*,1], *T. Gerersdorfer*[1], *H. Schume*[1], *W. Laube*[1], *F. Holawe*[2], *and T. Orfanus*[3]

[1]University of Natural Resources and Applied Life Sciences, Vienna, Austria
[2]University of Vienna, Vienna, Austria
[3]Institute of Hydrology, Slovak Academy of Sciences, Bratislava, Slovakia

## ABSTRACT

An accurate estimation of evapotranspiration is crucial for many applications in agrometeorology. However, the involvement of many influencing parameters in this complex process of mass flux makes it is difficult to establish a robust method for the estimation of representative values of potential and actual evapotranspiration. Especially, the influence of different spatial and temporal scales applied does not always allow a direct comparison between equations and even measurement methods. The amount of potential evaporation of water is an integrative effect of several meteorological parameters, such as radiation, temperature, air saturation pressure deficit and wind. The amount of evaporating water can be measured, for example, relatively easily by evaporimeters. Evaporimeters are cheap devices and can easily be used by untrained personnel to measure evaporation. In this study the measurements of Bellani plate and Livingston spherical atmometers are used to measure evaporation. In order to compare direct measurement methods of potential evapotranspiration by different types of evaporimeters for further comparison with indirect calculation methods from hourly to daily estimation of potential evapotranspiration, an experiment was established in the Marchfeld region of Austria. The atmometer results are compared with calculated evapotranspiration equations. The results should highlight the respective application potential of evaporimeters, their accuracy and response to calculated evapotranspiration.

[*] Corresponding author: E-mail address: josef.eitzinger@boku.ac.at, Phone: +43 1 476545622, Fax: +43 1 476545610

# 1. OVERVIEW AND HISTORY OF ATMOMETER DEVELOPMENT AND USE

Although it is difficult to identify a single parameter as the most important one in a complex system, evaporation comes near that. It interlinks the energy- and waterbalance and comes into play in every energy and water exchange between the atmosphere and all kinds of surfaces. But despite their relevance, evaporation is not as easy to measure or to calculate as it seems. During the historical development of scientific disciplines like hydrology, meteorology, geography, agriculture, oceanography, many different ways to handle evaporation have been developed. Thereby in the most evaporation is calculated from basic meteorological elements. Many equations have been developed and are in use today, each one prepared for a special situation of available climate elements and goals.

Beside scientific questions there are many important applications for evaporation measurements or calculations. Especially in agriculture under irrigation there is need in the amount of the consumptive use of different crops. But the further away from scientific research, where trained personnel may deal with the more complicated measurements, it is not possible to assume the same from farmers, who are mostly interested in the time and amount for irrigation under a prevailing weather situation. There, simple measurement devices are of more interest which should be easy to understand from a practical standpoint. During the history instruments have been developed to measure evaporation on a fairly simple basis. The simpler one is an open pan or tank. The best known of this class is the Class A pan, still in use today as a standard instrument in the weather service of different countries. Although these instruments are well understood in their evaporation behavior, their drawbacks limit their use as scheduling element for irrigation sprinklers. Another class of instruments is called atmometer. Atmometers are mainly paper or porous porcelain surfaces which evaporate. An overview about the early history of atmometers is given by [1] who promotes mostly these devices, especially his own sphere. The most important ones are the Wild evaporimeter [2], the Piche atmometer [3], the Cantoni, Bellani and Livingston atmometer [1]. Details about the later history can be found in [2].

The name atmometer is used interchangeably with evaporimeter. The Piche atmometer consists of a glass tube with a downward facing wet filter paper disk as evaporating surface. With the Bellani evaporation takes place from an upwards oriented flat porous ceramic disk, with a reservoir tube underneath. The Livingston atmometer has a spherical porous ceramic evaporating surface. Each type of atmometer measures the water evaporated from the surface in a given time. The drawbacks are manifold, but they are easy to use, cheap and could be used for irrigation scheduling. Although all of them measure evaporation, the exact meaning of what they actually measure is not easy to understand. It is some sort of evaporativity of the atmosphere [1], which is terminologically related to the potential evapotranspiration, but is surely not the same. Atmometer observations have been found at first difficult to interpret [4], but during the time many details about their physical behavior have been uncovered [5-9]. Besides Bellani, Livingston and others many more atmometers have been developed and some of them are still in use [10-19]. Atmometer measurements are sometimes used as substitutes for the aerodynamic term of the Penman-Monteith-equation [20-24]. The reason for that lies in the missing variables necessary to calculate reference or potential evapotranspiration. Additionally the difference between black and white coloured Bellani plates or Livingston spheres was used to estimate radiation [25,26,27,22].

Until today the usefulness of atmometers is shown for the most  part for irrigation scheduling and for the estimation of potential or reference evapotranspiration[28-36], but also to get a picture about the spatial behavior of evaporation [37,38,43]. The evaporation of atmometers is a function of all atmospheric variables involved in the evaporation process. Should an atmometer be used as part of the irrigation scheduling, it must be calibrated in each case against the specific atmospheric environment. A lot of investigations to compare the measurements of atmometers with calculated evaporation or evapotranspiration have been undertaken and also different types of atmometers have been compared in [5,27,39,40]

## 2. CASE STUDY RESULTS WITH ATMOMETERS/EVAPORIMETERS

In several measurement experiments different designed evaporimeters were compared as well as evaluated against various evapotranspiration equations under climatic conditions in North-East Austria and Vienna (annual precipitation about 600 mm, annual temperature about 10 °C).

### 2.1. Comparison of Different Designed Atmometers

Different designed atmometers (Fig. 1) were used to compare measured values with calculated evapotranspiration.

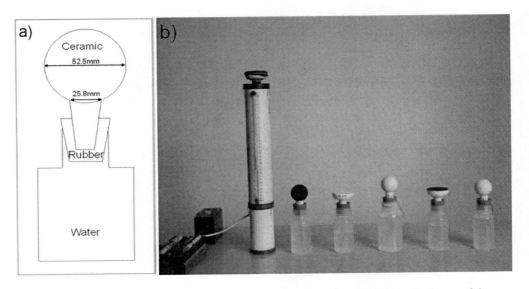

Figure 1. Type of evaporimeters which were used in the comparison study (b) and scheme of the spherical evaporimeter (a). In the picture, from the left: Automatic evaporimeter („ET-Gage"); Spherical Atmometers and Bellani Plate Atmometers: black-spherical ceramic, white-flat ceramic, white-spherical ceramic, black-flat ceramic (all: C&M Meteorological Supply, Colorado Springs, Colorado, USA).

The automatic type of evaporimeter (ET Gage system, C&M Meteorological Supply, Colorado Springs, Colorado, USA) has a convex (vaulted) evaporating ceramic surface, which is covered by green textile material to mimik albedo of various crop surfaces. The water flow through a pipe due to evapotranspiration from the surface is measured by a water flow counter, which signals can be registered by a datalogger. The ceramic spherical atmometers and Bellani plate atmometers (both black and white types) were adapted by the authors for simple manual measurements, where regular readings of the water level in a scaled transparent plastic bottle or regular weighting of the bottle are necessary. It represents, however, a very cost effective solution for the equipment. The evaporation surface of the ceramic spherical type is 80.1 cm² and of the Bellani plate atmometer 33.7 cm², respectively.

A comparison of the flat and spheric ceramic evaporimeter types shows significant higher evaporation rates of the flat types (Fig. 2). The water loss from atmometers is most influenced by wind and the turbulent exchange between the atmosphere and the evaporating surface [4]. The longwave radiation from the surrounding surfaces (e.g. soil or canopy surface) influences the spherical Livingston atmometers more than the flat Bellani plates. Differences in the lateral diffusion has an impact on the evaporation rates with higher evaporation rates for the smaller surfaces and is additionally influenced by the saturation deficit of the surrounding atmosphere [4]. It can be assumed, that the difference between the spheres and the plates is mainly related to the differences in the evaporating area and the influence of the different shapes on the dynamical characterstics of evaporation.

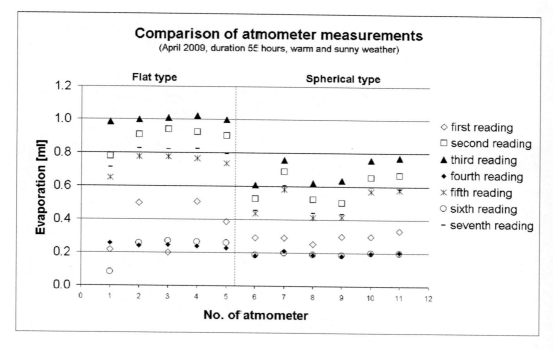

Figure 2. Comparison of absolute evaporation of the flat and spherical type atmometers (Fig. 1b) during a warm and sunny period in April 2009 (outdoor measurement). The replications represent the same type of atmometers.

Further, the flat type evaporimeters were compared with various equations for potential evapotranspiration as shown in Tab. 1 for indoor conditions. It can be seen that the parameterization of the equations, such as demonstrated for Dalton and Penman equation, can result in a significant range of results. However, the measured flat type evaporimeters shows the best agreement with the Dalton equation under our experimental conditions, whereas Penman for water surface parameterization shows a higher value.

**Table 1. Comparison of measured evaporation of flat black and white evaporimeter (Fig. 1) with various equations for evapotranspiration [41] (outdoor conditions).**

| Date | Method | Time | Atmometer Nr. 1 flat white weight [g] | E rate [g/h] | Atmometer Nr. 2 flat black [g] | E rate [g/h] |
|---|---|---|---|---|---|---|
| 29.09.2008 | | 14:40 | 460.1 | | 347.4 | |
| | | 16:40 | 456.6 | 1.75 | 343.4 | 2.00 |
| 30.09.2008 | | 10:00 | 443.0 | 0.78 | 329.6 | 0.80 |
| | Measured Evaporation [mm.d⁻¹] | | 6.30 | | 6.56 | |
| | Dalton - Richter [mm.d⁻¹] | | 5.85 | | | |
| | Dalton - Neusiedlersee [mm.d⁻¹] | | 6.71 | | | |
| | Dalton - warm lowlands [mm.d⁻¹] | | 5.52 | | | |
| | Penman [mm.d⁻¹] | | 5.21 | 8.23 | 6.99 | 7.99 |
| | simulated surface for $z$ and $\alpha$ | | $z$ and $\alpha$ of snow | $z$ and $\alpha$ of water | $z$ water and $\alpha$ snow | $z$ water and $\alpha$ soil |

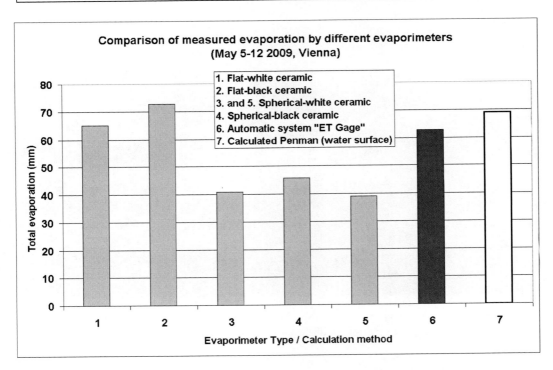

Figure 3. Comparison of evaporation rates of different evaporimeter types during calibration conditions (same height of measurements) in free atmosphere and the relation to the potential evaporation from open water surface by Penman [41].

Another comparison of evapotranspiration equations with the ceramic type of evaporimeters and the ET Gage system is shown in Fig. 3. Also here, the blackened flat atmometers show the highest values, which are also close to the calculated potential evapotranspiration for open water surface. The spherical type of the atmometers show the lowest values, whereas the measured value of the automatic system (ET Gage) with green fabric cover is close to the flat ceramic atmometers, but lower than the calculated evaporation by Penman from open water surface.

## 2.2. Using Evaporimeters to Detect the Influence of Hedgerows on Evapotranspiration

Daily evapotranspiration amounts measured by the digital ET Gage atmometers placed in 8 m, 20 m, and 80 m distances from a hedgerow (in the lee from the main wind direction) in a field experiment (Fig. 4).

Figure 4. Field experiment over alfalfa. Transect measurements including ET Gage evaporimeters to detect microclimatic impacts on different distances (Fig. 6) from a hedgerow.

The results of the measurements correlate well with calculated potential evapotranspiration values using Penman-Monteith and Turc equation within the period of measurement (Fig. 5). The meteorological station, representing field conditions without hedgerow impact on wind speed, was placed in 80 m distance from the hedgerow. Hence, not surprisingly, the best correlation was found between calculated potential evaporation and estimated evaporation by the atmometer placed in 80 m distance ($R^2 = 0.64$ for Penman) from the hedgerow.

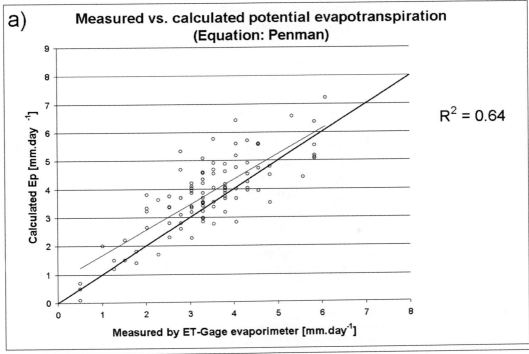

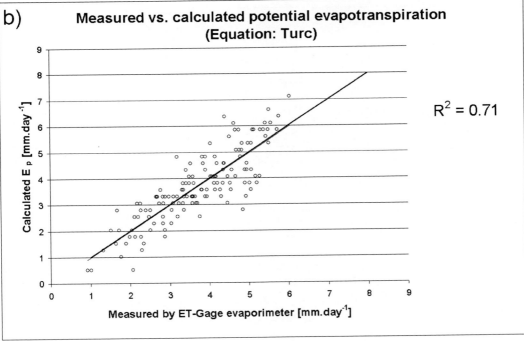

Figure 5. Comparison of ET Gage evaporimeter measurements with calculated potential evapotranspiration [41] over alfalfa canopy using the Penman (a) and Turc (b) method (Marchfeld, North-East Austria).

Calculations according to Turc provide the best approximations of the measured values of potential evapotranspiration by the automatic atmometers. This empirical equation is determined for semiarid and arid areas, but for the summer season it works well even in Germany [41]. It is usually used for calculation of evapotranspiration for dense canopies, especially grass. For these reasons we assume that this equation is suitable for the semi-arid Marchfeld region, too.

Considering the amount of data necessary to calculate evapotranspiration by Penman-Monteith, and very detailed physics of all processes involved, we recommend to use the Penman-Monteith grass reference evaporation equation as alternative [42] or some of locally calibrated and verified empirical equations (like that of Turc) to calculate potential evapotranspiration at regional scales. However, for a detailed analysis of local factors (like hedgerows) on microclimate, measurements with atmometers or some versions of Penman-Monteith equation are recommended.

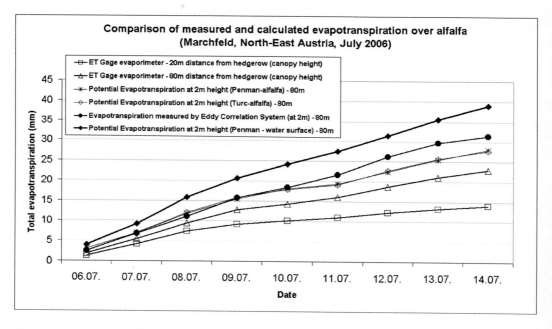

Figure 6. Comparison of ET Gage evaporimeter measurements at different distances from a hedgerow with evapotranspiration measurements from an Eddy Correlation system and evapotranspiration equations [41] in a field experiment over alfalfa.

In Fig. 6 the course of accumulated measured evapotranspiration by the ET Gage evaporimeters during a period of 10 consecutive days with mostly clear summer weather conditions is compared with the Penman-Monteith and Turc equation on the one side and an Eddy-Correlation system measurement on the other side. Understandably the evaporimeters at the different distances from the hedgerow show the impact of reduced wind speed in the lee. The closer to the hedgerow, the lower is the measured evaporation due to lower wind speed. It can be seen that the evaporimeter at 20 m distance from the hedgerow measured significant lower evaporation rates than at 80 m. However, also the ET Gage measurement at 80 m distance from the hedgerow does not reach the calculated evapotranspiration rates for alfalfa canopy at 2 m height, probably because the ET Gage evaporimeters measured evaporation close to canopy height where reduced wind speed and higher air humidity was observed.

For open field conditions (80 m from the hedgerow) the comparison with the equations shows that the Eddy Correlation System measured similar evaporation rates compared to the Penman and Turc equation for alfalfa canopy conditions (calculated only for time periods without precipitation). The potential evaporation calcualted by Penman for open water surface shows the highest values, which is in accordance to theory. It is, however, difficult to detect the method which estimates the real crop reference evapotranspiration most reliably in this experiment, which could be best verified and supplemented e.g. by lysimeter measurements.

## 3. CONCLUSION

Evaporimeters or atmometers are a useful tool for the detection or measurements of spatial variations of potential or reference evapotranspiration. Especially it is possible to use cheap manual atmometers, where there is need to place a great number of them within a specific area. As potential evapotranspiration is integrating a number of meteorological parameters, it can be effectively used for microclimatic analyses of local climate phenomena with some additional meteorological measurements. Although the measurement of relative variations between different measuring points is relatively simple, the estimation of absolute potential evapotranspiration by evaporimeters needs calibration against other methods, such as well calibrated evapotranspiration equations. If once calibrated, even the reference evapotranspiration of crops can be estimated.

## ACKNOWLEDGMENTS

The research presented in this chapter has been done under the project No. VEGA 2/0170/09 and Ernst-Mach-Stipendium der Aktion Osterreich - Slowakei fur Postdoktoranden (SK nach AT) No. ACM-2008-01832

## REFERENCES

[1]   B.E. Livingston, *Ecology* 16 (3), 438-472, (1935).
[2]   W. Brutsaert, D.Reidel Publishing Company: Boston, USA, 1982, 299 p., (1982).
[3]   C. Jelinek, J. Hann, *Z. Meteorologie* 8, 270-271, (1873).
[4]   E.I. Mukammal, *Proceedings of Hydrology Symposium* No.2: Evaporation, Toronto, Ontario. Queens Printer, Ottawa, 84-105, (1995).
[5]   J.A. Prescott, G.B. Stirk, *Austr. J. Appl. Sci.* 2, 243-256, (1951).
[6]   R. Roth, *Met Geo Bio* 11(1), 108-125, (1961).
[7]   J.V. Hoyningen-Huene, *Berichte des Deutschen Wetterdienstes* 148, 24 p., (1980).
[8]   A.S. Thom, J.L. Thony, M. Vauclin, *Quart. J. R. Met. Soc.,* 107, 711-736, (1981).
[9]   T.A. Fontaine, D.E. Todd, *Wat. Res. Bull.,* 29 (5), 785-795, (1993).
[10]  B. Ramsauer, *Wasserwirtschaft und Technik* 20-22, 189-200, (1936).

[11]  R.H. Waring, R.K. Hermann, *Ecology,* 47(2), 308-310, (1966).

[12]  J.C. Wilcox, *Wat Res Res* 3(2), 433-436, (1967).

[13]  W. Ceratzki, *Landbauforschung Völkenrode* 18(2), 93-98, (1968).

[14]  Th. Mosimann, *Arch. Met. Geoph. Biokl.*, Ser B 33, 289-299, (1983).

[15]  R. Williams, A. Zangvil, A. Karnieli, *Agric. For. Meteorol.,* 32, 217-224, (1984).

[16]  Th.W. Giambelluca, D.L. McKenna, P.C. Ekern, *Agric. For. Meteorol.,* 62, 109-125, (1992).

[17]  G.D. Worth, F. Holawe, G.N. McIntyre, *Theor. Appl. Climatol.,* 49, 263-265, (1994).

[18]  G.J. Kidron, *Weather* 60(9), 268-272, (2005).

[19]  G.J. Kidron, *Earth Surf. Proc. and Landforms* 34, 123-132, (2009).

[20]  J.L. Monteith, M. Unsworth, In: *Principles of Environmental Physics.* Butterworth-Heinemann, 291 p., (1991).

[21]  G. Stanhill, *Quart. J. Roy. Met. Soc.,* 88, 80-82, (1962).

[22]  A.C. Dilley, I. Helmond, *Agr. Meteorol.,* 12, 1-11, (1973).

[23]  G. Papaioannou, S. Kaloudis, P. Kerkides, *Agr. For Met.,* 82, 83-92, (1996).

[24]  G. Papaioannou, S. Kaloudis, P. Kerkides, *Int. J. Climat.,* 18, 1247-1260, (1998).

[25]  T.C. O`Connor, *Geof. pura e Appl.,* 30, 130-136, (1955).

[26]  T.C. O`Connor, *Geof. pura e Appl.,* 38, 154-156, (1957).

[27]  J.W. Shannon, *Amer. Soc. Civil. Engr.* 94, 309-320, (1968).

[28]  S. Uhlig, *Mitteilungen des Deutschen Wetterdienstes* 13(2), 24, (1955).

[29]  J. Altenhofen, In: Amer Soc of Agricultural Engr, editor. Advances in Evapotranspiration. St.Joseph, Michigan: *Amer. Soc. of Agricultural Engr.,* 177-184, (1985).

[30]  W.H. Van Zyl, D.M. DeJager, *Agric. For. Meteorol.,* 41, 65-75, (1987).

[31]  C.M. Feldhake, D.G. Boyer, *Agric. For. Meteorol.,* 42, 219-227, (1988).

[32]  M. Alam, T.P. Trooien, *Appl. Eng. Agr.,* 17(2), 153-158, (2001).

[33]  M. Alam, J. Elliott, *ASAE Ann Int Meet* 27-30 July, Las Vegas, 8p., (2003).

[34]  V. Magliulo, R. d'Adria, G. Rana, *Agr. For. Met.,* 63, 1-14, (2003).

[35]  S. Irmak, M.D. Dukes, M. Jacobs, *J. Irrig. Drain. Engrg.,* 131:2(164), (2005).

[36]  P. Gavilán, F. Castillo-Llanque, *Agr. Water Manage.,* 96, 465-472, (2009).

[37]  C.M. Feldhake, D.G. Boyer, *Agric. For Meteorol.,* 51, 211-222, (1990).

[38]  Th.W. Giambelluca, D. Nullet, *J. Hydrology,* 136, 219-235, (1992).

[39]  K. Heigel., *Met Rdsch*, 10(2), 101-107, (1957).

[40]  A.F.G. Jacobs, E.E. Linclaen Arriens-Bekker, *J Hydrology,* 60, 367-380, (1983).

[41]  DVWK (Hrsg.), *Ermittlung der Verdunstung von Land- und Wasserflächen. Merkblätter zur Wasserwirtschaft* 238. Bonn, Wirtschafts und Verl. Ges. Gas und Wasser, (1996).

[42]  G.A. Allen, L.S. Pereira, D. Raes, M. Smith, *Irrigation and Drainage* Paper No. 56, FAO, Rome, Italy, pp. 300, (1998).

[43]  G.N.McIntyre, F. Holawe and G. Worth, *Monash Publications in Geography 45,* IAG Conference 1993, Monash University Melbourne, 190-197, (1995).

# PART THREE – CLIMATE CHANGE IMPACT ON AGRICULTURE

In: Advances in Environmental Modeling and Measurements     ISBN: 978-1-60876-599-7
Editors: D. T. Mihailović, B. Lalić, pp. 183-194     © 2010 Nova Science Publishers, Inc.

*Chapter 17*

# CLIMATE CHANGE IMPACTS ON WINTER WHEAT AND MAIZE IN EUROPE

## *V.A. Alexandrov*[*]

National Institute of Meteorology and Hydrology, Sofia, Bulgaria

## ABSTRACT

Climate is a primary determinant of agricultural productivity. The impact of climate change on agricultural production is important at local, regional, national, as well as global scales. Any modifications of weather due to the impact of climate variability and change directly affect crop production. Global climate change will impact all economic sectors to some degree, but agricultural production is perhaps the most sensitive and vulnerable. Agriculture in Europe only accounts for a small part of the GDP, and the vulnerability in the overall economy to changes that affect agriculture are therefore low, however the local effects on society might be large. This study shows some model results on climate change impacts on selected crops across Europe. Changes in phenological dates and crop yields of winter wheat and maize are simulated by the RoIMPEL crop model. ATEAM climate data for the period 1991-2000 and climate change HADCM3 scenarios for the 21st century were engaged in the study.

## 1. INTRODUCTION

The Fourth Assessment IPCC report [1] concludes that the world's average surface temperature has increased by around 0.74 °C over the past 100 years. This figure is higher than the 2001 report's 100-year estimate of 0.6 °C due to the recent series of extremely warm years, with 11 of the last 12 years ranking among the 12 warmest years since modern records began around 1850. The warming trend throughout Europe is well established (+0.90 °C for 1901 to 2005).

---

[*] Corresponding author: E-mail address: Vesselin.Alexandrov@meteo.bg, Phone +359 2 9884494, Fax: +359 2 9884494

However, the recent period shows a trend considerably higher than the mean trend (+0.41 °C/ decade for the period 1979 to 2005). For the 1977 to 2000 period, trends are higher in central and north-eastern Europe and in mountainous regions, while lower trends are found in the Mediterranean region. Temperatures are increasing more in winter than summer. An increase of daily temperature variability is observed during the period 1977 to 2000 due to an increase in warm extremes, rather than a decrease of cold extremes. Precipitation trends are more spatially variable. Mean winter precipitation is increasing in most of Atlantic and northern Europe. In the Mediterranean area, yearly precipitation trends are negative in the east, while they are non-significant in the west. An increase in mean precipitation per wet day is observed in most parts of the continent, even in some areas which are becoming drier. Some of the European systems and sectors have shown particular sensitivity to recent trends in temperature and (to a lesser extent) precipitation:

- Upward shift of the tree line
- Phenological changes (earlier onset of spring events and lengthening of the growing season);
- increasing productivity and carbon sink during 1950 to 1999 of forests;
- Change in high mountain vegetation types and new occurrence of alpine vegetation on high summits
- Northern Europe: increased crop stress during hotter, drier summers; increased risk to crops from hail
- Britain, southern Scandinavia : increased area of silage maize - more favorable conditions due to warmer summer temperatures
- France: Increases in growing season of grapevine; changes in wine quality
- Germany: Advance in the beginning of growing season for fruit trees

Climate plays a fundamental role in agriculture because of its direct and indirect influence on production. Each physical, chemical and biological process determining agricultural activity is regulated by specific climatic requirements, and any deviation from these patterns may exert a negative influence. European agriculture, mainly oriented to production of high quality food, may be more susceptible to meteorological hazard impacts because it is based on highly developed farming techniques.

Global climate change will impact all economic sectors to some degree, but agricultural production is perhaps the most sensitive and vulnerable as climate is the primary determinant of agricultural productivity. World agriculture, whether in developing or developed countries, remains very dependent on climate resources [2,3]. For example, agriculture in Europe only accounts for a small part of the GDP (Gross Domestic Product), and the vulnerability in the overall economy to changes that affect agriculture is therefore low [4], however the local effects on society might be large. There is no doubt that the question of global and regional climate change as well as related impacts on agroecosystems is a major and important environmental issue facing the world at the beginning of the 21st century [5].That is why, the major goal of this investigation was to assess the climate change impacts on winter wheat and maize in Europe.

## 2. DATA AND METHOD

### 2.1. Climate Data and Emission Scenarios

The University of East Anglia developed a database of climate data for the 20th century within the framework of the ATEAM project. These data were based on a 10' grid for Europe with monthly time steps using observations for 1901-2000. ATEAM data for the period 1991-2000 were engaged in the study.

A set of GCM (global circulation model) output was applied in the study – this from the HadCM3 runs. HadCM3 is a coupled atmosphere-ocean GCM developed at the Hadley Centre, United Kingdom. It has a stable control climatology and does not use flux adjustment. The HadCM3 GCM dataset (for the time slices 2011-2020, 2041-2050 and 2071-2080) has a high spatial resolution - 10' latitude/longitude, which approximates to about 18 km ×18 km at the equator, with the east-west dimension decreasing to ~16 and ~9 km at 30 and 60° N and S, respectively. The high spatial resolution of the climate surfaces was obtained by applying the regional climate model RegCM3 and interpolation techniques such as thin-plate smoothing splines [6] with elevation, latitude and longitude as independent predictors.

Most of the scientists consider that the emissions of the carbon dioxide ($CO_2$) and the other so called "greenhouse gases", emitted in the atmosphere because of human activities such as industry and agriculture, may cause irreversible climate change. The $CO_2$ concentration in the atmosphere has increased by 31% since preindustrial times (i.e. about 1750) as a result of burning fuel, afforestation, etc. Increases in greenhouse gas concentrations since 1750 have led to a positive radiative forcing of climate, tending to warm the surface and to produce changes of climate.

By 2100 the world will have changed in ways that are difficult to imagine – as difficult as it would have been at the end of the 19th century to imagine the changes of the 100 years since. Each storyline assumes a distinctly different direction for future developments, such that the four storylines differ in increasingly irreversible ways. Together they describe divergent futures that encompass a significant portion of the underlying uncertainties in the main driving forces. They cover a wide range of key "future" characteristics such as demographic change, economic development, and technological change. For this reason, their plausibility or feasibility should not be considered solely on the basis of an extrapolation of current economic, technological, and social trends. Four qualitative storylines yield four sets of scenarios called "families": A1, A2, B1, and B2. Most of the recent climate change impact studies are focusing on the A2 storyline. The A2 storyline and scenario family describes a very heterogeneous world. The underlying theme is self-reliance and preservation of local identities. Fertility patterns across regions converge very slowly, which results in continuously increasing global population. Economic development is primarily regionally oriented and per capita economic growth and technological changes are more fragmented and slower than in other storylines. This study partially assumed also the B2 storyline. The B2 storyline and scenario family describes a world in which the emphasis is on local solutions to economic, social, and environmental sustainability. It is a world with continuously increasing global population at a rate lower than A2, intermediate levels of economic development, and less rapid and more diverse technological change than in the B1 and A1 storylines. While the

B2 scenario is also oriented toward environmental protection and social equity, it focuses on local and regional levels.


## 2.2. Roimpel Crop Growth Model

To define agricultural responses to climate, studies can be based on the application of simulation models. They can be used to describe the effect of climatic conditions on key agricultural aspects, including production, protection, fertilization, site selection, watering, etc. RoIMPEL is a modular simulation model of crop yields limited by soil -water and - nitrogen availability, using limited easy-to-map soil and weather data. Therefore, RoIMPEL is appropriate for GIS based regional and sub-regional land-use evaluation projects [7].

The minimum requirements for soil data in the RoIMPEL model are the soil texture and organic matter classes. Soil is considered as one reservoir partially filled with water. The zero level of the reservoir corresponds to the total soil water content at the wilting point for a soil layer corresponding to the maximum root front depth. The maximum volume of the reservoir is the maximum soil available water. Therefore, the actual water volume in the reservoir is the actual soil available water. The reservoir is filled with water from rainfall and discharged by crop transpiration. Should the water in the reservoir exceeds the maximum reservoir volume, an additional reservoir have start to fill with water. The water in this reservoir is the soil drainable water. This additional reservoir is filled by rainfall too, and discharged by drainage flow and evaporation. In a first approach, for limiting the number of input soil parameters, no restrictions on the maximum volume of water in this reservoir are imposed. This additional reservoir has a threshold corresponding to the wet water content limit for workability. If this threshold is passed the soil is not workable.

The RoIMPEL dynamics of the water budget elements (evaporation, transpiration, drainage) is computed using two algorithms: The first algorithm is a general balance equation for soil water in the maximum root-front-depth soil layer. The second algorithm uses Thornthwaite-Mathers approach computing the water balance elements for soil water contents less than the maximum available water, and travel time approach for drainage flow calculations for soil water contents greater than the maximum available water. Both algorithms require sharing of total actual evapo-transpiration in evaporation and crop transpiration. Ritchie's formula was used for this partition. Therefore, the dynamics of the leaves area index is the central driving process for soil water dynamics during vegetation period and, for biomass calculations. The dynamics of the leaves area index is computed using the maximum leaves area index and a build-in standard analytical function describing the relative leaves area index (i.e. the ratio between actual leaves area index and the maximum one) as related to the values of the development stage.

Nitrogen pools and dynamics are computed similar with EPIC algorithms considering only one soil layer having the thickness of the maximum root front depth. At the present stage of model development only nitrate forms are considered. The chemical kinetic equations describing fluxes of nitrogen between various pools in the soil are depending on soil temperature and soil water content. The simulation model includes the following processes of nitrogen in soil: mineralisation, immobilization, nitrate leaching and nitrogen crop uptake. Active and stable pools of soil nitrogen are considered. The dynamics of the crop residue and its associated nitrogen pool is considered in detail computing the decay rates for carbohydrate, lignin and cellulose-like materials. The concentration of nitrogen ($NO_3$) in soil solution is calculated for each day of simulation.

Climate data for RoIMPEL are provided by ATEAM project in a grid of 10×10' longitude × latitude covering all Europe. For each Soil Mapping Unit are associated the climate data corresponding to the closest grid point to the label point (weight centre of the polygon) of the Soil Mapping Unit.

RoIMPEL calculates the dynamic of state variables with a time step of 1 day. The data available from European scale grids have a time step of 1 month. Therefore, RoIMPEL incorporates build-in functions deriving daily weather data (temperature, rainfall, radiation) from monthly values of temperature and rainfall.

## 3. RESULTS

Significant summer warming in the western Balkan countries and Spain, projected by the HadCM3 model for 2080. Air temperatures during this time of the year are expected to increase between 5° and 8 °C over some of the countries in the southern European region. Although several uncertainties in relation to future precipitation exist, the HadCM3 model show precipitation slight increases during the winter and precipitation reductions during the summer in the region of the Central Europe. Summer precipitation is projected to decrease also into the eastern Europe. For example, in some areas in Romania its reduction would be up to 50% in 2080 (Fig. 1). In North Europe summer precipitation is expected to increase.

As the third generation of the Hadley Centre global coupled models (HadCM3) is skilful in reproducing currently observed major couplings, it was used as a tool for assessing how, and to what extent, these couplings are projected to change under human-induced climate change. A strong wintertime warming is projected to occur under the B2 and A2 scenarios from the Special Report on Emission Scenarios (SRES), particularly over northeastern Europe and in the A2 scenario. An overall increase (decrease) in the occurrence of warm (cold) events is also projected to occur in future scenarios, mainly due to the increase in mean temperatures (changes in variance are generally irrelevant). An eastward extension of the southern centre-of-action of the NAO towards the Mediterranean Basin is also projected to occur by the end of this century, yielding significant changes in the local/regional relationships between the occurrence of temperature extremes and this 'modified NAO'. Furthermore, projected changes in the surface large-scale forcing are associated with vertically coherent changes in the Northern Annular Mode in response to human-induced changes in radiative forcing.

All HadCM3 climate change scenarios used in the RoIMPEL simulation model projected a shorter vegetative and reproductive growing season for maize and winter wheat during the 21st century. These changes were caused by the predicted temperature increase of the climate change scenarios. Maturity dates for maize are expected to occur between 10 days and 30 days earlier in the 2050s (Fig. 2). The climate change scenarios for the 2080s projected a decrease in maize growing season by 15 to 40 days. This will cause a shift in harvest maturity dates for maize in southern Europe from September to August at the end of the 21st century.

a)

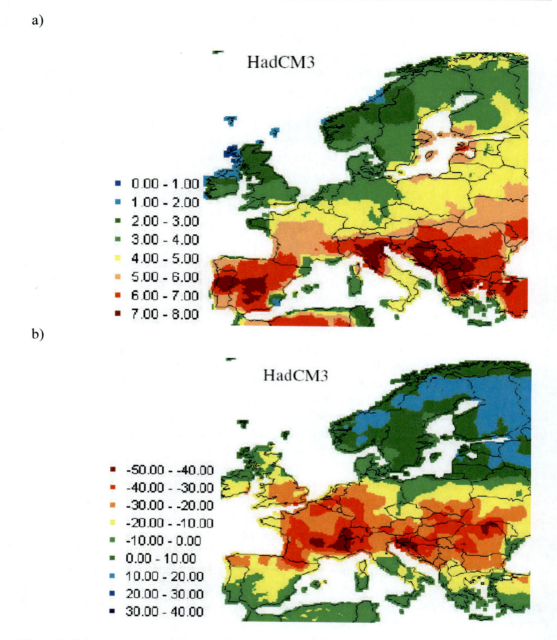

Figure 1. Changes in summer temperature (a: in °C) and precipitation (b: in %) for the HadCM3 climate model coupled with the A2 SRES scenario for 2080.

Winter wheat showed a decrease in growing season duration for the 2020s, varying between 3 days and 10 days. The transient HadCM3 climate change scenarios predicted that harvest for winter wheat would be approximately one to two weeks earlier in the 2050s, and between two to three weeks earlier in the 2080s (Fig. 3).

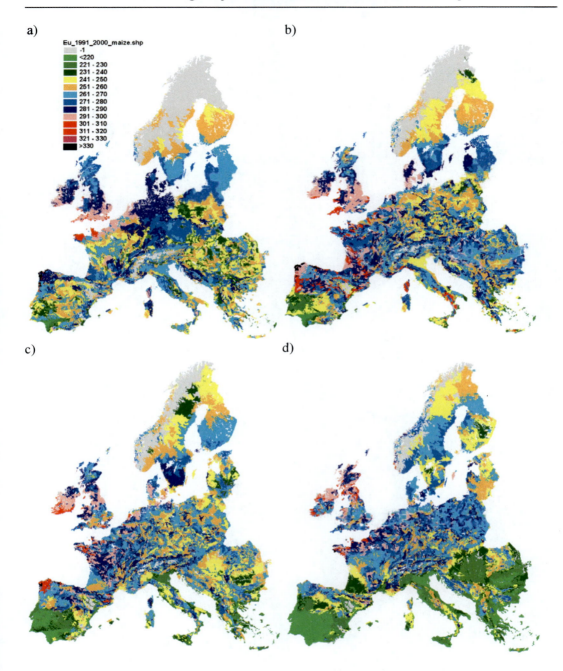

Figure 2. Maize maturity (in Julian days) under recent climate conditions (a: 1991-2000) and HadCM3 A2 climate change scenarios for the 21$^{st}$ century (b: 2011-2020; c: 2041-2050; d: 2071-2080).

a)

b)

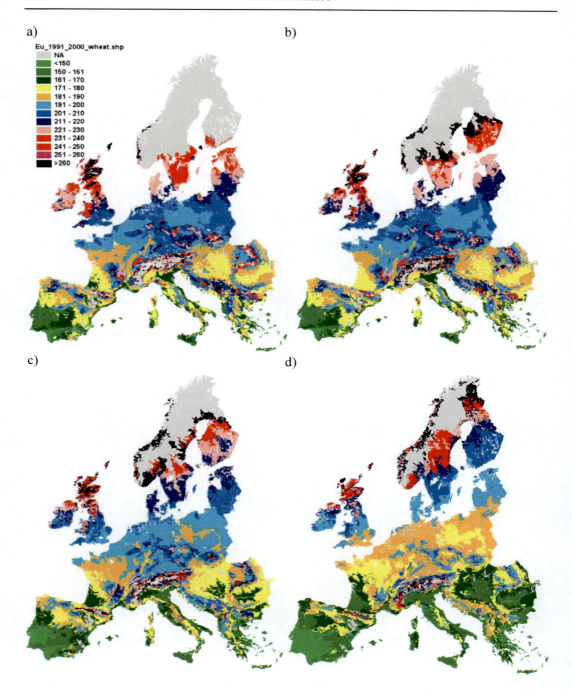

c)

d)

Figure 3. Winter wheat maturity (in Julian days) under recent climate conditions (a: 1991-2000) and HadCM3 A2 climate change scenarios for the 21$^{st}$ century (b: 2011-2020; c: 2041-2050; d: 2071-2080).

The yield changes of winter wheat and maize in Europe show different trends depending on the latitude, altitude, soil properties as well as the time slices during the current century (Fig. 4-6).

a)

b)

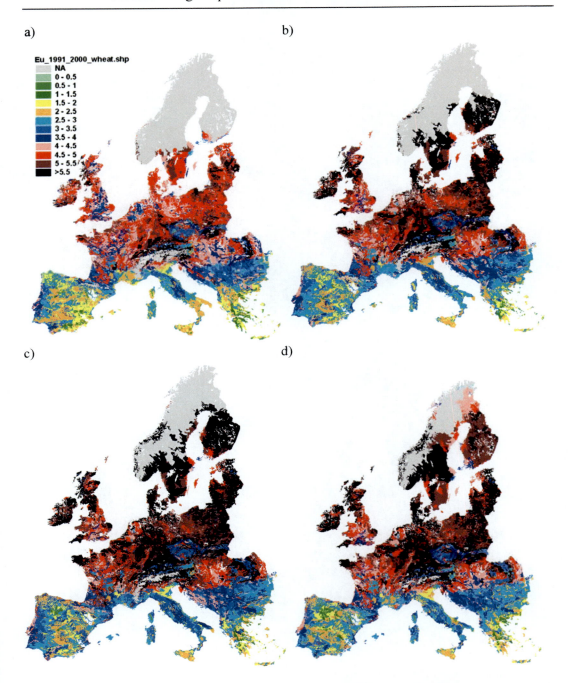

c)

d)

Figure 4. Winter wheat yield (in t ha$^{-1}$) under recent climate conditions (a: 1991-2000) and HadCM3 A2 climate change scenarios for the 21$^{st}$ century (b: 2011-2020; c: 2041-2050; d: 2071-2080).

a)                                          b)

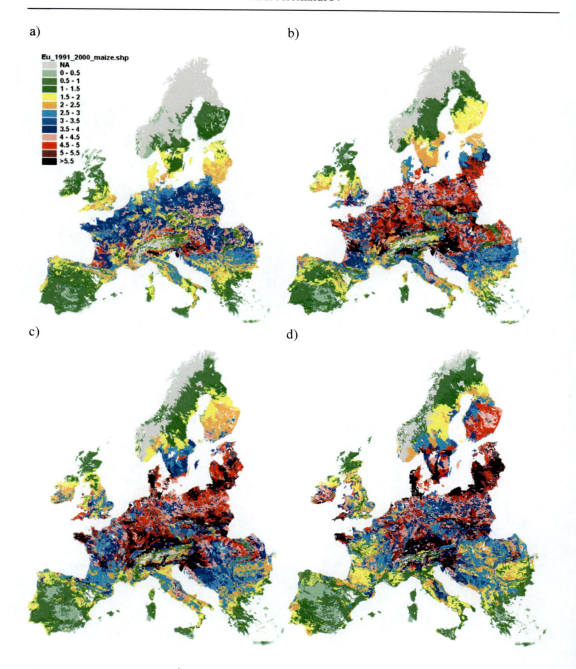

c)                                          d)

Figure 5. Maize yield (in t ha$^{-1}$) under recent climate conditions (a: 1991-2000) and HadCM3 A2 climate change scenarios for the 21$^{st}$ century (b: 2011-2020; c: 2041-2050; d: 2071-2080).

Significant increases in winter wheat yield are projected for the 21$^{st}$ century in the northern and central European countries with slight decreases/increases in the Mediterranean region. The major cause for this change in impact is that many crops, such as wheat belong to the group of C$_3$ crops, which are more sensitive to changes in $CO_2$ concentration than the group of C$_4$ crop, such as maize. Crop yield decreases in southern Europe (e.g. southwest France as well as areas in Romania and Bulgaria) would be observed for spring-sown crops such as maize. This crop is likely, therefore, to move to north or to higher altitude areas in the south. The HadCM3 A2 and B2 scenarios have relatively similar effects on crop yields (Fig. 5-6), although the A2 scenarios have involved more warming than the B2 ones.

a)                                                          b)

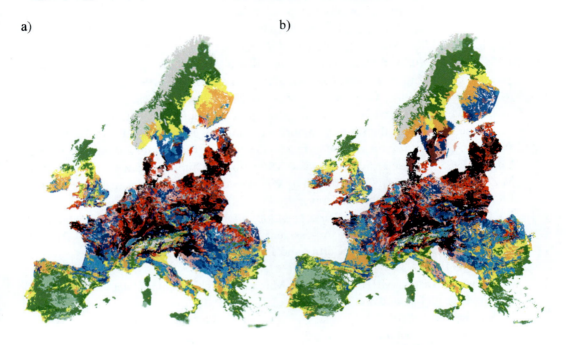

Figure 6. Maize yield (in t ha[-1]) under HadCM3 B2 climate change scenarios for the 21st century (a: 2041-2050; b: 2071-2080).

## 4. CONCLUSION

As the results show, warming will generally shorten the growing period of winter wheat and maize because of enhanced phenological development. As a result of expected warming and precipitation deficit some negative changes in maize yield in several areas in south Europe are projected. The $CO_2$ effect has a positive effect on winter wheat crop growth and its grain yield is projected to increase in most European regions.

## ACKNOWLEDGMENTS

The study was supported by the following EU projects funded by the EC in Brussels: ADAGIO, CECILIA, COST Action 734.

# REFERENCES

[1]    IPCC: *Climate Change 2007: The Physical Science Basis.* Contribution of Working Group I to the Fourth Assessment Report of the Intergovernmental Panel on Climate Change edited by S.Solomon, D. Qin, M. Manning, Z. Chen, M. Marquis, K.B. Averyt, M. Tignor and H.L. Miller. (Cambridge: Cambridge University Press, 2007), pp. 996.

[2]    T.E. Downing, (ed.). *Climate Change and World Food Security.* NATO ASI Series. Series I: Global Environmental Change, 37, Springer, 662 pp. (1996).

[3]    R. Watson, M. Zinyowera, and R. Moss (eds.), *Climate Change 1995 - Impacts, Adaptation and Mitigation of Climate Change.* Contribution of WG II to the Second Assessment Report of the IPCC, (Cambridge: Cambridge University Press, 1996)

[4]    J. Reilly, *Agriculture in a changing climate: Impacts and adaptation.* In: Climate Change 1995 - Impacts, Adaptation and Mitigation of Climate Change (eds R, Watson, M Zinyowera, R Moss). Contribution of WG II to the Second Assessment Report of the IPCC, (Cambridge: Cambridge University Press, 1996)

[5]    IPCC, Climate Change 2001. *Impacts, Adaptation and Vulnerability.* Contribution of Working Group 2 to the Third Assessment Report of the Intergovernmental Panel on Climate Change edited by McCarthy and J. James. (Cambridge: Cambridge University Press, 2001)

[6]    M. New, D. Lister, M. Hulme and I. Makin, A high-resolution data set of surface climate over global land areas. *Clim. Res.*, 21, 1–25 (2002).

[7]    E. Audsley, K.R. Pearn, C. Simota, G. Cojocaru, E. Koutsidou, M.D.A. Rounsevell, M. Trnka and V. Alexandrov, *En.Sci. &Poly.* 9(2), 148-162 (2006).

In: Advances in Environmental Modeling and Measurements    ISBN: 978-1-60876-599-7
Editors: D. T. Mihailović, B. Lalić, pp. 195-208    © 2010 Nova Science Publishers, Inc.

*Chapter 18*

# IMPACT OF CLIMATE CHANGE ON TUSCANY DURUM WHEAT QUALITY

## *S. Orlandini*[*1], *D. Grifoni*[2], *F. Natali*[1], *M. Mancini*[1], *and A. Dalla Marta*[1]

[1]University of Florence, Firenze, Italy
[2] CNR–Institute of Biometeorology, Firenze, Italy

## ABSTRACT

Meteorological conditions strongly affect agricultural activity, modifying plant responses and determining the quality and quantity of production. Moreover the analysis of these aspects on the basis of current meteo-climatic variability and change has a high importance, also in order to provide the growers with operational and forecasting tools to improve the management and planning of their production. On the basis of these considerations the present chapter has the aim of analyzing the relationship between meteorological conditions and the quality of durum wheat (*Triticum turgidum* L. var. *durum*) in terms of protein content. Weather conditions during growing season were described utilizing large-scale meteorological information, including climatic indices, presently available on internet sites (air temperature, cumulated precipitation, 500 hPa geopotential height, sea surface temperature, sea level pressure, North Atlantic Oscillation). The analysis was performed for the period 1996-2007 for Tuscany region, Central Italy. Moreover the analysis of trends was performed for meteorological data and indices from 1948 to 2007 in order to evaluate the effect of climate change. Results highlighted significant relationships between meteorological conditions and wheat quality. It was negatively correlated with precipitation cumulated along the growing period and positively correlated with spring air temperature. Teleconnections between quality data and 500 hPa geopotential height, sea surface temperature, sea level pressure and NAO index were also analyzed for the potential development of wheat-quality forecasting tools.

* Corresponding author: E-mail address: simone.orlandini@unifi.it, Phone: +39 055 3288257, Fax: +39 055 332472

# 1. INTRODUCTION

Before 1970 durum wheat (*Triticum turgidum* L. var. *durum*) was mostly diffused in the South of Italy, but thanks to EU contribution, its cultivation spread also in the Centre and in the North of the country. Actually, in Tuscany durum wheat is more diffuse than soft wheat (*T. aestivum*) with a cultivated area of about 135 000 ha representing about 15% of total cultivated surface (Tab. 1).

Differently from soft wheat, that is important for the production of flour for making bread, the cultivation of durum wheat is mainly related to the production of "semola", the primary ingredient of Italian pasta. The great role of durum wheat is not only due to the high national consumption of pasta, but also to the importance of Italian pasta for foreign markets. In fact, it represents a typical quality product exported almost worldwide. For these reasons, specific quality characteristic of kernels are required and they are mainly expressed through the type and content of protein in the grain. In general, durum wheat contains more protein than soft wheat [1], and the composition of gluten together with the vitreous consistency of kernels permits the production of "semola". Beside the percentage of protein and specific weight, moisture, gluten index and yellow index are sometimes also used for describing the durum wheat quality [2].

In Italy, the majority of durum wheat is sown in November and harvested within the first week of July. The shooting phase starts in April when the air temperature get 10-12 °C, while the ripening starts when air temperature reach 18-20 °C. Shooting, grain filling and ripening are the more important development stages that determine the quality of the grains, so that fertilization level and environmental condition during these periods can largely affect the quality characteristics of yield [3,4].

In particular, meteorological conditions have significant influence on the end-use quality characteristics of wheat. Several studies indicated the distribution of precipitation [5], late-season frosts [6], high air temperature during grain filling and its duration [7,8,9,4,10,11,12], as significant factors influencing variations in quality in terms of protein content and composition. In Australia, the cumulated precipitations are negatively associated with protein content of wheat in particular during period from May to September [13]; in China, spring temperature >30 °C increases the protein content [14], but heat stresses can cause a reduction of kernel weight and diameter [15]. A recent study analyses the effect of elevated atmospheric $CO_2$ that seem to have a negative influence on grain quality of wheat [16]. All these studies confirmed that meteorological conditions strongly affect wheat cultivation modifying plant responses and determining the quality of production, so that the analysis of meteo-climatic variability and change has a high importance.

Internet has increasingly been used to disseminate climate and meteorological data, given its rapid manipulation and display of information, interaction and feedback with the users and the reduction of costs. Internet allows for finding suitable applications providing free access to meteorological information with different spatial domains and temporal resolutions. Information provided by ground weather station, satellites, radars, soundings and weather forecasting models can be integrated to derive a complete description of meteorological and climatological variables and indices, such as air temperature, rainfall, North Atlantic Oscillation (NAO) index, sea surface temperature (SST), and geopotential height [17].

The relationships between meteorological variables and indices and quantity and quality of production has been investigated by many authors. In Spain, Gimeno et al. [18] analyzed the influence of El Nino Southern Oscillation (ENSO) and NAO phases on historical yields of important crop. Many studies, conducted in UK, demonstrated a relationship between the *T. aestivum* grain quality and the winter NAO [19-21] studying the relationship between three quality indices (Hagber falling number, specific weight and protein concentration) and January-February NAO index. Atkinson et al. [22] found that sunshine during grain growth and late summer precipitation during grain ripening are the most important meteorological factors determining specific weight of harvested wheat in UK. According to Kettwell et al., [23] the winter NAO has an effect on summer England and Wales cumulated precipitation and, consequently, on wheat quality, while Colman [24] suggested the association between sea surface temperature and NAO in UK.

The main objective of this chapter was to analyze the relationships between durum wheat quality and large-scale meteorological information freely available on the web, also considering the potential effect of climate change and variability.

**Table 1. Cultivated surface, production and yield of wheat in Tuscany, 1997-2008.
Source: Tuscany Region.**

|  | Cultivated surface (ha) | | Total production (q) | | Yield (q ha$^{-1}$) | |
|---|---|---|---|---|---|---|
|  | *T. aestivum* | *T. durum* | *T. aestivum* | *T. durum* | *T. aestivum* | *T. durum* |
| 1997 | 45 250 | 128 670 | 1 630 979 | 3 764 150 | 36.04 | 29.25 |
| 1998 | 36 800 | 127 910 | 1 399 600 | 4 177 900 | 38.03 | 32.66 |
| 1999 | 35 279 | 133 220 | 1 465 831 | 4 375 375 | 41.55 | 32.84 |
| 2000 | 30 979 | 133 291 | 1 309 282 | 4 172 235 | 42.26 | 31.30 |
| 2001 | 27 820 | 135 722 | 1 017 632 | 3 379 163 | 36.58 | 24.90 |
| 2002 | 28 160 | 160 782 | 1 097 107 | 4 882 750 | 38.96 | 30.37 |
| 2003 | 24 440 | 140 360 | 681 411 | 2 819 828 | 27.88 | 20.09 |
| 2004 | 21 210 | 184 638 | 868 598 | 6 690 743 | 40.95 | 36.24 |
| 2005 | 27 876 | 116 888 | 976 548 | 4 096 377 | 35.03 | 35.05 |
| 2006 | 27 525 | 96 495 | 932 685 | 3 057 194 | 33.89 | 31.68 |
| 2007 | 21 674 | 102 479 | 791 890 | 3 406 124 | 36.54 | 33.24 |
| 2008 | 25 189 | 150 440 | 935 415 | 5 055 195 | 37.14 | 33.60 |
| Mean | 29 350 | 134 241 | 1 092 248 | 4 156 420 | 37.07 | 30.96 |

# 2. MATERIALS AND METHODS

The research reported in this chapter was carried out in Tuscany, central Italy, where durum wheat represents an important crop for the production of quality Italian pasta.

The area is characterized by a typically Mediterranean climate, mainly affected by Azores and Russian anticyclones and by Mediterranean depressions. Precipitation is concentrated in spring and autumn with a dry and hot period in summer (annual rainfall around 750 mm, annual average temperature around 14.6 °C).

The protein content, expressed as percentage on dry matter, was chosen as quality index for durum wheat due to its strong relation to pasta production. Data, available from 1997 to 2007, were supplied by the Council for Research in Agriculture (CRA) for the most productive areas of Tuscany (provinces of Grosseto, Arezzo and Siena) and they were aggregated at regional scale for further analysis (Fig. 1). During considered period, nitrogen fertilization and crop management remained constant.

Figure 1. Study areas (Grosseto, Siena and Arezzo) of durum wheat in Tuscany (grey area).

Meteorological conditions of the study area were described through the reanalysis data that reprocessed and combined past multi-source observations with the output of weather forecast models in order to derive a more comprehensive spatial/temporal description of the environment at a global level. This method has changed the traditional approach to climatology, which was generally affected by a lack of available and continuous environmental information. Reanalysis information, available from 1948 onward, was provided by the NOAA-CIRES Climate Diagnostics Center, Boulder, Colorado, USA, from the website http://www.cdc.noaa.gov/ and processed by the NCEP/NCAR Reanalysis Project [25].

In particular air temperature, cumulated precipitation, 500 hPa geopotential height (altitude in meters where the air pressure corresponds to 500 hPa), sea surface temperature (SST) and atmospheric pressure were used.

Moreover, the correlation between wheat quality and NAO index was also investigated. The NAO index is based on the difference of normalized sea level pressure between the Azores and Iceland. The NAO can be described as a temporal fluctuation of the zonal wind strength across the Atlantic Ocean due to pressure variation in both the subtropical anticyclone belt and the subpolar low near Iceland. In the northern hemisphere the winter NAO index (December to March) shows a significant relationship with storm track, temperature and precipitation [26].

In the first part of this chapter, correlation analysis between wheat quality and air temperature and precipitation data over the study area were calculated by extracting meteorological data from the database (http://www.cdc.noaa.gov/) over Tuscany region.

Then, correlation maps between wheat protein content and 500 hPa geopotential height, SST and atmospheric pressure at surface level were used to verify the possible impact of large scale phenomena over the European and North-African areas on wheat quality of Tuscany.

The maps were created using the interactive plotting and analysis link from the website http://www.cdc.noaa.gov. It allowed to upload quality data and to calculate their correlation (teleconnection) with meteorological variables. In order to quantify the existing teleconnection inside the studied area and to define the regression functions during the highest correlation periods and areas, meteorological data were extracted from the database (http://www.cdc.noaa.gov/) and correlated with the wheat quality series.

All correlations were calculated on a monthly to a multi-monthly basis, also in relation to the different physiological stages of the crop. In particular, the periods investigated where the entire vegetative season, going from November to June, and its sub-periods of winter (December–February), spring (March–May) and the last two months of cultivation (May-June) during which the important physiological processes of grain filling and maturation take place.

## 3. RESULTS

For analyzing the relations between wheat quality and air temperature and cumulated precipitation, different multi-monthly combinations were considered from November to June, corresponding to the crop growing season. In particular, spring temperature (March-May) showed a positive effect on protein content, but the relation was not significant (Fig. 2). On the contrary, negative correlations were found between the final wheat quality and the cumulated precipitation over the growing season ($R^2$=0.38) and during winter ($R^2$=0.39), when shooting phase takes place (Fig. 3 and Fig. 4).

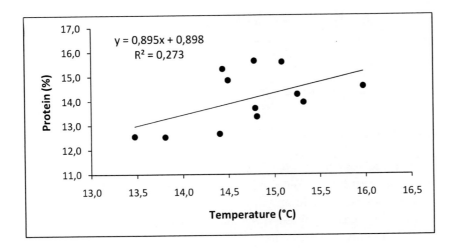

Figure 2. Linear regression between wheat quality and air temperature during spring (March–May) (1997–2008). Legend: $R^2$-determination coefficient.

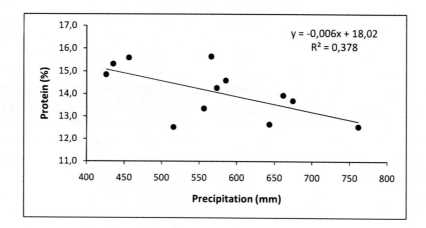

Figure 3. Linear regression between wheat quality and rainfall during the growing season (November–June) (1997–2008). Legend: $R^2$- determination coefficient.

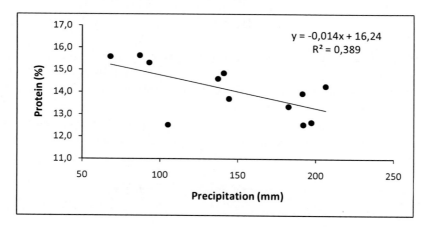

Figure 4. Linear regression between wheat quality and rainfall during winter (December–February) (1997–2008). Legend: $R^2$- determination coefficient.

The above results, obtained with the single meteorological variables at ground level, were in part confirmed by the analysis of 500 hPa geopotential height, SST and atmospheric pressure over the European and North-African areas. In fact, the quality of wheat was positively correlated to 500 hPa geopotential height over the Mediterranean Sea (mainly on the western portion) along the entire growing season (Fig. 5). Data were extracted for the November to June period over the Western Mediterranean (6 pixels defined by lat. 35 to 40; long. 0 to 7.5) and the correlation obtained was significant ($p<0.05$) with a determination coefficient of 0.4 (Fig. 6). This result confirmed the negative correlation between wheat quality and precipitation of the same period, since a high 500 hPa geopotential height in that area prevents Italian regions from Atlantic perturbations, leading to a drier growing season.

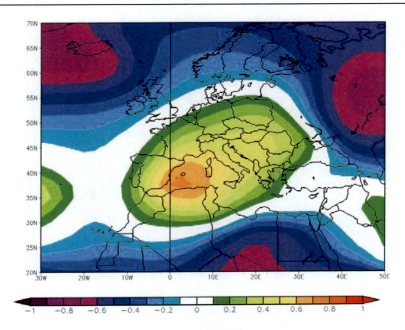

Figure 5. Correlation map between wheat quality and 500 hPa geopotential height of November to June period. Map provided by the NOAA-CIRES Climate Diagnostics Center, Boulder, CO (http://www.cdc.noaa.gov/) (1997–2008). Color scale reports correlation coefficient value.

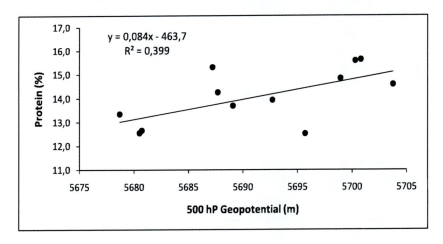

Figure 6. Linear regression between wheat quality and 500 hPa geopotential height over West Mediterranean for November to June period (1997–2008). Legend: $R^2$- determination coefficient.

Equally, sea level pressure data over the Mediterranean Sea (mainly on the North African region) was positively correlated to wheat protein content for the November to June period (Fig. 7). To better analyze the relation, pressure data of the period were extracted over the North African region (4 pixels defined by lat. 27.5 to 32.5; long. 15 to 20) and correlated to wheat quality in Tuscany. The correlation was positive and significant ($p<0.05$) with a $R^2$ of 0.43 (Fig. 8).

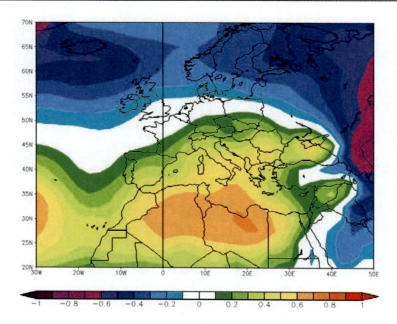

Figure 7. Correlation map between wheat quality and sea level pressure of November to June period. Map provided by the NOAA-CIRES Climate Diagnostics Center, Boulder, CO (http://www.cdc.noaa.gov/) (1997–2008). Color scale reports correlation coefficient value.

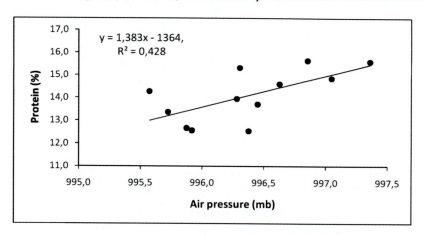

Figure 8. Linear regression between wheat quality and sea level pressure over North Africa for November to June period (1997 – 2008). Legend: $R^2$- determination coefficient.

Again, a higher sea level pressure in that region can contribute to maintain precipitation below the mean in the study area determining an increase in the quality.

A good relation was also found between the wheat protein content and the SST of central Mediterranean Sea (northern of Africa) for the April to June period (Fig. 9). The correlation between data extracted from this area (6 pixels defined by lat. 33.3 to 38.3; long. 11.3 to 18.8) and protein content was significant ($p < 0.05$, $R^2 = 0.38$) (Fig. 10). Concerning NAO index, positive correlations were found for winter months, in particular for February (p<0.05, $R^2$=0.45) (Fig. 11).

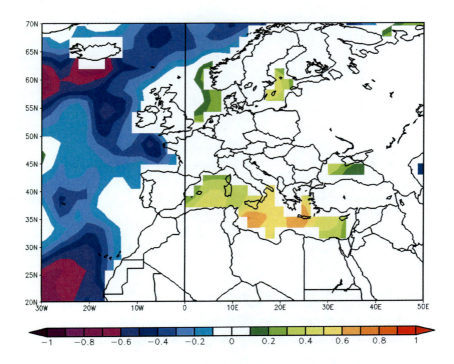

Figure 9. Correlation map between wheat quality and sea surface temperature (SST) of April to June period. Map provided by the NOAA-CIRES Climate Diagnostics Center, Boulder, CO (http://www.cdc.noaa.gov/) (1997 – 2008). Color scale reports correlation coefficient value.

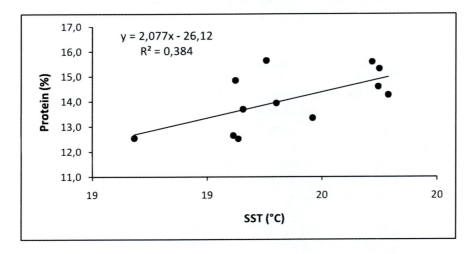

Figure 10. Linear regression between wheat quality and sea surface temperature (SST) over North Africa for April to June period (1997 – 2008). Legend: $R^2$- determination coefficient.

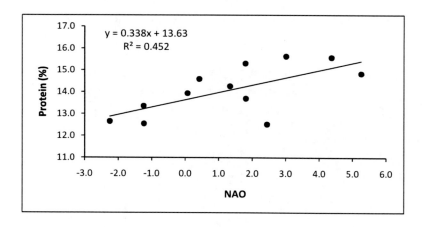

Figure 11. Linear regression between wheat quality and NAO in February (1997 – 2008). Legend: $R^2$-determination coefficient.

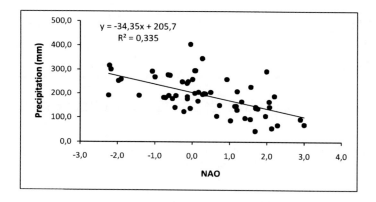

Figure 12. Linear regression between winter precipitation and winter NAO (December–February) (1948–2008). Legend: $R^2$- determination coefficient.

The relation between the meteorological index with the final wheat quality can be explained by the fact that NAO defines an atmospheric synoptic configuration limiting winter rainfall over Italian regions. In turn, winter precipitation has a negative effect on wheat quality (Fig. 4). Going into more depth of these relations, a highly significant correlation was found between winter NAO and winter precipitation in Tuscany for the period 1948-2008 ($p<0.001$, $R^2=0.33$) (Fig. 12) and a negative correlation was found between cumulated precipitation during winter period, when shooting phase is going on, and the quality of production ($p<0.05$, $R^2=0.39$) (Fig. 4).

All the results demonstrated that studied meteorological conditions, and particularly rainfall, are largely responsible for the quality of durum wheat in terms of protein content. For this reason the current climate change and variability can play a key role in the future modification of durum wheat quality. In fact, the analysis of the variables and indices used for the research, demonstrated significant trends over time (1948-2008). In particular, spring temperature showed a continuous and highly significant increase ($p<0.001$, $R^2=0.27$) (Fig.

13), while cumulated precipitation during wheat growing season had an opposite trend (p<0.001, $R^2$=0.17) (Fig. 14). For the same period, positive and highly significant trends were also shown by 500 hPa geopotential height and sea level pressure, with a determination coefficient of 0.42 and 0.34 respectively (Fig. 15 and Fig. 16). Instead, a more complicated behavior was shown by SST, for which the trend was negative from 1948 to 1979 ($R^2$=0.14) and positive from 1980 onward ($R^2$=0.15) (Fig. 17). This change in the SST trend is probably due to the delay with which an increase in sea temperature due to the atmospheric warming occurs. Concerning the global index of NAO, the regression analysis did not shown any trend (data not shown).

In general, the variability showed by the meteorological variables analyzed suggests a continuous increase in the quality of durum wheat due to the climate change related to the evidence of modifications towards conditions determining a high level of protein content (low rainfall and high temperature). Specific studies of longer series of quality data are necessary for the analysis of the effect of strongest climate changes, when extreme hot conditions or drought events will probably cause a reduction of wheat quality. The identification of critical thresholds will be a very crucial step to a better analysis of climate change impacts on durum wheat.

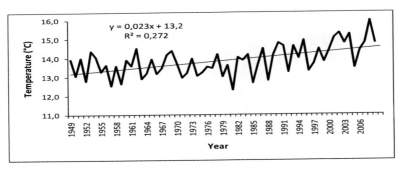

Figure 13. Trend of temperature of the March to May period (1948 – 2008). Legend: $R^2$- determination coefficient.

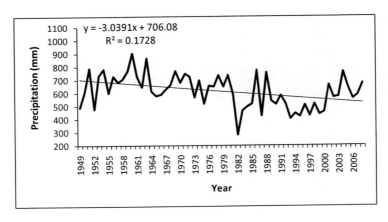

Figure 14. Trend of precipitation of the November to June period (1948 – 2008). Legend: $R^2$- determination coefficient.

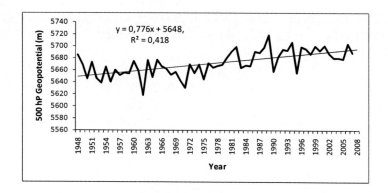

Figure 15. Trend of 500 hPa geopotential height over West Mediterranean of the November to June period (1948 – 2008). Legend: $R^2$- determination coefficient.

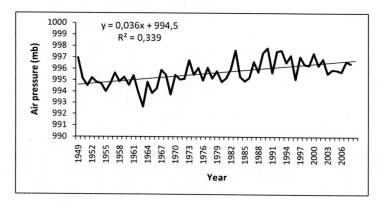

Figure 16. Trend of sea level pressure over North Africa of the November to June period (1948–2008). Legend: $R^2$- determination coefficient.

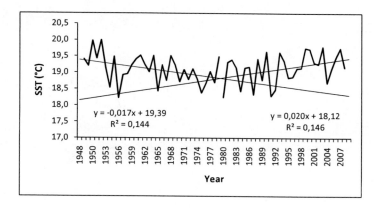

Figure 17. Trends of sea surface temperature (SST) over North Africa of the April to June period from 1948 to 1979 and from 1980 to 2008. Legend: $R^2$- determination coefficient.

# 4. CONCLUSION

The analysis reported in this chapter demonstrated the existence of strong relationships between meteorological conditions, described by large-scale meteorological information freely available on the WEB, and the quality of durum wheat in Tuscany. The strongest relations were found considering the entire growing season going from November to June. These results need further investigations in order to highlight possible relations to specific sub-periods according to the seasonal trend of durum wheat phenological development or physiological stresses, as well as the effect on protein quality composition. At the same time, different spatial scales (local, provincial, regional, etc.) should be analyzed with the aim to define more specific relations between field data and meteorological information. Moreover, for analyzing the effect of climate on wheat quality in the long period, the application of crop growth simulation models is desirable in order to create datasets not affected by particular trends due to the technological developments or variety improvements, typically characterizing historical series of field data. Finally, further studies should also clarify the possible effects that the interactions between climate and cropping techniques and management can have on the final quality. In fact, precipitation events or temperature extremes during critical periods can neutralize the effects of nitrogen fertilizations or chemical applications, as well as nitrogen cycle, with an indirect effect on the grain quality.

The importance of such studies is mostly related to the potential development of a wheat quality forecast system in order to supply cereal growers with useful information on the potential quality of the next production. The integration of these results with a climatic seasonal forecast, in fact, can represent the basis of a quality provisional system to support the sector of durum wheat production.

## ACKNOWLEDGMENTS

The authors wish to thank Fondazione Monte dei Paschi di Siena, Consorzio Agrario di Siena and COST734 Action for their financial, technical and scientific support to this research.

## REFERENCES

[1]  M. Bertelli, *Proceedings of Ricerca sulla filiera del pane e della pasta con semi antichi di cereali in agricoltura biodinamica,* Bologna, (2008).

[2]  G. Russell. *In Encyclopedia of Applied Plant Sciences,* 905-910 (2004).

[3]  O. Paredez-Lopez, M. Corravioubas-Alvarez, J. Barquin-Carmona. *Cereal Chem.,* 62, 427–432 (1985).

[4]  M. Ciaffi, L. Tozzi, B. Borghi, M. Corbellini, D. Lafiandra, *J. Cereal Sci.,* 24, 91–100 (1996).

[5]  H. Faridi, J.W. Finley, CRC *Critical Reviews of Food Science and Nutrition,* 28, 175–209 (1989).

[6]  G.L. Lookhart,. K.F. Finney, *Cereal Chem.,* 61, 496–499 (1984).

[7]   V.A. Johnson, P.J. Mattern, Nutritional quality of cereal grains: Genetic and Agronomic improvement edited by R.A. Olsen and K.J. Frey *Agronomy Monographs,* 28 Asa, Madison, WI.,1987, pp. 134–182

[8]   P.J. Randall, H.J. Moss, *J. Agric. Res.,* 41, 603–617 (1990).

[9]   C.W. Wrigley, C. Blumenthal, P.W. Gras, E.W.R. Barlow, Aust. *J. Plant Physiol.,* 21, 875–885 (1994).

[10]  M. Corbellini, M. G. Canevar, L. Mazza, M. Ciaffi, D. Lafiandra, B. Borghi, Aust. *J. Plant Physiol.,* 24, 245–260 (1997).

[11]  P.J. Stone, P.W. Gras, M.E.J. Nicolas, Cereal Sci., 25, 129–141 (1997).

[12]  C. Daniel, E.J. Triboi, *Cereal Sci.,* 32, 45–56 (2000).

[13]  A. Correl, J. Butler, L. Spouncer, C. Wrigley, Aust. *J. Plant Physiol.,* 21, 869-873 (1994).

[14]  J. Pan, Y. Zhu, W. Cao, T. Dai, D. Jiarg, *Plant Prod. Sci.,* 9, 323-333 (2006).

[15]  M.T. Labuschagne, O. Elago, E.J. Koen, *Cereal Sci.,* 49, 184–189 (2009).

[16]  P. Hogy, A.J. Fangmeier, *J. Cereal Sci.,* 3, 580–591 (2008).

[17]  D. Grifoni, M. Mancini, G. Maracchi, S. Orlandini, G. Zipoli, *Am. J. Enol. Vitic.,* 57, 339-346 (2006).

[18]  L. Gimeno, P. Ribera, R. Iglesias, L. de la Torre, R. Garcia, E. Hernandez, *Clim. Res.,* 21, 165-172 (2002).

[19]  H. Wanner, S. Bronnimann, C. Casty, D. Gyalistras, J. Luterbacher, C. Schmutz, D.B. Stephenson, E. Xoplaki, *Surv. Geophys.,* 22, 321-382 (2001).

[20]  J.W. Hurrell, Y. Kushnir, G. Ottersen, M. Visbeck, (Eds.) *Geophysical Monograph* 134. American Geophysical Union, Washington, DC, USA, (2003).

[21]  P.S. Kettlewell, R.B. Sothern, W.L.J. Koukkari, *Cereal Sci.,* 29, 205-209 (1999).

[22]  M.D. Atkinson, P.S. Kettlewell, P.D. Hollins, D.B. Stephenson, N.V. Hardwik, *Agr. Forest. Meteorol.,* 130, 27-37 (2005).

[23]  P.S. Kettlewell, D.B. Stephenson, M.D. Atkinson, P.D. Hollins, *Weather,* 58, 1-9 (2003).

[24]  A. Colman, *Int. J. CLimatol.,* 17, 1285-1300 (1997).

[25]  E. Kalnay, M. Kanamitsu, R. Kistler, W. Collins, D. Deaven, L. Gandin, M. Iredell, S. Saha, G. White, J. Woollen, Y. Zhu, M. Chelliah, W. Ebisuzaki, W. Higgins, J. Janowiak, K. C. Mo, C. Ropelewski, J. Wang, A. Leetmaa, R. Reynolds, R. Jenne, D. Joseph, Bull. *Amer. Meteor.,* 77, 437-471 (1996).

[26]  J.W. Hurrel, H. van Loon, *Clim. Change,* 36, 301-326 (1997).

In: Advances in Environmental Modeling and Measurements     ISBN: 978-1-60876-599-7
Editors: D. T. Mihailović, B. Lalić, pp. 209-222     © 2010 Nova Science Publishers, Inc.

*Chapter 19*

# CLIMATE CHANGE IMPACT ON SMALL GRAINS DISEASES APPEARANCE IN VOJVODINA REGION

## *R. Jevtić*[*1], *M. Telečki*[1], *B. Lalić*[2], *D.T. Mihailović*[2] *and M. Malešević*[1]

[1]Institute of Field and Vegetable Crops, Novi Sad, Serbia
[2]University of Novi Sad, Novi Sad, Serbia

## ABSTRACT

In the province of Vojvodina, biotic and abiotic factors were identified that may lead to significant yield losses. Their prevalence was directly correlated with climatic changes.

There is a strong correlation between the causal agents of powdery mildew and leaf rust, because the occurrence of one of the two pathogens prevents the other from occurring as a major outbreak. The present chapter introduces the concept of the Uredo-Teleuto Spore Coefficient (UTC). In *Puccinia coronata*, this coefficient shows the rapidity of transition from the uredo to the teleuto stage under the influence of temperature on reproductive organs of the pathogen. Based on the UTC values (0-1), five U/T categories were established. The most genotypes (54, or 22.6%) had UTC=1, i.e. a complete transition of *P. coronata* from the uredo stage to the teleuto one. Climatic changes have resulted in the dominance of pathogens that require higher temperatures for their development or are better able to adapt to drought conditions (*Septoria* spp., *Pyrenophora tritici-repentis*, *P. teres*, *Rhynchosporium secalis*). At phenophase 29-30, a correlation was found between the number of pycnides formed and infection severity by *Septoria tritici* in the first seven leaves. The correlation was complete in the variety Simonida (r=0.93) and very high in the variety Pobeda (r=0.88). The main causal agents of grain destruction in wheat are FHB and bunt, which may result in total yield losses. Abiotic factors that may significantly reduce grain yields are temperature conditions causing problems in the early stages of small grains development or stress at yield formation. The development of cultivars resistant to parasitic fungi is a very important measure of their control. Small grains cultivars for planting should be adapted and chosen based on resistance to abiotic and biotic factors, while the breeding strategy should be oriented towards developing genotypes adapted to stress factors.

* Corresponding author: E-mail address: jevtic@ifvcns.ns.ac.rs; Phone: +381 21 4898207, Fax: +381 21 4898222

# 1. INTRODUCTION

It is evident that certain climatic changes have been taking place in recent years. Global warming is one of them. Temperature has a potential impact on plant disease through both the host crop plant and the pathogen [1]. The risk of disease and pest damages to agricultural crops has increased significantly as a result of climatic changes. Climate change could have positive, negative or no impact on individual plant diseases. However, it can be foreseen that in some regions, under very strong temperature-precipitation change "signal", losses induced by increased infection potential of present and/or new diseases could be significant [2].

In Vojvodina and Serbia, climatic changes increase the incidence of small grains pathogens and influence their prevalence, adaptability and development cycle. The pathogen control principles used so far have been showing weaknesses in certain areas, bringing about the need for new methods of study under the new set of circumstances.

Small grains pathogens can be divided into three groups based on the symptoms and changes they cause in the plant being grown. These are: obligate parasites (*Puccinia* sp. and *Blumeria* sp.), organisms causing spot-type diseases (*Septoria* sp., *Pyrenophora* sp. and *Rhynchosporium*), and agents causing grain destruction (*Fusarium* sp.). According to the mechanisms established between the plant and the pathogen in the course of infection, the parasites can be classified as either obligate or facultative.

The causal agents of nonparasitic spots in small grains are most often a result of various abiotic factors, such as climatic changes and increased concentrations of ozone and carbon dioxide ($O_3, CO_2$), i.e. the greenhouse effect [3].

Studies conducted over a number of years in the Vojvodina region have shown that there is a large number of biotic and abiotic factors that may lead to significant yield losses. It is therefore necessary to understand their prevalence and direct correlation with climatic changes.

# 2. EFFECT ON BIOTROPHIC PARASITES

## 2.1. Powdery Mildew (*Blumeria /Erysiphe/ graminis*)

Powdery mildew is a disease occurring in warmer weather conditions preceded by occasional wet and cool spells. The conidia of this parasite germinate at high temperatures ranging from 1 to 30 °C without the presence of water, while the infection occurs at temperatures between 5 and 30 °C. Warm springs and summers promote the occurrence of the parasite.

In Vojvodina agroecological conditions, changes have been observed that are reflected in the greater severity of outbreaks of pathogens that are becoming prevalent in some parts of the country. In small grains, changes in the population and virulence of *Blumeria* (=*Erysiphe*) *graminis tritici* have been monitored via the sexual and asexual parts of the population.

In Vojvodina, the causal agent of powdery mildew of wheat develops a total of 15-18 generations, including the transitional period between the harvest and new planting when the so-called green bridge is formed [4]. After 30 asexual cycles of *Erysiphe graminis*, some cultivars may adapt to the pathogen [5,6].

Durability of resistance may be threatened, however, if the number of infection cycles within a growing season increases because of one or more of the following factors: increased fecundity, more pathogen generations per season, or a more suitable microclimate for disease development. This may lead to more rapid evolution of aggressive pathogen races [7].

During the 2000-2009 period, the highest degree of correlation was observed between population virulence in the years 2000 and 2003 (r=0.83) and 2002 and 2006 (r=0.83). In the same period, a complete correlation was found between resistance genes Pm17 and Pm2+6 (r=0.95), Pm2 and Pm2+ (r=0.92).

The effectiveness of the Pm resistance genes is correlated with temperature conditions. Wheat plant response to the pathogen is reflected in the number and size of the pustules forming on the leaves, which has as a result the existence of different infection types.

Race-specific resistance often gives complete protection, but most race-specific genes begin to lose effectiveness within 2-4 years [8]. Up against race-specific resistance, non-race resistance is incomplete but durable. It is characterized by retarding the rate of disease development and is also called partial resistance. Partial resistance to powdery mildew may involve one or several of the following components [9]: increased incubation or latent period (from inoculation to appearance of symptoms), reduced infection frequency (number of colonies per unit leaf area), reduced infectious period (the length of time during which the colony produces viable spores), reduced infection lesion size (colony size), reduced spore production (number of spores produced per unit leaf area over a particular length of time).

Partial resistance to powdery mildew (*Blumeria graminis* f.sp. *tritici*) of twenty winter wheat varieties and the susceptible control variety Barbee was tested under controlled conditions [10]. In order to assess the partial resistance of the varieties, the latent period ($LP_{50}$) and infection frequency (number of colonies per unit leaf area) were used. The highest degree of partial resistance that involved a long latent period and a low infection frequency was observed in the variety Dragana. The varieties Angelina, Barbara and NS 27/03 had a shorter $LP_{50}$, but similar infection frequencies; therefore, it seems likely that they also possess a high degree of partial resistance. There were significantly high negative correlations between $LP_{50}$ and infection frequency ($r=-0.755$) (Fig. 1). A similar correlation was found in studies of barley powdery mildew [11] and oat powdery mildew [12].

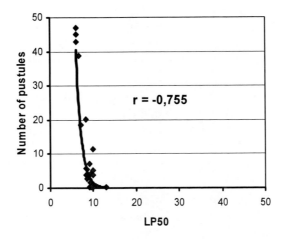

Figure 1. Exponential curve of correlation between $LP_{50}$ and infection frequency

Figure 2. *Blumeria graminis tritici* and *Puccinia triticina*

Identification of wheat varieties with partial resistance is of great importance for wheat breeding programmes, because this type of resistance has provided durable control of powdery mildew in cereals in several countries [13].

Multi-year data have shown that *B. graminis tritici* reaches a second peak of infection in the last few days of May in Vojvodina agroecological conditions. After that, the fungus begins to develop cleistothecia as a result of its sexual cycle and the risk of any major damage to crops practically vanishes. There is a direct link between the occurrence and severity of leaf rust and the causal agent of powdery mildew. The more severe the outbreak of powdery mildew is, the lower the incidence of leaf rust will be, and vice versa (Fig. 2).

## 2.2. Rusts of Small Grains (*Puccinia* spp.)

Rusts are caused by *Puccinia triticina* in wheat, *Puccinia hordei* in barley, and *Puccinia coronata* in oats. In Vojvodina, the occurrence of the rust-causing pathogens in small grains has been stagnating in recent years compared with the previous period. This is attributed to the earlier occurrence of spot-type diseases resulting in their earlier expansion across the leaf area, which accelerates aging and reduces leaf area duration. Compared with the previous period, these pathogens have been recently forming less generations and have been transitioning quickly from the uredo to the teleuto stage, which is a direct result of climatic changes.

The varying effectiveness of resistance genes depending on changes in temperature (temperature sensitive genes) is pronounced in the case of the causal agents of cereal rusts.

Examples include the Pg3 and Pg4 genes for resistance to the causal agent of oat stem rust [14], the Lr26 gene linked to resistance against the causal organism of wheat leaf rust (*Puccinia triticina*), and the generally increased occurrence of the causal agent of wheat yellow rust, *P. striiformis* [14].

Oat crops suffer significant damage from crown rust (*Puccinia coronata*) and stem rust (*P. graminis avenae*). Infections by these pathogens appear later in oat as compared to wheat and barley and are hence more severe in the spring genotypes of the crop. However, the effectiveness of the resistance genes (Pm and Lr, Pc ones) in a population is dependant on temperature fluctuations. The severity of the attacks by the pathogens is reflected in the different number and size of the pustules forming on the leaves, based on which different infection types are distinguished. By making a rapid transition from the stage of urediniospores to that of teliospores (Fig. 3), leaf rust causes less damage than expected.

At the Rimski Šančevi Experiment Field of the Institute of Field and Vegetable Crops, the severity of infection by the fungus *P. coronata* was assessed in 293 oat genotypes originating from 16 European countries. Experimental unit size was 2 m$^2$ and the assessment was carried out on June 16, 2008. Infection severity was estimated using a modified Cobb's scale (0-100%) [15]. The uredo-teleuto spore coefficient (UTC) was calculated based on the ratio of total leaf coverage by *P. coronata* to coverage by the teleutospores. The UTC shows the rapidity of transition from the uredo to the teleuto stage under the influence of temperature on reproductive organs of the pathogen. The frequency and distribution of the oat genotypes (Fig. 4) was determined based on the UTC. The most genotypes (54, or 22.6%) had UTC=1, i.e. a complete transition of *P. coronata* from the uredo stage to the teleuto one.

Figure 3. *Pucinia coronata*

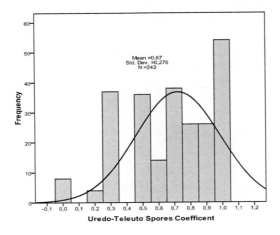

Figure 4. The frequency and distribution of the oat genotypes

Based on the UTC values (0-1), five U/T (Uredo/Teleuto stage) categories were established: Category I (UTC=0 ((U=U, for value T=0 and T=tR (trace)); Category II (UTC=0.1-0.4, for U>T); Category III (UTC=0.5, for U=2T); Category IV (UTC=0.6-0.9 for U=<T); and Category V (UTC=1 for U=T). In Category I, there is little or no transition from uredospores to teleutospores, so only the uredo stage is present (U=U), while in Category V, all uredospores have completely transitioned to the teleuto phase of *P. coronata* (U=T).

Disease resistance can be differentially affected by temperature. For example, cultivars of wheat on the UK Recommended List [16] were routinely tested against isolates of brown rust (leaf rust) (*Puccinia recondita*) at 10 °C and 25 °C for 20 years [17,18]. Generally about half showed differential resistance expression, either effective at 10 °C and not at 25 °C or vice versa [19]. Browder and Eversmeyer [20] also reported similar differential temperature responses in the same host–pathogen system, and both groups also demonstrated that the effect was not necessarily attributable simply to resistance gene expression, as isolates showed differential responses too. Similar temperature sensitivities have been reported previously for the same rust [21], *Puccinia striiformis* [22], and *Puccinia tritici* in oats [23].

In 1993/94 in Serbia and Vojvodina an epidemic of leaf rust occurred in wheat. According to Jevtic et al. [24], the main reasons were 59 days with rainfall and favorable temperatures (15-20 °C), susceptible genotypes, and volunteer wheat plants that enabled the maintenance and reproduction of the pathogen. In 2007 in Vojvodina, there was a severe outbreak of yellow rust, which was attributed to the inoculum arriving by air current from Romania to Vojvodina via the Carpathians [14].

Based on empirical climate–disease models established with a limited set of observational data, Jahn et al. [25] predicted that an increase in temperature combined with less precipitation could increase leaf rust of wheat and barley (*Puccinia triticina*), decrease infestation levels caused by foot rot and leaf blotch diseases, and cause no change in powdery mildew on small grains.

# 3. EFFECT ON CAUSAL AGENTS OF LEAF SPOTS

## 3.1. Leaf and Glume Blotches (*Septoria* spp.). (*Septoria tritici*, Perfect Stage *Mycosphaerella graminicola*; *Septoria nodorum* Perfect Stage *Leptosphaeria nodorum*).

Climatic changes have resulted in the dominance of pathogens that require higher temperatures for their development or are better able to adapt to drought conditions. This is the reason why fungi of the genus *Septoria* spp. have assumed the dominant role, causing significant damage.

The causal agent of leaf and glume blotches is currently considered one of the pathogens with the greatest impact on global wheat production and is the main wheat pathogen in most of Europe, North Africa, South America, and several other parts of the world.

The occurrence of these diseases is enabled by warm and wet conditions. The reproductive organs of the fungi, pycnidiospores, germinate at 2-37 °C. Major outbreaks of leaf and glume blotches in wheat occur during warm and wet springs and summers, causing significant yield losses.

The minimum temperature for germination is 2-3 °C, while the optimum and maximum ones are 20-25 °C and 33-37 °C, respectively. Infection in the field will stop if the temperature drops below 7 degrees for two consecutive days.

The pycnospores are released from the pycnides when the leaf is moistened for 30 minutes or more. The spores form in a thick, sticky substance that has high sugar and protein concentrations. These reserve substances enable the pycnospores to maintain moistness during dry spells.

During the wheat growing season, a number of secondary infections occur (seven to nine generations of the pathogen). The number of generations can be easily calculated based on incubation period length by month. The longest incubations occur in the autumn - 36, 28 and 25 days. In the spring, the length of the incubation period gradually decreases with increasing temperature until it reaches about 11 days in June. Infection in the field ceases if the temperature declines below 7 degrees for two consecutive days.

In 2006 at Rimski Šančevi, we studied 3 800 wheat genotypes and found that 2 064 (or 55.6%) of them had attack severity levels of 30% or more [26]. This translates into at least one third of the leaf area being affected by the spots caused by the parasite, which has direct influence on yields. The severity of *S. tritici* attack was greater in winter than in spring genotypes, leading to the conclusion that in the winter genotypes the primary infection occurred in the autumn.

In 2009 in several locations in Vojvodina, there were reports of deterioration of the lower wheat leaves due to early infections by the fungus *S. tritici*, resulting in a multitude of pycnides with pycnospores. This means that the primary infections occurred in the autumn of 2008, when the temperature conditions were optimal. The largest number of pycnides formed on the lower leaves closest to the ground. At phenophase 29-30, a correlation was found between the number of pycnides formed and infection severity in the first seven leaves. The correlation was complete in the variety Simonida (r=0.93) and very high in the variety Pobeda (r=0.88). *S. tritici* infection severity is most commonly estimated based on the ratio of necrotic leaf area to green leaf area [27].

## 3.2. Tan Spot of Wheat (*Pyrenophora tritici-repentis*)

This pathogen was described in Serbia in 1997 [28] when it occurred sporadically in a small number of locations in Vojvodina. In recent years, the occurrence of this spot has become more severe, which is attributed directly to the influence of climatic changes. The fungus needs high temperatures in order to grow. Depending on the type of toxin it exudes, *P. tritici-repentis* can produce three kinds of symptoms, ranging from small spots to chlorosis to complete necrosis of the leaves. More severe infections may result in a complete devastation of the leaf mass, with the necrosis spreading from the tip of the lamina down to the base. After analysing samples from several sites, it has been determined that the pathogen caused significant yield losses in the susceptible varieties of wheat in 2008, with the hard (durum) cultivars being the most susceptible.

Considering the climatic changes and the future importance of this pathogen in Vojvodina and Serbia, it is necessary to identify the sources of resistance to be used in further breeding work. In 2008 at Rimski Šančevi, a total of 1 238 winter wheat genotypes from different collections were tested in two groups. The first one consisted of varieties and lines from domestic breeding programs, while the second involved genotypes from different countries. A large number of genotypes were found to be highly resistant (VR and R), namely 391 (63.5%) domestic and 285 (45.8%) foreign ones. These genotypes can be successfully used as sources of resistance to *P. tritici-repentis*.

### 3.3. Net Blotch (*Pyrenophora teres*)

Weather conditions during the 2007/08 season favored the causal agents of spot-type diseases, the same as in the preceding growing season. The winter barleys were found to be infected with the causal organism of net blotch (*Pyrenophora teres*). In Vojvodina and Serbia, this pathogen causes net blotch as well as the spot form of the disease, which often leads to erroneous conclusions when identifying the pathogen in the field. Not all varieties of winter and spring barley that are commercially grown in Serbia have resistance to *Pyrenophora teres*, so this pathogen represented a significant problem in the country's barley production.

### 3.4. Barley Scald (*Rhynchosporium secalis*)

The occurrence of this pathogen is directly corellated with global warming and the resistance of barley cultivars as well as with the amount of the spontaneous flora inoculum (grass).

## 4. EFFECT ON AGENTS CAUSING GRAIN DESTRUCTION

### 4.1. Fusarium Head Blight (*Fusarium* spp.), *F. graminearum,* Perfect Stage *Gibberella zeae; F. moniliforme,* Perfect Stage *G. fujikuroi,* Etc.

The polyphagous species of the genus *Fusarium* are ubiquitous and attack small grains and maize as well as many other cultivated species and plants of the spontaneous flora. These parasitic fungi are favored by warm and wet weather and grow successfully at temperatures of 3~30 °C. They are typical parasites of weakness, as they successfully infect plants weakened by prolonged periods of drought and warm weather. Severe outbreaks of Fusarium disease and major damages occur during warm and dry summers that were preceded by a wet spring.

All the above wheat diseases have been occurring in Vojvodina with significantly increased severity in recent years, which used not to be the case. This can be partially attributed to the changes in climatic factors in the province, most notably the increased temperatures in spring and summer.

Head blight, caused by the fungi of the genus *Fusarium*, was found in large numbers in the varieties having awns, regardless of whether they were winter, facultative, or spring ones. The percentage of diseased spikes was directly correlated with planting date and preceding crop as well as with the coincidence of the ascospore release phase in the parasite and the flowering stage in the plant. Because of this, the control of this parasite did not produce the expected results in the commercial crops, as head blight appeared in some localities in spite of the fact that the crops were treated against the disease.

With the fungi of the genus *Fusarium*, Telečki and Jevtić [29] report finding a very strong negative correlation between 1 000-grain weight and the percentage of grains infected by *F. graminearum* in the hard wheat cultivar Dušan (r=-88.9) as well as a strong correlation of the same kind in the cultivar Durumko (r=-74.0). In 70% of cases, there is a greater risk of the occurrence of Fusarium diseases in fields that had maize or monoculture as the preceding crop. This is explained by the fungus entering the perfect stage on harvest residues and by the release of ascospores being at the peak at wheat flowering. However, if the crop phenophase fails to concide with favorable conditions for the development of the pathogen (warm and wet weather), individual varieties may often manage to avoid the attack (escape-type resistance). This is why the disease prognostication system is of great importance from the economic and environmental points of view.

Changes in crop rotations in response to climate change may also influence the future importance of specific pathogens. For example, if warming of northern latitudes enables forage maize to be grown in the rotation, then this will leave residues in which pathogens such as Fusarium Head Blight (FHB) could build up high levels of inoculum for subsequent wheat and barley crops [30].

## 4.2. Bunts (*Tilletia* spp.)

Wheat bunt is not a new but an old, almost forgotten disease that caused huge damage in 1993-1997. In 1997, it infected 100 000-150 000 tons of wheat seed, which, given the average yield of 4 tons recorded that year on state-owned land in the country, corresponds to 25 000-37 500 hectares worth of production [31].

The domestic scientific community had long held that teliospores of the causal agents of wheat bunt (*Tilletia* spp.) that are found on the seeds were the main source of the inoculum and that the critical period for the infection ended with the moment of emergence [32, 33]. Recently, however, significant new results have been obtained in this connection by Koprivica [34] in a study involving daily measurements of soil temperature during the growing of wheat under the conditions of artificial grain and soil infection and daily monitoring of conditions for the occurrence of infection. When wheat was infected by teliospores present on the seeds and in the soil, the critical period lasted 1-120 days after planting (r> +0,42). Temperatures during that period ranged from −1.8 to 13.1 °C. Maximum infection levels were achieved when the temperatures were within the 2.0-12.3 °C range, or 4.0-5.0 °C on average. The most plants were infected during the fourth ten-day period after planting, while a somewhat smaller number were infected in the sixth ten-day period. These findings have shown that in Serbian conditions the soil is the more important source of the inoculum and that infection by *Tilletia* sp. takes place during emergence.

# 5. EFFECT OF NONPARASITIC FACTORS

## 5.1. Influence of Ozone and Carbon Dioxide

In Vojvodina and Serbia, there has been no specific research conducted on the effects of $CO_2$ or $O_3$ on small grains pathogens. However, looking at the data in the literature, it is evident that these gases play an important role in the development cycles of certain pathogens and affect pathogen aggressiveness and rate of development, as the plant-host relationship is very active [6,7].

The causal agents of nonparasitic spots in small grains are most often a result of various abiotic factors, such as climatic changes and increased concentrations of ozone and carbon dioxide ($O_3$, $CO_2$), i.e. the greenhouse effect [3].

As a result of $CO_2$ influence, biotrophic parasites penetrate into plant tissue more rapidly [35,36], although resistance to the the causal agent of barley powdery mildew cannot be directly linked to the thickness of the waxy coating on the leaves [35]. The assumption is that increased $CO_2$ concentrations have a positive influence on rust penetration and development [37] but inhibit other biotrophs, most notably the causal agents of powdery mildews [35]. In the context of resistance to leaf pathogens, CO2 is also interesting because it can change the C:N ratio, which may have different effects on pathogenic fungi [38]. Increased $CO_2$ concentrations reduce N levels in wheat leaf cells by an average of 14% [39], which can be linked to decreased susceptibility to powdery mildew [40]. Following the penetration, the established colonies of *E. graminis* [35] grew faster under doubled $CO_2$. Increasing stand density in small grains increases the relative moisture content of the plants, which promotes the development of pathogens such as rusts, powdery mildews, leaf spots, and blights [37]. A change in microclimate may affect the growth, sporulation, spread, and infection severity of some leaf pathogens [7,41].

Krupa et al. [3] gave some examples of the effects of $O_3$ on plant diseases. There are some negative effects on fungal diseases such as reduced growth of uredia of *P. coronata* in oats, decreased hyphal growth and urediospore production of *P. graminis f. sp. tritici* on $O_3$-injured leaves of wheat, reduced rate of infection of *E. graminis* f. sp. *hordei* if exposed to sufficient $O_3$ during incubation, but enhanced colony size when infection is established.

## 5.2. Effect of Temperature

Climatic changes are most often explained by a rise in temperature. Regardless of whether they are high or low, excessive temperatures negatively affect plants and plant processes in the form of stress. In some years in Vojvodina, temperatures had a significant effect on overall small grains production. Those years are often characterized as being unfavorable for small grains production, which may mean that climatic changes had the most prominent effect in them.

- **Dry Seed Decay**. In 2000 at the location of Međa near Zrenjanin, a significant decay of wheat crops was recorded that was due to unfavorable conditions being present from planting to emergence. This period lasted for over six weeks, and planting depth was uneven. During that time, the crops were colonized by saprophytic fungi, most notably those of the genus *Penicillium* [42]. Dry seed decay, caused by *Penicillium* spp., occurs when winter wheat seeds are planted into a dry soil unfavorable for germination and emergence [43]. The decay occurs more often in semi-arid wheat-growing regions, where seeds stay in dry soil for several weeks or even months. During that time, they are colonized by saprophytic fungi, primarily those of the genera *Penicillium* and *Aspegillus*.

- **Frost.** In the 2002/03 crop season, deterioration of winter small grains was recorded. Of the 87 245 ha of winter barley sown in Serbia, 25-30% were winterkilled or damaged [44]. The largest damage was reported in the province of Vojvodina and was recorded at the following sites: Subotica, Bečej, Bačka Topola, Kikinda, Zrenjanin, Vršac and Pančevo. Around 10 000 ha of winter barley were lost in the province. Direct losses totaled 620 000 EUR, while the projected loss based on yield estimates exceeded 1 000 000 EUR [44].

- **Saprophytes.** A major outbreak of saprophytic fungi was recorded on small grains in Vojvodina in 2007 as a result of a mild winter, inadequate cultural practice, an absence of fertilizer use, and attacks by leaf aphids and the barley yellow dwarf virus (BYDV). The crops were in poor condition and the plants lost their immunity. As direct effects of climate change, high temperatures and a lack of precipitation in the spring led to plant decay and colonization by saprophytes. The damage was manifested as a change in spike color and grain color (black point), a reduced 1 000-grain weight, and a high toxin content. Percentage of seed fraction <2.2 mm was 41.4-47.3% and 1 000-kernel weight (g) was 16.9-18.2, depending on seed category, variety and location [45].

- **Reddening of leaves.** By the end of April, 2007, reddening of leaves of wheat varieties appeared most frequently in the area of Banat. The explanations of this appearance and its causes differed. However, changes in leaf, ligule and stem colour were due to abiotic or biotic factors (Mycoplasma) [45].

# 6. ADAPTATION MEASURES AND CONTROL OF WHEAT DISEASES

Adaptation to the occurrence of diseases caused by climatic changes can be viewed from several aspects in which a specific relationship exists between the plant (host) and the pathogen. It is likely that climate change will have positive, negative or neutral impact on specific host–pathogen systems [7]. Climatic changes alter plant physiological processes and resistance levels, while the pathogen adapts its life cycle and aggressiveness accordingly and expresses them through the degree of pathogenicity. The geographic distribution of the host and the pathogen changes, which results in a different interactive relationship, bringing about yield losses. This is what causes changes in the efficacy of the control measures implemented.

Climatic changes had the same effect on the occurrence and severity of small grains pathogens as in the previous season, enabling the predictability of their occurrence. This was especially true for the causal agents of spot-type diseases in wheat, barley, oat, and triticale, as in their case the timely application of chemical control measures can have an economic effect.

Climate change could affect the efficacy of crop protection chemicals in one of two ways [7]. First, changes in temperature and precipitation may alter the dynamics of fungicide residues on the crop foliage. Globally, climate change models project an increase in the frequency of intense rainfall events [39], which could result in increased fungicide wash-off and reduced control.

When using chemical control agents, one must take note of the pre-harvest interval (42 days for most chemicals) in order to leave the crop enough time after the treatment to prevent active ingredient residues from appearing in the grain and straw after harvesting.

The increasing severity and harmfulness of the above diseases makes it necessary to subject wheat to a greater number of fungicide treatments. There are fungicides in existence that successfully control these diseases and their mechanisms are based on the prolongation of leaf area duration (strobilurines). However, the increased number of chemical treatments significantly increases production costs and has a negative impact on the environment. A less expensive and environmentally friendlier alternative is to treat the seed with fungicides intended for seed-borne fungi (*Septoria* spp., *Fusarium* spp., etc.).

Modern systems of pest forecasting and reporting call for the use of mini weather stations. The development of a model for the correct timing of treatments that will result in cost-effective and economically justified fungicide use in small grains is under way. The model will incorporate parameters such as climate, preceding crop, cultural practices used, and cultivar-specific resistance to diseases.

# 7. CONCLUSION

Crop cultivation in an area under the influence of climatic changes forces man to develop new genotypes with adaptability to abiotic and biotic factors or to adapt the existing genotypes to said changes. To obtain these traits, germplasm from geographically distant areas in which such desirable traits are dominant needs to be used. This germplasm contains undesirable traits as well, most often susceptability to pathogens. The newly developed crop species or cultivar is now adapted to the growing conditions resulting from the climatic changes and begins to interact with the pathogen population. Because of this, a good risk assessment must be made to prevent disease outbreaks in a given area.

The development of cultivars resistant to the said parasitic fungi is a very important measure of their control. Other important measures include the planting of healthy seeds, crop rotation, irrigation, balanced fertilizer use, and other cultural practices. In order for the adaptation measures to be implemented successfully, the breeding process must be adapted to the newly arisen climatic changes from the points of view of both the plant and the pathogen.

# REFERENCES

[1]   C. Petzoldt, A. Seaman, *http://www.climateandfarming.org/pdfs/FactSheets/III.2* Insects.Pathogens.pdf (2006).

[2]   B. Lalic, D.T. Mihailovic, R. Jevtic, S. Jasnic, *Abstracts, 8th Annual Meeting of the EMS/7th ECAC,* 5, EMS 2008-A00468 (2008).

[3]   S. Krupa, M.T. McGrath, C.P. Andersen, F.L. Booker, K.O. Burkey, A.H. Chappelka, B.I. Chevone, E.J. Pell, B.A. Zilinskas, *Plant Dis.*, 85, 4-12 (2001).

[4]   R. Jevtić, Ph.D. Thesis, Novi Sad: Faculty of Agriculture, 1993. (in Serbian)

[5]   A.C. Newton, L. McGurk, *J. Phytopathol.*, 132, 328-338 (1991).

[6]   S. Chakraborty, S. Datta, *New Phytol.*, 159, 733-742 (2002).

[7]   S.M. Coakley, H. Scherm, S. Chakraborty, *Annu. Rev. Phytopathol.*, 37, 399–426 (1999).

[8]   H. Jørgensen, *Durability of Disease Resistance*, edited by T. Jacobs, J. E. Parlevliet (Dordrecht, the Netherlands: Kluwer Academic Publishers, 1993), pp. 159–76.

[9]   J.T. Kinane, P.W. Jones, *Eur. J. Plant Pathol.*, 106, 607-616, (2000).

[10]  M. Telecki, R. Jevtic, N. Hristov, N. Mladenov, M. Kalentic, *Conference Proceedings, Conventional and Molecular Breeding of Field and Vegetable Crops*, 290-293 (2008).

[11]  M.J.C. Asher, C.E. Thomas, *Plant Pathol.*, 33, 123-130 (1984).

[12]  I.T. Jones, *Annals of Applied Biology*, 90, 233-239 (1978).

[13]  D.Z. Yu, X.J. Yang, L.J. Yang, M.J Jeger, J.K.M. Brown, *Plant Breeding*, 120, 279-284 (2001).

[14]  R. Jevtić, Z. Jerković, S. Dencić, S. Stojanović, *Plant Doctor*, 4, 455-458 (in Serbian), (1997).

[15]  R.F. Peterson, A. B. Campbell, A. E. Hannah, *Canad. J. Res.*, C-26, 496-500 (1948).

[16]  HGCA (2003): www.hgca.com

[17]  E.R.L. Jones, B. C. Clifford, *United Kingdom Cereal Pathogen Virulence Survey 1985–2001 Annual Reports.* (1986–2002).

[18]  E.R.L. Jones, *United Kingdom Cereal Pathogen Virulence Survey 2003–2006 Annual Reports.* (2004–2007).

[19]  E.R.L. Jones, *United Kingdom Cereal Pathogen Virulence Survey 2002 Annual Report.*, 19–31 (2003).

[20]  L.E. Browder, M.G. Eversmeyer, *Phytopathology* 76, 1286–1288 (1986).

[21]  P.L. Dyck, R. Johnson, *Canadian Journal of Plant Pathology*, 5, 229–234 (1983).

[22]  Z.K. Gerecheter-Amitai, E. L. Sharp, M. Reinhold, *Euphytica*, 33, 665–672 (1984).

[23]  J.W. Martens, R.I.H. McKenzie, G.J. Green, *Can. J. Bot.*, 45, 451–58 (1967).

[24]  R. Jevtić, Z. Jerković, M. Pribaković, *Plant Doctor*, 1, 42-45 (in Serbian) (1995).

[25]  M. Jahn, E. Kluge, S. Enzian, *Asp. Appl. Biol.*, 45, 247–252 (1996).

[26]  M. Kalentić, R. Jevtić, M. Telečki, *Book of Abstracts, VIII Counseling on Plant Protection*, 32-33 (in Serbian), (2006).

[27]  Z. Eyal, A. L.Scharen, J. M. Prescott, M. Vanginkel, *The Septoria Diseases of Wheat. Concepts and Methods of Disease Management.* CIMMYT, Mexico, D.F (1987).

[28]  R. Jevtić, *Plant Doctor*, 5, 320-524 (in Serbian), (1997).

[29]  M. Telečki, R. Jevtić, *Book of Abstracts, VIII Counseling on Plant Protection*, 34-35 (in Serbian), (2006).

[30]  Maiorano, M. Blandino, A. Reyneri, F. Vanara, *Crop Protection*, 27, 182–188 (2008).

[31]  R. Jevtić, S. Stamenković, M. Malesević, *Plant Doctor,* 5, 524-526 (in Serbian), (1997).

[32]  M. Josifović, *Plant Pathology*. Beograd: Scientific book, 1964. (in Serbian)

[33]  M. Ivanović, D. Ivanović, *Plant Mycoses and Pseudomycoses*, 2nd edition, Beograd: P.P. DMV, 2001. (in Serbian)

[34]  M. Koprivica, *MSc. Thesis, Beograd-Zemun: Faculty of Agriculture*, 2004. (in Serbian)

[35]  J.M. Hibberd, R. Whitbread, J. F. Farrar, *Physiol. Mol. Plant Pathol.*, 48, 37–53 (1996).

[36]　J.M. Hibberd, R. Whitbread, J. F. Farrar, *New Phytol.*, 134, 309–315, (1996).

[37]　W.J. Manning, A. von Tiedemann, *Environ. Pollut.*, 88, 219– 45 (1995).

[38]　J. Goudriaan, J. C. Zadoks, *Environ. Pol'ut.*, 87, 215–224 (1995).

[39]　M.F. Cotrufo, P. Inescon, A. Scott, *Glob Change Biol.*, 4, 43–54 (1998).

[40]　G.B. Thompson, J.K.M. Brown, F.I. Wcodward, *Plant, Cell and Environment*, 16, 687-694 (1993).

[41]　S. Chakraborty, I. B. Pangga, J. Lupton, L. Hart, P.M. Room, D.Yates, *Environ. Pollut.*, 108, 381-387 (2000).

[42]　R. Jevtić, L. Panković, M. Milosević, M. Vujaković, *Plant Doctor,* 2, 121-125 (in Serbian)(2001).

[43]　B. Mathur, M. Cunfer, S*eed Born Diseases and Seed Health testing of Wheat*, Chapter 10, Copenhagen, (1993).

[44]　R. Jevtić, L. Panković, N. Pržulj, G. Mladenović, *Plant Doctor*, 4, 410-415 (in Serbian) (2003).

[45]　R. Jevtić, M. Telečki, M. Vujaković, M. Ignjatov, S. Statkić, *Plant Doctor*, 6, 418-425 (in Serbian), (2008).

In: Advances in Environmental Modeling and Measurements    ISBN: 978-1-60876-599-7
Editors: D. T. Mihailović, B. Lalić, pp. 223-231    © 2010 Nova Science Publishers, Inc.

*Chapter 20*

# IMPACT OF CLIMATE CHANGE ON AGRICULTURE IN NORTH-WEST RUSSIA AND ADAPTATION OPTIONS

## *M.V. Nikolaev*[*]

Agrophysical Research Institute, Russian Federation

## ABSTRACT

The impact of climate change on farm practice and distribution of crops within cultivable area of North-West Russia (55–65 °N, 20–60 °E) is analyzed.

The observed trends in seasonal temperature and precipitation series since 1961 indicate that the NW Russia's climate is getting warmer with some increase in wintertime precipitation. Such temperature and precipitation changes result in both beneficial (e.g., full ripening of warm-weather varieties) and adverse (e.g., increasing risk of rotting- and wetting out for winter crops; extending distribution of pest, diseases and weeds) effects on agriculture.

For assessing the impact of climate change on the NW Russia's agriculture for coming decades, the Last Interglacial climatic optimum is considered as a paleoanalog scenario of the global warming by 2020–2030, the conditions been compared with simulation results from transient GCMs for same "time slice". The input data include such climatic indicators as "winter severity" and "winter wetness" indices, effective temperature sums and soil moisture content as well as agronomical/technological parameters including regular dates of sowing and optimum fertilization. Moreover, the spatial analogs method is applied to changing climatic conditions.

Assessment results obtained evidence of both opportunities for cultivating more productive crops on the background of increasing fertilizer efficiency, and, on the other hand, deteriorating crop wintering in the regions with mild/moderate winters and potential acclimatization of some insect pest species in the more northern parts of NW Russia.

Regarding this, a number of feasible adaptation measures and strategies may be considered as follows: optimization of farm technologies and timing of farm operations; increasing cropping systems diversity by implementation of new crops into crop rotation systems; enlarging areas under snow mold resistant cultivars; improving tillage practice to suppress pest population and pathogens survivability; introducing entomophages and useful insects; diversification of environmentally sound chemicals for plant protection; etc.

[*] Corresponding author: E-mail address: clenrusa@mail.ru, Phone: +7 812 5341698, Fax: +7 812 5341900

# 1. INTRODUCTION

North-West Russia occupies more than 1/3 of the European territory of Russian Federation to the north of 55 °N. The Region's topography is characterized by plains and hills; also by high percent of forest-clad landscapes and bogginess. Fig. 1 illustrates the map of North-West Russia with indicated main regions within this territory.

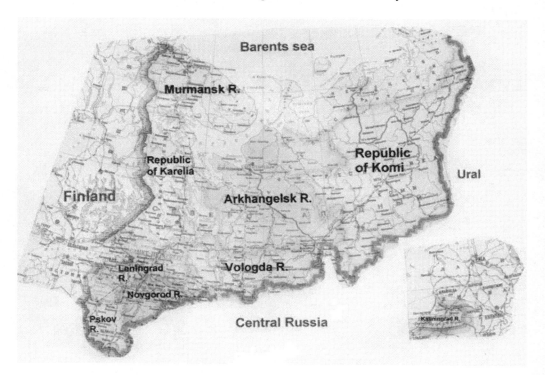

Figure 1. Territory of North-West Russia.

The NW Russia's climate is under the Gulf Stream influence and sporadic invasions of the Arctic air masses. Therefore, the type of regional climate is temperate, humid in the southern parts and cool temperate in the northern parts. The podzolic soils are predominated in soil cover. There are areas with gley soils and alluvial soils as well. Regional soils have low natural fertility, but very responsible to fertilizer applications.

The cultivable area is concentrated between 55–65 °N and 20–60 °E, and agriculture is presented by crop farming for potatoes, flax and fodder crops as well as cereal-, vegetable- and grassland farming. The basic crops are winter rye, spring barley, oats, potatoes, fiber flax and seed grasses. Wheat is cultivated in the southern parts of the Region only.

The climatic conditions which limit the cultivation practice diversity are thermal resources during growing season, whereas resources of moisture are in abundance.

Proceeding from the above, the NW Russia's territory may be subdivided into 3 agro-landscape (agroclimatic) zones, which are differentiated by heat provision:

1. Boreal forest zone (South of Murmansk Reg., central parts of Arkhangel'sk Reg. and Rep. of Komi; North of Rep. of Karelia);

2.  Subboreal forest zone (southern parts of Arkhangel'sk Reg., Rep. of Komi and Rep. of Karelia; North of Vologda Reg.);
3.  Forest zone, which is subdivided into 3 agro-landscape (agroclimatic) provinces:
    - Eastern province (South of Vologda Reg.);
    - Central province (Leningrad Reg., Novgorod Reg. and Pskov Reg.);
    - Western province (Kaliningrad Reg.).

## 2. OBSERVED CHANGES IN CLIMATE AND THEIR EFFECTS ON AGRICULTURE

The analysis of changes in temperature/precipitation conditions over the last four decades has confirmed that the NW Russia's climate is getting warmer. The evaluation of linear trends in air temperature series reveals the presence of upward trends, especially observed for winter/spring period, which are characterized by the increasing rate: 4.9–2.4 °C/ 40 years. The observed trends in precipitation series indicate some increase in precipitation totals due to increasing wintertime precipitation [1].

Climate warming is also associated with long-term changes in extreme temperatures. In NW Russia there is an evidence of the decreasing number of frost days which results reduction of frost killing events, especially for orchard plants. On the other hand, extremely high summer temperatures are recorded more frequently in recent decades than previously. Extremely hot summer conditions in the 1990s, nevertheless, influenced positively the farm practice since they contributed to full ripening of warm weather crops such as marrow- and tomato local cultivars.

In the last 50 years, the analysis of changes in accumulated effective temperatures ($\sum T > 10$ °C) shows, that their increment within the NW Russia's cultivable area makes up 80–100 °C, and for intensive crop growth period even 140 °C (see Fig. 2).

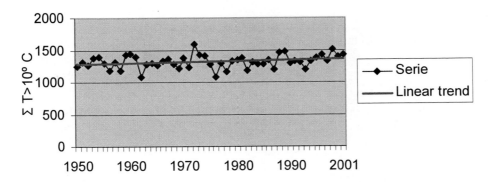

Figure 2. Changes in accumulated temperature for June-August at Petrozavodsk (Rep. of Karelia).

Meantime, the accumulated temperatures below 0 °C considerably decreased, and as a consequence the soil temperature at the depth of tillering node considerably increased by 2–3 °C. Then, the recurrence of rotting out in NW Russia increased by approx. 15–17% over the last 50 years [2]. Also wetting out phenomena became more frequent even in the large areas with adverse effect on crops.

Over the last decades, the insect population growth has been observed with strong attacks on crops. The rapid pest infestation into large areas is registered more frequently than before; several species migrate northward. For example, the area of occupation and acclimatization (due to mild winters) by such potato pest as Colorado beetle has moved to 63 °N,, including southern parts of Arkhangel'sk Reg., Rep. of Karelia and Rep. of Komi. In fact, this pest became ordinary for the NW Russia's potatoes farming [3].

A number of pathogens not specific for the NW Russia's conditions is been enlarged in relation to climate change. The new diseases are *pyrenosphoriosis* on winter wheat and grow rust on oats. The harmfulness of such leaf disease as *helmintosphoriosis* on barley has increased by 3.5 times in recent years [4]. Snow mold infects winter cereals annually is affecting from 53% to 100% of plants. Besides, potato diseases, *bacteriosis* on fiber flax and *coccomycosis* on cherry tree are frequently registered to north of 60 °N. (e.g., in Vologda Reg.).

The effects of climate change result in weed flora spread. We can find green amaranth, which was considered a southern weed, in crops north 59 °N (e.g., in Leningrad Reg.). *Echinochloa crus-galli* has widely spread in NW Russia as well as *Cirsium arvense* did [5].

## 3. POSSIBLE IMPACT OF FORTHCOMING CLIMATE CHANGE ON AGRICULTURE

To assess the impact of climate change on the NW Russia's agriculture in forthcoming decades, the Last Interglacial climatic optimum is considered as a paleoanalog scenario of the global warming by 2020–2030, these conditions been compared with simulation results obtained from transient GCMs for the same "time slice".

This scenario is based on paleoclimatic data, and scenario estimates are in good agreement with the observed trends in changing climatic conditions in NW Russia during the last five decades.

Thus, the scenario estimates indicate an increment in $\sum T > 10$ °C up to 200–400 °C within the NW Russia's cultivable area and, as a result, an elongation in the period with temperatures above this temperature threshold. The increase in effective temperature sums and the growing season length are of great importance for the cultivation practice, in particular, in the potential distribution of crops and cultivars. According to the existing methodologies [6], accumulated effective temperatures can be compared with bioclimatic temperatures which are necessary for successful principal phases of crop development and maturity.

Prospective changes in specialization of cash crops production in different agro-landscape zones and provinces with predicted changes in thermal conditions by 2020–2030 is shown in Tab. 1. Such changes result in the opportunities to switch to more later-season cultivars and also to grow new crops (e.g., buckwheat, sugar beet and ultra early- ripening maize hybrids).

**Table 1. Prospective changes in specialization of farm production under climate change in NW Russia.**

| Agro-landscape zone (province) | $\Sigma T > 10\ °C$ at current climate | Specialization in farm production under current climate conditions | $\Sigma T > 10\ °C$ by 2020–2030 | Specialization in farm production by 2020–2030 (possible change) |
|---|---|---|---|---|
| Boreal forest (64–67 °N) | 1050–1350 | Legume-grass mixtures. Ultra early- ripening oat and barley cultivars (cultivation in alluvial plains only). | 1400–1700 | Extending the diversity of legume-grass mixtures. Switching to early- and mid-ripening oat and barley cultivars. |
| Subboreal forest (61–64 °N) | 1400–1600 | Early-ripening winter rye cultivars. Early-ripening potato cultivars. | 1700–1900 | Switching to mid- and later-ripening winter rye and potato cultivars. Introducing early-ripening spring wheat cultivars. |
| Forest (eastern) (59–60 °N) | 1600–1750 | Early-ripening spring and winter wheat cultivars. Early-ripening fiber flax cultivars. | 1850–2000 | Switching to mid-ripening spring and winter wheat cultivars. Introducing early-ripening buckwheat cultivars. |
| Forest (central) (56–60 °N) | 1700–2000 | Early- and mid-ripening potato cultivars. Early- and mid-ripening spring and winter wheat cultivars. | 1950–2200 | Introducing early-ripening sugar beet cultivars |
| Forest (western) (54–55 °N) | > 2200 | Early- and mid-ripening winter wheat cultivars and maize hybrids for silage | > 2350 | Introducing ultra early-ripening cultivars of maize for grain (or new maize hybrids) |

There are other opportunities for cultivation practice in some parts of NW Russia. They consist in:

- switching to mid- and later-ripening cultivars of peas (e.g., within Boreal- and Subboreal forest zones);
- switching to early- and mid-ripening cultivars of sunflower for silage (e.g., within Eastern forest province);
- switching to mid- and later-ripening cultivars of fiber flax (e.g., within Central forest province);
- switching to later-ripening cultivars of cereal crops (e.g., within Western forest province).

The simulation results from GCMs such as ECHAM, HadCM3 and GFDL give estimates in close agreement with potential changes in accumulated effective temperatures according to the paleoanalog scenario [7].

Raising of new crops and cultivars is also expected on the background of high efficiency of $N_2$, $P_2O_5$ and $K_2O$ consumption by plants due to predicted increase in the soil moisture content. Estimates have been obtained for soil moisture content using heat/water balance model based on M.I.Budyko's method of computing the evaporation from land surface [8].

Thus, the expected growth of moisture in soils up to 6–8% by 2020–2030 may contributes to increasing in the NPK optimum up to 5–7%, which in turn ensures an additional yield of, e.g., winter wheat up to 7%; and spring wheat up to 5%, respectively [7].

Simultaneously, the predicted earlier temperature rise above 5 °C in spring and later temperate fall below 5 °C in autumn may provide earlier spring sowing and later autumn sowing. By 2020–2030 within cultivable area of NW Russia spring wheat sowing should be moved from 15 to20 days earlier than regular dates; winter wheat sowing should be postponed by 2 weeks.

As an indicator of winter severity for the NW Russia's climate it is convenient to use the value of mean monthly temperature in the coldest month ($T_{jan}$). It has been found that there is a strong correlation between changes in $T_{jan}$ and minimum negative temperatures, including mean monthly minimum temperatures and absolute minimum temperatures. The predicted increase in $T_{jan}$ up to 5–7 °C, and hence, the relevant increase in minimum negative temperatures will contribute to decrease in frost killing risks for orchard plants (e.g., apple trees, cherry trees and others), especially in the eastern parts of NW Russia due to decrease in bark injuries by severe frosts.

It should be noted that frost killing of field crops in the NW Russia's climate is rare thanks to the sufficient snow cover depth. However, it should be expected that there will be increase in rotting- and wetting out of winter crops by 2020-2030.

Therefore, as an winter wetness indicator it is proposed

$$W_w = \sum P \big/ 0.1 * \sum T , \qquad (1)$$

where: $\sum P$ is the precipitation sums for cold period (mm); $\sum T$ is the accumulated temperatures for cold period (°C). Long-term field experiments show that when $W_w \approx 1$, we have favorable conditions for crop wintering, excluding the years with sharp temperature drops during cold period. Thus, the dimensionless indicator may be given as

$$K_w = W_{wobs} \big/ W_{wopt} , \qquad (2)$$

where: $W_{wobs}$ is the mean annual value; $W_{wopt}$ is the unity.

Tab. 2 gives $K_w$ estimates which are compared with the frequency of rotting- and wetting-out (two left columns). This frequency is the percent of years, when the losses of cereal plants after wintering (due to overall effect of rotting- and wetting out) took place in the more than 20% of planted area to the early spring [4]. As it follows from two right columns of the table, it is expected that will be a significant increase in rotting- and wetting out risks for winter rye and winter wheat due to predicted more mild and damp winters. On average, the losses of winter cereals may increase by 13–15% by 2020–2030.

Certainly, for separate analysis of these unfavorable factors impact on crop wintering, more detailed methodologies will be required. These methodologies should take into account the depth of snow cover and the length of its stay as well as hydro-physical characteristics of soils (e.g., full water capacity of soil under saturation, etc.).

**Table 2. Possible changes in frequency of rotting- and wetting out under changing wetness of winters in NW Russia.**

| Agro-landscape zone (portion) | $K_w$ (at current climate) | Years with strong effect of rotting- and wetting out, % (at current climate) | $K_w$ (by 2020–2030) | Years with strong effect of rotting- and wetting out, % (by 2020–2030) |
|---|---|---|---|---|
| Boreal forest (western) 64–67 °N, 30–40 °E | 1.65 | 19 | 2.74 | 28 |
| Subboreal forest (western) 61–64 °N, 30–40 °E | 1.90 | 21 | 2.88 | 29 |
| Subboreal forest (middle) 61–64 °N, 40–50 °E | 1.56 | 15 | 2.08 | 22 |
| Subboreal forest (eastern) 61–64 °N, 50–60 °E | 1.34 | 11 | 1.72 | 18 |
| Forest 54–60 °N, 20–40 °E | 2.30 | 23 | 3.14 | 31 |

Meanwhile, the expected shift in distribution of crops and cultivars will cause the penetration of pests, pathogens and weed flora into new areas and also potential acclimatization of several insect pest species in the more northern parts of the NW Russia's territory. Therefore, the spatial analogs method has been developed for defining the areas vulnerable to potential risk of crop damage by insect pests, diseases and weeds with climate warming process [9–11]. This approach is based on the analysis of analog regions under current and future climate regimes according to the following criteria:

- similarity in annual course of daily temperatures;
- similarity in annual precipitation amounts;
- similarity in soil type and fractional composition;

(wide range of field crops adaptation to the light factor taken into consideration).

Fig. 3 shows a possible 'transfer' of agroclimatic conditions from present-day analogs to potential analogs along the NW Russia's territory, which is characterized by humid climate and podzolic type of soil cover. In this approach the Last Interglacial climatic optimum is considered as a paleoanalog scenario of the global warming by 2020–2030 [12].

Then, comparison was made of spatial analogs (Fig. 3) with those by O.D. Sirotenko and V.N. Pavlova, determined for more southern regions within European territory of Russia [13]. Their approach is based on HadCM3 and GFDL simulation results for 'time slice' 2020–2030, and the following criteria are used:

- similarity in the values of accumulated temperatures above 10 °C;
- similarity in the values of evaporation deficit during the period with temperature above 10 °C;
- similarity in the values of mean monthly temperature in the coldest month.

Despite discrepancies between analogue criteria and climate prediction options, the vector directions are from south-west to north-east, i.e. from warmer regions to cooler regions [14].

Figure 3. Possible 'transfer' of agroclimatic conditions within territory of NW Russia under development of global warming by 2020–2030.

## 4. CONCLUSION

For forthcoming decades, the estimates obtained above testify of the following feasible adaptation measures and strategies in crop management practice: (i) adjustment of farm operations timing (e. g., by transfer of regular dates of sowing to earlier dates); (ii) optimization of recommended use of fertilizers for changing soil moisture conditions; (iii) step-by-step switching from early-season cultivars to mid- and later-season cultivars; (iv) increasing the crop rotation systems diversity by introduction of new cultivars/varieties and different crops; (v) enlarging the areas under orchard plants in Subboreal belt due to more favorable conditions for wintering; (vi) widening the areas under snow mold resistant cultivars in the regions with high risks of rotting- and wetting- out (otherwise to switch from winter crops to summer crops); (vii) increasing the portion of cultivars highly resistant to pests and viruses, and also improving tillage practice to suppress pest population and pathogen's survivability; (viii) introduction of some useful flora species from southern regions to northern regions for the purpose of establishing reservation for acclimatization of introduced entomophages and new useful insects.

Strategy for diversification of pesticides, fungicides and herbicides for further applying in the regions potentially vulnerable to new pests, pathogens and weeds also may be proved, however, considering their high toxicology, and thus the selective application.

# REFERENCES

[1] M.V. Nikolaev, I.B. Uskov and V.B. Minin, Thesis Collection of the 8th Int. Ecological Forum *"The Baltic sea Day"*, St. Petersburg: 'Dialog' Issue, pp. 282–284 (2007).

[2] V.A. Moiseychik, N.A. Bogomolova, T.A. Maksimenkova, A. I. Strashnaya, *Consequences of global climate change far agricultural sector of economy*, edited by A.L. Ivanov, Moscow: Russian Academy of Agricultural Sciences Issue, pp. 127–154 (2004).

[3] S.R. Fasulati, *Proceedings of the Regional Scientific Conference*, pp. I-171–I-177 (2007).

[4] A.P. Matveeva, *Proceedings of the Crop Protection Conference: Pests, Diseases and Weeds*, pp. 63–67 (2003).

[5] N.N. Luneva and E.V. Filippova *Proceedings of the Int. Conference Information systems of diagnostics monitoring and forecasting the major weed plants, pests and disease of agricultural crops*, All- Russian Institute of Plant Protection Issue, pp. 63–65 (2008).

[6] D.I. Shashko, *USSR's agroclimatic resources*, Leningrad: Gidrometeoizdat, (in Russian) 1985.

[7] M.V. Nikolaev, Almanac Field Investigator, *Field Research for Sustainable Development of Agriculture and Countryside St. Petersburg:* NW Russia's Institute of Agricultural Engineering and Electrification Issue, pp. 7–9 (2008).

[8] M.I. Budyko, *Climate and Life,* Leningrad: Gidrometeoizdat, (in Russian) 1971.

[9] M.V. Nikolaev, V.B. Minin, *Baltic21 Newsletter,* 2, 9–10 (2000).

[10] M.V. Nikolaev, *IAMFE News*, 2, 7–8 (2002).

[11] M.V. Nikolaev, V. P. Yakushev, *Consequences of global climate change far agricultural sector of economy*, edited by A. L. Ivanov, Moscow: Russian Academy of Agricultural Sciences issue, 2004, pp. 274–299.

[12] M.V. Nikolaev, *Research and investigations for empirical basis of landscape adapted agricultural systems planning, St. Petersburg: Institute of Nuclear Physics issue,* 2007, pp. 147–153.

[13] O.D. Sirotenko, V.N. Pavlova, *Meteorology and hydrology*, 6, 89-99 (in Russian), (2003).

[14] M.V. Nikolaev, *Slovak Meteorological Journal,* 10 (2), 75–80 (2007).

In: Advances in Environmental Modeling and Measurements  ISBN: 978-1-60876-599-7
Editors: D. T. Mihailović, B. Lalić, pp. 233-243  © 2010 Nova Science Publishers, Inc.

*Chapter 21*

# ADAPTATION OPTIONS TO CLIMATE CHANGE IMPACTS IN EUROPEAN AGRICULTURE

## *J. Eitzinger*[*1]*, G. Kubu*[1]*, S. Thaler*[1]*, J. Glauninger*[1]*,*
## *V.A. Alexandrov*[2]*, A. Utset*[3]*, D.T. Mihailović*[4]*, B. Lalić*[4]*, M. Trnka*[5]*,*
## *Z. Zalud*[5]*, D. Semeradova*[5]*, D. Ventrella*[6]*, D.P. Anastasiou*[7]*,*
## *M. Medany*[8]*, S. Altaher*[8]*, J. Olejnik*[9]*, J. Leśny*[9]*, N. Nemeshko*[10]*,*
## *M.V. Nikolaev*[11]*, C. Simota*[12]*, and G. Cojocaru*[12]*

[1] University of Natural Resources and Applied Life Sciences, Vienna, Austria
[2] National Institute of Meteorology and Hydrology, Sofia, Bulgaria
[3] Agrarian Technological Institute of Castilla and Leon, Valladolid, Spain
[4] University of Novi Sad, Novi Sad, Serbia
[5] Mendel University of Agriculture and Forestry, Brno, Czech Republic
[6] Instituto Sperimentale Agronomico, Bari, Italy
[7] Institute of Environmental Research and Sustainable Development, Athens, Greece
[8] Central Laboratory for Agricultural Climate, Giza, Egypt
[9] August Cieszkowski Agriculture University of Poznan, Poznan, Poland
[10] State Hydrological Institute, St. Petersburg, Russia
[11] Agrophysical Research Institute, Petersburg, Russian Federation
[12] TIAMASG Foundation, Romania

## ABSTRACT

Ongoing climate change will significantly change agricultural production conditions in Europe during the next decades. An early recognition of risks and implementation of adaptation strategies is crucial as anticipatory and precautionary, adaptation is more effective and less costly than forced, last minute, emergency adaptation or retrofitting. Results of climate change impact and adaptation studies often show considerable

---

* Corresponding author: E-mail address: josef.eitzinger@boku.ac.at; Phone: +43 1 476545622, Fax: +43 1 476545610

different results, depending on the spatial scale of regionalization. However, for a decision maker, only a high spatial resolution of related study results is useful as it can represent local conditions and its spatial variability much better. Therefore the ADAGIO project (adagio-eu.org) was designed to focus on regional studies in order to uncover regional specific problems. In this context a bottom-up approach is used beside the top-down approach of using scientific studies, involving regional experts and farmers in the evaluation of potential regional vulnerabilities and adaptation options. Results of the regional studies and gathered feedback from experts and farmers show in general that (increasing) drought and heat is the main factor of agricultural vulnerability not only in the Mediterranean region, but also in the Central and Eastern European regions. Another important aspect is that the increasing risk of pest and diseases may play a more important role for agricultural vulnerability than assumed before, however, till now this field is only rarely investigated in Europe. An important aspect is also that there are increasing regional differences in the crop production potential in Europe due to climate change and that positive or negative impacted agricultural systems can vary in a relatively small spatial scale, depending on the specific limiting environmental conditions such as climate or soil conditions (especially in complex terrain). Although dominating risks such as increasing drought and/or heat are similar in most regions, the vulnerabilities in the different regions are very much influenced by characteristics of the dominating agroecosystems and prevailing socio-economic conditions. Most important adaptation options in Europe concern changes in crop and soil management, pest and disease management as well as land use options at different scales. The feasibility of many adaptation options, however, is strongly influenced by regional socio-economic conditions, which can vary significantly within regions and countries in Europe.

# 1. INTRODUCTION

Weather and climatic conditions are the most important production factors for agriculture. Farming (and their actors, the farmers) within any agroecosystem therefore seeks to adapt to these prevailing conditions as much as possible. Farm technologies and methods of farm management play a major role in this adaptation process in both the short and the long term. Farming is normally optimized for different purposes with varying priorities, such as producing food with maximum quantity and quality, securing farmer's income, reducing production risks [1]. Because of ongoing climate change, the optimization of farming techniques and methods is very critical for the productivity of various agricultural production systems. In the context of climate change also additional factors become more important, which is the effective use of farming inputs (energy, fertilizers, machinery, etc.) and natural resources (water, soil, crops, local climate) in order to enable sustainable agricultural production.

Available farm technologies are often closely linked to specific management options, which will therefore be considered in the following analysis. These options for the various agricultural systems are always embedded within the given socioeconomic, policy and trading framework within and between countries and regions and these can vary widely. This framework is an important consideration when identifying measures to adapt to weather and climate conditions and has a strong influence on the adequacy of measures for adapting farm technologies [2,3]. This background should be kept in mind when applying general adaptation recommendations to a region with specific agricultural systems and conditions. In all agroecosystems since farming began farmers have developed specific strategies, mainly the use of different farm technologies and related management options, to survive in the given environment, but for various reasons not always with sustainability in mind. However, the development or improvement in farm technologies has been responsible for most of the increases in productivity and yields in agricultural production worldwide, beside the impact of the socioeconomic environment and agricultural infrastructure. This trend should continue [4] and could potentially outrange, for example, any negative effects of climate change impacts on food production in many regions (especially in those which are still underdeveloped).

Under the conditions of climate change, the proper management of water resources by application of appropriate farm technologies and methods will play a major role in many European regions, mainly due to increasing summer droughts. Crop water use efficiency and water use efficiency of whole crop rotations as well as irrigation systems are identified in many studies as critical issues. Studies of European agricultural systems conclude that there is strong evidence in climate change scenarios, especially for soils with low soil water storage capacity or no groundwater impact to the rooting zone, that irrigation or water-saving production techniques (e.g. by introducing mulching systems, adapting crop rotation), will be important requirements in future climate conditions in most Mediterranean, Central European and Eastern European crop production regions for crops to attain their yield potential [5].

Summer crops in general will be more vulnerable and dependent on soil water reserves, as the soil water or higher groundwater tables during the winter period cannot be utilized as much as by winter crops. Evapotranspiration losses during summer due to higher temperatures would increase significantly in whole Europe. Significant negative yield effects for several crops and significant additional water use for irrigation (up to 60–90%) might be expected in the Mediterranean and South-East European region especially at locations with low soil water availability due to climate change. According to [6], reduced water availability in Mediterranean countries as a consequence of climate change and variability might be the most important climate risk for crop yields, especially if extreme weather events would increase. An European study [7] draws a similar conclusion, remarking on the need for future studies on the effectiveness of irrigated agriculture in Southern Europe. There are however many other aspects of regional climate change impacts on agriculture and related adaptation options. For example, the changing phenology of crops, especially for perennial crops, would lead to different crop management regimes such as for fertilizing regime, crop maintenance, yielding techniques and others. Special emphasis should be taken on crop pest, disease and weed management as there are significant shifts expected in ecological niches with consequences to regional crop damage risks.

In many simulation studies focusing on climate change impacts on crop production in European agricultural regions, mostly only simple adaptation measures such as possible changes in sowing dates (earlier sowing dates) and cultivar selection (e.g. selecting slower maturing varieties) were investigated [8], showing that these measures often have the potential to significantly reduce negative impacts on crop yields. Adaptation of planting density and fertilizing can have similar effects [9]. Many studies confirm that simple and low-cost technologies can significantly reduce the negative effects of climate warming scenarios and extreme weather on crop yields [10,11]. Many of these adaptation options often are already applied by farmers, as they are type of autonomous adaptation. However, these could be not enough in many cases and are depending on the type of agricultural production. For example, arable crop production is seen as less vulnerable due to the flexibility in crop selection and management. Whereas permanent cropping systems such as orchards or especially grassland and dairy production are less flexible because of economic or ecological limitations such as long term planned investments, unfavorable farm size structure or unfavorable soil and terrain conditions. Also agroecosystems, which depend on infrastructure beyond the farm level, such as irrigation infrastructure or regional water resources for irrigation could be more vulnerable if these infrastructure services fail or are underdeveloped due to bad socioeconomic conditions. Some of these aspects are discussed in the following chapters for selected European countries, based on findings from the ADAGIO project.

## 2. CRITICAL FIELDS OF AGRICULTURAL ADAPTATION OPTIONS IN EUROPE

**Table 1. List of the ADAGIO countries and the dominating agricultural systems for which feasible adaptation options were investigated.**

| Country | Low farming intensity | Medium farming intensity | High farming intensity | Character of farming structure |
|---|---|---|---|---|
| Austria | | X | X | Small scale agriculture; high number of organic farms; dominating grassland production systems |
| Spain | | X | X | Irrigation dependent farms; high intensity of inputs |
| Bulgaria | X | X | | Weak irrigation systems infrastructure; overaging of farmers; giving up of small scale farms |
| Serbia | | X | | Large regional differences of farm structures |
| Czech Republic | | | X | Large scale farming structure |
| Italy | | X | X | Small and medium scale farming structure |
| Greece | | X | | Small and medium scale farming structure |
| Egypt | X | X | | Specific multi-cropping systems with high inputs but low overall intensity; small scale farming |
| Poland | X | X | | Partly small scale farming structure; large regional differences |
| Russia | X | | X | Large scale farming structure; infrastructure problems |
| Romania | X | | X | Large scale farming structure; giving up of small scale farms |

In order to analyze recommendations for adaptation strategies in various agricultural systems a distinction between the most important and climate-sensitive agricultural resources to be managed, such as water, soil (including nutrients), crop (including management) and microclimatic conditions in relation to low, medium and high agricultural input systems should be made [1]. Of course, many farm technology optimization strategies can affect more than one of these resources at the same time. Low input systems may be characterized as small farm structures and with low income in a less developed socioeconomic environment as is found in many developing regions in Eastern Europe (almost no financial reserves for investment in farm technologies available). Medium input systems might be characterized as small farm structures with acceptable farm income in a good socioeconomic environment, as in small farms in Western Europe (limited financial reserves for investment in farm technologies available). High input systems might be characterized as farms with high income levels in any socioeconomic environment, where there is theoretically no limitation to investment in new farm technologies. Countries in and around Europe include all of the mentioned agriculture systems with the low input systems dominating in Egypt, Romania, Bulgaria or Poland. Medium input systems are found in most of the countries including Austria, Greece or Italy and the high input systems dominate mostly in Western countries (Tab. 1), although in any country can be found each of the types.

## 2.1. Adaptation of Crop and Soil Management

Agricultural practices can strongly impact soil functions (e.g. soil fertility, soil water holding capacity) in the short and long term, and farming technologies and management can play an important role in these processes. Soil functions can react very quickly to agricultural practices. Unfortunately this can lead to rapid and irreversible degradation of soil functions and further to desertification, which has become a significant problem in many agroecosystems in the world. For example, improper irrigation schemes and use of salinated irrigation water can lead to increasing salinity of soils, making them unusable for agricultural production. Climate change and climate variability may especially affect soil erosion, such as by increasing heavy precipitation. In almost all agroecosystems soil erosion, caused by various factors, leads to a decrease in soil fertility and hence to a reduction in crop productivity because of loss of organic matter, nutrients and lower water-holding capacity. In temperate regions with high-input systems heavy machinery, often in combination with slowly developing crops and soil cover, contributes to soil compaction, decreasing water infiltration, increasing runoff and therefore water erosion. In Europe these problems are apparent with sugar beet and maize, where soils are not covered for a long time in spring and heavy machinery has often irreversible affect on soil structure during the frequently wet harvest periods in the autumn. This problem accelerates with increasing slopes of fields, as are frequently found in Europe. Perennial crops in various climatic regions such as vineyards and orchards, which are often grown in hilly regions, are also subject to water erosion, especially during extreme precipitation events.

Crop yield and crop production within a certain territory can be seen as an interaction of many factors. However, crops adapted to certain conditions are an important local resource for crop productivity with a significant influence on yield risk. Crops can respond nonlinearly to changes in their growing conditions, exhibit threshold responses and be subject to combinations of stress factors that affect their growth, development and yield. Thus, climate variability and changes in the frequency of extreme events are important for yield and the stability and quality from year to year. Higher temperature and precipitation variability increase the risk of lower yield, as many experimental and simulation studies have shown [12]. Over the generations farmers have selected the best cultivars for their use, creating locally well adapted crops, some of which are still in use in agricultural systems and are an important genetic resource for modern crop breeding. Farmers can not only change crops and cultivars but also modify crop management, by changing the sowing date according to the expected seasonal weather, for example. However the effectiveness of each adaptation option is closely related to the magnitude of change of climate conditions with the change of cultivar being able to mitigate less severe changes and the introduction of new crop (or cropping pattern) might become suitable under larger climate shifts. An example for the expected large shifts in agricultural production zones is shown in Fig. 1 for the federal district of Upper

Austria, which will lead to significant shift of cropping patters within the next decades and related recommendations for adaptation.

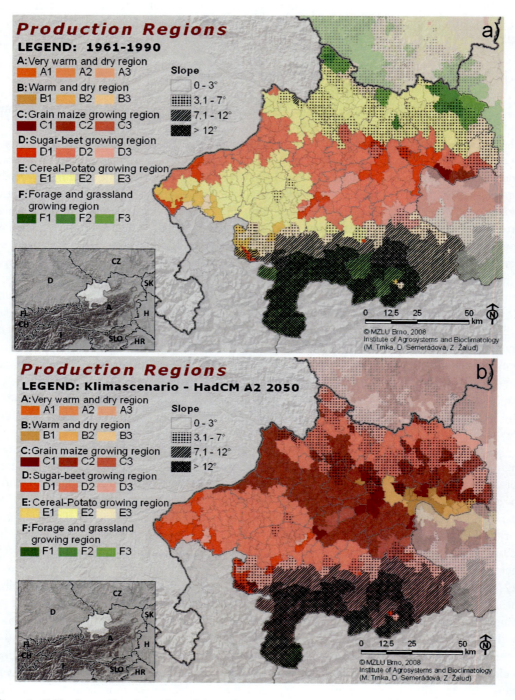

Figure 1. Shift of agroclimatic zoning of the region Upper Austria for the baseline period 1961-1990 using thresholds according to the Trnka et al [13] (a) compared to the 2050s using HadCM model from AR4 (b).

Many of the recommendations provided to farmers for adaptation of crop and soil management in order to reduce production risks or for a better use of the production potential (including selection of cultivars, crop rotation schemes or timing of field operations) have been since early 20th century based on long term agroclimatic conditions using many various zoning schemes [14]. It is however rarely realized that during past few decades the basic assumption allowing for the agroclimatic zoning i.e. that the agroclimatic conditions remain stable in the long-term, has been shattered by the ongoing climate change [15]. When these changes are not reflected and agroclimatic zoning updated, it might have negative consequences both for farmers as well as for the environment by application of potentially biased adaptation measures. While the risks of using climatically inappropriate fertilization schemes, crop rotation or cultivars are well known, it should be realized that the creeping shifts of agroclimatic zones make many of the widely used practices obsolete or even unsustainable at the areas where the same approach constituted "good practice" just one generation ago. As farmers understand well the concept of agroclimatic zones, the estimates of their shift under climate change could prove to very effective modes of communication of the impacts of climate change on agriculture between them and research community. Beside these aspects many detailed adaptation measures for crop and soil management in Europe can be given.

**Table 2. List of pests which are considered to increase due to climate warming in Central Europe (in bold significant observed ones).**

| German name | Species | Affected crops/plants |
|---|---|---|
| Gemeiner Grashüpfer | *Chorthippus longocornis* | all |
| Blasenfüße / Thripse | (thrips) many | many |
| Amerikanische Rebzikade | *Scaphoideus titanus* | wine |
| Winden-Glasflügelzikade | *Hyalesthes obsoletus* | wine |
| Blattläuse | (aphids) many | many |
| Getreidewanzen | *Eurygaster* sp., *Aelia* sp. | cereals |
| Drahtwürmer | *Agriotes* sp. | many |
| Getreidehähnchen | *Oulema melanopus* and *O. gallaeciana* | cereals |
| Kartoffelkäfer (potato beetle) | *Leptinotarsa decemlineata* | potato |
| Buchdrucker | *Ips typographus* | forest trees |
| Erdflöhe (soil flee) | many | many |
| Stängelrüssler | *Ceutorhynchus napi* and *C. quadridens* | rape |
| Rübenrüssler | *Bothynoderes punctiventris* u.a. | sugar beet |
| Engerlinge | *Melolontha* sp., *Phyllopertha* sp. | many crops and grassland |
| Getreidehalmwespe | *Cephus pygmeus* | cereals |
| Baumwollkapselwurm | *Helicoverpa armigera* | many |
| Maiszünsler (corn borer) | *Ostrinia nubilalis* | maize |
| Westl. Maiswurzelbohrer (Western Corn Rootworm) | *Diabrotica virgifera virgifera* | maize |
| Bekreuzter Traubenwickler | *Eupoecilia ambiguella* | wine |
| Apfelwickler | *Cydia pomonella* | apple |
| Schwammspinner | *Lymantria dispar* | oak |
| Kastanienminiermotte | *Cameraria ohridella* | chestnut |
| Fritfliege | *Oscinella frit* | cereals, maize |
| Gemeine Spinnmilbe | *Tetranychus urticae* | many |
| Feldmaus (mouse) | *Microtus arvalis* | many |
| Wühlmaus (mouse) | *Arvicola terrestris* | many |
| Wildschwein (wild pig) | *Sus scrofa* | many |

## 2.2. Adaptation of Pest, Disease and Weed Management

Similar to a shift in climatic crop production conditions, ecological niches for pests, diseases and weeds are observed. Especially thermophile insects are observed to become a higher damage potential (e.g. due to more generations or spatial shift, higher overwintering rates) (Tab. 2). Also a shift of weeds is observed from colder to warmer regions. For occurrence of diseases there are several trends depending on the complex life cycles of each species. The risk for farmers in this context is the unknown future of the developments of various pests, diseases and weeds, and the relatively fast change of these developments under warming climate. Adaptation to these biotic damaging factors include therefore especially an effective monitoring and advising services for farmers as these changes are highly specific for different agroecosystems and climatic regions.

## 2.3. Adaptation of Agricultural Land Use (Changing Production Systems)

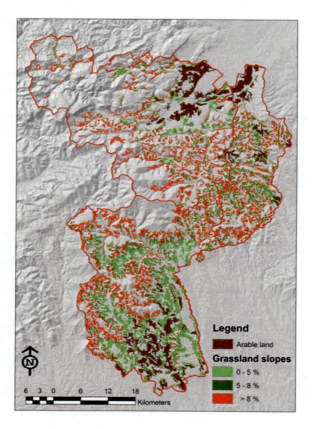

Figure 2. Limitation of soil cultivation in current grassland regions of an district in Eastern Austria (red colors represent slopes >7° which are not suitable for a change to arable fodder production).

Changes of agricultural land use mainly are related to a change of soil cultivation, which can significantly affect landscape functions and natural resources. Managed permanent grassland systems (in combination with dairy farming) are an important part of European agricultural systems and landscapes. However, they are under risk in regions below about 800mm precipitation under conditions of increasing summer droughts. Because of the fact and that grassland production is much less flexible for adaptation options at different levels due to several reasons, it is considered as the most critical sector and most emphasis has to be paid for feasible adaptation options in the related regions. For example, for regions where a change to crop production or other alternatives by changing land use is difficult due to terrain or soil conditions, there are only few potential adaptation options possible for farming (Fig. 2).

Other potential land use changes are from grassland production to orchards and vineyards or to perennial woods for biomass production. These options also affect landscape significantly and could be limited by social acceptance, e.g. in tourism regions. Currently such regions often show a reforestation trend due to a lack of alternatives and income sources for farmers (e.g. in the Alpine region).

## 2.4. Main Recommendations and Limitations for Adaptation in European Agriculture

Most important recommended adaptation options for European agroecosystems include:

Short term measures:

- Soil water conservation techniques (mulching, reduced and minimum tillage);
- Improve water use efficiency of crops and crop rotations (especially Mediterranean regions);
- Improve, change or introduce effective irrigation scheduling techniques and methods (e.g. reduce flood irrigation, apply deficit irrigation);
- Change to heat tolerant cultivars;
- Change cultivars and crops according temperature demands;
- Change sowing date and shift timing of field works;
- Improve, introduce monitoring systems for pest and diseases;
- Adaptation in crop rotation (e.g. more winter crops in dry regions);
- Adapted crop fertilization (timing, salinity control, ensure potassium content under drought conditions);
- Ensure frost protection methods (and for hail in some regions);
- Ensure protection methods against soil erosion and degradation;
- Effective insurance system (ideally supported by government);
- Adapted animal stables to heat waves, ensuring power generation, increasing hygienic measures.

Medium and long term measures:

- Improve or establish irrigation infrastructure;
- Breeding of adapted cultivars (esp. for higher water use efficiency and heat stress);
- Improving soil conditions e.g. by enhancement of organic contents in soils;

- Crop diversification (farm and regional scale);
- Increasing storage capacities (fodder);
- Change land use and/or production system (e.g. cereals to maize, grassland to vineyards, grassland or crop production to energy biomass production);
- Increase small farm size structure;
- Landscape structure improvements against evapotranspiration (lowering wind speed by hedegrows or agroforestry systems, in some flat semi-arid regions);
- Introduce effective farm based or regional monitoring techniques and warning systems (weather extremes and medium term forecasting, pest and disease management);
- To ensure higher market price stability for agric. products (improves planning of adaptation options) by using appropriate tools (not only political measures); eg. organic farming; terroir characteristics for wine quality aspects.

To downscale recommended adaptation options several regional limitations have to be considered:

- Structural changes are mainly driven by economic reasons rather than by climatic driven reasons (strong decrease of income per work unit (esp. Poland), too small farm sizes (Austria, Poland), complex terrain and high production costs (Austria), too low income at small farms (esp. related to family business) leads to abandoning small farms (Austria, Poland) or reduction of agricultural used land (Poland);
- Farmers of small farms are less experienced in agricultural production in general (often part time depending on other incomes) leading to a decreasing success or interest in farming;
- Adaptive capacity of small farms seems to be better in well developed countries with better infrastructure (or well established local market) (such as in Austria, where already many small farms could successfully change to ecological production or alternatives/niche). Eastern countries are much less flexible in that sense, probably also by the missing political support, low financial resources, not well developed infrastructures, fewer possibilities of additional incomes beside agriculture at the same location;
- Bad existing or destroyed infrastructure (esp. irrigation systems) and less financial resources for improvements;
- Too less water available in the region for additional irrigation (partly an infrastructure problem);
- Too high costs of certain adaptation options;
- Terrain and soil limitations for changing agricultural land use;
- No market (or still no) and market price uncertainties leads to uncertainties in success of esp. mid term adaptation options (e.g. change of land use or production system);
- labor and time pressures.

# 3. CONCLUSION

To develop adaptation options for European agriculture needs a regionalization approach and involvement of local Know-How on limiting factors as there is a wide variety of agricultural production as well as socioeconomic conditions in Europe. Still much research has to be done in order to detect regional aspects and potentials for adaptation under consideration of sustainable agricultural production and food security. However, main aspects and problems in Europe are related to water resources for agricultural production and main shifts in agricultural production zones due to the warming trend. This will lead to a shift in production potentials and type of agroecosystems over Europe, where especially regions with weak socioeconomic conditions and farming structure are under risk. Adaptation measures are therefore not only important at the farm level, but especially at the policy levels in order to provide resources for adaptive capacity for ensuring sustainable agricultural production and regional food security.

## REFERENCES

[1]   J. Eitzinger, A. Utset, M. Trnka, M., Z. Zalud, M. Nikolaev, I. Uskov, In: M.V.K. Sivakumar, R. Motha, (Eds.), *Managing Weather and Climate Risks in Agriculture*, 554p; Springer, Berlin, (2007).

[2]   Q.P. Chiotti, T. Johnston, *J. Rural Stud.,* 11 (3), 335–350, (1995).

[3]   P. Reidsma, PhD Thesis Wageningen University, Wageningen, *The Netherlands*, p. 204, (2007).

[4]   M.D.A. Rounsevell, S.P. Evans, P. Bullock, *Clim. Change.,* 43 (4), 683–709, (1999).

[5]   J. Eitzinger, M. Stastná, Z. Zalud, M. Dubrovsky, *Agr. Water Manage.,* 61, 195-217, (2003).

[6]   J.E. Olesen, M. Bindi, *Eur. J. Agron.,* 16, 239–262, (2002).

[7]   *European Environmental Agency (EEA), EEA Report No 2/2004.*

[8]   V. Alexandrov, J. Eitzinger, V. Cajic, M. Oberforster, M., *Glob. Change Biol.,* 8(4), 372-389, (2002).

[9]   N.M. Holden, A.J. Brereton, *Agric. Forest Meteorol.,* 122, 175-191, (2004).

[10]  W.E. Easterling, M. Apps, *Clim. Change,* 70, 165–189, (2005).

[11]  M.J. Salinger, M.V.K. Sivakumar, R. Motha, *Clim. Chang.,* 70, 341–362, (2005).

[12]  J.R. Porter, M.A. Semenov, M.A., *Phil Trans R Soc Lond B Biol Sci* 360 (1463), 2021–35, (2005).

[13]  M. Trnka, J. Eitzinger, D. Semeradova, P. Hlavinka, J. Balek, M. Dubrovsky, G. Kubu, P. Stepanek, S. Thaler, Z. Zalud, *Clim. Change,* (in press), (2009).

[14]  D. Rijks, In: *Handbook of Agricultural Meteorology.* Ed.: J.E.Griffiths, Oxford Univ. Press., pp. 231-244, (1994).

[15]  E.D. Assad, H.S. Pintor, J.Z. Junior, *Pesquisa Agropecu. Bras.,* 39, 1057-1064, (2004).

In: Advances in Environmental Modeling and Measurements    ISBN: 978-1-60876-599-7
Editors: D. T. Mihailović, B. Lalić, pp. 245-254    © 2010 Nova Science Publishers, Inc.

*Chapter 22*

# AGRO-CLIMATIC POTENTIAL OF LANDSCAPE IN CONDITIONS OF CLIMATE CHANGE IN SLOVAKIA

## B. Šiška[*1], J. Takáč[2], and P. Nejedlík[3]

[1]Department of Biometeorology and Hydrology, SAU Nitra, Nitra, Slovakia
[2]Soil Science and Conservation Research Institute, Bratislava, Slovakia
[3]Slovak Hydrometeorological Institute, Bratislava, Slovakia

## ABSTRACT

Meteorological and phenological data from the territory of Northern Carpathian were evaluated for two periods according to the $CO_2$ concentration in the atmosphere (1961–1990 and 2061–2090). Climatic data from the database of Slovak Hydrometeorological Institute were used as a reference data for 1961-90 ($1xCO_2$). A calculation of energy and water balance, phenological development and agroclimatic productive potential was done for the defined period limited by daily mean air temperature T >10 °C (GS 10). The selection of the stations entering GIS analysis was based on the geographical position of the stations as well as on the plant production. This is limited by the altitude of about 900 m a.s.l. and represents an acreage of 45 000 km². Selected stations represent four agriculturally productive types. Current GCMs for the Central European area show an increase of air temperature, changes in precipitation distribution and decline of water balance. As the growing season will prolong a rise of air temperature will most probably causes a significant increase in the productive potential. The precipitation regime will change and higher frequency of drought will be the most significant characteristic influencing the crop production. The regions where the precipitation and potential evapotranspiration are balanced will move from 550 m a.s.l. to 700 m a.s.l. This fact, together with the increases of air temperature, will probably affect both the zonality of growing areas of some crops (especially maize) and crop rotation. Slovak territory belongs to one of the European watershed and the precipitations represent the only water coming to this territory. Thus, keeping water in the country will became an urgent issue in close future.

Changing climatic conditions will evoke significant changes in the acreage of growing of particular crops and crop rotations, as well as the invasion and gradation of

* Corresponding author: E-mail address: bernard.siska@uniag.sk,  Phone: +421 905 944679, Fax: +421 376514707

pests. The phenomenon of climate change is real, and we have to take it into account. It is necessary to accept effective adaptive measures leading towards sustainable agriculture under the conditions of changing climate.

# 1. INTRODUCTION

Climate conditions have become the most important factor influencing variability of field crop yields in Slovakia nowadays. Effective adaptive measures to reduce the lost of plant production can be proposed only after regional analyses of impacts of present and future climatic conditions is done. An increase of the annual mean air temperature by about 1 °C has occurred at most climatic stations in Slovakia during the last century. On the other hand, annual precipitation has decreased by about 10% in the lowlands of Slovakia (Danubian and East Slovakian lowlands) during this period. Precipitation totals varied also in mountainous regions, but no significant trend was found during the last century [1]. Increased air temperatures and shortage of precipitations which are frequently cumulated into heavy rains during the growing season created the conditions for drought occurrence, especially in the lowlands of Slovakia. According to the outputs of the general circulation models (GCM), this trend is also predicted for the future climate. These facts call for analysis of drought occurrence under conditions of climate change in the territory of the Slovak Republic.

Impacts on the agroclimatic potential of landscapes in condition of climate change is evaluated by a comparison of changes of atmospheric parameters of present (meterological data from the years 1961–1990) and future climates [1,2] especially during the growing seasons. Photosynthetically active radiation (PAR), daily mean air temperature sums ($TS$ in °C), precipitation totals ($R$ in mm), potential evapotranspiration ($E_0$ in mm), and actual evapotranspiration ($E$ in mm) were analyzed for the growing season.

According to the natural climate variability and the duration of drought, several levels of drought can be defined [3,4]. Climatic water balance is also frequently used as a criterion for evaluation of drought conditions in Central Europe [5-8].

This criterion was also used for agroclimatic regionalization of the Slovak Republic during the periods of 1931–1960 [9] and 1961–1990 [10].

# 2. REGIONAL AND/OR LOCAL CONDITIONS

Regional conditions of the Slovak Republic are influenced first of all by the altitudinal profile of Slovakia. Basic characteristics according to temperature and water balance conditions are given in Tab. 1.

Actual agro-climatic regionalization is evaluated according to meteorological data from the years 1961-1990. This regionalization fits very well to traditional agro-regions (production zones) of the Slovak Republic. Spatial distribution is given in Fig. 1. Warm macro-regions cover conditions of maize and sugar beet production agro-regions, moderately warm macro-region fit potato growing agro-regions, and cold macro-regions fit with mountainous production agro-regions.

**Table 1. Criteria of agro climatic regionalization of the Slovak republic according to air temperature sums and climatic water balance [10] and relating agro-regions.**

|   | TS10 | | $E_0$-R | | Agro region |
|---|---|---|---|---|---|
| 1 | Cold | < 2000 | - | < 0 | Mountainous |
| 2 | Moderately warm | 2000 – 2400 | - | 0 – 50 | Potato |
| 3 | | 2400 -2600 | Wet | 50 – 100 | Sugar beet |
| 4 | Warm | 2600 – 2800 | Wet – normal | 100 – 150 | |
| 5 | | 2800 – 3000 | Dominantly dry | 150 – 200 | Maize |
| 6 | | Dry | | > 200 | |

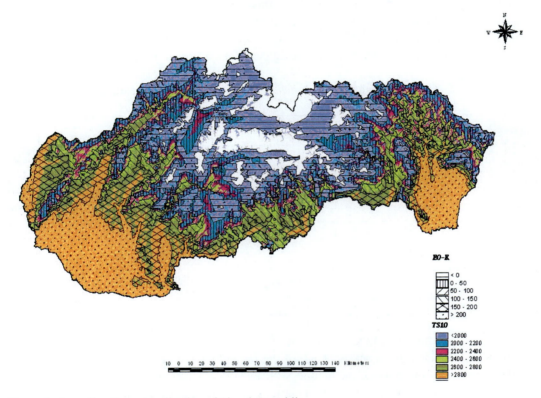

Figure 1. Agroclimatic regionalization of Slovak Republic.

# 3. DATA AND METHODS

Climatic data from the database of SHMI in Bratislava were used for calculation in the reference period 1961-1990 (present climate - concentration $1 \times CO_2$) data referring to climate change conditions ($2 \times CO_2$) were generated according to the GCMs [1]. Two periods of years related to the concentration of $CO_2$ in the atmosphere were evaluated as given in Tab. 2.

**Table 2. $CO_2$ concentrations used in the evaluation.**

| $CO_2$ concentration | | Time slice |
|---|---|---|
| $1xCO_2$ | 330 ppm | 1961–1990 |
| $2xCO_2$ | 660 ppm | 2061–2090 |

Phenological development of the particular crop was considered for growing seasons limited by daily mean air temperature T>10 °C. This period is characterized by changes of daily mean air temperature sums ($TS$ in °C), precipitation totals ($R$ in mm), potential ($E_0$ in mm) and actual evapotranspiration ($E_0$ in mm) and climatic water balance.

Climatic stations used for GIS analyses in this report were selected both from the point of view of altitude (up to 900 m a.s.l. – upper border of plant production) and also according to their spatial distribution. The evaluated acreage represents 45 000 $km^2$ – 90% of the total area of Slovakia. Selected stations represent four agro-regions as given in Tab. 3.

**Table 3. Agricultural zones and related climatic stations.**

| Agricultural regions (productive type) | Altitude (m a.s.l.) | Climatic stations | Altitude (m a.s.l.) |
|---|---|---|---|
| Maize | < 200 | Somotor | 100 |
| | | Hurbanovo | 115 |
| | | Nitra | 143 |
| | | Piešťany | 165 |
| | | Kamenica n/C. | 178 |
| Sugar beet | 200 – 300 | Rimavská Sobota | 214 |
| | | Prievidza | 260 |
| | | Košice | 230 |
| Potato | 300 – 500 | Bardejov | 304 |
| | | Sliač | 330 |
| Mountainous | >500 | Liptovský Hrádok | 640 |

Spatial evaluation is realized in the raster model of geodata. Through the interpolation technique is calculated the spatial change of the individual average meteodata. It is used the regularized spline interpolation technique with tension and kriging. Resolution component will be comparison of both results interpolations and selection of the most suitable surface. By the interpolation created surface is than possible to divide by reclassification to the zones, those determinate spatially the specific range of values.

# 4. RESULTS

## 4.1. Growing Season

Duration of the growing season is an important factor influencing energy and water balance conditions. GS 10 is limited by a biological temperature minimum (by daily average air temperature T≥10 °C) [11]. It basically represents the period of biomass production of the main crops like maize (*Zea mays* L.), sugar beets (*Beta vulgaris* L.) and other plants of temperate zones.

From trend lines of the onset and end of GS10, it is predicted that the onset would accelerate significantly (by about 28 days) in climate conditions $2xCO_2$ in the entire altitudinal profile (Fig. 2). This fact has serious effects on over-wintering field crops (winter wheat (*Triticum vulgare* L.) and seed rape (*Brassica napus* L.)). The growing season will be shifted to the months with lower input of solar radiation with negative effects on biomass production. Higher temperatures also influence evaporation and evapotranspiration and consequently droughts can occur earlier than in conditions of $1xCO_2$ climate. Duration of the GS 10 typical for maize agro-regions in the present climate $1xCO_2$ is 175 days and more. Those conditions will occur on 80% of the total agricultural acreage in climate conditions $2xCO_2$, and duration of GS 10 can exceed 200 days in the lowlands up to 200 m a.s.l..

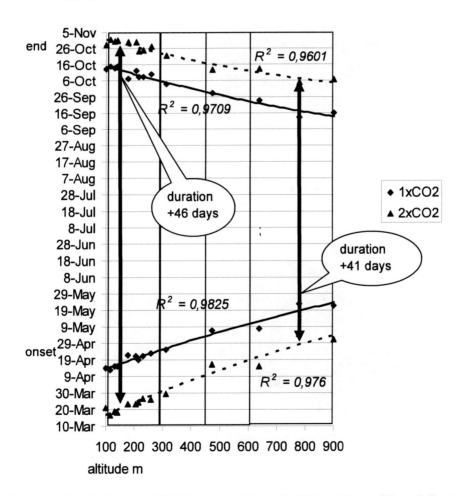

Figure 2. Onset and end of growing GS10 in present climate ($1xCO_2$) and in condition of climate change ($2xCO_2$) in dependence on altitude in Slovakia.

## 4.2. Air Temperature

Air mean temperature sums GS10 will increase by 23% in the lowlands of Slovakia under climate condition $2xCO_2$ (Station Hurbanovo). However, the relative increase of temperature in sub-mountain regions would be about 45%. The TS10>2 800 °C was found on the acreage of 11 136 $km^2$ (25%) in climate conditions $1xCO_2$. This value will most probably occur in the area bigger than 30 000 $km^2$ under climate conditions represented by $2xCO_2$ (67%).

This will enlarge the growing area of crops demanding higher temperature totals not only in the lowlands, but also in sub-mountainous uplands up to 650 m. On the other hand, water demand will rise, too, and drought can occur in bigger areas.

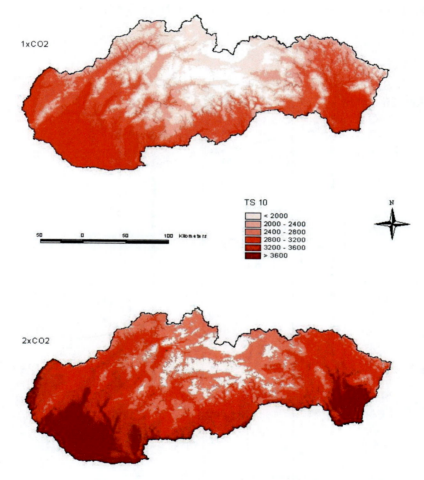

Figure 3. Daily mean air temperature sums in conditions of climate $1xCO_2$ and $2xCO_2$.

## 4.3. Precipitation and Evapotranspiration

Precipitation totals are influenced by the altitudinal profile of Slovakia. Generally, there is expected an increase of precipitation (R) for climate conditions $2xCO_2$: 65-80 mm (15-

20%) in the lowlands and by 65-128 mm (12-20%.) in northern part of the Slovak Republic. During GS10 all agro-regions should receive rainfall R>390 mm in climate conditions $2xCO_2$. This fact should favorably influence a production potential of some crops especially in higher altitudes (e.g. winter wheat, spring barley, forage crops and grass-land). However, the potential is also influenced by number and time distributions of rainfall. The number of days with rainfall has decreased and the number of periods of drought has increased in the lowlands by about 4% in each decade since 1960 [12]. Except for it, precipitation should be evaluated in the context of evapotranspiration. Rainfall increases will not cover the evapotranspiration demands of plants in hot lowland conditions.

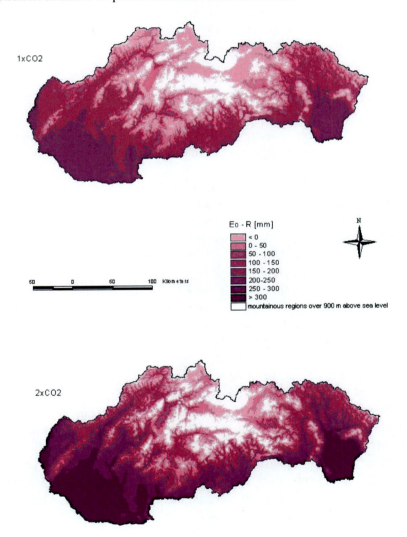

Figure 4.Climatic water balance (E0-R) in mm in conditions of $1xCO_2$ and $2xCO_2$.

Supposed air temperature increases during GS10 will cause the increase of $E_0$ in the entire area of the Slovak Republic under climate conditions $2xCO_2$. $E_0$ will increase by 150 mm, i.e. almost at 25% on the south of Slovakian lowlands. $E_0 > 500$ mm can be expected in the whole cultivated area, and $E_0$ more than 800 mm can be expected in the hottest localities of the Slovak Republic (the lowermost localities of Slovakia). Extremely high $E_0$ totals call for effective management of water resources and development of irrigation in the most areas of the Slovak Republic in order to eliminate unfavorable effects of drought on crop production.

The climatic water balance (difference between potential evapotranspiration and rainfall) is significantly changing with changes of $E_0$ and $R$ in the altitudinal profile. More significant changes of climatic index were found in lowland conditions of south Slovakia (+30%) under climate conditions of $2xCO_2$. Zero values of the index will shift from altitude 550 to 650 meter above sea level. There was found an increase of the index climate by 90–100 mm in the lowlands (+32 to +45%) under $2xCO_2$. Zero values of the index will shift from altitudes of 550 m to 700 m.

# 5. CONCLUSION

Only four agro-technical measures are considered as effective adaptations to negative effects of climate change (including droughts) in the conditions of the Slovak Republic [13].

- Change of crop. This step can bring a positive effect in sub-mountain regions in which the shortage of water will be rather moderate. Increasing temperature comfort in higher altitudes will enable growing the crops, which are nowadays typical for the hottest Slovak regions. Strong representation of maize in crop rotations is supposed in future climate conditions. Maize is able to overcome periods with lack of water during the vegetative period [14].
- Change of variety. Other cereals, which are dominating in plant production in Slovakia nowadays, will call for a change of varieties. Current winter wheat varieties are not enough drought-resistant, and could reach their maturity in climate change conditions about 4 weeks earlier [11]. Season of wintering is likely to become a risk. A warm winter can cause sudden decreases of temperatures that will likely become more frequent during the growing season, and so damage caused by frost will have to be taken into account by selecting new varieties.
- Modification of sowing date term. According to the results of modeling, it can be concluded that the sowing term of spring barley is suitable to adapt to average day temperature $T > 5$ °C in the agro-climatic conditions of Slovakia [14].
- Irrigation systems. Expansion of irrigation systems is currently one of the most frequently considered adaptive measures to mitigate drought effects. Using irrigation systems, however, requires sufficient amount of water, and it is likely that the needs of field crops will be satisfied only partly.

Agro climatic conditions were evaluated against the background of temperature and water balance during growing seasons limited by daily mean air temperature $T > 10$ °C (GS10). GS10 were characterized by daily mean air temperature sums (TS in °C), precipitation totals ($R$ in mm), potential evapotranspiration ($E_0$ in mm) and climatic water balance. As a base for agroclimatic regionalization (zonation) was proposed according to meteorological data from the years 1961-1990.

High totals of potential evapotranspiration during so short a time period as GS10 can evoke the situation when drought will appear in the lowlands of the Slovak Republic more frequently. This fact should be considered in future selection of the proper varieties of field crops. Effective management of water resources and irrigation can reduce the negative effects of increased evapotranspiration on the production.

## ACKNOWLEDGMENTS

This study was made with the help of grant project VEGA 1/4427/07: Design of new agroclimatic regionalization of plant production in condition of changing climate in Slovakia and FP6 project CECILIA.

## REFERENCES

[1]   M. Lapin, M. Melo, I. Damborská, *Scenarios of several physically plausible climatic elements (in Slovak). MoE SR Bratislava,* NCP SR 11, pp. 5-30 (2001).

[2]   L.O. Mearns, C. Rosenzweig and R. Goldberg, *Mean and variance change in climate scenarios: methods, agricultural applications and measures of unceirtinities.Clim. Chan.,* 35(4), 367-396, (1997).

[3]   M.J. Hayes, M.D. Svoboda, D.A. Wilhite, O.V. Vanyarko, *Monitoring the 1996 Drought using the standardized Precipitation Index. Am. Meteor. Soc.,* 80, 429-438, (1999).

[4]   R.R. Heim, *A Review of Twentieth-Century Drought Indices Used in the United States. Am. Meteor. Soc.* 83, 1149-1165, (2002).

[5]   Ditmarová, Ľ., Kmeť, J., Střelcová, K., Gőmőry, D., *Effects of drought on selected physiological parameters of young beech trees under stress conditions. Ekológia,* 25, 1-11, (2006).

[6]   M. Dubrovský, M. Trnka, M. Svoboda, M. Gates, D. Wilhite, Z. Žalud, D. Semerádová, *Drought conditions in the Czech republic in present and changed climate. Proceedings of the European Geophysical Union,* 25-29, (2005).

[7]   T. Hlásný, P. Baláž, *The climatic water balance of Slovakia based on the FAO Penman-Monteith evapotranspiration (in Slovak).Geographical Journal,* 60 (1), 15-30, (2008).

[8]   J. Tomlain, *Distribution of evapotranspiration in the territory of Slovakia in the period* 1961-1990. Podzemná voda, Vol. III., No. 1, SAH Bratislava, pp. 5-23 (in Slovak with English resume) (1997).

[9]   M. Kurpelová, J. Coufal, J. Čulík, *Agroclimatic Conditions of ČSSR. Príroda,* Bratislava, (in Slovak with English, German and Russian summary) (1975).

[10]  B. Šiška, F. Špánik, *Agroclimatic regionalization of Slovak territory in condition of changing climate. Meteorological Journal,* 11(1-2), 61-64, (2008).

[11]  B. Šiška, J. Takáč, *The impact of climate change on plant production conditions in Slovakia.* In: National climate program of the Slovak Republic: Climate change impacts

and adaptation measures. Bratislava, Slovak Hydrometeorological Institute 12, pp .103-109, (2008).

[12]  F. Špánik, D. Igaz, J. Čimo, *Periods of drought in agroclimatic conditions of Danubian lowland. In: Water for life – water as an element,* Agrofilm, Nitra, pp. 67-72. (in Slovak with English resume), (2006).

[13]  F. Špánik, B. Šiška, *Biometeorology,* VES SPU Nitra, 2004, pp. 1-227. (in Slovak with English resume), (2004).

[14]  J. Takáč, B. Šiška, *Climate change impact on spring barley yield in Slovakia. Bioclimatology and Natural hazards,* edited by Střelcova, K. et al.: Springer-Verlag 2009, pp. 283-288

In: Advances in Environmental Modeling and Measurements        ISBN: 978-1-60876-599-7
Editors: D. T. Mihailović, B. Lalić, pp. 255-265        © 2010 Nova Science Publishers, Inc.

*Chapter 23*

# CLIMATE INDICATOR ANALYSIS SPECIALIZED FOR VITICULTURAL RESEARCHES

## *M. Ladányi*[*]

Corvinus University of Budapest, Budapest, Hungary

## ABSTRACT

While the probability of extreme high grapevine production has increased with climate change in Hungary, the risk of production quantity and quality has also considerably increased. Surveying the possible reasons and consequences of risk increase climate change and its expected positive and negative impacts on viticulture of Hungary were considered. As a result of a synthesized analysis of international and national literature and practice there were fixed some weather indicators which may significantly define grapevine production from quality and/or quantity aspect.

A data management software was developed especially for our indicator research and it can be used as a tool to reveal how the trends of the examined indicators have been changing with time. Based on RegCM scenarios as well as specially generated weather data we defined the expected change of the plant specific weather indicators in the future. The possible impacts of the changing indicators on the production quality and quantity are described. Finally, some important conclusions for Hungary that can be built in the national climate change prevention and adaptation strategy are formulated.

## 1. INTRODUCTION

Grapevines can only be grown across a fairly narrow range of climates for optimum quality and production. Hungary is now situated at near the north of suitable land for grapevine growing, in a region where climate change can bring for viticulture both positive and negative effects. The area of Hungarian vineyards is 2% of cultivated area; 5-6% of GDP and 10% of agricultural exports are due to grapevine production. Ripening is quite slow

---

[*]  Corresponding author: E-mail address: marta.ladanyi@uni-corvinus.hu, Phone: +361 4826261, Fax: +361 4669273

because of moderate radiation; taste and flavour accumulation is good. According to the observations in the last decades as well as to the regional climate change models (RegCM), Carpathian basin is expecting definitely significant temperature increase and precipitation decrease in the growing season together with several anomalies (drought, frost, storm, wind, flood, hail etc.). Moreover, phenology, pest and disease occurrence, water availability may also change and bring new challenges in the future. It means that this region belongs to the highly vulnerable areas in Europe and not only viticulture but several other agricultural sectors are concerned in this problem. Both national and international climate change impact studies, however, predict spatial shifts of viticulture suitability [1-6]. While the probability of extreme high vine production has increased with climate change, the risk of production quantity and quality has also considerably increased. Dry and hot summers with great amount of precipitation in winter and spring as well as frost events after bud initialization force us to research the possible impacts of climate change more extensively because the stakeholders in viticulture might soon need radical and quick adaptation response.

## 2. MATERIALS AND METHODS

### 2.1. Data

Historical weather data with minimum, maximum and average temperature, precipitation and sunshine hours daily data as well as grapevine production data for several Hungarian regions from 1964 to 2000 and detailed grapevine production data from 2000-2006 were used. For the scenario approach we applied GCMs of GFDL (Geophysical Fluid Dynamics Laboratory, USA) which were downscaled to Hungary and refer to about 2030 and 2060 as well as CRU control data base with reference time series 1901-2000, Prudence monthly data with reference time series 2071-2100 (based on Hadley Centre, A2, B2 scenarios), Prudence control data (reference time series 1961-90) and finally monthly data of Tyndall Centre with reference period 1901-2000 (CRU) and 2001-2100 (A1, A2, B1, B2 scenarios) which was provided by Mitchell et al. (2004) with 10' resolution. The resolution of the downscaled Prudence data is 5 km [4,5,8,9]. Data management and evaluation were made by WIN-MET software that was developed for our special demand by Szenteleki et al. (2007a, b) [6, 21].

### 2.2. Weather Generator C2W

There were available historical and control daily weather data for the baseline periods 1961-90 or 1901-2000. Moreover, there were available RegCM scenarios with reference period 2071-2100. For the period in between, however, we needed a weather generator the weather data of which can somehow connect the two periods. We do not say that the climate changes proceeds in this way, this was just an approximated approach for the time in the near future. We needed it because stakeholders can be persuaded only if we draw a possible scheme of near future as well. To this, we used C2W [10] which is aimed at disaggregating climatological means and anomalies into realistic weather processes. The weather parameters were calculated by a multiple linear fit connecting the baseline and the far future parameters.

The parameters were then normalized by the probit normalization method. Then a first order autoregressive model was fitted to the normalized parameters. By way of Monte-Carlo simulations it was assured that the means of the simulated data converge statistically to the given parameters. The practical work of data extraction and generation was made by Solymosi and Kern [11].

# 3. RESULTS

## 3.1. Production Risk Increase Approach

The risk increase of grapevine production was proved by a simplified variant of the general stochastic dominance criterion [12,13]. Under the assumption of a negative exponential utility function $U$, certainty equivalent $CE$ was calculated as the inverse of $U$. We represented the graph of certainty equivalent $CE$ depending on the absolute risk aversion. With this method we proved that in every examined grapevine production region of Hungary the risk of production increased between 1964 and 2000, independently to the rate of risk aversion and to the fact that some of the examined regions are quite different from each other with respect to their mesoclimates, terrains as well as grapevine production structures. In some regions the rate of increase became even quicker (Fig. 1). In order to see the trends, the time interval 1964-2000 was split into four parts: 1964-76, 1970-82, 1976-88 and 1988-2000 and the risk of vine production was elicited for each interval.

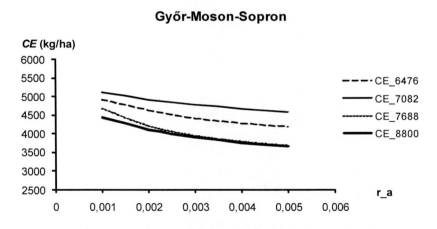

Figure 1 Stochastic efficiency for vine production in Győr-Moson-Sopron County with respect to 1964-76, 1970-82, 1976-88, 1988-2000. If we represent the graph of certainty equivalent depending on the absolute risk aversion, the highest curve indicates the less risky time series.

## 3.2. Plant Specific Weather Indicator Approach

As Hungary has relatively dry climate, soil plays a relatively smaller role in grapevine production because wine quality is determined mainly by temperature and precipitation, therefore, in our next survey, we considered temperature and precipitation/humidity effects, only.

### 3.2.1. Temperature Sensitivity of Grapevine and Regional Expectations for the Future

Temperature effect on grapevine quality and quantity is not a question, however, it can be very different in different phonological phases and when accompanied by different other circumstances (e.g. high/low precipitation and/or humidity, radiation, wind, etc.). Let us consider the most important ones.

In early bud development relatively high temperature improves fruitfulness. After the initialization of bud development frost can severely damage the potential fruiting load. At budburst the plant is quite sensitive to temperature fluctuation and the number of flowers increases under cool temperature. Near flowering high temperature reduces fruitfulness while low one reduces fruit set which means practically that grapevine is sensitive on temperature during the whole spring.

During veraison extreme heat events, especially associated with hot winds and low humidity can cause serious damages, at most risk are red varieties and berries that are well exposed. Warm summer, nevertheless, decreases the risk of diseases.

Extremely high temperature while ripening results in general poorer quality must concerning with low acid and pH content increase as well as phenolic content of the must. In very hot environment earlier maturity can happen shortly after the warmest month which is quite unfavourable for plant function. Under cool circumstances, nevertheless, wines become to be fresher, more acidic and finer in bouquet and aroma. Depending on varieties, the optimum daily average temperature is between 17-26 °C in this period. Daytime temperature over 30 °C can be very harmful, especially when accompanied by hot nights.

Low variation in temperature around the mean in the last month before harvest helps grapevine to pick up great flavour, aroma and pigmentation. The optimum mean temperature is about 15-21 °C in this period and 10-15 °C around harvest. High temperature, however, results higher soluble sugar content in grape together with high alcohol content and less fine taste and aroma in wine. In case the temperature is extremely high in this period (over 33 °C), transpiration and photosynthesis is impeded and sugar assimilation is reduced.

If the daytime mean temperature is high in harvest season, photosynthesis and net assimilation are suppressed and it can result an inflated estimate of grape maturity.

If the autumn temperature is high in post harvest season, re-accumulation of carbohydrates prior to defoliation is improved, thus bud and inflorescence differentiation is improved and spring growth in the following year is supported.

**Table 1. Expected changes of extreme temperature indices after 2071 in Hungary, according to Prudence A2 scenario [14].**

| Extreme indices | The rate of change |
|---|---|
| Number of summer days when the daily maximum temperature is above 25 °C | +39% |
| Number of hot days when the daily maximum temperature is above 30 °C | +91% |
| Number of extremely hot days when the daily maximum temperature is above 35 °C | +250% |
| Number of icy days when the daily minimum temperature is under -10 °C | -83% |
| Number of frost days when the daily minimum temperature is under 0 °C | -65% |
| Number of hot night days when the daily minimum temperature is above 20 °C | +625% |

All impacts of warming are of concern to Hungary as in our region (Carpathian Basin) A2 and B2 scenarios predict relatively higher warming compared to global rates. Though warming is the lowest in spring, we expect it to be higher than 3 °C (A2) or 2,5 °C (B2). Warming is the highest in summer (over 4 °C) and autumn but it is not lower than 3 °C in winter, either. Warming nevertheless is expected to come with unequally distribution and with serious extremes in summer (long hot and dry periods) and at nights (Tab. 1) which has an impeding impact to acidity retention.

### 3.2.2. Precipitation and Humidity Sensitivity of Grapevine

The best environment for grapes is even rainfall distribution, moderate temperature and sufficient sunshine with sufficient soil moisture stores or irrigation. Hungary, however, is not belonging to the regions with optimal circumstances. In general, in the last 10-20 years vineyards in Hungary have been suffering from relatively arid, hot and low humidity summer climate. Therefore, transpiration demands outstrip root water uptake thus even with adequate soil moisture grapevines close stomata and cease photosynthesis to conserve moisture. As the saturation deficit increases, the moisture: carbon dioxide ratio increases thus growth (yield) per unit of water transpired is decreased.

Grapevine is quite sensitive to both precipitation and humidity. The minimum level of rainfall or irrigation is of 500 mm or higher, especially if the growing season is characterised by high evapotranspiration rates. The ideal relative humidity is 50-65% for the ripening of grapes for table wine and 40-50% for fortified wines. More than sufficient relative humidity may result fungal infections. In spring grapevine is very susceptible to moisture stress. Heavy rain may promote vigorous growth which suppresses bud differentiation and fruit setting by causing overshading.

In case there is adequate moisture available till veraison, yield is higher and final sugar content is lower. If there is severe moisture stress in the few weeks up until and after veraison, both berry and flavour developments are endangered. Nevertheless, some moderate water stress can be favourable for colour and flavour by limiting berry size easing vegetative growth.

After veraison and before harvest moisture stress may reduce photosynthesis and thus the movement of sugar to the berry but may also increase the movement of potassium from the leaves to the fruit. The higher potassium: sugar ratio tends to increase must pH and results lower must and wine quality. Excess rain in this period, however, may cause berry splitting, especially in hotter, drier climates with delayed ripening even in hot climates. In this case, as a risk management strategy grape growers usually harvest the immaturate grapes to avoid even greater loss.

If there is insufficient moisture available after harvest and prior to leaf fall, root growth, photosynthetic activity and assimilation for the following vintage are reduced which endanger a vigorous, even budburst and early growth in the following spring.

## 4. DISCUSSION OF THE RESULTS

Based on international literature and Hungarian experts' opinion as well as circulation models with different scenarios' predictions together with case studies we have drawn up a list of the most important plant specific weather indicators for grapevine with Hungarian location.

The indicators were classified as:

- Extreme indicators: number of extremely hot ($T_{max}$>35 °C), hot ($T_{max}$>30 °C), summer ($T_{max}$>25 °C), frost ($T_{min}$<0 °C), icy ($T_{min}$<-10 °C), hot night ($T_{min}$>20 °C), spring frost and fall frost days as well as the length of frost free period with several spring frost indices.
- Temperature indicators: Gladstones' biologically effective growing degree days, Winkler and Huglin indices, mean July, mean January temperature, winter severity and latitude temperature indices, growing season average, average maximum, average minimum, harvest maximum, harvest average, winter minimum, ripening average temperature, cool night index as well as daily temperature range indices [15-17].
- Precipitation indicators: annual, blooming, summer, winter, growing season, ripening rainfall, dryness index and number of growing season rainy days.
- Complex indicators: radiation, sunshine hours, Branas heliothermic index, Ribereau-Gayon-Peynaud index [18,19].

We do not state that production (quality and quantity) is exactly determined by these factors and there can not be other important indicators. Nevertheless, we proved that grapevine production is highly correlated with these factors and there has been detected a very strong, mainly very obvious connection between years with high/low amount and/or quality of production indices (°Brix, pH, ripening index based on acid indices) or production loss and the values of the weather indicators in the historical data. Therefore, if we learn the expected trends of indicators more or less, we can conclude the production as well as the expected risk in the future. [20,21].

Though the demand of detailed analysis of the indices is far beyond this chapter, we set out some remarkable changes we expect.

## 4.1. Extreme Indicators

Because of the quite high rate of the expected autumn and winter warming in Hungary, the risk of autumn and winter frost decreases considerably, however, the risk of spring frost increases, mainly because of early frost free days and earlier initialization of bud development and flowering. According to Kurtural (2006) [22] spring frost index classification, based on time interval 1901-2000, e.g. Tokaj is belonging to the regions with moderate (11-13) frost risk with 9 years of high values (above 13.5); Sopron is belonging to the one with low (<11) frost risk with 11 years of moderate and 4 years of high values and with quite high variance. If we calculate spring frost index from Prudence A2 and B2 scenario data, the trends for both regions are increasing. The increase is significant. Moreover, both regions reach in some years their spring frost index value of 15 which is extremely high and happened never before 2000.

## 4.2. Temperature Indicators

According to the Winkler index classification of the viticultural climatic regions [16,23], Sopron and Tokaj grapevine production regions of Hungary are belonging to the first (below 1390 °C) and the second (1391-1670 °C) coolest classes based on historical temperature data of 1901-2000. Both regions, however, are expected to be belonging to the fifth (warmest) regions (over 2220 °C) up to 2070 based on A2 and B2 scenarios' data of Prudence. Compare this with the fact that the fifth class corresponds to the current Winkler index values of e.g. Split (South-Croatia), Palermo (Italy) or Algiers (Algeria). According to the classification due to Tonietto and Carbonneau (2004) [24], moreover, we can conclude that up to 2070 Hungarian grapevine growing regions may shift from temperate class (over 1800 °C and under 2100 °C) to hot class (over 2400 °C and under 3000 °C). It means that, supposed that humidity, radiation and wind circumstances allow it, regions producing now Riesling, Pinot Noir, Chardonnay, Merlot or Cabernet franc may become to be suitable for Cabernet Sauvignon, Grenache or even all cultivated varieties as there is no more constraint to ripen them. Till the end of the century, however, the values of Huglin index may exceed the needs of even the late varieties resulting high risk of production.

We have shown that present site classification in Hungary is changing with climate change since because of warmer springs and thus earlier bud break and flowering, the growing season length increases significantly in Hungary.

## 4.3. Precipitation Indicators

Summer rainfall (mm) is very important as besides warming, precipitation in expected to decrease in summer significantly, during the growing period of grapevine. There is no significant change of the annual rainfall (mm) indices of Tokaj and Sopron proved. However, the case of summer rainfall (mm) indices is quite different. We can detect significant decrease and, meantime, an increase in variability. It means that climate change brings us not only much hotter but also much drier summers to Hungary with increasing risk of low-probability – high impact events.

The number of growing season rain days, moreover, provides us alarming information about the (unbalanced) distribution of future precipitation. The risk of drought would be considerably higher in Hungary even if precipitation were not predicted to decrease over the growing period. Thus, if we ad that summer precipitation deficit is expected to be up to around 30% (A2) or 15% (B2), we expect that the increase of evapotranspiration rates leads to the reduction in available soil moisture in our region where water is already scarce, therefore the risk of drought is expected to be extremely high.

## 5. CONCLUSION

According Prudence A2/B2 scenarios, we summarize the trends of Hungarian climate and their impacts on grapevine production up to and after 2070.

- Increasing mean temperature. The rate of increase is the greatest in summer (A2: 4.5-5.1 °C or B2: 3.7-4.2 °C). Winter dormancy will be reduced. Warmer and longer growing seasons and season's shift of 6-25 days earlier over numerous varieties and locations are expected. Ripening will begin earlier during the hotter summer months. Higher temperatures at ripening may depress quality and will shorten the harvest window for premium quality wines. Because of more rapid phenological development, suitable locations of varieties with long time growers' experience are expected to be shifted northward, while current grape growing regions may shift into another maturity type.

- Increasing winter-spring (A2: 0-37%, B2: 3-27%) while decreasing summer-autumn precipitation (A2: 3-33%, B2: 0-20%). Less water is likely to be available, due to either or both increased evapotranspiration and lower precipitation, and yield/quality variability is likely to increase creating a higher economic risk for the producer.

- More frequent and serious anomalies, longer extreme periods as well as increased seasonal variability are expected to occur.

- Warming during also the dormant periods is detected. The number of winter/frost days decreases significantly, nevertheless, late frost risk increases because of early vegetation period start. The presence and/or intensity of pests and diseases may change.

- Increasing uncertainty due to delayed ecological and economical feedback is of high possibility.

- Both extremely positive and negative production can cause great economical risk.

It is obvious that Hungarian grapevine production depends highly on the magnitude, rate and distribution of future warming, precipitation and extreme events. The issue is likely mostly about adaptation:

- New types are under plantation and development on experimental fields of regions of flat and downy production (Kecskemét, Tokaj, Eger). New species are under breeding. New sites are under evaluation.

- Formerly, grapevines were mostly not irrigated in Hungary, thus there may be a substantial risk in terms of more frequent and more severe droughts with negative effects on yield and quality. Irrigation has to be introduced in several sites. Complex management is needed on sites with scarce water resources. The way of soil cover should be modified on exposed sites. The rate of sunburn risk has to be considered when defining the way of pruning. Economical analysis is needed before investments.

- Current integrated pest management strategies may not be useful any more because of warmer dormant periods. New technologies and management practices are needed to be put into action in order to mitigate the risk caused by pests and diseases.

- Regarded the new situation of grape growers in Hungary, the support and insurance systems have to be revised. An information and alert system for grape growers has to be developed.

Further on we aim to create and analyze combined (temperature - precipitation) indicators as well as indicators controlled by functions of special heat sums, in order to handle the changing vegetation seasons more flexible. As grapevine production needs several long-term decisions, we also plan a variety-specific impact study and a detailed adaptation strategy approach to improve the decisiveness of the stakeholders.

## ACKNOWLEDGMENTS

Our work was supported by ADAM GOCE 018476 EU6 project.

## REFERENCES

[1]    J. Gladstones *Viticulture and Environment Winetitles* Adelaide, Australia (1992).

[2]    G.V. Jones, E. Duchene, D. Tomasi, J. Yuste, O. Braslavska, H. Schultz, C. Martinez, S. Boso, F. Langellier, C. Perruchot, G. Guimberteau, *http://www.sou.edu/geography/jones/Publications/ (2005).*

[3]    G. V. Jones *Whitman College Working Paper* 7, (2007).

[4]    J. Bartholy, R. Pongrácz, R. *Global and Planetary Change*, 57, p. 83–95. (2007a).

[5]    J. Bartholy, R. Pongrácz, Gy. Gelybó, B. Szintai, P. Szabó, Cs. Torma, A. Hunyady, P. Kardos *Geophysical Research Abstracts,* 9, CD-ROM. (2007b).

[6]    K. Szenteleki, E. P. Botos, A. Szabó, Cs. Horvath, L. Martinovich, Z. Katona, *Proceedings of EFITA Conference, CD-ROM (2007a)*

[7]    T. Mitchell, T. R. Carter, P. Jones, M. Hulme, *Tyndall Centre Working Paper* 55 (2004)

[8]    J. H. Christensen, *Prediction of Regional scenarios and Uncertainties for Defining European Climate change risks and Effects* – Final Report. DMI. 269p. (2005).

[9]    M. New, M. Hulme, P. Jones, *J. Clim.*, 12, 829–856 (1999).

[10]   G. Bürger, *Clim. Res.*, 8, 183-194, (1997).

[11]   N. Solymosi, A. Kern, Á. Maróti-Agócs, L. Horváth, K. Erdélyi, *Environ. Model. .Softw.*, 23(7),  948-949 (2008).

[12]   J. B. Hardaker, R. B. M. Huirne, J. R. Anderson, G. Lien, G. *Coping with Risk in Agriculture.* 2nd edn. (CABI Publishing, 2004).

[13]   M. Ladányi, É. Erdélyi, Environmental, *Health and Humanity Issues in the Down Danubian Region,* edited by D.T. Mihailovic & M. V. Miloradov (World Scientific, 2008) p. 245-255.

[14]   R. Pongrácz, J. Bartholy, Proceedings of 87th AMS Annual Meeting CD-ROM (2007).

[15]   J. Gladstones, Proceedings of 5th Intl. Symp. *Cool Climate Vitic. Oenol.* p. 1-10. (2000)

[16]   M.A. Amerine, A.J. Winkler, *Hilgardia*, 15(6), 493-674. (1944)

[17]   P. Huglin, *Biologie et ecologie de la vigne.* (Payot Lausanne, Paris, 1986).

[18]   J. Branas, G. Bernon, L. *Levadoux, Eléments de viticulture générale.* (Dehan, Montpellier, 1946).

[19]   P. Ribéreau-Gayon, G Guimberteau, *Vintage Reports*, 1988-1997.

[20]   M. Ladányi, É. Erdélyi, K. Szenteleki, *Proceedings of EFITA, CD-ROM (2007).*

[21] K. Szenteleki, M. Ladányi, É. Szabó L. Horváth, L. Hufnagel, N. Solymosi, A. *Révész, Proceedings of EFITA, CD-ROM (2007b)*.

[22] S.K. Kurtural, *http://www.uky.edu/Ag/Horticulture/siteselection.pdf.* (2006).

[23] C. Riou, *European Commission* (1994).

[24] J. Tonietto, A. Carbonneau, *Agricultural and Forest Meteorology*, 124, p. 81-97. (2004).

# INDEX

**F**

**G**

## H

## I

## N

## Q

## R

## S